Vermont

Vermont

Christina Tree & Sally W. Johnson

Principal Photography by Kim Grant

The Countryman Press ✳ Woodstock, Vermont

TENTH EDITION

DEDICATION

Laura Howe
—C. T.

Stephen C. Terry and William West Terry
—S. W. J.

We welcome your comments and suggestions. Please use the card enclosed in this book to contact us.

Tenth Edition

ISSN 1523-9462
ISBN 0-88150-608-7

Maps by Moore Creative Design, © 2004 The Countryman Press
Cover and interior design by Bodenweber Design
Text composition by PerfecType, Nashville, TN
Cover photograph © William H. Johnson

Published by The Countryman Press,
P.O. Box 748, Woodstock, Vermont 05091

Distributed by W. W. Norton & Company, Inc., 500 Fifth Avenue,
New York, NY 10110

Printed in the United States of America

10 9 8 7 6 5 4 3 2 1

EXPLORE WITH US!

We have been fine-tuning *Vermont: An Explorer's Guide* for the past 21 years, a period in which lodging, dining, and shopping opportunities have more than quadrupled in the state. As we have expanded our guide, we have also been increasingly selective, making recommendations based on years of conscientious research and personal experience. What makes us unique is that we describe the state by locally defined regions, giving you Vermont's communities, not simply its most popular destinations. With this guide you'll feel confident to venture beyond the tourist towns, along roads less traveled, to places of special hospitality and charm.

WHAT'S WHERE

In the beginning of the book you'll find an alphabetical listing of special highlights, with important information and advice on everything from antiques to weather reports.

LODGING

Prices: Please don't hold us or the respective innkeepers responsible for the rates listed as of press time in 2004. Some changes are inevitable. We do not include the 9 percent state room and meals tax in rates unless stated. Many lodging establishments also add a gratuity to their listed rate, something we try to note but do not always catch. It's best to check ahead of time.

Smoking: State law bars smoking in all places of public accommodation in Vermont, including restaurants, and even in bars that don't qualify as "cabarets."

RESTAURANTS

Note the distinction between *Dining Out* and *Eating Out*. By their nature, restaurants listed in the *Eating Out* group are generally inexpensive.

KEY TO SYMBOLS

⚭ **Weddings.** The wedding-ring symbol appears beside establishments that frequently serve as venues for weddings and civil unions.

🏆 **Special Value.** The special-value symbol appears next to lodging and restaurants that combine high quality and moderate prices.

🐾 **Pets.** The dog-paw symbol appears next to lodgings that accept pets (usually with a reservation and deposit) as of press time.

🦋 **Child-friendly.** The kids-alert symbol appears next to lodging, restaurants, activities, and shops of special appeal to youngsters.

♿ **Handicapped access.** The wheelchair symbol appears next to lodging, restaurants, and attractions that are partially or fully handicapped accessible.

We would appreciate your comments and corrections about places you visit or know well in the state. Please use the card enclosed in this book, or e-mail Chris: ctree@traveltree.net.

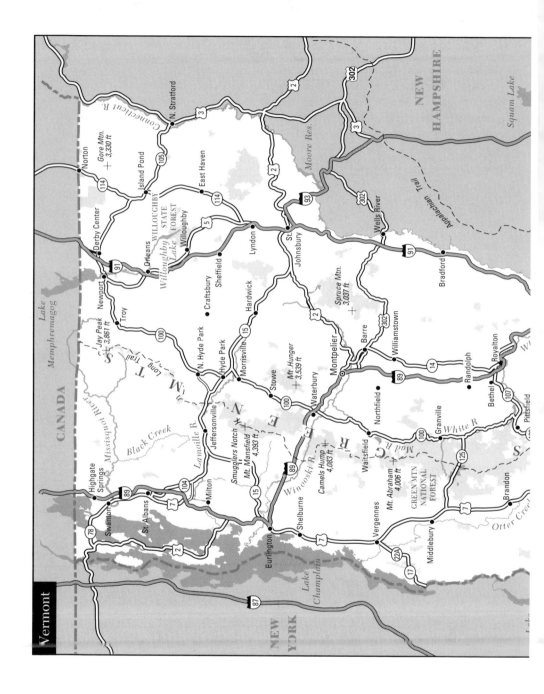

Vermont

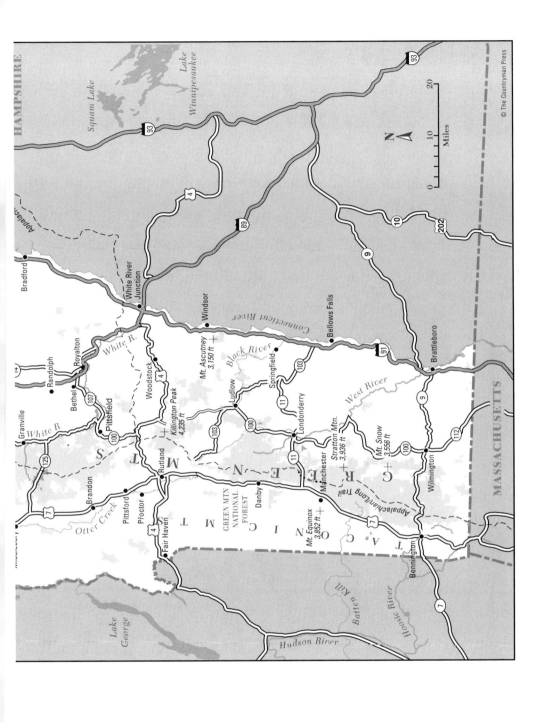

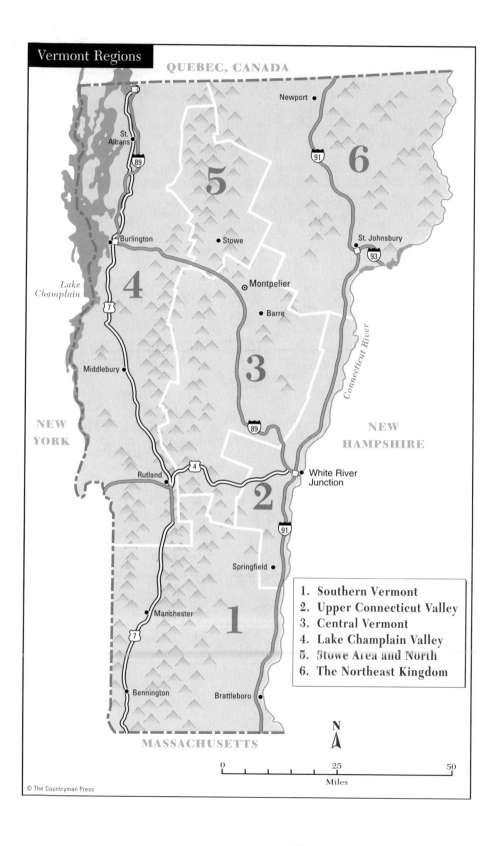

Vermont Regions

QUEBEC, CANADA

Newport

St. Albans

89

Burlington

Stowe

⊙ Montpelier

Barre

Lake Champlain

Middlebury

7

5

4

3

St. Johnsbury

93

Connecticut River

91

6

NEW YORK

NEW HAMPSHIRE

Rutland

4

White River Junction

89

2

91

Springfield

Manchester

7

1

Bennington

Brattleboro

MASSACHUSETTS

N

1. Southern Vermont
2. Upper Connecticut Valley
3. Central Vermont
4. Lake Champlain Valley
5. Stowe Area and North
6. The Northeast Kingdom

0   25   50

Miles

© The Countryman Press

CONTENTS

INTRODUCTION

Welcome to the Green Mountain State and this 10th edition of the most comprehensive guide to its distinctive landscape, character, and places to see and stay. No other portrait of Vermont gathers so much practical information between two covers—so much, in fact, that even Vermonters find it useful.

We have divided the guide into areas whose boundaries usually coincide with those of the local chambers of commerce. Each section begins with a verbal snapshot of the area against a historical background, followed by advice on sources of information, getting around, things to see and do, and descriptions of just about every legal form of recreation, from skiing, horseback riding, sailing, hiking, swimming, canoeing, and golf to llama trekking and white-water rafting.

Then we give capsule descriptions of places to stay, representing roughly two-thirds of the resorts, inns, B&Bs, and farm stays—but omitting most motels. We try to be descriptive and reasonably candid about what we like and don't like. We visit regularly and we describe many reasonably priced options, some of them real gems that are found in no other book.

We critique upscale restaurants *(Dining Out)* and the everyday options *(Eating Out)*, plus good delis, bakeries, and coffeehouses. Local entertainment, shops worth walking into, and special events round out coverage of virtually every city and town, and most villages.

Vermont is within a few hours' drive of 35 million people, and its popularity as a destination is growing. In summer visitors seem to find their way to every corner. In winter they converge on those areas that offer the best alpine and cross-country skiing in the East. On fall foliage weekends, traffic congeals in places, and visitors without reservations find themselves sleeping in spare bed-rooms. At that time of year it's best to come midweek—with reservations and this book. Vermont, after all, invented "foliage season" 50 years ago and has been promoting its autumn colors as a drive-through spectacle ever since. In the process it has developed a better system (see *Foliage* in "What's Where") for lodging "leaf-peepers" at peak periods than is found in other New England states.

Ironically, Vermont's fame as an autumn and winter destination has upstaged its original tourist season. Vermont's summer is soft, still, and deep, almost secre-tive. While traffic jams New England's coastal resorts, Vermont's roads and

A NOTE ON LODGING LISTINGS
We do not charge innkeepers to be included in this book. It's worth noting that a large percentage of lodging guides charge lodging places a "processing fee," anywhere from $250 to $2,500—and that the web is also paid advertising. Within this edition we supply hundreds of web sites, but we feel strongly that the Internet has increased rather than obviated the need for an honest, opinionated guidebook based on actual snoop-around rather than virtual research. Sure, this is the best search engine to visiting Vermont, but it's also much more: a combination of critical, current sleuthing and a sense of how to convey what's out there, based on decades of exploring and describing the Green Mountain State.

widely scattered lodging places are relatively quiet. Wooded paths and swimming holes are never far but rarely obvious.

Whatever the season, this book is about exploring beyond highways and tourist routes. Mud season aside, Vermont is best viewed from its vast network of unpaved roads. Whether it's a cross-country ski network or crafts studio, a farm or B&B, a waterfall, covered bridge, or corn maze, we have supplied countless lures to lead you into as well as around Vermont.

Contrary to its image, Vermont's landscape varies substantially from north to south and even more from east to west. Rather than following the tried-and-true tourist routes (east–west Routes 9 and 4 and north–south Route 100), we suggest that (weather permitting) you drive the dramatic but well-surfaced "gap" roads (see *Gaps, Gulfs, and Gorges* in "What's Where") east or west across the state's relatively narrow width, bundling very different landscapes—mountain valleys and the broad sweep of farmland along Lake Champlain—into a few hours' drive.

While focusing on all the state's regions through the same lens (our format), we fervently hope that this book conveys the full spectrum of Vermont's beauty: the river roads of the Upper Valley, the high rolling farmland around Tunbridge and Chelsea, the glacially carved, haunting hills of the Northeast Kingdom, and the limestone farmsteads of Isle La Motte. Villages range from the self-consciously painted and pampering old resorts of Stowe, Woodstock, and Manchester to the equally proud but quiet villages of Craftsbury Common, Chelsea, and Newfane and the Victorian brick streetscapes of Brattleboro and Burlington.

Despite the inevitable inroads of today's shopping-center culture, Vermont has mostly preserved the character of the rural countryside that causes pangs of nostalgia in many urban visitors. Currently, for every acre of open land paved for a parking lot, at least 10 acres are added to the holdings of the Vermont Land Trust and are shielded from development. The administrators of Act 250, the state's pioneering land-use program, also still exercise sensible controls over new commercial development, deflecting sporadic efforts in the legislature to dilute the act's provisions. Vermonters, prudently and in a spirit of thrift, have not torn

TOURISM IN VERMONT

Contrary to common belief, tourism (for lack of a better word to describe the phenomenon of visitors "from away") is an integral part of Vermont's history, one that has affected its landscape—not just since the '50s but for 150 years.

Before the Civil War, southerners patronized mineral spas along the Connecticut River in Brattleboro and Newbury, and after the war Vermont's burgeoning railroads teamed up with the state's Board of Agriculture to promote farm vacations. Railroad guides also promoted Newport, with its elegant four-story Lake Memphremagog House ("one of the largest and finest hotels in New England"), and Lake Willoughby ("one of the most remarkable places in the continent"). Carriage roads were built to the top of Jay Peak, Mount Mansfield, and Mount Equinox, and of course there was a summit hotel atop Mount Mansfield (the highest peak in the state) as well as a large hotel beside the Green Mountain Inn in Stowe Village.

In the 1850s the Equinox House was recognized as one of New England's leading hotels. By 1862 the *Manchester Journal* could report that the previous summer, "Every house in the village was as full as a 'Third Avenue car,' almost entirely New Yorkers." Woodstock was equally well known in the right Manhattan circles by the 1890s.

All 19th- and early-20th-century visitors arrived by train (the exception being those who crossed Lake Champlain by ferry), and Vermont was slower than many other states to provide roads suitable to touring. The flood of 1927 washed out a number of major highways and bridges. In 1936 the proposal for building a federally funded, 260-mile Green Mountain Parkway the length of the state—passing just below the crests of Pico, Killington, and several other peaks—was roundly defeated in a public referendum.

After World War II, however, Vermont launched what may be the world's first and most successful campaign to turn off-season into peak season.

"If you can pick and choose, there is no better time for a motor trip through Vermont than in autumn," Abner W. Coleman wrote in the first issue of *Vermont Life*, a state publication. The autumn 1946 article continued: "To the color photographer, Vermont during the autumn months offers delights indescribable. Should film become more plentiful this year, hundreds of camera enthusiasts will be roaming around these hills, knocking themselves out in a

down the past. Abandoned farmhouses have been restored, and in a score of towns, adaptive preservation techniques have been thoughtfully applied to convert obsolete mills to other uses.

Vermont has never been a "rich" state. Except for machine tools, the industrial revolution skipped over it; as one political scientist noted, we leaped from happy frenzy of artistic endeavor. For the autumn woods run the entire spectrum's course, from the blazing reds of the maple through the pale yellows of beech and birch to the violet of far-off mountain walls." The story was illustrated with the first of many vividly hued photos for which *Vermont Life* remains famous.

While Vermonters can't claim to have invented skiing, the state does boast America's oldest ski resorts. In the 1930s skiers began riding rope tows up slopes in Woodstock, at Pico, and on Mount Mansfield; after World War II Stowe became "Ski Capital of the East." Patrons at Mad River Glen built the country's first slope-side lodging, and in the early '60s nearby Sugarbush opened with the East's first bottom-of-the-lifts village. In ensuing decades more than a dozen Vermont ski areas have evolved into year-round resorts, several (Stowe, Sugarbush, and Killington) spawning full-fledged communities. Stowe and Warren were towns before they were resorts.

Vermont's ski communities mirror (in reverse) the story of its mill towns. Whereas mills were positioned on waterfalls—and no longer need the water to generate power—ski resorts have grown around mountains chosen for their good terrain and "dependable" snowfall. Only in recent years has it become apparent that access to enough water—to make snow—is crucial.

The question of whether skiing or any other manifestation of "tourism" (again that inadequate term) contributes to the preservation or destruction of the Vermont character and landscape can be argued interminably. But the fact is that it has been here for 150 years. Today Vermont inns and B&Bs outnumber farms, and Vermont visitors outnumber cows.

Today's visitor is more likely than not to be welcomed by ex-visitors: More than 40 percent of the state's population of 608,827 has come "from away," a post–World War II phenomenon that has profoundly affected the cultural and political landscapes.

Much has been made of the proverbial "Vermont mystique," that indefinable quality of life and character. It is, we are happy to report, alive and well, especially along the back roads and in villages and hamlets where "neighboring" still reigns. While the portrait of the legendary Vermont Yankee—frugal, wary, taciturn, sardonic—has faded somewhat in today's homogenized culture, independent-minded Vermonters (many of them ex-"tourists") take care of each other, tolerate eccentricities, and regard the world with a healthy skepticism.

"cow chips to microchips." Nevertheless, a few 19th-century family fortunes were made from lumber, wool, marble, and railroads. Tangible evidence of those entrepreneurs can be found in half a dozen stately homes that survive as inns, notably the Inn at Shelburne Farms, The Castle in Proctorsville, and the Hartness House in Springfield.

The 14 years of sovereignty as an independent country between 1777 and 1791 stamped Vermont with the indelible "contrary country" brand. Many examples of this spirit animated the state's subsequent history, from the years when Ethan Allen's Rabelaisian Green Mountain Boys wrested independence from the grip of Hampshiremen and 'Yorkers as well as from "The Cruel Minestereal Tools of George ye 3d," and blunted the British invasion of the Champlain Corridor. This spirit was later responsible for the abolitionist fervor that swept the state in the years before the Civil War and impelled Vermonters to flock to the colors in record numbers when President Lincoln called for troops. They voted their consciences with much the same zeal when, in both world wars, the legislature declared war on Germany, in effect, before the United States did; and when Vermont and the United States observed their bicentennials in 1976–77, debates about secession drew crowds to the state's town halls!

The Authors

A flatland author, born in Hawaii, raised in New York City, and living near Boston, Chris Tree claims to be a professional Vermont visitor. Her infatuation with the state began in college.

"The college was in Massachusetts, but one of my classmates was a native Vermonter whose father ran a general store and whose mother to whom Chris has dedicated this edition knows the name of every flower, bird, and mushroom. I jumped at her invitations to come 'home' or to 'camp' and have since spent far more time in Vermont than has my friend. As a travel writer for the *Boston Globe,* I have spent more than 30 years writing newspaper stories about Vermont towns, inns, ski areas, and people. I interviewed John Kenneth Galbraith about Newfane, Pearl Buck about Danby. I rode the Vermont Bicentennial Train, froze a toe on one of the first inn-to-inn ski treks, camped on the Long Trail and in state parks, paddled a canoe down the Connecticut, slid over Lake Champlain on an iceboat as well as paddling it in a kayak, soared over the Mad River Valley in a glider, and hovered above the Upper Valley in a hot-air balloon. I have also tramped through the woods collecting sap, ridden many miles with Vermont Transit, led a foliage tour, collided with a tractor, and have broken down in a variety of places."

Sally West Johnson was born near Philadelphia and grew up in northern Maryland, but her family on the West side had long and deep ties to Vermont, in particular her mother, who spent much of her childhood as well as her college years in Middlebury. For years the Johnson family—five children and two adults—would load into the family car for their annual 2-week ski vacation at Stowe. Those trips strongly influenced her decision to attend Middlebury College (class of 1972) and to move back to Vermont in 1979 after 7 years in the wilds of Manhattan.

A journalist, Johnson spent years covering stories for the *Rutland Herald* that took her to every nook and cranny of Vermont. She has also written about Vermont for the *New York Times* and the *Boston Globe Magazine.* She is married to Stephen Terry, a native of Windsor, Vermont; and their son, Will, also can claim native status. They live in a restored 1800 Cape on the outskirts of Middlebury.

"Somehow, even as a kid, I knew I wanted to make my home here, without necessarily knowing what I would do to make a living. For me, the appeal of Vermont is in both its beauty and its human scale; we all tend to know each other up here, which keeps the politicians honest and the neighbors neighborly. To the extent we can capture that ethos and share it with visitors, I will feel that this book has achieved its goals."

Chris and Sally are deeply indebted to Peter Jennison, a sixth-generation Vermonter, who was born on a dairy farm in Swanton, attended one-room schoolhouses, and graduated from Middlebury College. After 25 years in the publishing business in New York City, he became a "born-again" Vermonter, returning to his native heath in 1972 and founding The Countryman Press. Peter coauthored this book during its first eight editions, and many of the best words in it remain his.

Chris wishes to thank Betsy Gentile and William Hays in Brattleboro, Pat Fowler in Bellows Falls, Thom and Joan Gorman and Susan Roy in the Mad River Valley, Beth Kennett of Rochester, the Upper Valley's Susan and Les Motschman, Killington's Kim Jackson, Jay and Karen Keller of Chelsea, Sarah Cook of Hardwick, and Margaret Ramsdell of Craftsbury, and Diane Konrady of the Vermont Department of Tourism and Marketing. Special thanks to Gordon Pine of Woodstock and Darcie McCann of the Northeast Kingdom Chamber.

Sally would like to thank Brian Harwood of Stowe, Barbara Thomke of Smugglers' Notch, Anne Weber of Arlington, and the many staffers at local chamber of commerce offices for their generous assistance.

Both authors are grateful to Ann Kraybill for launching this update and to Jennifer Thompson for shepherding it to fruition with the help of our ever-speedy and supportive copy editor Laura Jorstad.

Christina Tree
Sally W. Johnson

WHAT'S WHERE IN VERMONT

AREA CODE The area code for all of Vermont is **802.**

AGRICULTURAL FACTS AND FAIRS
Some 1.34 million acres of the state's total of 6 million acres are devoted to agriculture. The farmhouse and barn are still a symbol of Vermont, and a Vermont vacation should include a farm visit, whether to buy syrup, cheese, wool, or wine, maybe to pick apples or berries, tour the dairy operation, or to stay for a night or a week. Finding farms can be an excuse to explore unexpectedly beautiful backcountry.

Of course a "farm" isn't what it used to be. Just 1,525 of Vermont's 6,800 farms are now dairy, compared with 10,000 dairy farms 40 years ago. Even so, the average size of dairy herds has increased: With just 15 percent as many dairy farms, the state produces more than twice as much milk as it did 45 years ago. Vermont farms today are more likely to raise goats or llamas, beef cattle or sheep, not to mention Christmas trees and flowers, vegetables, fruit, or trout. Bear in mind that before cows, there were sheep. In the 1830s and '40s, meadowland was far more extensive, and was populated by millions of sheep. When the Civil War ended, so did the push for wool blankets, and a significant number of sheep farms were wiped out. Luckily railroads were expanding to every corner of the state in the 1870s, and railroad companies teamed up with state agriculture departments to promote farms to "summer boarders."

Now farmers are once again looking to visitors as well as to new forms of agriculture to maintain their farms. Within "What's Where" we suggest how to find a variety of agricultural

Robert Eddy

products, from apples to wine. Request a packet of brochures from the Vermont Agency of Agriculture (802-828-2416; 116 State Street, Drawer 20, Montpelier 05620-2901; www.vermontagriculture.com) or contact the Vermont Farms! Association (www.vermontfarms.org; 1-888-892-6748).

The **Champlain Valley Exposition** (www.cvfair.com) in Essex (lasting an entire week around Labor Day) is by far the state's largest agricultural fair. **Addison County Fair and Field Days** in early August in New Haven, as well as the **Orleans County Fair** in Barton (5 days in mid-August) and the **Caledonia County Fair,** always the following weekend in nearby Lyndonville, all feature ox, pony, and horse pulling as well as a midway, live entertainment, and plenty to please all ages. The **Bondville Fair** (2 days in late August) in southern Vermont is also the genuine thing, the **Vermont State Fair** (802-775-5200) in Rutland (9 days in early September) is big, and the **Tunbridge World's Fair** (4 days in mid-September) is the oldest and most colorful of them all (www.tunbridgefair.com). See also in this chapter *Apples, Cheese, Christmas Trees, Farmer's Markets, Farms Open to the Public, Farm Stays, Gardens, Maple Sugaring, Pick Your Own, Sheep and Wool,* and *Wine.*

AIR SERVICE **Burlington International Airport** (802-863-1889) currently offers most of the scheduled (largely commuter) service in Vermont. Carriers include: **Delta Express** (1-800-221-1212), **Continental Express** (1-800-525-0280), **Northwest Airlink** (1-800-

225-2525), **JetBlue** (1-800-538-2583) with reasonable fares to New York's JFK International Airport, **United Airlines** (1-800-241-6522), connecting with most U.S. points via Chicago, and **USAirways Express** (1-800-428-4322), which also serves **Rutland State Airport** and **Lebanon Regional Airport** (603-298-8878), in New Hampshire just across the river from White River Junction. **Bradley International Airport** in Windsor Locks, Connecticut, is served by major carriers and handy to much of central and southern Vermont (www.bradleyairport.com), while busy **Albany Airport** (www.albanyairport.com) in New York is convenient for much of the western part of the state. **Manchester (New Hampshire) Airport** (www.flymanchester.com) is the largest airport in northern New England, with many domestic and some international flights.

AIRPORTS Click on www.vermontair ports.com for details about Vermont's 17 public-use airports, just two (see above) with scheduled flights but all accessible to private and some to charter planes. Request a copy of the *Vermont Airport Directory* from the Vermont Agency of Transportation (802-828-5754).

AMTRAK Amtrak service (1-800-USA-RAIL; www.amtrak.com) has improved dramatically in recent years. Amtrak's **Vermonter** runs from Washington to Montreal with stops (at decent hours both north- and southbound) in Brattleboro, Bellows Falls, Claremont (New Hampshire), Windsor, White River Junction, Randolph, Montpelier, Waterbury, Burlington, and St. Albans. The **Adirondack** runs up the western shore of Lake Champlain en route from Manhattan to Montreal and stops at Port Kent, New York, across from the ferry to Burlington. The **Ethan Allen Express** connects Rutland with New York City (with special weekend ski-season runs and bus shuttles to Killington and Okemo) and Albany. All Vermont trains carry bicycles and skis in the baggage car.

ANTIQUARIAN BOOKSELLERS The **Vermont Antiquarian Booksellers Association** (VABA; www.valley .net/~vaba) publishes a pamphlet list of its more than 50 member stores, available in those stores.

ANTIQUING A pamphlet guide, *Antiquing in Vermont,* listing more than 120 members of the Vermont Antiques Dealers' Association (www.vermontada.com), is available by sending a double-stamped, self-addressed, business-sized envelope to Elizabeth Harley—VADA, 88 Reading Farms Road, Reading 05062. The association sponsors an **annual antiques show** in September. Major concentrations of dealers can be found in Bennington, Burlington, Dorset, Manchester, Middlebury, Woodstock, and along Route 30 in the West River Valley. The **Weston Antiques Fair,** usually the first weekend in October, is the state's oldest and still one of its best. The state's largest group dealers are in Quechee and East Barre.

APPLES During fall harvest season the demand is not only for bushel baskets already filled with apples but also for an empty basket and the chance to climb a ladder and fill it with the many varieties of apples grown in Vermont—primarily in the

Champlain Islands, the Champlain Valley around Shoreham, and the lower Connecticut River Valley between Springfield and Brattleboro. Listings of orchards can be found under descriptions of these areas in this book and by requesting a map/guide to farms from the Vermont Apple Marketing Board (www.ver montapples.org) through the Agency of Agriculture (802-828-2416; 116 State Street, Montpelier 05620-2901). From the earliest days of settlement through the mid-1800s more apples, it's said, were used for making hard cider and brandy than for eating and cooking. In 1810 some 125 distilleries were producing more than 173,000 gallons of apple brandy annually. Today wineries and cideries are once more making apple wines (see *Wine*).

ART GALLERIES Vermont's principal collections of art (painting, sculpture, and decorative arts) are found in the **Bennington Museum** (www.ben ningtonmuseum.com; works by Grandma Moses); the **Robert Hull Fleming Museum** at the University of Vermont, Burlington; the **Middlebury College Museum of Art;** the **St. Johnsbury Athenaeum**

Christina Tree

and Art Gallery (www.stj athenaeum.org); the **Shelburne Museum** (www.shelburnemuseum .org) in Shelburne; the **Chaffee Art Gallery,** Rutland; the **Southern Vermont Arts Center** (www.svac.org), Manchester; the **Thomas Waterman Wood Art Gallery,** Montpelier; the **Helen Day Art Center** in Stowe; the **Chester Art Guild** in Chester; and the **Chandler Gallery** in Randolph. Brattleboro, Manchester, Woodstock, and Bellows Falls offer an unusual number of private galleries. Burlington and Brattleboro sponsor open gallery tours the first Friday of every month; Bellows Falls, on the last Friday. The Vermont Museum & Gallery Alliance maintains an excellent web site: www.vmga.org.

ARTS COUNCILS Vermont's local arts councils organize films, festivals, and concerts throughout the year. Those listed here are the largest and sources of cultural happenings in their areas: **Arts Council of Windham County,** Brattleboro (802-257-1881); **Catamount Arts** (802-748-2600; www.catamountarts.com) in St. Johnsbury; **Crossroads Arts Council,** Rutland (802-775-5413); **Onion River Arts Council,** Montpelier (802-229-9408); **Pentangle Council on the Arts,** Woodstock (802-457-3981; www.pen tanglearts.org). The overall information source is the **Vermont Arts Council** (802-828-3291; 136 State Street, Montpelier 05633-6001; www.vermontartscouncil.org).

AUCTIONS Most major upcoming auctions are announced in the Thursday edition of Vermont news papers, with a listing of items that will be up for bid. Auctions may be scheduled at any time, however, during summer months, advertised primarily on local bulletin boards and in shop windows. Among well-known auctioneers and auction houses: **William Dupras** of Randolph Center; **Butch Sutherland,** Woodstock; **C. W. Gray** of East Thetford, every Monday night, year-round (livestock); and **Arthur Hicks,** Hicks' Commission Sales, Morrisville.

BALLOONING Year-round flights are offered by **Balloons of Vermont** (802-291-4887), based in Quechee; inquire, too, at the **Stoweflake Resort** in Stowe (802-253-7355). Ascents are also offered by **Brian Boland** at Post Mills Airport (802-333-4883) and **Balloons Over New England** (1-800-788-5562). The **Annual Balloon Festival** in Quechee is held in June during Father's Day weekend.

BARNS Many barns along the highways and byways have distinctive touches, such as ornate Victorian cupolas, and still more are connected to farmhouses in the "extended" architectural style that served as shelter for the farmers' trips before dawn in deep snow. Just a dozen round barns survive in Vermont, all built between 1899 and World War I. The concept of the round barn is thought to have originated with the Shakers in Hancock, Massachusetts, where the original stone barn, built in 1824, is now the centerpiece of a museum. The Vermont survivors include: the **Moore barn** in East Barnet; the **Hastings barn** in Waterford; the **Metcalf barn** (Robillard Flats) in Irasburg; the **Parker barn** in Grand Isle, converted into a housing center for the elderly; two barns in Coventry; the **Powers barn** in Lowell; the **Parker barn** in North Troy; one in Enosburg Falls; and **Southwick's** in East Calais. In Waitsfield the **Joslin round barn** is now a cultural center with a swimming pool in its bowels, attached to the **Inn at Round Barn Farm;** in Strafford the **Round Barn Farm,** a 350-acre working dairy farm, takes guests. Round-barn addicts should check at local general stores for exact location and to secure permission to photograph the structures. Among other Vermont barns open to the public are the vast, five-story, 416-foot-long, Norman-style **Farm Barn** and the impressive stable and coach barn at Shelburne Farms in Shelburne. The round barn once in Passumpsic has been moved to the Shelburne Museum. Two lively, illustrated guides are *A Field Guide to New England Barns and Farm Buildings* by Thomas Visser and *Big House, Little House, Back House, Barn: The Connected Farm Buildings of New England* by Thomas Hubka (both from the University Press of New England).

BED & BREAKFASTS The hundreds of B&Bs we have personally inspected are listed under their respective locations in this book; they range from working farms to historic mansions, $55–350 per room.

BICYCLE TOURING In Vermont the distance via back roads from swimming hole to antiques shop to the next inn is never far. John Freidin, author of *25 Bicycle Tours in Vermont* (Backcountry Guides), introduced the whole notion of guided bike tours for adults back in 1972. Woodstock-based **Bike Vermont** (1-800-257-2226;

VBT

www.bikevt.com) is now by far the state's largest, most respected inn-to-inn tour outfitter, offering a "sag wagon," renting 21-gear hybrid bikes, specializing in small (under 20) groups and a wide variety of Vermont destinations. Guided camping tours (with a sag wagon) are offered by **POMG (Peace of Mind Guaranteed) Bike Tours of Vermont** (802-434-2270; www.pomgbike.com). **Vermont Bicycle Touring** (1-800-245-3868; www.vbt.com) offers inn-to-inn biking tours to several destinations. **Cycle-Inn-Vermont** (802-228-8799; Box 243, Ludlow 05149) is an association of innkeepers whose establishments are a comfortable bike ride from each other. Participants are largely on their own, but rental equipment is available and baggage is transferred from inn to inn.

Bicycle paths continue to grow and multiply in Vermont. Stowe's **"Rec" Path** (5.3 miles) and easy rentals make it an ideal place to sample the sport. The **Burlington Bike Path** follows the shore of Lake Champlain for 8 miles (rentals available); from South Burlington there's another 15 miles. The 26-mile **Missisquoi Rail Trail** follows an old railbed from St. Albans to Richford; the **Bennington Historic Bike Route** leads bikers around local sights; and the 34-mile **D&H Recreation Trail** follows an abandoned railroad bed almost 20 miles from Castleton to West Rupert, with the remainder in New York State. Within each chapter we have described sources for local bike rentals. Note that many inns and outfitters offer shuttle service from Amtrak stops. See also *Mountain Biking*.

BIRDING While the hermit thrush, the state bird, is reclusive and not too easy to spot, Vermont offers ample opportunities for observing herons and ducks, as well as raptors like owls, hawks, falcons, ospreys, even bald eagles. It's home to more than 240 species of birds. Outstanding birding areas include the **Missisquoi National Wildlife Refuge** (802-868-4781) in Swanton, the **Dead Creek Wildlife Refuge** (802-759-2398) in Vergennes, and the 4,970-acre **Victory Basin** east of St. Johnsbury. The 255-acre **Green Mountain Audubon Nature Center** in ·Huntington (802-434-3068) is open year-round; inquire about guided walks and special programs (www.the compass.com/audubon). The neighboring **Birds of Vermont Museum** (802-434-2167) in Huntington is well worth checking out, an exceptionally well-mounted display (in their natural habitats) of lifelike carvings of over 200 species, showing both male and female plumage, all the work of master carver Bob Spear of Colchester. The **Vermont Institute of Natural Science (VINS)** has a new nature center beside Quechee Gorge (802-457-2779) that's open year-round, with owls, hawks, eagles, and other raptors in residence and a full program of naturalist walks and flight programs.

BOATING A booklet, *Laws and Regulations Governing the Use and Registration of Motorboats,* is available from the Vermont State Police, Marine Division, in Williston (802-878-7111). Click onto www.boatsafe .com/vermont. (See also *Canoeing and Kayaking, Connecticut River,* and *Whitewater.*)

BOAT EXCURSIONS If you don't own a yacht, there are still plenty of ways to get onto Vermont rivers and lakes. Possible excursions include the ***Belle of Brattleboro*** (802-254-1263; www.belleofbrattleboro.com), which plies the Connecticut from Brattleboro, and **Peacemaker Cruises** (603-445-2371), which sails a scenic reach of the river above Bellows Falls; the ***Spirit of Ethan Allen II*** (802-862-8300), an excursion vessel based in Burlington; the ***M/V Carillon*** (802-897-5331), which offers narrated cruises from Larrabees Point in Shoreham up and down Lake Champlain near Fort Ticonderoga; and the ***M/V Mountain Mills*** (802-464-2975), which sails on Lake Whitingham. For details, check under respective locations in this book. See also *Ferries.*

BOOKS In addition to the books we mention in specific fields or on particular subjects, here are some of the most useful current titles: *The Vermont Atlas and Gazetteer* (DeLorme); and *Vermont Place Names: Footprints in History*, by Esther Swift (Vermont Historical Society). *The Roadside History of Vermont*, by Peter Jennison (Mountain Press), is an informal narrative of what happened where and when along main travel routes. *Hands on the Land: A History of the Vermont Landscape*, by Jan Albers, published by the MIT Press for The Orton Family Foundation, is also essential reading for anyone truly interested in understanding why Vermont looks the way it does. Lovers of natural history should seek out *The Nature of Vermont* by Charles Johnson (University Press of New England). For children, *Vermont: The State with the Storybook Past*, by Cora Cheney (New England Press), is the best. A basic reference directory is *The Vermont Yearbook*, published by the National Survey, Chester. Civil War buffs will be rewarded by Howard Coffin's *Full Duty: Vermonters in the Civil War; Nine Months to Gettysburg: Stannard's Vermonters and the Repulse of Pickett's Charge;* and *The Battered Stars: One State's Civil War Ordeal During Grant's Overland Campaign* (all The Countryman Press).

Our favorite current Vermont fiction writer is unquestionably Howard Frank Mosher of Irasburg, whose evocative novels include *Disappearances, Northern Borders, Where the Rivers Flow North,* and *A Stranger in the Kingdom;* the last two are now also films. Joseph Citro is the author of several books about occult occurrences and ghost stories in the state, including *Green Mountains, Dark Tales* (University Press of New England). The Brattleboro-based mysteries of Archer Mayor, including *Open Season* and other titles in his Joe Gunther police-procedural series, are gaining momentum. And look for the charming little *Art of the State: Vermont* by Suzanne Mantell (Abrams). For a charming narrative guide to some off-the-beaten-path attractions, seek out *Off the Leash: Subversive Journeys around Vermont* by Helen Husher (The Countryman Press). *Northeastern Wilds* (AMC books), by Stephen Gorman, features stunning photography and includes informative text about Vermont's segment of the Northern Forest.

BREWERIES Civil War–era Vermont was New England's leading hops-producing state; in the United States only New York surpassed its production. In the late 19th century, however, temperance movements and other factors virtually eliminated its beer and wine industries. But Vermont brewing is back. Check out www .vermontbrewers.com. **Magic Hat**

Kim Grant

Brewing Co. (802-558-BREW) in South Burlington, **Harpoon Brewery** (1-888-HARPOON) in Windsor, and **Otter Creek Brewing** (1-800-473-0727) in Middlebury offer tours and tastings, while **Black River Brewing** (802-228-3100) in Ludlow, **Long Trail Brewing** (802-672-5011) in West Bridgewater, **McNeil's Brewery** (802-257-9102) in Brattleboro, **Jasper Murdock's Alehouse** at the Norwich Inn (802-649-1143), **The Shed** (802-253-9311) in Stowe, and **Trout River Brewing Co.** (802-626-3984) in Lyndonville all serve their own brews. **Rock Art Brewery** (802-635-9758) in Johnson welcomes visitors by appointment.

BUS SERVICE Vermont Transit. For a current timetable, contact Vermont Transit Co., Inc. (802-864-6811; in New England: 1-800-451-3292, but within Vermont 1-800-642-3133; 106 Main Street, Burlington 05401; www.vttransit.com). Outside New England contact Greyhound. The major routes are (1) up the western side of the state from New York City and Albany via Bennington, Rutland, and Burlington to Montreal; (2) from Boston via White River Junction and Burlington to Montreal; you can connect to St. Johnsbury and Newport. Read the timetable carefully, and you will find that most corners of the state of Vermont—and a number elsewhere in northern New England—are served. Inquire about service to and from the Manchester (New Hampshire) Airport. Children under 12 travel at half price; one child under 5 can travel free. The 345 Pine Street terminal in Burlington offers ample parking but is not downtown. At this writing the Montpelier terminal is a battered trailer off State Street. *Note:* A passport is required to cross into Canada by bus.

CAMPS, FOR CHILDREN For information about more than 50 Vermont summer camps for boys and girls, contact the **Vermont Camping Association** (1-888-VTCAMPS; www.vermontcamps.org).

CAMPGROUNDS A *Vermont Campground Guide* advertising more than 70 private campgrounds and describing more than 30 state park campgrounds is published by the Vermont Campground Association (www.campvermont.com) and is available from the Vermont Department of Tourism (1-800-VERMONT). A handy Vermont state parks descriptive listing is available from Vermont State Parks (802-241-3655), 103 South Main Street, 10 South, Waterbury 05671-0501. Their web site (www.vtstateparks.com) is excellent, describing each park in detail with maps of the camping areas. State facilities include furnished cottages, unfurnished cabins, lean-tos, and tent and trailer sites. Fees vary with the class of the area; in 2004 the range is $14–23, with cottages available on a weekly basis. Reservations can be made up to 11 months in advance. Phone weekdays, 9–4: 802-479-4280 or 1-888-409-7579; within this book each park is described as it appears geographically. Vermont state park campsites are all screened by trees from neighboring sites and are well maintained. Many offer organized programs such as hikes, campfire sings, films, and lectures. Most parks are relatively uncrowded, especially midweek; the most popular parks are Branbury, Stillwater, Groton Forest, Quechee Gorge, and Lake St. Catherine.

There are nine designated campsites within the 300,000-acre **Green Mountain National Forest** (sites are available on a first-come, first-served basis for a maximum 14-day period at a modest charge). Camping is also permitted, without fee or prior permission, but before you pitch your tent visit one of the district ranger offices; see *Green Mountain National Forest.* The U.S. Army Corps of Engineers, New England Division, maintains more than 100 campsites near flush toilets, showers, and swimming at Ball Mountain Lake in Jamaica; for details phone 802-874-4881.

CANOEING AND KAYAKING

Organized canoe and kayaking trips have increased in recent years. **BattenKill Canoe** (1-800-421-5268) in Arlington offers day trips and inn-to-inn tours throughout the state; **Clearwater Sports** (802-496-2708) in Waitsfield offers guided tours, instruction, and special expeditions, as does **Umiak Outdoor Outfitters** (802-253-2317) in Stowe. **Vermont Canoe Touring Center** (802-257-5008) in Brattleboro offers canoe rentals, shuttle service, and river

VDT

camping on the Connecticut, just as **North Star Canoes** (603-542-5802), based in Cornish, New Hampshire, does for the scenic reach above the covered bridge, one particularly rich in camping spots (see "Upper Connecticut Valley"). **Wilderness Trails** (802-295-7620) in Quechee offers similar trips on the neighboring stretch of the river, also on nearby ponds and on the White River. The stretch of the Lamoille River around Jeffersonville is served both by **Smugglers' Notch Canoe Touring,** based at the Mannsview Inn (1-800-937-6266), and by **Green River Canoe** (802-644-8336), based at Smugglers' Notch Resort.

Fish Vermont, a map/guide free from the Vermont Fish and Wildlife Department (802-241-3700; 1-800-837-6668; 103 South Main Street, 10 South, Waterbury 05671-0501), notes ponds, lakes, and put-in places. A *Winooski River Canoe Guide* is $3.95 if you pick it up; $4.95 by mail from the Winooski Valley Park District, Ethan Allen Homestead, Burlington 05401. Recommended books: Roioli Schweiker's third edition of *Canoe Camping Vermont and New Hampshire Rivers* (Backcountry Guides) is a handy guide, and the *AMC River Guide: Vermont/New Hampshire* (AMC Books) is good for detailed information on canoeable rivers. (See also *Connecticut River* and *Whitewater.*)

CANOE AND KAYAK RENTALS

Rentals are available from the canoe outfitters listed above and from the boat rental sources described in each chapter.

CATAMOUNT TRAIL You may not want to ski the 300 miles from

Massachusetts to Canada, but it's nice to know that you can—along the longest cross-country ski trail in this country. Since 1984, when three young skiers bushwhacked their way the length of Vermont, the Catamount Trail has been evolving. The nonprofit Catamount Trail Association (CTA) now numbers almost 1,600 members. Over the years countless permits and dozens of easements have secured use of private and public lands. Bridges have been built, trailhead parking created, and a newly updated 8th edition of *The Catamount Trail Guidebook* ($18.95) maps and describes each of the trail's 31 segments. The excellent web site includes a "trip planning" section with suggested places to stay along the way. Contact the CTA at 802-864-5794; 1 Main Street, Suite 308A, Burlington 05401. Members receive a regular newsletter and discounts at participating touring centers. Also see *Skiing, Cross-Country.*

CHEESE In recent years Vermont's production of cheese has increased to more than 100 million pounds annually and has become more varied, with sheep and goat as well as cow cheeses winning top national and international honors. Check out all the following producers on Vermont Cheese Council's informative web site, www.vtcheese.com. Of course a century ago most Vermont towns had a cheesemaker to which farmers brought the day's surplus milk. **Crowley Cheese** (802-259-2340; 1-800-683-2602), established in 1882 and billed as "the oldest continuously operated cheese factory in the U.S.," is the only survivor of this era, and welcomes visitors to its wooden factory just west of Ludlow on Route

103 in Healdville (open weekdays 8–4; store open daily). This distinctive cheese is creamier than cheddar and still made the traditional way. **Cabot Creamery** (802-563-2231) in Cabot is the state's biggest, most famous producer, with a modern plant turning out 12 million pounds of cheese a year. It includes a visitors center (open daily, year-round) and offers plant tours; it also operates an annex in Waterbury Center, south of Stowe. Cabot continues to maintain quality as well as quantity.

Award-winning **Vermont Shepherd Cheese** (802-387-4473), a rich, tangy sheep's milk cheese from Westminster, opens its "cave" to visitors at certain times (call); the nearby **Westminster Dairy** at Livewater Farm (a variety of delicious hard and soft cow cheeses) is open daily 7–7. **Grafton Village Cheese Company** (1-800-472-3866) in Grafton had its beginnings around 1890 and was resurrected by the Windham Foundation in 1966; visitors view the cheesemaking from outside, through a picture window. The **Plymouth Cheese Company** (802-672-3650) was founded in 1890 by Colonel John Coolidge, father of President Coolidge, and at this writing plans to soon resume producing its old-fashioned

Kim Grant

Vermont granular curd cheese. The **Taylor Farm** (802-824-5690) in Londonderry (southern Vermont) is making a reputation with its Gouda, and **Woodcock Farm** in Weston has won top national honors for its European-style sheep cheese. Also in southern Vermont **Peaked Hill Farm** in Townshend welcomes visitors at convenient times. In Randolph Center, minutes off I-89 exit 4 at **Neighborly Farms** (802-728-4700), you can walk down a hallway and view cows on one side and cheesemaking on the other (open Monday through Saturday, 10–5). **Vermont Butter & Cheese Company** in Websterville makes a wide variety of tantalizing goat cheeses, and **Blythedale Farm** (802-439-6575) in Corinth produces a variety of soft cheeses (a fine Vermont Brie, a Camembert, a Green Mountain Gruyère, and Jersey Blue), but neither is open to visitors. **Sugarbush Farm** (802-457-1757), set high on a hill in Woodstock, smokes and packages several varieties of cheddar cheese and welcomes visitors.

At **Shelburne Farms** (802-985-8686; open daily, year-round), in Shelburne near Burlington, prize-winning cheddar is made from the milk of a single herd of Brown Swiss cows. In New Haven, **Orb Weaver Farm** (802-877-3755) produces a creamy, aged, Colby-type cheese made in small batches, entirely by hand (available in 2-pound wheels and 1-pound waxed wedges). In the northwest corner of the state goat cheese is made at **Willow Hill Farm** (802-893-2963) in Milton and at **Lakes End Cheeses** (802-796-3730) in Alburg. In nearby Highgate Center visitors are welcome at **Green Mountain Blue Cheese** (802-868-

4193). Also see *The Cheeses of Vermont: A Gourmet Guide to Vermont's Artisanal Cheesemakers*, by Henry Tewksbury (The Countryman Press), which includes a map of cheesemakers that welcome visitors.

CHILDREN, ESPECIALLY FOR Look for the ✿ symbol throughout this book; it designates child-friendly attractions as well as lodging and dining. Alpine slides delight children of all ages at **Bromley** (where there is also a DévalKart Ride), and **Pig Dog's Fun Park** (www.bromley.com) as well as **Stowe** (www.stowe.com) and at Pico, part of the **Killington/ Pico Adventure Center** (www .killington.com) that includes water slides, a climbing wall, an in-line skate park, mountain biking, guided hikes, and more. Alpine lifts, which operate in summer, are also a way of hoisting small legs and feet to the top of some of Vermont's most spectacular summits. In Stowe **Mount Mansfield,** Vermont's highest peak, and **Killington Peak,** second highest in the state, are accessible via gondola on weekdays. **Jay Peak,** commanding as dramatic a view as the others, is accessible on aerial tram (www.jaypeak resort.com). In southern Vermont, **Stratton**'s gondola runs daily all summer and fall.

Santa's Land in Putney is the only commercial attraction geared specifically to children.

The **Shelburne Museum** (www.shelburnemuseum.org) has many exhibits that please youngsters, as does the **Fairbanks Museum and Planetarium** (www.fairbanks museum.org), St. Johnsbury, which is filled with stuffed animals, birds, and exhibits from near and far. The **Montshire Museum of Science**

Kim Grant

and Fairs, Farms Open to the Public, Farm Stays, Boat Excursions, and *Railroad Excursions.*)

CHRISTMAS TREES Christmas tree farms are plentiful throughout the state and most open after Thanksgiving, inviting customers to come tag the tree they want, leaving it to cut until the last moment. Check the Vermont Agency of Agriculture web site, www.vermontagriculture .com, for a listing of growers and www.vermontfarms.org for a list of the more imaginative marketers. These include **Redrock Farm** (1-866-685-4343; www.christmas-trees.net) in Chelsea, and **Elysian Hills** (802-257-0233; www.elysian hillsfarm.com) in Dummerston, where you can pick out a tree in summer or fall and have it shipped to you at Christmas anywhere in the continental United States the day it's cut. (If you do this, judging from our own experience, schedule delivery for the beginning of the week and at least a week before Christmas.) In recent years bed & breakfasts and inns have teamed up with farms to offer preholiday lodging packages that include a fresh Christmas tree (contact the Vermont Chamber of Commerce: 802-223-3443; www.vtchamber.com). For a do-it-yourself experience, contact the Green Mountain National Forest Service in Rochester (802-767-4261) and inquire about tagged trees you can cut for a nominal fee.

CIVIL UNIONS In the first year (2001) that Vermont sanctioned civil unions between couples of the same sex, 2,479 such ceremonies were performed, with almost twice as many females as males taking vows. Only 479 couples were from Vermont. The

(www.montshire.org) in Norwich is a real standout, with hands-on exhibits explaining many basic scientific mysteries plus a 2-acre outdoor exhibit inviting plenty of water experiments (bring a towel) and a beautiful riverside walk. **ECHO at the Leahy Center for Lake Champlain** (www.echocenter.org) is a new science center and aquarium featuring 2,200 live fish, amphibians, and reptiles with hands-on exhibits for kids 3 through 17. The **Billings Farm & Museum** (www.billingsfarm.org) and **Vermont Institute of Natural Science** (www.vinsweb.org), both in Woodstock, are child pleasers.

Over the past few years, as ski areas have come to compete for family business, most ski resorts have developed special programs for children; see the description for each ski area in the text. In summer a number of ski areas, notably **Smugglers' Notch** (www.smuggs.com), offer full day-camp programs for children. The **Tyler Place Family Resort** (802-868-4000) in Highgate Springs and the **Basin Harbor Club** (www.basin harbor.com) in Vergennes are family-geared resorts with children's programs. (See also *Agricultural Facts* post office in the central Vermont village of Gaysville has become a favorite venue for wedding pictures. Throughout this guide, we indicate venues that specialize in weddings and civil unions with the wedding-ring symbol ⚭.

COLLEGES For information about all the state's colleges and universities, contact the **Vermont Higher Education Council** (802-878-7466; P.O. Box 47, Essex Junction 05453-0047; www.vtcolleges.org). Also check out the **Association of Vermont Independent Colleges** web site: www.Vermont-icolleges.org.

CONNECTICUT RIVER New England's longest river rises near the Canadian–New Hampshire border and forms the border between that state and Vermont for some 255 miles. Not far below its source, it has been dammed into a series of lakes: five in New Hampshire's North Country above Pittsburg and two, Moore and Comerford Reservoirs, near St. Johnsbury. The 145 miles between Barnet and Brattleboro is punctuated by six dams, each creating deep pools that turn the river into a series of placid, narrow lakes. Check out the Brattleboro, Bellows Falls, and Upper Valley chapters for canoe and kayak rentals and boat excursions. *Boating on the Connecticut River* is a detailed guide available by sending a self-addressed envelope to the Connecticut River Scenic Byway Council (603-826-4800; P.O. Box 1182, Charlestown, NH 03603). The commission also maintains an excellent web site, www.ctrivertravel.net.

COVERED BRIDGES The state's 110 surviving covered bridges are marked

WOODSTOCK

Kim Grant

on the official state map, on our maps, and are described in the appropriate chapters of this book under *To See*. Bridge buffs should secure a copy of *Covered Bridges of Vermont* by Ed Barna (The Countryman Press). The new **Vermont Covered Bridge Museum** in Bennington features a theater production, dioramas, interactive exhibits, and a covered railroad with covered railroad bridges (www.vermontartscenter.org).

CRAFTS More than 1,500 Vermonters make their living from crafts. There are also more than 100 retail crafts venues in the state, ranging from local shops to fine galleries. The dazzling **Vermont State Craft Center** at Frog Hollow in Middlebury and its branch stores in Manchester and Burlington each has its own educational program. The new **Vermont State Craft Gallery** in Windsor is well worth checking out. Crafters also sell their wares at frequent events, ranging from farmer's markets and church bazaars to juried crafts shows and festivals. Within this book we have described outstanding local crafts studios, galleries, and shops as they appear geographically and have also included major crafts festivals. Best of all is the **Open Studio Weekend,** held annually Memorial Day weekend, with more than 200 artisans in almost as many locations. Request a copy of the *Vermont Crafts Studio Tour Map,* available at information centers and on request from the Vermont Crafts Council (802-223-3380; P.O. Box 938, 104 Main Street, Montpelier 05601-0938; www.vermontcrafts.com).

CUSTOMS INFORMATION Vermont shares a 90.3-mile border with the Canadian province of Quebec. Since September 11 all border crossings have become far more strict; even in Derby Line (Vermont), where it's tempting to walk the few steps into Stanstead (Quebec) to a restaurant, repercussions can be serious. Travelers other than American or Canadian must present a valid tourist visa, and pets are required to have a veterinarian's certificate showing a recent vaccination against rabies. For detailed information contact the U.S. Customs District Office in St. Albans (802-524-6527), in Montreal (514-636-3875), or in Toronto (416-676-2606).

DINERS Vermont will not disappoint diner buffs. Hearty meals at reasonable prices can be found at the **Miss Newport** (good coffee), East Main Street, Newport; and at **Henry's Diner** (known for its Yankee pot roast, lobster roll, and generally good three squares) and the **Oasis,** both on Bank Street, Burlington. **Libby's Blue Line Diner,** Route 7 (just off I-89, exit 16), Colchester, is upscale and popular (you might dine on an eggplant burger). The **Parkway Diner** at 1696 Williston Road, South Burlington, is known for its Greek salad, lobster roll, and Parkway Special: roast beef on a pumpernickel roll. **Halfway House** on Route 22A, a few miles north of Shoreham Village, a local gathering spot, is open 5 AM–8 PM daily. The **Miss Lyndonville Diner** on Bond Street, Lyndonville, is admired for its pies (a breakfast special) and has been augmented by the nearby **Miss Vermont** (Route 5, St. Johnsbury Center), though lines are still long on Sunday morning. **Anthony's Restaurant** on Railroad Street in St. Johnsbury has expanded and is wheelchair accessible but still offers great food at great prices.

Just off 1-91 in Wells River the **P&H Truck Stop** is open 24 hours, 7 days a week, serving large, reasonably priced diner food quickly and cheaply. The **Wayside Restaurant and Bakery** (exit 7; follow signs for Route 302 and it's on your left) south of Montpelier, open 6:30 AM–9:30 PM daily, has expanded gradually over the years to become Vermont's ultimate family restaurant. **The Farmer's Diner,** 240 North Main Street in Barre, specializes in locally-grown food. **Blue Benn Diner,** 102 Hunt Street in Bennington, serves imaginative vegetarian as well as standard diner fare. Add to these the **Farina Family Diner,** Route 4 in Quechee Gorge Village; **Green Mountain Diner,** Main Street in Barre; **Cindy's Diner,** St. Albans; and **Don's Diner,** Bennington.

T. J. Buckley's in Brattleboro may look like the battered vintage Worcester diner it is, but inside oak paneling gleams and the fare (dinner only, and only by reservation) is recognized as some of the best in the state. West Brattleboro also offers the **Chelsea Royal Diner,** west on Route 9, which, while a bit heavy on diner decor, is still a good family bet (wheelchair accessible). In Chester there is the **Country Girl Diner. Miss Bellows Falls Diner** is on the National Register of Historic Places; the equally historic **Windsor Diner** has been nicely restored, and the **Fairlee Diner** in Fairlee is the real thing. The state's newest addition is the **Springfield Royal Diner and Precision Valley Corvette Museum,** a 1955 diner that stood in Kingston, New York, until the chrome classic was moved to Springfield in 2003 and a showroom filled with vintage Corvettes was tacked on. The food is great. Check these establishments out in their respective chapters. (Also see *Highway Roadfood.*)

EMERGENCIES Try **911** first. This simple SOS has finally reached most corners of Vermont. Within this book we have furnished the number of the medical facilities serving each area in each chapter. For state police phone 802-655-3435, for poison 802-658-3456, and for dental emergencies 1-800-640-5099.

EQUESTRIAN SPORTS Horses have become nearly as much a part of the Vermont landscape as the famous black-and-white Holsteins, and a dedicated equine aficionado can find plenty to see from late spring well into fall. At the moment Vermont has three polo clubs: **Sugarbush Polo**

Leight Johnson

Club (802-496-8938), based in the Mad River Valley and Middlebury; **Green Mountain Polo Club** (Hildene: 802-362-1788), near Manchester; and **Quechee Polo Club** (802-295-7900). All hold games on Saturday and Sunday during summer (usually at 1 PM); most games are free. The **Vermont Summer Horse Festival** (www.vermonthorse.org), the largest of several hunter-jumper shows around the state, takes place at the Harold Beebe Farm in East Dorset from early July through early August. The **Vermont Quarter Horse Association** (whinny.org/horseshow) hosts shows around the region in summer. The VQHA season begins the first weekend of June at the Tunbridge Fairgrounds in Tunbridge. The **Green Mountain Horse Association** in South Woodstock holds **Dressage Days** in mid-July; see www.usdf.org/calendars for a complete list of dressage events. One of the newest equine activities to hit Vermont is driving. Pleasure-driving events are recommended for spectators; the web site is www.americandrivingsociety.org.

EVENTS Almost every day of the year some special event is happening somewhere in Vermont. Usually it's something relatively small and friendly like a church supper, contra dance, community theatrical production, concert, or crafts fair. We have worked up our own *Special Events* for each region, and listings can also be found in various ways on the state's travel web site, www.vermontvacation .com. Still, many of the best events are like fireflies, surfacing only on local bulletin boards and in the Thursday editions of local papers. In Burlington check out the free and fat *Seven Days,* a funky weekly listing of local arts and entertainment, available everywhere in town.

FACTORY OUTLETS Within the book we have mentioned only a small fraction of the factory outlets of which we are aware. Our bias has been to favor distinctly made-in-Vermont products. Among our favorites: **Johnson Woolen Mills** (outstanding wool clothing for all ages) in Johnson; **Bennington Potters** (dinnerware, planters, and more) in Bennington and Burlington; **Vermont Marble** in Proctor; and **Weston Bowl Mill** in Weston. **Townshend Furniture** in Townshend is a long-established furniture factory worth checking, and **Shackleton Furniture** in Bridgewater, **Pompanoosuc Mills** in East Thetford, and **Copeland Furniture** in Bradford all sell seconds in their workshops. Manchester is known for its concentration of outlet stores specializing in quality clothing. **Simon Pearce** in Quechee and Windsor sells seconds of his gorgeous glassware at good prices.

FARMER'S MARKETS From mid-June through early October you can count on finding fresh vegetables, fruit,

honey, and much more at farm prices in commercial centers throughout the state. Click on www.vermontagricul ture.com for a complete list. Major market venues include Burlington, Enosburg, Morrisville, Newport, St. Johnsbury, Norwich, Fair Haven, Middlebury, Montpelier, Rutland, Brattleboro, Manchester, Waterbury, Windsor, and Woodstock.

FARMS OPEN TO THE PUBLIC For a list of farms open to the public for tours, to sell their products, or for farm stays, check out the Vermont Farms! Association web site, www.vermontfarms.org.

FARM STAYS A century ago hundreds of Vermont farms took in visitors for weeks at a time. "There is no crop more profitable than the crop from the city," an 1890s Vermont Board of Agriculture pamphlet proclaimed, a publication noted by Dona Brown in *Inventing New England* (Smithsonian, 1995). Articles advised farmers on how to decorate, what to serve, and generally how to please and what to expect from city guests—much as B&B literature does today. Our own family found a farm stay so enriching that we returned year after year and are happy to see that the phenomenon is on the increase again. Within the book we have listed those farms that we have personally visited. For a list you can click on the Vermont Farms! Association's web site, www.vermontfarms.org.

Maple Crest Farm (802-492-3367) in Shrewsbury deserves special mention because it remains in the same family who have been taking in guests on this working farm since the 1860s. In Rochester **Liberty Hill Farm** (802-767-3926) has pioneered

Kim Grant

the resurgence in farm stays by proving how successful they can be, and **Harvey's Mountain View** (802-767-4273), while no longer a working farm, still welcomes visitors precisely as it has for generations. **Allenholm Farm** (802-372-5566) in South Hero offers a B&B in the midst of a major apple orchard. **Round-Robin Farm** (802-763-7025), way off Sharon's beaten track, and **Emergo Farm Bed and Breakfast** (802-684-2215), on the edge of Danville Village, are also genuine working farms. **Hollister Hill Farm** (802-454-7725) in Marshfield invites guests to participate in sugar making and take home the results of their labors, while **Rooster Ridge Farm** (802-472-8566) in Wolcott, **The Parent Farmhouse** (802-524-4201) in Milton, and **Pie in the Sky** in Marshfield (802-426-3777) are all working farms/B&Bs. At the other extreme is lakeside Shelburne Farms, the state's most elegant farm, also the site of its most elegant inn: the **Inn at Shelburne Farms** (802-985-8686).

FERRIES On Lake Champlain a number of car-carrying ferries ply back and forth between the Vermont and New York shores, offering splendid views of both the Green Mountains and the Adirondacks. The northernmost, the **Plattsburgh Ferry,** crosses from Grand Isle, Vermont, on Route 314 (year-round; 15-minute passage). From Burlington the **Lake Champlain Transportation Co.** services Port Kent, New York (1 hour), and the **Essex Ferry** travels between Charlotte, Vermont, and Essex, New York (20 minutes). All three of these are operated by the Lake Champlain Transportation Company (802-864-9084), descendant of the line founded in 1828 claiming to be "the oldest steamboat company on earth." Near the southern end of the lake, the **Fort Ticonderoga Ferry** (802-897-7999) provides a scenic shortcut between Larrabees Point, Vermont, and Ticonderoga, New York. This small, car-carrying ferry makes the 6-minute crossing continuously between 8 AM and 9 PM during the summer season, less frequently in spring and fall. Service runs from late April through the last Sunday in October. Officially, the Fort Ti Ferry has held the franchise from the New York and Vermont legislatures since 1799.

FIDDLING Vermont is the fiddling capital of the East. Fiddlers include concert violinists, rural carpenters, farmers, and heavy-equipment operators who come from throughout the East to gather in beautiful natural settings. The **Northeast Fiddling Association** (802-728-5188) publishes newsletters that list fiddling meets around the state. Annual fiddling events include the **Crackerbarrel Fiddle Festival,** Newbury, and the **National Championship Fiddle Contest** in Barre, usually the last Friday and Saturday in September.

Fiddle festivals tend to start around noon and end around dusk.

FILM Three Vermont filmmakers have produced some notable low-budget films in recent years. Jay Craven's dramatizations of Howard Frank Mosher's novels—*Where the Rivers Flow North* and *A Stranger in the Kingdom*—are not only good films but evocative of life in the Northeast Kingdom not too long ago. Nora Jacobson's *My Mother's Early Lovers* rings true throughout. By the same token John O'Brien's films, *Vermont Is for Lovers, Man with a Plan,* and *Nosey Parker,* go right to Vermont's still very real rural core. *Man with a Plan* actually launched its hero's real-life political campaign in 1998: To the amazement of the country, retired Tunbridge dairy farmer Fred Tuttle not only defeated a wealthy carpet-bagger for the Republican nomination but won a respectable percentage of the vote for a U.S. senatorial seat. (Sadly, Tuttle died in 2003.)

FISHING Almost every Vermont river and pond, certainly any body of water serious enough to call itself a lake, is stocked with fish and has one or more access areas. Brook trout are the most widely distributed game fish. Visitors ages 15 and over must have a 5-day, a 14-day, or a nonresident license good for a year, available at any town clerk's office, from the local fish and game warden, or from assorted commercial outlets. Because these sources may be closed or time consuming to track down on weekends, it's wise to obtain the license in advance from the **Vermont Fish and Wildlife Department** (802-241-3700; www.vtfishandwildlife.com). Request an application form and ask for a copy of *Vermont Guide to Fishing,* which details every species of fish and where to find it on a map of the state's rivers and streams, ponds, and lakes. Boat access, fish hatcheries, and canoe routes are also noted.

Orvis Company, which has been in the business of making fishing rods and selling them to city people for more than a century, also maintains an outstanding museum devoted to fly-fishing. Many inns, notably along Lake Champlain and in the Northeast Kingdom, offer tackle, boats, and advice on where to catch what. **Quimby Country** (802-822-5533; www.quimbycountry.com), with a lodge and cabins on Forest and Great Averill Pond; **Seymour Lake Lodge** (802-895-2752; www.seymourlake lodge) in Morgan; and **Seyon Ranch** (802-584-3829) on Noyes Pond in Groton State Forest have all catered to serious fishermen since the 19th century. Landlocked salmon, rainbow trout, brown trout, brookies, and lake trout are all cold-water species plentiful in the Northeast Kingdom's 37,575 acres of public ponds and 3,840 miles of rivers and streams. For guiding services check in those chapters. Warm-water species found elsewhere

Kim Grant

in the state include smallmouth bass, walleye, northern pike, and yellow perch.

Federal fish hatcheries can be found in **Bethel** (802-234-5241) and **Pittsford** (802-483-6618), and state hatcheries are in **West Burke** (802-467-3660), **Bennington** (802-442-4556), **Grand Isle** (802-372-3171), **Roxbury** (802-485-7568), and **Salisbury** (802-352-4471). Ice anglers can legally take every species of fish (trout only in a limited number of designated waters) and can actually hook smelt and some varieties of whitefish that are hard to come by during warmer months; the **Great Benson Fishing Derby** held annually in mid-February on Lake Champlain draws thousands of contestants from throughout New England. The **Lake Champlain International Fishing Derby,** based in Burlington (call 802-862-7777 for details), is a big summer draw. Books to buy include *The Vermont Atlas and Gazetteer* (DeLorme), with details about fishing species and access; the *Atlas of Vermont Trout Ponds* and *Vermont Trout Streams,* both from Northern Cartographics Inc. (Box 133, Burlington 05402); and *Fishing Vermont's Streams and Lakes* by Peter F. Cammann (Backcountry Guides). Within this book we have listed shops, outfitters, and guides as they appear within each region. **Vermont Outdoor Guide Association** (1-800-747-5905) represents qualified guides throughout the state; check out their informative web site, www.adventureguidesvt.com.

FOLIAGE Vermont is credited with inventing foliage season, first aggressively promoted just after World War II in the initial issues of *Vermont Life.*

The Department of Tourism (see *Information*) maintains a foliage "hot line" and sends out weekly bulletins on color progress, which is always earlier than assumed by those of us who live south of Montpelier. Those in the know usually head for northern Vermont in late September and the first week of October, a period that coincides with peak color in that area as well as with the **Northeast Kingdom Fall Foliage Festival.** By the following weekend central Vermont is usually ablaze, but visitors should be sure to have a bed reserved before coming, because organized bus tours converge on the state. By the Columbus Day weekend, when what seems like millions of families within driving distance make their annual leaf-peeping expedition, your odds of finding a bed are dim unless you take advantage of those chambers of commerce (notably Middlebury, Woodstock, Brattleboro, Manchester, Central Vermont, and St. Johnsbury) that pride themselves on finding refuge in private homes for all comers. During peak color, we recommend that you avoid Vermont's most heavily trafficked tourist routes; there is plenty of room on the back roads, especially those unsuited to buses. We strongly suggest exploring the high roads through Vermont's "gaps" (see *Gaps, Gulfs, and Gorges*) during this time of year.

GAPS, GULFS AND GORGES
Vermont's mountains were much higher before they were pummeled some 100,000 years ago by a mile-high sheet of ice. Glacial forces contoured the landscape we recognize today, notching the mountains with a number of handy "gaps" through which men eventually built roads to

get from one side of the mountain to the other. Gaps frequently offer superb views and access to ridge trails. This is true of the **Appalachian, Lincoln, Middlebury,** and **Brandon Gaps,** all crossing the Long Trail and linking Route 100 with the Champlain Valley; and of the Roxbury Gap east of the Mad River Valley. Note, however, that the state's highest and most scenic gap of all is called a *notch* (**Smugglers Notch** between Stowe and Jeffersonville), the New Hampshire name for mountain passes. Gaps at lower elevations are *gulfs,* scenic passes that make ideal picnic sites: Note **Granville Gulf** on Route 100, **Brookfield Gulf** on Route 12, and **Williamstown Gulf** on Route 14. The state's outstanding gorges include: 163-foot-deep **Quechee Gorge,** which can be viewed from Route 4 east of Woodstock; **Brock-way Mills Gorge** in Rockingham (off Route 103); **Cavendish Gorge,** Springfield; **Clarendon Gorge,** Shrewsbury (traversed by the Long Trail via footbridge); **Brewster River Gorge,** south of Jeffersonville off Route 108; **Jay Branch Gorge** off Route 105; and (probably the most photographed of all) the **Brown River** churning through the gorge below the Old Red Mill in Jericho.

GARDENS Vermont's growing season is short but all the more intense. Commercial herb and flower gardens are themselves the fastest-growing form of agriculture in the state, and many inns and B&Bs pride themselves on their gardens. Lodging places with especially noteworthy gardens include the **Basin Harbor Club** in Vergennes, the **Inn at Shelburne Farms** in Shelburne, **Judith's**

Garden B&B and **Blueberry Hill,** both in Goshen, and the **Jackson House** in Woodstock. **Historic Hildene** in Manchester also features formal gardens. Within this book we describe our favorite commercial gardens as they appear under *Selective Shopping.* For a listing of commercial nurseries click onto www.vermont agriculture.com/links).

GENERAL STORES Still the hub of most small Vermont communities, general stores retain some shreds of their onetime status as the source of all staples and communication with the outside world. The most famous survivor is the **Vermont Country Store** in Weston and Rockingham, a genuine family business that has expanded into a Vermont version of L.L. Bean. Still, its thick catalog is a source of long underwear and garter belts, Healthy Feet Cream, shoe trees, and gadgets like a kit that turns a plastic soda bottle into a bird feeder. "The General Store in Vermont," an oral history by Jane Beck, is available from the Vermont Folklife Center in

Christina Tree

Middlebury. Within this book we have described our favorite general stores as they appear geographically.

As we updated this 10th edition of our guide we couldn't help noting how this genre is changing: The best of the old-timers survive in Stowe (where Shaw's is still the "real thing"), Barton, Greensboro Village, West Danville, Marshfield, Sharon, and Norwich (among many others), but new owners tend to add café tables, armchairs, fine wines, baked items, and specialty foods and products; a couple now employ full-time chefs. For an overview check out the newly formed **Vermont Alliance of Independent Country Stores** at www.vaics.org.

GOLF More than 60 Vermont golf courses are open to the public, and more than half of these have 18 holes, half a dozen of them justly famed throughout the country. A full program of lodging, meals, and lessons is available at Mount Snow, Killington, Okemo, Stratton Mountain, Sugarbush, and Stowe. The Woodstock Inn, Lake Morey Inn, and others also offer golf packages. The Manchester area boasts the greatest concentration of courses. Sixty-seven courses are identified on the *Vermont Attractions Map;* for detailed descriptions and editorials see the glossy annual magazine *Vermont Golf* (1-800-639-1941; www.playnortheast golf.com). Also see www.vermontvaca tion.com.

THE GREEN MOUNTAINS Running 160 miles up the spine of this narrow state, the Green Mountains themselves range in width from 20 to 36 miles, with peaks rising to more than 4,000 feet. A part of the Appalachian

Mountain chain, which extends from Alabama to Canada's Gaspé Peninsula, they were once far higher. The Long Trail runs the length of the range, and Route 100 shadows its eastern base. Also see *Hiking and Walking* and *Gaps, Gulfs, and Gorges.*

GREEN MOUNTAIN CLUB See *Hiking and Walking.*

GREEN MOUNTAIN NATIONAL FOREST The Green Mountain National Forest encompasses 850,000 Vermont acres managed by the USDA Forest Service. It's traversed by 900 miles of trails, including the **Appalachian Trail** and the **Long Trail,** which follows the ridgeline of the main range of the Green Mountains (see *Hiking and Walking*). The forest harbors six wilderness areas. Use of off-road recreational vehicles is regulated. Information—printed as well as verbal—about hiking, camping, skiing, berry picking, and bird-watching is available from the ranger stations in **Manchester Center** (802-362-2307), **Middlebury** (802-388-4362), and **Rochester** (802-767-4261). Request a free "mini map" from the **Green Mountain National Forest** (802-747-6700; 231 North Main Street, Rutland 05701). All four offices maintain visitors centers, open weekdays 8–4:30; Rochester is open 8–4 except Sunday, weekdays only off-season.

HANDICAPPED ACCESS The wheelchair symbol & indicates lodging and dining places that are handicapped accessible.

HIGH SEASON "High season" varies from Vermont community to community and even within a community such as Manchester (one side of town is nearer the ski resorts; the other is geared more to summer). While "foliage season" represents peak price as well as color everywhere, a ski condo can easily cost four times as much in February as it does in July. Meanwhile, a country inn may charge half its July price in February.

HIGHWAY ROADFOOD As we have cruised Vermont's interstates over the years, we have developed patterns of exiting for food at places where (1) food is less than a mile from the exit, and (2) food is good, and we strongly favor diners and local eateries over fast-food chains. Needless to say, wherever there's food, there's gas (no pun intended). All the following restaurants are described in their respective chapters.

Along **I-91,** south to north: *Exit 2* is handy to the many choices in downtown Brattleboro and to the **Chelsea Royal Diner,** west on Route 9. *Exit 4:* The **Putney Inn** is good for all three meals; around the corner is **Curtis' Barbecue,** and just up Route 5 is the **Putney Diner.** *Exit 15:* The **Fairlee Diner** is just north. *Exit 16:* **The Hungry Bear** is just off I-91; the **Bradford Village Store** in the middle of the village serves hot soups and deli sandwiches (try for the window seat), while for dinner there's **Colatina Exit** and **Perfect Pear Café.** *Exit 17:* **P&H Truck Stop** is worth a stop. *Exit 23:* Turn north onto Route 5 to find the **Miss Lyndonville Diner.** *Exit 25:* **Miss Newport Diner.**

Along **I-89:** *Exit 3:* **Eaton's Sugar House** is right off the exit. *Exit 7:* Follow signs to Route 302 and the **Wayside Restaurant and Bakery,** a real find, is on your left. *Exit 10:* Turn left, then left again, and you are in the middle of Waterbury at **Arvad's.** *Exit 14W:* Burlington is just down the hill, worth a detour. *Exit 14E:* Turn right on Williston Road and head away from town to find **Al's French Frys.** *Exit 16:* **Libby's Blue Line Diner** is right there and great. Also see *Diners.*

HIGHWAY TRAVEL INFORMATION See *Information.*

HIKING AND WALKING More than 700 miles of hiking trails web Vermont—which is 162 miles long as the crow flies but 255 miles long as the hiker trudges, following the **Long Trail** up and down the spine of the Green Mountains. But few hikers are out to set distance records on the Long Trail. The path from Massachusetts to the Canadian border, which was completed in 1931, has a way of slowing people down. It opens up eyes and lungs and drains compulsiveness. Even die-hard backpackers tend to linger on rocky outcrops, looking down on farms and steeples. A total of 98 side trails (175 miles) meander off to wilderness ponds or abandoned villages; these trails are mostly maintained, along with the Long Trail, by the **Green Mountain Club** (802-244-7037; www.greenmountainclub.org), founded in 1910. The club also maintains 70 shelters, many of them staffed by caretakers during summer months. The club publishes the *Long Trail Guide,* which gives details on trails and shelters throughout the system, as well as the *Day Hiker's Guide to Vermont.* These and other guides are sold in the club's **Hiker's Center** (4711 Waterbury Road, Waterbury Center 05677; open 9–5 daily). The **Appalachian Trail Conference** (P.O. Box 807, Harpers Ferry,

©Sports File/Dennis Curran

WV 25425) includes detailed descriptions of most Vermont trails in its *Appalachian Trail Guide to Vermont and New Hampshire,* and a wide assortment of trails are nicely detailed in *50 Hikes in Vermont* (Backcountry Guides).

Backpackers who are hesitant to set out on their own can take a wide variety of guided hikes and walks. **Adventure Guides of Vermont** (1-800-747-5905; www.adventure guidesvt.com) and **Vermont Outdoor Guide Association** (1-800-425-8747; www.voga.org) can put you in touch with guides and adventure-geared packages throughout the state. Organized tours are offered by **Umiak Outdoor Outfitters** (802-253-2317), based in Stowe. In the Ludlow area several inns also offer support services (route planning, baggage transfers) as well as meals and lodging; check out www.vermont inntoinnwalking.com. Within this book we suggest hiking trails as they appear geographically. Also note the recent proliferation of trail systems: In the Northeast Kingdom check out **Kingdom Trails** in East Burke, the **Vermont Leadership Center** near

Island Pond, and the **Hazen's Notch Association Trails** (www.hazens notch.org). We should also note that both Killington and Sugarbush offer ridge hiking from the top of their lifts. (See also *Birding, State Parks, Mountain Biking,* and *Nature Preserves.*)

HISTORY Vermont is a small state, but it has had a dramatic life. In essence, the whole state is a living history museum, even though most towns were settled after the Revolution. Many, often overlapping, land grants issued by the royal governors of both New Hampshire and New York were not finally sorted out until 1791, when Congress admitted Vermont as the 14th state, after 14 years as an independent republic.

The Abenaki presence in Vermont is far more pervasive than was acknowledged until very recently. Today's **St. Anne's Shrine on Isle La Motte** memorializes Champlain's first landfall on the lake that bears his name; the site was certainly an Indian village and by 1666 a mission as well as a fort. It was abandoned in 1679 but remains an evocative place. A colossal granite statue of Champlain depicts an unnamed Indian guide at his feet. Nearby in present-day Swanton, the Indian village of Missisquoi became a mission village, a way stop for Abenaki headed for Montreal. Abenaki life is presented in an exhibit at the **Abenaki Tribal Museum and Cultural Center** (802-868-2559), 100 Grand Avenue, Swanton; open Monday through Friday 9–4 (but call ahead). Abenaki settlements are also recorded at Otter Creek, and the 18th-century tavern at **Chimney Point State Historic Site** in Addison has a well-mounted display that explains the territory's Native American and French colonial heritage. In Newport the new lakeside state office building displays the **Memphremagog Historical Society's** exhibit on northern Vermont Abenaki people, from Paleolithic through current times, and at **Fort at Number Four** in Charlestown, New Hampshire (see "The Upper Valley"), a community in which settlers and Indians lived side by side, the reconstructed fort exhibits Native American artifacts from the Connecticut River Valley.

Bennington, chartered by the avaricious Governor Benning Wentworth in 1749, the first chartered town west of the Connecticut River in the New Hampshire Grants, became the tinderbox for settlers' resistance to New York's rival claims, confirmed by King George in 1764. The desperate grantees found a champion in the protean Ethan Allen from Connecticut. This frontier rebel—land speculator, firebrand, and philosopher—recruited the boisterous Green Mountain Boys militiamen, who talked rum and rebellion at the Catamount Tavern in **Old Bennington,** roared defiance of the 'Yorkers, and then fought the British. Ethan's rambunctious life is reflected in the **Ethan Allen Homestead,** the farm north of Burlington where he died in 1789.

In Westminster, on the bank of the Connecticut River, the 1775 **"Massacre"** was thought, incorrectly, to have been the first armed engagement of the Revolution. But the death of William French, shot by a 'Yorker sheriff ("The Cruel Minestereal Tools of George ye 3d"), galvanized opposition to both New York and England, leading to a convention in

Westminster in January 1777, where Vermonters declared their independence of everyone.

Formal independence was declared the following July, upriver in Windsor, where delegates gathered in Elijah West's tavern (now **The Old Constitution House**). They adopted a model constitution, the first to abolish slavery, before rushing off to attack the British, who had retaken Fort Ticonderoga. (While in Windsor, visit the **American Precision Museum,** a landmark reflecting early gun makers and the heyday of the machine tool industry.)

Since its discovery by Samuel de Champlain in 1609, Lake Champlain has been not only one of the nation's most historic waterways, but a strategic corridor in three wars as well. The French controlled the lake until 1759, when Lord Jeffery Amherst drove them out of Fort Carillon (now **Ticonderoga**) and then captured Montreal. In the American Revolution, the British used the lake as an invasion route to divide the colonies, but were thwarted when Ethan Allen's Green Mountain Boys captured Fort Ticonderoga in 1775.

Facing Ticonderoga across the lake's narrowest channel, the **Mount Independence State Historic Site** near Orwell dramatizes the struggle that ended with the decisive British defeat at Saratoga in 1777. As Burgoyne's British troops marched south, the only battle of the Revolution to have been fought on Vermont soil is commemorated at the **Hubbardton Battlefield** near Castleton, where a small force of Green Mountain Boys under Colonel Seth Warner stopped a far larger British contingent. The invaders were soon repulsed again in the battle of

Bennington—actually fought in New York—marked by the **Bennington Battle Monument** and by exhibits in the **Bennington Museum.**

The lake also figured in naval warfare when Benedict Arnold and a quickly assembled American flotilla engaged a heavier British squadron off Plattsburgh, New York, in the battle of Valcour Island in October 1776. One of Arnold's small gunboats, the *Philadelphia,* sunk by the British, was salvaged in 1935 and reposes in the Smithsonian. An exact replica is moored at the **Lake Champlain Maritime Museum** at Basin Harbor near Vergennes. A number of ships and other artifacts of that battle have been found buried in the mud on the lake bottom in recent years. In 1814 the British again tried to use Lake Champlain as an invasion route. Thomas McDonough moved his headquarters from Burlington to Vergennes and a shipyard at the mouth of Otter Creek. His small fleet barely managed to defeat British ships at Plattsburgh Bay, a bloody engagement that helped end the War of 1812.

With Vermont in the vanguard of the antislavery movement of the 1840s, the Underground Railroad flourished, notably at **Rokeby,** the home of the Robinson family in Ferrisburgh, now a museum.

Evidence of the state's extraordinary record in the Civil War and its greater-than-average number of per capita casualties may be seen in the memorials that dot most town and village greens. How Vermonters turned

Vermont Historical Society

The Vermont Historical Society presents
VERMONT HISTORY
Expo 2004
June 26–June 27, 10 a.m.–5 p.m.
Tunbridge, Vermont

A Weekend Celebration of Vermont's Story

the tide of battle at Cedar Creek is portrayed in Julian Scott's huge and newly restored painting that hangs in the **State House** in Montpelier. The anniversary of the October 1864 **St. Albans Raid,** the northernmost engagement of the Civil War, is observed annually.

There are few 18th-century structures in the state, but the settlers who poured in after 1791 (the population nearly tripled, from 85,000 to 235,000 in 1820) built sophisticated dwellings and churches. **Dorset, Castleton, Chester** (Old Stone Village), **Middlebury, Brandon, Woodstock,** and **Norwich** are architectural showcases of Federal-style houses. Several historic, outstandingly splendid mansions built by 19th-century moguls are open to the public: the **Park-McCullough House,** North Bennington; the **Wilburton Inn** and **Hildene,** Manchester; **The Castle Inn,** Proctorsville; **Wilson Castle,** West Rutland; the **Marsh-Billings-Rockefeller National Historical Park,** Woodstock; and **The Inn at Shelburne Farms** (built by Lila Vanderbilt Webb and William Seward Webb), Shelburne.

Vermont's congressional delegations, especially in the 19th century, have always had more influence in Washington than the size of the state might indicate. For example, the **Justin Morrill Homestead** in Strafford, a spacious Gothic Revival house, reminds us of the distinguished career of the originator of the Land Grant Colleges Act, who served in Congress from 1855 to 1898.

State and local historical societies have faithfully preserved the cultural evidence. The **Vermont Historical Society Museum** (www.vermont history.org), reopened after a complete makeover and expansion in 2004, is housed in a replica of the Pavilion Hotel that stands beside the Vermont State House in Montpelier. The society also maintains a research library with changing special exhibits in Barre. Arts, crafts, architecture, and transportation are featured in the **Shelburne Museum** in Shelburne. In Woodstock the **Billings Farm & Museum** re-creates a model 1890s stock farm and dairy and the **Marsh-Billings-Rockefeller National Historical Park** traces the state's environmental history. Outstanding collections of the ways people lived and worked can be found in town historical societies, notably the **Farrar Mansur House** in Weston, the **Sheldon Museum** in Middlebury, and the **Dana House** in Woodstock. For a lively, popular story of the state from its origins to the present, read Peter Jennison's *Roadside History of Vermont* (Mountain Press). A pamphlet guide to Vermont state historic sites, operated by the Division for Historic Preservation, is available at information centers throughout the state, and the sites are also profiled, along with events and historic roadside markers, at www.historic vermont.org. See also *Historical Societies.*

HISTORICAL SOCIETIES The attics of every town, historical societies are frequently worth seeking out, but because most are staffed by volunteers, they tend to be open just a few hours a week, in summer. Of Vermont's 251 towns, 184 have historical societies; we have tried to give accurate, current information on them within each chapter. The Vermont Historical Society publishes a free booklet, *Passport to Vermont*

History, listing hours and contact phones for more than 170 . Information is also found at www.vermonthistory.org. Outstanding local historical societies are found in **Brattleboro, Brownington, Newfane,** and **Middlebury.** *Note:* On the last weekend of June the Vermont Historical Society sponsors the **Vermont History Expo,** held at the fairgrounds in Tunbridge, billed as "a celebration of Vermont's Story as Told by the Keepers of Its Treasures and Traditions." It includes a full schedule of folk songs, lectures, demonstrations, and other live entertainment as well as displays.

HUNTING The *Vermont Digest of Hunting, Fishing and Trapping Laws* and a useful *State of Vermont Hunting Map* are available from the Vermont Fish and Wildlife Department (802-241-3700; 103 South Main Street, 10 South, Waterbury 05671-0501; www.vtfish andwildlife.com). Of special interest to nonresidents: a reasonably priced, 5-day small-game license. The ruffed grouse or "partridge" is the state's most abundant game bird, while woodcocks, or "timberdoodles," are found throughout the state. The wild turkey is considered "big game"—as hunters will understand when they try to bag them (in-season in October and May). October is bow-and-arrow season for white-tailed deer, and November is buck season. Black bear and moose populations are both healthy, but hunting regulations vary with the year.

ICE CREAM Vermont's quality milk is used to produce some outstanding ice cream as well as cheese. The big name is, of course, **Ben & Jerry's,**

INFORMATION

The **Vermont Department of Tourism and Marketing** (1-800-VERMONT) offers vacation planning, information packets, seasonal conditions, and an excellent web site: www.vermontvacation.com. Their business office (802-828-3237) is 6 Baldwin Street, Montpelier 05633-1301. Request: (1) *Vermont's Official Attractions Map and Guide,* a road map with symbols locating attractions, covered bridges, golf courses, state parks and historic sites, ski areas, public boat and fishing access ramps, and more.

(2) *Vermont Travelers Guidebook* (spring–summer and fall) and *Vermont Winter Guide,* helpful and current magazine-format guides published by the **Vermont Chamber of Commerce** (802-223-3443), which maintains its own useful web site: www.vtchamber.com. You can also request the *Vermont Historic Sites Guide,* the *Vermont Farms* brochure, and the *Vermont Campground Guidebook;* from the chamber you can request a pamphlet guide to country inns and B&Bs. We have noted local chambers of commerce town by town in each chapter of this book under *Guidance.* In towns not served by a chamber, inquiries are welcomed by the town clerk. First-time visitors may be puzzled by Vermont's Travel Information System of directional signs, which replace billboards (banned since 1967, another Vermont first). Stylized symbols for lodging, food, recreation, antiques and crafts, and other services are sited at intersections off major highways.

Kim Grant

Interstate welcome and information centers with pay phones and bathroom facilities are generally open 7 AM–11 PM and marked on the state map. At the Massachusetts border, northbound at Guilford on I-91, the state's largest and most complete **Welcome Center** (802-254-4593; open 24 hours) displays Vermont products and exhibits. Other I-91

Christina Tree

welcome centers, open daily, are northbound at **Bradford** (802-222-9369), southbound at **Lyndon** (802-626-9669), and at **Derby Line** (802-873-3311). At the junction of I-91 and I-89 (in downtown White River Junction) the **White River
Junction Welcome Center** (802-281-5050), housed in the Amtrak station, is open
varying hours. Along I-89 welcome centers are found at **Sharon,** north- and
southbound; at **Randolph,** northbound (802-524-0015) and southbound (802-524-
0018); at **Williston** southbound (802-879-2360); and north of Burlington both
north- and southbound in **Georgia.** At the Canadian border you'll find a major
welcome center at **Highgate** (802-868-3244, 7 AM–11 PM). There's also an inviting
welcome center just over the state line on I-93 at **Waterford** (802-748-9368, 7
AM–11 PM), as well as visitors centers at the New York–Canadian border on
Route 2 in **Alburg** (802-796-3980, open 10–6) and on the New York border on

Steve Cook

Route 4A in **Fair Haven** (802-265-
4763, open 7 AM–9 PM). In
Montpelier the **Capital Region
Visitors Center,** 134 State Street
(802-828-5981, open 9–5 daily), is
the source of statewide information.
AAA Emergency Road Service:
1-800-222-4357.

For road conditions contact 1-800-
429-7623 or www.vermontroads
.com. New in 2004: Dial 511 from
any phone in Vermont. Also see
Highway Roadfood and *Weather
Reports.*

proud producers of what *Time* has billed "the best ice cream in the world." Their plant on Route 100 in Waterbury (featuring factory tours, free samples, real cows, and a gift shop full of reproductions in every conceivable shape) has quickly become one of the state's most popular tourist attractions. Other good Vermont ice creams include **Seward's** in Rutland, **Wilcox Brothers** in Manchester, **Page's** in West Brattleboro, **Umbleby's** in Bridgewater, the **Mountain Creamery** in Woodstock, and the **Brown Cow** in Newport.

INNS It's safe to say that we have visited more Vermont inns, more frequently, than anyone else living today. We do not charge for inclusion in this book, and we attempt to give as accurate and detailed a picture as space permits. We quote 2003–04 rates—which are, of course, subject to change. Summer rates are generally lower than winter (except, of course, at lake resorts); weekly or ski-week rates run 10–20 percent less than the per diem price quoted. Many inns insist on MAP (Modified American Plan—breakfast and dinner) in winter but not in summer. Some resorts have AP (American Plan—three meals), and we have shown EP (European Plan—no meals) where applicable. We have attempted to note when 15 percent service is added, but you should always ask if it has been included in a quoted rate and whether an additional local tax is added. Always add the 9 percent state tax on rooms and meals. It's prudent to check which, if any, credit cards are accepted. Many lodging places now insist on minimum 2- or 3-day stays during busy seasons. Within the text, special icons highlight lodging places offering exceptional value 🏆, those that appeal to families ✐, those that are handicapped accessible ♿, those that accept pets 🐾, and those that specialize in weddings and civil unions ⚭.

LAKES The state famed for green mountains and white villages also harbors more than 400 relatively blue lakes: big lakes like **Champlain** (150 miles long) and **Memphremagog** (boasting 88 miles of coastline, but most of it in Canada), smaller lakes like **Morey, Dunmore, Willoughby, Bomoseen,** and **Seymour.** Lakes are particularly plentiful and people sparse in Vermont's Northeast Kingdom. A century ago there were many more lakeside hotels; today just a handful of these classic summer resorts survive: **Quimby Country** in Averill, **Highland Lodge** in Greensboro, the **Tyler Place** in Highgate Springs, the **Basin Harbor Club** near Vergennes, and the **Lake Morey Inn Resort** in Fairlee. There are half a dozen smaller, informal inns on scattered lakes, but that's about it. Still, you can bed down very reasonably within sound and sight of Vermont waters either by renting a cottage (more than half of those listed

Kim Grant

in *Four Season Vacation Rentals,* available from the Vermont Department of Tourism and Marketing, are on lakes) or by taking advantage of state park campsites on **Groton Lake, Island Pond, Maidstone Lake, Lake Bomoseen, Lake Carmi, Lake Elmore, Lake St. Catherine,** and **Silver Lake** (in Barnard). On Lake Champlain, there are a number of state campgrounds, including those on **Grand Isle** (accessible by car) and **Burton Island** (accessible by public launch from St. Albans Bay). See *Campgrounds* for details about these and the free campsites on **Ball Mountain Lake,** maintained by the Army Corps of Engineers. There is public boat access to virtually every Vermont pond and lake of any size. Boat launches are listed on the state map.

LIBRARIES The small village of Brookfield boasts the state's oldest continuously operating public library, established in 1791. Most libraries that we mention here date, however, from that late-19th-century philanthropic era when wealthy native sons were moved to donate splendidly ornate libraries to their hometowns. Notable examples are to be found in **Barre, Chester, Ludlow, Wilmington, Rutland, Newport, Woodstock, St. Johnsbury,** and **Brattleboro**. For research, the **Vermont Historical Society Library** in Barre is a treasure trove of Vermontiana and genealogical resources, as is the **Wilbur Collection** of the Bailey-Howe Library at the University of Vermont and the **Russell Collection** in Arlington. Three of the Vermont state colleges—Castleton, Johnson, and Lyndon—have collections of Vermontiana in the Vermont Rooms of their libraries.

LLAMA TREKKING Check out **Green Mountain Expeditions** (802-368-7147) in Whitingham; **Northern Vermont Llama Co.** (802-644-2257) in Waterville; the **Stowe Llama Ranch** (802-253-5118); **Cold Hollow Llamas** (802-644-5846) in Belvidere; **On the Loose Expeditions** (1-800-688-1481) in Huntington; **Apple-cheek Farm** (802-888-4482) in Hyde Park; **Maple Leaf Llamas** (802-586-2873) in Craftsbury Common; **Heart of Vermont Llama Hikes** (802-889-9611) in Tunbridge; and **Woodstock Llama Trekking** (802-457-3722) in Woodstock/Quechee.

MAGAZINES *Vermont Life* (1-800-284-3243; www.vtlife.com), the popular and colorful quarterly published by the Agency of Development and Community Affairs and edited by Tom Slayton, is an outstanding chronicle of Vermont's people and places, featuring distinguished photographers. *Vermont Magazine* (www.vermontmagazine.com), the upbeat, statewide bimonthly launched in 1989, covers major issues, townscapes, products, and personalities, and reviews inns and restaurants. *Seven Days* (802-864-5684; www.sevendaysvt.com), Burlington's free weekly tabloid of area arts and entertainment, is far more than a calendar of events.

MAPLE SUGARING Vermont produces an average of 400,000 gallons of maple syrup each year, more than any other state. No fewer than 2,400 maple growers tap an average of 1,000 trees each. About a quart of syrup is made per tap; it takes 30 to 40 gallons of sap to make each gallon of syrup. The process of tapping trees and boiling sap is stubbornly known as *sugaring,* rather than *syruping,* because the end product for early settlers was sugar. Syrup was first made in the early 19th century, but production flagged when imported cane sugar was easy to come by. The Civil War revived the maple sugar industry: Union supporters were urged to consume sugar made by free men and to plant more and more maples.

We urge visitors to buy syrup direct from the farm that has produced it any time of year (finding the farm is half the fun), but also to seriously consider making a special trip to a sugarhouse during sugaring season. It's then, not autumn, that sugar maples really perform, and it's a show that can't be viewed through a windshield. Sugaring season begins quietly in February as thousands of Vermonters wade, snowshoe, and snowmobile into their woods and begin "tapping," a ritual that may have changed technically as plastic tubing has replaced buckets, but the timing hasn't. Traditionally, sugaring itself begins on Town Meeting Day (the first Tuesday in March). The fact is, however, that sap runs only on those days when temperatures rise to 40 and 50 degrees during the day and drop into the 20s at night. And when the sap runs, it must be boiled down quickly. What you want to see is the boiling process: sap churning madly through the large, flat evaporating pan, darkening as you watch. You are enveloped in fragrant steam, listening to the rush of the sap, sampling the end result on snow or in tiny paper cups. Sugaring is Vermont's rite of spring. Don't miss a sugar-on-snow party: plates of snow dribbled with hot syrup, accompanied by doughnuts and dill pickles.

A *Vermont Maple Syrup Map,* available by phoning 1-800-VERMONT, lists and pinpoints producers who agree to be open on **Maple Open House Weekend** in mid-March. See www.vermont.com/maple for similar information and a list of producers who ship. The **Vermont Maple Festival,** held the latter part of April in St. Albans, is a 3-day happening that includes tours through the local sugarbush (802-524-5800). At **Maple Grove Farm** of Vermont, "the world's largest maple candy factory" in St. Johnsbury, factory tours are offered Monday through Friday year-round, and there is a maple museum and gift shop. Videos on maple are also shown in the **New England Maple Museum** in Pittsford and in the maple museum at

Kim Grant

Sugarmill Farm in Barton. Within this book we list maple producers in the areas in which they are most heavily concentrated. There are many more than found on any formal lists. Ask locally.

MAPS *Vermont's Official Attractions Map and Guide* (see *Information*) is free and extremely helpful for general motoring but will not suffice for finding your way around on the webs of dirt roads that connect some of the most beautiful corners of the state. Among our favorite areas where you will need more detail: the high farming country between Albany, Craftsbury, and West Glover; similar country between Chelsea and Williamstown; south from Plainfield to Orange; and between Plymouth and Healdville. There are many more. We strongly suggest securing a copy of *The Vermont Atlas and Gazetteer* (DeLorme) if you want to do any serious back-road exploring, or *The Vermont Road Atlas and Guide* (Northern Cartographics); both are widely available at bookstores, gas stations, and general stores. Among the best regional maps for anyone planning to do much hiking or biking are those published by Map Adventures (www.mapadventures.com). Also see *Hiking and Walking.*

MONEY Don't leave home without MasterCard or Visa, the two credit cards that are far more readily accepted in Vermont than American Express or personal checks. Each inn has its own policy about credit cards and checks.

MOUNTAIN BIKING Several ski areas offer lift-assisted mountain biking.

The **Mount Snow Bike School and Touring Center** (802-245-SNOW) was the first, offering 45 miles of trails, some served by lifts. **Stratton Sports** (802-297-2200; 1-800-STRATTON), at Stratton Mountain, rents mountain bikes and offers a variety of terrain. In the Burlington area, **Bolton Valley** (802-434-3444) and the **Catamount Family Center** (802-879-6001) both offer extensive cross-country trail networks and rentals. **Killington** (www.killington .com) and **Jay Peak Resort** (www.jay peakresort.com) also permit mountain biking on ski trails, accessible via lifts.

In recent years, however, Vermont mountain biking options have dramatically broadened beyond the state's ski mountains as the potential for its hundreds of miles of dirt and Class 4 roads as well as cross-county trail systems has been recognized. The **Craftsbury Outdoor Center** (www.craftsbury.com) up in the Northeast Kingdom was the first place to rent mountain bikes and offer guided tours over dirt and abandoned logging roads. A former prep school now devoted to running and rowing as well as biking in summer and cross-country skiing in winter, it's set in high, rolling farm country with mountain views. There's another magnificent trail system in the Burke Mountain area: **Kingdom Trails,** a 100-mile mix of trails maintained by a nonprofit organization. Pick up a map and day pass at the **East Burke Sports Shop** (802-626-3215), or visit www.kingdomtrails.org. In Randolph you can arrive with your bike via Amtrak and take advantage of the **Three Stallion Inn**'s network of trails. In southeastern Vermont the **West Hill Shop** (802-387-5718) publishes its own map to an extensive network of singletrack trails and forgotten roads.

We describe inns and bike shops that offer bike rentals in almost every chapter, but here we should mention **Blueberry Hill Inn** (1-800-448-0707), set high in Goshen with easy access to trails in the Moosalamoo region of the Green Mountain National Forest and to Silver Lake. The nominally priced *Topographic Maps & Guides,* produced by Stowe-based Map Adventures (802-253-7489; www.mapadventures.com), are useful map/guides outlining rides in various parts of Vermont: the Burlington and Stowe areas, the White River Valley, the Upper Valley, and southern Vermont, among others. **Adventure Guides of Vermont** (1-800-425-8727) is the way to find a guide, and maintains an excellent web site: www.voga.org. See also *Bicycle Touring.*

MOUNTAINTOPS While Vermont can boast only seven peaks above 4,000 feet, there are 80 mountains that rise more than 3,000 feet and any number of spectacular views, several of them accessible in summer and foliage season to those who prefer riding to walking up mountains. **Mount Mansfield,** which at 4,343 feet is the state's highest summit, can be reached via the Toll Road and a gondola. The mid-19th-century road brings you to the small Summit Station at 4,062 feet, from which the 0.5-mile Tundra Trail brings you to the actual summit. The Mount Mansfield gondola, an eight-passenger, enclosed lift, hoists you from the main base area up to the Cliff House (serving light meals all day), from which a trail also heads up to the Chin. **Killington Peak,** Vermont's second highest peak at

4,241 feet, can be reached via a 1.2-mile ride on a gondola that takes you to a summit restaurant and a nature trail that even small children can negotiate. **Jay Peak,** a 3,861-foot summit towering like a lone sentinel near the Canadian border, is accessible via a 60-passenger tram (daily except Tuesday), and a "four-state view" from the top of **Stratton Mountain** is accessible via the ski resort's six-passenger gondola, Starship XII (daily in summer and fall). Other toll roads include the Auto Road to the 3,267-foot **Burke Mountain** in East Burke, the Toll Road to the 3,144-foot summit of **Mount Ascutney** in Ascutney State Park, and the road to the top of **Mount Equinox** in Sunderland. There are also chairlift rides to the tops of **Bromley** (you don't have to take the alpine slide down) and **Mount Snow** (weekends in summer, daily in foliage season).

MUD SEASON The period from snowmelt (around the middle of March) through early May (it varies each year) is known throughout the state as mud season for reasons that few visitors want to explore too deeply. It's worth mentioning that dirt roads can turn quickly into boggy quagmires, and travel off the main roads in this season can be challenging.

MUSEUMS Vermont museums vary from the immense **Shelburne Museum**—with its 36 buildings, many housing priceless collections of Americana, plus assorted exhibits such as a completely restored lake steamer and lighthouse—to the **American Precision Museum** in Windsor, an 1846 brick mill that once

BRATTLEBORO MUSEUM & ART CENTER Kim Grant

produced rifles. They include a number of outstanding historical museums (our favorites are the **Sheldon Museum** in Middlebury, the **Old Stone House Museum** in Brownington, and the **Dana House** in Woodstock) and some collections that go beyond the purely historical: **Bennington Museum** (famed for its collection of Grandma Moses paintings as well as early American glass and relics from the Revolution) and the **Fairbanks Museum and Planetarium** in St. Johnsbury. The **Billings Farm & Museum** in Woodstock shows off its blue-ribbon dairy and has a fascinating, beautifully mounted display of 19th-century farm life and tools. The **Vermont Museum & Gallery Alliance** maintains an excellent web site: www.vmga.org. Within this book, we have included all museums in their respective areas.

MUSIC The Green Mountains are filled with the sounds of music each summer, beginning with the **Discover Jazz Festival** (www.discover jazz.com), more than 100 concerts

held over a week around Burlington in early June. In Putney a late-June-through-July series of three evening chamber music concerts each week is presented in the **Yellow Barn** (1-800-639-3819). In July and August options include the internationally famous **Marlboro Music Festival** (802-254-2394; www.marlboromusic.org) at Marlboro College, presenting chamber music on weekends, and the **Vermont Mozart Festival** (802-862-7352), a series of 20 concerts performed at a variety of sites ranging from beautiful barns at the University of Vermont and Shelburne Farms to a Lake Champlain ferry and including some striking classic and modern churches and a ski area base lodge. The **Killington Music Festival** (802-773-4003) is a series of Sunday concerts at Ramshead Lodge in July and August, and the **Manchester Music Festival** (802-362-1956; 1-800-639-5868) brings leading performers to various venues around Manchester. Also well worth noting: the **Central Vermont Chamber Music Festival** (802-728-9133) at the Chandler Music Hall in Randolph in mid-August, **Summer Music School** in Adamant (802-229-9297), concerts at the Town House in Hardwick by the **Craftsbury Chamber Players** (1-800-639-3443), and in Stowe, for a week in late July, at the **Performing Arts Festival** (802-253-7321).

Other concert series are performed at the **Southern Vermont Arts Center** (Thursday and Sunday, 802-362-1405); at the **Fine Arts Center,** Castleton State College (802-468-4611, ext. 285); at the **Dibden Auditorium,** Johnson State College (802-635-2356); and at **Middlebury College Center for the Arts** (802-388-3711, ext. SHOW). The **North**

Country Concert Association (43 Main Street, Derby Line 05830) schedules performances at sites throughout the Northeast Kingdom lake area. The **Vermont Symphony Orchestra,** oldest of the state symphonies, figures in a number of the series noted above and also performs at a variety of locations, ranging from Brattleboro's Living Memorial Park and the State House lawn to Wilson Castle, throughout the summer. In Weston the **Kinhaven Music School** (802-824-3365) offers free concerts on summer weekends. The **Vermont Bach Festival** (802-257-4523), sponsored by the Brattleboro Music Center with performances in local churches and at Marlboro College, is a fitting climax to the season. See also *Fiddling.*

NATURE PRESERVES The **Vermont Land Trust** (www.vlt.org), founded in 1977, is dedicated to preserving Vermont's traditional landscape of farms as well as forest (it has helped protect more than 400 farms), and many local land trusts have acquired numerous parcels of land throughout the state. Many of the most visitor-friendly preserves are owned by **The Nature Conservancy,** a national nonprofit conservation organization that has preserved close to 7 million acres throughout the United States since its founding in 1951. Contact The Nature Conservancy (802-229-1105), 27 State Street, Montpelier 05602.

OPERA HOUSES Northern New England opera houses are a turn-of-the-20th-century phenomenon: theaters built as cultural centers for the surrounding area, stages on which lecturers, musicians, and vaudeville acts, as well as opera singers, performed. Many of these buildings have long since disappeared, but those that survive are worth noting. The **Hyde Park Opera House,** built in 1910, has been restored by the Lamoille County Players, who stage four annual shows—one play, two musicals, and an annual foliage-season run of *The Sound of Music.* The **Barre Opera House,** built in 1899, is an elegant, acoustically outstanding, second-floor theater, home of the Barre Players; productions are staged here year-round. In Derby Line, in the second-floor **Opera House** (a neoclassical structure that also houses the Haskell Free Library), the audience sits in Vermont watching a stage that is in Canada. The **Chandler Center for the Arts** in Randolph and the **Vergennes Opera House** in Vergennes have been restored for varied uses.

PETS We note lodging places that accommodate pets with the symbol ☘. We should note that while traveling with a dog or cat generally tends to rule out the possibility of staying in inns or B&Bs, some of Vermont's most elegant inns do permit them: the **Inn on the Common** in Craftsbury, **Topnotch** in Stowe, the **Basin Harbor Club** in Vergennes, the **Woodstock Inn and Resort** in Woodstock, and the **Waybury Inn** in East Middlebury.

PICK YOUR OWN Strawberry season is mid- to late June. Cherries, plums, raspberries, and blueberries can be picked in July and August. Apples ripen by mid-September and can be picked through foliage season. For specifics on where, see *Apples* and *Farms Open to the Public.*

QUILTS A revival of interest in this craft is especially strong in Vermont, where quilting supply and made-to-order stores salt the state. The **Vermont Quilt Festival** (www.vqf.org) is held for 3 days in late June in Northfield, including exhibits of antique quilts, classes and lectures, vendors, and appraisals. **Shelburne Museum** has an outstanding quilt collection, and the **Billings Farm & Museum** holds an annual show.

Kim Grant

RAILROAD EXCURSIONS The **Green Mountain Railroad** (802-463-3069; 1-800-707-3530; www.rails-vt.com) runs a number of excursion trains around the state. The Green Mountain Flyer, named for the fastest train on the old Rutland Railroad, runs between Bellows Falls on the Connecticut River and Chester (13 miles), with special foliage runs for another 14 miles to Ludlow and seasonal Santa Claus runs before Christmas.

RENTAL COTTAGES AND CONDOMINIUMS *Four Season Vacation Rentals*, an annual booklet available from state information centers (Vermont@cyberrentals.com), lists upward of 200 properties, most of them either lakeside cottages or condominiums near ski areas but also including a variety of other housing, ranging from wooded summer camps by streams to aristocratic brick mansions with priceless views. *Vermont Rentals Magazine* (802-228-7158), 110 Main Street, Ludlow, is also available on request. Regional rentals are listed in each chapter.

RESTAURANTS Culinary standards are rising every day: You can lunch

simply and inexpensively nearly everywhere and dine superbly in a score of places. Fixed-price menus (prix fixe) have been so noted. We were tempted to try to list our favorites here, but the roster would be too long. Restaurants that appeal to us appear in the text in their respective areas. Note that we divide restaurants in each chapter into *Dining Out* (serious dining experiences) and *Eating Out* (everyday places). See also *Highway Roadfood*.

ROCKHOUNDING The most obvious sites are **Rock of Ages Quarry and Exhibit** in Barre and the **Vermont Marble Company Exhibit** in Proctor, both with interactive exhibits. Vermont fossils, minerals, and rocks may be viewed at **Perkins Geology Hall,** University of Vermont, Burlington; and the **Fairbanks Museum** in St. Johnsbury. An annual **Rock Swap and Mineral Show** is held in early August, sponsored by the Burlington Gem and Mineral Club. Gold, incidentally, can be panned in a number of rivers, notably Broad Brook in Plymouth; the Rock River in Newfane and Dover; the Williams River in Ludlow; the Ottauquechee River in Bridgewater;

the White River in Stockbridge and Rochester; the Mad River in Warren, Waitsfield, and Moretown; the Little River in Stowe and Waterbury; and the Missisquoi in Lowell and Troy.

SHEEP AND WOOL Specialty sheep and alpacas are multiplying quickly in Vermont. A number of farmers specialize in processing wool and fiber. Check www.vermontsheep.org and www.vtllama.com. The **Vermont Sheep and Wool Festival,** featuring sheep shearing, spinning, weaving, and plenty of sheep, is held in October.

SHIPWRECKS Well-preserved 19th-century shipwrecks are open to the public (licensed divers) at three underwater historical preserves in Lake Champlain near Burlington. Check with the **Lake Champlain Maritime Museum** in Vergennes, which is charting underwater remains.

SKIING, CROSS-COUNTRY The **Vermont Ski Areas Association** lists 29 cross-country centers in their *Vermont Winter Guide.* For descriptions and conditions click on www.xcountryski-vermont. Within this book we have described each commercial touring center as it appears

Kim Grant

geographically. Given the dearth of natural snow in recent years, checking current conditions is now more important than ever. Vermont's most dependable snow can be found on high-elevation trails in **Stowe,** at **Craftsbury Outdoor Center** in Craftsbury Common, **Hazen's Notch** in Montgomery Center, **Bolton Valley Resort** (between Burlington and Stowe), **Burke Mountain Cross-Country** in East Burke, and **Blueberry Hill** in Goshen. **Mountain Top Inn** and **Mountain Meadows,** both in Chittenden (handy to Killington and Rutland), and **Grafton Ponds** in Grafton offer some snowmaking. All the cross-country ski centers mentioned above are located on the 300-mile **Catamount Trail,** a marked ski trail that runs the length of the state (see *Catamount Trail*). *Adventure Skiing,* a map/guide to cross-country trails in the Stowe/Bolton/Underhill area, is useful (802-253-7489). Inn-to-inn tours are possible between **Craftsbury Center Resort** and **Highland Lodge** in Greensboro; **Trapp Family Lodge** and **Edson Hill Manor** in Stowe; **Chipman House** in Ripton and **Churchill House Inn** in Goshen; and between **Village Inn** of Landgrove and **Nordic Inn** in Londonderry. **Mad River Glen** and **Bolton Valley** are two alpine resorts that specialize in telemarking. The Vermont Chamber of Commerce and *Vermont Living* magazine publish a glossy *Vermont Winter Guide* (available free at www.vtchamber.com). Also see *State Parks* and *Green Mountain National Forest.*

SKIING, DOWNHILL Since the 1930s, when America's commercial skiing began with a Model-T Ford engine

Sandy Macys

pulling skiers up a hill in Woodstock, skiing has been a Vermont specialty. Fifteen ski areas are members of the Vermont Ski Areas Association and accessible with daily updated snow conditions and weather on the web site www.skivermont.com. The Vermont Chamber of Commerce publishes a glossy *Vermont Winter Guide* (available free at www.vtchamber.com). Daily lift tickets are, of course, not the cheapest way to ski; all resorts deeply discount multiday lifts and lodging packages, and there are discounts for ordering ahead online. **Killington/Pico,** the largest ski resort in the East, and **Mount Snow,** Vermont's second largest area, are owned by the American Skiing Company; lift tickets and passes at one are honored at the others, and at ASC resorts in New Hampshire and

Maine. **Sugarbush,** which was an ASC property, has been returned to local ownership. A number of long-established Vermont ski areas have become self-contained resorts. Both **Bolton Valley** and **Smugglers' Notch** cater to families; **Okemo, Stratton,** and **Sugarbush** offer varied skiing and facilities, appealing to a full range of patrons. Though no longer Vermont's biggest, **Stowe** remains Ski Capital of the East when it comes to the quantity and quality of inns, restaurants, and shops. We have described each ski area as it appears geographically. A 24-hour snow-condition report for the state is available by calling the **Vermont Skiing Today SnowLine:** 802-229-0531 (November through June); or, again, you can check www.skivermont.com.

SLEIGH RIDES Sleigh rides are listed under *To Do* as they appear geographically in the book.

SNOWBOARDING An international sport first popularized by Burton Snowboards (born in Manchester, long since moved to Burlington, where we list details about its factory store), snowboarding lessons, rentals, and special terrain parks are offered

THE INN AT MOUNTAIN VIEW FARM
Marilyn Pastore

at every major Vermont ski area except Mad River Glen (the only holdout in the East).

SNOWMOBILING Vermont's 3,900 miles of well-marked, groomed trails are laced in a system maintained by the **Vermont Association of Snow Travelers (VAST).** VAST's corridor trails are up to 8 feet wide and are maintained by 150 local snowmobile clubs; for detailed maps and suggestions for routes, activities, and guided tours, contact the group at 802-229-0005; 41 Granger Road, Berlin 05641; www.vtvast.org. Also check www .snowmobilevt.com. Thanks to insurance laws, snowmobile rentals and tours are, however, few. The Northeast Kindgom in general and Island Pond in particular are geared to snowmobiling, with storage facilities and a wide choice of lodging handy to trails. The Northeast Kingdom Chamber of Commerce (802-748-3678; 1-800-639-6379; www.nekchamber.com) publishes a snowmobiling map/guide to the area.

SNOWSHOEING Snowshoeing is experiencing a rebirth in Vermont, thanks to the new lightweight equipment available from sources like Tubbs Snowshoe Company in Stowe. Virtually all ski touring centers now offer snowshoe rentals, and many inns stock a few pairs for guests.

SOARING **Sugarbush Soaring** (802-496-3730; Sugarbush Airport, Warren), in the Mad River Valley, is known as one of the prime spots in the East for riding thermal and ridge waves. The Sugarbush Airport is a well-established place to take glider lessons or rides or simply to watch the planes come and go. The **Fall**

Wave Soaring Encampment held in early October draws glider pilots from throughout the country. Gliders and airplane rides are also available at the **Stowe-Morrisville Airport** (802-888-5150) and **Post Mills Aviation** in Post Mills (802-333-9254), where soaring lessons are also a specialty, along with simply seeing the Connecticut Valley from the air.

SPIRITUAL CENTERS/RETREATS **Karmê Chöling Shambhala Buddhist Meditation Center** (802-633-2384; www.karmecholing.org) is a long-established retreat in Barnet with many special programs. **Yoga Vermont** in Burlington (802-660-9718; www.yogavermont.com) draws Ashtanga yoga practitioners from throughout the country. The **Maple Forest Monastery and Green Mountain Dharma Center** in Hartland is the scene of a major retreat (families welcome) the first week in July (802-434-1103; www.plumvillage.org), and the **Weston Priory** (802-824-5409; www.weston-priory.org) in Weston is a longtime Benedictine monastery known for its music and offering retreats.

STATE PARKS Vermont's more than 50 exceptionally well-groomed state parks include camping and/or day-use facilities, and are so diverse an assortment of properties that no one image applies. Within this book we attempt to describe each as it appears geographically. Vermont state parks are also detailed in an exceptional web site (**www.vtstateparks.com**) and are part of the **Department of Forests, Parks and Recreation** (802-241-3665; 103 South Main Street, Waterbury 05671-0603), which manages more than 157,000 acres of state land, offering opportunities for hunting, fishing, cross-country skiing, mountain biking, snowmobiling, and primitive as well as supervised camping. Also see *Campgrounds.*

SUMMER SELF-IMPROVEMENT PROGRAMS Whether it's improving your game of tennis or golf, learning to take pictures or to weave, cook, identify mushrooms, fish, or bike, or simply to lose weight, there is a summer program for you somewhere in Vermont. See *Tennis, Golf, Canoeing and Kayaking,* and *Fishing* for lodging and lesson packages. Intensive language programs are offered at **Middlebury College** (among the offerings are Arabic and Japanese, as well as more standard ones; www.middlebury.edu), and a writers' conference is held at its Bread Loaf summer campus. Senior citizens can take advantage of some outstanding courses offered at bargain prices (which include lodging) as part of the **Elderhostel** program. For details, write to Elderhostel, 11 Avenue de Lafayette, Boston, MA 02111; www.elderhostel.org. The state's oldest, most respected crafts program is offered by **Fletcher Farm Craft School** (Ludlow 05149): off-loom weaving, creative needlework, quilting, pottery, raku, and stained glass, plus meals and lodging (minimum age 18). The **Vermont Studio Center** (802-635-7000) in Johnson has a national reputation. Working visual artists and writers come to renew their creative wellsprings or to explore completely new directions during intensive sessions that feature guidance and criticism by some of the country's premier artists. **Craftsbury Outdoor Center** in

Craftsbury (www.craftsbury.com) has summer programs for all ages in running and sculling.

SWIMMING On the *Official Vermont Attractions Map,* you can pick out the 36 day-use areas that offer swimming, most with changing facilities, maintained by the Vermont State Department of Forests, Parks and Recreation (www.vtstateparks.com). Similar facilities are provided by the Green Mountain National Forest at Hapgood Pond in Peru, and the U.S. Army Corps of Engineers has tidied corners of its dam projects for public use in Townshend and North Springfield. There are also public beaches on roughly one-third of Vermont's 400 lakes and ponds (but note that swimming is prohibited at designated "Fishing Access Areas") and plenty on Lake Champlain (see Burlington, Charlotte, Colchester, Georgia, and Swanton). Add to these all the town recreation areas and myriad pools available to visitors and you still haven't gone swimming Vermont-style until you've sampled a Vermont swimming hole. These range from deep spots in the state's ubiquitous streams to 100-foot-deep quarries (**Dorset Quarry** near Manchester and **Chapman Quarry** in West Rutland are famous) and freezing pools between waterfalls (see "Sugarbush/Mad River Valley"). We have included some of our favorite swimming holes under *Swimming* in each section but could not bring ourselves to share them all. Look for cars along the road on a hot day and ask in local general stores. You won't be disappointed.

TENNIS Vermont claims as many tennis courts per capita as any other state in the union. These include town recreation facilities and sports centers as well as private facilities. Summer tennis programs, combining lessons, lodging, and meals, are offered at **Ascutney, Bolton Valley, Killington,** the **Village at Smugglers' Notch, Stratton, Topnotch Resort** in Stowe, and at the **Bridges** in Sugarbush. Check *Tennis* in each area.

THEATER Vermont's two long-established summer theaters are both in the Manchester area: the **Dorset Playhouse** and the **Weston Playhouse.** The **Green Mountain Guild** presents a series of summer musicals at the Killington Playhouse. Other summer theater can be found in Castleton, in Saxtons River, in Waitsfield (the **Valley Players**), in Warren **(Phantom Theater),** in Stowe (the **Stowe Playhouse** and the **Lamoille County Players** in Hyde Park), and **Northern Stage** at the Briggs Opera House in White River Junction. There's also the **Lost Nation Theater** in Montpelier. The **Flynn Theater** in Burlington and the **Paramount Theater** in Rutland are the scene of year-round live entertainment as well as film.

TRAINS See *Amtrak* and *Railroad Excursions.*

VERMONT PUBLIC RADIO Stations for those addicted to National Public Radio can be found throughout the state on the FM dial (click onto www.vpr.net). In the Burlington area, tune into WVPS (107.9), in the Windsor area to WVPR (89.5), in the Rutland area to WRVT (88.7); WVPA (88.5) is in St. Johnsbury; and WBTN (94.3), in Bennington.

WATERFALLS Those most accessible and worth accessing include (north to south): the falls at **Brewster River Gorge,** Route 108 in Jeffersonville and, farther south off Route 108 (the Mountain Road) in Stowe, **Bingham Falls** (an unmarked pull-off on the north side of the road); a trail leads downhill to the falls and gorge, recently conserved and deeded to the state. In Stowe also look for **Moss Glen Falls,** a 125-foot drop off Route 100. (About 3 miles north of the village, turn right onto Randolph Road, then right again on Moss Glen Falls Road; park at the area on the left just before a 90-degree turn across from a narrow bridge and look for the well-worn trail.) Beware **Big Falls** in Troy (directions are in our Jay Peak chapter): The top of this series of drops and cascades is a dramatic but rather scary spot; they represent the largest undammed waterfall on any major Vermont river (the Missisquoi). Also in northern Vermont: the **Great Falls of the Clyde River** in Charleston; **Duck Brook Cascades** in Bolton; **Little Otter Creek Falls** in Ferrisburgh; the seven falls on the **Huntington River** in Hanksville; **Shelburne Falls** in Shelburne; and **Cadys Falls** in Morrisville.

On the east–west roads linking the Champlain Valley with Route 100 (see *Gaps, Gulfs, and Gorges*), several falls are worth noting. On Route 17 look for the parking area, picnic table, and a short trail leading to the 45-foot **Bartlett Falls** in Bristol Memorial Park. On Route 125 check out Middlebury Gorge in East Middlebury; in Hancock don't miss 35-foot **Texas Falls,** well marked and a great picnic spot. North on Route 100 from Hancock also look for 45-foot **Moss Glen Falls** in Granville

VDT

www.neuswaterfalls.com, a site for which we thank Dean Goss.

WEATHER REPORTS For serious weather travel information in Vermont, check with the Vermont highway department's weather line: 802-828-2648. Listen to *An Eye on the Sky* on Vermont Public Radio (see *Vermont Public Radio* for stations; www.fairbanksmuseum.com). In the show, produced by the Fairbanks Museum and Planetarium, Mark Breen and Steve Maleski make their reports on life's most constant variable both entertaining and informative. The Vermont Chamber of Commerce web site (www.vermontvacation.com) also carries current weather information.

Gulf; here a boardwalk leads back to the falls, passing **Little Moss Glen Falls.** In the Upper Valley of the Connecticut River look for **Cow Meadows Ledges** in Newbury, the falls on the **Waits River** by Route 5 in the village of Bradford, and **Glen Falls,** a 75-foot drop in Fairlee almost opposite the fishing access on Lake Morey Road.

In southern Vermont look for **Buttermilk Falls** (a popular swimming hole) in Ludlow; the **East Putney Falls** and **Pot Holes;** and, our favorite of all, 125-foot **Hamilton Falls** in Jamaica, cascading down a schist wall with pools (responsible for more than one death over the years). Ask locally for directions to 160-foot **Lye Brook Falls** in Manchester. It's best accessed via a trail from Jamaica State Park off Routes 30/100. Most of these sites can be located on the invaluable *Vermont Atlas and Gazetteer* (DeLorme); also check

WEB PAGES In this edition we have hundreds of web sites within each region. Among the most helpful statewide sites are the following: **www.vermontvacation.com** is maintained by the Vermont Department of Travel and Tourism, with many informational leads and links; the Vermont Outdoor Guide Association maintains the best overall site for activities of every kind in the state: **www.voga .org; www.vtstateparks.com** includes locator maps and special programs related to state parks; **www .scenesofvermont.com** is an independently published mine of general information and links. The Vermont Chamber of Commerce is found at **www.vermontvacation.com**, while the Vermont Lodging and Restaurant Association maintains **www.visitvt .com.** This book is probably the single best directory to Vermont web sites, listing them by subject in this chapter and as they appear geographically throughout the book.

WEDDINGS Destination weddings have become big business in Vermont, so big and so ubiquitous that we use the wedding-ring symbol ∞ to designate lodging places that specialize in them. Contact www.vermontweddingguide.com or 1-800-860-5813 to request a free copy of the promotional *Vermont Wedding & Resource Guide* (remember, it's all advertising). One great wedding site that doesn't make these listings is **Grand Isle Lake House** (802-865-2522) in the Champlain Islands, a turn-of-the-20th-century summer hotel currently maintained by the Preservation Trust of Vermont. Also see *Civil Unions*.

WHITEWATER During white-water season beginning in mid-April, experienced canoeists and kayakers take advantage of stretches on the **White,** the **Lamoille,** and the **West Rivers,** among others. **White-water rafting** is also available on the **West River** during spring dam releases.

WINE Vermont has traditionally made apple and other fruit wines, but recently two wineries in the very northern reaches of the state have begun planting, harvesting, and fermenting grapes, with respectable results. These are **Boyden Valley Winery** (802-644-8151)—also good for premium apple wines—in Cambridge, and **Snow Farm Vineyard and Winery** (802-372-9463; www.snowfarm.com) in South Hero. **North River Winery** (802-368-7557; www.vtnatural.com), Vermont's long-established vintner, produces fruit wine, while the **Ottauquechee Valley Winery** (802-295-9463) in Quechee, **Flag Hill Farm** (802-685-7724) in Vershire, **Grand View Winery** (802-456-7012) in East Calais, and **Putney Mountain Winery** (802-387-4610) in Dummerston all make cider and apple wine. The newest addition is **Shelburne Vineyard** (802-734-1386; www.shelburnevineyard.com), which leases land from Shelburne Farms but operates as a separate enterprise.

THE INN AT MOUNTAIN VIEW FARM

Marilyn Pastore

Southern Vermont

THE LOWER CONNECTICUT AND
WEST RIVER VALLEYS

MOUNT SNOW/WILMINGTON AREA

BENNINGTON AREA

MANCHESTER AND THE MOUNTAINS

BELLOWS FALLS, SAXTONS RIVER,
AND GRAFTON

OKEMO VALLEY REGION

Kim Grant

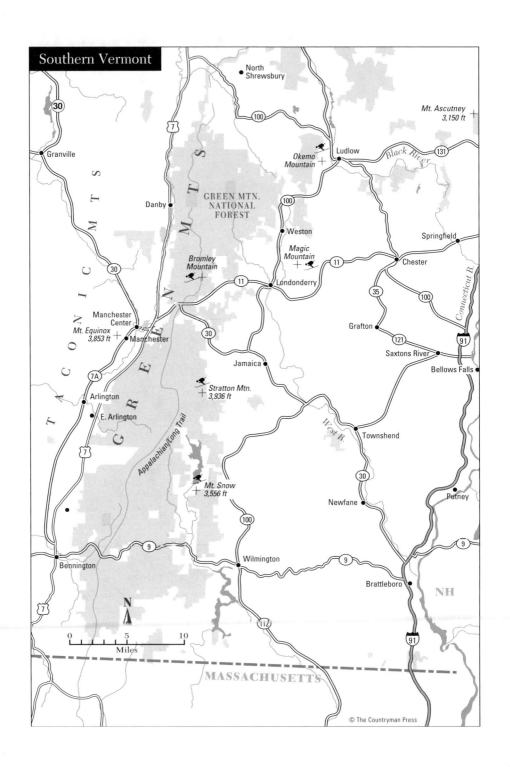

Southern Vermont

North Shrewsbury

Mt. Ascutney
3,150 ft

Granville

Ludlow

Black River

131

Okemo Mountain

GREEN MTS

Danby

GREEN MTN.
NATIONAL
FOREST

Weston

Springfield

Bromley Mountain

Magic Mountain

Chester

Londonderry

TACONIC MTS

Manchester Center

Mt. Equinox
3,853 ft

Manchester

Grafton

Saxtons River

Connecticut R.

Jamaica

Bellows Falls

Arlington

Stratton Mtn.
3,936 ft

E. Arlington

West R.

Townshend

GREEN

Appalachian/Long Trail

Mt. Snow
3,556 ft

Newfane

Putney

Bennington

Wilmington

Brattleboro

NH

MASSACHUSETTS

N

0   5   10
Miles

© The Countryman Press

THE LOWER CONNECTICUT
AND WEST RIVER VALLEYS
INCLUDING BRATTLEBORO, PUTNEY, NEWFANE, TOWNSHEND, AND JAMAICA

Wedged between the Green Mountains and the Connecticut River, Vermont's southeastern corner is a visually varied, richly layered, poke-around kind of place. Brattleboro, in its southern corner, is the commercial and cultural hub, contrasting with the classic white-clapboarded, green-shuttered towns of Newfane, Townshend, and Jamaica, which are strung like pearls along the West River, and with equally rural Putney, up along the Connecticut. Back roads web the area, connecting villages in unexpected and sometimes heart-stoppingly beautiful ways.

Many of Brattleboro's movers and shakers are former members of the communes that once flourished in the nearby hills. It's an earnest, yeasty community in which the spirit of the '60s continues to build. The supermarket is a co-op showcasing Vermont cheeses; the movie house is a restored art deco theater. Downtown Victorian-era blocks house a mix of traditional and counterculture shops, and include an unusual number of bookstores, galleries, restaurants, and coffeehouses.

While it's one of the most accessible, this is far from the most touristed corner of Vermont. Beyond the widely scattered country inns, antiques dealers, and crafts shops lie swimming holes, and hiking trails that lead to unexpected vistas. The confluence of the Connecticut and West Rivers at Brattleboro is itself a beautiful, placid place to paddle.

GUIDANCE **Brattleboro Area Chamber of Commerce** (802-254-4565; www.brattleborochamber.com), 180 Main Street, Brattleboro 05301, is good for walk-in information (open year-round, Monday through Friday 8–5, Saturday 10–2). It maintains seasonal information booths staffed by knowledgeable senior citizens on Route 5 at the common, just north of the junction with Route 30. Public **restrooms** are in the Robert S. Gibson Garden building on Main Street at the light, across from High Street (Route 9). Also see www.brattleboro.com.

Putney has its own first-rate web site: www.putney.net, featuring its many artists and artisans, as well as lodging and dining. The **West River Valley** towns along Route 30 maintain www.westrivervalley.com.

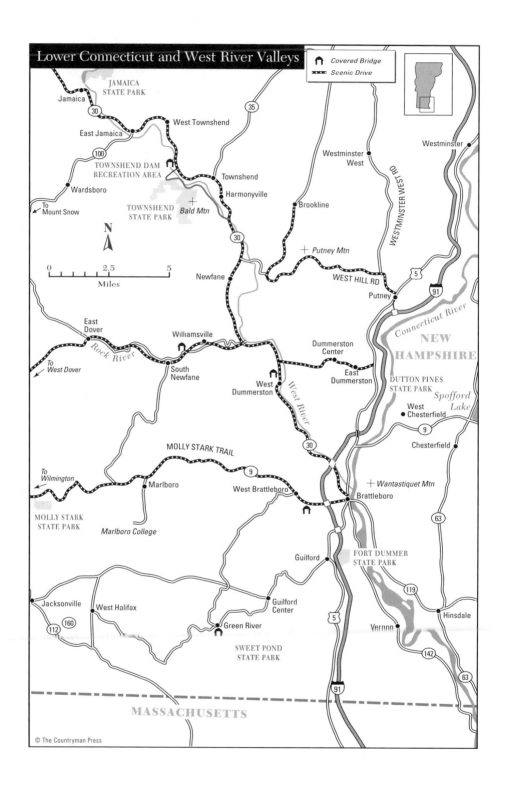

Lower Connecticut and West River Valleys

Covered Bridge
Scenic Drive

JAMAICA STATE PARK
Jamaica
30
East Jamaica
West Townshend
35
100
Westminster West
Westminster
TOWNSHEND DAM RECREATION AREA
Townshend
Wardsboro
Harmonyville
To Mount Snow
TOWNSHEND STATE PARK
Bald Mtn
Brookline

N

0   2.5   5
Miles

30
Putney Mtn
Newfane
WEST HILL RD
Putney
5
91

East Dover
Williamsville
Dummerston Center
NEW HAMPSHIRE
Rock River
To West Dover
South Newfane
West Dummerston
East Dummerston
DUTTON PINES STATE PARK
Spofford Lake
West Chesterfield

West River
9
Chesterfield

MOLLY STARK TRAIL
30
To Wilmington
Marlboro
9
West Brattleboro
Wantastiquet Mtn
Brattleboro
MOLLY STARK STATE PARK
Marlboro College
63

FORT DUMMER STATE PARK
Guilford

Jacksonville
West Halifax
Guilford Center
Hinsdale
112
160
Green River
5
Vernon
142
SWEET POND STATE PARK
63
91

Connecticut River

WESTMINSTER WEST RD

MASSACHUSETTS

© The Countryman Press

The **Southern Vermont Regional Market Organization** (1-877-887-2378; www.southernvermont.com) maintains a good web site for the entire region and sends out printed material.

Note: **The Southeast Vermont Welcome Center,** I-91 in Guilford (open daily 7 AM–1 AM), is the state's most elaborate visitors center (restrooms).

Newspapers: The *Brattleboro Reformer* (802-254-2311) publishes a special Thursday calendar that's the best source of current arts and entertainment. Also check out *The Observer* (802-874-4360), a weekly.

GETTING THERE *By bus:* **Greyhound/Vermont Transit** offers service from New York and Connecticut. **Peter Pan Bus Company** serves Boston via Springfield. The bus stop is on Route 5 at its junction with Route 9 west.

By train: **Amtrak** (1-800-USA-RAIL) trains from Washington, DC, and New York City stop at the old downtown railroad station, now a museum.

GETTING AROUND **Brattleboro Taxi** (802-254-5411) will meet trains and buses. **Thomas Transportation** (1-800-526-8143) offers shuttle service to Boston's Logan Airport, Hartford's Bradley Airport, and Manchester Airport.

Parking: Main Street has metered parking; side streets are possible. A large parking area (Harmony Place) in the rear of the Brooks House is close to shops on High, Elliot, and Main Streets; access is from High Street (Route 9). Brattleboro's new Transportation Center offers multilevel parking with access from Elliot or Flat Streets. Another large lot runs between High and Grove Streets.

WHEN TO GO In winter skiers tend to speed through up Route 30 to Stratton or across Route 9 to Mount Snow, but in summer this is a favorite area both for day-tripping (from Boston, western Massachusetts, and Connecticut) and for longer stays in the many gracious inns and B&Bs. The annual Strolling of the Heifers through downtown Brattleboro the first week in June is a big draw, and "Marlboro Season" (early July through early August) brings chamber music lovers, but other than that there is no single event or locale, just general beauty and many ways to enjoy it. Foliage brings more day-trippers, and it's wise to avoid the obvious roads (Routes 9 and 30). Luckily, there are many options (see *Scenic Drives*).

MEDICAL EMERGENCY Emergency service is available by calling **911.**

Brattleboro Memorial Hospital (802-257-0341), 17 Belmont Avenue, Brattleboro. **Grace Cottage Hospital** (802-365-7357), Route 25, Townshend.

✳ Towns and Villages

Brattleboro. This largely 1870s brick and wrought-iron town is the commercial hub for rural corners of three states. (Population swells from 12,000 at night to 30,000 by day.) It's a mix of native Vermonters, former commune members, and young people who keep arriving to study at one of several nearby educational institutions, including the burgeoning Brattleboro Music Center. Each year some

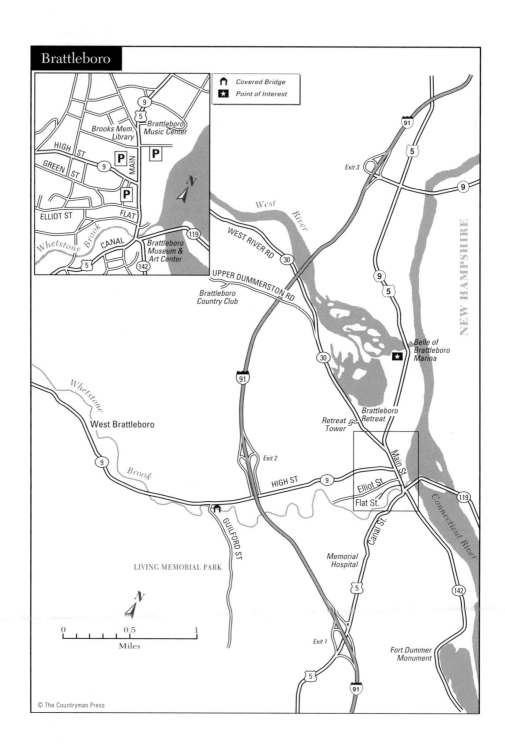

Brattleboro

Covered Bridge
Point of Interest

Brooks Mem. Library
Brattleboro Music Center

HIGH ST
GREEN ST
MAIN
ELLIOT ST
FLAT

Whetstone Brook
CANAL

Brattleboro Museum & Art Center

West River

WEST RIVER RD

UPPER DUMMERSTON RD

Brattleboro Country Club

Exit 3

NEW HAMPSHIRE

Belle of Brattleboro Marina

Whetstone

West Brattleboro

Brook

Brattleboro Retreat
Retreat Tower

Exit 2

HIGH ST

Elliot St.
Flat St.
Main St.

Connecticut River

LIVING MEMORIAL PARK

GUILFORD ST

Memorial Hospital

Canal St.

Exit 1

Fort Dummer Monument

0   0.5   1
Miles

© The Countryman Press

200 enroll in graduate programs at World Learning, begun in 1932 and best known for its Experiment in International Living program (now the School for International Training). Galleries, bookstores, boutiques, alternative shops, and restaurants now outnumber traditional stores. Sam's Outdoor Outfitters, Brown & Roberts Hardware, and Miller Brothers-Newton continue to thrive, but antiques and crafts stores have replaced former downtown anchors. On the first Friday of every month two dozen galleries and studios now host a Gallery Walk.

During its long history, this town has shed many skins. The site of Fort Dummer, built in 1724 just south of town, has been obliterated by the Vernon Dam. Gone, too, is the early-19th-century trading and resort town; no trace remains of the handsome, Federal-style commercial buildings or the two elaborate hotels that attracted trainloads of customers who came to take their water cures. The gingerbread wooden casino in Island Park and the fine brick town hall, with its gilded opera house, are gone, but the great slate-sided sheds in which hundreds of thousands of Estey organs were made are slowly being restored; one houses the new Estey Organ Museum.

Still, a motorist bogged down in the perpetual Main Street bottleneck notices Brooks House, built splendidly in 1869 as an 80-room hotel, once frequented by Rudyard Kipling, now converted to housing, offices, and shops. A couple of blocks down, the 1930s art deco Latchis Hotel has been restored inside as well as out; around the corner, Elliot Street is lined with specialty shops and restaurants.

Brattleboro is full of pleasant surprises. The former railroad station is now the Brattleboro Museum and Art Center. The Connecticut River is accessible by both excursion boat and rental canoe and can be viewed from a hidden downtown park and the new Robert H. Gibson River Garden, a weatherproofed public space (with public restrooms). Live theater, music, and dance are presented without hoopla. The fanfare seems to be reserved for the annual winter carnival, begun eons ago by Fred Harris, who also founded the Dartmouth Winter Carnival and the U.S. Eastern Amateur Ski Association.

Kim Grant

Along Route 30 in the West River Valley

Newfane. A columned courthouse, matching Congregational church, and town hall—all grouped on a handsome green—are framed by dignified, white-clapboard houses, including two elegant inns. When Windham County's court sessions began meeting in Newfane in 1787, the village was about the same size it is now: 20 houses and two hotels. But in 1787, the village was

2 miles up on Newfane Hill. Beams were unpegged and homes moved to the more protected valley by ox-drawn sleighs in the winter of 1824.

Newfane inns have been famous for more than a century, at first because the whitewashed jail accommodated 25 paying guests, feeding them (as an 1848 poem says) "good pies and oyster soup" in the same rooms with inmates. By the time this facility closed (in the 1950s), the Old Newfane Inn—which incorporates much of its original hilltop structure—was beginning to acquire a reputation for gourmet fare. Economist John Kenneth Galbraith, a summer resident in the area since 1947, helped publicize the charms of both the village and the inn—whose onetime chef eventually opened the Four Columns Inn at the rear of the green. Newfane Village is more than a place to dine, sleep, and stroll. It is the site of one of the state's oldest and biggest Sunday flea markets, and the immediate area offers an unusual number of antiques shops. Beyond the stores and the remnants of the railway station (which served the narrow-gauge Brattleboro–Londonderry line from 1880 to 1936) is a fine old cemetery.

Newfane has bred as well as fed famous people. You'll learn about some of them in the exceptional **Historical Society of Windham County** (802-365-4148), Route 30, south of the common (open Memorial Day through mid-October, Wednesday and Sunday noon–5, and for special events). It looks like a brick post office. Displays change, but the most interesting is the story of John Wilson (see Brookline, below).

Brookline. Half as wide as it is long, Brookline is sequestered in a narrow valley bounded by steep hills and the West River. (Turn off Route 30 at the Newfane Flea Market.) Its population of 410 is four times what it was 50 years ago but a small fraction of what it was in the 1820s and '30s, when it supported three stores, three schools, two hotels, and a doctor. Those were the decades in which its two landmark brick buildings were constructed. One is a church, but the more famous is a round schoolhouse, said to be the only one in the country—and also probably the only school designed by a crook.

NEWFANE VILLAGE

Kim Grant

John Wilson never seems to have mentioned his past career as Thunderbolt, an infamous Scottish highwayman. In 1820 the obviously well-educated newcomer designed the circular schoolhouse. He gave it six large windows, the better (it was later noted) to allow him to see whoever approached from any side. Wilson taught for only a term before moving to the neighboring (and more remote) town of Dummerston, just about the time that an Irish felon, "Lightfoot" Martin, was hanged in Cambridge, Massachusetts. In his confession (reprints are sold at the historical society), Martin fingered

Wilson as his old accomplice, but with no obvious effect. Not long thereafter, Wilson added "Dr." to his name and practiced medicine in Newfane, then in Brattleboro, where he married, fathering a son before his wife divorced him "because of certain facts she learned." When he died in 1847, scars on Wilson's ankles and neck suggested chains and a rope. Today several of Thunderbolt's pistols are preserved by the historical society and in Brattleboro's Brooks Library.

TOWNSHEND GREEN

Kim Grant

Unfortunately, the round schoolhouse is now virtually never open. In 1928 the town's first eight grades moved down the road to the current wooden schoolhouse. As the population dwindled through the '30s, '40s, and '50s, the building was used for town meeting, but that assemblage is now held in the vestry of the Baptist church, Brookline's second landmark. Built in 1836, the church has been beautifully restored, thanks to fund-raising efforts like the annual Musicale Sunday, usually held late in July, sponsored by the Ladies Benevolent Society.

Townshend. The next village green north on Route 30 is a full 2 acres, complete with Victorian-style gazebo. It's bordered on one side by a classic white 1790 Congregational church flanked by lovely clapboard houses, on others by a columned and tower-topped stucco town hall of the Leland and Gray Union High School (founded as a Baptist seminary in 1834), and by a clapboard commercial block. On the first Saturday in August the common fills with booths and games to benefit Grace Cottage Hospital, which has grown, unbelievably, out of the back side of a rambling old village home. (Known for the quality of its service, this is Vermont's first hospital to have installed a birthing bed.) West Townshend, farther along Route 30, is a three-corners with a photogenic church and general store.

The town also harbors stuffed-toy and furniture factories, a state park, a public swimming area, Vermont's largest single-span covered bridge, 15 cemeteries, and several good places to stay and to eat.

Jamaica. A small village clustered around its white Congregational church (1808) on Route 30, Jamaica is the kind of place you can drive through in 2 minutes, or stay a week. The village buildings are few but proud, and there is swimming and plenty of hiking as well as camping in **Jamaica State Park.** The village, which lies within the bailiwick of Stratton Mountain's resort community, also offers some surprisingly good shopping.

North along Route 5
Putney. This village's riverside fields have been heavily farmed since the mid–18th century, and its hillsides produce more than one-tenth of all the state's

apples. Putney is an unusually fertile place for progressive thinking, too. Back in the 1840s it spawned a group who practiced Bible Communism, the sharing of all property, work, and wives. John Humphrey Noyes, the group's leader, was charged with adultery in 1847 and fled with his flock to Oneida, New York, where they founded the famous silverplate company. Known today for experimental education rather than religion, Putney is the home of the Putney School, a coed, college preparatory school founded in 1935, with a regimen that entails helping with chores, including raising animals. Landmark College is the country's only fully accredited college specifically for dyslexic students and those with other learning disabilities. The Greenwood School, a prep school for dyslexic boys, and the Oak Meadow School, a pioneering support service for homeschooling, are also in town. In July the **Yellow Barn Music School and Festival** is housed in a barn behind the library; concerts are staged there and at other local venues throughout the month.

Putney Village is tiny but offers some interesting shopping, augmented on the first weekend after Thanksgiving by the annual **Putney Artisans Craft Tour,** for which dozens of established craftspeople open their back-roads studios. Putney's scenic roads are also well known to serious bicyclists, and Putney Mountain (see *Hiking*) is beloved by both hikers and mountain bikers.

Putney's native sons include the late George Aiken, who served as governor before going on to Washington as a senator in 1941, a post he held until his retirement in 1975. Frank Wilson, a genuine Yankee trader who was one of the first merchants to enter Red China, built the first of his **Basketvilles,** "The World's Largest Basket Stores," in the village. The **Putney Historical Society** (802-387-5862), housed in town hall, is open by appointment.

South on Route 5

Guilford. Back-roaded by I-91 (which has no exit between Brattleboro and Massachusetts), this old agricultural town rewards with quiet rural scenery any-

Kim Grant

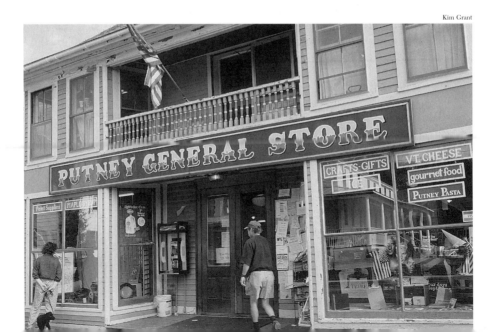

one who drives or pedals its roads. Check out **Sweet Pond State Park,** a former 125-acre estate with a large pond, good for swimming and boating, and circled by a nature path. Labor Day weekend is big here, the time for the old-fashioned **Guilford Fair** and for the annual 2-day, free concerts sponsored by Friends of Music at Guilford (802-257-1961) in and around the **Organ Barn.** The **Guilford Historical Society,** open Memorial Day through Columbus Day, Tuesday and Saturday 10–2 and by appointment (call Addie Minott at 802-254-5910), maintains exhibits in the 1822 town hall, in the 1837 meetinghouse, and in the 1797 one-room brick schoolhouse.

✳ To See

MUSEUMS The **Brattleboro Historical Society** (802-258-4957) maintains a "history room" (a restored 1800s classroom), and more than 7,000 photographs dating from the mid-1800s. It's on the third floor of the Municipal Building (230 Main Street; open Thursday 1–4 and Saturday 9–noon). Note the new Estey Organ Museum under *To See* and pick up the leaflet that describes the architectural walking tour of Main Street. The International Center on the 200-acre campus of **World Learning** (802-257-7751) on Kipling Road (off Route 5 just north of town), offers much the same view across the valley to Mount Monadnock that Rudyard Kipling enjoyed from Naulakha during the years that he lived there (1892–96).

&. **Brattleboro Museum and Art Center** (802-257-0124; www.brattleboromuseum.org), 10 Vernon Street (corner of Canal and Route 119), Brattleboro. Open mid-May through December, Tuesday through Sunday noon–6; $3 per adult, $2 for seniors and students, free under 12. The town's 1915 rail station makes a handsome home for changing exhibits that have varied widely in recent years, from quilts to architecture to contemporary art. Inquire about frequent lectures related to the exhibits, family workshops and events, concerts, and "twilight" guided walks.

Brooks Memorial Library (802-254-5290), 224 Main Street (open daily except Sunday), mounts changing exhibits of regional art and has a fine collection of 19th-century paintings and sculpture, including works by Larkin G. Mead, the Brattleboro boy who first achieved national renown by sculpting an 8-foot-high angel from snow one night and placing it at the junction of Routes 30 and 5.

Estey Organ Museum (802-258-2363; www.esteyorganmuseum.org), 108 Birge Street (rear), Brattleboro. Open June through Columbus Day, weekends 1–5. Brattleboro's famed Estey Organ Co., once the town's largest employer, produced thousands of organs each year between 1846 and its demise in 1960. This fledgling museum, founded in 2002, is currently housed in a former engine house, a large airy, well-lit space in which exhibits trace the history of organs in general and of Estey organs in particular. There are examples of reed organs from the 1860s and the ornately carved parlor organs found in countless Victorian homes. There are also the pipe organs Estey made for small churches throughout the county, and finally there are electronic organs, highly innovative when they first appeared. It's a fabulous story, and one that's been waiting for decades to be told. Eventually the museum will include sound as well as visuals. The Engine House is the smallest of four buildings that are eventually planned to house the museum. They are surrounded by the Estey Company's other cast, slate-sided sheds.

See also Historical Society of Windham County in Newfane under *Villages*.

COVERED BRIDGES In Brattleboro the reconstructed **Creamery Bridge** forms the entrance to Living Memorial Park on Route 9. North on Route 30 in West Dummerston, a Town lattice bridge across the West River is the longest still-used covered bridge in the state (for the best view, jump into the cool waters on either side; this is a popular swimming hole on a hot summer day). The **Scott Bridge,** Vermont's longest single-span bridge, stands by Route 30 in West Townshend just below the Townshend Dam, but it's closed to traffic. The region's oldest covered bridge spans the Rock River between Williamsville and South Newfane. The Green River in Guilford also boasts a covered bridge.

FOR FAMILIES ♪ **Retreat Farm** (802-257-2240), 350 Linden Street, Route 30 just north of Brattleboro. Open Memorial Day through October, Wednesday through Sunday 10–4. Admission: $5 for 12 and over, $4 under 12. Brattleboro Retreat's working dairy farm, now owned by the Grafton-based Windham Foundation, also includes llamas, pigs, emus, lambs, sheep, goats, oxen, donkeys, horses, chickens, kittens, shaggy Highland cattle, and a cow that visitors are invited to milk. A gift shop features farm-related toys and Grafton Village Cheese.

♪ **Butterfly Heaven** and **D&K's Little Petting Farm** (802-874-4160; www.dkgarden.com), Route 30, Jamaica. Open year-round daily, 9–5 May through October, 9–3 in winter; the petting farm is seasonal. $6 adult to either the Butterfly Heaven or Petting Farm, $8 for both, less for children and seniors.

GREEN RIVER BRIDGE AND GREEN RIVER FALLS IN GUILFORD

Alois Mayer

Dale and Karen Ameden began by creating a garden center featuring more than 1,000 varieties of perennials and acres of display gardens. They then added a petting farm with chicks, ducks, bunnies, Shetland sheep, pygmy goats, a Holstein calf, and more. Now they've built another big greenhouse and filled it with the plants butterflies love, along with paths, seats, and a jungle habitat for tropical birds at the far end. The result is enchanting. In all the complex covers 11 acres.

There are more farms to visit listed under *Selective Shopping*.

♪ **Santa's Land** (802-387-5550; 1-800-726-8299), Route 5, Putney.

Open daily 10–5 Memorial Day through Labor Day, then weekends, weather permitting, until Christmas. Designed for children ages 2–8, this Christmas theme village includes an Igloo Pancake House, Christmas shops, Santa's home, reindeer, kiddie rides, barnyard and unusual animals, a Ferris wheel, Santa's Express Train, and, of course, Santa.

✿ **Connecticut River Fish Ladder,** Vernon. The New England Power Company's 984-foot fish ladder helps American shad and Atlantic salmon return to their spawning grounds—51 pools in a 35-foot vertical rise. Best viewing is from late May through mid-July, daily 8–5.

Also see the Southern Vermont Natural History Museum at Hogback Mountain (west of Brattleboro) in "Mount Snow/Wilmington Area" and the Nature Museum of Grafton in "Bellows Falls, Saxtons River, and Grafton."

SCENIC DRIVES The hilly, heavily wooded country between the West and Connecticut River Valleys is webbed with roads, most of them dirt. Our favorites include:

Putney Mountain Road to Brookline. At the Putney General Store on Route 5, turn left onto Westminster West Road and left again about a mile up the hill onto West Hill Road. Not far above the Putney School, look for a dirt road on your right. It forks immediately; bear right to Putney Mountain. Trees thicken and sunlight dapples through in a way that it never seems to do on paved roads. Chipmunks scurry ahead on the hard-packed dirt. The few drivers you pass will wave. The road curves up and up—and up—cresting after 2.1 miles. Note the unmarked parking area on your right (see Putney Mountain under *Hiking*). The road then snakes down the other side into Brookline.

The **Molly Stark Trail**—Route 9 between Brattleboro and Bennington—is dedicated to the wife of General John Stark, hero of the battle of Bennington. The 17-mile stretch west from Brattleboro passes by Marlboro, climbing high over Hogback Mountain before winding down into Wilmington. Very scenic but heavily trafficked during foliage season.

West Dummerston to West Dover. Beautiful in a car or on a bike, the 13 miles between Route 30 and Route 100 form a shortcut from Newfane to Mount Snow. Turn west off Route 30, 2 miles north of the covered bridge. Follow the Rock River (in summer, clumps of cars suggest swimming holes) west from West Dummerston and Williamsville, on through the picturesque village of South Newfane (the general store is a source of picnic fare); detour 0.5 mile into the old hill village of Dover, very different from West Dover down on busy Route 100.

Route 30 from Brattleboro to Jamaica (you can loop back on Route 100 and take either of the two routes sketched above) shadows the West River, passing two covered bridges and going through the exceptionally picturesque villages of Newfane and Townshend, as well as by the Townshend Dam (good for swimming). Both villages offer first-rate crafts and antiques.

East Dummerston to West Dummerston. A handy shortcut from Route 5 to Route 30 (or vice versa), just 2 miles up one side of a hill to picturesque Dummerston Center and 2 miles down the other. This was long known in our family as the Gnome Road because of the way it winds through the woods to Vermont's longest (recently refitted) traffic-bearing covered bridge. It's generally known as the East/West Road.

Brattleboro to Guilford Center to Halifax and back. This can be a 46-mile loop to Wilmington and back; ask locally for shortcuts back up to Route 9. Take Route 5 south from Brattleboro to the Guilford Country Store (selling sandwiches), then right into Guilford Center. Continue for 0.5 mile and bear right on Stage Road to Green River with its covered bridge, church, and recently restored crib dam. Bear right at the church (before the bridge) and then left at the Y; follow Green River Road (along the river) and then Hatch School Road into Jacksonville. To complete the loop, see *Scenic Drives* in "Mount Snow/Wilmington Area."

✳ To Do

BICYCLING Some 200 miles of dirt and abandoned roads, along with miles of off-road trails, add up to a well-established mecca for bicyclists. The **Putney Bicycle Club,** the oldest in Vermont, organizes weekly (hard-core) mountain bike tours. Check with the **West Hill Shop** (802-387-5718; www.westhillshop.com), open daily, I-91 exit 4, across from the Putney Inn. Since 1971 the hub of biking information throughout this area, the shop has published its own map, detailing four tours as well as Class 4 roads and off-road routes. It also provides mountain bike rentals. **Brattleboro Bicycle Shop** (802-254-8644; 1-800-BRAT-BIKE; www.bratbike.com), 178 Main Street, offers repairs, day rentals (hybrids), and plenty of advice about where to use them. **Burrows Specialized Sports** (802-254-9430), 105 Main Street in Brattleboro, also offers bike sales, rentals, and repairs.

Also see "Manchester and the Mountains."

THE CONNECTICUT RIVER VALLEY IS LINED WITH FARMS.

Kim Grant

BOATING Vermont Canoe Touring Center (802-257-5008; vtcanoe@sover.net), 451 Putney Road, Brattleboro. Located on the West River at the cove at Veterans Memorial Bridge, Route 5, just north of the junction with Route 30. Open daily Memorial Day weekend through Labor Day weekend 9–7, weekends in spring and fall. John Knickerbocker rents canoes and kayaks, and offers shuttle service, guided trips, and wilderness camping on the river. The 32 miles from Bellows Falls to the Vernon Dam is slow-moving water, as is the 6-mile stretch from below the dam to the Massachusetts border.

Connecticut River Tours (802-254-1263; www.belleofbrattleboro.com), Putney Road, Brattleboro. The 49-passenger, mahogany-trimmed *Belle of Brattleboro* offers several kinds of cruises Wednesday through Sunday and holidays, Memorial Day through Columbus Day.

Whitewater on the West River. Twice a year, once in spring and again in September, the Army Corps of Engineers releases water from the Ball Mountain Dam (802-874-4881) in Jamaica, creating whitewater fit for national kayak championships. The races are no longer run here, but commercial white-water rafters as well as white-water kayakers and canoeists take advantage of the flow, especially in fall, when many of the region's other white-water courses are dry.

Townshend Outdoors (802-365-7308), Route 30 south of Townshend Village. Open weekends in summer, otherwise by appointment. Ann Griswold's consignment shop for sports equipment has canoes and kayaks, which can also be rented for use at the nearby Townshend Recreation Area (the dam) and other nearby lakes. You can rent tubes for use in the river, too. (The shop also sells and rents skis and snowshoes.)

FISHING In the **Connecticut River** you can catch bass, trout, pike, pickerel, and yellow perch. There is an access on Old Ferry Road, 2 miles north of Brattleboro on Route 5; another is from River Road on the New Hampshire shore in Westmoreland (Route 9 east, then north on Route 63). For fishing boat rentals contact the **Marina Restaurant** (802-257-7563).

The **West River** is a source of trout and smallmouth bass; access is from any number of places along Route 30. In Vernon there is a boat access on **Lily Pond;** in Guilford on **Weatherhead Hollow Pond** (see the DeLorme *Vermont Atlas and Gazetteer*).

GOLF **Brattleboro Country Club** (802-254-9864), Upper Dummerston Road, has recently expanded to 18 holes and includes a full driving range, practice areas, and instructional range. The **Windham Golf Club** (802-825-2517), Popple Dungeon Road in Windham, offers 18 holes. Also see Mount Snow and Stratton ski resorts under *Downhill Skiing;* both offer golf schools and 27 holes.

HIKING **In Brattleboro** a pleasant path up to the Retreat Tower, a 19th-century overlook, begins beside Linden Lodge on Route 30. Another trail follows the West River along the abandoned **West River railroad bed.** Access is off Route 5 north of town; take the second left turn after crossing the bridge. **Wantastiquet Mountain,** overlooking Brattleboro from across the Connecticut River in New Hampshire, is a good 1½-hour hike from downtown, great for picnics and views of southeast Vermont. See also Fort Dummer State Park under *Green Space* for a wooded trail south of town overlooking the Connecticut, and Townshend State Forest for a steep trek up Bald Mountain.

Putney Mountain between Putney and Brookline, off Putney Mountain Road (see *Scenic Drives*), is one of the most rewarding 1-mile round-trip hikes anywhere. A sign nailed to a tree in the unmarked parking area assures you that this is indeed Putney Mountain. Follow the trail that heads gently uphill through birches and maples, then continues through firs and vegetation that change remarkably quickly to the stunted growth usually found only at higher elevations. Suddenly you emerge on the mountain's broad crown, circled by a deep-down satisfying panorama. The view to the east is of Mount Monadnock, rising in lonely magnificence above the roll of southern New Hampshire, but more spectacular is the spread of Green Mountain peaks to the west. You can pick out the ski trails on Haystack, Mount Snow, and Stratton.

Jamaica State Park offers a choice of three interesting trails. The most intriguing and theoretically the shortest is to Hamilton Falls, a 125-foot cascade through a series of wondrous potholes. It's an obvious mile (30-minute) hike up, but the return can be confusing. Beware straying onto Turkey Mountain Road.

Black Mountain Natural Area, maintained by The Nature Conservancy of Vermont (802-229-4425). Cross the covered bridge on Route 30 in West Dummerston and turn south on Quarry Road for 1.4 miles. The road changes to Rice Farm Road; go another 0.5 mile to a pull-off on the right. The marked trail begins across the road and rises abruptly 1,280 feet to a ridge, traversing it before dropping back down, passing a beaver dam on the way back to the river. The loop is best done clockwise. Beautiful in laurel season.

HORSEBACK RIDING **West River Stables at Meadowbrook Farm** (802-365-7668), Hill Road, Brookline. Roger Poitras has built a barn and ring across the way from the West River Lodge and offers English riding lessons featuring "centered riding" (using the Alexander technique), dressage, and jumping. **Winchester Stables** (802-365-9434), River Road in Newfane, also offers lessons. For trail rides see "Mount Snow/Wilmington Area" and "Manchester and the Mountains."

RAILROAD EXCURSION The **Green Mountain Flyer** (802-463-3069), based just north of this area in Bellows Falls, offers a 26-mile run in-season. (See "Bellows Falls, Saxtons River, and Grafton.")

SWIMMING ✐ **Living Memorial Park,** west of downtown Brattleboro on Route 9, offers a public pool (mid-June through Labor Day). In the West River Valley at the **Townshend Lake Recreation Area** (802-874-4881) off Route 30 in West Townshend you drive across the top of the massive dam, completed in 1961 as a major flood-prevention measure for the southern Connecticut River Valley. Swimming is in the reservoir behind the dam, with a human-made beach and gradual drop-off, good for children. Changing facilities provided; small fee. The **West River** itself offers a few swimming holes, notably under the West Dummerston covered bridge on Route 30 and at Salmon Hole in Jamaica State Park. **Hamilton Falls,** accessible from the park, and **Pikes Falls,** also in Jamaica (ask directions locally), are favorite swimming holes, but not advised for children. Just off Route 30, a mile or so up (on South Newfane Road), the **Rock River** swirls through a series of shallow swimming spots; look for cars. In Guilford there is swimming at **Sweet Pond State Park** (802-257-7406), a former 125-acre estate with a large pond circled by a nature path. Also handy to Brattleboro, **Wares Grove** is across the Connecticut River in Chesterfield, New

Hampshire (9 miles east on Route 9, the next left after the junction with Route 63). This pleasant beach on Spofford Lake is good for children; you'll find a snack bar and makeshift changing facilities.

❋ Winter Sports

CROSS-COUNTRY SKIING **Brattleboro Outing Club Ski Hut** (802-254-4081), Upper Dummerston Road, Brattleboro. Trails through woods and a golf course, 16 km machine tracked, rentals, instruction. In **Living Memorial Park** (802-254-4081), Brattleboro, a 6 km trail through the woods is not only set but also lighted for night skiing. **West Hill Shop** (802-387-5718), I-91, exit 4 (across from the Putney Inn), is the source of cross-country information for the Putney area. **Townshend Outdoors** (802-365-7309), Route 30 south of Townshend Village, rents cross-country skis and snowshoes. **Jamaica State Park** in Jamaica (see *Green Space*) offers marked trails.

See also Grafton Ponds in "Bellows Falls, Saxtons River, and Grafton."

DOWNHILL SKIING The big ski areas are a short drive west into the Green Mountains, either to **Mount Snow** (Route 9 from Brattleboro and then up Route 100 to West Dover—see "Mount Snow/Wilmington Area") or up Route 30 to **Stratton** (see "Manchester and the Mountains").

SLEIGH RIDES **Fair Winds Farm** (802-254-9067), Upper Dummerston Road, and the **Robb Family Farm** (802-254-7664; 1-888-318-9087), 827 Ames Hill Road, both offer sleigh rides within minutes of downtown Brattleboro. See also *Farms to Visit*.

SNOWMOBILING See "Mount Snow/Wilmington Area."

❋ Green Space

Fort Dummer State Park (802-254-2610), Guilford. Located 2 miles south of Brattleboro on South Main Street. There are 61 campsites, including 10 lean-tos, and a dump station, a playfield, and a hiking trail through hardwoods with views of the river valley.

✍ **Jamaica State Park** (802-874-4600), Jamaica. This 758-acre wooded area offers riverside camping, swimming in a great swimming hole, a picnic area, and an organized program of guided hikes. An old railroad bed along the river serves as a 3-mile trail to the Ball Mountain Dam, and an offshoot mile-long trail leads to Hamilton Falls. A weekend in spring and again in fall is set aside for white-water canoe races. There are 61 tent/trailer sites and 18 lean-tos. A large picnic shelter is handy to the swimming hole; a playground includes swings, a teeter-totter, and slides.

Ball Mountain Lake (802-874-4881), Jamaica. This 85-acre lake, created and maintained by the U.S. Army Corps of Engineers, is a dramatic sight among the wooded, steep mountains, conveniently viewed from the access road off Route 30. Over 100 campsites are available on Winhall Brook at the other end of the reservoir, open mid-May through Columbus Day; it's accessible off Route 100 in South Londonderry. For reservations phone 1-877-444-6777. A controlled release from this flood dam provides outstanding canoeing on the West River below Jamaica each spring and fall (see *Boating*).

Townshend State Park (802-365-7500), Townshend, marked from Route 30 south of town. Open early May through Columbus Day. Up a back road, an attractive, classic '30s Civilian Conservation Corps (CCC) stone-and-wood complex with a picnic pavilion. This is really an 826-acre state forest with 41 acres reserved for the park. The camping area (30 campsites, four lean-tos) is near the start of the 2.7-mile (steep) climb to the summit of Bald Mountain; trail maps are available at the park office.

Dutton Pines State Park (802-254-2277), Brattleboro. On Route 5, 5 miles north of town, this is a picnic area with a shelter.

Living Memorial Park, just west of Brattleboro on Route 9. This is an unusual facility for any community. It includes a swimming pool (mid-June through Labor Day), ice-skating rink (early December through mid-March), tennis courts, playground, camping sites, lawn games, a nine-hole golf course, and a ski hill serviced by a T-bar.

See also Sweet Pond State Park under *Swimming*.

✳ Lodging

COUNTRY INNS 🐾 ♿ **Four Columns Inn** (802-365-7713; 1-800-787-6633; www.fourcolumnsinn.com), Newfane 05345. This Greek Revival mansion, built in 1830 by General Pardon Kimball to remind his southern wife of her girlhood home, fronts on Newfane's classic green. The 15 guest rooms vary from merely country elegant ($125–150) to deluxe (with gas fireplace, $155–175) to extravagant suites (two-person whirlpool or soaking tub typically with a view of the gas fireplace, $190–340). The very best suite fills the space above the four columns, formerly a porch, with a Jacuzzi overlooking the green. While it's set in a splendid village, the inn backs onto 150 steep and wooded acres, good for walking or snowshoeing. Dining is a big attraction (see *Dining Out*), and facilities include a swimming pool. Roll-away $25. Rates increase in foliage season. Breakfast included. $10 extra for pets.

♿ **Windham Hill Inn** (802-874-4080; 1-800-944-4080; www.windhamhill .com), West Townshend 05359. High above the West River Valley, this 1825 brick farmhouse, presently owned by Joe and Marina Coneeny, is a luxurious retreat. Several of the 21 guest rooms have soaking tub, private deck, Jacuzzi, fireplace, or gas stove, and all have private bath and phone. All are carefully furnished with antiques and interesting art. Eight are in the White Barn Annex, some with a large deck looking down the valley. Common space in the inn itself includes a music room with grand piano and an airy sunporch with wicker. Two sitting rooms are country elegant with wood-burning fireplace, Oriental carpets, and wing chairs, and the dining room also has a fireplace, a formal dining table, and tables for two (see *Dining Out*). There's a nicely landscaped pool overlooking the mountains and tennis court. The 160-acre property also includes an extensive network of hiking paths, groomed as cross-country trails in winter (when the frog pond freezes for skating). Inquire about weddings, both inside (there's a small conference center in the barn) and outside (for up to 75 guests). $195–345 per couple B&B plus $50 in foliage season.

☙ **Three Mountain Inn** (802-874-4140; 1-800-532-9399; www.three mountaininn.com), Route 30, Jamaica 05343. This 1790s inn in the middle of a classic Vermont village has recently undergone a complete makeover by David Hiler with help from Bill Oates and Heidi Bredfeldt. There are seven upstairs rooms and seven in neighboring Robinson House, all newly decorated, several with whirlpool tub and eight with gas or wood fireplace or stove. Sage Cottage in the garden now features a Jacuzzi tub, gas fireplace, two skylights and a stained-glass window, surround sound, and, of course, a TV/VCR. Common space includes the old tavern room with its large hearth and a cozy corner bar. There are two small but elegant dining rooms (see *Dining Out*) and a new private dining room/meeting space. The gathering room with its big hearth is charming. Jamaica State Park and its trails are a short walk, and Stratton Mountain, with its 27-hole golf course, is a short drive. From $145 for small rooms in the inn to $295 for the ground-floor two-room Jamaica Suite with French doors in the bedroom and sitting rooms opening onto the patio; $325 for the cottage; breakfast is included. Add $20 during foliage season and holidays.

Old Newfane Inn (802-365-4427; 1-800-784-4427) Route 30, Newfane 05345. Closed in November and April.

THE VIEW FROM THE LAWN OF THE WINDHAM HILL INN

Christina Tree

Closed Monday. Under the same ownership for more than 30 years, this inn has changed little in the past two decades. The long, low-beamed dining room was a part of the original inn built up on Newfane Hill, and there is a seemly sense of age and a formal atmosphere. The eight spotless guest rooms and two suites are furnished with antiques; $135–175 double (the high end is for a suite with living room, bath, and bedroom). The inn is best known for outstanding French-Swiss cuisine (see *Dining Out*).

Chesterfield Inn (603-256-3211; 1-800-365-5515; www.chesterfield inn.com), P.O. Box 155, Chesterfield, New Hampshire 03443. On Route 9, 2 miles east of Brattleboro. The original house served as a tavern from 1798 to 1811 but the present facility is contemporary, with a large attractive dining room, spacious parlor, and 13 guest rooms and two suites divided between the main house and the Guest House. All rooms have sitting area, phone, controlled heat and air-conditioning, optional TV, and wet bar, and some have a working fireplace or Jacuzzi. Innkeepers Phil and Judy Hueber have created a popular dining room and a comfortable, romantic getaway spot that's well positioned for exploring southern Vermont, as well as New Hampshire's Monadnock region. $150–275 includes a full breakfast.

BED & BREAKFASTS

In Brattleboro 05301

🐾 ♂ **Forty Putney Road** (802-254-6268; 1-800-941-2413; frtyptny@sover .net), at that address. Just north of the town common and within walking distance of downtown shops and restaurants, this house with steeply pitched, gabled roof is said to be patterned on a French château. It was built in 1930 for the director of the neighboring Brattleboro Retreat. Lowell and Lindsay Hanson, the new owners, are avid gardeners and usually found tending the landscaped grounds. Five tastefully furnished guest rooms, each with phone, TV, and private bath, include a two-room suite and a two-room cottage with a gas fireplace and full kitchen. There's a cozy pub serving guests a wide selection of beer and wine. We would request one of the rear two rooms overlooking the gardens, away from Route 5 (Putney Road), but front rooms are air-conditioned so noise is muted. Common space is plentiful and attractive, and landscaped grounds with working fountains border the West River. The $110–230 double rates include a full breakfast served, weather permitting, on the garden patio. The fireplace suite is $180 and the cottage, $230 double. Dogs and children welcome.

1868 Crosby House (802-257-4914; 1-800-528-1868; www.crosbyhouse .com), 175 Western Avenue. A mansion built in 1868 and set in landscaped gardens, this is a special place with a marble fireplace and baby grand piano in the parlor and superb detailing, augmented by cabinets and other examples of highly skilled woodworking by Lynn Kuralt's late husband, Tom. Each of the three guest rooms is well thought out and has a fireplace and magnificent bed and bath; Winifred's Summer Retreat has both a paneled fireplace and a double whirlpool with separate shower. There are also two studio suites with cathedral ceilings and garden views and two suites, one with a fireplace. $120–150 includes a full, heart-healthy breakfast served in the oak-paneled dining room or continental, served in your room.

The Artist's Loft B&B and Gallery (phone/fax: 802-257-5181; www.theartistsloft.com), 103 Main Street. Artist William Hays and his wife, Patricia Long, offer a middle-of-town spacious, colorful suite with a private entrance, queen-sized bed, and river view (private bath). This is a great spot if you want to plug into all that Brattleboro offers in the way of art, music, dining, and shopping; Patricia and William delight in sharing their knowledge about their adopted town. Their web site features an extensive area guide. $118–158 includes continental breakfast.

Meadowlark Inn (802-257-4582; 1-800-616-6359; www.meadowlark innvt.com), Orchard Street, P.O. Box 2048. The town of Brattleboro includes some surprisingly rural corners, like this maple-walled ridge road. The large farmhouse, set in lawns with vista views, has been recently renovated by new innkeepers Lucia Osiecki and Deborah Jones. Common space includes a wrap-around screen porch as well as a large living room. The yard offers a shady garden with Adirondack chairs, a hammock, and several tables with umbrellas. Rooms are divided between the main house and an 1870s coach barn with its own central area warmed by a hearth and decorated by a rural mural. All rooms have private bath and phone. In the Main House, the Pine Room has a king bed, fireplace, TV, and views all around ($160); in the coach house, two have Jacuzzi and views of the woodland garden. The coach house also has two more luxurious rooms with king bed, views, and refrigerator. The innkeepers are culinary school graduates who enjoy creating a fresh and bountiful breakfast with a choice of hot entrées and freshly baked goods. $105–160.

In Putney 05346
∞ ⅙ **Hickory Ridge House** (802-387-5709; 1-800-380-9218; www .hickoryridgehouse.com), 53 Hickory Ridge Road South. An 1808 brick mansion, complete with Palladian window, set on 12 acres on a country road near the Connecticut River (with walking/cross-country ski trails). There are six airy guest rooms in the inn and a two-bedroom cottage (two baths and full kitchen facilities, a wood-burning fireplace in the sitting room), painted in soft, authentic colors. They come with and without fireplace, but all have private bath, phone, and (hidden) TV/VCR. The original Federal-era bedrooms are large, with Rumford fireplaces, and there's an upstairs sitting room. A first-floor room is handicapped accessible. The neighboring two-bedroom cottage can be rented as whole or as separate rooms. The new owners, Miriam and Cory Greenspan, are seasoned travelers. A swimming hole lies within walking distance, and cross-

country touring trails are out the back door. $125–205 per couple includes a full breakfast, perhaps banana pancakes or orange French toast.

Ranney-Crawford House (802-387-4150; 1-800-731-5502; www.ranney-crawford.com), Westminster West Road. Arnie Glim, innkeeper of this 1810 brick Federal-style house on a quiet country road surrounded by fields, is an enthusiastic bicyclist who knows all the local possibilities for both touring and mountain biking. Four attractive guest rooms (private baths) are $125–155, including a three-course breakfast.

Beckwood Pond (802-254-5900; 1-877-670-5900; www.beckwood pond.com), 1107 Route 5. Alan and Helene Saxby are an Anglo-American couple who have lived on both sides of "the pond" and bring warmth and sophistication to this 1803 house, creating a very special place to stay. The five guest rooms are furnished with art and family antiques; the two-room suite features an intricately carved French bed from the early 1800s. All have European duvets and private bath. The 15 acres, 5 of tiered gardens and 10 of woodland with trails, are good for cross-country skiing. $120–165 includes a three-course breakfast and tea, coffee, wine, and other refreshments. Appropriate for children over age 10.

In the West River Valley
❦ **West River Lodge** (802-365-7745; www.westriverlodge.com), 117 Hill Road, Newfane 05345, off Route 30. This may be the only Vermont farmhouse-turned-inn that's still dwarfed by its weathered red barn, one that hasn't been turned into "carriage house suites." Instead, since the 1930s, the inn has catered

to horse lovers. Innkeepers Ellen and Jim Wightman carry on the equestrian tradition (horses are boarded) but also welcome anyone who finds their way here, just a couple of miles but seemingly worlds away from Route 30. Instead of a pool, there is a swimming hole (10 feet deep with a totally private beach) on the West River. Riding lessons are still offered across the street. There are eight guest rooms. $110–130 with private bath, $75–90 shared, including a full breakfast.

♠ **Boardman House** (802-365-4086; 1-888-366-7182), village green, Townshend 05353. We like the friendly feel of this 1840s Greek Revival house tucked into a quiet (away from Route 30 traffic) corner of one of Vermont's standout commons. Sarah and Paul Messenger offer five attractive guest rooms (one can be a suite) with private bath. There's also a two-bedroom suite, a parlor, and an airy, old-fashioned kitchen. Breakfast usually includes fresh fruit compote and oven-warm muffins with a creative main dish. $70–75 for rooms, $110–120 for a suite.

♠ **Ranney Brook Farm** (802-874-4589; RBFrmBB@sover.net), Route 30, West Townshend. Set back in wooded grounds, this comfortable old house is just up the road from boating and swimming at Townshend Dam. It's an informal, relaxing place with a piano in the den, a "great room" in the rear (a 1790s barn), and a dining room in which a full breakfast is served family-style. Residents include a dog, two cats, and a parrot. The four rooms are upstairs; two have private bath. Diana Wichland is innkeeper; her husband, John, manages Miller Brothers-Newton, a long-

established clothier in Brattleboro. $65–75 (no surcharge for foliage season).

♠ ✍ **Ascent of Nature** (802-874-4424; www.ascentofnature.com), 23 Turkey Mountain Road, Jamaica 04543. Becky Sue and Tom Tolbert have turned this 1850s farmhouse into an informal B&B. Sited near the junction of Routes 100 and 30, it's not that far from either Stratton or Mount Snow. Turkey Mountain Road runs up alongside the property and leads up into the woods, a great place to walk. The three simply but nicely furnished rooms share one bath. The woodstove in the kitchen actually heats the kitchen and is used to prepare morning muffins. $75–95 includes full breakfast.

♠ **Rock River Bed & Breakfast** (802-348-6301; www.rockriverbb .com), 408 Dover Road, South Newfane 05301. Off the beaten path, between the West River and Mount Snow Valleys and on the edge of a small village, Chris and Nissa Petrak share their 1795 house with guests lucky enough to find them. Two guest rooms are upstairs under the eaves, and the prize room is downstairs off the dining room, overlooking the gardens and Rock River. All rooms are furnished with family antiques and original art; the reasonable rates ($65–95 in low season, $75–110 in high) include a full breakfast.

In Guilford 05301

⊕ **Green River Bridge House** (802-257-5771; www.greenriver bridgehouse.com), Green River. Joan Seymour has totally rehabbed a vintage-1791 house next to the covered bridge in this classic back-roads village. It's full of whimsical touches, like a former confessional as the reception window and specially designed ceilings to display her collection of crystal chandeliers. Amenities range from Jacuzzis to hair dryers. There are three guest rooms with private bath. Gardens and lawn stretch back along the river, with a "meditation garden," a venue for weddings. $165–235 per couple includes a full breakfast, organic by prearrangement. Inquire about renting the whole house. Appropriate for children over 14 years.

OTHER LODGING 🌹 Latchis Hotel (802-254-6300; www.latchis.com), 50 Main Street, Brattleboro 05301. This downtown, art-deco-style hotel first opened in 1939 and was resurrected after a thorough restoration. It remained in the Latchis family until 2003, when it was acquired by the Brattleboro Arts Initiative (BAI), a local group dedicated to turning the hotel's magnificent theater into a performance center. Push open the door into the small but spiffy lobby, with its highly polished terrazzo marble floors. Surprises in the rooms include restored 1930s furniture, air-conditioning, and soundproof windows (a real blessing). Rooms are cheerful, brightly decorated, all with private bath, phone, fridge, and coffeemaker. The 27 rooms and 3 two-room suites are accessible by elevator. The rooms to request are on the second and third floors, with views down Main Street and across to Wantastiquet Mountain. The hotel is so solidly built that you don't hear the traffic below. For Windham Brewery and Lucca Bistro, both in the hotel, see *Dining Out*, and for more about the theater see *Entertainment*. Rates are from $55 in the off-season ($75 in summer) for double rooms to

$145–175 for suites, including continental breakfast.

🌹 🐾 🎣 ♿ **The Putney Inn** (802-387-5517; 1-800-653-5517; www.putney inn.com), Putney 05346. One of the oldest farmhouses in the area, this red-clapboard landmark was built by the first settlers. In the early 1960s, when the land was divided for construction of I-91, it was sold to local residents, who renovated the farmhouse without disturbing the posts and beams or the central open hearth. Plants and antiques add to the pleasant setting of the entry and large dining rooms. Twenty-five air-conditioned guest rooms occupy a motel-like wing, each with Queen Anne reproductions, bath, color TV, and phone. Pets are permitted but "must be smaller than a cow and not left alone in the rooms." The complex is set in 13 acres, with views of the river valley and mountains. Staff are helpful and friendly and the restaurant is first-rate, with New England fare featuring local products (see *Dining Out*). At $88–158 per couple (children free under age 14) with a

THE ART DECO LATCHIS HOTEL IN DOWNTOWN BRATTLEBORO

Kim Grant

RUDYARD KIPLING AND NAULAKHA

Rudyard Kipling first visited Brattleboro in the winter of 1892 and determined to build himself a house high on a hill in Dummerston (just north of the Brattleboro line), on property owned by his wife's family. The young couple then headed for Samoa to see Robert Louis Stevenson but got no farther than Yokohama, when their bank failed, taking virtually all their money. Returning to Vermont, they rented a cottage while building Naulakha; the name is a Hindi word meaning "great jewel." The shingled house is 90 feet long but only 22 feet wide, designed to resemble a ship riding the hillside like a wave. Its many windows face east, across the valley to the New Hampshire hills with a glimpse of the summit of Mount Monadnock. Just 26 years old, Kipling was already one of the world's

best-known writers, and the two following years here were among the happiest in his life. Here he wrote the *Jungle Books.* Here the local doctor, James Conland, a former fisherman, inspired him to write *Captains Courageous* and also delivered his two daughters. Kipling's guests included Sir Arthur Conan Doyle, who brought with him a pair of Nordic skis, said to be the first in Vermont. Unfortunately, in 1896 a highly publicized falling-out with his dissolute brother-in-law drove the family back to England. They took relatively few belongings from Naulakha, and neither did the property's two subsequent owners, who used it as a summer home. Happily, in 1992 it was acquired by The Land-

RUDYARD KIPLING IN HIS STUDY AT
NAULAKHA, CIRCA 1895

farmer's breakfast," this is one of the best values around. $10 pet fee.

CAMPGROUNDS See *Green Space* for information on camping in Fort Dummer State Park, Jamaica State Park, Ball Mountain Lake, and Townshend State Park.

✳ Where to Eat
DINING OUT

In Brattleboro
T. J. Buckley's (802-257-4922), 132 Elliot Street. Open Thursday through Sunday 6–9. Reservations suggested. From the outside this small (eight tables) but classic red-and-black

FROM THE ORIGINAL ARCHITECTURAL DRAWING OF NAULAKHA, WHERE RUDYARD KIPLING LIVED FROM 1893 TO 1896

mark Trust USA, which rewired, repaired, and replumbed it (a new septic system was required) but otherwise preserved every detail of the home as Rudyard and Carrie Kipling knew it. Though the house is not available for functions and rarely for tours, it can be rented for $1,300–3,000 per week and, depending on the season, for a few days at a time. There are four bedrooms (three baths). Some 60 percent of the present furnishings are original, including a third-floor pool table. A game of tennis, anyone, on the Kipling court? Or how about curling up with the *Jungle Books* on a sofa by the fire, only a few feet from where they were written? Or steeping in Kipling's own deep tub? For details about renting Naulakha, contact The Landmark Trust USA (802-254-6868), c/o 707 Kipling Road, Dummerston 05301. *Rudyard Kipling in Vermont: Birthplace of the* Jungle Books by Stuart Murray (Images from the Past) offers an excellent description of Kipling's relation to and portrayal of the area.

1920s Worcester diner looks unpromising, even battered. Inside, fresh flowers and mismatched settings (gathered from yard sales) brighten the tables, walls are oak paneled, and chef-owner Michael Fuller prepares the night's fish, chicken, and beef (vegetarian is also possible) in the open kitchen behind the counter.

Fuller buys all produce locally, and what's offered depends on what's available: On a July day the menu included bluefin tuna with roast lobster stock, carrots, celery, and fresh horseradish root, served with a risotto with a ginger-pheasant stock; and a chicken breast with white truffle and goat Fontina, served with flageolet beans (white) with fresh artichoke and julienned Romano beans. The $30–35 entrée includes salad; appetizer and dessert are extra. The wine list ranges $20–85. No credit cards, but personal checks are accepted.

Peter Haven's (802-257-3333), 32 Elliot Street. Open from 6 PM Tuesday through Saturday. Just 10 tables in this nifty restaurant decorated with splashy artwork, and with an inspired menu to match. Chef owned for more than 15 years and a universal favorite. The evening's entrées might include pasta del mar (a nest of linguine with a creamy pesto sauce topped with shrimp, scallops, and artichoke hearts), tenderloin with blue cheese and walnut butter, and a tortellini with Andalusian sausage and always fresh seafood. Entrées $20–26, including salad. Credit cards accepted.

Max's (802-254-7747; www.maxs restaurant.com), 1052 Western Avenue, West Brattleboro. Open for dinner Wednesday through Sunday from 5:30. When it changed hands in fall 2003, former sous chef Adam Silverman became chef, perpetuating the menu and ambience that have won this attractive restaurant an enthusiastic following. The menu is large, with many appetizer and pasta choices that change frequently. Specialties that tend to stick include the grilled filet mignon with roasted shallots, a Gorgonzola mashed potato brick, shiitake mushrooms, and grain mustard, finished with a red wine reduction. Entrées $14–26. The wine list is large and reasonable.

Letamaya Restaurant (802-254-2352; www.cooknatural.org), 51 Main Street. Open Tuesday through Saturday 5–9:30. Chef Hiroshi Hayashi, well known in Boston and New Hampshire's Monadnock region for his previous restaurants, has opened this attractive storefront restaurant featuring an "epicurean collage" of dishes, all prepared from scratch and using local ingredients. Appetizers include soups and nori rolls, and entrées ($16–19.95) might include ginger-marinated chicken toasted then simmered with vegetables and served over noodles in ginger sauce, or spinach tortellini stuffed with Parmesan cheese and served with a homemade tomato sauce and fresh vegetables. Organic wines and beers are served.

Lucca Bistro (802-254-4747), 6 Flat Street. Open for dinner except Tuesday. Abel Anaya-Lucca hails from Ponce, Puerto Rico, but the large menu in this cheerful bistro reflects many accents, most notably French. Dishes are so varied that everyone at a table tends to order something different and then sample. Servings are more than generous. Choices might range from eggplant layered with fire-roasted red peppers, red onions, portobello mushrooms, basil, fresh mozzarella, and sauce Provençal to filet mignon with a petit ragout of fresh chanterelles in a savory tart, smoked bacon whipped potatoes, and sauce bourguignon. Entrées $12.95–19.95. "Small Plates" $7.95–10.

✒ ὆ **Riverview Café** (802-254-9841; www.riverviewcafe.com), 36 Bridge Street. Open for lunch, dinner, and a Sunday brunch buffet. The big news here is the (seasonal) rooftop seating with the best dining view of the Connecticut River along its 410-mile length; there's also a downstairs deck and, of course, windowside dining.

Owner-chef Tristam Toleno, a graduate of the New England Culinary Institute, worked in New York before transforming this longtime standby into an informal but sophisticated restaurant with a mainstream menu, including fish-and-chips, steak, and applewood-smoked spicy pork spareribs. Full liquor license and regional microbrews on tap. Entrées $7–19.95.

39 Main Street (802-254-3999; www.39main.com). Open Thursday through Monday from 5:30; seasonally for Sunday brunch. Down at the southern end of Main Street across from the Latchis Theater, chef-owner Matthew Miner offers a zany decor and tapas-style eclectic dishes. Small samplings are $5–9 and entrées $11–14; the average is $22 per person, plus drinks.

Along Route 30
The Four Columns Inn (802-365-7713; www.fourcolumnsinn.com), Route 30, Newfane. Serving 6–9 nightly except Thursday; Sunday brunch 11–2; reservations suggested. Chef Greg Parks has earned top ratings for his efforts, served in a converted barn with a large brick fireplace as its centerpiece. The emphasis is on herbs (homegrown), stocks made from scratch, and locally raised lamb and trout (the latter from the adjacent pond). While the menu changes frequently, it might include grilled salmon fillet and shrimp with coconut milk, kaffir lime leaves, lemongrass, and green curry, or seared venison loin with a spiced zinfandel glaze and sun-dried cherries. Entrées $25–34.

Old Newfane Inn (802-365-4427), Route 30, Newfane Village. Open for dinner nightly except Monday. Reser-

THE RIVERVIEW CAFÉ (FORE-GROUND) OFFERS DINING OUT OVER THE CONNECTICUT RIVER.

vations requested. The low-beamed old dining room is country formal. Chef-owner Eric Weindl is widely known for his Swiss-accented Continental menu with entrée choices like roast duckling au Cointreau à l'orange or rack of lamb for one ($19–32).

Windham Hill Inn (802-874-4080; 1-800-944-4080; www.windhamhill .com), West Townshend. The exceptionally attractive, candlelit Frog Pond Dining Room overlooking a pond is open to the public for dinner (6–8:30) by reservation. You could opt for the four-course prix fixe dinner for $45 or order à la carte from a menu that might include beef carpaccio as an appetizer, grilled salmon fillet with rice and spicy cucumber, and a roasted eggplant tart filled with Vermont chèvre and tomatoes, served with wilted spinach and roasted summer vegetables. Entrées $27–31.

Three Mountain Inn (802-874-4140), Route 30, Jamaica. Dinner by reservation only. While enjoying a candlelit dinner in front of the fireplaces in the two small dining rooms of this 18th-century village house, it's easy to imagine that you're in a colonial tavern. As we go to press, the chef has recently changed but the menu, while altered daily, retains some signature dishes such as pan-fried foie gras as an appetizer, as well as main courses like grilled venison medallions with cider and chestnut sauce, and free-range Long Island duck breast with spicy cherry tomato jam. There's a $50 prix fixe, but items can be ordered à la carte. Entrées $29–34.

🍴 **Asta's Swiss Restaurant** (802-874-8000), 3894 Main Street, Jamaica 05343. Open for dinner 5–10 except Wednesday; also for Sunday brunch 10–2. Chef-owner Michel de Preux is Swiss and has a sure touch with everything he prepares, from turkey breast snizel (topped with lemon, caper, and anchovies) and roast half duckling à l'orange (finished with an orange green peppercorn sauce) to filet mignon café de Paris (topped with mustard, herbs, and spice butter, and served with rösti potatoes). There are options for vegetarians, such as falafel with garlic tahini, cucumber salad, hummus, and pita chips; also look for Swiss specialties like fondue and raclette (both cheese and meat) and choucroute garnie. Sunday brunch offers plenty of egg dishes plus pastas, salads, even grinders. All entrées come with bread and salad. The ambience is warm. $8.95–24.95. Wine and beer.

Elsewhere

🍴 *ঌ* **The Putney Inn** (802-387-5517; 1-800-653-5517), just off I-91, exit 4, in Putney. Open for all three meals. An 18th-century house is now a popular restaurant. Executive chef Kevin Takei, a Culinary Institute of America graduate (with high honors), has worked with The Four Seasons and takes pride in featuring local, seasonal produce. The dinner menu combines classic New England dishes such as roast breast of turkey with herbed apple stuffing with the likes of shellfish bouillabaisse and Colorado lamb osso buco (a summer cassoulet with fresh beans). Traditional favorites include reasonably priced options like turkey and vegetable potpie in a bread bowl, and macaroni and cheese Vermont-style (with Grafton Village extra-sharp cheddar). Entrées $14–22.50; from $11 for lighter fare. Lunch is also popular, with offerings that might include baked five-onion and apple soup, and an herb-shallot grilled chicken breast.

EATING OUT

In Brattleboro

ঌ **The Marina Restaurant** (802-257-7563; www.vermontmarina.com), Route 5 just north of the West River bridge. Open daily April through mid-October, less frequently off-season. Situated at the confluence of the West and Connecticut Rivers, this place has a great view and maximizes it, with a screen porch and patio as well as a recently expanded deck; in winter there's fireside dining. The reasonably priced menu includes plenty of seafood and vegetarian choices at both lunch and dinner, but also burgers. Full liquor license. A great place to enjoy a margarita while watching the sunset.

Shin La Restaurant (802-257-5226), 57–61 Main Street. Open 11–9, closed Sunday. Yl'soon Kim is the dynamo behind this attractive Korean restaurant, really a standout that has evolved over its years at this storefront. It's known for homemade soups, dumplings, and other Korean fare and includes a sushi bar.

Amy's Bakery Arts Café (802-251-1071), 113 Main Street. A good lunch spot. There are river views from tables in the back of this attractive storefront café, and the food is appealing, too: spinach and cheese croissants, salads, and sandwiches, some with meat but plenty without.

Back Side Cafe (802-257-5056), Green Street Extension. Open weekdays for breakfast and lunch, dinner Thursday through Saturday nights; Sunday brunch. A great place for breakfast if you like an omelet with lots of fresh garlic or homemade salsa. Lunch features homemade soups, salads, deli sandwiches, and bagels; dinner runs from burgers to roast chicken, with a full bar featuring Vermont beers. Brunch both Saturday and Sunday.

Brattleboro Food Co-op (802-257-0236), 2 Main Street, Brookside Plaza. Open Monday through Saturday 8–9, Sunday 9–9. An outstanding natural foods market and deli worth checking out for its stellar choice of Vermont cheese—but while you're there, take advantage of the Café and Juice Bar featuring creative smoothies, first-rate sandwiches, and salads.

India Palace Restaurant, 69 Elliot Street. Open daily for lunch and dinner, both reasonably priced for authentic Indian curries, tandoori, and biryani dishes. The list of Indian breads alone is long, and the menu is immense. Dinner specials include multicourse meals priced from $12.50 (vegetarian) to $35.95.

Sarkis Market DeliCafe (802-258-4906), 50 Elliot Street. Open for lunch and dinner (until 8), for take-out and eat-in. A great source of stuffed grape leaves, spinach pies, lamb stew, homemade baklava, and falafel pockets.

Thai Garden (802-251-1010), 7 High Street. Open daily for lunch (11:30–3) and dinner (5–10). Sign of the times! For many years this was the site of Dunkin' Donuts, but in 2003 it was replaced by this representative of a small chain, best known for its popular restaurant in Williamstown, Massachusetts. Dishes typically feature Thai basil and crisp vegetables. Try the Goi See Mee, fried crispy yellow noodles with chicken and shrimp, onions, carrots, mushrooms, and bamboo shoots. Wine and beer are served.

Mole's Eye Café (802 257-0771), corner of Main and High Streets. A popular local hangout serving soups, chili, and sandwiches all day, with a full bar and frequent live and lively music until 1 AM.

⚓ **Gillies Seafood Restaurant and Raw Bar** (802-257-9900), 209 Canal Street. Open Tuesday through Sunday 4–9, longer hours in summer. Whoever the fish buyer is here, he's good. The specialty is Atlantic seafood. Try the crabcakes and chowder. Children's menu.

⚓ **Brattleboro Farmer's Market.** If you happen into town around noon on a sunny Wednesday or Saturday, head for the farmer's market. On Wednesday it's downtown off Main Street by the Merchants Bank Building (look for the parking lot right there), with food vendors next to a small park overlooking the river. On Saturday it's just west of town by the Creamery Bridge. A live band and crafts, as well as produce vendors, are usually on hand.

Along Putney Road and in Putney

⚓ **Top of the Hill Grill** (802-258-9178), 632 Putney Road. Open mid-April through mid-November for lunch and dinner. You have to be looking for this unusual BBQ place. It comes up fast after the bridge, heading north on Route 5 out of town. You order, get a card, and then sit at a picnic table or in the weatherproofed outdoor dining space (with restrooms) until your card is called (I was Queen of Hearts). The specialties are apple-smoked chicken and hickory-smoked pulled pork and ribs, but you can also get a tempeh burger, roll-up, salad, or hot dog.

Curtis' Barbeque (802-387-5474). Summer through fall, Wednesday through Sunday 10–dusk. Follow your nose to the blue school bus parked on Route 5 in Putney, just off I-91, exit 4. Curtis Tuff cooks up pork ribs and chicken, seasoned with his secret barbecue sauce, also foil-wrapped potatoes, grilled corn, and beans flavored with Vermont maple syrup. By far the best barbecue in the Northeast!

Putney Diner (802-387-5433), Main Street. Open 6 AM–8 PM daily. Another pleasant option in the middle of Putney Village, open for all three meals. Good for Belgian waffles, Philly cheese steak, and homemade vegetable lasagna, super sandwich plates, salads, chicken-fried steak, grilled liver and onions, even burritos and tacos. Pastries made daily. Children's menu.

Putney Food Co-op (802-387-5866), Route 5 just south of the village. Open for lunch at 11. This is a great, quick lunch stop at a supermarket-sized cooperative with a pleasant café area: daily soups, salads, and deli.

Along Route 30
Rick's Tavern (802-365-4310), just south of Newfane Village. Open daily for lunch and dinner, music Saturday nights. Daily blackboard specials, pizza, homemade desserts, microbrews.

Townshend Country Inn (802-365-4141), Route 30, Townshend. Open for dinner nightly (except Wednesday) year-round; also May through October for a Sunday buffet brunch. Said to have been a summer home for Grandma Moses, this pleasant restaurant specializes in roast Vermont turkey and offers a full menu at reasonable prices, pub menu. Check out the Sunday buffet.

Wildflower Cafe & Bakery (802-365-9300), 2041 Route 30, Townshend. Open for breakfast, lunch, and Sunday brunch. What a great addition to the West River Valley! Ann Doherty has created a winner of a place, right were it's needed: homemade soups of the day and specials like a grilled portobello sandwich with roasted red peppers, pesto, and chèvre on a roll, and an Angus beef burger. Brunch is heavy on omelets; also smoked salmon with bagel and cream cheese, breakfast sandwiches, ginger crêpes with brown sugar, pear, and cranberry. Pastries are a specialty, including tiramisu and seven-layer wonder bars.

The Townshend Dam Diner (802-874-4107), Route 30, 2 miles north of the Townshend Dam. Open 5 AM–8 PM. Breakfast all day. Homemade French toast, home fries, muffins and biscuits, the "best dam chili," soups, and bison burgers (from the nearby East Hill Bison Farm), dinner staples like roast turkey, spaghetti, and garlic bread, daily specials.

Along Route 9 west
The New England House (802-254-6886), West Brattleboro west of

I-91, exit 2. Open for dinner Wednesday and Thursday 4:30–9, Friday and Saturday 4:30–10, Sunday noon–8. Formerly The Jolly Butcher, this popular restaurant is now family owned as well as family geared. It was acquired in 2003 by the Kerber family after their Falls River Inn in Bernardston, Massachusetts (a few exits south on I-91) burned to the ground. The menu features seafood as well as meat dishes and fresh greens and vegetables, also a choice of regular and small portions.

Ziter's Deli (802-257-4994), 201½ Western Avenue (Route 9), West Brattleboro. Open Monday through Saturday 7–6, Sunday 8–6. A deli and café featuring great designer sandwiches like Vermont veggie on a pita and chicken Caesar wrap; also salads, chili, and soups, as well as house-made meat loaf and fresh-baked breads and pastries.

Chelsea Royal Diner (802-254-8399), Route 9, West Brattleboro. Open 6 AM–9 PM. A genuine '30s diner that's been moved a few miles west of its original site (it's a mile west of I-91, exit 2). Plenty of parking and diner decor, serving breakfast all day as part of a big menu; also plenty of daily specials.

WINE AND BREWS **McNeil's Brewery** (802-254-2553), 90 Elliot Street, Brattleboro. Open at 4 Monday through Thursday and at 2 Friday and Saturday. This brewery in the town's original firehouse, a mecca for beer and ale lovers, has medals to show for its variety of brews, including lagers, traditional cask-conditioned real ales, and barley wines.

Windham Brewery (802-254-4747), 50 Main Street, Brattleboro (in the Latchis Hotel). There's a pub menu to go with the ales, porters, and lagers on tap that are made on the spot.

Mocha Joe's (802-257-7794), 82 Main Street, Brattleboro. Coffee is taken seriously here, roasted as well as brewed. Live music on weekends.

Coffee Country (802-257-0032), on the Harmony parking lot, Brattleboro. Good coffee, good food.

Twilight Tea Lounge (802-254-8887), under 51 Main Street, Brattleboro. Open Wednesday through Sunday, noon to varying hours. A barbershop for 75 years, this pleasant space is filled with mismatched tables and chairs and the aroma of rare teas. A cooperative, the venue for Thursday-night poetry and music.

Putney Mountain Winery (802-387-4610), at Scott Farm, Rudyard Kipling Road, Dummerston. Music professor and composer Charles Dodge has established a sensational reputation for the quality of his sparkling apple wines. Tastings are offered on weekends at Basketville in Putney and increasingly in the licensed tasting room at Scott Farm, open for special events.

❋ Entertainment

The Latchis Theater (802-254-5800; www.latchistheater.com), Main Street, Brattleboro, shows first-run films. For film buffs, this 900-seat movie house with three screens is itself a destination. Apollo still drives his chariot through the firmament on the ceiling; walls are graced with Doric columns, and the lobby floor bears the zodiac signs in multicolored terrazzo. This gloriously beautiful art deco theater is now owned by the Brattleboro Arts Initiative, a group dedicated to transforming it into a performing arts center with a gradually increasing number of live arts shows.

Sandglass Theater (802-387-4051; www.sandglasstheater.org), Kimball Hill, Putney. October through Christmas and April and May, frequent summer performances in a variety of local venues. Based in a barn in Putney Village, the resident theater company performs original work combining live theater with puppetry. Also hosts guest performers.

Hooker-Dunham Arts Center (802-254-9276), 139 Main Street, Brattleboro. Call and check out what's going on at this middle-of-town venue. Offerings include theater, music, film, and lectures, and there's always a gallery show.

Whittemore Theater at Marlboro College (802-257-4333), Marlboro, is the setting for frequent presentations.

Kipling Cinemas (at Fairfield Plaza, Route 5 north of Brattleboro), a multiplex, also shows first-run films.

MUSIC **Yellow Barn Music Festival** (802-387-6637; 1-800-639-3819; www.yellowbarn.org), Putney. Begun in 1969, this is a series of 25 chamber music concerts in July and early August. Performances are in a 150-seat barn located behind the public library in Putney Village. Artists include both well-known professionals and students from leading conservatories.

Brattleboro Music Center (802-257-4523; www.bmcvt.org), 15 Walnut Street, Brattleboro. Housed in a former convent, this burgeoning music school sponsors a wide variety of local musical events and festivals, including a Spring Festival of oratorios and pageants such as a winter/spring Cham-

ICE CREAM ✔ **Page's Ice Cream** (802-254-3826), Route 9, West Brattleboro. Easy to miss in the strip (beside the New England House), this yellow-clapboard ice cream stand has been a landmark for more than 50 years. Its ice cream is said to be lower in saturated fats and calories than commercial brands but that's not the point. It tastes good. We haven't tried all 14 flavors but can recommend the fresh peach, black raspberry, and sweet cream.

ber Music Series. Periodic concerts are presented by the Windham Orchestra, by the Community Chorus in area churches, and, most notably, the **New England Bach Festival.** The festival, a series of more than a dozen October concerts and lectures, has been held since 1969 in area churches and chapels, featuring choral performances conducted by the Swiss-born Blanche Moyse (founder of the Music Center in 1951). It's reviewed and celebrated as one of the Northeast's major annual musical events.

Vermont Jazz Center (802-254-9088), 72 Cotton Mill Hill, Studio 222, South Main Street, Brattleboro, stages frequent musical, vocal, and jazz happenings.

Friends of Music at Guilford (802-257-1961; 802-257-1028), Guilford. A series of concerts throughout the year at various locations. Note the free Labor Day weekend concerts under *Special Events.*

Also see the Marlboro Music Festival in "Mount Snow/Wilmington Area."

✳ Selective Shopping

ANTIQUES

In Brattleboro

Twice Upon a Time (802-254-2261), 63 Main Street. Open Monday through Saturday 10–6, Friday until 8, Sunday noon–5. "I always wanted a consignment shop that would be able to display anything that anyone wanted to give me," says Randi Crouse, proprietor of this truly amazing shop that now fills the entire three-level space created in 1906 for the E. J. Fenton Department Store. In the '50s it was chopped into smaller storefronts, but the two-story-high Corinthian columns, bubble glass, and wooden gallery are back, a setting for clothing, antique furniture, and furnishings. The markdown schedule is patterned on that of Filene's Basement. More than 100 dealers and a total of 4,000 consignors are represented. If there's something special you're looking for, chances are Crouse can find it.

The Alley Cat Antiques Etc. (802-257-5502), 16 Elliot Street, mixes vintage clothing and antiques.

Along Route 30

More than two dozen dealers are found along this route. Pick up a copy of their pamphlet guide at the first place you stop. They include:

Newfane Flea Market (802-365-4000), just north of Newfane Village. Sundays, May through October. Billed as the largest open-air market in the state; usually 100 tables with assorted junk and treasure.

Jack Winner Antiques (802-365-7215; www.winnerantiques.com), Newfane. Specializing for over 30 years in 18th- and 19th-century formal and country furniture, equestrian antiques, and hunting prints.

Auntie M's Attic (802-365-9796), Route 30, south of Newfane Village. Open May through October, Thursday through Monday. A nice selection of antique china, furniture, glass, lamps, linens, and prints.

Nu-tique (802-365-7677), Newfane Village. Open May through October and by appointment. Books, including New England histories, poetry, military, children's; also old lamps, glass, sheet music, records.

Riverdale Antiques (802-365-4616), Route 30, Harmonyville (between Newfane and Townshend). Open year-round, daily 10–5. More than 60 dealers selling quality antiques and collectibles.

Townshend Auction Gallery (802-365-4388), Route 30, Townshend. Over 30 years Kit Martin and Art Monette have established a solid reputation for their frequent auctions.

Old Corker's Antiques (802-874-4172; www.oldcorkersantiques.com), Route 30, Jamaica. Open May through October, most days 10–5. Skip Woodruff specializes in antique fishing equipment and books, also snowshoes and the rustic furniture he makes himself. A great stop!

ART AND CRAFTS GALLERIES *Note:*
The first Friday of each month is Gallery Walk in Brattleboro: open house with refreshments and music at downtown businesses that hang works by local artists and at studios as well as at formal galleries, usually 5:30–8:30.

Windham Art Gallery (802-257-1881), 69 Main Street, Brattleboro. Open Wednesday through Sunday noon–5, weekends until 7:30. Exhibits by members of an outstanding artists' cooperative, also source of the Arts Council of Windham County quarterly publication *Arts in the Season*, which lists current theater, poetry readings, and gallery shows throughout southeastern Vermont.

Artist's Loft Gallery (phone/fax: 802-257-5181), 103 Main Street, Brattleboro. Realistic Vermont landscapes as well as portraits and other worth-checking oils by William Hays.

Vermont Artisan Designs (802-257-7044), 106 Main Street, Brattleboro. Open daily. Ever-expanding to fill three floors of a former department store, southern Vermont's outstanding contemporary crafts gallery displays the work of 300 artisans. Melange, a collection of interesting small shops, and Kitchen Sync, a culinary boutique, are part of this complex.

Gallery in the Woods and Dante's Infurniture (802-257-4777; www.galleryinthewoods), 143 Main Street, Brattleboro. For decades Dante and Suzanne Corsano have drawn patrons to their rural gallery

JENNY BLUE POTTERY AND CRAFTS IN JAMAICA
Christina Tree

(see "Mount Snow/Wilmington Area") to view Dante's furniture and Suzanne's ceramic creations. This new downtown venue also features nationally known painters and artists in a variety of media.

Borter's Jewelry Studio (802-254-3452; www.bortersjewelry.com), 103 Main Street, Brattleboro. Gemstones; silver and gold jewelry handcrafted into stunning settings on the premises.

The Art Building, 127 Main Street, Brattleboro, houses a dozen studios, open irregularly and for Gallery Walk. Visitors are welcome to stroll up any day and see whose door is open. The **River Gallery School** (802-257-1577) offers frequent classes and workshops here.

In Putney
Note: **The Putney Craft Tour** (www.putneycrafts.com), held for more than 25 years the weekend after Thanksgiving, showcases the work of two dozen craftspeople working within a dozen miles of Putney. An open-house atmosphere prevails.

Richard Bissell Fine Woodworking (802-387-4416), Signal Pine Road. Open Monday through Friday 8–5. Exceptional Shaker-inspired furniture, cabinetry, Windsor chairs.

Joshua Gold Pottery (802-387-2116), Westminster West Road, 3.7 miles north of Putney Village. Open July through January 1, Friday through Sunday 11–4 and by appointment. Fine, seemingly simple, functional, and sculptural pottery pieces noteworthy for the sophistication of their shapes and glazes. Worth a detour.

Brandywine Glassworks (802-387-4032), Fort Hill Road. Robert Burch handblows glass in his studio (call to see what he's doing); seconds of distinctive paperweights and other likely gifts are sold.

Along Route 30
Taft Hill (802-865-4200), Harmonyville (Townshend). Open daily 11–5. Gifts and furnishings, featuring fine hand-painted glass and china created here at Crest Studio.

Jennie Blue (802-874-4222; www.vermontpottery.net), Jamaica Village. Open 9:30–5 daily except Tuesday. Local potter Susan Leader's bright, irresistible plates, vases, and pots with cheerful designs are the specialty here; also personalized wedding plates and a nice selection of local pottery and crafts.

Elaine Beckwith Gallery (802-874-7234), Routes 30/100, Jamaica Village. Open daily except Tuesday. Some 30 artists in a variety of styles and media are represented.

BOOKSTORES **The Book Cellar** (802-254-6026; www.vtbookcellar .com), 120 Main Street, Brattleboro. An outstanding, long-established, full-service bookstore, particularly strong on Vermont and New England titles.

Everyone's Books (802-254-8160), 25 Elliot Street, Brattleboro. This is an earnest and interesting alternative bookstore, specializing in women's books; also a great selection of children's and multicultural titles.

Collected Works Books & The Cafe Beyond (802-258-4900; www.collectedworksbookstore.com), 29 High Street, Brattleboro. An attractive, full-service bookstore with rooms that ramble on and back into the café. Not a bad place to spend a rainy day.

Old & New England Books (802-365-7074), West Street, Newfane. Open May through October. A delightful browsing place with an interesting stock of books old and new.

Heartstone Books (802-387-2100), at the junction of Route 5 and West Hill Road in Putney. Open daily 10–6. Housed in the restored old tavern at the center of Putney Village, a full-service bookstore that invites browsing, with a frequently working hearth in the adjacent café.

Brattleboro Books (802-257-0177; www.brattleborobooks.com), 34 Elliot Street. Open 9:30–6 daily except Sunday. An extensive selection of used and out-of-print books; over 70,000 titles fill two storefronts. Browsing encouraged.

Green Mountain Spinnery (802-387-4528; 1-800-321-9665; www.spinnery.com), just off I-91, exit 4. Open Monday through Friday 9–5:30, Saturday 10–5:30. Labor Day through Thanksgiving, also Sunday noon–4. Founded as a cooperative more than 20 years ago, this is a real spinning mill in which undyed, unbleached fibers—alpaca, mohair, wool, and organic cotton—are carded, spun, skeined, and labeled. You can buy the resulting yarn in various plies in natural and 55 dyed colors. No chemicals are used. More than 40 original patterns are shown in the catalog. The store also carries buttons, and knitting and spinning supplies.

Basket's Bookstore/Paperback Palace (802-258-4980), 48 Harmony Place, Brattleboro, a trove of used paperbacks.

SPECIAL SHOPS

In Brattleboro

Delectable Mountain (802-257-4456), 125 Main Street. Fine-fabric lovers make pilgrimages to Jan Norris's store, widely known for its selection of fine silks, all-natural imported laces, velvets, cottons, and upholstery jacquards. It also offers a wide selection of unusual buttons.

Brattleboro Food Co-op (802-257-0236), 2 Main Street, Brookside Plaza. Open Monday through Saturday 8–9, Sunday 9–9; deli and fresh-baked products. The cheese counter could just be the best showcase for Vermont cheese in the state; cheeses from around the world are also knowledgeably selected and presented (note the "cheese of the week"), and there's local produce, grains, wines, and a café.

Adavasi Imports (802-258-2231), 8 Flat Street. Shram and Elissa Bhanti keep prices low because they are also wholesalers, traveling to northwest India to buy their fabrics: linens and clothing hand blocked with natural vegetable dyes; silk saris for $25; cotton rugs; and a wide variety of crafted items and jewelry. It's an exotic, fragrant emporium that keeps expanding.

Tom & Sally's Handmade Chocolates (802-254-4200), Route 30. Locally made and worth a taste.

A Candle in the Night (802-257-0471), 181 Main Street. Donna and Larry Simons have built up a vast knowledge as well as inventory of Oriental and other handcrafted rugs over the decades.

Beadnicks (802-257-5114), 115 Main Street. Beads, baubles, whimsical wonders.

In Putney

Basketville (802-387-5509), Route 5. Open daily 8 AM–9 PM in busy seasons, 8–5 in slack seasons. The first of "The World's Largest Basket Stores" now scattered along the East Coast, it's also one of the oldest crafts producers in the state. Founded by Frank Wilson, an enterprising Yankee trader in the real sense, this is a family-run business. The vast store features woodenware, wicker furniture (filling the entire upstairs), wooden toys, and exquisite artificial flowers as well as traditional baskets and myr-

Sam's Outdoor Outfitters (802-254-2933; www.samsoutfitters.com), 74 Main Street. Open 8–6, until 9 on Friday, closed Sunday. The business that Sam Borofsky started in 1934 now fills two floors of two buildings with a full stock of hunting, camping, and sports equipment. Prices are reasonable, but people don't shop here for bargains. The big thing is the service—skilled help in selecting the right fishing rod, tennis racket, or gun. There are also name brand sports clothes and standard army and navy gear. On the first day of deer hunting season (early November), the store opens at dawn and serves a hunter's breakfast (it also sells licenses). *Tip:* There's free popcorn every day, all day.

iad other things, large and small. *Note:* Check out the Columbus Day weekend Basketville Seconds Sale.

Silver Forest of Vermont (802-387-4149), in the center of the village. A clothing and accessories store, recently expanded to fill two floors, worth checking out.

Along Route 30

Newfane Country Store (802-365-7916), Newfane. Quilts, Vermont cheese and maple syrup, plus toys and Christmas ornaments. The quilts and other quilted things are truly outstanding.

Lawrence's Smoke House (802-365-7751), Newfane. Corncob-smoked hams, bacon, poultry, fish, meats, and cheese are the specialties of the house. Catalog and mail order.

Jamaica Country Store (802-874-9151), Jamaica Village. Just a real country store, selling cheese, syrup, and souvenirs along with everything else.

FARMS TO VISIT One of the state's concentrations of farms and orchards is here in the lower Connecticut River Valley, some offering "pick your own," others welcoming visitors to their farm stands, sugaring houses, or barns. Call before coming.

Note: **Brattleboro Farmer's Market** is held May through late October, Wednesday 10–2 at Merchants Bank Square across from the post office, and Saturday 9–2, Route 9 in West Brattleboro. This lively community coming-together showcases crafts and produce. Food vendors and, frequently, music and flowers are part of the scene.

Southern Vermont Working Farms, a map/guide available from the Wind-

ham County Natural Resources Conservation District (802-254-5323), locates more than a dozen farms in this area.

Apples, maple sugar, and more
Green Mountain Orchards (802-387-5851; www.greenmountain orchards.com), 130 West Hill Road, Putney. Open daily in-season. Pick-your-own apples and blueberries; cider available in-season. Open in winter, selling apples. Christmas trees, local crafts, and produce also sold.

Robb Family Farm (802-254-7664; 1-888-318-9087; www.robbfamily farm.com), 827 Ames Hill Road, Brattleboro. This 420-acre dairy farm has been in the same family since 1907, and visitors are welcomed here in a number of ways and in all seasons. In spring the sugarhouse is a fragrant, steamy place; year-round it's also the Country Shop (open Monday through Saturday 10–5, Sunday 1–5, closed Wednesday), stocked with maple products and floral items. Visitors are also welcome in the barn, moved here from Halifax in 1912 (50 of the 100-head herd are presently milked). Inquire about a Day on the Farm, beginning with breakfast, also about hayrides, sleigh rides, hiking, and the Apple Fritter Fest in October.

Harlow's Sugar House (802-387-5852; www.harlowssugarhouse.com), Route 5 north of Putney Village. Open March until late December, Harlow's is one of the most visitor-oriented operations. The Sugar House lets you watch maple production in-season, and there's a film and maple museum; the big store sells their own syrup and honey and offers pick-your-own apples, blueberries, and strawberries. The produce stand features a wide variety of apples in-season.

Walker Farm (802-254-2051; www.walkerfarm.com), Route 5, Dummerston. A 200-year-old farm and garden center (open April 15 through fall, 10–6), specializing in hard-to-find annuals and perennials and garden books by local authors. A full line of produce June through Thanksgiving, featuring their own organic vegetables and local fruit. Display gardens, and calves for petting.

Dutton Berry Farm and Stand (802-365-4168), farm stand on Route 30, Newfane. This is a large, varied stand featuring produce from the family's Dummerston farm, Christmas trees, much more.

Dwight Miller & Son (802-254-9158), 581 Miller Road, East Dummerston. Open daily year-round. Syrup and seasonal pick-your-own apples, strawberries, and peaches, blueberries and raspberries, also selling pears, plums, and organic produce.

Elysian Hills Tree Farm (802-257-0233; www.elysianhillsfarm.com), 209 Knapp Road, Dummerston. Bill and

Mary Lou Schmidt maintain this 100-acre tree farm (available for tagging in October) and also raise rhubarb (harvested May through June), much of which goes to make wine at the Putney winery.

Olallie Daylily Gardens (802-348-6614; www.daylilygarden.com), 129 Augur Hole Road, South Newfane. Open early May through Labor Day weekend, daily 10–5 except Tuesday. No charge for self-guided tours, but a 2-hour guided tour is $5. Pink irises in mid-June; daylilies June, July, and August through September. PYO organic blueberries in July and August. Garden shop and potted plant nursery. Inquire about Daylily Festival.

Cheese

Vermont Shepherd (802-387-4473; www.vermontshepherd.com), Patch Road, Westminster West. Vermont Shepherd holds one of the country's top awards for its distinctive, hand-pressed, sweet, creamy sheep's milk cheese. It's made April through October, then aged 4 to 8 months and available mid-August until the year's supply runs out in spring. Call for appropriate visiting times.

Westminster Dairy at Livewater Farm (802-387-5110), 1289 Westminster West Road. Don't fail to stop! Pull in behind the farmhouse and check out the shop, a source of certified organic cheeses made from the farm's Jersey cows. We bought a delicious Italian-style Tomme; softer cheeses are also available.

Peaked Mountain Farm (802-365-4502), 1541 Peaked Mountain Road, Townshend. Call first. In an idyllic locale high above the West River Valley, Ann and Bob Works make sheep's

HARLOW'S FARM STAND IN PUTNEY

Christina Tree

VERMONT SHEPHERD FARM IN WESTMINSTER WEST

Kim Grant

milk cheese: Camembert, Tomme, and several other varieties. Call before visiting.

FACTORY OUTLETS

Townshend Furniture (802-365-7720), Route 30, Townshend. Open weekdays 10–4, weekends until 5. Handcrafted, sturdy, attractive furniture made on the premises is sold at discount. Cherry Shaker and country pine are specialties.

Big Black Bear Shop at Mary Meyer (802-365-4160; 1-888-758-BEAR; www.bigblackbear.com), Route 30, Townshend, west of the village. Open daily. The original location of Vermont's oldest stuffed-toy company. More than 500 designs, 20–70 percent off.

The Outlet Center (802-254-4594; 1-800-459-4594; www.vermontout lets.com), Canal Street, Brattleboro; exit 1 off I-91. Open daily 9:30–8 except Sunday 10–6. This former factory building that once produced handbags is an old-fashioned factory outlet center with 15 varied stores, worth checking.

✳ Special Events

February: **Brattleboro Winter Carnival,** with many events in Living Memorial Park—a full week of celebrations, climaxed by the Washington's birthday cross-country ski race.

May–October: The **Brattleboro Area Farmer's Market,** Saturday on Route 9 at the Creamery Covered Bridge and Wednesday downtown. **Memorial Day Dawn Dance,** 8 PM–7 AM in Brattleboro.

First Saturday of June: **Strolling of the Heifers** down Main Street, Brattleboro, along with a Dairy Fest and marketplace, Heifer Ball.

Late June: Dummerston Center **Annual Strawberry Supper,** Grange Hall, Dummerston.

July–August: **Yellow Barn Music Festival** in Putney (see *Entertainment*).

July 4: A big **parade** winds through Brattleboro at 10 AM; games, exhibits, refreshments in Living Memorial Park; **fireworks** at 9 PM.

Last Saturday of July: Annual **sale and supper** sponsored by the Ladies Benevolent Society of Brookline; an old-fashioned affair with quality crafts.

Last weekend of July: Events in Brattleboro both days climaxed by the **Riff Raff Regatta** Sunday, a raft competition off the Marina Restaurant at the confluence of the West and Connecticut Rivers.

First Saturday of August: **Grace Cottage Hospital Fair Day**—exhibits, booths, games, rides on the green in Townshend. Free concert series on Newfane common.

September: **Labor Day Dawn Dance,** 8 PM–7 AM, Brattleboro. Labor Day weekend in Guilford is observed both with the old-style **Guilford Fair** and with the annual 2-day music festival in **Guilford's Organ Barn** (802-257-1961). Concerts are free. **Whitewater on the West River,** Jamaica State Park; see *Boating.* **Heritage Festival Benefit** in Newfane, sponsored by the Newfane Congregational Church. **Putney**

Artisans Festival, Putney Town Hall. **Apple Days** (last weekend) in downtown Brattleboro.

October: **Newfane Heritage Fair** on Columbus Day—crafts, dancing, raffle, sponsored by the Newfane Congregational Church.

Mid-October: The **Apple Pie Festival** in Dummerston features hundreds of Dummerston's famous apple pies, also crafts, at the Dummerston Center Congregational Church and Grange. **New England Bach Festival,** a series of major concerts in area churches sponsored by the Brattleboro Music Center (802-257-4523; see *Entertainment*). The annual **Pumpkin Festival** on Townshend common features biggest-pumpkin and best-pumpkin-pie contests, plenty of vendors, food.

Weekend after Thanksgiving: **Putney Craft Tour**—some two dozen local studios open to the public, geared to Christmas shopping.

Early December: **Christmas Bazaar** on the common, Newfane.

MOUNT SNOW/
WILMINGTON AREA

Mount Snow made its splashy debut as a ski destination in 1954. Reuben Snow's farm was transformed by ski lifts and trails, lodges, a skating rink, and an immense, floodlit geyser. Ski lodges mushroomed for miles around, varying in style from Tyrolean to 1950s futuristic. By the early '70s bust had followed boom, and the ski area was absorbed by one company after another. Acquired in 1994 by the American Ski Company, Mount Snow now incorporates Haystack, a long-established ski area in its own right, a few miles down the valley. Both have standout golf courses.

West Dover is a picturesque lineup of church, inn, and town offices, but much of the 9 miles of Route 100 between Wilmington and Mount Snow is a visual history of the ups and downs of the ski industry since the late '50s. Look closely, however, and you will find plenty to please. Perhaps because the valley's visitors come overwhelmingly from the New York City area, a number of inns and restaurants are several cuts above average. Beyond this narrow corridor, mountains rise on all sides. The village of Dover is a knot of white-clapboard buildings on the crest of a hill, a few miles east but palpably farther away. Forest surrounds Route 100 north to the classic village of Wardsboro, south to the delightfully back-roaded towns of Jacksonville and Whitingham, and east to the college town of Marlboro, site of the world-class Marlboro Music Festival in July and August.

Although the surrounding hills were once lumbered extensively, they are now hauntingly empty. Two former logging villages actually lie at the bottom of sizable Harriman and Somerset Reservoirs, which have transformed the Deerfield Valley into one of the wateriest parts of Vermont, good for fishing, walking, boating, and swimming.

GUIDANCE **Southern Vermont Regional Marketing Organization** (1-877-887-2378; www.southernvermont.com) maintains a good web site and is a source of printed area information.

Mount Snow Valley Chamber of Commerce (802-464-8092; 1-877-887-6884; www.visitvermont.com) maintains a major Vermont Information Center on West Main Street in Wilmington (Route 9 west, seven doors from the junction of

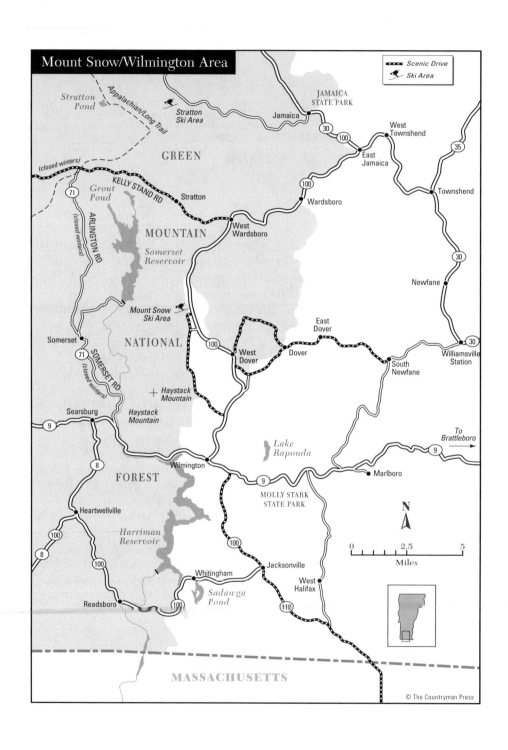

Mount Snow/Wilmington Area

Scenic Drive
Ski Area

Stratton Pond

Appalachian/Long Trail

Stratton Ski Area

JAMAICA STATE PARK

Jamaica

West Townshend

GREEN

30

100

35

East Jamaica

Townshend

(closed winters)

KELLY STAND RD

71

Grout Pond

Stratton

100

Wardsboro

30

MOUNTAIN

West Wardsboro

ARLINGTON RD

(closed winters)

Somerset Reservoir

Newfane

Mount Snow Ski Area

East Dover

Somerset

NATIONAL

100

West Dover

Dover

30

71

SOMERSET RD

(closed winters)

South Newfane

Williamsville Station

Haystack Mountain

Searsburg

Haystack Mountain

To Brattleboro

9

Lake Raponda

9

8

Wilmington

FOREST

9

Marlboro

Heartwellville

MOLLY STARK STATE PARK

N

100

Harriman Reservoir

0   2.5   5
Miles

8

100

100

Whitingham

Jacksonville

West Halifax

Readsboro

100

Sadawga Pond

110

MASSACHUSETTS

© The Countryman Press

Routes 9 and 100). Pick up the useful *Mount Snow Valley Visitor's Guide.* The *Deerfield Valley News,* a local weekly, is a good source for current events.

GETTING THERE The obvious route to Mount Snow from points south and east is I-91 to Brattleboro, then Route 9 to Wilmington. There are also two scenic shortcuts: (1) Route 30 north from Brattleboro 11.1 miles to the marked turnoff for Dover; follow the road through the covered bridge in South Newfane past Dover to West Dover; (2) turn off I-91 onto Route 2 in Greenfield, Massachusetts; follow Route 2 for 3.6 miles to Colrain Road (turn at Duck Pond Tavern) and proceed 17.3 miles to Jacksonville, where you pick up Route 100 into Wilmington.

From New York City: **Edventures Bus Service** (802-464-2810; 212-921-9161).

GETTING AROUND **The MOO-ver** (802-464-8487) is a free community bus service operated by the Deerfield Valley Transit Association (DVTA). It connects points of interest in the valley, along Route 100 from the Deerfield Valley Health Center in Wilmington, picking up passengers at DVTA stops 7 AM–10 PM. Look for its Holstein cow logo.

WHEN TO GO High season is Christmas through February; in March snow is less dependable here than in other parts of the state. Golfers arrive in June, and in July and August both Art on the Mountain at Haystack and the Marlboro Music Festival draw a cultured crowd. Summer is, however, very low-key. Foliage usually fills every inn and restaurant during October's first three weekends.

MEDICAL EMERGENCY Emergency service is available by calling **911.**

✳ To See

SCENIC DRIVES **East along the Molly Stark Trail.** Wilmington is midway between Bennington (21 miles) and Brattleboro (20 miles) on Route 9, which is dedicated to the wife of General John Stark, hero of the battle of Bennington. Five miles east of Wilmington you come to Hogback Mountain. Formerly a ski area, this is now a major overlook, said to offer a 100-mile view (weather dependent) facing south. This is also the site of the **Southern Vermont Natural History Museum** (802-464-0048; open Memorial Day through late October, 10–5). Larger than it looks from the outside, it displays mounted specimens of more than 500 New England birds and mammals in 80 dioramas, the collection of taxidermist Luman R. Nelson. When we visited, live exhibits included two hawks and four hoot owls.

Marlboro. Continue along the Molly Stark Trail east some 5 miles to the turnoff to Marlboro Village, home of Marlboro College. From mid-July until mid-August its campus is the venue for the Marlboro Music Festival. The **Marlboro Historical Society** (802-464-0329), with its collection of pictures, old farm tools, and antique furniture, is housed in the Newton House, and the 1813 one-room schoolhouse on Main Street is open in July and August, Sunday 2–5. See *Selective Shopping* for the studios of notable Marlboro craftspeople. Continue into Brattleboro and return via the Dover Hill Road or follow the road past the college to the T, turn right, and you are soon in Jacksonville. See the following tours.

Jacksonville and Whitingham. From Wilmington follow Route 100, past Flames Stable and the turnoff for Ward's Cove, south 6 miles to the village of Jacksonville. At the junction of Route 100 and Route 112 stop by **Stone Soldier Pottery** (802-368-7077), open daily, known for its distinctive contemporary designs. Just down Route 112 is the **North River Winery** (802-368-7557) on Route 112 (open daily 10–5, except January through May, when hours are Friday through Sunday 11–5), dedicated to producing fruit wines. We can speak for the full-bodied apple-blueberry, neither too dry nor too sweet. Green Mountain apple, cranberry-apple, and a number of other blends are offered (free samples come with the tour). Follow Route 100 another 1.5 miles south and turn left onto Town Hill Road (marked for the Brigham Young Monument) into Whitingham. At the top of Town Hill a monument commemorates the Mormon prophet who led his people into Utah and is hailed as the founder of Salt Lake City. He was born on a hill farm here, the son of a poor basket maker. The view takes in surrounding hills; there are picnic benches, grills, a playground, and a parking area. Continue down the hill to Brown's General Store and turn right. Look on the right-hand side of the road near the top of this hill for a small marker that proclaims this to be the homestead site of Brigham Young: BORN ON THIS SPOT 1801 . . . A MAN OF MUCH COURAGE AND SUPERB EQUIPMENT. (BRIGHAM YOUNG FATHERED 57 CHILDREN BY 16 OF HIS 20 WIVES.) Before leaving the village, note the "floating island" in the middle of Sadawga Pond. Whitingham was once a busy resort, thanks to a mineral spring and its accessibility via the Hoosic Tunnel and Wilmington Railroad. The old railroad bed is now a 12-mile walking trail along this remote shore of Lake Whitingham. (Continue 1 mile south on Route 100 beyond the store, and take a right onto Dam Road; park and walk across the dam. Note the "Glory Hole," a large concrete overflow funnel that empties into the Deerfield River.)

Dover Hill Road, accessible from Route 100 via either Dorr Fitch Road in the village of West Dover or East Dover Road farther south (just below Sitzmark). The road climbs steeply past the tiny village center of Dover.

GREEN MOUNTAIN HALL IN WHITINGHAM

Christina Tree

KELLY STAND ROAD

Kim Grant

Here you could detour onto Cooper Hill Road for a few miles to take in the panorama of mountains. On an ordinary day, you can pick out Mount Monadnock in New Hampshire beyond Keene. You can either loop back down to Route 100 via Valley View Road, or continue down the other side of the hill through East Dover to the general store, covered bridge, and picturesque village center in South Newfane, following the Augerhole Road back to Route 9—or, if you're out for a real ride, continuing to Route 30, then south to Brattleboro and back to Wilmington on Route 9.

Handle Road runs south from Mount Snow, paralleling Route 100, turning into Cold Brook Road when it crosses the Wilmington line. The old farmhouses along this high, wooded road were bought up by city people to form a summer colony in the late 1880s. It's still a beautiful road, retaining some of the old houses and views.

Arlington–Kelly Stand Road heads west from West Wardsboro through the tiny village of Stratton. At 6.3 miles the Grout Pond turnoff is clearly marked and leads 1.3 miles to the pond. Hiking trails loop around the pond, through the woods, and continue to Somerset Reservoir. Beyond this turnoff is the monument to Daniel Webster, who spoke here to 1,600 people at an 1840 Whig rally. The hiking trail into Stratton Pond that begins just west of the monument is the most heavily hiked section of the Long Trail. It's possible (your vehicle and conditions permitting) to return to Route 9 through the Green Mountain Forest via the Arlington–Somerset Road (closed in winter). Roughly halfway down you pass the turnoff for Somerset Reservoir.

✳ To Do

AIRPLANE RIDES **North Air** (802-464-2196), Mount Snow Airport off Country Club Road, West Dover, offers scenic air rides.

BOATING **Green Mountain Flagship Co.** (802-464-2975), Route 9 west from Wilmington. Richard Joyce offers seasonal excursions on Lake Harriman aboard the M/V *Mt. Mills*, a twin-stacked pontoon vessel accommodating 65. Joyce caters to bus groups, but there are usually at least half a dozen seats left over. His narration of the logging history of the area is often accompanied by live music. Canoes and kayaks can be rented, too.

High Country Marine (802-464-2108; 1-800-627-7533), Route 9, on Lake Harriman, rents jet boats or pontoon boats, wake boards, ski tubes.

Zoar Outdoor (1-800-532-7483; www.zoaroutdoor.com), Charlemont, Massachusetts. The Deerfield River flows south into Massachusetts, where a regular dam releases power white-water rafting that's exciting enough to satisfy most jocks but doable for children. This long-established outfitter also rents kayaks and sit-on-top canoes for lower stretches of the river. Charlemont is about 40 minutes south of Wilmington via Route 8A.

Equipe Sport (802-464-2222), on the Mount Snow Access Road in West Dover, rents canoes and kayaks.

BOWLING **North Star Bowl and Mini Golf** (802-464-5148), Route 100, Wilmington, opens daily at noon for candlepin bowling; videos and pool tables, too.

CHAIRLIFT **Mount Snow** (1-800-245-SNOW). The lift operates on weekends in summer and daily throughout foliage season.

DAY CAMPS ✐ **Mount Snow Day Camps** (802-464-3333), Mount Snow. Mini Camp (age 6 weeks to 12 months), Kids Camp (ages 5–8), and Sports Camp (ages 9–12) run during summer, Monday through Friday 9–4. Activities include swimming, chairlift rides, arts and crafts, nature hikes, field trips, and more.

FISHING The **Deerfield** is known for rainbow and brook trout (the season is the second Saturday in April through October). The remote Harriman Bypass Reach, a 4.5-mile stretch of the river between the dam in Whitingham and Readsboro, is a good bet. Fly-fishermen can readily find guides. Note **Taddingers/ Orvis Fly Fishing School and Guiding Service** (802-464-6263), Route 100 north, Wilmington.

Harriman Reservoir is stocked with trout, bass, perch, and salmon; a boat launch is located off Fairview Avenue.

Somerset Reservoir, 6.5 miles west of Wilmington, then 10 miles north on the Somerset Road, offers bass, trout, and pike. There is a boat launch at the foot of the 9-mile-long lake. Smaller **Sadawga Pond** in Whitingham and **Lake Raponda** in Wilmington are also good for bass and trout; there is a boat launch on the former. Fishing licenses ($7) are available at Bill's Bait Shop, Whitingham; from the Wilmington town clerk; and at the Orvis dealership at Taddingers, Wilmington.

GOLF **Mount Snow Country Club** (802-464-4254). Billing itself as "The Original Golf School," this program has been evolving since 1978. Weekend and 2- to 5-day midweek golf school packages are offered May through September; the 18-hole, Cornish-designed championship golf course is also open on a daily basis.

Haystack (802-464-8301), Mann Road, off Cold Brook Road, Wilmington; clubhouse, 18 holes designed by Desmond Muirhead, full pro shop, recently upgraded with rave reviews.

Sitzmark Golf & Tennis Club (802-464-3384), Wilmington; 18 holes, club and cart rentals. No tee times.

HIKING Along with the trails in Molly Stark State Park (see *Green Space*) and a short, self-guided trail atop Mount Snow, there are a number of overgrown roads leading to ghost towns. The Long Trail passes through the former logging town of Glastenbury (261 residents in 1880), and a former colonial highway in **Woodford State Park** (see "Bennington Area") leads to a burying ground and 18th-century homesites. Somerset is another ghost town. The Hogback Mountain Overlook on Route 9 is the starting point for a hike up the old ski area access road to the Mount Olga fire tower. Inquire at the Mount Snow Valley Chamber of Commerce about accessing the 12-mile trail along the undeveloped shore of **Lake Whitingham.** Also see Grout Pond under *Green Space.*

Forest Care Nature Walks (802-254-4717). Lynn Levine leads popular group and individual treks in summer and fall, discussing the ecology and wildlife in the area. Reservations needed a week ahead.

HORSEBACK RIDING ✿ **Flames Stables** (802-464-8329), Route 100 south, Wilmington. Western saddle trail rides, half-hour wagon rides, pony rides for young children.

Mountain View Stables (802-464-0615), Higley Hill Road, Wilmington. One-hour guided trail rides, English and Western saddles.

Whitingham Farm (802-368-2620) offers wagon rides using their Percheron/Morgan team, Blitz and Blaze.

✿ **Brookside Stables** (802-464-0267), Route 100 north of Wilmington. Pony rides for the kids.

HUNTING **Hermitage Sporting Clays and Hunting Preserve** (802-464-3511), Wilmington, consists of 200 acres and provides guided shoots with dogs, or you can try your hand at a round of 100 sporting clays. It is possible to use your own dog for a shoot. Reservations required. Pheasant hunts cost $295–395 per day.

LLAMA TREKKING **Green Mountain Expeditions** (802-368-7147), Whitingham. Joy Powell arranges picnic llama treks from June into October.

MOUNTAIN BIKING The **Mountain Bike School and Touring Center** at Mount Snow (1-800-245-SNOW) bills itself as "America's first and foremost mountain bike school." It includes the Crisports Bike Shop with rentals and repairs and 45 miles of trails with lifts servicing a portion. Inquire about lodging/biking packages, clinics, and guided tours.

Alpine Traders (802-464-8010), Route 100, West Dover. Open daily 8–6. Sales and rentals of Reflex mountain bikes.

Equipe Sport (802-464-2222), on the Mount Snow Access Road in West Dover, rents bikes and helmets in addition to offering guided rides.

SWIMMING There are several beaches on 11-mile-long Harriman Reservoir, also known as Whitingham Lake. **Mountain Mills Beach** is 1 mile from Wilmington

Village, posted from Castle Hill Road. **Ward's Cove Beach** is on Route 100 south of Wilmington—turn right at Flames Stables and follow signs. Inquire locally about less publicized places.

Sitzmark Lodge (802-464-3384), north of Wilmington on Route 100, has a pool that's open to the public free of charge. Snacks and a bar are available poolside.

TENNIS The municipal courts at **Baker Field** in Wilmington are open to the public; also eight courts at Sitzmark (see above).

✳ Winter Sports

CROSS-COUNTRY SKIING **Hermitage Ski Touring Center** (802-464-3511), Wilmington. Outstanding 35 km, machine-tracked network (50 km total) includes a ridgetop trail with superb views and elevations of 1,867–3,556 feet. Instruction, rental, repair, telemark guided tours.

The **White House Winter Activity Center** (802-464-2135), Wilmington. A total of 25 km of tracked trails meander through the woods at elevations of 1,573–2,036 feet. Snowshoes are also available, and there's snow tubing down the hill the inn stands on. Instruction, rentals, lodging, ski weeks.

Timber Creek Cross Country Touring Center (802-464-0999), West Dover. Just across Route 100 from the entrance to Mount Snow, a high-elevation, wooded system of trails that hold their snow cover; rentals, instruction available.

Prospect Mountain Cross Country Touring Center (802-442-2575), Route 9, Woodford, features 40 km of groomed trails with special trails for snowshoeing and a comfortable base lodge with a fireplace, home-cooked food, and baked goods. Trail fees are $15 for adults, $12 for juniors and seniors. Rentals. Because of its elevation, Prospect Mountain often has snow when other areas are bare.

DOWNHILL SKIING/SNOWBOARDING ♂ **Mount Snow/Haystack** (information: 802-464-3333; snow report: 802-464-2151; reservations: 1-800-245-SNOW; www.mountsnow.com), West Dover. Owned by the American Skiing Company, the 767-acre area offers some 2,100 "on mountain" beds. There are five distinct areas here: the Main Mountain, the expert North Face, the Sunbrook Area, Carinthia Slopes, and Haystack (open weekends and holidays only). The vertical drop is 1,700 feet. The area also features two half-pipes and four terrain parks. Base area facilities include lodges, rental/repair shops, retail, and more. See the chapter introduction for the resort's history. *Lifts:* 23 chairlifts—3 high-speed and 1 fixed quad, 10 triples, 4 doubles. There are also two surface lifts and three Magic Carpets. *Ski/snowboard trails:* 132, including 33 "easier," 66 "more difficult," 26 "advanced," and 2 "double black diamonds." There are also 139 acres of hand-cleared "Tree Terrain." *Snowmaking:* 85 percent of the mountain. *Facilities:* Five base lodges, an upper lodge near the summit, the Snow Barn (nightclub with entertainment, dancing), and the Natural Life Center spa. *Ski school:* 85 instructors, Perfect Turn teaching methods—two clinics. *For children:* Perfect Kids; Mountain Camp (7–12); Mountain Riders (7–12); Snow Camp (4–6); Cub Camp (3-year-olds); Child Care (6 weeks–5 years). *Rates:* **Mount**

Snow, weekdays adult $57 (weekends $64), young adult $55, junior/senior $42. **Haystack:** adult $45, junior/senior $32. *Special events:* Thanksgiving and Christmas vacations; Fireworks and Torchlight Extravaganza; January, Snowmobile Snowcross; February, Budweiser Aerial Assault and Boarderfest; March, Annual Reggae Festival. See www.mountsnow.com for a full schedule.

DOGSLEDDING **Snowdoggin' Inc.** (802-380-2200), P.O. Box 151, East Dover, offers dogsled rides through the Green Mountains.

SLEIGH RIDES Sleigh rides are offered at **Adams Farm** (802-464-3762), Wilmington, with a refreshment stop at a cabin in the woods. They are also offered at **Flames Stables** (802-464-8329) on Route 100, south of Wilmington, and at **Whitingham Farm** (802-368-2620) in Whitingham.

SNOWMOBILING **High Country Snowmobile Tours** (802-464-2108; 1-800-627-SLED) in Wilmington and **Twin Brooks Snowmobile Tours** (802-442-4054; 1-888-616-4054) in Woodford, both on Route 9 west, offer rentals and guided tours. **Sitzmark** (802-464-5498) on Route 100 north in Wilmington is now a snowmobile touring center.

✳ Green Space

Molly Stark State Park (802-464-5460), Route 9 east of Wilmington Village. This 158-acre preserve features a hiking trail through the forest to 2,415-foot Mount Olga, from which there is a panoramic view. The 34 campsites include eight lean-tos. See *Campgrounds* in "What's Where" for state park fees and reservations.

Grout Pond Recreation Area (802-362-2307), west of West Wardsboro, off the Arlington (aka Kelley Stand) Road. A 1,600-acre piece of the Green Mountain National Forest designated for hiking, picnicking, fishing, boating, and camping. In summer a ranger resides at the Grout Pond Cabin, and campsites are available on a first come, first-served basis (6 vehicle sites, 11 walk-in campsites, and 4 sites accessible by canoe). Twelve miles of trails, which circle the pond and connect with Somerset Reservoir, are open in winter for skiing (they are not groomed). At the north end of the pond there are five picnic sites.

✳ Farms to Visit

✐ **Adams Farm** (802-464-3762; www.adamsfamilyfarm.com), 15 Higley Hill Road, off Route 100, Wilmington. A sixth-generation, exceptionally visitor-friendly farm. Its Petting Farm (open daily except Tuesday July through Labor Day, then weekends through Columbus Day) includes Rosie, the sow, in her swimming pool; Mr. McGregor's garden rabbits; a miniature horse; and goats, sheep, peacocks, turkeys, and geese. Visitors can gather fresh eggs, milk a goat, ride a tractor or pony, explore bear caves, or jump in the hay. Special events include a moonlight hayride and a sheep-shearing festival. In winter there are horse-drawn sleigh rides. Inquire about afternoon tea. The **Far Store** and **Quilt and Fiber Arts Loft** features things locally crafted and otherwise produced.

Wheeler Farm (802-464-5225), Route 100 north of Wilmington Village. A third-generation working farm with Jersey and Dutch belted cows. Maple syrup is produced and sold, along with maple cream and sugar.

Boyd Family Farm (802-464-5618), East Dover Road, Wilmington. A working hillside farm, with pick-your-own flowers June through September, then pumpkins and Christmas wreaths.

North River Winery. See Jacksonville and Whitingham in *Scenic Drives*.

Ridgeway Red Deer Farm (802-368-2556), Whitingham. A working deer farm that sells red deer meat products, antlers, and much more. Tours at 10 AM and 2 PM.

✳ Lodging

This area can sleep more than 10,000 visitors on any one night, primarily in condominiums and ski lodges. The **Mount Snow Valley Chamber of Commerce** maintains a reservation line that includes inns as well as B&Bs (1-877-887-6884; www.visit vermont.com); the **Mount Snow Region Vacation Information Center** (1-800-451-MTSNOW, ext. 40; www.mountsnow-vt.com) operates a similar year-round service. Our listings focus on the inns and B&Bs.

RESORT ✍ **The Grand Summit Resort Hotel** (802-464-6600; 1-800-451-4211; www.mountsnow.com), 89 Mountain Road, Mount Snow 05356. At the base of the ski lifts, this 187-room, condo hotel/conference center features one to three-bedroom suites (many with kitchen) as well as the usual hotel rooms. Amenities include an outdoor pool and hot tubs, child care and arcade, and, of course, the adjacent ski lifts and, in summer, the golf and mountain biking programs. **Harriman's Restaurant** is open for breakfast and dinner; the **Grand Country Deli** has take-out. Rates vary seasonally as well as for midweek and weekend stays: $137–528 for a double. Valet parking costs $15 per night.

INNS

In Wilmington 05363
♿ **The White House of Wilmington** (802-464-2135; 1-800-541-2135; www.whitehouseinn.com). Built in 1915 on a knoll off Route 9 as a summer residence for Martin Brown, founder of Brown Paper Company, this is a Colonial Revival mansion. Adam Grinold recently took over running the inn from his father, Bob. Public rooms are huge, airy, and light but also manage to be warm in winter—with the help of yawning hearths. In all seasons guests gather around the sunken bar. A total of 25 rooms, including 3 suites, are divided between the main house and the cottage. Two rooms have a balcony with fireplace, plus two-person whirlpool tub; two have a terrace with fireplace and whirlpool tub. There's a 60-foot outdoor pool and a small indoor pool with sauna. In winter 43 km of cross-country trails are out the door. A full breakfast is included in the rates, and dinner (see *Dining Out*) is served, along with a buffet Sunday brunch and a skiers' lunch in winter. Cash or checks preferred for accommodations. Rates range from $118–262 per room in low season to $150–284 per room in high season, plus 10 percent gratuity. Discounts on nonholiday midweek stays in both facilities.

🦆 ♂ ♿ **Misty Mountain Lodge**
(802-464-3961; www.mistymountain
bandb.com), 326 Stowe Hill Road.
Just 16 people can be accommodated
in this informal old farmhouse set
high on a hillside. There are six rooms
(four with private bath, two with
shared); one has a jetted whirlpool
bath, and one is handicapped
approved. Meals are served family-
style, and children feel welcome. Vic
and Donna Ruiz, the current owners,
perpetuate the genial atmosphere for
which this place is known. Guests can
walk, cross-country ski, or relax by
one of the gardens on the property, or
settle down with a book by the fieldstone fireplace in the living room.
$100–125 per couple; children 7 and
under are free.

Nutmeg Inn (802-464-3351; www
.nutmeginn.com), P.O. Box 1899.
Gerry and Susan Goodman's delightful 18th-century roadside farmhouse
on Route 9 west is a B&B that feels
like an inn. It's on the edge of the village and offers 10 rooms, each nicely
decorated with wallpaper, quilts, and
braided rugs; four spacious one- and
two-bedroom suites with fireplace and
color TV/VCR and two-person
whirlpool. All rooms and suites have
central air-conditioning. There is a
cozy living room, library, and BYOB
bar, plus three intimate dining rooms
for full, complimentary breakfasts.
Food is important here. Summer
$119–209 double; fall $149–299; winter $139–269.

∞ **The Hermitage Inn** (802-464-
3511; www.hermitageinn.com), Coldbrook Road. Innkeeper Jim McGovern
collects wines and art for this unusual
and popular hostelry, which combines
fine dining with cross-country skiing
and pheasant hunting. There are 15

guest rooms in the inn and another 14
a mile down the road in the former
Brook Bound, which now serves as an
annex. All rooms have private bath.
Rates vary widely: from $60–125 dou-
ble in Brook Bound, B&B, to $89–175
double, B&B, in the inn, plus 15 percent gratuity.

∞ **The Red Shutter Inn** (802-464-
3768; 1-800-845-7548; www.red
shutterinn.com), Route 9. Lucylee and
Gerard Gingras preside over this big,
gracious, 1890s house on the edge of
the village with nine nicely furnished
guest rooms including two suites with
fireplace, one with a double whirlpool
tub. The dining room, furnished with
an assortment of old oak tables, has a
good reputation and is open to the
public (see *Dining Out*). From $130
double for cozy rooms in the carriage
house to $260 for the spacious two-
room Courtemanche Suite in the main
house, B&B.

In West Dover 05356

The Inn at Sawmill Farm (802-
464-8131; 1-800-493-1133;
www.theinnatsawmillfarm.com),
Crosstown Road and Route 100.
Closed early April through mid-May.
Rod Williams is an architect, his wife,
Ione, an interior decorator, and their
son, Brill, an accomplished chef.
Together the team has created one of
Vermont's most elegant inns, a world-
class hideaway in the Relais &
Châteaux category, filled with
antiques and splendid fabrics. The
dining room is exceptional (see *Dining Out*). In summer, flowers are
everywhere, inside and out; there is a
swimming pool, a tennis court, and
two trout ponds. There are 21 beautifully appointed guest rooms, each different, 10 with working fireplace.
$400–850 per room MAP.

  ♿ **Deerhill Inn** (802-464-3100; 1-800-99-DEER9; www.deerhill .com), 14 Valley View Road. Chef-owner Michael Allen has won raves for his dining room (see *Dining Out*) as well as for his 15 luxurious rooms and suites, some in the old farm-house, others in a newer wing. From the latter—especially on the galleried second floor—you enjoy a smashing view of Haystack and Mount Snow. One comfortable sitting room adjoins the tiny bar and two spacious dining rooms, walled with the work of local artists; upstairs is another big lounge for guests, plus a library nook. In summer, flowers abound inside and out and around the patio of the new swimming pool. A lot happens here, too, especially during the valley's pre-Christmas festivities. Weekends $130–250 B&B; MAP rates (an additional $80) are available except in holiday or foliage seasons.

Doveberry Inn (802-464-5652; 1-800-722-3204; www.doveberryinn .com), Route 100. A spacious, well-built inn on Route 100 near the Mount Snow access. There's a comfortable, large living room with fireplace and wine bar. Upstairs, each of the eight rooms is immaculate and bright, with private bath and full vanities (some of them copper), also with cable TV and video player, one with a fireplace and balcony. Request a back room overlooking the woods. The recent expansion added on three more rooms with whirlpool tub, fireplace, and king or queen bed. Innkeepers Michael and Christine Fayette are culinary school graduates and prepare all the northern Italian cuisine (see *Dining Out*). $90–110 daily per room with full breakfast in fall, $110–150 in winter, $90–110 in spring, and $80–105 in summer. MAP is available on request.

⚁ **West Dover Inn** (802-464-5207; www.westdoverinn.com), P.O. Box 1208, 108 Route 100. Built as the village inn in 1846 and now on the National Register of Historic Places, Ed Riley's handsome inn includes modern amenities and antique appointments in each of its 12 guest rooms, 5 of which are fireplace suites with whirlpool tub. All rooms have private bath and cable TV. Guests enjoy a common room, with fireplace, as well as a publike cocktail lounge and casual fine-dining restaurant (see *Dining Out*). B&B rates: $100–175 per couple in summer; $120–225 in foliage season. Some minimum stays required during holiday periods. Children 12 and over.

In East Dover 05431

⚁ ♻ **Cooper Hill Inn** (802-348-6333; 1-800-783-3229; www.cooper hillinn.com), P.O. Box 146, Cooper Hill Road. High on a hilltop on a quiet country road with one of the most spectacular mountain panoramas in New England, this sprawling inn run by Gordon and Carolyn Lucas has 10 guest rooms, all with private bath, including two-room family suites, living room, dining room, game room, and roomy covered porch. B&B rates: $130–190 per room on fall and winter weekends, $110–160 on weekends in spring and summer.

BED & BREAKFASTS ⚁ ♿ **The Four Seasons Inn** (802-464-8303; 1-877-531-4500; www.thefourseasons inn.com), 145 Route 100, West Dover 05356. Ann and Barry Poulter have renovated this historic inn, adding four-poster bed, Jacuzzi, and fireplace in many of the 15 rooms, all with private bath. Room rates of $120–235 in low season, $150–325 in high season, include a full breakfast.

☙ **Austin Hill Inn** (802-464-5281; 1-800-332-7352; www.austinhillinn.com), Box 859, Route 100, West Dover 05356. John and Debbie have 11 rooms with private bath, with 3 large enough to accommodate more than two. Their specialty is Murder Mystery Weekends that involves a full weekend package and a four-course dinner on Saturday night. Room rates are $115 in low season, $135–195 in high season, including breakfast and afternoon refreshments.

Trail's End, A Country Inn (802-464-2727; 1-800-859-2585; www.trailsendvt.com), 5 Trail's End Lane, Wilmington 05363, off East Dover Road. Unusual spaces in this ski lodge include a library and game room, a large living room with a two-story, fieldstone fireplace, and a dining space with large, round, hand-carved pine tables. The 13 rooms all have private bath, and 4 have wood-burning fireplace; the two fireplace suites also have canopy bed, refrigerator, microwave, and Jacuzzi. In summer, check to see how your room is cooled. Facilities include a clay tennis court, a nicely landscaped heated pool, and paths leading out into the gardens and up the hill to the pond. Guests have access to their own fridge, a plus in summer when no one wants to stray too far from the pool. Rates per room with breakfast: low season $110–160, high season $130–190.

∞ ☙ ♪ **The Inn at Quail Run** (802-464-3362; 1-800-34-ESCAPE; www.theinnatquailrun.com), 106 Smith Road, Wilmington 05363. Nicely positioned above the valley,

this ski lodge/inn with 11 rooms is known for its breakfasts. Served in a flagstone-floored sunporch with mountain views, the morning menu might include a lobster-and-Boursin or crabmeat-and-avocado omelet, or lemon-orange ricotta pancakes with a special maple-glazed bacon (the public is welcome for a prix fixe of $12.95). Common space is ample and includes a large living room with a piano and fireplace, as well as a small, inviting bar. Amenities include a heated pool and nine-person Jacuzzi. Children and pets are welcome on the lower level of the inn (the coolest in summer). Summer $90–170; fall $105–200; ski season $105–180.

☙ **Whetstone Inn** (802-254-2500; www.whetstoneinn.com), 5550 South Road, Marlboro 05344. Handy to the Marlboro Music Festival, this is a 1786 tavern with a Palladian window, part of the cluster of white-clapboard buildings—including the church and post office—that form the village core. Innkeepers Jean and Harry Boardman have been here more than 20 years, and there's a casually comfortable feel to the place. Most guests have been here before and have their own favorite rooms, of which there are 12, 7 with private bath and 3 with kitchen. Singles with private bath run $40–70; doubles, $65–85. Breakfast, served daily, is extra, as is dinner, which is served on weekends and selected weekdays. There's swimming in a spring-fed pond.

☙ **Shearer Hill Farm** (802-464-3253; 1-800-437-3104; www.shearerhillfarm.com), Shearer Hill Road off Route 9, 5 miles southeast of the village in Halifax. Keep going on this back road, bearing left at the fork, to Bill and Patti Pusey's simple, restored

200-year-old farmhouse a stone's throw from the Massachusetts border. Three rooms in the main house have private bath; there is an annex with a ground-floor room and kitchenette, plus two bedrooms and a sitting room upstairs, all with private bath. The pleasant large living room in the farmhouse has a VCR library. $90 double, $70 single with continental breakfast buffet. Cross-country skiing on the grounds.

The Candlelight Bed & Breakfast (802-368-2004; www.candlelight bandb.com), 3358 Route 100, Jacksonville 05342. Fran and Peter Madden run this attractive three-room B&B set above a rural stretch of Route 100; two guest rooms feature fireplaces; $100 per couple includes breakfast.

CONDOS AND LODGES Mount Snow Lodging (802-464-7768; 1-800-451-4211). A general reservation service that includes condos at the base of the mountain, the Grand Summit Hotel, and the Snow Lake Lodge.

Snowresort Rentals (802-464-2177; 1-800-451-MTSNOW), Mountain Park Plaza, West Dover, has extensive listings of vacation homes and condos, ranging from small studios to five-bedroom condos for daily, weekend, monthly, or seasonal rentals.

CAMPING See Molly Stark State Park and Grout Pond Recreation Area in *Green Space*.

OTHER The Amos Brown House, the oldest house in the back-road town of Whitingham, is currently under restoration by nonprofit Landmark Trust USA. The brick Cape-style farmhouse, built around 1800,

with connected barn and sheds, is set in 30 acres of meadow and sugarbush on a quiet dirt road. For details about renting the house, contact Landmark at 802-254-6868.

✳ Where to Eat

DINING OUT The Inn at Sawmill Farm (802-464-8131), Route 100, West Dover. Open for dinner only, 6–9:30. The main dining room is the interior of a former barn, with fine chintz and old portraits. The linen-covered tables are set with sterling and fresh flowers; there is also a smaller, sun- and plant-filled dining room. The 34,000-bottle wine cellar was given the Grand Award from *Wine Spectator*. Specialties include Key West snapper with lobster risotto, or seared moulard duck breast with prunes and lentils; there is also a wide choice of appetizers and irresistible desserts. One of the best in the state. Entrées $32–38.

Deerhill Inn (802-464-3100) 14 Valley View Road (off Route 100), West Dover. Michael Allen presides over the kitchen of this luxurious establishment, offering prix fixe and à la carte menus. You might begin a prix fixe ($45) menu with arugula fettuccine and continue with olive-oil-poached swordfish or magret of moulard duck with currants and pecans. Desserts are delectable.

The Hermitage Inn (802-464-3511) Coldbrook Road, Wilmington. A popular, highly regarded restaurant with two dining rooms, fine art on the walls, and a mixture of arm- and wing chairs that all make for the elegance due the dishes. You might begin dinner with homemade venison sausage or game bird pâté, proceed to chicken amandine, boneless trout, or the game bird selection, with a wine chosen from among 2,000 labels. Sunday brunch. Entrées $15–30.

Le Petit Chef (802-464-8437), Route 100 north, Wilmington. Open for dinner daily except Tuesday. Elegant French dining in an old roadside house. This is a local favorite. Chef-owner Betty Hillman's French-accented menu might include *poisson* Mediterranean (shellfish poached in a zesty broth) and *côte de veau grillée* (grilled veal rib seasoned with herbs and a balsamic glaze, with straw potatoes and roasted stuffed tomato). Entrées $18–28.50. Reservations a must.

Doveberry Inn (802-464-5652), Route 100, West Dover. Closed Tuesday. This elegant inn is chef owned, and the accent is authentic northern Italian. The à la carte menu might include fennel and leek risotto followed by Gorgonzola and then wood-grilled veal chop. The Italian wine list is large. Entrées $19–31.

West Dover Inn (802-464-7264), Route 100, West Dover. The dining room at the West Dover Inn has a distinctive and seasonally changing menu. It might include curried crabcakes for starters, then applewood-smoked pork tenderloin. Entrées $17–28.

Two Tannery Road (802-464-2707), 2 Tannery Road, Route 100, West Dover. Open Tuesday through Sunday. The building itself is said to date in part from the late 1700s, when it stood in Marlboro, Massachusetts, and has moved several times within this valley, serving for a while as a summer home for Theodore Roosevelt's son. The bar began service in the original Waldorf Astoria (present site of the Empire State Building). The food is highly rated, with a large

à la carte menu that might include the Tannery Two, jumbo Acadian shrimp paired with grilled Cajun salmon; or the Nutty Vermonter, a ham-and-cheese-stuffed chicken breast with an almond crust. Entrées $23–30. On Thursday a complete dinner is the same price as an entrée.

The Red Shutter Inn (802-464-3768), Route 9, Wilmington. Closed Monday. The pleasant, oak-filled dining room provides a locally acclaimed "night-out" atmosphere. Appetizers usually include escargots with wild mushrooms or baked Brie with fresh fruit, and entrées range from fresh Long Island duckling with raspberry sauce to linguine with chicken and shrimp. $19.50–26.

The White House of Wilmington (802-464-2135), Route 9 east, Wilmington. The wood-paneled dining room is warmed by a glowing hearth. The menu is extensive and usually includes a veal chop, Parmesan-crusted sea scallops, filet mignon, and semiboneless stuffed duck with mandarin orange and wild blueberry melba. $22–31.

DOWNTOWN WILMINGTON

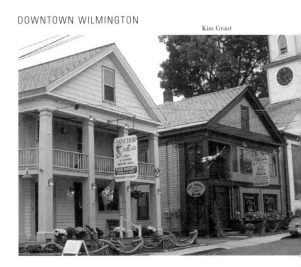
Kim Grant

EATING OUT ✒ **Poncho's Wreck** (802-464-9320), South Main Street, Wilmington. Open daily for dinner; lunch and brunch Saturday and Sunday. Early-bird menu 4–6. A pubby, nautical atmosphere; specialties are Mexican dishes, seafood dishes, and steaks. Frozen drinks and a wide selection of beer. Try Poncho's Combo. Tends to fill up, so it's advisable to come very early or late. Inquire about live entertainment.

✒ **Dot's Restaurant** (802-464-7284; 802-464-6476), Wilmington, is open 5:30 AM–8 PM, until 9 PM Friday and Saturday. This is a cheerful, pine-sided place in the middle of the village. There's a long Formica counter as well as tables, a fireplace in back, and wine by the glass. Stop by for a bowl of the hottest chili in New England. The soup and muffins are home-made, and the Reubens are first-rate. Its sibling is on Route 100 in Mountain Park Plaza.

✒ **Skyline Restaurant** (802-464-3536), Route 9, Hogback Mountain, Marlboro. For more than 40 years Joyce and Dick Hamilton have operated this restaurant with "the 100-mile view." The knotty-pine dining room has worn, shiny tables, fresh flowers, and a traditional New England menu. In winter there's a fire. Specialties include homemade soups; home-baked brownies, pies, and turnovers; and a Vermonter sandwich.

✒ **Anchor** (802-464-2112), 8 South Main Street, Wilmington. Lunch and dinner, Sunday brunch. Same ownership as Poncho's. This is an informal fish place with a raw bar, fried clams, and daily specials like fried salmon slices in bacon and a sautéed mixed grill with lemon-pepper sauce, plus ribs; also a full menu of cocktails.

The Roadhouse Restaurant (802-464-5017), Route 100, Wilmington. Open for dinner daily except Wednesday. Considered one of the better deals in the valley because all dinners ($18.75–23.75) come with soup, bread, salad, and dessert, and the food is good. Entrées might include sautéed pork tenderloin, roast duckling with orange sauce, fresh Boston scrod, and pasta dishes.

✒ **Alonzo's Pasta and Grille** (802-464-2355), at the Crafts Inn, West Main Street, Wilmington. Open daily for lunch and dinner, breakfast on weekends. "Create-your-own-grill" specials (teriyaki steak, Andouille sausage, for example); homemade pastas.

Mildred's Fine Foods Deli (802-464-1224), Route 9, Wilmington Village. Open 11–5. A source of standout deli sandwiches and wraps; eat in or take on a picnic.

BREWS Bean Heads (802-464-1208), Main and River Streets, Wilmington. Espresso, cappuccino, bagelry, soup, and sandwiches.

Maple Leaf Malt & Brewing (802-464-9900), 3 North Main Street, Wilmington. Open for lunch and dinner, full bar. The local microbrew in an attractive space, full bar, weekly entertainment.

✳ Entertainment

Memorial Hall Center for the Arts (802-464-8411), lodged in the McKim, Mead, and White–designed theater next door to the historic Crafts Inn, Wilmington. The center sponsors frequent theatrical, musical, and community events.

Mountain Park Cinema (802-464-6477), Route 100, West Dover, has two movie theaters for first-run films; matinees on rainy weekends.

APRÈS-SKI During ski season the following places feature live entertainment or DJs on most nights; in summer they come to life on weekends: On Route 100, between Wilmington and Mount Snow, look for **Deacon's Den** (802-464-9361), and **Snow Barn Entertainment Center** (the old Rubin's Barn at Mount Snow). The **Billiard Sanctuary** (802-464-9975), Route 100, has music every Friday and Saturday. **Mo Jazz,** under the Village Pub on South Main Street in Wilmington, has music on Friday and Saturday nights 9–midnight.

✳ Selective Shopping

ANTIQUES **Wilmington Antique & Flea Market** (802-464-3345), junction of Routes 9 and 100. Open May through October, Saturday and Sunday. Bills itself as southern Vermont's largest outdoor flea market.

Left Bank Antiques (802-464-3224), Routes 9 and 100, Wilmington. Country furniture, old paintings, and prints.

ARTISANS AND CRAFTS **Quaigh Design Centre** (802-464-2780), Main Street, Wilmington. This is a long-established showcase for top Vermont crafts; imported Scottish woolens are also a specialty. Lilias MacBean Hart, the owner, has produced a Vermont tartan. There's also lots of Vermont artist Mary Azarian's work.

John McLeod, Ltd. (802-464-8175), Route 9, Wilmington. Unusual wooden shapes to decorate your home (clocks, mirrors, cutting boards) are sold in the showroom of this woodworking shop on the western verge of the village; open daily. McLeod has expanded his operation to fill six buildings.

Turnpike Road Pottery (802-254-2168), Marlboro. Open Saturday 1–4. Malcolm Wright makes distinctive wood-fired pottery.

Applewoods (802-254-2908), Marlboro. Open June through September 1,

SUMMER MUSIC FESTIVAL
Marlboro Music Festival, Persons Auditorium, Marlboro College. (For advance tickets write to Marlboro Music Festival, 135 South 18th Street, Philadelphia, PA 19103; 215-569-4690; after June 6 call the Marlboro box office, 802-254-2394; www.marlboromusic.org.) Concerts, primarily chamber music, are offered on Friday, Saturday, and Sunday, early July through mid-August. This unusual "festival" is a 7-week gathering of 70 or so world-class musicians who come to work together. It is held on this rural campus because Rudolf Serkin, one of its founders, owned a nearby farm. Pablo Casals came every year from 1960 to 1973. Some concerts are sold out in advance, but you can frequently find good seats before the performance (chairs are metal, and regulars bring cushions). There are (almost) always bargain-priced seats in the tent just outside the auditorium's sliding glass doors.

weekends 10–4 and by appointment. David and Michelle Holzapfel create amazing furnishings from burls and other wood forms.

Gallery in the Woods and Dante's Infurniture (802-464-5793), 1825 Butterfield Road (off Route 9), Marlboro. Dante Corsano makes widely respected tables, dressers, armoires—whatever you need. The lines are simple, and the craftsmanship is so exceptional that the pieces are striking. His wife, Suzanne, crafts equally striking pottery lamps in a range of soft hues. Many other artists are also featured. There's a new gallery in downtown Brattleboro as well; see "Lower Connecticut and West River Valleys."

Craft Haus (802-464-2164), Stowe Hill Road, Wilmington. Set high on a hillside, this is a gallery in Ursula Tancrel's home. The big attractions are works by folk artist Will Moses and Ursula's cloisonné and enamel-plated jewelry, which sells for far higher prices in urban stores. Open weekends 10–5 and at other times by appointment.

Kaos Fine Art Gallery (802-464-1414; www.kaosgallery.com), corner of Route 100 and Route 9, Wilmington. A slick new gallery featuring the works of its cofounders, Miki Boni, known for her portraits, and Karen Baker, a landscape artist.

More galleries: Pick up an *Art Galleries* map/guide to the burgeoning number of galleries.

BOOKSTORES Bartleby's Books and Music (802-464-5425), North Main Street, Wilmington, is a cheerful shop for new books (mostly paperbacks), greeting cards, cassettes, and compact disks.

Austin's Antiquarian Books (802-464-3727), Route 9 west, Wilmington.

R&S Kurland Fine Books (802-464-9670), 59 Davis Drive, Wilmington. Mid-May through mid-October. First editions, New Englandiana, Americana, Civil War.

SPECIAL SHOPS Taddingers (802-464-6263), Route 100, Wilmington. Seven specialty shops under one roof: antiques and fine prints, exclusive decorative accessories, Christmas Room, Nature Room, and an Orvis dealership, with gear for fly-fishing, fly-tying, and shooting, plus sponsorship of 1- and 2-day fishing schools.

Manyu's Boutique (802-464-8880), Main and River Streets, Wilmington, has casual, contemporary clothes and accessories for women.

Down in the Valley (802-464-2211), West Main Street, Wilmington. A long-established, genuinely off-price ski- and sportswear shop, featuring fleece outerwear.

Klara Simpla (802-464-5257), Route 9 west, Wilmington. A "holistic country store" with a following stretching the length of Route 9. Vitamins, homeopathic remedies, natural foods, a wide selection of books, and, of course, Birkenstock sandals are available. Upstairs are weekly sessions in massage therapy, yoga, chiropractic, acupuncture; also special workshops in such topics as nutrition and dowsing.

1836 Country Store Village (802-464-5102), West Main Street, Wilmington, has an eclectic stock of decorative brasses, pierced-tin lanterns, cotton calicoes, quilting supplies, cheese, and the usual souvenirs.

Pickwell's Barn (802-464-3198; www.pickwellsbarn.com), West Main

ART ON THE MOUNTAIN

A 9-day exhibit, late July through early August at Haystack (802-464-8671). One of the largest and best gatherings of craftspeople and their wares, displayed in Haystack's unusual glass-and-wood base lodge, daily 10–5.

Street, Wilmington, has pottery, clocks, prints, colorful glassware, Vermont wines, and specialty foods.

SweDenNor Ltd. (802-464-2788), Route 100, West Dover. A long-established store with a wide selection of Scandinavian, contemporary, and country furniture; also lamps, paintings, and gifts.

☀ Special Events

Late January: **Harriman Ice Fishing Derby** on Lake Whitingham (802-368-2773).

Easter weekend: Nondenominational **sunrise service** on Mount Snow's summit with continental breakfast. Eggs hidden all over the mountain, good for prizes.

July 4 weekend: A very big celebration in these parts with fireworks, parades, et cetera.

July through mid-August: **Marlboro Music Festival** (802-254-2394; see *Entertainment*).

August: **Deerfield Valley Farmers Day** (802-464-8092), Wilmington—an old-fashioned agricultural fair with midway, livestock exhibits.

November 25–December 25: "Nights Before Christmas" celebration—wreath sales, fashion shows, concerts, Festival of Lights, holiday tour of country inns, Living Nativity, and other events in the Mount Snow Valley.

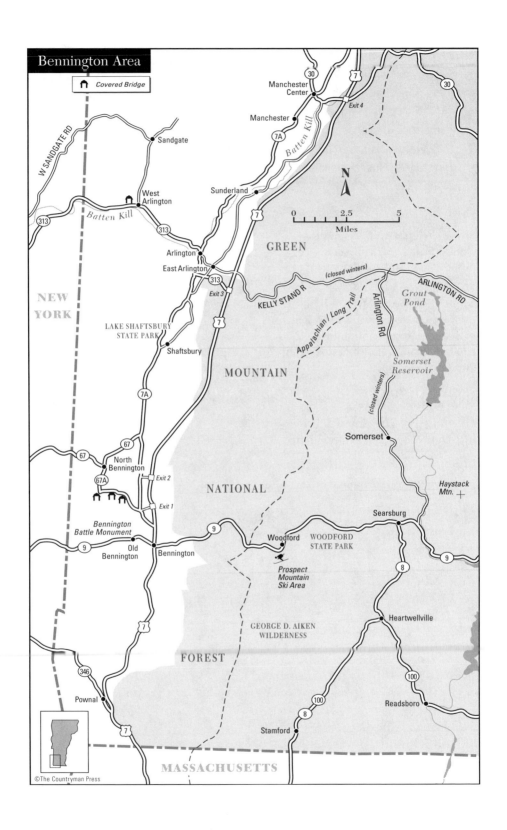

Bennington Area

⌂ Covered Bridge

Manchester
Center

30

7

Exit 4

Manchester

7A

Batten Kill

30

W SANDGATE RD

Sandgate

N

0   2.5   5
Miles

West
Arlington

Sunderland

Batten Kill

313

7

GREEN

313

Arlington

313

East Arlington

NEW
YORK

Exit 3

KELLY STAND R

(closed winters)

Appalachian / Long Trail

Arlington Rd

ARLINGTON RD

*Grout
Pond*

LAKE SHAFTSBURY
STATE PARK

7

MOUNTAIN

*Somerset
Reservoir*

Shaftsbury

(closed winters)

7A

Somerset

67

Haystack
Mtn. +

67

North
Bennington

67A

Exit 2

NATIONAL

Searsburg

Exit 1

9

Woodford

WOODFORD
STATE PARK

8

9

*Bennington
Battle Monument*

9

Old
Bennington

Bennington

Prospect
Mountain
Ski Area

7

GEORGE D. AIKEN
WILDERNESS

Heartwellville

346

FOREST

100

Pownal

100

Readsboro

7

8

Stamford

MASSACHUSETTS

©The Countryman Press

BENNINGTON AREA

Vermont's southwest corner is dominated by Bennington, the state's fifth largest town, which is undergoing something of an industrial renaissance while retaining its historic luster. This growth has, in turn, led to a general improvement in places to stay and eat. The first town settled west of the Connecticut River in the New Hampshire Grants in 1749 and named for avaricious Governor Benning Wentworth, Bennington became a hotbed of sedition when the "Bennington Mob," or Green Mountain Boys, formed in 1770 at Fay's Catamount Tavern under the leadership of Seth Warner and Ethan Allen to expel both the 'Yorkers (who claimed the territory) and, later, the British.

The battle of Bennington (more precisely, the battle for Bennington) on August 16, 1777, deflected General Burgoyne's occupation of the colonies when New Hampshire general John Stark's hastily mobilized militiamen beat the tar out of Colonel Baum's overdressed Hessians on high ground near the Walloomsac River, across the New York border.

Today Bennington is nationally known as the home of distinguished Bennington College, established in the early 1930s, as well as Southern Vermont College, headquartered in the Everett Mansion. It is also remembered fondly by collectors of Bennington pottery.

GUIDANCE A good visitors guide to Bennington County is provided by the **Bennington Area Chamber of Commerce** (802-447-3311; 1-800-229-0252; www.bennington.com), 100 Veterans Memorial Drive, Bennington 05201, which also has a well-supplied information center. The **Regional Marketing Organization** (RMO) can be reached at 1-800-362-4144; www.thegreenmountains.com.

GETTING THERE *By car:* Bennington lies at the convergence of Routes 7, 7A, 9, 67, and 67A. Going north can be confusing; watch the signs carefully to choose between the limited-access Route 7 to Manchester and the more interesting but slower historic Route 7A to Shaftsbury and Arlington.

By bus: **Vermont Transit** from Albany or hubs in Connecticut and Massachusetts.

MEDICAL EMERGENCY Emergency service is available by calling **911.**

Southwestern Vermont Medical Center (802-442-6361), 100 Hospital Drive, Bennington.

✴ To See

Historic Bennington Walking Tours, self-guided with a keyed map/brochure from the chamber of commerce—also available at www.bennington.com—that describes Old Bennington, including the 306-foot, blue limestone shaft of the Bennington Battle Monument, dedicated in 1891; all the fine early houses along Monument Avenue; the Old Academy; Old First Church; the Burying Ground, where five Vermont governors and Robert Frost repose; and the venerable Walloomsac Inn, now a private home. A second walking tour of the downtown area includes the 1898 railroad depot (now a restaurant), constructed of blue marble cut to resemble granite; old mills; and Victorian homes.

Bennington Battle Monument (802-447-0550), Old Bennington. Open mid-April through October, daily 9–5, this Sandy Hill dolomite limestone shaft commemorates General John Stark's defeat of General Burgoyne's invading British and Hessian forces at Walloomsac Heights, 5 miles to the northwest, on August 16, 1777.

MUSEUMS Bennington Museum (802-447-1571; www.bennington museum.com), West Main Street, Route 9, Bennington. Open daily 9–6 June through October; 9–5 November through May. This distinguished and growing collection features memorabilia from the battle of Bennington, including the oldest American Revolutionary flag in existence, plus early American glass, furniture, dolls and toys, historic Bennington pottery (notably an extraordinary 10-foot ceramic piece created for the 1853 Crystal Palace Exhibition), and a luxury 1925 Wasp touring car, the only surviving model of the rare automobiles made by Karl Martin in Bennington.

THE OLD FIRST CHURCH IN OLD BENNINGTON
Kim Grant

Particularly popular is a gallery of the largest collection of paintings by Grandma Moses (Anna Mary Robertson, 1860–1961), who lived in the vicinity. There's a gift shop and genealogical library. Admission.

The Park-McCullough House (802-442-5441), near Route 67A in North Bennington. Open for tours late May through October and December, daily 10–3 except Tuesday and Wednesday. Admission: $8 for

THE PARK-MCCULLOUGH HOUSE IN NORTH BENNINGTON

Kim Grant

adults, $7 for seniors, $5 for students. A splendid, 35-room Victorian mansion built in 1865 by Trenor W. Park, a forty-niner who struck it rich as a lawyer in California and later as a railroader. He built the house on part of the farm owned by his father-in-law, Hiland Hall, a representative to Congress and governor of Vermont. Park's son-in-law, John G. McCullough, became governor of Vermont in 1902 and raised his family in this capacious house. It has been open to the public since 1965 and is on the National Register of Historic Places, functioning as a community arts center. There's an appealing children's playhouse replica of the mansion and a stable full of carriages; also a gift shop, lunch counter, afternoon tea on the veranda.

Bennington Center for the Arts (802-442-7158; www.vermontartscenter.org), Route 9 at Gypsy Lane, houses four visual arts galleries and a theater for the Oldcastle Theatre Company, which performs May through December.

The Shaftsbury Historical Society, Route 7A, is gradually developing a cluster of five historic buildings, including two schools. Open summer weekends 2–4 and serendipitously when the curator happens to be handy.

Hemmings Old-Fashioned Filling Station (802-442-3101), 216 Main Street, Bennington. Open daily 7 AM–10 PM. A full-service classic Sunoco filling station and convenience store with vintage vehicle displays and a quasi-museum selling auto-related memorabilia.

Robert Frost Stone House (802-447-6200; www.frostfriends.org), 121 Route 7A, Shaftsbury. Open Tuesday through Sunday 10–5. Admission is $5 for adults, $2.50 for those 18 and under. This site features galleries in the house where the poet lived and worked and is only minutes away from Frost's grave in Bennington. The grounds of the museum evoke Frost's poems with their stone walls, birches, and apple trees.

Vermont Covered Bridge Museum (802-442-7158; www.vermontartscenter
.org), Route 9 (West Road), Bennington. Video theater, dioramas, railroad displays, interactive exhibits, stories of ghosts and war and lost love.

WINERY North River Winery (802-442-9463), Route 9, Bennington, in
Camelot Village. This outlet for the North River Winery in Jacksonville is open
daily for tastings, 9:30–5:30.

COVERED BRIDGES Three stand just off Route 67A in North Bennington: **Silk
Road, Paper Mill Village,** and the **Burt Henry.** There are two more in Arlington, and a driving tour of all five is available through the chamber.

✳ To Do
CANOEING BattenKill Canoe Ltd. (802-362-2800; 1-800-421-5268), River
Road, off Route 7A, Arlington, is the center for day trips—with van service—
canoe camping, instruction, rentals, and equipment. Customized inn-to-inn tours
arranged.

FARM VISITS Shaftsbury Alpacas (802-447-3992), 12 South Stateline Road,
Shaftsbury. Sandy and Johan Harder invite you to spend a day as an alpaca
farmer—or just to shop in the Alpaca Shack for throws, slippers, outerwear, and
more.

GOLF AND TENNIS Mount Anthony Country Club (802-447-7079), 180
Country Club Drive (just below the Battle Monument): 18-hole golf course, tennis and paddle courts, pool, lunch and dinner (802-442-2617).

HORSEBACK RIDING Kimberly Farms Riding Stables (802-442-4354), 1524
Myers Road, Shaftsbury, offers trail rides, lessons, hayrides, inn-to-inn tours, and
an overnight horse camp.
Miles to Go (802-442-4354), Shaftsbury. Julia and Richard Hines offer trail
rides and other horsey activities.
Lively's Livery (802-447-7612; www.livelyslivery.com), 193 Crossover Road,
Bennington. Horse-drawn carriage service, wagon rides, sleigh rides, bridge tours.

SKIING ♪ Prospect Mountain (802-442-2575; 802-442-5283), Route 9 east of
Bennington. An intimate, friendly, family ski area, with cross-country (25 km),
downhill, and telemark facilities, ski school, rentals and repairs, learn-to-ski
packages, group rates, cafeteria, and bar. Moderate prices for all.

SNOWMOBILING Twinbrooks Tours (802-442-4054; 1-888-616-4054) in
nearby Woodford offers snowmobile rentals, trail maps, and guided tours.

✳ Green Space
Lake Shaftsbury State Park (802-375-9979), 10.5 miles north on Route 7A, has
swimming, picnicking, boating, and a nature trail on 26-acre Lake Shaftsbury.

✦ **Woodford State Park** (802-447-7169), Route 9 east of Bennington. This 400-acre area includes 104 camping sites, 16 of them with lean-tos, swimming in Adams Reservoir, a children's playground, picnic spots, canoe and rowboat rentals.

✳ Lodging

INNS The Four Chimneys Inn (802-447-3500; 1-800-649-3503; www.fourchimneys.com), 21 West Road (Route 9), Old Bennington 05201. This stately, 1910 Colonial Revival home, once the estate of Phillip Jennings, offers 11 luxurious rooms, all with private bath, TV, and phone, some with fireplace and Jacuzzi. The owners, Harold and Christine Cullison, keep the grounds beautifully landscaped. Rates $105–205 double B&B, depending on the season. (See also *Dining Out*.)

BED & BREAKFASTS South Shire Inn (802-447-3839), 124 Elm Street, Bennington 05201. This turn-of-the-20th-century Victorian mansion is a most attractive guest house, featuring 10-foot ceilings with plaster moldings, a library with a massive mahogany fireplace, an Italianate formal dining room, and comfortable bedrooms furnished with antiques. The five guest rooms in the main house, some with fireplace, have private bath; two can be joined as a suite. Four newer rooms, with Jacuzzi and TV, have been added in the old carriage house. $110–190 with breakfast; older children preferred.

⊙ ♿ **Molly Stark Inn** (802-442-9631; 1-800-356-3076; www.molly starkinn.com), 1067 East Main Street, Bennington 05201. Reed Fendler offers nine cozy bedrooms, all with private bath, some with Jacuzzi and/or woodstove, decorated with Americana, antiques, and quilts; wrap-around porch. $80–125 in the main house; $160–175 for the three guest cottages with Jacuzzi; lower off-season. Rates include full breakfast. Children over 10.

Alexandra B&B (802-442-5619; 1-888-207-9386; www.alexandra inn.com), historic Route 7A at Orchard Road, Bennington 05201. Alex Koks and Andra Erickson, former proprietors of the Four Chimneys, and Daniel Tarquino have redecorated this attractive 1859 farmhouse. The 12 guest rooms with private bath have an English country-house atmosphere. Alex Koks is a master chef, so breakfasts are very special. $100–150.

⊙ ♿ **The Henry House** (802-442-7045; 1-888-442-7045; www.henry houseinn.com), 1338 Murphy Road, North Bennington 05257. Don and Judy Cole have six beautiful guest rooms, four with private bath, in this restored historic place, built in 1769 on 25 acres, complemented by four common rooms. Among the guest rooms, the Ballroom, with its vaulted 14-foot ceiling, four-poster canopy bed, and a sitting area with working fireplace, is the most notable ($135). The others are also distinctive: $85–135 year-round, including breakfast. Pets may be kept in the garage or crated. Children over 12 are welcome.

Samuel Safford Inne (802-442-5934; www.samuelsaffordinne.com), 722 Main Street, Bennington 05201. Sandy Redding runs her B&B out of the oldest house in Bennington

Village, built by Lieutenant Colonel Samuel John Safford; it was restored during the Victorian period. She has five guest rooms, some with private bath, and serves a full breakfast. Rates range $78–135.

HoneyBee B&B (802-447-2941), P.O. Box 306, Church Street, Shaftsbury 05262. A beautiful 1840 Victorian home with a large front porch, five comfortable bedrooms, and three working fireplaces. Full breakfast included. $70–125.

MOTELS **Vermonter Motor Lodge** (802-442-2529), Route 9 (West Road), Bennington 05201. This motel, 2 miles west of Old Bennington, is an attractive mini resort with nicely decorated rooms and cabins, cable TV, room phone, swimming, boating, bass pond, **Sugar Maple Inne Restaurant;** $55–90 per room.

Paradise Motor Inn (802-442-8351; www.theparadisemotorinn.com), 141 West Main Street, Bennington 05201, close to the Bennington Museum, has 76 rooms and a nice restaurant on the premises; $55–128.

Knotty Pine Motel (802-442-5487; www.knottypinemotel.com), 130 Northside Drive (Route 7A), Bennington 05201. The locals use this motel to put up their guests, which is always a good sign. There's a pool and a restaurant right next door. The clean, well-kept rooms range $63–77 in summer, $79–95 in fall.

Kirkside Motor Lodge (802-447-7596; www.thisisvermont.com/kirkside), 250 West Main Street (Route 9 west), Bennington 05201. The Kirkside offers 25 individually decorated guest rooms in a completely smoke-free, downtown setting. Room rates $54–119.

Catamount Motel (802-442-5977; 1-800-213-3608), 500 South Street, Bennington 05201. This downtown motel has 17 large, comfortable rooms with HBO, an in-room fridge, and an outdoor pool. Rates $50–100.

Harwood Hill Motel (802-442-6278; www.abnl.net/harwoodhill), 898 Harwood Hill Road, Bennington 05201. Planted right on top of a scenic hilltop in Bennington, its location right across the street from an apple orchard makes it a good choice for apple-blossom season (spring) and apple-picking time (fall). There are 16 rooms, some with refrigerator. Rates $45–75.

OTHER LODGING **Greenwood Lodge & Campsites** (802-442-2547; www.campvermont.com/greenwood), P.O. Box 246, Bennington 05201, 8 miles east of town on Route 9. Open mid-May through late October. This rustic lodge/hostel and its 40 campsites occupy 120 acres in Woodford, adjacent to the Prospect Mountain ski area. There are dorms for American Youth Hostel members and private family rooms; bring your own linen or sleeping bags. Three small ponds for swimming, boating, and fishing. There are hiking trails at Prospect Mountain. Inquire about the inexpensive rates.

Camping on the Battenkill (1-800-830-6663; www.campvermont .com/battenkill), 48 Camping on the Battenkill, Arlington 05250. This quiet family campground right along the Batten Kill River has more than a dozen campsites with showers, another 43 with water and electric hook-up, and 9 just for tents.

✳ Where to Eat

DINING OUT **The Four Chimneys Inn** (802-447-3500), 21 West Road (Route 9), Old Bennington. Open Wednesday through Sunday for dinner in a gracious dining room and an enclosed porch. Dinner could begin with blini ($10) or gnocchi ($8) and continue with duck roulade stuffed with morels ($28), an "Atkins-friendly" filet mignon served with a number of vegetables ($30), or an Australian veal chop ($35).

Pangaea (802-442-7171), 1 Prospect Street, North Bennington. Open Tuesday through Sunday for dinner beginning at 5. The appetizer menu includes lamb and roasted garlic ravioli ($8), and a goat cheese flan with caramelized Gewürztraminer ($9). Your entrée might be filet mignon and roast quail over mushroom risotto ($28), or calamari fra diavolo tossed with squid ink pasta and finished with basil ($21).

Bennington Station (802-447-1080), 150 Depot Street, Bennington. Open for lunch and dinner daily. Train buffs love this place—a splendidly converted Romanesque railroad station built in 1897 of rough-hewn blue marble for the Bennington & Rutland Railroad. The exceptionally attractive restaurant features a collection of historic photos. For lunch you could have the Club Car, the Rail Splitter, or the Depot (railroad-worker-sized sandwiches). The dinner menu includes roast duck ($18), boneless apricot pork chops ($15), and Sam Adams pie—Angus beef topped with garlic mashed potatoes ($14).

Mount Anthony Country Club (802-442-2617), 180 Country Club Drive. The original clubhouse once housed a military boarding school that burned in 1957. Golf or no golf, you can now enjoy at lunch or dinner in this scenic setting just below the Bennington Battle Monument. For lunch try the Chinese pot stickers ($8), the fish-and-chips ($10), or the Italian calzone ($8.50). For dinner chef Grant Brown does a nice job with seafood Alfredo ($19), salmon baked on a cedar plank ($20), or almond-crusted pork loin ($18). There's also room here for a banquet.

McMorland's Steak and Seafood (802-442-7500), 782 Harwood Hill, Bennington. Executive chef Brian McMorland's menu features a broiled seafood platter ($18), a McMorland's cut of prime rib ($20), or a filet mignon and lobster surf and turf ($26). For dessert the bread pudding with lemon sauce and the chocolate confusion cake are both house favorites.

EATING OUT 🍴 **Blue Benn Diner** (802-442-5140), Route 7, near Deer Park, Bennington, open from 6 AM; breakfast all day, or lunch, which combines "road fare" with more esoteric items like eggs Benedict, tabbouleh, falafel, and herb teas.

Alldays & Onions (802-447-0043), 519 Main Street, Bennington. Open every day for breakfast, lunch, and dinner. The range of choices runs from bakery items and full breakfasts to gourmet pastas, deli sandwiches, and dinner entrées. There's outdoor seating in warm weather and live weekly entertainment.

Kevin's at Mikes Place III (802-442-0122), 27 Main Street, North Bennington. With soup, salads, burgers, steaks, and lots of hot snacks, this is everything a sports bar should be—and there's a full dinner menu.

Fortune Cookie Chinese Restaurant (802-447-1111), 218 Northside Drive, Bennington. For those times when you need a change, this is decent Chinese food at decent prices. The Special Beef comes highly recommended.

Carmody's Restaurant (802-447-5748), 421 Main Street, Bennington. This is Bennington's Irish pub that also offers family dining and take-out. It's open 7 days a week, 11:30 AM–midnight. The food is distinctively Irish American.

Stagecoach Grill (802-823-5200), 2848 Route 7, Pownal. Open Tuesday through Sunday 4:30–9 PM. The Stagecoach menu features chicken and pasta, steaks and ribs, seafood, burgers, and sandwiches.

Rattlesnake Cafe (802-447-7018), 230 North Street, Bennington. Choose your margarita, pardner. You can have a Cadillac, a Snake Bite, a Gold, a Bennington Blue, a Frozen Raspberry, or an Over the Top. Also lots of beer and Mexican food, including plenty of different kinds of nachos to accompany the liquid refreshment.

✳ Entertainment

Oldcastle Theatre Company (802-447-0564; www.oldcastle.org), Box 1555, Bennington. This accomplished theater company offers a full summer season of plays in the Bennington Center for the Arts. May through December.

✳ Selective Shopping

Camelot Village (802-447-0039), located just west of Old First Church on West Road in Bennington, can keep a shopper happy for a long time. The village has been growing over the years. It now includes the **Antique Center,** displaying the antiques and collectibles from more than 135 area dealers, and the **Craft Center** (802-447-0228), featuring the work of more than 250 regional artisans. **Fan-Tastic Gifts Country Store** offers homemade fudge, Vermont foods, maple products, and all sorts of gift items. **Bennington Cider Mill** carries an extensive collection of specialty foods in addition to housing **Kay's Country Bakery,** where the muffins, cobblers, crisps, breads, cookies, and pies are homemade every day. Kay also makes soup and sandwiches. Other stores include **Granite Lake Pottery, Occasional Flowers, Magic Sleigh, John McLeod Ltd.,** and **Vermont Soap & Candle.** There's even food, so you can spend a long time here.

BOOKSTORE **Bennington Bookshop** (802-442-5059), 467 Main Street. Vermont books, adult and children's titles, cards.

CRAFTS SHOPS **Hawkins House** (802-442-6463), 262 North Street (Route 7), Bennington, is a crafts market complex for the work of some 400 artisans in silver and gold, unusual textiles, handblown glass, pottery, quilts, cards, books, music, prints and woodcuts, stained glass, candles, and more. Open daily except Christmas and New Year's.

Oak Bluffs Cottage Pottery (802-823-5161), Route 7, 8 miles south of Bennington, has a full range of stoneware, baskets, and lamps.

Mahican Moccasin Factory (802-823-5294), Route 7, 5 miles south of Bennington, features a variety of deerskin, elk, and cowhide footwear, made in Pownal.

Bennington Potters Yard (802-447-7531), downtown on County Street, Bennington, is the high-tech place to get contemporary Bennington pottery, Catamount glass, and well-designed ovenproof cookware manufactured in North Bennington.

GALLERIES **Images from the Past** (802-442-3204), West Main Street, Bennington. Open daily April through December, winter weekends. Fascinating ephemera: postcards, prints, holograms, historic house boxes.

Bennington Center for the Arts. See *Museums.*

Fiddlehead at Four Corners (802-447-1000), 338 Main Street, Bennington. Glass, ceramics, jewelry, fiber, animation, furniture, Judaica, Dr. Seuss art.

SPECIAL SHOPS **The Chocolate Barn** (802-375-6928), Route 7A north of Shaftsbury, is an unusual combination: two floors of antiques, plus 56 varieties of hand-dipped chocolates, fudge, and special orders from antique candy molds. (There's another store at Routes 30 and 100 in Jamaica.)

✿ **Apple Barn & Country Bake Shop** (802-447-7780). Near Bennington, there are cornfield mazes starting in September and haunted mazes for Halloween. Watch out for the pumpkin-eating dinosaur.

International Herbs (802-442-7870) in Bennington is one of the most complete herbal shops in the East, with herbs of every description packed into a relatively small space.

✳ Special Events

Late May: **Bennington Mayfest** is a street festival with crafts and entertainment.

May–October: **2nd Friday Open Gallery Night.** The second Friday of each month, galleries all over the area are open 5–8 PM with receptions, special sales, and an opportunity to meet the artists.

June 1–2: **NAFA Flyball Tournament,** Southern Vermont College Athletic Center, Bennington.

June–August: **Lake Paran Music Series.** Contact the Bennington Chamber of Commerce for information.

July: **Annual Bennington Museum Antique Show** (see *Museums*). **Pownal Valley Fair**—exhibits, antique tractor pull, bingo, music, fireworks, petting zoo, and more. **Summer in the Park**—free concert series.

Mid-August: **Bennington Battle Day Weekend.**

Mid-September: **Antique and Classic Car Show,** Willow Park, Bennington.

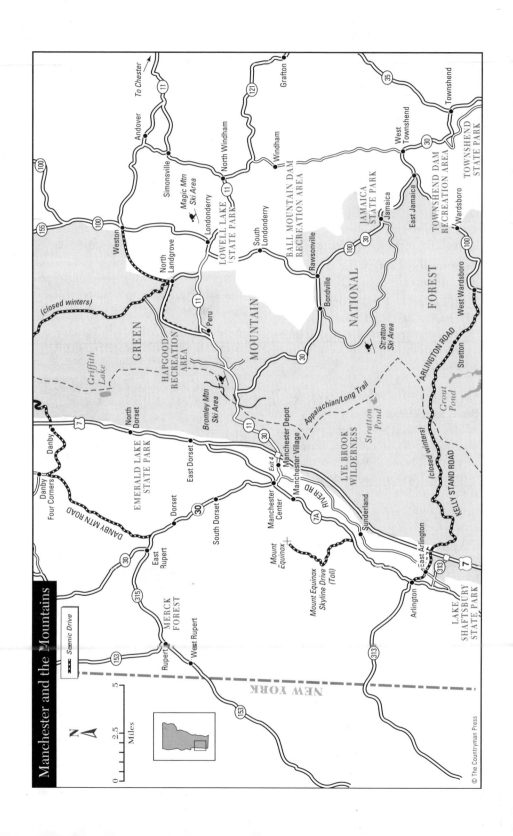

Manchester and the Mountains

• • • • • Scenic Drive

N
▲
Miles
0   2.5   5

© The Countryman Press

NEW YORK

To Chester

Andover

Simonsville

Magic Mtn
Ski Area

Londonderry

North
Windham

Windham

Grafton

Townshend

Weston

North
Landgrove

South
Londonderry

LOWELL LAKE
STATE PARK

BALL MOUNTAIN DAM
RECREATION AREA

Rawsonville

Jamaica

East Jamaica

West
Townshend

TOWNSHEND DAM
RECREATION AREA

Wardsboro

TOWNSHEND
STATE PARK

(closed winters)

Peru

HAPGOOD
RECREATION
AREA

Griffith
Lake

GREEN

MOUNTAIN

Bondville

NATIONAL

Stratton
Ski Area

FOREST

West Wardsboro

ARLINGTON ROAD

Stratton

North
Dorset

Bromley Mtn
Ski Area

Manchester Depot

Appalachian/Long Trail

Stratton
Pond

Grout
Pond

Danby

East Dorset

Manchester
Village

LYE BROOK
WILDERNESS

(closed winters)

KELLY STAND ROAD

Danby
Four Corners

EMERALD LAKE
STATE PARK

Exit 4

Manchester
Center

Manchester

Dorset

South Dorset

RIVER RD

Sunderland

East Arlington

DANBY MTN ROAD

East
Rupert

Mount
Equinox

Mount Equinox
Skyline Drive
(Toll)

Arlington

SHAFTSBURY
STATE PARK

MERCK
FOREST

Rupert

West Rupert

LAKE

JAMAICA
STATE PARK

MANCHESTER AND THE MOUNTAINS

INCLUDING ARLINGTON, DORSET, DANBY, LANDGROVE, LONDONDERRY, PAWLET, PERU

No Vermont community has changed more dramatically in recent years than Manchester. A summer resort since the Civil War, Manchester has also long been a place to stay while skiing at nearby Stratton and Bromley and on southern Vermont's most dependably snowy cross-country trails.

What's new is the breadth and depth of shopping in this proud old town: upward of 50 top-brand outlet stores and another 50 or so specialty stores and galleries. Manchester is also home to some of Vermont's best restaurants and places to stay, including one of its grandest resorts. Furthermore, the town is positioning itself as a cultural center for the state with the spectacular Southern Vermont Arts Center, the Riley Rink at Hunter Park with its lengthy list of summer concerts, and two of the state's premier summer theaters, the Dorset Playhouse and the Weston Playhouse.

The white-columned, tower-topped, 180-room Equinox is as much a part of Manchester's current appeal as it was in the 1850s, the era in which the town's status as a resort was firmly established. Mrs. Abraham Lincoln and her two sons spent the summers of 1863 and '64 at the Equinox, booked again for the summer of '65, and reserved a space for the entire family the following season. The president, unfortunately, never made it.

Other presidents—Taft, Grant, Theodore Roosevelt, and Benjamin Harrison—came to stay at the Equinox, but it was Lincoln's family who adopted the village. Robert Todd Lincoln, who served as secretary of war under President Garfield, minister to Britain under Harrison, then president of the Pullman Palace Car Company, selected Manchester Village as his summer home, building Hildene, the lavish mansion that's now such an interesting place to visit. Other opulent "summer cottages" are sequestered off River Road and nearby country lanes.

Manchester Center and Village are both down in the wide Valley of Vermont, but Mount Equinox, a stray peak from New York's Taconic Range, thrusts up a full 3,800 feet from the village, rising right from the back of its namesake hotel.

Luckily the 1930s Work Progress Administration plan to carve ski trails on Mount Equinox never panned out, and Manchester Village retains its serene, white-clapboard good looks. The hotel faces the Congregational church and gold-domed Bennington Courthouse, and the few tasteful stores include a branch of Frog Hollow, Vermont's premier crafts shop. Public buildings trail off into a line of mansions, spaced along marble sidewalks.

Discount shopping begins 0.25 mile downhill in Manchester Center, a village with a different zip code and zoning. The center was "Factory Point" in the 19th century, when sawmills, marbleworks, and a tannery were powered by the Batten Kill River's flow.

Fears that the former Factory Point might become Vermont's future factory outlet capital began in the mid-1980s, with the opening of a trendy wood-and-glass shopping complex at the traffic heart of town, the junction of Routes 7A and 11/30—known locally as "Malfunction Junction."

The strip malls, however, haven't materialized. Instead, outlets along Route 7A fill old homes and house-sized compounds, blending nicely with shopping landmarks like the Orvis Retail Store, a spacious new building done in the style of a country lodge, which has been supplying the needs of fishermen and other sporting folk since 1856.

The Green Mountains rise even within Manchester town limits to 3,100 feet on the east, then roll off into heavily forested uplands punctuated by picturesque villages like Peru, Landgrove, Weston, and Londonderry, all noteworthy for cross-country skiing and equally appealing in summer. Dorset and Danby are also well worth a visit.

GUIDANCE Manchester and the Mountains Regional Chamber (802-362-2100; 1-800-362-4144; www.manchestervermont.com), 5046 Main Street, Manchester Center. This white-clapboard chamber of commerce information booth is walled with pamphlets, good for general walk-in information. The chamber does not make reservations but does keep a running tally on space in member lodging places and on short-term condo and cottage rentals.

Stratton Mountain maintains a reservation and information service (in-state: 802-297-2200; 1-800-STRATTON) and serves some 20 lodges, condo clusters, and inns on and around Stratton.

In winter the **Bromley Village Lodging Service** (1-800-865-4786; www .bromley.com) also makes reservations for condominiums.

The Arlington Chamber of Commerce has merged with the Manchester Chamber, but it maintains a self-serve information booth on Route 7A open May through October.

Dorset Chamber of Commerce (802-867-2450; www.dorsetvt.com), P.O. Box 121, Dorset 05251.

Londonderry Chamber of Commerce (802-824-8178) maintains an information booth and office in the Mountain Marketplace (the Londonderry shopping center) at the junction of Routes 11 and 100.

GETTING THERE *By car:* From Bennington, US 7 to Manchester is a limited-access highway that's speedy but dull, except for viewing Mount Equinox. You get a more interesting taste of the area, especially around Arlington, by clinging to historic Route 7A. From the southeast, the obvious access is I-91 to Brattleboro, then Route 30 north. And from the Albany–Troy area, take US 7 heading east into Vermont, where it becomes VT 9 east. In the center of Bennington, take VT 7 north to exit 4, or follow historic Route 7A.

By bus: **Vermont Transit** offers good service from New York and Montreal to Manchester; connections with Boston are via Williamstown, Massachusetts, or Rutland.

MEDICAL EMERGENCY Emergency service is available by calling **911.**

Northshire Medical Associates (802-362-4440), Manchester Center. **Manchester Family Medical Clinic** (802-362-1263), Route 7A, Manchester. **Mountain Valley Medical Clinic** (802-824-6901), Route 11, opposite the Flood Brook School, 2 miles west of Londonderry, 3 miles east of Peru. **Carlos Otis Clinic** (802-297-2300), at Stratton Mountain. **Tri Mountain Rescue Squad** (802-824-3166) serves Bondville, Landgrove, Peru, and Stratton.

✳ Villages

In addition to Manchester, the area's picturesque places include Arlington, 7 miles south along Route 7A; Weston, 15 miles to the northeast; Dorset, 8 miles to the northwest; Pawlet, another 7 miles to the north on Route 30; and Danby, 8 miles north of Dorset and 10 miles east of Pawlet.

Although never formally the capital of Vermont, **Arlington,** on Route 7A, was the de facto seat of government during most of the Revolutionary period. Fearing British attacks in the north, Vermont's first governor, Thomas Chittenden, moved south from Williston, liberated a Tory property in Arlington (the area known as Tory Hollow), and conducted affairs of state from there. Arlington recently was voted the most historic village in Vermont.

Many older visitors to Arlington fondly remember Dorothy Canfield Fisher, the author of 50 immensely popular, warmhearted novels and a judge of the Book-of-the-Month Club for 25 years. Another famous resident was illustrator Norman Rockwell, who lived in West Arlington from 1939 to 1953. Many of his illustrations of small-town Americans were done in and around Arlington.

Dorset. This pristine village is visible evidence that it takes money to "prevent the future." A fashionable summer refuge for years, few signs of commerce mar its state of carefully

NEAR MANCHESTER

Kim Grant

manicured nature. Today's tranquillity, making it a haven for artists and writers as well as the affluent, contrasts sharply with the hotheaded days of its youth. In 1776 the Green Mountain Boys gathered in Cephas Kent's tavern and issued their first declaration of independence from the New Hampshire Grants, signed by Thomas Chittenden, Ira Allen, Matthew Lyon, Seth Warner, and other Founding Fathers of Vermont. Today the Dorset Inn, said to be the state's oldest continuously operating hostelry, is the village focal point, along with the Dorset Playhouse, one of New England's most venerable summer theaters. The first marble to be quarried in North America came from Dorset, and one quarry is now a popular swimming hole. There is also a nine-hole golf course, the private Dorset Field Club (billed as the state's oldest), and a fine choice of places to stay.

Pawlet. Not far north of Dorset, this hamlet on Route 30 is an unexpected delight, with a mix of architectural styles in the buildings that cling to the rather steep slopes leading up from Flower Brook, over which Johnny Mach's General Store extends. Gib Mach has harnessed the rushing brook to a turbine that generates his electricity and has built a glass-topped counter at the end of a store aisle through which you can peer down at the water surging through the narrow gorge below. Next door, a former railroad station is now the Station Restaurant and Ice Cream Parlor, and a clutch of nearby shops is worth investigating.

Danby. A bypassed hamlet on Route 7 between Dorset and Wallingford, Danby is a vintage village known for fine marble quarries and as home base for Silas Griffith, an 1850s lumber baron who was Vermont's first millionaire. In the 1960s novelist Pearl Buck bought seven buildings in the village and began to renovate them, and since her death inns, restaurants, and some intriguing shops have opened here.

Weston. A mountain crossroads that's a logical hub for exploring all of southern Vermont, this village of just 500 souls looms large on tourist maps. It's the home of one of the country's oldest and best summer theaters and the Vermont Country Store, New England's number one nostalgia outlet. The oval common is shaded with majestic maples, and a band plays regularly in the bandstand. Free summer concerts are presented by the Kinhaven Music School high on a back road; visitors are also welcome at Weston Priory, a small community of Benedictine monks, nationally known for the music sung and played at Sunday liturgies. Weston was actually one of the first villages in Vermont to be consciously preserved. The theater, the unusually fine historical collection in the Farrar Mansur House, and (indirectly) the Vermont Country Store all date from the "Weston Revival" of the 1930s. Today it offers exceptional lodging and dining as well as theater and shopping.

✳ To See

MUSEUMS & **Southern Vermont Arts Center** (802-362-1405; www.svac.org), West Road, Manchester Center. Open all year, Tuesday through Saturday 10–5, Sunday noon–5. Nonmembers, $6; students, $3; members and children under 13, free. The Elizabeth deC. Wilson Museum, which opened in July 2000, is a work of art in itself with its soaring, light-filled galleries that house some first-class touring shows of paintings, sculpture, prints, and photography. Concerts and lectures are held in the adjacent, 430-seat Arkell Pavilion; there are other special events throughout the year. Light lunches are served in the Garden Café (see *Eating Out*), and there are extensive trails through the woods, among them a botany trail featuring rock formations, 67 varieties of wildflowers, and birches. Limited handicapped accessibility.

The American Museum of Fly Fishing (802-362-3300; www.amff.com), next to Orvis on Route 7A, Manchester Village. Open weekdays 10–4; admission $3, students free. The museum displays the beautiful flies of Mary Orvis Marbury as well as more than 1,000 rods and reels made by famous rod builders and owned by such luminaries as Daniel Webster, Bing Crosby, Ernest Hemingway, and Presidents Hoover and Eisenhower. Don't miss it.

Norman Rockwell Exhibition (802-375-6423), Route 7A, Arlington. Open May through October 9–5, otherwise 10–4. Admission. Housed in a Hudson River Gothic church are some 500 of the artist's *Saturday Evening Post* cover illustrations and prints. There's a 20-minute film, and a gift shop.

The **Dr. George A. Russell Collection of Vermontiana,** believed to be the third largest such collection, is housed in quarters behind the Martha Canfield Public Library, Arlington. Although not a museum (there are no displays), the collection is open to the public on Tuesday or by appointment with the curators, David and Mary Lou Thomas (802-375-6307). Dr. Russell, the country doctor immortalized in the Rockwell print that hangs in thousands of doctors' offices, collected Vermontiana for most of his long life and left his collection to the town. The collection includes Dorothy Canfield Fisher materials, a large selection of Norman Rockwell's work, many photographs from the period 1860–90, an extensive selection of town and country histories for Vermont and neighboring states, and a wealth of genealogical materials (deeds, letters, wills, account books, and diaries) for both the Arlington area and the state as a whole.

The Martha Canfield Public Library, Route 7A, Arlington (named for Dorothy Canfield Fisher's grandmother). From June 15 through foliage season the library holds a book sale under a tent on its lawn, Friday and Saturday 10–5 and Sunday 1–5. Books are sold at prices from 15¢ to 50¢, and records and jigsaw puzzles are also available at moderate prices. During peak holiday seasons, the sale is sometimes held weekdays as well.

HISTORIC HOMES ⅍ **Historic Hildene** (802-362-1788; www.hildene.org), Route 7A, Manchester Village. Mid-May through October, 9:30–4. $10 adults, $4 youths 6–14. Limited handicapped accessibility. An impressive house among historic houses, this 24-room Georgian Revival manor is set on 412 acres, including formal gardens and paths that lead down into the Battenkill Valley. Bring a picnic lunch and plan to stay half the day. The tour begins with a wagon ride to the Carriage Barn, now a sophisticated visitors center with a slide show about Robert Todd Lincoln. You learn that he first came to the village as a boy with his mother for a stay at the Equinox House; his father was assassinated before the family could return, as they had intended, the following summer. It was Todd's law partner who later persuaded him to build this summer home adjacent to his own mansion. Todd died here in 1926, and members of the family lived here until 1975. Guides are familiar with at least one Lincoln and with the true character of the authentically furnished house. Tours include the restored formal gardens and a brief demonstration of the 1,000-pipe organ, which can be played both manually and with one of 240 player rolls on hand. Picnic tables outside command a view of the valley below, and there are numerous trails to stroll or—in winter, when the Carriage Barn becomes a warming hut—to explore on skis. In summer, Sunday-afternoon polo matches are a popular spectator sport. Inquire about organ concerts and other special events.

& **Farrar Mansur House** (802-824-4399), village green, Weston. Open weekends Memorial Day through Columbus Day; in July and August, Wednesday through Sunday 1–4. Fee. Limited handicapped accessibility. Even if you have never set foot inside a historic house, make an exception for this one, built in 1797 as a tavern with a classic old taproom and seven fireplaces. Thanks to 1930s Work Progress Administration (WPA) artists, murals of Weston in its prime—in the 1840s it was twice the size it is today—cover the living room walls, and a number of primitive portraits hang in adjoining rooms, which are filled with furniture and furnishings donated by Weston families. Upstairs in the old ballroom, a rendition of townspeople dancing—each face is painted to resemble a specific resident—conjures the spirit of a town that knew how to have fun.

Weston Mill Museum, at the junction of Routes 100 and 155, Weston. Memorial Day through Columbus Day, daily 10–5. Donations requested. This is a working restoration of a vintage mill. Note the work of David Claggett, a skilled tinmaker who uses 18th-century methods to create exceptional chandeliers, lanterns, sconces, and folk art.

SCENIC DRIVES **Mount Equinox** (802-362-1114). The summit of Mount Equinox is 3,825 feet high. Most of the mountain is owned by the Carthusian monks who occupy the monastery, which you can see from the top. A toll road (open May through November; $6 per car and driver; $2 per passenger) climbs

HISTORIC HILDENE, ROBERT TODD LINCOLN'S SUMMER HOME

Kim Grant

more than 5 miles from Route 7 to the top. This can be a spectacular ride on a clear day, even more dramatic if the mountain is in the clouds and the road keeps disappearing in front of you. Be sure to drive back down in low gear and in total sobriety. There are also trails to the top.

Green Mountain National Forest Road Number 10, Danby to Landgrove. Closed in winter. The longest (14 miles) and most isolated of these byways, the road (beginning in Danby) climbs through the White Rocks Recreation Area, crossing a number of tempting hiking paths as well as the Long Trail. There are some fine views as you continue along, and you might want to picnic somewhere in the middle of the forest, as we did by a beaver pond. The road follows Tabor Brook down into Landgrove, itself a tiny, picturesque village.

Peru to Weston. From the village of Peru, an enticing, wooded road is paved as far as Hapgood Pond, then continues smoothly through Landgrove, a minuscule village with an outstanding inn (open to the public for dinner), set in rolling fields. The way to Weston is clearly marked.

East Rupert to Danby. Danby Mountain Road is the logical shortcut from Dorset to Danby, and it's quite beautiful, winding up and over a saddle between Woodlawn Mountain and Dorset Peak. Well-surfaced dirt, with long views in places. If you're coming from East Rupert, be sure to turn right at Danby Four Corners and follow Mill Brook into Danby.

Kelley Stand Road. From Route 7A, follow the East Arlington Road past Candle Mill Village and continue until you cross a one-lane bridge. Turn right onto Kelley Stand Road, which is a great foliage-viewing trip all the way to Stratton. Closed in winter.

✳ To Do

BICYCLING In Manchester, mountain bike, hybrid bike, and touring bike rentals and touring information are available from **Battenkill Sports Cycle Shop** (802-362-2734; www.battenkillbicycle.com), open Monday through Saturday 9:30–5:30, in the Stone House, junction of Routes 7 and 11/30.

Stratton Sports (802-297-2200; 1-800-STRATTON), at Stratton Mountain, rents mountain bikes and offers terrain ranging from paved roads to cross-country ski trails and (for expert bikers) a combination of service and ski trails down from the summit (the gondola hoists bikes as well as riders to the top); guided tours.

Equipe Sport and Mountain Riders (802-297-2847), junction of Routes 30 and 100 in Rawsonville; also on the Mount Snow Access Road in West Dover (802-464-2222) and in the Village Square at Stratton Mountain (802-297-3460).

CAMPING **Green Mountain National Forest** (802-362-2307), District Ranger Office, Manchester. A public information office serving the southern third of the 275,000-acre Green Mountain National Forest is located on Routes 30 and 11 east of Manchester; open year-round, Monday through Friday 8–4:30. Maps and details are available about where to fish, hike, cross-country ski, and camp. All national forest campsites are available on a first-come, first-served basis.

Emerald Lake State Park (802-362-1655), North Dorset. On Route 7, this area offers 105 campsites, including 36 lean-tos, also hiking and nature trails, among them a 3.4-mile, round-trip trek to a natural bridge.

Hapgood Pond Recreation Area, Peru. Acquired in 1931, this was the beginning of the Green Mountain National Forest. There is swimming, fishing, and limited boating on the 7-acre pond. Removed from the picnic ground and beach are 28 campsites (first come, first served). A pleasant 8-mile forest trail threads through the woods.

Greendale Campground, 2 miles north of Weston on Route 100. There are 14 sites.

Camping on the Batten Kill. See "Bennington Area."

Dorset RV Park (802-867-5754), Route 30, Dorset. Open April through November. Hot showers, flush toilets, electric and water hook-ups, laundry and camp store.

See also *Green Space* in "The Lower Connecticut and West River Valleys" for details about Jamaica State Park.

CANOEING The **Battenkill** makes for satisfying canoeing in spring; the Manchester-to-Arlington section is relatively flat water, but it gets difficult a mile above Arlington.

BattenKill Canoe Ltd. (802-362-2800), Route 7A in Arlington. An outfitter offering inn-to-inn canoe trips throughout the state and as far afield as Costa Rica and England, also rents canoes and offers shuttle service on the Batten Kill.

DRIVING

Country Pursuits Centre (802-362-7873), Manchester Village. Includes the Land Rover Driving School, Junior Off-Road, and the Fly Fishing School. An off-road instructional course and classroom area has been constructed for the driving school, and expert instructors are on hand to offer tips on driving both on- and off-road. Junior Off-Road is for children of all ages. Fly-fishing lessons and guided trips.

Backroad Discovery Tours (802-362-4997; www.backroaddiscovery.com). Sharon O'Connor will pile a maximum of six guests (plus snacks) into the back of her open Jeep to show you the back roads and byways of the Manchester–Arlington area, stopping along the way to give you a taste of local history. She also knows the best spots for sunset viewing.

FISHING Fly-fishing has been serious business in the Batten Kill since the mid–19th century. The Orvis Company began manufacturing bamboo rods in Manchester Village near the spot where they are still produced.

The **Batten Kill** is generally recognized as Vermont's best wild trout stream; access is available at a number of places off Route 7A. Brown trout can also be found in **Gale Meadows Pond,** accessible via gravel road from Route 30 at Bondville. **Emerald Lake** in North Dorset is stocked with pike, bass, and perch; rental boats are available at the state park facility.

Orvis Fishing Schools (802-362-3622; 1-800-235-9763; www.orvis.com), *the* name in fly-fishing instruction as well as equipment; 3-day courses are offered twice weekly April through August. Instruction is also available at nine locations around the country as well as several international venues.

Southern Vermont Fly Fisherman (1-800-682-0103). Chuck Kashner's guide service includes rods, reels, waders, flies, and a meal on full-day trips.

Battenkill Anglers (802-362-3184) is a Thomas & Thomas–sponsored fly-fishing school and outfitter.

Peter Basta (802-867-4103), P.O. Box 540, Dorset 05251, offers guide service and on-stream instruction.

Marty Oakland (802-375-6663) guides and teaches fly-fishing in addition to running **Quill Gordon,** a small B&B that caters particularly to fisherpersons.

GOLF The 18-hole **Gleneagles Golf Course** at the Equinox Country Club (802-362-3223), Manchester Center, which was established in the 1920s for guests of the Equinox House, has in more modern times undergone a $3 million renovation and is open to the public. The **Dormy Grill** at the Gleneagles Club-house also offers pleasant noontime dining.

The Stratton Golf School (802-297-2200; 1-800-843-6867) offers weekend and midweek sessions, including professional instruction, use of the 27-hole course at the Stratton Mountain Country Club, and a special 22-acre "training site." A good and reasonably priced seasonal lunch is available at the club.

Windham Golf Club (802-875-2517), Popple Dungeon Road, Windham. An 18-hole course, built on the site of one of New England's largest and oldest po-tato farms. Facilities include a pro shop, carts, dressing rooms, and showers. The **Clubhouse** serves a Vermont country breakfast on weekends; salads, sand-wiches, and burgers at lunch; and a tavern menu from 3:30 until closing.

The Practice Tee (802-362-3100), Route 7, Manchester Center. Open in-season, weather permitting, weekdays 9–7, weekends and holidays 8–7; lessons available.

HIKING From the Green Mountain National Forest District Office, request hik-ing maps for **Lye Brook Wilderness,** a 14,600-acre preserve south of Manches-ter with a 2.3-mile trail to the Lye Brook Waterfalls and the **Long Trail.** This Massachusetts-to-Quebec path doubles as the Appalachian Trail throughout the area; portions of the trail make good day hikes, either north over Bromley Mountain or south over Spruce Peak from Routes 11 and 30. The most heavily hiked stretch of the entire trail is the relatively level trek in from Kelley Stand Road to Stratton Pond; there are three shelters in the immediate area, and swimming is permitted. **Griffith Lake,** accessible from Peru and Danby, is a less crowded swimming and camping site on the trail. For details, consult the Green Mountain Club's *Long Trail Guide.*

Mount Equinox. Details about the rewarding, 6-mile Burr and Burton Trail from Manchester Village to the summit are available in *Day Hiker's Guide to Vermont* (Green Mountain Club). At 3,825 feet, this is the highest mountain in the state that is not traversed by the Long Trail. See also Equinox Preservation Trust under *Green Space.*

Tracks of Vermont (802-645-1938; www.explorevt.com), P.O. Box 252, Weston 05161. Organized day trips and longer outings.

HORSEBACK RIDING, ETC. **Horses for Hire** (802-297-1468), South Road, Rawsonville. Trail rides, sleigh rides, and riding lessons, even in winter, weather permitting; $30 per person for a 1-hour ride. Half-day trips also available. English riding.

Karl Pfister (802-824-6320), Landgrove. Fall foliage carriage and wagon rides available by reservation.

Sun Bowl Ranch (802-297-9210), at Stratton Mountain Resort, offers trail rides, donkey rides, lessons, junior riding camps, and overnight rides. Letitia and John Sisters also operate **Mountain View Ranch** (802-293-5837) in Danby, open mid-October through mid-June for trail rides.

Chipman Stables (802-293-5242), Danby Four Corners. Trail rides and lessons, both Western-style. Trail rides are $30 per person.

Petticoat Junction (802-362-3885) in Manchester offers carriage, wagon, sleigh, and small-group trail rides through the woods and meadows of Manchester.

HUNTING **Orvis Company** (802-362-3622; 1-800-548-9548) of Manchester offers 2-day shooting courses ($990) and 3-day programs ($1,250) from August through mid-October. Hunters move in groups of 5 through 10 stations in a simulated hunting course. Tuition includes guns and ammo, but not lodging.

The **British School of Falconry** (802-362-4780) at the Equinox hotel, Manchester Village, offers introductory lessons, hawk walks, and pheasant hunting with hawks and falcons at the Tinmouth Hunting Preserve in Wallingford.

MOUNTAIN RIDES ⊘ **Bromley Mountain** (802-824-5522; www.bromley.com), Route 11, Peru (6 miles east of Manchester). This 3,284-foot-high mountain offers excellent views of Stratton and Equinox Mountains. It's traversed by the Long Trail and is also accessible by hiking the ski trails from the midpoint exit on the chairlift. This lift, serving the alpine slide, is open Memorial Day through mid-October, weather permitting, on weekends 10–5 and daily July through Labor Day 9:30–6 (fee). The Bromley Alpine Slide, the longest in this country, is a great ride with fabulous views whatever your age. The DévalKarts and the Bromley Thrill Sleds (similar to a winter luge) are big draws for the teen set. You'll also find miniature golf, a 24-foot climbing wall, space bikes, the Big Splash, a parabounce, the "trampoline things," and an extreme zip line. Lunch, snacks, and drinks are available at the base lodge.

⊘ **Stratton Mountain** (802-297-2200; 1-800-STRATTON; www.stratton.com) offers a four-state view from its summit, accessible by Starship XII gondolas from the ski resort (Route 30, Bondville). The gondolas run daily in summer and fall, 9:30–4:15. And there's lots of summer action in its Adventure Zone—a skate park, a climbing wall, boulders, and a cave.

NATURE WALKS AND WORKSHOPS ✐ **Vermont Institute of Natural Science** (VINS), in partnership with the Equinox Preservation Trust (802-362-4374), offers natural history walks and programs for adults, families, and children. The programs run year-round, geared to the season. $4–5 per adult, $1–2 for children.

SWIMMING Dana L. Thompson Recreation Area (802-362-1439), Route 30 north, Manchester, is open daily in summer, but hours for general swimming are limited; nominal fee.

Dorset Quarry, aka Norcross-West Quarry, off Route 30 on Kelly Road between Manchester and Dorset (turn across from Mountain Weavers), is a deep, satisfying pool but not recommended for children. It's private property, but the owners will allow it to be used by members of the public who treat it respectfully.

✐ **Hapgood Pond** in Peru, with its sand and calm, shallow drop-off, is favored by families with young children.

Emerald Lake State Park (802-362-1655), Route 7, North Dorset, offers clear lake swimming.

See also *Green Space.*

TENNIS ✐ **Stratton Mountain** (802-297-2200; 1-800-STRATTON; www.stratton.com) offers weekend and midweek clinics. There are 15 outdoor and 4 indoor courts. *Note:* Stratton Mountain offers full daycare and day camp in summer for children (6 weeks–10 years old) of parents enrolled in the golf and tennis programs. A Junior Tennis Day Camp is also offered weekdays for children 7–15.

Dana L. Thompson Recreation Area, Manchester. Public courts are available with weekly memberships or on a per-hour basis.

Equinox Hotel Tennis (802-362-4700), Route 7A, Manchester Village. Three Har-Tru courts are open to the public for an hourly fee.

Dorset Tennis Club (802-362-2236), Route 7A, 4 miles north of Manchester. Indoor court; lessons.

TRAIN RIDES ✐ **The Vermont Valley Flyer** (802-463-3069; 1-800-707-3530), operated by the Green Mountain Railroad Corp., makes three round-trips a day between Manchester Depot and North Bennington from the Fourth of July through mid-October. $14 for adults, $10 children 3–12.

THE DORSET QUARRY

Kim Grant

CROSS-COUNTRY SKIING **Viking Nordic Centre** (802-824-3933; www.viking nordic.com), 615 Little Pond Road, Londonderry. Trail fee: $14 full day, $10 seniors; children 12 and under ski free. The Viking trail system now includes 40 km of groomed trails, 3 km lighted. There is a rental and retail shop, lessons, and a café serving drinks, light breakfasts, and lunches. The **Viking Nordic Guest House** also offers four bedrooms at the center; $55 per person per night includes breakfast and trail pass.

Wild Wings Ski Touring Center (802-824-6793), North Road, Peru. Trail fee. Tracy and Chuck Black run a family-oriented touring center located within the boundaries of the Green Mountain National Forest, 2.5 miles north of Peru. Trails are narrow, geared to beginning and intermediate skiers. This area tends to get a heavier snowfall than other local touring centers; the 24 km of groomed, one-way trails are at elevations between 1,650 and 2,040 feet. Instruction and rentals.

Stratton Ski Touring Center (802-297-2200), Stratton Mountain. Trail fee. Based at the Sun Bowl, a 30 km series of groomed loops plus adjoining backcountry trails. Guided backcountry tours as well as a variety of other tours are offered.

Hildene Ski Touring Center (802-362-1788), Manchester. The Lincoln Carriage Barn serves as a warming hut for this system of 12 km of groomed and mapped trails on the estate built by Robert Todd Lincoln. Trails meander through woods and fields on a promontory overlooking the Battenkill Valley between Mount Equinox and Lye Brook Wilderness. Lessons and equipment are available.

Equinox Ski Touring Center (802-362-3223) has 35 km of groomed trails and tracked terrain, snowshoeing, instruction, and rentals. This network includes trails on the golf course, up through the forests of the Equinox Preservation Trust, and around Equinox Pond.

DOWNHILL SKIING ✍ **Bromley** (802-824-5522), 3984 Route 11 in Peru, 8 miles east of Manchester. Founded in 1937 by Fred Pabst of the Milwaukee brewing family, this is among the oldest ski areas in the country. It was also one of the first to have snowmaking, snow farming, a slope-side nursery, and condominiums. It retains its own following of those who like its friendly atmosphere and sunny trails. Boarders will enjoy Snowboard Heaven Terrain Park. *Lifts:* 10: 1 high-speed detachable quad, 1 fixed-grip quad, 4 doubles, 1 T-bar, 2 Mighty-Mites, and Magic Carpet. *Trails:* 43 trails—35 percent intermediate, 34 percent beginner, 31 percent expert. *Vertical drop:* 1,334 feet. *Snowmaking:* 80 percent of terrain from base to summit. *Facilities:* The base lodge offers two cafeterias as well as more formal areas. Skiers unload right at the base lodge; the driver then parks in an area across Route 11 and rides back on a shuttle bus. Valet parking is another option. *Ski school:* Ski and snowboard school. *For children:* The Bromley Learning Center includes Mighty Mites for ages 6 weeks–3 years, Mighty Moose for ages 3–5, and PigDog's Ski & Snowboard Mountain Club for 6- to

12-year-olds. *Rates:* $54 adults, $46 teens, $35 juniors, weekends; midweek, $46 adults, $38 teens, $32 juniors.

✤ **Stratton** (1-800-STRATTON; ski report: 802-297-4211; boarder line: 802-297-4545). Located atop a 5-mile access road from Route 30 in Bondville, Stratton is an unusually well-groomed mountain. This goes for its trails, facilities, lodges, and clientele. It ranks high among Vermont's major ski resorts, a big mountain with two separate areas: the original North Face, otherwise known as Stratton Village, and the distinctly sunnier Sun Bowl, the newer of the two. Thanks to the quantity of lifts, skiers are generally dispersed over the trail network. Stratton Village, a complex that includes a variety of shops, a dozen restaurants, a 91-room condo hotel, a 750-car garage, and 170 condominiums, dwarfs the base facility. A sports center includes a 25-yard-long pool, whirlpool, indoor tennis courts, racquetball courts, exercise equipment, and a lounge. There's also a new Under 21 Club offering après-ski entertainment for the teen set.

A lot happens here in summer, too: There's a 70-foot climbing wall; a skate park with jumps, ramps, and rails; and an indoor family FunZone.

Lifts: 16: a 12-passenger gondola, four 6-passenger high-speed detachable, four quads, one triple, one double chair, two surface lifts, and three Magic Carpets. *Trails and slopes:* 90. *Terrain parks:* Six, including the pro Power Park and Power Superpipe, designed and built with the stamp of approval from Stratton snowboarder and Olympic medalist Ross Powers. The superpipe is 420 feet long, with walls of 17–22 feet. Skiers and riders must earn access to Stratton's biggest park by completing a safety awareness session. *Vertical drop:* 2,003 feet. *Snowmaking:* 90 percent. *Facilities:* Restaurant and cafeteria in the base lodge, also cafeterias midmountain and in Sun Bowl Ranch. Chapel of the Snows at the parking lot, a little Bavarian-style church, has frequent nondenominational and Roman Catholic services. A shuttle bus brings skiers from inns on the mountain to the base lodge. Also a clinic, sports center, and shops and restaurants in the base area Village Square. *Ski school:* Ski and snowboard lessons. *For children:* Childcare Center for ages 6 weeks–3 years; Mountain Riders 5–8 and 9–18. A separate base lodge and new slope-side meeting place for KidsKamp; combined ski and play programs are offered—Little Cubs (age 4–6), Big Cubs (7–12), Junior Newcomers (7–12). *Rates:* $59 per adult midweek, $72 weekends and holidays; $52 midweek and $60 weekends for young adults and seniors. Many special multiday packages.

🐾 ✤ **Magic Mountain Ski Area** (802-824-5645), Londonderry. Skiing and riding. A weekend lift ticket is $42, midweek $32. Tubing is big here at the Ala Kazaam Tube Park with its own tow, and Magic is the only resort in the area that offers it.

ICE SKATING **Riley Rink at Hunter Park** (802-362-0150), a paradise for music lovers in summer and sports enthusiasts in spring, is transformed into an Olympic-sized ice-skating rink in winter.

SLEIGH RIDES **Karl Pfister** (802-824-6320) in Landgrove offers the most remote, romantic sleigh ride around.

Other options include **Sun Bowl Ranch** (802-297-9210) at Stratton Mountain Resort (see *Horseback Riding*), the **Equinox** hotel (see *Lodging*), **Merck Forest and Farmland Center** (see *Green Space*), **Petticoat Junction** (802-362-3885) in Manchester, and the **Taylor Farm** (802-824-5690), operated by cheesemakers Jon and Kate Wright on Route 11 in Londonderry. (The benefit here is that you can buy some of their wonderful cheese at the same time.)

SNOWMOBILING A *Winter Recreation Map,* available free from the Green Mountain National Forest District Ranger Office (802-362-2307), Manchester, shows trails presently maintained in this area by the Vermont Association of Snow Travelers. **Classic Snow Tours** (802-824-6628), based at the Pinnacle Sun & Ski Lodge, junction of Routes 11 and 30, Manchester, offers tours and rentals. **Twin Brooks Tours** (802-442-4054) is located in nearby Woodford.

✳ Green Space

✎ **Equinox Preservation Trust** (802-362-4700), Manchester Village. A not-for-profit organization created in 1993 by Equinox Resort Associates and administered through the Vermont Land Trust and The Nature Conservancy. Some 850 acres on Mount Equinox are now a user-friendly preserve. Secure a map/guide to the trail system (a portion is open to cross-country skiers) and inquire about the nature walks and seminars offered year-round, some geared to children, in conjunction with the Vermont Institute of Natural Science. Horseback riding and mountain biking are also permitted on the ski trails in summer and fall. Be sure at least to walk the 1.2-mile loop through the hardwoods around Equinox Pond. *Note:* All parking for access to the trust property is at the parking lot of the Equinox hotel.

✎ **Merck Forest and Farmland Center** (802-394-7836), Route 315, Rupert. Some 2,800 acres of near wilderness were set aside in the 1950s as a foundation by George Merck of the Merck Drug Company. The area is now maintained through donations, and the forest offers year-round walks, talks, and facilities: foot and horse trails, picnic areas, a spring-fed swimming pond, 12 shelters, a farm museum, and a sugarhouse that produces 400 gallons of syrup. The **Merck Forest Summer Camp** has six 1-week sessions for children. Reservations are required for overnight use of the shelters. An extensive network of trails is marked for cross-country skiing.

Grout Pond, west of the village of Stratton, marked from Kelley Stand Road. Deep in the Green Mountain National Forest, this is a great spot for a picnic, complete with grills and a small beach.

See also *To Do—Camping.*

✳ Lodging

INNS AND BED & BREAKFASTS

In Manchester
♿ **The Inn at Ormsby Hill** (802-362-1163; 1-800-670-2841; www.ormsbyhill.com), 1842 Main Street, Manchester Center 05255. The inn is 2 miles southwest of Manchester Village on Route 7A, set in 2.5 acres of rolling lawns. The best views are from the back of the house. This gracious, elegant manor was the home of Edward Isham—Robert Todd Lin-

RESORT The Equinox (802-362-4700; 802-362-1595; 1-800-362-4747; www.equinoxresort.com), Route 7A, Manchester Village 05254. The white-columned inn comprises 17 distinct parts that have evolved over the past 229 years. It's still evolving. In the mid-1980s it was revamped from its foundations up, an unavoidable process that left it sound but, many said, soulless. Thanks to a 1990s infusion of funds, the 136 rooms and 47 suites, most of them spacious and furnished in pine reproductions, have acquired modern plumbing and a brighter, more country-inn feel. The **Charles Orvis Inn** next door is composed of suites, each with a cherry-paneled kitchen, oak floors, gas fireplace, and separate living room and bedroom. Common rooms include a paneled bar, billiards room, and meeting space. The inn's public spaces are extensive and quite magnificent, the grandest in Vermont. Meals are memorable (see *Dining Out*). Facilities for which guests pay extra include the recently revamped 18-hole golf course, a fitness center with outdoor and indoor pool, touring bikes, a 14-acre stocked trout pond, tennis courts, a cross-country ski network, snowmobiling, hunting with falcons, and learning to drive Land Rovers ecologically off-road. You might want to make sure before booking that your stay does not coincide with one of the business groups that can preempt the public spaces. $279–639 for a double at the Equinox during peak season, $50 less in regular season; $609–899 at the Charles Orvis Inn. Inquire about midweek and MAP packages.

THE EQUINOX

coln's law partner—and his family's home for 100 years. Its connection to Hildene is strong, spiritually and aesthetically. Innkeepers Chris and Ted Sprague have 10 guest rooms and obviously enjoyed distinctively decorating each in Waverly prints and exceptional antiques, all with fireplace and two-person Jacuzzi. The spacious Taft room, with its wood-burning fireplace and huge four-poster, is the unofficial honeymoon suite, but every one of the rooms is romantic enough to qualify. The downstairs Library suite is handicapped accessible. Common space includes a formal parlor and an inviting library lined with bookshelves that hold many of Isham's personal volumes. The huge, many-windowed dining room with ornately carved hearth is the scene of bountiful breakfasts featuring, perhaps, strawberries with crème fraîche and wild mushroom risotto with sliced ham, capped with desserts like rhubarb crumble with vanilla ice cream. $255–320 on weekends, $195–260 weekdays, more on holidays.

The Inn at Manchester (802-362-1793; 1-800-273-1793; www.innat manchester.com), 3967 Main Street, Manchester 05254. A gracious old home, set back from Main Street, with an expansive front porch, big windows, gables, and a restored, vintage-1867 carriage house in back. The 18 rooms, all with private bath and air-conditioning, are named for flowers and herbs. There are also four suites, three with working fireplace. The dining room and parlors are imaginatively and comfortably furnished, and there is a TV and game room, warmed by an antique wood-stove. Summer brings use of the pool

in the back meadow and plenty of wicker on the flowery porch. Children over 8 are welcome. Ron and Mary Blake are the new owners of the inn. Rates are $129–249 per room, including breakfast and afternoon tea.

✿ **Manchester Highlands Inn** (802-362-4565; 1-800-743-4565; www.high landsinn.com), P.O. Box 1754, 216 Highland Avenue, Manchester Center 05255. Patricia and Robert Eichorn call their spacious Victorian inn "Manchester's best-kept secret." Recently repainted a Victorian gray with rose and plum accents, it's on a quiet side street, a short walk from all the shops and restaurants but with an away-from-it-all feel, especially on the back porch and lawn (with its pool), both of which command an expansive view of Mount Equinox. The 15 guest rooms, all with private bath, are nicely decorated with family antiques and personal touches, many with canopy beds. Common space includes a comfortable living room, a wicker-filled sunroom, and a TV room (with a library of movies to feed the VCR). In winter the loss of the pool and porch is assuaged by the basement Remedy Room, with its bar and games—connected by "the tunnel" (decorated with guest graffiti) to the rooms in the carriage house, which, incidentally, are usually reserved for families. A very full breakfast featuring morning glory muffins, maybe lemon soufflé pancakes and cheddar soufflés, is served, plus home-baked afternoon snacks and tea. $115–179 double; $15 more in foliage and holiday weeks.

1811 House (802-362-1811; 1-800-432-1811; www.1811house.com), P.O. Box 39, Manchester Village 05254. "A place to feel pampered" is the way the owners of this magnificent building describe what they offer. Parts of this mansion date from the 1770s. It has been an inn since 1811, except for a few years during which it was owned by President Lincoln's granddaughter Mary Lincoln Isham. Public rooms are as elegant as any to be found in New England, and the 13 guest rooms are in keeping, each with private bath, 7 with wood-burning fireplace. Innkeepers Bruce and Marnie Duff and Cathy and Jorge Veleta dispel any stuffiness in this rarefied world. The cozy pub, replete with dartboards and a wide selection of single-malt scotches, is open to the public 5:30–8. An expansive lawn and newly redesigned English-style gardens overlook the Gleneagles Golf Course. A wonderful full breakfast is included in the room rate, from $140 per person for a cozy double to $280 per person for a suite with a king-sized four-poster canopy bed, fireplace, and sitting room. Rates include gratuity. Children over 16 are welcome. Off-season rates available.

Reluctant Panther Inn & Restaurant (802-362-2568; 1-800-822-2331; www.reluctantpanther.com), 17–39 West Road, Manchester 05254. Renowned for its gourmet fare (see *Dining Out*), this mauve, yellow-shuttered village home also has 13 rooms, with five suites in the adjacent Porter House, each decorated with bright wallpaper and antiques. Seven rooms and all the suites have fireplace. Many suites feature two wood-burning fireplaces—one in front of the two-person whirlpool bath and a second in the bedroom. All have private bath, room phone, and cable TV. Breakfast is served to guests only, and, with the exception of dining hours, the living room and unique pubs

make a peaceful and pleasant retreat. Innkeepers are Maye and Robert Bachofen. The inn is open year-round; the restaurant is open every day but Sunday through summer, weekends in fall and winter, and closed from March through May. $159–479 per room includes breakfast and dinner. No children under age 14.

The Village Country Inn (802-362-1792; 1-800-370-0300; fax: 802-362-7238; www.villagecountryinn.com), Box 408, Route 7A, Manchester 05254. This century-old, three-story Main Street inn has a long piazza lined with wicker and rockers. There are 33 rooms (18 suites and luxury rooms), 1 with Jacuzzi, some with gas fireplace, all with private bath, and many recently refurbished in lace, antiques, and chintz. Outside is a formal garden and gazebo, swimming pool, and patio; inside, an informal tavern and formal dining room. Rates, including breakfast, are $129–345 for a double, with a special dinner price for guests.

∞ **Wilburton Inn** (802-362-2500; 1-800-648-4944; www.wilburton.com), River Road, Manchester 05254. This is a brick, baronial, turn-of-the-20th-century mansion set up a hill and well off the main road on expansive grounds with long views of the Battenkill Valley. Common rooms are richly paneled and the living room is immense, complete with piano, comfortable window seats and couches, Oriental rugs, and an enormous hearth. Owners Georgette and Albert Levis's abiding interest in the human psyche and conflict resolution have resulted in what they call "the Museum of the Creative Process," located on the 20-acre grounds. The house itself offers four suites and five bedrooms; there are also 25 rooms in outlying cottages, better suited to families, as they offer more privacy and direct access to the seemingly limitless lawn—which harbors a pool and tennis courts. Breakfast is served at wrought-iron, glass-topped tables in the Terrace Room, and dinner, in the Billiard Room, is reminiscent of an exclusive men's club. Open year-round, $115–300 per couple including a full breakfast and afternoon tea. Weddings are a specialty here.

The Inn at Willow Pond (802-362-4733; outside Vermont: 1-800-533-3533; www.innatwillowpond.com), Box 1429, Manchester Center 05255. Located 2.3 miles north on Route 7A, this inn run by Kay and Ron Bauer offers 40 spacious guest rooms and suites in three separate, contemporary, Colonial-style buildings on a hillside overlooking the Manchester Country Club's golf course. The 18th-century Meeting House reception building contains the lofty main lounge, conference facilities, a fitness center with exercise equipment, two saunas, and a library. There's also an outdoor lap pool and a restaurant in a renovated 1770 house (see *Dining Out*). The larger guest rooms feature a fireplace and sitting area. Winter rates are $158 (for a small suite) to $348 for multiroom suites with a fireplace and full living room; all include continental breakfast. Full breakfast is served in the restaurant on weekends and holidays. Midweek and special off-season weekend rates available.

River Meadow Farm (802-362-1602), P.O. Box 822, Sugarhouse Lane, Manchester Center 05255. Off by itself down near the Batten Kill south of Manchester Village, this is a beautiful old farmhouse with barns,

built around 1797 and purchased in the 1820s by Manchester for use as a "poor farm." There are five bedrooms sharing two and a half baths, and guests have the run of the downstairs with its welcoming kitchen, pleasant living room, and dining room. Outside there is fishing on the Batten Kill plus ample space to hike, snowshoe, and cross-country ski—with a splendid view of Mount Equinox. Pat Dupree is a longtime Manchester resident who enjoys orienting her guests. Rates are $35 per person, full breakfast included.

Seth Warner Inn (802-362-3830; www.sethwarnerinn.com), P.O. Box 281, Manchester Center 05255. This imposing vintage-1800 house is set back from Route 7A, southwest of Manchester Village, and it's a beauty —carefully restored by Stasia and Lee Tetreault. Rooms with open beams and stenciling are furnished in antiques and curtained in lace. Five bright guest rooms have country quilts, canopy bed, and private bath. Common space includes a gracious living room, a hall library, and the dining room, in which guests gather for a full breakfast. $110 (summer) and $120 (fall) per room including breakfast.

The Battenkill Inn (802-362-4213; 1-800-441-1628; www.battenkillinn.com), P.O. Box 31, Manchester 05254. This 1840 Victorian farmhouse sits at the foot of the Mount Equinox Skyline Drive and backs onto meadows that stretch down to the Batten Kill. The 11 guest rooms all have private bath and are furnished with antiques, and the common rooms include two sitting rooms and two small dining rooms—plenty of space to relax in. One room with a double bed and fireplace is fully handicapped accessible. Your hosts are Cliff and Donna Ward. $135–180 per couple includes a full breakfast and complimentary hors d'oeuvres. Springtime midweek specials are available. No children under 10, please.

In Arlington 05250

∞ **The Arlington Inn** (802-375-6532; 1-800-443-9442; www.arlingtoninn.com), 3904 Route 7A in the center of Arlington, occupies the 1848 Greek Revival mansion built by Martin Chester Deming, a Vermont railroad magnate, and has been used as an inn off and on since 1889. The new owners are Eric and Elizabeth Berger. The 12 rooms and six suites in the main house and former carriage barn are spacious and furnished with Victorian antiques, and there's a formal parlor. Sylvester's Study on the ground floor is particularly impressive. There are six units, including two suites, in the adjacent 1830 parsonage; they have Drexel cherry four-posters and sleigh beds, TV, and air-conditioning. The inn is also known as a popular spot for dinner (see *Dining Out*), and the gardens make a great spot for weddings or civil union ceremonies. Rates per room are $125–350, including a full breakfast. MAP also available. Open all year.

∞ ♪ ♿ **West Mountain Inn** (802-375-6516; www.westmountaininn.com), on Route 313 west of Arlington. Open year-round. A large, rambling former summer home with splendid views of the mountains and valley, converted and expanded into an inn. The 22 attractive rooms, 9 of which are suites, are named for famous people associated with Arlington, and a copy of Dorothy Canfield

Fisher's *Vermont Tradition* is in every room. Breakfast and dinner are served daily; Sunday brunch on certain holidays (see *Dining Out*). The inn's property includes more than 5 miles of walking and cross-country ski trails, a bird sanctuary, seasonal gardens, and llamas in residence. A number of special events are featured, such as a St. Lucia Festival of Lights in early December, Leek and Fiddlehead Days in early May, and Ethan Allen Days (Father's Day weekend). Amie Emons is the innkeeper. $169–275 for two MAP in low season, $228–305 for two MAP in high season. There are also three town houses at the Historic Mill on the property.

♪ **Hill Farm Inn** (802-375-2269; 1-800-882-2545; www.hillfarminn.com), 458 Hill Farm Road. Located off Route 7A north of the village, this historic farmstead, owned and managed by Al and Lisa Gray, is set on 50 acres of land bordering the Batten Kill River. The 1830 main building, 1790 guest house, and four seasonal cabins hold a total of 15 rooms, all with private bath. Licensed for beer and wine. Double rooms are $105–190, including full country breakfast. Children are welcome at special rates.

The Inn on Covered Bridge Green (802-375-9489; 1-800-726-9480; fax: 802-375-9046; www.coveredbridgegreen.com), 3587 River Road. Fans of Norman Rockwell can now actually stay in his former home, a pretty white 1792 colonial next to a red covered bridge on the village green where Ethan Allen mustered his Green Mountain Boys. The inn offers nine bedrooms, all with private bath (four have two-person spa tubs), and two cottages.

There's swimming, canoeing, and fly-fishing in the Batten Kill, just a few hundred feet from the inn. The full country breakfasts are events, served on bone china with Waterford glass and silver. Rates range $140–250.

⊙ **Country Willows B&B** (802-375-0019; http://countrywillows.com), 332 East Arlington Road. Anne and Ron Weber run this tidy, 1850s village historic landmark with five spacious guest rooms with private bath (two with claw-footed tubs), decorated in Victoriana. The West Mountain Room has a fine view, fireplace, and sitting area. The Dorset Suite is a two-bedroom, one-bath suite that can accommodate parents with school-age children. There is a wraparound porch and a hammock for two. Rates of $110–160 per double include full country breakfast, possibly Anne's French toast served with Ron's secret-recipe apple compote.

✤ **Ira Allen House** (802-362-2284), (1-888-733-8666), Box 251, Route 7A. Ray and Sandy Walters run this smartly renovated old roadside home where Ira and Ethan Allen once lived. The inn has nine guest rooms, some set up for families. The inn's property across Route 7A fronts the Batten Kill, good for trout fishing and, for the warm-blooded, a dip in a 10-foot-deep swimming hole. $110–150 per room with full breakfast.

⊙ ✤ **Green River Inn** (802-375-2272; 1-000-040-2212, www.green riverinn.com), 3402 Sandgate Road, Sandgate 05250 (off Route 313, 4 miles west from Route 7A, Arlington), has 14 renovated guest rooms, all with private bath, some with whirlpool and fireplace; sunroom, deck, and special children's room. Jim and Betsy Gunn have a lot of ideas about what to do

outdoors on their 450 acres. $90–200 B&B.

In Danby 05739

⊙ ✿ ✤ ♿ **Silas Griffith Inn** (802-293-5567; 1-800-545-1509), 178 Main Street, is the renovated 1891 mansion that once housed Vermont's first millionaire. George and Carol Gaines own this comfortable inn with its restored hardwood floors and carved bird's-eye, curly maple, and cherry woodwork. The 15 guest rooms, all with private bath, are divided between the main house and the converted carriage house, all furnished with antiques. You might want to request the room with the round porch (but no closet), or the room with the huge bed—one of several rooms that can be combined into a family suite sharing one bath. Common rooms include a large living room, well stocked with books, and a front parlor with TV, accessed by a wonderful "moon gate" door. The restaurant (in the carriage house) is locally popular (see *Dining Out*). Danby's intriguing shops are just down the street, and there are some outstanding hiking trails just a few minutes' drive into the Green Mountain National Forest; Emerald Lake State Park is just 3 miles down Route 7. The inn's own 11 hilltop acres include a pool. Rates range $159–349, including full breakfast; discounts for weekdays and for a stay of several days.

The Quail's Nest (802-293-5099; 1-800-599-6444; www.quailsnest bandb.com), Box 221, 81 South Main Street, is a homey, pleasant B&B in an 1835 house. Terry Parker and Chris Hardaway offer six guest rooms, all with private bath, furnished with antiques and handmade country quilts. There's a comfy living room and an interesting gift store out back. $70–115 includes a full breakfast.

In Dorset 05251

The Dorset Inn (802-867-5500), 8 Church Street. A national historic site and the state's most venerable hostel ry (in continuous operation since 1796) faces Dorset's historic green. It has been stylishly renovated by its owners, Sissy Hicks, former chef at the Barrows House, and Gretchen Schmidt. Known for its excellent cuisine (see *Dining Out*) and relaxing atmosphere, the inn has 30 guest rooms. It's within walking distance of antiques shops and the theater and offers a lineup of front-porch rockers from which you might not want to stir. $95–145 in low season, $145–200 in high season. All rates include breakfast, and some include dinner.

☀ ♿ **The Barrows House** (802-867-4455; 1-800-639-1620; www.barrows house.com), Box 98. This exceptional mini resort on Route 30, now owned by Linda and Jim McGinnis, features attractive, flexibly arranged accommodations (18 rooms, 10 suites) in the main house and 7 rooms in adjacent buildings. The early-19th-century house is a short walk from the center of this historic village, but there is an out-in-the-country feel to the 12-acre grounds, which include a gazebo, heated outdoor swimming pool, sauna, and two tennis courts. In summer, bikes are available; golf and hiking are nearby. In winter, cross-country ski equipment is available. There are comfortable sitting rooms in the main house and the bigger cottages, where large families or several friendly couples can be lodged. A convivial bar is wallpapered to resemble a private library. Dogs are

welcome in two separate accommodations. The dining room and a guest room in one of the outer buildings are wheelchair accessible. The dining room is outstanding (see *Dining Out*). $205–300 per couple, including breakfast and dinner; B&B rates also available.

♂ ♿ **Inn at West View Farm** (802-867-5715; 1-800-769-4903; www.innatwestviewfarm.com), Route 30, just south of Dorset, is a small, well-groomed lodge with an appealing personality, once the focus of a 200-acre farm, now known especially for its exceptional cuisine. (Under the direction of chef Raymond Chen, the dining room—see *Dining Out*—remains the focal point of the inn.) Christal Siewertsen is the innkeeper. The inn has a very pleasant living room with a fireplace in the old front parlor; common space also includes an inviting, wicker-filled sunporch. One downstairs room has been fitted for handicapped access, and the nine upstairs rooms are all furnished comfortably with cheerful paper and bright, crisp fabrics; all rooms are

THE DORSET INN

Kim Grant

air-conditioned. Rates are $110–200, including full breakfast.

Marble West Inn (802-867-4155; 1-800-453-7629; www.marblewest inn.com), Dorset West Road. This Greek Revival house has seven marble columns on its marble front porches, and there are marble walkways and three marble fireplaces. It offers eight well-decorated guest rooms (one a two-room suite with fireplace), an inviting living room, and a piano room that is the scene of impromptu concerts. The stencil work in the entrance hallway and on stairway walls is exceptional, and the high ceilings and bull's-eye moldings are pleasant reminders of an earlier era, as is the gracious hospitality of owners Bonnie and Paul Quinn. Guests mingle in the library for drinks (BYOB) and conversation. Rates are $90–175 per couple, including a candlelit, gourmet breakfast and afternoon tea. A 15 percent service charge is added. Please, no pets or children under 12.

∞ **Cornucopia of Dorset** (802-867-5751; 1-800-566-5751; www.cornu copiaofdorset.com), 3228 Route 30, P.O. Box 307. This turn-of-the-20th-century home is one of Vermont's more elegant B&Bs. Donna Butman offers five meticulously decorated, air-conditioned bedrooms in the main house, each with canopy or four-poster bed, phone, and private bath; three have fireplace. There is also a cottage. The solarium, walled in glass, overlooks gardens and a manicured back lawn. Guests can also relax in the library or small living room, both with a fireplace, and on a back terrace under an awning. The cottage suite in the rear is a beauty, with a loft bedroom (with skylights), living room with fireplace, kitchen, and sundeck.

The multicourse breakfast may feature puff pancakes, gingerbread waffles, or quiche Lorraine. A welcoming flute of champagne and a morning tray of coffee or tea are among the many amenities. Rooms are $200–300 for a double, $180–270 in low season.

Dovetail Inn (802-867-5747; 1-800-4-DOVETAIL; www.dovetailinn .com), Route 30. An 1800s inn on the Dorset green with 11 bedrooms (all with private bath), run by Jean and Jim Kingston. Breakfast is served in the Keeping Room or in guest rooms. $65 for the smallest double room in low season; $195 for a two-room suite with a fireplace and TV, sleeping up to four. Ask about midweek rates.

In Weston 05161
Judge Wilder Inn (802-824-8172), 25 Lawrence Hill Road. A classic, Federal-style brick house, beautifully transformed into a B&B. There are seven guest rooms, most with private bath, several with early-19th-century stenciling, each with a different decor. There's a huge hearth in the dining room, where a full breakfast is served; there's also an attractive library and living room and a full bar. All the sights of Weston are within an easy walk, and there's a waterfall across the street. $90–135 per couple B&B. No children under age 12. No smoking.

🐾 ✒ & **Colonial House Inn & Motel** (802-824-6286; 1-800-639-5033; www.cohoinn.com), 287 Route 100. A rare and delightful combination of nine motel units and six traditional inn rooms (shared baths), connected by a very pleasant dining room, a comfortable, sunken sitting room with dried flowers hanging from the rafters, and a solarium overlooking the lawn; there's also a fully equipped game room. Innkeepers Kim and Jeff Seymour (Kim is the daughter of former owners John and Betty Nunnikhoven) make all ages feel welcome, and most guests are repeats. Rates include memorable, multicourse breakfasts. Dinners are served family-style ($19.95). The inn is 2 miles south of the village, with lawn chairs facing a classic farmscape across the road; most guest rooms overlook a meadow. Rooms are $40–108 B&B; extra charges for children and singles. Ramp available for wheelchairs.

☙ **The Darling Family Inn** (802-824-3223; www.thedarlingfamily inn.com), 815 Route 100. An 1830s house, exquisitely furnished with family antiques by Joan and Chapin Darling. The five guest rooms have private bath, canopy bed, fine quilts, and artistic touches. There are wide-plank floors throughout, and Joan has expertly painted the walls. Full country breakfasts, by candlelight, are included in the rates. In summer the pool adds a nice touch. $90–145 per couple, including breakfast, except for guests in the two attractive cottages up on the hill (where pets are welcome).

Inn at Weston (802-824-6789; www.innweston.com), P.O. Box 66, Route 100. Bob and Linda Aldrich own this 13-room establishment that offers lodging in the main inn, the Coleman House, or the Carriage House. There's a gourmet dining room (see *Dining Out*) with live music, a deck, and a gazebo. $165–305 in the main inn and the Coleman House, $275–335 in the Carriage House.

☙ **Johnny Seesaw's** (802-824-5533; 1-800-424-CSAW; www.jseesaw.com), 3574 Route 11. Built as a dance hall in 1920 and converted into one of Vermont's first ski lodges, this is a wonderfully weathered, comfortable place. Within walking distance of the slopes in winter, it offers tennis and a pool in summer. There are 28 rooms—doubles, master bedrooms with fireplace in the main house, and family suites—also four cottages with fireplaces, good for large families and small groups. There is a licensed pub (see *Dining Out*); "Yankee cuisine" dinners are à la carte and have a French accent. The living room boasts Vermont's first circular fireplace. Rates are $80–130 per room, high season $100–200 per room B&B; add 15 percent service. Pets are okay.

✎ **The Wiley Inn** (802-824-6600; 1-888-843-6600; www.wileyinn.com), P.O. Box 7, Route 11, just 1 mile from Bromley. Its core is an 1835 house containing a delightful living room with fireplace, library, and dining room. A motel-like wing, now refurbished, includes two rooms with fireplaces within view of the whirlpool tubs in the bathrooms. Jerry and Judy Goldman extend a special welcome to families with the configuration of a number of rooms, as well as a game room with an online computer, TV, piano, and toys. Couples, on the other hand, may prefer the suitably quiet and romantic rooms in the original part of this rambling inn, with its total of eight rooms and four two-bedroom suites, all with private bath. Summer facilities include a backyard heated pool and play area; there's also a year-round outside hot tub. The inn's relatively small and attractive dining room is currently the Bromley Beach, an Italian bistro open weekends and holidays. Rooms for two, including breakfast, are $115–175 in summer and fall; suites, $135–195 on winter weekends excluding holidays; the first child 12 or under is free in parent's room.

In Landgrove 05148

⚭ 🐾 🐕 🎣 **The Landgrove Inn** (802-824-6673; 1-800-669-8466; www.landgroveinn.com), 132 Landgrove Road. Tom and Maureen Checchia recently bought this red-clapboard building that rambles back and around, beginning with the 1820 house, ending an acre or two away. The "Vermont continuous architecture" draws guests through a handsome lobby, past 16 rooms with private bath that meander off in all directions, through the inviting Rafter Room Lounge (huge, filled with games and books), to the attractive dining room in the original house. Our favorite rooms are tucked up under the eaves in the oldest part of the inn, papered in floral prints and furnished with carefully chosen antiques but with new baths. Many rooms are well suited to families, who also will appreciate the heated pool, tennis court, trout pond, lawn games, and paddle tennis court. In winter you can take a sleigh ride or step out onto the 15-mile cross-country trail system that leads through the picturesque village of Landgrove (just a church, former school, and salting of homes cupped in a hollow), on into surrounding Green Mountain National Forest. Bromley Ski Area is just 6 miles away, and Stratton is a 20-minute drive. Breakfast is an event here, served in the wood-beamed dining room with a many-windowed wall overlooking the garden. The dining room is open to the public 5 nights a week. Dining is by candlelight, with a choice of six entrées prepared by a well-respected local chef (see *Dining Out*). $95–235 per couple with full breakfast.

⚭ **The Macartney House** (802-824-6444; www.MacartneyHouse .com), 24 Vermont Route 11. James and Elaine Nelson-Parker's forested retreat (this used to be the Meadowbrook Inn) has seven guest rooms, all with private bath, some with fireplace and/or whirlpool tub, plus comfortable lounging areas. Their 26 km trail system is available to guests in all seasons for hiking, biking, nature walks, and cross-country skiing. Rates range $120–280 all year long, with a gourmet breakfast included. Children over 16.

In and around Londonderry

Frog's Leap Inn (802-824-3019; 1-887-FROGSLEAP; www.frogs leapinn.com), 7455 Route 100, Londonderry 05148. One of the oldest inns in the area, this is a classic Colonial, built in 1842 and set well back from the road above a sloping lawn. The estate-like place has an excellent dining room, 32 acres of pasture and forests with 1.5 miles of hiking and cross-country trails, an outdoor heated swimming pool, and a tennis court. There are eight rooms with private bath in the main house, and another eight (four of which are suites) with private bath in the annex, plus the Tad Pool House, which has a large two-bedroom suite with a kitchen and a deck overlooking the pool. B&B rates ($89–114 per room for two) include a full breakfast. Rates for the Tad Pool House and the Forest Glen House are $260 without housekeeping.

♦ ✍ ♿ **The Londonderry Inn** (802-824-5226; 1-800-644-5226; www .londonderryinn.com), 8 Melendy Hill Road, South Londonderry 05155. On a knoll overlooking the West River, this 1826 dairy farm has been a country inn since 1940. The 24 guest rooms—some are suites—are decorated with folk-art-painted furniture and Chagall-inspired paintings on the walls, patchwork quilts and teddy bears on every bed. The large, bright public rooms include a huge stone fireplace, spring-fed pool, tropical birds, billiards room, movie room, and Maya's antique bell collection. Fresh-baked cookies are available every afternoon. Full hot vegetarian buffet breakfast and afternoon tea are included in the room rates. Innkeepers Chrisman and Maya Kearn are glad to help guests plan daily itineraries. Children are welcome. Gift shop on premises. Room rates are the same all year and run $136–176 for two with breakfast. By the way, guests make their own beds.

MOTELS Palmer House Resort (802-362-3600; 1-800-917-6245; www.palmerhouse.com), P.O. Box 657, Manchester Center 05255. A luxury motel with 50 rooms and suites with color TV, free coffee, a heated indoor lap pool, whirlpool, and sauna, plus fishing in a private, stocked trout pond, tennis, and a nine-hole golf course; there's an adjacent restaurant. Continental breakfast is included in room rates of $75–175, $160–300 for suites, depending on the season.

♿ **The Manchester View** (802-362-2739; 1-800-548-4141; www.man chesterview.com), P.O. Box 1268, Route 7A, Manchester Center 05255. Tom and Pat Barnett own this place just north of town with marvelous views. Thirty-five rooms with fridge, 3 two-bedroom suites, and 7 one-bedroom suites (most with fireplace, living room, and two-person Jacuzzi); also handicapped-accessible units. A former barn now holds a breakfast room. Facilities include a heated outdoor pool in summer. Golf and tennis available at nearby Manchester Country Club. Rates are $85–235 based on double occupancy, $185–270 for suites.

♦ ✍ **Swiss Inn** (802-824-3442; 1-800-847-9477; www.swissinn.com), 249 Route 11, Londonderry 05148. From its exterior, this looks like a standard motel, but once inside, the differences are appealing. Joe and Pat Donahue feature Swiss dishes in their dining room (see *Dining Out*). Nineteen rooms, all with private bath, are large enough to accommodate families, and public space includes a library as well as a sitting room and bar. There's also an outdoor pool. $69–109 per room includes a full breakfast.

The Barnstead Inn (802-362-1619; 1-800-331-1619; www.barnsteadinn .com), Box 998, Manchester Center 05255. Just up Bonnet Street (Route 30), two blocks from the amenities of town, this is a genuine former hay barn converted into 14 motel units. It's all been done with consummate grace and charm, with many small touches like braided rugs and exposed old beams (but no room phones). There is also an outdoor pool and hot tub. $90–170 with breakfast on weekends.

The Weathervane (802-362-2444; 1-800-262-1317), Route 7A, Manchester 05254. Set back from the road with two picture windows in each of its 22 large units, each room has TV, free coffee, and hot chocolate. There is a "courtesy room" with books, games, and magazines, as well as a putting green and a heated pool. $76–150 per couple, with breakfast in summer.

CONDOMINIUMS AND SKI LODGES

Stratton Mountain Inn (1-800-STRATTON; www.stratton.com), 61 Middle Ridge Road, Stratton Mountain 05155, with 125 rooms and suites, is the largest lodging facility on the mountain. Rooms have private bath, phone, and TV, and facilities include a large dining room, saunas, and whirlpools. On winter weekends room rates start at $179 per night. The on-site **Stone Chimney Grill** offers breakfast and candlelit dining.

Stratton Condominiums (1-800-STRATTON), Stratton Mountain 05155. Roughly 250 of the resort's condominium units are in the rental pool at any given time, in a range of sizes and shapes; they run $79–109 per person per day with lift ticket midweek. Weekend rates per unit start at $299. All resort guests have access to the sports center and its indoor pool, exercise machines, and racquetball and tennis courts (a fee is charged).

Liftline Lodge (1-800-STRATTON), Stratton Mountain 05155. This traditional 77-room European-style lodge is close to Stratton's lifts and village shops and restaurants. Two restaurants. Lift and lodging $59 per person midweek. Weekends from $139 per room.

Long Trail House (1-800-STRATTON), Stratton Mountain 05155. The newest Stratton property has a heated pool, hot tub, and sauna. Weekend and holiday rates start at $259 per night.

Bromley Village (802-824-5458; 1-800-865-4786), P.O. Box 1130, Manchester Center 05255, is a complex of attractive one- to four-bedroom units adjacent to the ski area. Summer facilities include a pool and tennis courts. In winter you can walk to the lifts; there is also a shuttle bus. Call for rates.

CAMPGROUNDS See *To Do—Camping* for campground options in the area.

✳ Where to Eat

DINING OUT Chantecleer (802-362-1616), Route 7A, East Dorset. Open 6–closing, closed Tuesday. Long respected as one of Vermont's outstanding restaurants, Swiss chef Michael Baumann's establishment is known for nightly game specials, whole Dover sole Chantecleer, and Australian roast rack of lamb (both $35). Leave room for profiterole de maison or coupe Matterhorn. The setting is an elegantly remodeled old dairy barn with a massive fieldstone fireplace. There is an extensive wine list. Reservations essential.

Forty nine forty main street (802-362-9839), 4940 Main Street, Manchester. Lunch and dinner daily 11 AM–closing. Entrées range from a Black Angus burger for $8 to ropa vieja Cuban beef stew for $15 or Zarensuella seafood stew for $19.

Inn at Weston (802-824-6789; www.innweston.com), Route 100, Weston. Executive chef Max Turner has made this a favorite. You might begin with sushi maki roll or seared Hudson Valley foie gras, then move on to Alaskan halibut seared in pink peppercorns or Long Island duckling marinated in five spices. Seatings begin at 5:30. Entrées $27–34.

Wilburton Inn (802-362-2500; 1-800-648-4944; www.wilburton.com), River Road, Manchester Village. Dinner in the mansion's baronial Billiard Room is an event. You might start with beef carpaccio drizzled with truffle oil, and move on to grilled black grouper and PEI mussels or seared peppered yellowfin tuna on a bed of tabbouleh. And then there's always dessert. Monday is grill night on the terrace, weather permitting.

Three Clock Inn (802-824-6327; www.threeclockinn.com), Middletown Road, South Londonderry. Dinner daily except Monday. Reserve and request directions. Owner Serge Roche and his chef-partner, Michael Kloeti, work their magic in a rustic dining space with low beams and glowing hearths. The à la carte menu changes frequently but might include grilled skate wings ($22) or veal emmince Zurichoise ($23). Desserts might include a warm pear tart or crème caramel à l'orange ($7). A complete dinner is $38. There is an extensive wine cellar. Cooking classes are offered by Chef Michael.

Mistral's at Toll Gate (802-362-1779), off Routes 11/30 east of Manchester. Open for dinner daily except Wednesday. Reservations recommended. Chef Dana Markey and his wife, Cheryl, run this longtime dining landmark located in the old tollhouse once serving the Boston-to-Saratoga road. During warm-weather months a brook rushes along just under the windows. The menu might include tournedos of veal morel, salmon cannelloni, or sautéed veal pesto with fusilli. All are accompanied by a very long wine list. Entrées $22–30.

The Barrows House (802-867-4455), Route 30, Dorset. Open for dinner nightly from 6. In a spacious, rather formal country dining room and its attached conservatory, both conscientiously appointed, diners can select from an à la carte menu that changes seasonally; nightly specials are also offered. Maine crabcakes or vegetable strudel might be followed by pan-roasted veal Sinatra or hazelnut-crusted Arctic char. Entrées are $15–29, with "lighter-side entrées" as an option.

Inn at West View Farm (802-867-5715; 1-800-769-4903), 2928 Route 30, Dorset. Open for dinner Thursday through Monday. The Auberge Room is exceptionally attractive, and the food is dependably good. Chef Raymond Chen's entrées range $21–28 and might include braised short ribs, paupiette of halibut, or coriander-crusted venison.

The Black Swan (802-362-3807), Route 7A, Manchester Village (next to the Jelly Mill). Open for dinner daily except Wednesday. The food in this crisply decorated and managed old brick Colonial house is a treat for the senses. A representative dinner might begin with chilled calamari salad or broiled Greenlip mussels topped with garlic butter, and proceed to Nana's fried chicken with pan gravy ($16.25) or almond-crusted flounder ($18.50). Lighter fare is served in the **Mucky Duck Bistro.**

Silas Griffith Inn (802-293-5567), 178 Main Street, Danby. This attractive, informal dining room, with a hearth and walls decorated with antique kitchen gadgets, is in the converted carriage house. On holiday weekends prix fixe dinners range $30–50.

Reluctant Panther (802-362-2568), 39 West Road, Route 7A, Manchester

Village. Open for dinner nightly except Tuesday and Wednesday, weekends only in late fall and winter. The greenhouse dining room is particularly pleasant and can be the setting for a memorable evening. The menu might include choucroute garnie, pot-au-feu, or Wiener schnitzel prepared by Swiss-born chef Robert Bachofen. The wine list is extensive. Prix fixe dinners are $45; à la carte is also available.

The Perfect Wife (802-362-2817), Routes 11/30, 1 mile east of the Route 7 overpass. Open Tuesday through Sunday 5–10 for dinner. Amy Chamberlain features locally raised chicken with chèvre and eggplant, sesame-crusted tuna, or the Howling Wolf vegetarian special. There's live music in the tavern every weekend. Entrées $5.95–22.

The Dorset Inn (802-867-5500; 1-877-367-7389), 8 Church Street, Dorset. Open daily for breakfast, lunch, and dinner. Chef Sissy Hicks can be relied on for outstanding New England fare. Dinner entrées include duck confit with wild rice and plum chutney ($21.75), or eggplant crêpes rolled with spinach and ricotta ($13.75). Entrées $13–26.

The Equinox (802-362-4700), Route 7A, Manchester Village. Dinner is served in the formal, vaulted Colonnade dining room; a prix fixe Sunday brunch is a tradition for residents and visitors. The attractive Marsh Tavern is open for breakfast, lunch, and dinner daily, serving hearty soups, salads, pastas, and such specials as Devonshire shepherd's pie, lobster ravioli, Yankee pot roast, and various seafood selections at moderate prices, with live entertainment on weekends. The Dormy Grill serves lunch outside daily on the deck in warm weather with a dinnertime lobsterfest Thursday through Saturday in summer. Entrées $10–24 in the Marsh Tavern.

Bistro Henry (802-362-4982), 1942 Routes 11/30, Manchester. Open for dinner daily except Monday. Dina and Henry Bronson run this Mediterranean-style dining room with a casual atmosphere, a full bar, and a *Wine Spectator* award for excellence. You might begin with a vegetable and Vermont goat cheese tart, then dine on the risotto of the day or quail stuffed with foie gras. Entrées are $16–30.

The Restaurant at Willow Pond (802-362-4733), Route 7 north of Manchester Center. A restaurant in a restored 1770s farmhouse. Dinner every night (but check in the off-seasons). The menu is "authentic" northern Italian. You might begin with a spinach salad, or grilled eggplant with a three-cheese-and-spinach stuffing and a fresh diced tomato and porcini mushroom sauce. Entrées include linguine alla pesto ($12.95) and veal piccata ($19.95).

Swiss Inn (802-824-3442), Route 11, Londonderry. Open to the public for dinner daily except Wednesday, the Swiss Inn has a strong local following. While ownership is no longer Swiss, the current owner-chef seems to have the right touch with such dishes as Geschnetzeltes (veal à la Swiss), beef fondue, and chicken Lugano (chicken breast dipped in a Gruyère cheese batter); also Continental dishes like shrimp à la Marseilles and veal Marsala. Fondues are a specialty. Entrées run $13–23.

Johnny Seesaw's (802-824-5533; 1-800-424-CSAW), Route 11, Peru. A Prohibition-era dance hall, then one of New England's first ski lodges, this atmospheric inn is well worth a dinnertime visit even if you don't happen to be staying there. The extensive menu usually includes a choice of veal and seafood dishes and pork chops Vermont-style, but huge prime rib of beef is the house special (children can always get hamburgers or pasta as well as half-sized portions). Adult entrées $12.95–19.95. Soft music played live on weekends.

✔ **The Landgrove Inn** (802-824-6673), 132 Landgrove Road, Landgrove. Dinner by reservation Wednesday through Sunday. This fine old inn is off by itself up dirt roads at the edge of a tiny village. Meals are by candlelight in a delightful old dining room with windows overlooking the garden. You might begin with a delectable butternut squash, apple, and onion soup, then dine on roast duck with blueberry sauce or rack of lamb. Entrées $18–28. Children's portions and delicious desserts.

🍴 **Ye Olde Tavern** (802-362-0611), 214 North Main Street, Manchester Center. Open daily from 11:30 AM for lunch and 5 PM for dinner. A 1790 tavern theoretically specializing in "authentic American" dinner dishes like roast tom turkey and pot roast, but seafood fettuccine is also on the menu, and the Tavern Seafood Stew is laced with vermouth, tomato, and fennel ($19). The several veal specialties all are priced at $21–24, and there's lots of prime rib ($22). One of the better values in town.

The Arlington Inn (802-375-6532), Route 7A, Arlington. There's a mauve-walled formal dining room and the more casual Deming Tavern. From a recent menu, you could select steamed mussels as an appetizer, and continue to Arlington Inn mixed grill or cedar-planked salmon. Entrées $22–30.

West Mountain Inn (802-375-6516), River Road, Arlington. Chef Larry Vellucci's dining room is open to the public by reservation 6:30–8:30 PM, Sunday through Friday, featuring a $42 prix fixe menu that might include pan-seared Chilean sea bass, spinach and roasted red pepper ravioli, or a Black Angus filet mignon.

See also the "The Lower Connecticut and West River Valleys" for Three Mountain Inn in Jamaica.

EATING OUT

In and around Manchester

The **Garden Café** at the Southern Vermont Arts Center (802-362-4220), West Road, Manchester Village. Open for lunch May through mid-October, Tuesday through Saturday 11:30–2, Sunday noon–2. The food is fine and the setting is superb: a pleasant indoor room or the outside terrace, both with views over the sculpture garden and down the mountain to Manchester Village.

Al Ducci's Italian Pantry (802-362-4449; 1-800-579-4449), Elm Street, one block up Highland Avenue from Routes 11/30, Manchester Center. An authentic Italian deli; eat in or take out. Daily specials, plus the best supply of specialty cheeses and artisan breads in the region. Open daily until 6 PM. Closed Tuesday.

Little Rooster Cafe (802-362-3496), Route 7A south, Manchester Center. Breakfast and lunch from 7 AM; closed Wednesday. An offshoot of Chantecleer (see *Dining Out*), an "eclectic European café" serving exquisite waffles and omelets, café au lait and cappuccino, baguette sandwiches.

Expensive by breakfast and lunch standards, but special.

Laney's Restaurant (802-362-4456), Routes 11/30, Manchester Center. Open from 5 PM, this is a festive, kid-friendly spot, specializing in exotic pizzas from a wood-fired brick oven, Adam's Ribs (baby back pork ribs), Gone with the Wind (pork and beef ribs), and Oliver Twist (pasta primavera); draft beer in frosted mugs.

Maxwell's Flat Road Grill (802-362-3721), Routes 11/30, Manchester Center, across from r. k. Miles. Diner food done well, everything from popcorn chicken and quesadillas to chili and big burgers. For dinner you might try crabcakes or horseradish-crusted salmon. All entrées are less than $15, some considerably less.

Sherrie's Cafe (802-362-3468), Routes 11/30, Manchester. Open 8–3, this café serves great breakfasts, homemade soups, sandwiches, salads, and desserts.

Best Diner (802-362-8171), Routes 11/30, Manchester Depot. Very good food (the milk shakes are literally the best) at good prices in this upscale part of the world. Give it a try, especially with kids.

Gourmet Café and Deli, Route 7A, Manchester Center. Tucked back into one of Manchester Center's many shopping centers, this café offers great salads and sandwiches, plus a pleasant terrace to eat on in warm weather.

Candeleros (802-362-0836), Main Street, Manchester Center, is a Mexican cantina open daily for lunch and dinner; there's a pleasant outdoor patio in summer.

The Buttery (802-362-3544), second floor at the Jelly Mill, Route 7A, Man-

chester Center. An attractive, welcoming spot for lunch or brunch daily, starting at 10 AM: eggs Benedict or Blackstone, chicken salad with currants, soups, and sinful desserts.

Up for Breakfast (802-362-4204), 710 Main Street, Manchester. Breakfast Monday through Friday 7–noon, weekends 7–1. Bright, art-decked space with tables and a counter, an open kitchen, and blackboard menu specials—maybe a sausage, apple, and cheddar omelet, trout with eggs and hash browns, or wild turkey hash—and innovative specials later in the day as well. Worth climbing the stairs.

Mika's (802-362-8100), Avalanche Motor Lodge, Routes 11/30, Manchester. Open daily for lunch and dinner until 10 PM for fans of traditional Chinese and Japanese cuisines; the full-service sushi bar has a local following.

Village Fare Café & Bakery (802-362-2544), on Union Street just below the Equinox, Manchester Village, is open daily 6:30 AM–4 PM, from 7:30 on Sunday. Breakfast and lunch, artisan breads, and baked goods.

For pizza: **Christo's** (802-362-2408) on Main Street; **Marilyn Bruno's** (802-362-4469) on Center Hill; and **Manchester Pizza House** (802-362-3338) in the Manchester Shopping Center all offer high-quality pizza as well as salads, subs, grinders, and Italian lunches and dinners. All are in Manchester; all serve beer and wine and will deliver locally.

Elsewhere
Jonathon's Table (802-375-1021), Route 7A, Arlington. Keep your eyes peeled for the sign; the place is worth your trouble. Cheerful and done in lots of natural wood, Jonathon's Table

is attracting both a local and a tourist crowd. Jonathon serves Veal Jonathon with a sherry and mushroom sauce and Vermont rainbow trout as well as steak, ribs, and pasta. The prices are moderate and the food is good.

White Dog Tavern (802-293-5477), Route 7 north of Danby. Open for dinner Wednesday through Sunday. This is an 1812 farmhouse with a central chimney and three fireplaces, each serving as the focal point of a dining room. There's a cheery bar, and an outdoor deck in summer. The blackboard menu includes clams, shrimp, and the house special— chicken breasts à la Tom, served up with herbs, garlic, and melted cheese over spaghetti. Options might include blackened catfish and clams zuppa ($14–18).

Downstairs at the Playhouse (802-824-5288), Weston Playhouse, on the green in Weston. Open for dinner on theater nights beginning at 5:30; 5 on Sunday. A pleasant dining room by the falls, good, and then you're there. Reserve. (See also *Entertainment*.)

🍴 **The Barn Restaurant and Tavern** (802-325-3088), Route 30, Pawlet. Open daily for dinner June through October. This is a genuine old barn with a huge fireplace and a view of the Mettawee River. A large menu offers something for everybody, but it's best known for seafood and steaks. There's also a salad bar and children's menu. Moderate.

Jake's Marketplace Café (802-824-6614), Mountain Marketplace at the junction of Routes 100 and 11, Londonderry. A local institution with a lively sports lounge, a lunch counter, and a pleasant pink dining room. Overstuffed sandwiches, salads, homemade soups, burgers. Pasta,

steak, fish, personal pizzas ($11–21) are the dinner offerings. Lunch served only on weekends.

Gran'ma Frisby's (802-824-5931), Route 11 east of Londonderry. Open for lunch and dinner. When Magic Mountain Ski Area is open, you're lucky to get in the door of this wonderfully pubby place. Known for its fries and fresh-dough pizza, this is a friendly, reasonably priced find any time of year.

The Station Restaurant and Ice Cream Parlor (802-325-3041), School Street, Pawlet. Open 6 AM– 3 PM in winter, later in summer. If you think about it, railroad depots make perfect diners—with the counter and a row of stools down the length of the building and tables along the sides. This classic 1905 depot was moved here from another town and positioned above a babbling brook. It's a particularly pleasant place. Coffee cups bearing regulars' names hang by the door.

🍴 **Mulligans** (802-297-9293) at Stratton Mountain also has a Manchester Village locale (802-362-3663). This spacious, pleasant, family-priced restaurant is open for lunch and dinner; good for burgers, sandwiches, salads, and dinner options like Thai basil chicken and lobster and seafood manicotti. Children's specials include a Ninja Turtle Burger and Gorilla Cheese. There's a baked stuffed lobster special on Monday and Tuesday ($11.95 for a single), an Evening in Paris on Thursday ($12.95), and so on.

Out Back at Winhall River (802-297-FOOD), Route 30, Bondville, serves dinner daily from 5 PM, lunch on weekends, with live music on Saturday, eight beers on tap, a lengthy wine list, a children's menu, a pool table, and a game room.

The Bryant House (802-824-6287), Route 100, Weston. Now owned by the neighboring Vermont Country Store, this fine old house belonged to one family—the Bryants—from the time it was built in 1827 until the family line petered out. Upstairs, a special room is set aside to look as it did in the 1890s. There are plenty of salads, sandwiches, and Vermont-style chicken pie. Lunch served 11:30–3. Try the homemade pie.

ICE CREAM AND SNACKS **Wilcox Brothers Dairy** (802-362-1223), Route 7A south, Manchester. Some of the creamiest, most delectable flavors in Vermont are made in this family-owned and -run dairy, available at the grocery store and in a variety of local restaurants. The dairy bar doesn't have a name, but it's 7 miles south of the blinking light in Manchester on the west side of the road.

Mother Myrick's Ice Cream Parlor & Fudge Factory (802-362-1560), Route 7A, Manchester Center. Open daily 11 AM–midnight in summer; fountain treats, cappuccino, sumptuous baked goods, and handmade chocolates and fudge concocted daily.

✳ Entertainment

MUSIC **Vermont Symphony Orchestra** (1-800-VSO-9293), Riley Rink at Hunter Park, on Route 7A, Manchester Center, serves as the distinguished orchestra's permanent summer home. When it's not on tour, especially around the Fourth of July weekend, the symphony's concerts in the arena are major events. The acoustics are fine, and one side of the arena swings up and open to permit

part of the audience to picnic on a grassy bank.

Kinhaven Music School (802-824-3365), Lawrence Hill Road, Weston, a nationally recognized summer camp for young musicians, presents free concerts by students July through mid-August, Friday at 4 and Sunday at 2:30. Faculty perform Saturday at 8 PM. Performances are in the Concert Hall, high in the meadow of the school's 31-acre campus. It still looks more like a farm than a school. Picnics are encouraged.

Strattonfest (802-297-0100), Stratton Mountain, July and August. This series usually includes folk, jazz, classical, and country-western music on successive weeks.

Manchester Music Festival (802-362-1956; 1-800-639-5868), West Road, Manchester Center. A 7-week series of evening chamber music concerts in July and August, with performances at the Southern Vermont Art Center's Arkell Pavilion, Burr and Burton's Smith Center for the Arts, and the First Congregational Church in Manchester; also fall and winter performances in Manchester and Dorset.

THEATER **Dorset Playhouse** (802-867-5777; www.dorsettheatrefestival .com), Cheney Road, Dorset. The Dorset Players, a community theater group formed in 1927, actually owns the beautiful playhouse in the center of Dorset and produces winter performances there. In summer the Dorset Theatre Festival stages new plays as well as classics, performed by a resident professional group 6 days a week from June through late September.

Weston Playhouse (802-824-5288; westonplayhouse.org), 703 Main

Street, Weston. Not long after the Civil War, townspeople built a second floor in their oldest church on the green and turned the lower level into a theater, producing ambitious plays such as Richard Sheridan's *The Rivals*. Theatrics remained a part of community life, and in the 1930s, a summer resident financed the remodeling of the defunct church into a real theater. Now billed as "the oldest professional theater in Vermont," the Weston Playhouse has a company composed largely of professional Equity actors and routinely draws rave reviews. Quality aside, Weston couldn't be more off-Broadway. The pillared theater (the facade is that of the old church) fronts on a classic village common and backs on the West River, complete with a waterfall and Holsteins grazing in the meadow beyond. Many patrons come early to dine "Downstairs at the Playhouse" and linger after the show to join cast members at the Cabaret (reservations often necessary). Performances are every night except Monday (plus Wednesday and Saturday matinees), late June through Labor Day weekend, plus a fall production. Tickets run $27–38.

THE WESTON PLAYHOUSE   Kim Grant

FILM Manchester Twin Cinema (802-362-1229), Manchester Center.

✳ Selective Shopping

ANTIQUES SHOPS See *Special Events* for area antiques shows and festivals.

Gristmill Antiques (802-375-2500), Old Mill Road, East Arlington, in Candle Mill Village. Ethan Allen's cousin, Remember Baker, built a gristmill on Peter's Brook in 1764. Two hundred years later it became a candle factory. Now the building is an inviting shop representing several area dealers with an emphasis on 1800s and early-1900s period antiques. **Hayloft Collectibles** is just next door. Open daily 10–5 from July through mid-October.

The Farm Antiques (802-375-6302), on Route 313 west of Route 7A. Eighteenth- and 19th-century country painted furniture and accoutrements as well as folk art. Open year-round by appointment.

Carriage Trade Antiques Center (802-362-1125), Route 7, north of Manchester Center. Open daily, displaying quality antiques representing more than 50 dealers.

Weston Antiques Barn (802-824-4097), open daily except Wednesday. One mile north of the village. A multiple-dealer shop.

Carlson Antiques (802-867-4510), on the Dorset green. This two-story shop offers early American and Victorian furniture, paintings, glass, and china, plus textiles such as antique needlepoint pillows, hooked rugs, and fine linens. Closed Tuesday.

Danby Antiques Center (802-293-5990), Main Street, Danby. Open 10–5 daily April through December;

Thursday through Monday from January through March. Displays American country and formal furniture and accessories from 24 dealers in 11 rooms and the barn.

Equinox Mountain Antiques Center (802-362-5459), Route 7A, Sunderland. Thirty-five dealers on two floors. Open 10–5 daily.

Comollo Antiques (802-362-7188; www.vtantiques.com), 4686 Main Street, Manchester Center. Furniture, paintings, and accessories. Open daily (except Wednesday) 10–5.

ART GALLERIES West Wind Fine Art (802-366-8126), 7352 Main Street, Route 7A north, Manchester Center, is an excellent recent addition to the Manchester art scene. The gallery represents work by some fine American painters, including Richard Schmid and Nancy Guzik.

Artists Guild Gallery (802-362-4450), the Farmhouse at Manchester Marketplace, Manchester Center. A gallery of regional furniture makers, photographers, artists, and craftspeople.

Southern Vermont Arts Center (see *Museums*). In addition to solo shows held throughout the year, the SVAC hosts a Members' Show in early summer and a National Fall Exhibition. There are also outdoor sculpture shows May through October, and other special exhibits in winter.

Gallery North Star (802-362-4541), Route 7A, Manchester Village. Open daily 10–5. An offshoot of the Grafton gallery, showcasing Vermont-based artists.

Peel Gallery (802-293-5230), Route 7, 2 miles north of Danby Village. Represents 50 American artists whose

works are dramatically displayed in a restored 18th-century barn. Shows and receptions are scheduled between Memorial Day and Columbus Day. Among those represented are several nationally known artists. The gallery is open daily (except Tuesday) 10–5 year-round; open daily in July and August.

Tilting at Windmills Gallery (802-362-3022; www.tilting.com), Routes 11/30, Manchester Center. Open daily. An unusually large gallery with a wide selection of market-geared art.

Todd Gallery (802-864-5606; www.toddgallery.com), southern edge of the village of Weston. Housed in an 1840s carriage barn, this attractive gallery displays owner Robert Todd's watercolors of Vermont and Ireland. Also whimsical photography, original sculpture, and unusual pieces crafted by Vermont artists. Closed Tuesday and Wednesday.

Beside Myself Gallery, Lathrop Lane, 4 miles north of Arlington off Route 7A. Open May 15 through October 15, daily 2–5 or by appointment, this gallery displays the work of contemporary regional artists: paintings, handmade paper, sculpture, and collages.

BOOKSTORES ✍ The Northshire Bookstore (802-362-2200), Main Street, Manchester Center. Open Sunday and Monday 10–7, Tuesday through Saturday 10–9. Highly regarded as one of the most complete bookstores in New England. The Morrows have filled the venerable Colburn House with a wide range of unusually well-displayed volumes, and in summer books overflow onto the porch. An amazingly wide range of adult titles, children's books, and records are featured, along with an extraordinarily comprehensive stock of current and classic paperbacks. The store and the Manchester Historical Society cosponsor frequent author lectures and book signings. The Morrows recently doubled the size of the store and incorporated used and antiquarian books into the Northshire. They also opened the **Spiral Press Café** (802-362-9944), which serves three meals plus coffees, pastries, and other goodies.

CRAFTS SHOPS Frog Hollow at the Equinox (802-362-3321; www.frog hollow.org), a few doors north in the Equinox complex, is the third Vermont State Crafts Center, showcasing the work of state artisans, painters, sculptors, furniture makers, and jewelers.

The Porter House of Fine Crafts (802-362-4789), Green Mountain Village Shops, Manchester Center. Open daily 10–6. Unusual jewelry and handcrafts, clothing, toys, fabric art, kitchenware, alternative music.

Dorset Craft Center (802-362-8123), Route 30, Dorset. An old farmhouse has been converted into a studio showroom for baskets, pottery, candles, woodenware, stained glass, and quilts.

D. Lasser Ceramics (802-824-6183), 6405 Route 100, Londonderry. Open daily 9–6. A studio showroom with potters doing their thing, and shelves—inside and out—filled with bright pitchers and platters, bowls and vases, mugs and plates, all highly original and affordable. We're delighted with the multicolored "stix" we bought that hold either candles or flowers.

Vitriesse Glass Gallery (802-824-6634), Route 100, Weston Village.

Open daily except Tuesday. Lucy Bergamini's intricate glass-bead jewelry is very special. The gallery also carries richly colored blown-glass vessels, goblets, and perfume bottles.

Danby Marble Company (802-293-5425), Route 7 north of Danby Village, open daily May through October and from November 20 through December 30. At first glance this is just another array of marble bookends, lamps, chessboards, candleholders, trivets, and vases. Look more closely, though, and you'll find that this is a showcase for marble from throughout the East. (Danby itself is the site of what's billed as "the largest underground marble quarry in the world.") Tom Martin, owner of this store, cuts marble to whatever sizes and shapes you may desire.

Weston House Quilt Collection (802-824-3636), Route 100, Weston Village. Joanne and Richard Eggert have assembled one of the state's standout selections of both hand- and machine-made quilts and quilting fabrics, books, and notions.

Susan Sargent Designs (802-366-8017), Route 100, Weston Village. Open daily. The store features Sargent's striking designs woven into rugs, pillows, and throws. Other rugs, spreads, and curtains are also carried.

FACTORY OUTLETS Manchester merchants refuse to call these stores "outlets." Prices are slightly higher than at factory stores, but they're lower than retail. The list is lengthening quickly.

Manchester Commons and **Manchester Square,** the glass-and-wood anchor complex at and near the junction of Route 7A and Routes 11/30 in Manchester Center, presently house: Giorgio Armani, J. Crew, Baccarat,

Boston Traders, Brooks Brothers, Coach, Cole Haan, Crabtree & Evelyn, Garnet Hill, Dansk, Joan & David, Ellen Tracy, Jones New York, Donna Karan, Tommy Hilfiger, Movado, Polo/Ralph Lauren, Seiko, and Timberland, among others.

Equinox Square, a smaller complex tucked behind Friendly's, houses Burberry's and Christian Dior, among others.

Manchester Marketplace Outlet Shops (next to Dexter Shoe) harbors more shops.

Designer Outlets Center, also on Route 7A south near its junction with Routes 11/30, houses six more shops, including Anne Klein and Van Heusen.

J. K. Adams Co., Factory and Factory Store, Route 30, has a complete line of its fine wood products: sugar maple butcher blocks, knife racks, spice racks, cheese and carving boards, with complementary accessories. Discounted "seconds" on the second floor.

GENERAL STORES **The Vermont Country Store** (802-824-3184), Route 100, Weston Village. Open year-round, Monday through Saturday 9–5, but 9–6 from July through October. Established by Vrest Orton in 1946 and billed as America's first restored country store, this pioneer nostalgia venture also includes one of the country's first mail-order catalogs. The original store (actually an old Masons Hall) has since quintupled in size and spilled into four adjacent buildings. The specialty of both the catalog (which accounts for 75 percent of the company's business) and the store is the functional item that makes life easy, especially anything that's difficult to find nowadays—jumbo metal hairpins, hardwood coat hangers, slippery-elm throat lozenges, garter belts. Lyman, the present Orton-in-charge, has a penchant for newfangled gadgets, such as a plastic frame to hold baseball caps in dishwashers. He's a zealot when it comes to basics that seem to have disappeared, and he frequently finds someone to replicate them, as in the case of the perfect potato masher. The store's own line of edibles features the Vermont Common Cracker, unchanged since 1812, still stamped out in a patented 19th-century machine.

The Weston Village Store (802-824-5477), Route 100, Weston. Open daily. A country emporium catering to visitors.

J. J. Hapgood Store (802-824-5911), off Route 11, Peru. Daily 8:30–6. Nancy and Frank Kirkpatrick's genuine general store has a potbellied stove, old-fashioned counters filled with food, and some clothing staples; geared to locals as well as tourists.

Peltier's General Merchandise (802-867-4400), Route 30, Dorset Village. A village landmark since 1816: staples and then some, including almost any kind of fish on request, baking to order, Vermont products, wines, and gourmet items like hearts of palm and Tiptree jams. Because there are no lunch or snack shops in Dorset, this also serves the purpose; good for picnic fare.

Mach's General Store (802-325-3405), Route 30, Pawlet Village. The focal point of this genuine old emporium is described under Pawlet (see *Villages*), but the charm of this family-run place goes beyond its water view. Built as a hotel, it's filled with a wide variety of locally useful merchandise.

SPECIAL SHOPS **Orvis Retail Store** (802-362-3750), Route 7A, Manchester Center, supplying the needs of anglers and other sportsmen since 1856. Known widely for its mail-order catalog, Orvis has opened a luxurious new retail store done in the style of a country lodge but still specializing in the fishing rods made in the factory out back; also other fishing tackle and gear, country clothes, and other small luxury items—from silk underwear to welcome mats—that make the difference in country, or would-be country, living.

Herdsmen Leathers (802-362-2751), Manchester Center. Open daily, year-round, calling itself "New England's finest leather shop": coats, boots, shoes, and accessories; watch for sales.

Two Sisters (802-362-5112; 1-877-362-5112), 4676 Main Street, Manchester. Home furnishings including desks, lamps, dressers, furniture, slipcovers, and just about anything else you could think of for your home.

Jelly Mill Marketplace (802-362-3494; www.jellymill.com), Route 7A, Manchester Center. Open daily. The Marketplace includes the Jelly Mill Shop, the House Works, the Jewel of the Mill, and the Toy Shoppe.

Equinox Village Shops. This cluster of historic buildings across from the Equinox hotel in Manchester Village includes the Claire Murray Shop and Irish Too, a collection of Irish gifts and clothing.

Equinox Nursery, Route 7A, south of Manchester. An outstanding farm stand and nursery managed by three generations of the Preuss family; good for picking vegetables, berries in-

season. Especially famous in fall for the 100,000 pounds of pumpkins it produces, also for its display of scarecrows and pumpkin faces. Sells pumpkin bread, pie, ice cream, and marmalade, along with other farm stand staples, annuals, perennials, and shrubs. During January and February the family usually makes 1,000 jars of jams and jellies.

East Arlington is a charming hamlet of specialty shops across the street from **Candle Mill Village.** There's the **Happy Cook,** the **Rosebud Toy Company,** the **Bearatorium,** the **Village Peddler,** and the **Scandinavian Country Shop.**

Vermont Country Bird Houses (802-293-5991), Main Street, Danby. Imaginatively hand-carved birdhouses in various architectural styles, with

PELTIER'S IN DORSET

Kim Grant

steeples, cupolas, bell towers, and the like, by Jim Kardas. Open daily.

✳ Special Events

March: Spring skiing, sugaring.

April: Trout season opens; Easter parades and egg hunts at ski areas. White-water canoeing on the West River (see "Lower Connecticut and West River Valleys").

May: **Vermont Symphony Orchestra** performs at Hunter Park; Hildene opens.

June: **Strawberry festivals** in Dorset; the annual **Antique and Classic Car Show** at Hildene and **vintage sports car climb** to Equinox Summit; **Hildene Peony Festival.**

July: Manchester and Dorset host an **old-fashioned Fourth,** a daylong celebration that culminates in fireworks. The **Vermont Summer Festival Horse Show** comes to Manchester for 3 weeks.

July–mid-August: **Kinhaven Music School** concert series; **Dorset Playhouse** and **Weston Playhouse** open; a **major antiques show** is held at Hildene Meadows in even years, at Dorset in odd ones. **Manchester Music Festival.** The **Vermont Sym-**

phony Orchestra takes up residence at Hunter Park. **Strattonfest** at Stratton Mountain Resort.

August: **Southern Vermont Crafts Fair**—juried exhibitors, entertainment, food, and music at Hildene. **Wine & Food Festival** (second week) at Stratton Mountain Resort. **Norman's Attic** in Arlington is a townwide tag sale. **Storytelling Festival** (late August) at Stratton Mountain.

September: The month is chock-full of antiques shows around the area; the biggest is the annual **Vermont Antiques Dealers Association Show** at Riley Rink in Hunter Park. **Peru Fair**—just 1 day (the fourth Saturday), considered one of Vermont's most colorful (and crowded), it includes a pig roast, crafts, food, and entertainment. **Stratton Quilt Festival.**

October: **Weston Antiques Show** (first weekend), one of the state's oldest and most respected, staged in the Weston Playhouse. **Hildene Foliage Art & Craft Festival** (first week) at Hildene Meadows.

November: Harvest dinners and wild game suppers abound; check local papers and bulletin boards.

December: **Christmas Prelude** (first three weekends)—weekend events in Manchester including Vermont's largest potluck dinner, **Candlelight Tours of Hildene** (between Christmas and New Year's)—sleigh rides, refreshments in the barn, music on the organ. A **tour of the historic inns** of Manchester Village takes place the first two Saturdays of December. There's a **Winter Solstice Walk** at Merck Forest in Rupert.

THE EQUINOX NURSERY IN MANCHESTER
Kim Grant

BELLOWS FALLS, SAXTONS RIVER, AND GRAFTON

Some 40 years ago Grafton, a derelict back-roads village, was restored to picturesque perfection. Now it's nearby Bellows Falls that's reviving as a lively arts center. The two are, however, very different places. In contrast to Grafton's steepled church and stagecoach inn, the icons in Bellows Falls are a brick, Florentine-style tower and a 1920s diner.

A village of 3,165 residents within the town of Rockingham (total population: 5,309), Bellows Falls is a late-19th-century brick mill and railroad center sited at one of the largest drops in the entire length of the Connecticut River. Its buildings cascade, too, down glacial terraces so steep that steps connect the brick downtown with Victorian homes above and with surviving mill buildings down by the river. Geologists tell us that 400 to 600 million years ago two continents collided and separated at this site. Local historians say that it's no accident that this was a sacred place for Native Americans, as evidenced by carvings still visible at the foot of the Great Falls.

One of America's first canals, built in 1802 to ease river traffic around the great falls, still flows behind downtown shops, and passenger trains still rumble through the tunnel built in 1851 beneath the village square. Bellows Falls remains an Amtrak stop; rail buffs can switch here to the Green Mountain Flyer for an excursion up along the Connecticut and then the Williams River to Chester. But without a car, or at least two wheels, you will miss Grafton, the Old Rockingham Meeting House, and Saxtons River, a delightfully unrestored village that's also in the town of Rockingham, one with a first-rate summer theater.

GUIDANCE **Great Falls Regional Chamber of Commerce** (802-463-4280; www.gfrcc.org), housed in the spiffy new Waypoint Visitor Center (restrooms) on Depot Street (near the Amtrak station), is open daily 10–4. It serves the Walpole, New Hampshire, as well the Bellows Falls area. Pick up the *Guided Walking Tour* and *Building on the Past* pamphlets. The best web site for Bellows Falls tourist info is www.bellowsfalls.org.

In **Grafton** the Daniels House Gift Shop/Café (802-843-2255; www.windhamfoundation.org), behind the Old Tavern, is open daily, year-round except March and April, and doubles as a town information center with public restrooms. Pick up a walking tour brochure.

SOUTHERN VERMONT

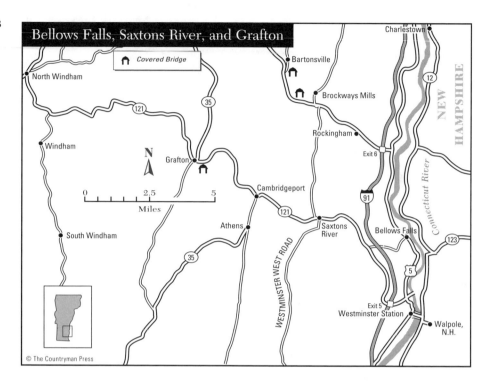

Bellows Falls, Saxtons River, and Grafton

Covered Bridge

Charlestown

Bartonsville

North Windham

Brockways Mills

NEW HAMPSHIRE

Windham

Rockingham

Grafton

Exit 6

Cambridgeport

Connecticut River

Miles

Athens

Saxtons
River

Bellows Falls

South Windham

Exit 5
Westminster Station

Walpole,
N.H.

© The Countryman Press

Southern Vermont Regional Market Association (1-877-887-2378; www.southernvermont.com). Maintains a web site and sends out printed material for this entire region.

GETTING THERE *By bus:* **Vermont Transit** buses from points in Connecticut and Massachusetts stop at Bellows Falls (at Fletcher's drugstore in the square).

By train: **Amtrak** trains stop at Bellows Falls en route to New York City and Washington. Call 1-800-USA-RAIL.

WHEN TO GO Grafton's Christmas-card look draws winter guests, but serious cross-country skiers should know that snow here can be iffy. In spring water surges over the dam in Bellows Falls, but summer brings theater to Saxtons River and it's the preferred season on both sides of the Connecticut River. Still, it's pretty quiet, with the exception of July 4 and foliage season.

MEDICAL EMERGENCY Emergency service is available by calling **911**.

Bellows Falls Health Center (802-463-1360).

✳ Villages

Bellows Falls. Viewed from above the dam at Bellows Falls, the Connecticut River resembles a glassy, narrow lake. The view from below the village, however, is very different. Instead of thundering falls, what you usually see is a power station between two narrow water channels and several bridges. The Bellows Falls Canal Co. was the first in the country to obtain a charter, and it was an amazing feat easing flatboats through a series of locks, substantially expanding navigation up the Connecticut. The creation of the canal also formed the island separating the village from the Connecticut River, which for much of the year is now reduced to a modest cascade, dropping through the 0.5-mile gorge beneath the dam. It's on the island that the 1920s railroad station stands, serving Amtrak and the Green Mountain Flyer.

In 1869 William Russell developed the novel idea of making paper from wood pulp, using logs floated down from both sides of the river. He went on to found International Paper. The canal was put to work powering mills, and it still powers turbines generating electricity.

Despite major fires, much of the village architecture dates from the 1890s, the period depicted in a building-sized mural just south of the square. Rockingham Town Hall, with its Florentine-style tower, includes the town-owned New Falls Cinema and Fletcher's Drug, the bus stop. The surrounding square is lined with a lively mix of shops and restaurants.

Bellows Falls is also known as the home of Hetty Green (1835–1916), who parlayed a substantial inheritance into a $100 million fortune; she was called the Witch of Wall Street, to which she traveled by day coach, looking like a bag lady in threadbare bombazine. The **Bellows Falls Historical Society** (802-463-4270) in the **Rockingham Free Library and Museum,** Westminster Street, is open summer Fridays 2–4 or by appointment. The **Adams Grist Mill** (open July through October, Saturday and Sunday 1–4) ground grain from 1831 until 1961; the old machinery is all in place.

Grafton. Prior to the Civil War, Grafton boasted more than 1,480 residents and 10,000 sheep. Wool was turned into 75,000 yards of Grafton cloth annually; soapstone from 13 local quarries left town in the shape of sinks, stoves, inkwells, and foot warmers. But then one in three of Grafton's men marched off to the Civil War, and few returned. Sheep farming, too, "went west." An 1869 flood destroyed the town's six dams and its road. The new highway bypassed Grafton. The town's tavern, however, built in 1801,

GRAFTON TOWN HALL

Kim Grant

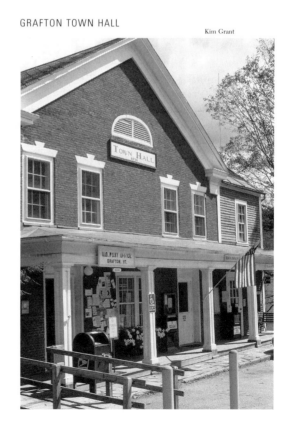

Kim Grant

entered a golden era. Innkeeper Marlan Phelps invested his entire California gold rush fortune in adding a third floor and double porches, and his brother Francis organized a still-extant cornet band. Guests included Emerson, Thoreau, and Kipling; later both Woodrow Wilson and Teddy Roosevelt visited.

By 1940, however, the Tavern was sagging, and nearly all the 80-some houses in town were selling—with plenty of acreage—for just $3,000–5,000. It wasn't until 1963 that Matthew Hall, a summer resident descended from of the town's first pastor, hit on a suitable use for the fortune his aunt Pauline Fiske had left for a worthy cause. Incorporated in 1963, the resulting Windham Foundation first focused on the town's rotting core, restoring the store, a **blacksmith shop,** and the **Old Tavern** (see *Lodging*). It went on to revive the cheese factory, to bury the village wiring, and eventually to acquire many buildings and 2,000 acres with marked footpaths on which visitors can walk or cross-country ski down past the pond, into the woods, and home again. In the Daniels House behind the Tavern, pick up a pamphlet *Walking Tour of Grafton.* The **Grafton History Museum** (802-843-1010; www.graftonhistory .org), 147 Main Street, is open daily during foliage season, weekends and holidays Memorial Day through Columbus Day 10–12 and 2–4 (admission).

✔ The **Nature Museum** (802-843-2111; www.nature-museum.org), on the Townshend Road just south of the village, is open weekends year-round 10–4. It focuses on local flora and fauna, with hands-on exhibits for children, including an underground tunnel; there are also trails to hike. The **Grafton Village Cheese Company** (802-843-2221; www.graftonvillagecheese.com) on the Townshend Road is open Monday through Friday 8:30–4, Saturday and Sunday 10–4; cheesemaking weekdays 8–11. To produce its Covered Bridge Cheddar, vats of fresh milk are heated and the curd is cut by hand, tested, drained, milled, salted, molded, and pressed before aging.

Saxtons River, like Bellows Falls, is a village in the town of Rockingham. Said to be named for a surveyor who fell into the river and drowned, it's best known as the home of the Vermont Academy (founded in 1876, a private prep school since 1932). This village of 541 souls is also not a bad place to stay, eat, and shop. The **Saxtons River Historical Museum** (802-869-2566; open summer Sundays 1–4:30) is housed in a former Congregational church built in 1836 at the western end of the village. Its collection includes art, tinware, toys, Civil War memorabilia, and a furnished Victorian parlor and kitchen.

Walpole, New Hampshire. Few villages are as historically and physically linked (by two bridges) as Bellows Falls and Walpole, New Hampshire. Bellows Falls is named for Walpole's founder, Colonel Benjamin Bellows, who owned land on both sides of the river. Walpole's village is a white wooden classic, graced by fine old churches and dozens of clapboard mansions, set high on a plateau above the river. Some buildings date from the early and mid–19th century, when this was a popular summer resort with several large inns. Louisa May Alcott wrote here, and Emily Dickinson visited. James Michener came to research the chapter of *Hawaii* about a departing missionary family. Current creative residents include filmmaker Ken Burns. The **Walpole Historical Society** (603-756-3308; open May through October, Wednesday and Saturday 2–4) is exceptional. Also see *Lodging* and *Where to Eat*.

✳ To See

COVERED BRIDGES There are four covered bridges in the area: two in Bartonsville (1.5 miles north of Route 103 and the other east off Route 103); one in Grafton; and one in Saxtons River off Route 121, noteworthy for its "flying buttresses" (replaced in 1982).

ALONG THE CONNECTICUT RIVER IN BELLOWS FALLS ⌀ The **Fish Ladder and Visitors Center** (802-463-3226) of the New England Power Company on Bridge Street in Bellows Falls is one of a series of ladders constructed on the Connecticut River to return Atlantic salmon and American shad to their native spawning grounds.

ROCKINGHAM MEETING HOUSE
Vermont's oldest unchanged public building is off Route 103 between Chester and Bellows Falls, and open Memorial Day through Columbus Day, 10–4. Built as a combination church and town hall in 1787, this Federal-style structure stands quietly above its graveyard. It's striking inside and out. Inside, "pigpen"-style pews each accommodate 10 to 15 people, some with their backs to the minister. The old burying ground is filled with thin old markers bearing readable epitaphs.

ROCKINGHAM MEETING HOUSE

Kim Grant

✎ **Native American petroglyphs.** On the Vermont side of the river, visible from the Villas Bridge. Etched into two separate rock surfaces you see a series of round heads. Note the prominent figure with a neck and shoulders and rays or feathers, assumed to denote power. Said to date in age anywhere from 300 to 2,000 years, the carvings were reportedly created by the Abenaki tribe who fished at the foot of the falls. Unfortunately they have been eroded by logging and railroad blasting and years ago were painted bright yellow to make them easier to see.

✳ To Do

BICYCLING Grafton Ponds (802-843-2400; www.graftonponds.com) in Grafton rents mountain bikes for use on dirt roads radiating from the village and on its cross-country trails.

BOATING *Peacemaker* **Cruises** (603-445-2371), 22 West Street, North Walpole, New Hampshire. Just across the bridge from Bellows Falls, Bill Gallagher offers regularly scheduled (late May through mid-October, weekends at 2) 2-hour cruises on *Peacemaker*, his canopied pontoon boat. The cruise takes you upriver between cornfields, past Herrick's Cove, a particularly beautiful spot at the confluence with the Williams River. Chances are you'll spot a blue heron in the cove and swallows soaring and swooping by the dozens around their nests in the riverbank. The boat accommodates 16, and is available for charters.

GOLF Bellows Falls Country Club (802-463-9809), Route 103, Rockingham. Scenic nine-hole course; clubhouse with bar and lunchroom.

Windham Country Club (802-875-2517; www.windhamgolf.com), 6802 Popple Dungeon Road. Formerly Tater Hill, 18 holes with a pro shop.

RAILROAD EXCURSION ✎ **Green Mountain Flyer** (802-463-3069; 1-800-707-3530; www.rails-vt.com), 54 Depot Street, Bellows Falls. Round-trips available Tuesday through Sunday in summer; daily during foliage season. Inquire about special runs. Based in the same handsome 1920s railroad station that serves Amtrak, this excursion is operated by the Green Mountain Railroad; its rolling stock includes some turn-of-the-20th-century cars. The 13-mile (one-way) route is along the Connecticut River, past covered bridges, then up the Williams River and through wooded rock cuts, which include the spectacular Brockway Mills gorge.

A MURAL IN DOWNTOWN BELLOWS FALLS

Christina Tree

SWIMMING ✦ **Grafton Swimming Pond,** Route 121, 1 mile west of the village, is an oasis for children.

CROSS-COUNTRY SKIING AND SNOWSHOEING **Grafton Ponds** (802-843-2400; www.graftonponds.com), Townshend Road, Grafton. You'll find 30 km of trails groomed both for skating and classic strides, meandering off from a log cabin warming hut, over meadows, and into the woods on Bear Hill. Snowmaking on 5 km, rentals, and instruction, plus ice skating, snow tubing, and trails specifically for snowshoeing.

✴ Lodging

INNS ∞ ♿ **The Old Tavern** (802-843-2231; 1-800-843-1801; www.old-tavern.com), Main Street, Grafton 05146, where Routes 35 and 121 intersect. The brick core of this splendid building dates from 1788, but the double-porched facade is mid–19th century. The stylish interior (vintage 1965) tastefully re-creates a formal early American setting. More than 40 rooms are divided among the inn and nearby houses, a few of which can be rented in their entirety. Guest rooms have private bath, but no TV or air-conditioning. Common rooms are formal and elegant. The Phelps Barn has a fireplaced lounge. In summer there are nearby tennis courts, platform tennis courts, and a sand-bottomed swimming pond; in winter, cross-country skiing. Youngsters are welcome in some cottages. Pets are not permitted, but you can bring your horse (there's a stable). $135–245 per room, $260–390 per suite, depending on the room and season. Inquire about houses sleeping eight or nine people.

∞ **Inn at Saxtons River** (802-869-2110; www.innsaxtonsriver.com), Main Street, Saxtons River 05154. This vintage-1903 inn with a distinctive square, five-story tower has an attractive streetside pub and a large, popular dining room (see *Dining Out*). New owners Christopher Wolf and Stuart Pease are currently in the process of redoing the 16 rooms (all with private bath). $110–135 per couple, including breakfast. Inquire about packages.

The Walpole Inn (603-756-3320; www.walpoleinn.com), Main Street, Walpole, New Hampshire 03608. Recently rehabbed, this 1760s tavern, best known for its dining, offers eight comfortable, sparely, and tastefully furnished upstairs guest rooms, some with gas fireplace. $135–165.

BED & BREAKFASTS **Readmore Bed & Breakfast & Books** (802-463-9415; www.readmoreinn.com), 1 Hapgood Street, Bellows Falls 05101. New in 2002. Dorothy and Stewart Read's splendid, Victorian house was named one of the 10 prettiest country homes in America by the *Ladies Home Journal* in 1899. The entryway is truly splendid, with a magnificent hearth, a windowed wall, and an oval opening in the middle of the ceiling to the floor above. Four of the five guest rooms are unusually spacious, all with private bath, air-conditioning, TV, radio/CD players, and feather beds, some with Jacuzzi and fireplace. The Reads are antiquarian-book dealers; rooms are themed with appropriate books (gardening, history, and so on). $150–270 includes a very full breakfast.

∞ **Inn at Cranberry Farm** (1-800-854-2208; www.cranberryfarminn .com), 61 Williams River Road (off Route 103), Chester 05143. Despite the postal address, this appealing inn is in the town of Rockingham not far from the Rockingham Meeting House, with property that extends to the Williams River. Built as an inn in the 1990s, it's been recently acquired and renovated by Carl Follo and Pam Beecher. There are 11 guest rooms and 3 two-room suites (with whirlpool tub and fireplace). The airy design of the inn, with its spacious common areas, lends itself to groups and weddings (there's a pond right outside). $139–149 for rooms, $219 for the suites.

✔ **River Mist B&B** (802-463-9023; 1-888-463-9023; www.river-mist.com), 7 Burt Street, Bellows Falls 05101. On a quiet street, this Queen Anne Victorian (1895)—recently turned "painted lady"—is high Victorian inside and out, reflecting the way the town's one-time mill owners lived. Michael, Verone, and Roger offer four lacy guest rooms with private bath, plenty of personal attention, and a very full breakfast—perhaps quiche and baked apples or stuffed French toast. $80–100 year-round, $120–150 during foliage.

✔ **The Inn at Woodchuck Farm** (802-843-2398; woodchuckhill.com), Middletown Road, Grafton 05146. Open most of the year. This 1780s farmhouse sits high on a hill, on a back road above Grafton. The porch, well stocked with comfortable wicker, has a peaceful, top-of-the-world feel, and there are views from the elegant living room and dining room, too. Operated as an inn by the Gabriel family for more than 30 years, it offers six rooms, four of them corner rooms with private bath (one with a fireplace) in the main house. In the west wing, an upstairs studio has its own kitchen and glass doors that open onto a private deck with views of the woods. Downstairs is a spacious suite with a king-sized canopy bed and a fridge, microwave, and coffeemaker sequestered in a hand-carved armoire. By the pond, the old barn has been rejigged to offer some great spaces. You can have either a double room with fireplace, two rooms with fireplace, or the whole barn with a two-story living room, woodstove, kitchen, and view of the pond. Spruce Cottage offers privacy and seclusion. Furnished in antiques, it's fully equipped and sleeps up to seven people ($375 per day). There's a sauna in the woods next to the pond, which is good for swimming, fishing, and canoeing, and the 200 rolling acres are laced with walking trails. No smoking. $89–260 B&B.

The Inn at Valley Farms (1-877-327-2855; www.innatvalleyfarms .com), 633 Wentworth Road, Walpole, New Hampshire 03608. An elegant farmhouse dating from 1774, set on a 105-acre organic farm. Common rooms are elegant, and there's an inviting sunporch and gardens. In addition to attractive guest rooms and suites in the house, you'll find a pair of three-bedroom cottages. $130–145 for rooms, $165 for the two-room garden suite and for the cottages. Guests can pick their own produce and flowers in-season or visit with the farm's cashmere goats, Angora rabbits, pigs, cows, and pets.

✳ Where to Eat

DINING OUT Oona's (802-463-9830), 15 Rockingham Street, Bellows Falls.

Open Monday through Saturday for lunch and dinner, live entertainment Thursday, jazz and folk music Saturday, tapas and guitar music Wednesday. Oona Madden's storefront restaurant is the heart of the new Bellows Falls. It's colorful and comfortable, with an eclectic menu that changes daily, moderate at lunch and upscale at dinner. It might include pan-seared lamb chops with an orange-brandy demiglaze, and a creamy barley risotto with shiitake and portobello mushrooms, sea scallops, cheddar, crisp bok choy, and beets. Entrées $17.50–25.50.

The Old Tavern (802-843-2231), Main Street, Grafton, serves breakfast and dinner daily in the formal dining rooms or in the more casual Pine and Garden rooms. Reviews celebrate the food and wine to be sampled in this formal old dining room amid fine portraits and Chippendale chairs. A spring menu might include roast lamb chop with morels, fiddleheads, and a white wine demiglaze with herbed popover and sautéed green beans. The wine list is both extensive and reasonably priced. Entrées $24–31.

Inn at Saxtons River (802-869-2110), Main Street, Saxtons River. Open for dinner except Monday; Sunday brunch in summer. This attractive inn's dining room gets mostly good reviews. The à la carte menu is unusually large. You might dine on pan-seared salmon fillet with leek confit, crispy onion, roasted garlic, and mashed potatoes; pan-roasted breast of duck; or grilled miso-marinated portobello mushroom with spicy peanut noodles, sautéed veggies, and ginger. Entrées $17–24. This is

GRAFTON'S OLD TAVERN

Kim Grant

the obvious spot to dine before productions at the Saxtons River Playhouse around the corner.

☞ **Leslie's** (802-463-4929), Rockingham, Route 5 just south of I-91, exit 6. Open nightly except Tuesday. Reservations appreciated. John Marston opened his restaurant in a 1790s tavern back in 1985 and continues to create new and eclectic dishes, fusing many influences with experience and using as much home-grown produce as possible. Veal and organically raised chicken are served a variety of ways, and there's always a vegetarian plate. Signature dishes include a pork and crab napoleon (layerings of crab and pork medallions) served in a mushroom cream sauce, and his Thai-style shrimp curry. Entrées $16–25.

Worth crossing the river for

The Walpole Inn (603-756-3320; www.walpoleinn.com), Main Street, Walpole, New Hampshire. Open for dinner. A traditional, beamed dining room with nicely spaced tables and a menu with an enviable reputation. The summer menu might range from a crispy duck and ginger salad to seafood Newburg (lobster, shrimp, and scallops) in puff pastry with jasmine rice: $17–28. The specialty, served Friday and Saturday, is herb-crusted prime rib.

The Restaurant and Café at Burdick Chocolates (603-756-2882; www.laburdick.com), 47 Main Street, Walpole, New Hampshire. Café open 7 AM–8 PM daily (until 6 Sunday and Monday); restaurant open Monday through Saturday noon–2:30 for lunch, Tuesday through Saturday 5:30–9 for dinner, and Sunday for brunch 10–3. This is home base for the nationally known chocolatier with

cafés in Cambridge and Edgartown, Massachusetts. The restaurant offers an upscale lunch as well as dinner menu. The menus change daily; on an October day the lunch menu included pan-seared scallops with red pepper coulis, green beans, and lentils, as well as steamed mussels in a spicy tomato broth with *pommes frites* (entrées $9–11.50); on the dinner menu was grilled Black Angus rib-eye steak with bordelaise sauce, served with Parmesan polenta and arugula (entrées $15–19.75). The café menu features pastries to complement the house chocolates.

EATING OUT *Note:* Also see Oona's (under *Dining Out*) for lunch.

Happy Cat Cafe (802-376-6446), 13 Rockingham Street, Bellows Falls. Open daily 9–3. Jenny Veitch has created a great little café. Stop by weekday mornings for latte or chai tea and baked goods, or lunch on the soup or quiche of the day, salads or design-your-own sandwiches. On Sunday morning, breakfast sandwiches and omelets are served. Freshly baked LaBrea breads are also sold.

Log Jam Restaurant (802-463-3337; 1-800-9-LOGJAM), 117 Rockingham Street, Bellows Falls (across from Brooks). Open Tuesday through Saturday for dinner; check for lunch. Fully air-conditioned. This is all about flapping-fresh fish, but steaks are on the menu, too.

Miss Bellows Falls Diner (802-463-9800), 90 Rockingham Street, Bellows Falls. Open daily from 6 AM through dinner. Inside and out this Worcester Diner #771 is still pure, unhokey 1920s.

Joy Wah (802-463-9761), Rockingham Road (Route 5), Bellows Falls.

Full-service Chinese fare in a Victorian farmhouse perched on a knoll overlooking the Connecticut River; includes all the familiar dishes on its lengthy menu. Open daily for lunch and dinner.

♪ **Anatolia** (802-869-7778), 33 Main Street, Saxtons River. Open daily 11–10:30. As the name suggests Somet and Michrican Eroglu are from Turkey, hence the gyro plate offered along with a variety of pizzas, grinders, burgers, and pastas. Anatolia recently migrated to Saxtons River from Bellows Falls and offers free delivery from Grafton to Bellows Falls and points south.

China Wok (802-463-9885), 92 Rockingham Street, Bellows Falls. Open daily for lunch and dinner. No MSG and a pleasant atmosphere combine with a wide, reasonably priced selection.

Golden Egg (802-869-2300), 16 Main Street, Saxtons River. Open Tuesday through Saturday 7–2:30, dinner Friday 5–8:30. In addition to the breakfast and lunch basics are plenty of Mexican offerings: breakfast burritos, huevos rancheros, tacos, quesadillas, and more. Great local rep.

Daniels House Café (802-843-2255), Townshend Road, Grafton. Just behind the Old Tavern and attached to the village's information center/gift shop. Open for lunch with soups, salads, and sandwiches.

✷ Entertainment

THEATER AND FILM ♪ **Saxtons River Playhouse** (802-869-2030), Westminster West Road, Saxtons River Village. Late June through August, musicals and popular plays, Monday through Saturday at 8 PM;

Sunday at 7. Also some matinees and children's theater on Thursday and Friday at 2, as well as after-show cabarets.

New Falls Cinema (802-463-4766), on the square in Bellows Falls, operated by the Rockingham recreation department, shows first-run flicks Friday through Tuesday for $3 ($1.50 on bargain days). This fine old vaudeville house is also the venue for live performances.

Front Porch Theater Company (802-463-9791; www.frontporch theater.org). A community theater group performs in town hall during the school year. Not to be confused with **The Front Porch Summer Entertainment Series,** which features varied musical and performance groups, usually staged Friday at 7 PM on various Bellows Falls porches. For details, contact Village Square Booksellers (see *Selective Shopping*).

MUSIC The **Flying under Radar Series** folk music Thursday evening at Oona's Restaurant is now a stop on the national folk music circuit.

The **Grafton Cornet Band** performs in either Grafton or Chester (some-

THE MISS BELLOWS FALLS DINER
Alan Fowler

times in Townshend) on summer weekends.

ARTS Main Street Arts (802-869-2960), Main Street, Saxtons River. This local arts council sponsors dance and musical performances, parades, cabarets, recitals, and a midwinter solstice celebration (The Revels) as well as art classes and the Jelly Bean crafts shop.

✳ Selective Shopping

ANTIQUES SHOPS Grafton Gathering Places Antiques (802-875-2309), 748 Eastman Road, open year-round daily except Tuesday. A two-story country barn filled with early country and period furniture and accessories. **Sign of the Raven** (802-869-2500), Route 121 east (Main Street), Saxtons River. Open 10–5 (by chance or appointment—call ahead). Antiques and fine American paintings.

GALLERIES

In Bellows Falls
Note: The third Friday of every month, April through December, Bellows Falls stages an Art Gallery Walk 5–8 PM. In addition to the galleries listed below, changing artwork is also displayed in Oona's Restaurant, Green's Fresh Fruits & Vegetables (on Village Square), and Village Square Booksellers.
Three Rivers Gallery (802-463-1991), Canal Street in the Exner Block. A showcase for the best of local art, custom furniture, and decorative accessories.
Spheris Gallery (802-463-2220; www.spherisgallery.com), 59 The Square. Open Tuesday through Saturday 10–5:30. Cynthia Reeves has

recently moved her sophisticated gallery here from Walpole. Top contemporary artists are featured.
The Richter Gallery Arts & Antiques (802-463-2049; www.richtergallery.com), 2 Village Square; also 3 Westminster Street. Open daily. Stephen Zeigfinger has solved the perennial artist's problems—regular income and studio space. Having bought and sold art and antiques since 1967, he is now focusing on his own art, which he works on while also staffing one of the two antiques-filled stores. His wife, Allison Richter, a custom framer, maintains the handsome frame and print shop across the way.
The Framery of Vermont (802-463-3295), 115 Rockingham Street. The particular focus here is the Connecticut River Valley, its landscape, flora, and fauna.
Great River Arts Institute (802-463-3330; www.greatriverarts.org), 95 Rockingham Street. Workshops in writing and a variety of visual arts are offered. Check current calendar for lectures, special events. Changing art exhibits.

In Saxtons River and Grafton
Gallery North Star (802-843-2465; www.northstar.com), 151 Townshend Road, Grafton Village. Open daily except Tuesday. Six rooms in this Grafton Village house are hung with landscapes and graphic prints, oils, watercolors, and sculpture.
Jud Hartmann Gallery (802-843-2018), by the Brick Church on Main Street, Grafton. Open 10–5 mid-September through foliage season and again in December for the holidays. Hartmann began his career as a sculptor in Grafton and has since won

national acclaim for his bronze renditions of Native Americans. He divides his time among studios here, in Maine, and in the Southwest.

CRAFTS **Jelly Bean Tree** (802-869-2326), Main Street, Saxtons River. Open April through December, daily noon–5. A crafts cooperative run by local artisans and carrying the work of many more on consignment: pottery, macramé, leather, weaving, batik, and hand-sewn, -knit, and -crocheted items.

Coyote Moon Jewelry & Imports (802-463-9529), 11 Canal Street, Bellows Falls. Open daily except Sunday. Intriguing gifts from throughout the world with an emphasis on Mexico, and sterling-silver jewelry.

SPECIAL SHOPS **Vermont Country Store** (www.vermontcountrystore .com), Route 103, Rockingham Village. An offshoot of the famous Vermont Country Store in Weston, this is also owned by Lyman Orton and houses a Common Cracker machine, which visitors can watch as it stamps out the hard round biscuits. The store also sells whole-grain breads and cookies baked here, along with a line of calico material, soapstone griddles, woodenware gadgets, natural-fiber clothing, and much more. There's also an upstairs bargain room.

Village Square Booksellers (802-463-9404; www.villagesquarebooks .com), 32 The Square, Bellows Falls. Open Monday through Saturday 9–6, Friday until 7, and Sunday 10–3. Patricia Fowler's independent, full-service bookstore offers poetry readings and other special programs, and also features local photography by Alan Fowler and changing work by local artists.

Sam's Outdoor Outfitters (802-463-3500; www.samsoutdoor.com), 78 The Square, Bellows Falls, bills itself as "the biggest little store in the world." A branch of the Brattleboro store but still big.

Caboose Corner (802-463-4575), 676 Missing Link Road, Route 5, Bellows Falls. Open year-round, Wednesday through Sunday noon–8. Model trains and accessories in an old Rutland Railroad caboose.

Allen Brothers Farms & Orchards (802-722-3395), 6-23 Route 5, 2 miles south of Bellows Falls. Open year-round, daily, 6 AM–9 PM. Offers pick-your-own apples and potatoes in-season, also sells vegetables, plants and seeds, honey, syrup, and Vermont gifts.

Also see Grafton Village Cheese Company, described under *Villages*.

✳ Special Events
Note: Check www.bellowsfalls.org for current happenings.

May–December: Downtown **Bellows Falls Art Walk,** third Friday of each month.

July 4 weekend: A big **parade** in Saxtons River and fireworks supplied by the Lisai family.

Early August: **Old Home & Transpo Days,** Bellows Falls. A full weekend of events—railroad excursions, live entertainment, art show, Rockingham Meeting House Pilgrimage, more fireworks.

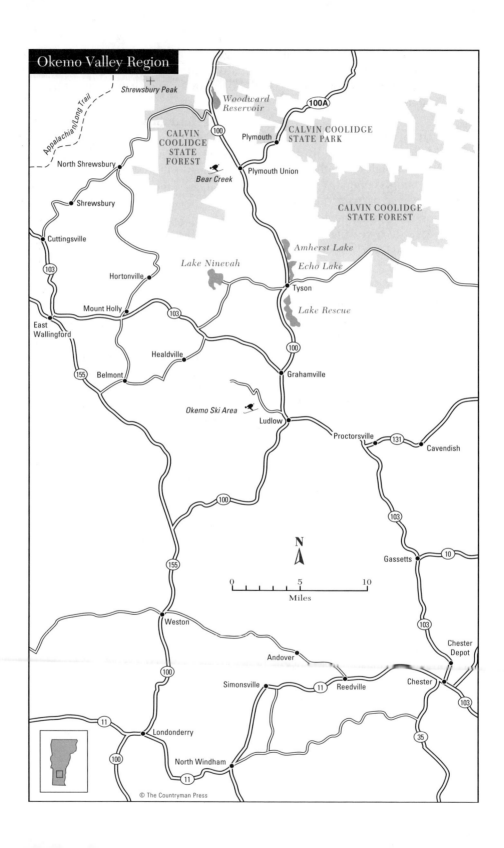

Okemo Valley Region

Shrewsbury Peak
Appalachian/Long Trail
Woodward Reservoir
100A
CALVIN COOLIDGE STATE FOREST
Plymouth
CALVIN COOLIDGE STATE PARK
North Shrewsbury
100
Bear Creek
Plymouth Union
Shrewsbury
CALVIN COOLIDGE STATE FOREST
Cuttingsville
103
Amherst Lake
Echo Lake
Lake Ninevah
Hortonville
Tyson
Mount Holly
103
Lake Rescue
East Wallingford
Healdville
100
155
Belmont
Grahamville
Okemo Ski Area
Ludlow
Proctorsville
131
Cavendish
100
103
N
Gassetts
10
5
0   5   10
Miles
155
103
Weston
Chester Depot
100
Andover
11
155
Simonsville
Reedville
Chester
103
11
Londonderry
35
100
North Windham
11

© The Countryman Press

OKEMO VALLEY REGION
INCLUDING LUDLOW AND CHESTER

O kemo is the name of a mountain, not a valley, but it's a popular ski mountain and in this is this era of "branding" the label applies to a large and varied region. Okemo towers 3,300 feet above Ludlow, a lively village on the eastern edge of the Green Mountains. North of town Route 100 threads a chain of lakes, through a steep-sided valley, and Route 103 angles off to climb west through Mount Holly to Belmont or Hortonville and Shrewsbury, beautiful high country. To the east Route 131 follows the Black River through the small mill villages of Proctorsville and Cavendish, and Route 103 shadows the Williams River south to Chester, the region's other handsome old crossroads community.

GUIDANCE **Okemo Valley Regional Chamber of Commerce** (802-228-5830; www.okemovalleyvt.org), P.O. Box 333, Ludlow 05149. This walk-in information office in the Marketplace, across from Okemo Mountain Access Road on Route 103 (look for the clock tower), has menus, events listings, and lodging brochures. The chamber also maintains a seasonal information booth on the green in Chester (802-875-2939). Restrooms both places. Request the current issue of the *Okemo Valley Regional Guide*. For lodging in the Chester area, also check out www.chesterlodging.com; for other area lodging, www.okemo.com.

GETTING THERE *By bus:* **Vermont Transit** (802-862-9671) stops two times per day in Ludlow at the Okemo Marketplace en route from Boston to Rutland.

By air: See "Rutland and Lower Champlain River Valley" for service from Boston.

GETTING AROUND **George's Shuttle Service** (1-800-208-3933), based in Weathersfield, provides transport by reservation to and from the railroad stations in Bellows Falls and Rutland and airports throughout New England.

Okemo Mountain Resort (802-228-4041) offers a free shuttle to the village during peak times in ski season.

Ludlow Transport is a free shuttle service that runs several routes throughout Ludlow and the surrounding area. The service operates Monday through Friday. Pick up the schedule at the chamber of commerce.

WHEN TO GO Nearby lakes make Ludlow as much of a summer place to be as Chester and the hill towns. In winter, Okemo is the big draw; cross-country skiers also head for Andover and Shrewsbury.

MEDICAL EMERGENCY Emergency service is available by calling **911.**

Ludlow Health Center (802-228-4362), 8 Main Street, is open daily with emergency care. **Springfield Hospital** (802-885-2151), 25 Ridgewood Road, Springfield, offers 24-hour emergency care. Also see "Rutland and the Lower Champlain River Valley."

✳ Town and Village

Ludlow (population: 2,700) boomed with the production of "shoddy" (fabric made from reworked wool) after the Civil War, a period frozen in the red brick of its commercial block, Victorian mansions, magnificent library, and academy (now the Black River Museum). In the wake of the wool boom, the General Electric Company moved into the steepled mill at the heart of town and kept people employed making small-aircraft engine parts until 1977. Okemo opened in 1956, but for years it was a sleeper—a big mountain with antiquated lifts on the edge of a former mill town. Ski clubs nested in the Victorian homes, and just a few inns catered to serious skiers. Tim and Diane Mueller bought the ski area in 1982, and it has been evolving ever since as one of New England's most popular ski resorts, known for the quality of its snowmaking, grooming, and on-mountain lodging and other facilities. A major golf course has recently been added that doubles as a full-service cross-country ski center.

The effect on Ludlow has been dramatic. The old General Electric plant has been turned into condominiums. Other lodging options as well as restaurants have multiplied. For a sense of Ludlow B.O. (Before Okemo) visit the **Fletcher Library** (802-228-8921), Main Street, Ludlow. Open Monday through Friday 10–5:30, Saturday 10–1 and 6:30–8:30, it offers reading rooms with fireplaces; old-style, green-shaded lights; and 19th-century paintings of local landscapes. The **Black River Academy Historical Museum** (802-228-5050), at the corner of Smith and High Streets, is open June through Labor Day, Tuesday through Sunday noon–4, then through mid-October just Friday and Saturday, same hours. $2 adults, free under age 12. A steepled, brick school building, built in 1889, the academy's reputation drew students from throughout New England. One large room is dedicated to President Calvin Coolidge, class of 1890. Other rooms in the four-story building are filled with exhibits about mining, lumbering, railroading, farming, and other segments in the history of the Black River Valley.

Lake Pauline and Lake Rescue harbor rental cottages, as do Lake Ninevah in nearby Mount Holly and Echo and Amherst Lakes, which are just north of the town line. In warm-weather months, however, Ludlow's big attraction is its location and abundant rental housing stock, making it an ideal base from which to explore much of southern and central Vermont.

Chester (population: 2,700) encompasses three distinct villages within a few miles, each of them worth noting. The village of Chester itself is a beauty, sited at the confluence of three branches of the Williams River and of five major roads. Its stringbean-shaped village green is lined with shops and restaurants, including the double-porched old Fullerton Inn. Across the street (Route 11) is a fine old brick schoolhouse, its ground floor now occupied by the **Chester Art Guild** (802-875-3767; staffed daily by volunteers from June through October), with changing exhibits and frequent special events. Upstairs the **Chester Historical Society** (802-875-6211; open June through October, Saturday and Sunday 2–5) presents the town's colorful history, including the story of Clarence Adams, a prominent citizen who broke into more than 50 businesses and homes between 1886 and 1902 before being apprehended.

Don't miss Chester's **Stone Village** up on North Street (Route 103): a double line of 30 buildings faced in gneiss, a rough-hewn, gleaming mica schist quarried from nearby Flamstead Mountain. Cool in summer, warm in winter, stone houses are a rarity in New England. All of these are said to have been built by two brothers in the pre–Civil War decade, with hiding spaces enough to make them a significant stop on the Underground Railroad.

Midway between Main and North Streets is **Chester Depot,** a pleasant old traffic center that resembles neither of these places. The well-kept Victorian depot serves as the northern terminus for the Green Mountain Flyer (see *To Do*), spilling more than 100 passengers at a time to browse and stroll.

SCENIC DRIVE From Ludlow head north 2 miles on Route 100, then west on 103 for 5 miles to Healdville and the sign for the Crowley Cheese Factory. In the 1880s every Vermont town had its cheese factory to process surplus milk, but Crowley Cheese, which the family had begun making in the 1820s, was distributed up and down the East Coast. The three-story wooden building, built in 1882 by Winfield Crowley, is now billed as America's oldest cheese factory. It's a 2-mile detour down a side road but well worth the effort. Visitors are welcome weekdays, 8–4, to watch the shower-capped employees "cutting," "raking," and otherwise turning 5,000 pounds of fresh milk into 500 pounds of cheese (see *Selective Shopping*).

CROWLEY CHEESE FACTORY IN HEALDVILLE

Christina Tree

Route 103 climbs on to **Mount Holly,** then continues anther 5 miles to Cuttingsville. U.S. senator Jim Jeffords lives nearby and can frequently be found at the Over Easy Restaurant. Turn up the road ("Town Hill") posted for Shrewsbury, a gem of a town with dense forest and long vistas, seemingly on the roof of this area that straddles central and southern Vermont. **Shrewsbury Center** is marked by a white wooden church set back on a knoll beside two face-to-face taverns, now both B&Bs. One of these, Maple Crest Farm, remains in the same family that built it in 1808 and has been taking in guests since the 1860s. Although the dairy herd is gone, this is still a working farm with more than 30 head of beef cattle and some 300 acres in hay. Stop and take in the view and the quiet. In **North Shrewsbury,** 2 more miles up the hill, is the **W. E. Pierce General Store** (presently closed), with a '50s gas pump out front. A sign across the road points to Meadowsweet Herb Farm just down Eastham Road. Here Polly Haynes sells the herbal blends and vinegars, potpourri, party dips, and more and maintains display gardens (see *Selective Shopping*). The farm's brochure directs visitors back down dirt roads to Mount Holly, but adventurous and careful drivers (with good brakes) should head back up to North Shrewsbury and take the right just past the store. This is **CCC Road,** one of Vermont's steepest and most scenic routes, open in summer only. It's 6 miles seemingly straight down— with superlative mountain and valley views—to Route 100 in Plymouth.

Turn south (right) onto Route 100 for 2 miles and left onto Route 100A to **Plymouth Notch,** perhaps the first rural Vermont village to appear in publications throughout the world—on August 2, 1923, the day Calvin Coolidge was sworn into office here as the 30th U.S. president. It's now the **Calvin Coolidge Historic Site** (for a full description, see "Killington/Plymouth Area"). Make your way back to Route 100; from Plymouth it's a scenic 9-mile ride south past a chain of lakes to Ludlow.

✳ To Do

BIKING Mountain Cycology (802-228-2722), Ludlow, across from the Grand Union. No rentals but equipment, repair, guidebooks, and local advice as well as sales.

Bike Vermont (1-800-257-2226; www.BikeVermont.com) offers a choice of inn-to-inn tours in this area.

BOATING Echo Lake Inn (802-228-8602), Route 100, Tyson, rents canoes and other boats to guests only. Rentals are also available at **Camp Plymouth State Park** (802-672-3612) off Route 100 in Tyson. Nearby Lake Ninevah is quieter, with some beautiful marshes and woods. **Hawk Inn and Mountain Resort** (802-672-3811) in Plymouth also rents boats.

FISHING Public access has been provided to Lake Rescue, Echo Lake, Lake Ninevah, Woodward Reservoir, and Amherst Lake. Fishing licenses are required except under age 16. The catch includes rainbow trout, bass, and pickerel. There is also fly-fishing in the Black River along Route 131 in Cavendish, and the 6-mile stretch from the green metal bridge in Downers to the covered bridge is stocked and maintained as a trophy trout section, stocked each spring with 1.5-pound brown trout and 18-inch rainbows.

GOLF The **Okemo Valley Golf Club** (802-228-1396), Fox Lane, Ludlow. An 18-hole championship "heathland-style" course featuring wide fairways with dips, ripples, rolls, and hollows said to suggest Scottish links. The Golf Academy also utilizes an 18-acre outdoor Golf Learning Center with a 370-yard-long driving range and four practice greens. Also look for the Golf Operations & Academy Center, with a 6,000-square-foot indoor practice area, a computerized virtual golf program, classrooms, and changing rooms with showers. The Club House includes a fully stocked Pro Shop and Willie Dunne's Grille (see *Eating Out*).

Windham Golf Club (802-875-2517; www.windhamgolf.com), 6802 Popple Dungeon Road, Windham (off Route 11, not far from Chester). An 18-hole course with a pro shop and practice range.

Crown Point Country Club (802-885-1010), Weathersfield Center Road, Springfield. An 18-hole course with pro shop, golf lessons, driving range, restaurant, and banquet facilities.

HORSEBACK RIDING AND HORSE-DRAWN RIDES **Cavendish Trail Horse Rides** (802-226-7821), Twenty Mile Stream Road, Proctorsville, offers guided tours and pony rides. Trail rides are offered at **Hawk Inn and Mountain Resort** on Route 100 in Plymouth (see "Killington/Plymouth Area"). **Ludlow Carriage Company** (802-228-5283) offers scenic carriage rides in summer and fall, Wednesday, Thursday, and Saturday 6–9 PM. Every half hour the ride begins at Gazebo Park, tours the village of Ludlow, and crosses the Black River. $30 per ride for up to four adults.

RAILROAD EXCURSION ✿ **Green Mountain Flyer** (802-463-3069; 1-800-707-3530; www.rails-vt.com), 54 Depot Street, Bellows Falls. From late June through Labor Day, one daily round-trip; twice daily during foliage season. $12 round-trip for adults, $8 per child 3–12. Rolling stock includes some turn-of-the-20th-century cars. The 13-mile (one way) route to Chester Depot is along the Connecticut River, past covered bridges, then up the Williams River and through wooded rock cuts, which include the spectacular Brockway Mills gorge.

SELF-IMPROVEMENT VACATIONS **Fletcher Farm School for the Arts and Crafts** (802-228-8770), Route 103 east, Ludlow. Operated since 1948 by the Society of Vermont Craftsmen, this old farmstead on the eastern edge of town offers dorm-style lodging and pleasant studio space for the 150 classes held during July and August. Subjects include early American decoration, stained glass, basketry, weaving, woodcarving, quilting, oil and watercolor painting, spinning, and rug hooking and braiding. Meals are family-style.

SWIMMING ✿ **West Hill Recreation Area** (802-228-2849), West Hill off Route 103 in Ludlow, includes a beach (with lifeguard) on a small, spring-fed reservoir; also a snack bar and playground/picnic area.

Buttermilk Falls, near the junction of Routes 100 and 103. This is a swimming hole and a series of small but beautiful falls (turn at the VFW post just west of the intersection).

✿ **Camp Plymouth State Park** (802-672-3612), off Route 100 at Tyson. Beach on Echo Lake, picnic area, food concession, volleyball, horseshoes, and playground, but no lifeguard.

Star Lake in the village of Belmont in Mount Holly is also a great place for a swim.

✳ Winter Sports

CROSS-COUNTRY SKIING Okemo Valley Nordic Center (802-228-8871), junction of Routes 100 and 103, Ludlow. A café and a rental shop are surrounded by the open roll of the golf course; there are also wooded and mountain trails adding up to 28 km (including 20 km of skating lanes), plus 10 km of dedicated snowshoe trails. The clubhouse offers a fireplace, restaurant and lounge, changing rooms, and showers. Rentals. $18 adult, $15 junior.

Also see Grafton Ponds in Grafton (in "Bellows Falls, Saxtons River, and Grafton") and Viking Nordic Centre in Londonderry (in "Manchester and the Mountains").

DOWNHILL SKIING ✎ **Okemo** (information: 802-228-4041; snow reports: 802-228-5222; reservations: 1-800-78-OKEMO; www.okemo.com). A big mountain (boasting Vermont's fourth highest vertical drop), Okemo is a destination ski and snowboard resort with a small-resort feel. Jackson Gore is the big news for the 2003–04 season, with a $55 million base area infrastructure and trail network scheduled to debut. The Jackson Gore Inn is a new lodging option, with its own fitness center, restaurants, and other amenities. Jackson Gore, Okemo's fifth peak, has 16 trails adding 30 percent more terrain to the resort.

Overall, Okemo is far larger than it looks from its base. Surprises begin at the top of the initial chairlifts, where you meet a wall of three-story condominiums and find your way down to the spacious Sugar House base lodge—from which the true size of the mountain becomes apparent. This is a ski area of many parts. Beginners and lower-intermediate skiers can enjoy both the lower southwest and upper northeast sides of the mountain—entirely different places in view and feel.

A VIEW OF OKEMO MOUNTAIN AND ITS TRAILS

From the summit, beginners can actually run a full 4.5 miles to the base. Expert skiers, on the other hand, have the entire northwestern face of the mountain, served by its own chair. There are also a number of wide, central fall-line runs down the face of Okemo. World Cup is a long and steep but forgiving run with sweeping views down the Black River Valley to the Connecticut River. Solitude Peak, with snowmaking on eight trails served by a quad chair, is another haven with long cruisers, bump runs, beginner terrain, and the Solitude Village. Recent enhancements include a 420-foot-long superpipe and a recently renovated Snow Stars Center for kids.

Lifts: 18: 9 quad chairs (including 3 high-speed), 3 triple chairs, and 6 surface lifts. *Trails and slopes:* 113 trails and glades covering 600 acres—25 percent novice, 50 percent intermediate, 25 percent advanced expert. *Vertical drop:* 2,150 feet (highest in southern Vermont). *Snowmaking:* Covers 95 percent of trails (495 acres). *Facilities:* Base lodge with cafeteria; midmountain Sugar House base lodge with cafeteria; summit lodge and cafeteria; Solitude Day Lodge. *Note:* **Gables,** in the Solitude Day Lodge, run by the New England Culinary Institute, is not your usual cafeteria (open 11–3). *Ski school:* Okemo's Cutting Edge Learning Center is staffed by 250 instructors. Children's programs include Snow Star Skiers (age 4–7), Young Mountain Explorers (7–12), and Get Altitude (3–16). Children's snowboard programs are Snow Star Riders (5–7) and Young Riders (7–12). Ski and snowboard programs include Women's Ski Spree and Adult Snowboard Camps. Senior discounts available on group lessons; an Adaptive Program includes discounted ski and snowboard lessons (reservations required) and tickets. The state-approved Penguin Day Care Center serves children 6 weeks–8 years and offers supervised indoor and outdoor activities. A Mini Stars ski program is also available for ages 3 and 4. Inquire about Kids' Night Out evening programs, available 6–10 PM in-season. *Lift tickets:* Adult $59 midweek, $65 weekend; ages 13–18, $51 midweek, $55 weekend; 7–12, $38 and $42. Kids 6 and under ski free. Savings on multiday tickets are substantial.

SNOWMOBILE RIDES *⌀* **Okemo Snowmobile Tours** (802-422-2121; 1-800-FAT-TRAK; www.snowmobilevermont.com) at Okemo Mountain Resort. The "Mountain Tour" is a casual tour through the woods (good for small children), while the "Radical Ride" is an adventurous half-hour journey for beginner through expert.

✳ Lodging

RESORTS **Okemo Mountain Resort** (802-228-4041; 1-800-78-OKEMO; www.okemo.com) is a ski resort that's open year-round, with nearly 700 on-mountain condominiums and a new 18-hole golf course as well as a variety of weatherproofed sports facilities. See *Condominiums* (below) and *Downhill Skiing* (above).

Also see Hawk Inn and Mountain Resort in Plymouth, described in "Killington/Plymouth Area."

INNS ∞ **The Andrie Rose Inn** (802-228-4846; 1-800-223-4846; www.andrieroseinn.com), 13 Pleasant Street, Ludlow 05149. Michael and Irene Maston preside over this complex on a quiet back street with unexpectedly luxurious rooms and suites and a reputation for fine dining. The inn itself is a turn-of-the-20th-century house in which the old detailing has been carefully preserved, but the feel—thanks to skillful decor and skylights—is light-filled and cheerful. Five of the nine upstairs guest rooms have whirlpool tub, and all are furnished with antiques and designer linens. Summit View features a skylight framing the summit of the mountain. Next door the Federal-style Guesthouse contains townhouse suites geared to families (each with kitchen facility and washer/dryer) as well as suites for two; also next door is Solitude, an 1840s Greek Revival building with seven luxury suites featuring bedside whirlpool tub for two facing a gas fireplace. See *Dining Out* for details about the $38 per-person prix fixe menu. Guests in the main house breakfast in the dining room, while those without kitchen facilities in the neighboring buildings receive breakfast in a basket. Amenities include shuttle service to and from Okemo. Rates are $90–350 in low season, $120–725 in high season.

⊙⊙ **The Inn at Water's Edge** (802-228-8143; 1-800-706-9736; www.innatwatersedge.com), 45 Kingdom Road, Ludlow 05149. The aforementioned water is Echo Lake, and Bruce and Tina Verdrager have taken full advantage of the location, offering canoeing and fly-fishing as well as bicycles for guests. The 11 rooms and suites are well appointed, many with Jacuzzi. Doc's English Pub is a good spot for lounging, and guests may sit down to a four-course candlelit dinner each evening. Rates are $175–275 MAP; the B&B rate is $50 less per room.

⊙⊙ **Echo Lake Inn** (802-228-8602; 1-800-356-6844; www.echolakeinn .com), Route 100 in Tyson, but the mailing address is P.O. Box 154, Ludlow 05149. One of the few survivors of the many Victorian-style summer hotels (although parts of the building predate the Victorian era) that once graced Vermont lakes, the inn is four stories tall with a long white porch, lined in summer with pink geraniums and red rockers. Now winterized, it offers 23 rooms, all with private bath, and seven condo units in the adjacent Carriage House. The living room is homey and informal, with hooked rugs and wooden chairs grouped around the fireplace and TV. There's also the inviting Stone Tavern and a low-beamed dining room (see *Dining Out*), both open to the public. Summer facilities include tennis courts and a pool. At the dock on Echo Lake across the road, rowboats and canoes are available to guests. $99–269 B&B, more on holidays and in foliage season. Inquire about MAP rates and special packages.

The Fullerton Inn (802-875-2444), 40 The Common, P.O. Box 188, Chester 05143. Brett and Nancy Rupp now own this big, old-fashioned, 1920s-style hotel, and they have renovated guest rooms, adding sitting rooms and ceiling fans. Common space includes the immense old lobby, a huge stone fireplace, and Ye Olde Bradford Tavern as well as the formal dining room (see *Dining Out*) and a sunny breakfast room. $99–159 double.

⊙⊙ **The Castle** (802-226-7222; 1-800-697-7222; www.thecastle-vt.com), P.O. Box 207, Routes 131 and 103, Proctorsville 05153. Quarry and timber baron Allen Fletcher, elected governor of Vermont in 1913, built this imposing neo-Jacobean stone manor on a knoll, importing European artisans in 1901 for the oak and mahogany woodwork and detailed cast-plaster ceilings. Weddings are the specialty here, with facilities to accommodate many guests. The 10 rooms are regal, 6 with gas or wood-burning fireplace and 2 with whirlpool bath. Also see *Dining Out*. Rates $149–300; ask about ski-and-stay packages in winter.

BED & BREAKFASTS

In the Ludlow area
The Governor's Inn (802-228-8830; 1-800-GOVERNOR; www.thegover

ECHO LAKE

Kim Grant

norsinn.com), 86 Main Street, Ludlow 05149. Open year-round except December 23–26. William Wallace Stickney, governor of Vermont 1900–1902, built this Victorian house with its ornate slate, hand-painted fireplaces. Now it's owned by Jim and Cathy Kubec. The eight upstairs guest rooms are furnished with antiques, and a suite features a whirlpool bath and sitting area. The living room is small but elegant; full bar service is offered to guests in the den. Dinner, prepared by Cathy, is an elegant, six-course event that takes place on Saturday night and special occasions, and is for guests only. Breakfast is served in a cheery back room, warmed by the sun and a woodstove. Tea takes place in the front parlor. Cathy also does picnic baskets with a little prior notice, and she runs very popular cooking weekends. $165–315 B&B

double in fall and winter, $109–239 in regular season; add $90 per couple MAP; add 18 percent dinner gratuity.

✿ **The Okemo Inn** (802-228-8834; out of state: 1-800-328-8834; www.okemoinn.com), junction of Routes 100 north and 103, Ludlow 05149. Open year-round except for 2 weeks in April and November. Ron Parry has been here longer than any other local innkeeper, and this 1810 home is well kept and effortlessly welcoming. There are 11 nicely furnished guest rooms, most with two double beds, all with private bath. In the living room a table in front of the hearth is made from old bellows, and the dining room has low, notched beams; there's also a TV room, a sauna, and in summertime a pool. $110–150 per day B&B for two people. Inquire about ski, golf, and crafts packages. There are also winter rental B&B

packages for skiers who just can't get enough.

&. **The Golden Stage Inn** (802-226-7744; 1-800-253-8226; www.golden stageinn.com), 399 Depot Street, P.O. Box 218, Proctorsville 05153. Sandy and Peter Gregg are at the helm of this handsome, historic house. An inn in the 18th century, it belonged to the Skinner family for 100 years, beginning in 1830. There is a suite and eight guest rooms, one named for the writer and performer Cornelia Otis Skinner. Dining areas include the solarium, the inn's greenhouse. The inn is centrally air-conditioned, and a swimming pool is set in gardens. $69–250 B&B, MAP available.

✍ **Okemo Lantern Lodge** (802-226-7770; 1-800-732-7077), P.O. Box 247, 329 Main Street, Proctorsville 05153, a former mill owner's mansion, is rich in ornately carved butternut and stained glass. The dining room takes center stage downstairs. Dody Button offers 10 guest rooms, ranging from small to large enough for a king-sized bed; all have private bath. Our favorites are on the third floor. In warm-weather months the inn is popular with bicyclists and families; it's a casual, comfortable inn with a swimming pool out back. $90 B&B, $140 MAP.

In Chester 05143
Quail Hollow Inn (802-875-2794; 1-888-829-9874; www.quailhollowinn .com), 225 Pleasant Street. This inn on Route 11 in Chester offers six guest rooms, all with private bath. Room rates run $95–150 in high season, $85–150 in low season, including breakfast.

Park Light Inn (802-875-4417; 1-888-875-4417; www.parklightinn .com), 232 Depot Street. Steve and Karen Cox offer five guest rooms, three with private bath. The rooms have themes—Yellowstone, Central Park, Boston Harbor, and more. $110–135 in low season, $135–155 in high season (more on holidays), including Karen's bountiful breakfast.

✍ **Henry Farm Inn** (802-875-2674; 1-800-723-8213; www.henryfarminn .com), 2206 Green Mountain Turnpike. There's a nice out-in-the-country feel to this old place, set in 50 rolling acres. Larger than other farmhouses of the period, it was built in 1760 as a stagecoach stop and retains its pine floors, beehive oven, and sense of pleasant, uncluttered simplicity. The nine rooms are large, all with small bathroom. Two of the rooms are suites with kitchen. What you notice are the quilts and the views. A path leads to the spring-fed pond up the hill, and a swimming hole in the Williams River is just across the road. Inquire about frequent quilting workshop weekends. Your hosts are Patricia and Paul Dexter and their enterprising son Joseph. Children welcome. $90–155 includes a country breakfast.

Stone Cottage Collectables (802-875-6211), 196 North Street. Chris and Ann Curran are your hosts at this 1840 stone house in Chester's Stone Village historic district. Three sitting rooms are furnished with antiques and collectibles; you'll also find a pleasant patio, deck, and garden. There are two guest rooms with private bath, but the find here is a glorious queen-bedded room with fireplace created by the late owner, best-selling author Olivia Goldsmith (*The First Wives Club*). Room rates, including full breakfast, are $80–100.

The Currans also operate a shop here, featuring radios and tubes, cameras, and stamps as well as antiques.

&. **Inn Victoria** (802-875-4288; 1-800-732-4288; www.innvictoria .com), 321 Main Street. Yellow brick with purple shutters, a mansard roof, and columned porch, this showy Victorian has seven antiques-furnished guest rooms and a suite (sleeping six to eight). All rooms have queen-sized bed, three have Jacuzzi, and the first-floor garden room is handicapped accessible. Jack and Janet Burns have added an outdoor hot tub and deck, and serve tea. No children under 15, please. From $110 for a small room to $215 for a suite, breakfast included.

The Chester House (802-875-2205; 1-888-875-2205; www.chesterhouse inn.com), 266 Main Street, on the green. Common space includes a keeping room with fireplace (beer and wine are served). There are seven rooms in all. Room 1 has a queen bed and a whirlpool bath; Room 2, queen bed plus steam bath and sitting area; Room 4, queen bed, sitting area, and whirlpool. All have telephone and air-conditioning. Paul Anderson and Randy Guy are your hosts. $95–189 B&B.

& **Hugging Bear Inn & Shoppe** (802-875-2412; 1-800-325-0519; www.huggingbear.com), 244 Main Street. A teddy bear lover's haven with bears on the beds of six guest rooms (private bath). The place teems with them: teddy bear wallpaper, teddy bear sheets and shower curtains, and more than 6,000 stuffed bears in the shop behind the kitchen. Georgette Thomas believes that people don't hug enough. Everyone is invited to hug any bear in the house, and the atmosphere here is conta-

giously friendly. Rates are $65–95 single, $90–155 double. Full breakfast is included.

Night With A Native Bed & Breakfast (802-875-2616; www.chesterlodging.com), P.O. Box 327, 266 Depot Street. Doris Hastings is a sixth-generation Vermonter who obviously enjoys accommodating guests in a house that conveys a lively interest in many things. The two small, antiques-decorated bedrooms have private bath. Breakfast is included. $75–95 per couple. Children 12 and over.

Up in the hills

🐾 *&* **The Inn at High View** (802-875-2724; www.innathighview.com), 753 East Hill Road, Andover 05143. An attractive inn set high on 72 acres of East Hill, with some of the best views of any inn in Vermont. A portion of the house dates from the 18th century, but it's been a ski lodge for decades, one of the first to cater to cross-country skiers; there is a 15 km trail network out the back door. In summer a pool is set in the rock gardens. There are six rooms and two suites (each two rooms), all very attractively furnished and named for fictional cats. Request a room with access to the hot tub. There's also a sauna. A game room in the basement is fitted with videos and games for kids; there's a gazebo out on the lawn for weddings. Hosts Greg Bohan and Sal Massaro enjoy an enthusiastic repeat business. Saturday nights during the ski season, Sal cooks elegant Italian fare ($30; BYOB). $135–170 for rooms, $185–265 for suites, includes breakfast. Pets possible.

☉ **Crisanver House** (802-492-3589; 1-800-492-8089; www.crisanver.com), 1434 Crown Point Road, Shrewsbury

Maple Crest Farm (802-492-3367), RR Box 120, Cuttingsville 05738. This handsome, white-brick farmhouse sits high on a ridge in the old hilltop center of Shrewsbury. It was built in 1808 as Gleason's Tavern and is still in the same family—they began taking in guests in the 1860s and have done so off and on ever since. The Smiths offer three antiques-filled rooms (the front ground-floor room with a half bath is our favorite) sharing two baths, and two charming apartments that can accommodate small families. "Every piece of furniture has a story," says Donna Smith—and she knows each one. Ask about a rocking chair or spool bed, and you'll begin to sense who has lived in this unusual house down through the years. Books and magazines are everywhere, focusing on local and Vermont tales and history. The Smiths raise beef cattle and hay, and are noted for the quality of their maple syrup, produced in the sugarhouse at the peak of the hill; the same sweeping view can be enjoyed in winter on cross-country skis. You can walk off in any number of directions. $55–85 per room. Breakfast is included. No credit cards.

MAPLE CREST FARM

Christina Tree

05738. Set high on 115 acres of woods and meadows, with panoramic views, this is a find—but it's booked many weekends for weddings. The 1802 portion of this house has recently been restored and offers eight attractive guest rooms, all with down comforters and pillows, exposed beams, original art, robes, and individual heat control. The casually elegant living room has a fireplace and grand piano, and a downstairs game room has table tennis and a pool table. Innkeepers Carol and Michael Calotta also have two mini suites in the neighboring cottage, and a barn has been designed to accommodate 120 people for weddings and parties. In summer there's a heated pool; in winter, cross-country skiing. $90–185 for rooms with shared bath, $110–225 with private bath, $140–320 for mini suites, including afternoon tea, full breakfast, and shuttle service from the Rutland airport, bus stop, and train station. Inquire about dinner, available with advance notice for $35 per person.

Balm of Gilead B&B (802-492-7010), 774 CCC Road, Shrewsbury 05738. Sarah Schiermeyer offers the Pink Suite, the Blue Suite, and the Green Room for $200–350, depending on the season. She serves breakfast and afternoon tea most of the year, and dinner in the high season. The great room has a Steinway grand piano and a billiards table. The views out the windows are of mountains, mountains, and more mountains.

The Buckmaster Inn (802-492-3720; www.buckmasterinn.com), 20 Lottery Road, Shrewsbury 05738. Built as the Buckmaster Tavern beside the Shrewsbury church in 1801, the house is owned by Richard and Elizabeth Davis, who have lightened and brightened its decor. Eight to 10 guests can be accommodated in four rooms (private bath). There is a spacious living room, a library with fireplace and TV, and a long, screened-in porch that's especially inviting in summer and fall. The Davises are enthusiastic hosts who can tell you what to see and do. $105 for any double includes a continental-plus breakfast featuring home-baked goodies.

Out in the country
⊚🐾♿ **The Inn at Cranberry Farm** (802-463-1331; www.cranberry farminn.com), 61 Williams River Road, Chester 05143. Set in 60 acres off by itself near Brockway Mills, a contemporary lodge with an open-beamed, two-story living room and library obviously designed for numbers—ideal for weddings, but couples are very welcome. There are 11 guest rooms, all with private bath, some handicapped accessible, some with fireplace. $150–225 includes a full breakfast and tea.

🐾 ♿ **Old Town Farm Inn** (802-875-2346; 1-888-232-1089; www.otfi.com), 665 Vermont Route 10, Chester 05143. This former "Town Farm" is in Gassetts, a village midway between Chester and Ludlow. Long known to families as a reasonably priced ski lodge, the old place with its wide-board floors has been nicely rehabbed by Michiko and Alex Hunter. There are now eight comfortable guest rooms, all with private bath. It's set in 11 acres with a pond. $79–139 with breakfast. This is also now a popular place to dine on sushi (see *Dining Out*).

Rowell's Inn (802-875-3658; 1-800-728-0842), Route 11, Simonsville, Andover 05142. Open year-round.

This distinctive, double-porched, brick stage stop has been serving the public off and on since 1820. Michael Bregnoli and Susan McNulty offer seven comfortable guest rooms with private bath, one with a working fireplace. Two spacious spaces on the third floor have been carved from the old ballroom, furnished grandly with antiques and Oriental rugs. Located midway among Londonderry, Weston, and Chester, the inn is off by itself with some fine walks and cross-country skiing out the back door. $120–175 B&B; a four-course, single-entrée dinner is offered Friday and Saturday nights during ski season.

🐾 ✍ **The Combes Family Inn** (802-228-8799; 1-800-822-8799), 953 East Lake Road, Ludlow 05149. Ruth and Bill Combes have celebrated their 23rd anniversary as innkeepers, welcoming families to their peaceful 1891 former dairy farm home. There are 11 guest rooms, all with private bath—6 in the farmhouse and 5 in an attached unit (where pets are allowed). B&B double rates are $65 spring, $94 summer, $114 winter. Ruth's hearty Vermont-style dinners are available nightly by reservation at $16 per adult and $8 for kids.

Stone Hearth Inn (802-875-2525; www.thestonehearthinn.com), 698 Route 11 (1 mile west of the village), Chester 05143. Under the ownership of Chris Clay and Brent Anderson, this rambling 1810 farmhouse is a comfortable, informal place. The 10 guest rooms all have private bath; common space includes a library, sitting room, and recreation room with games, TV, and a hot tub. The tavern at one end of the inn is fully licensed with a pool table and casual menu. $119–149 double, B&B.

Whitney Brook (802-226-7460; www.whitneybrook.com), 2433 Twenty Mile Stream Road, Proctorsville 05153. Jim and Ellen Parrish welcome guests to their pretty 1870 farmhouse on a quiet road. There are four guest rooms, three with queen beds and one with a double and a single. Two rooms have private bath, two share. Guests enjoy a private living room downstairs and a sitting room upstairs. $60–115 per room includes full breakfast.

Popple Fields (802-875-4219; www.popplefields.com), 1300 Popple Dungeon Road, P.O. Box 636, Chester 05143. It took Conrad Delia 10 years (1989–1999) to build this amazing reproduction 18th-century house, and it's a beauty, remarkable for its beauty and detailing, right down to a Colonial-style bar. It's way out on a back road, set in 18 rolling acres. There are four guest rooms, two with private bath, and Conrad has made much of the furniture, too (he operates a Windsor chair and cabinet shop on the premises). Marylin Delia serves a full buffet breakfast in the large country kitchen. No children under 15, please. $100–150.

MOTELS Best Western (802-228-8188; www.bestwesternludlow.com), 93 Main Street, Ludlow 05149. Years ago Fire Chief Rick Harrison built a 14-unit motel onto the back of his 1825 home. It's now a 48-unit motel with a range of rooms and suites, from antiques decorated to contemporary. All units have phone, cable TV, full bath, and in-room coffee, and there's a pool. $90–225 in foliage season, $90–300 in ski season.

Clarion Hotel, Cavendish Pointe (802-226-7688; 1-800-438-7908;

www.okemocavendishpointe.com),
Route 103, Cavendish 05142. A contemporary motor inn with 72 fairly
large rooms. Facilities include an
indoor pool, hot tub/spa room, and
game room; there's also a
restaurant/bar open only during ski
season. $69–230.

All Seasons Inn Motel (802-228-
8100; 1-888-228-8100), 112 Main
Street, Ludlow 05149. A mansard-
roofed house in the middle of the village has been turned into 17 units, all
with cable TV, phone (with voice
mail), and refrigerator; 6 have kitchenette. Free shuttle-bus service.
$85–135 during foliage-season week-
ends, $125–175 on ski-season week-
ends with a 2-night minimum.

Timber Inn Motel (802-228-8666;
www.vacationinvermont.com/timber),
112 Route 103 south, Ludlow 05149.
This 18-room cedar and knotty-pine
motel on the Black River is a short
shuttle-bus ride to Okemo—and the
shuttle is free. Hot tub and sauna in
winter, heated outdoor pool in summer. $49–99.

CONDOMINIUMS **Okemo Mountain
Resort** offers nearly 700 condominium units, all booked through the
Okemo Mountain Lodging Service
(802-228-5571; 1-800-78-OKEMO;
RFD 1, Ludlow 05149). Obviously
they are far cheaper in summer than
winter. They include: **Jackson Gore
Inn,** a new lodge in the recently
opened Jackson Gore area; and
Okemo Mountain Lodge, a three-
story hotel at the entrance to the
resort, really a cluster of 55 one-
bedroom condos, each with a sleeping
couch in the living room. There's a
compact kitchen with eating counter
and a fireplace; enough space for a

couple and two children. **Kettle
Brook** has one-, two-, and three-
bedroom units, all nicely built, salted
along trails. **Winterplace,** set high on
a mountain shelf, consists of 17 buildings with a total of 250 units ranging
in size from two bedrooms to three
bedrooms plus a loft. Residents have
access to a fitness center with indoor
pool. **Solitude Village** is a ski-in/ski-
out complex of one- to five-unit condos and town houses plus a lodge with
indoor/outdoor heated pool and a
service area with a restaurant, ski
shop, and children's learning center.
Ledgewood Condominiums are
three- and four-bedroom units with
garages accessed by their own trail.
Rentals also are available through
Strictly Rentals (1-800-776-5149;
www.strictlyrentals.com) in downtown
Ludlow.

✳ Where to Eat

DINING OUT **Nikki's** (802-228-7797),
Routes 100/103, Sunshine Market
Place, Ludlow. Dinner nightly from 5.
Operated by Bob Gilmore since 1976,
Nikki's has evolved into one of the
premier restaurants in the Okemo
Valley. The exposed wood and brick
walls are garnished with stained and
beveled glass, and there are booths,
an inviting bar area, and gleaming
coffee machines. One table is downstairs in the wine cellar. New England
bouillabaisse (fresh salmon, littleneck
clams, and scallops in a simmering
tomato seafood broth) is a specialty,
and the osso buco con orecchiette is
said to be excellent. The wine selection is exceptional. Entrées $15–28.

Echo Lake Inn (802-228-8602;
1-800-356-6844; www.echolakeinn
.com), Route 100 north in Tyson.
Open to the public for dinner. The

dining room, with print wallpaper and shades of mauve, is attractive. Chef Kevin Barnes has established an enviable reputation over the past decade. His menu ranges from spinach cannelloni to sautéed ostrich medallions in lingonberry sauce. Entrées $17–25.

The Castle (802-226-7222), intersection of Routes 131 and 103, Proctorsville. Open for dinner Thursday through Saturday. The interior of this stone mansion is a rich blend of American oak, Mexican mahogany, and French marble. Feast on beef Wellington or lobster Armagnac. Entrées $37–49.

The Andrie Rose Inn (802-228-4846; www.andrieroseinn.com). Open to the public by reservation Friday and Saturday with a set, four-course dinner at $38 per person. Chef-owner Irene Maston's menu on a summer Friday included a choice of Cavendish Farm quail with nectarine and plum stuffing in an Asian-spiced sauce, or seed-crusted halibut fillet in roasted garlic and red pepper broth.

Fullerton Inn (802-875-2444), 40 The Common, Chester. Open nightly Tuesday through Saturday. This pleasant dining room is surprisingly casual with a varied menu ranging from focaccia bread pizza to steak Oscar. Live entertainment on Saturday night.

Tokai-Tei Japanese Restaurant at the Old Town Farm Inn (802-875-2346, 1 888 232-1089), 665 Vermont Route 10, Chester. Open Thursday through Sunday 5–9 by reservation. Halfway between Chester and Ludlow isn't exactly where you expect to find a first-rate Japanese restaurant, but that's where Michiko Hunter presides over the kitchen of this old family-geared lodge, turning out tan-talizing and reasonably priced sushi. Entrées include *gyu-aspara maki* (beef asparagus roll) and *buta niku no shoga yaki* (gingered pork). It's BYOB, and desserts include green tea or red bean ice cream and Japanese snow white jelly, all made at the inn.

Also see **The River Tavern** at Hawk Inn and Mountain Resort in Plymouth, in "Killington/Plymouth Area."

EATING OUT

In Chester
Raspberries and Tyme (802-875-4486), on the green. Open daily, serving delectable breakfasts 8–11; lunches 11–closing; dinner 5–9. The only problem with this place is getting in. In summer, even with the porch tables, it's frequently a crunch, so come early or late. Great salads, simmering soups, and a wide choice of sandwiches are named for a variety of village establishments. The Misty Valley Books veggie bagel (spinach, tomato, grated carrots, broccoli, and sprouts with hummus on their own garlic-herb spread under melted Vermont cheddar) is a best seller. Lisai's Market Reuben burger is memorable.

Baba-A-Louis Bakery (802-875-4666), Route 11 west, Chester. Closed April and November, as well as Sunday and Monday, but otherwise open 7 AM–6 PM. This is the other great lunch option in town, a long-established bakery with an open kitchen and self-serve lunch fare that includes soups and a salad bar as well as quiche and panini. Breakfast options include sticky buns and cinnamon twists, and no one leaves without a loaf of this top-drawer bakery's specialty breads.

Country Girl Diner (802-875-2650), junction of Routes 11 and 103, Chester. An authentic Silk City diner made in Patterson, New Jersey, in the early '40s. It's a homey, popular spot open Monday through Saturday 6 AM–8 PM, Sunday 7 AM–8 PM. Classic diner with classic diner fare.

Rose Arbor Tea Room (802-875-4767), just off the green, Chester. Tea served daily 10–5 except Monday. A combination gift store and tearoom. Coffee and lemonade are also served to accompany the chicken salad with fruit garnish and diablo chocolate cake.

In and around Ludlow

Harry's Cafe (802-259-2996), Route 103, Mount Holly. Open daily 5–10. Trip Pierce took the funky old Backside Restaurant and turned it into a light, airy space with good art and a woodstove. The menu is wildly eclectic, but Thai food is a specialty.

Sam's Steakhouse (802-228-5622), 91 Route 103, just east of downtown Ludlow. Open for dinner nightly with midweek specials. Known for filet mignon you can cut with a butter knife, excellent seafood, a good salad bar, and sinful desserts.

Willie Dunne's Grille (802-228-1387), at the Okemo Valley Golf Club & Nordic Center, Route 100. Open year-round for lunch and dinner, serving surprisingly affordable and good food. Two windowed walls open to views of the pond and the 18th green.

Ludlow Cooking Co. (802-226-7251), 29 Main Street, Ludlow. Open 11–10. Good for sandwiches, deli items, and rich desserts, mostly Italian-style dinner menu (also meals-to-go), but homestyle stuffed cabbage is a specialty.

DJ's Restaurant (802-228-5374), 146 Main Street, Ludlow. Open from 4:30 for dinner. A downtown eatery that's been upscaled, best known for its broiled scallops and shrimp, extensive salad bar, and nightly specials.

Cappuccino's Cafe (802-228-7566), 41 Depot Street, Ludlow, serves dinner Wednesday through Sunday; reservations suggested. Chef-owner Steve Degnan and his wife, Dawna, have created a pleasant ambience and a varied menu of pasta, seafood, beef, chicken, and nightly specials; full bar.

✍ **Pot Belly Restaurant and Pub** (802-228-8989), 130 Main Street, Ludlow. Open for dinner nightly and lunch most days. First opened in a storefront in 1974, this zany place has expanded into a great space; good for live entertainment (swing and blues bands, jug band music, and rock 'n' roll on weekends), and victuals ranging from popcorn shrimp, Pot Belly chicken, or ribs to chocolate peanut butter pie. A Belly burger or the Cajun chicken sandwich is a good bet at lunch, and you can always get a Belly burger at dinner, too.

Java Baba's Slow Food Café (802-228-4131), at the base of the Okemo Access Road, features overstuffed chairs and couches, serves fresh-baked muffins and pastries, homemade soups, sandwiches, salads, desserts, and a variety of coffee drinks.

BREWS **Black River Brewing Company** (802-228-3100), Route 103, Proctorsville, makes several ales, porters, and stouts (among them Big Buck, Fish Tale, Long Term Disability, and Stump Jumper), which can be sampled and downed in its English pub. Wings and sweet potato chip nachos are among the specialties. Children's menu, late-night menu, live entertainment.

✳ Selective Shopping

ANTIQUES SHOPS

In Chester

Stone House Antiques (802-875-4477), Route 103 south, is an antiques mall with 125 dealers and a touristy collection of country crafts. Open daily 10–5. See also Stone Cottage Collectables under *Bed & Breakfasts.*

William Austin's Antiques (802-875-3032), 42 Maple Street, Chester. A full line of antique country furniture and collectibles.

ART GALLERIES **Chester Art Guild**
(802-875-4373), on the green, Chester (see the description under *Town and Village*).

Crow Hill Gallery (802-875-3763), Flamstead Road, Chester. This is a great excuse to ride up Crow Hill; the contemporary gallery shows the work of Jeanne Carbonetti and other local artists. Open Wednesday through Saturday 10–5, Sunday by appointment.

Grist Mill Gallery of Fine Art (802-875-3415), just off Route 103, Chester Depot. This distinctive old red gristmill lends itself nicely to exhibit space for Allison Kibbe's original landscapes. Open 10–4 weekdays, 10–5 on weekends.

Beach Tree Gallery (802-875-6225; www.beachtreegallery.com), on the green, Chester. Displaying local artwork and fine crafts from around New England, the gallery is owned and operated by watercolorist Elaine Reed and photographer Pamela Nelligan. Workshops and demonstrations throughout the year. Open daily 10–5.

BOOKS AND MAPS **Misty Valley Books** (802-875-3400; www.mvbooks.com), on the green, Chester, open daily except Monday. An unusually friendly, well-stocked bookshop; browsing is encouraged and book and author readings are frequent, making it a lively cultural center.

The National Survey (802-875-2121), Chester Village, off the green. Open Monday through Friday 9–5, Saturday 10–4. Founded in 1912 by two sons of Chester's Baptist minister, the National Survey publishes maps for many states, foreign governments, industries, and other groups throughout the world. The store carries a large selection of maps, also old brochures.

Over Andover (802-876-4348; call for directions), open July through October, Thursday through Monday 11–5 and weekends year-round. A barn full of rare and unusual used books (specialties include King Arthur, Thomas Merton, and C. S. Lewis).

CRAFTS **Bonnie's Bundles** (802-875-2114; www.bonniesboundles dolls.com), Stone Village, Route 103, Chester. Open weekends and by appointment. Housed in an 1814 stone house, a doll lover's find. Bonnie Waters handcrafts wonderfully original dolls.

Craft Shop at Fletcher Farm (802-228-4348), 611 Route 103, east of Ludlow. Open late June through mid-September, 9:30–5, and weekends from Memorial Day. Work by members of the Society of Vermont Craftsmen.

FOOD AND FLOWERS **Crowley Cheese Factory and Shop** (1-800-

683-2606; www.crowleycheese-vermont.com), Route 103, 5 miles northwest of Ludlow. See *Scenic Drive* for the history of this exceptional cheese, which is sharper and creamier than cheddar. The factory (802-259-2340) is open Monday through Friday 8–4, and the shop (802-259-2210) on Route 103, which carries other Vermont products as well, is open daily 10–5:30.

Meadowsweet Herb Farm (802-492-3565; www.meadowsweetherbfarm.com), 1130 Eatham Road, North Shrewsbury. See *Scenic Drive*. The shop in this 1860 farmhouse features herb wreaths, potpourri, and culinary blends as well as herbal soaps, gift baskets, and more. Perennial herbs and geraniums are grown year-round in the solar greenhouse and sold as seedlings. A picnic bench overlooks the gardens, open daily 9–5, May through October and holidays.

Green Mountain Sugar House (802-228-7151), Route 100, 4 miles north of Ludlow. You can watch syrup being produced in March and April; maple candy is made throughout the year on a weekly basis. This is also a place to find freshly pressed cider in September. The gift and produce shop is open daily 9–6 "most of the time."

Black River Produce (802-226-7484), Route 103 in Proctorsville. The purveyor of fruits and vegetables to the area's best restaurants, an exceptional source of fruit, vegetables, fresh breads, cheese, seafood, and flowers, excellent prepared foods, lobsters steamed to go, chowder and fish-and-chips on Friday.

Singleton's Store (802-226-7666), downtown Proctorsville. A long-established family-run grocery store just east of Route 103 on Route 131

in the middle of Proctorsville has kept abreast of the demands of the area's condo owners while continuing to cover the basics: a Vermont liquor store, fishing and hunting licenses, rods and reels, guns and ammo, sporting goods, outdoor wear and boots, plus fine wines, choice meats, a standout deli, and a gun shop; the specialty of the house is smoked and marinated meat (an average of 350 pounds of meat sold per day).

Crow's Bakery, Route 131, Proctorsville. A full array of delicious homemade breads, pastries, desserts, and heart-warming soups.

Belmont General Store, across the street from Star Lake in Belmont Village. Former Nikki's Restaurant chef Chris Kelly and his wife, Louisa, have turned this general store into a source of homemade bread and pastries, lunch and dinner menus to go, as well as local eggs and other produce.

SPECIAL SHOPS **Vermont Industries Factory Store** (802-492-3451; 1-800-826-4766), Route 103 in Cuttingsville, open daily 10–5:30. A big barn full of hand-forged, wrought-iron products—freestanding sundials, sconces, candleholders, corn dryers, hanging planters, chandeliers, and a wide range of fireplace accessories. The distinctive floor lamps sell for substantially more in stores throughout New England.

Clear Lake Furniture (802-228-8395; www.clearlakevt.com), 322 Route 100 north, Ludlow. The workshop and showroom for elegantly simple custom-made pieces in cherry, curly maple, oak, and walnut by Brent Karner and Frank Procopio. Open Monday through Saturday 9–6, Sunday noon–5.

Conrad Delia, Windsor Chair Maker (802-875-4219), Popple Dungeon Road, Chester. After a long career as a home builder on Long Island, Conrad Delia studied with several New England chair makers before opening his own shop. Call to schedule a visit.

Inn Victoria Teapot Shop (802-875-4288), 321 Main Street, Chester. Teapots in all shapes and sizes and tea accessories.

Forlie-Ballou (802-875-2090), off Main Street, Chester Village. Worth checking. Suzy Forlie and Mary Ballou carry a fine selection of women's clothing and accessories.

✳ Special Events

February–March: **Okemo Winter-Fest** includes "the Ludlow Olympics"—tobogganing, snow sculpture contest, fireworks, ski races, and torchlight parade. Call 802-228-4041 or 802-228-6110 for details.

July 1: **Fletcher Farm Arts and Crafts Fair,** Route 103, Ludlow; **St. Joseph's Carnival; horse show and community picnic,** Chester.

August: **Chester Outdoor Art Show. Vermont State Zucchini Festival,** Ludlow—4 days of "zucchini madness" include a costume parade, Z-buck auction, and other events. **Thursday-evening concerts** on the Chester green all month.

Last weekend of September: **Fall Crafts Fair,** Chester.

Early December: **Victorian Christmas Walk and Parade,** Ludlow.

December: **Overture to Christmas** (usually the second Saturday), Chester. Tree lighting and a candlelight caroling procession from church to church.

Upper Connecticut Valley

UPPER VALLEY RIVER TOWNS

WOODSTOCK/QUECHEE AREA

Kim Grant

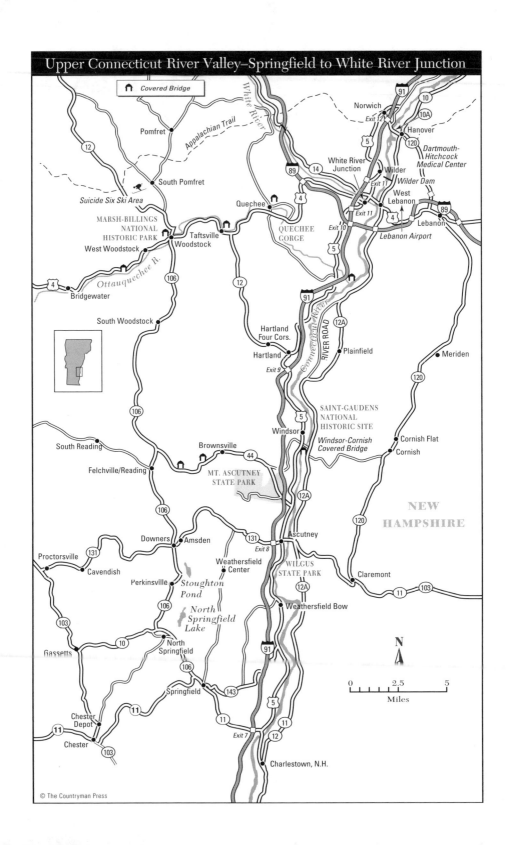

Covered Bridge

White River

Appalachian Trail

91
10

Norwich
Exit 12
10A

Pomfret

12

Hanover

5
120

Dartmouth-
Hitchcock
Medical Center

South Pomfret

White River
Junction

89
14

Wilder

Suicide Six Ski Area

Wilder Dam

Exit 11

West
Lebanon

MARSH-BILLINGS
NATIONAL
HISTORIC PARK

Quechee

4

Taftsville
Woodstock

Exit 11

4

89

West Woodstock

QUECHEE
GORGE

Exit 10

Lebanon

Ottauquechee R.

106

12

Lebanon Airport

4

Bridgewater

91

5

South Woodstock

12A

River Road

Hartland
Four Cors.

Plainfield

Meriden

Hartland

Connecticut River

120

Exit 9

SAINT-GAUDENS
NATIONAL
HISTORIC SITE

5

South Reading

Brownsville

44

Windsor

Windsor-Cornish
Covered Bridge

Cornish Flat

Felchville/Reading

MT. ASCUTNEY
STATE PARK

Cornish

106

12A

NEW

120

HAMPSHIRE

Downers
Amsden

131

Ascutney

Proctorsville
131

Exit 8

WILGUS
STATE PARK

Cavendish

Weathersfield
Center

Claremont

Perkinsville

Stoughton
Pond

12A

11
103

103

106

North
Springfield
Lake

Weathersfield Bow

Gassetts
10

North
Springfield

91

N

106

Chester
Depot

Springfield

143

0   2.5   5

11

5

Miles

11

11

Chester

Exit 7

12

103

Charlestown, N.H.

© The Countryman Press

UPPER VALLEY RIVER TOWNS

The Upper Valley ignores state lines to form one of New England's most beautiful and distinctive regions. Its two dozen towns are scattered along the Vermont and New Hampshire banks of the Connecticut River for some 20 miles north and south of Dartmouth College.

Upper Valley is a name coined in the 1950s by a local daily, the *Valley News*, to define its two-state circulation area. The label has stuck, interestingly, to the same group of towns that, back in the 1770s, attempted to unite politically. But the Dartmouth College–based supporters of their "New Connecticut" were thwarted by larger powers, namely New York and New Hampshire, along with the strident Vermont independence faction, the Green Mountain Boys. On July 2, 1777, delegates met at Elijah West's tavern in Windsor to declare Vermont a "free and independent state," bounded on the east by the Connecticut River.

The Upper Valley itself prospered, a fact that's obvious from the exquisite Federal-era meetinghouses and mansions still salted through this area. The river belongs to New Hampshire, thanks to a decree by King George III that still holds, which means that the state is responsible for maintaining the bridges. Of the dozens of bridges that once connected the two states, only 10 survive, but they include the longest historic covered bridge in the United States (connecting Windsor with Cornish). The Upper Valley area phone book includes towns on both sides of the river (it's a local call back and forth, although the area code is now needed), and Norwich and Hanover's Dresden School District reaches well into Vermont. Several Independence Day parades start in one state and finish across the bridge in the other. And the Montshire Museum, founded on the New Hampshire side of the river and now splendidly rooted on the Vermont bank, combines both states in its name.

The cultural center of the Upper Valley remains the Dartmouth campus in Hanover, graced with a major theater and museum. With the nearby medical complex and the West Lebanon shopping center strip (a popular escape route from Vermont's sales tax), it forms a genuine hub, handy to the highways radiating, the way rail lines once did, from White River Junction. Since the 1820s, the area's industrial core has traditionally been at its southern end, in Springfield and

Windsor, both of which have produced far more than their share of inventors. At the northern end of the valley summer camps have lined the shores of Lakes Morey and Fairlee for more than a century.

Beyond these redbrick towns and old resort enclaves, farms still spread comfortably along the river, all the way from Weathersfield Bow to a similar oxbow in Newbury. They are backed in places by steep hills, including Mount Ascutney, a monadnock thrusting 3,144 feet straight up from the banks of the river (site of both a state park with a summit road and a self-contained ski resort). The stretch of both road (Route 5) and river north from Wilder Dam to Newbury offers unexpected vistas of the White Mountains, and its inns cater to bicyclists, canoeists, and kayakers.

Thanks to decades of acquisitions, greenups, and cleanups by numerous conservation groups, the Connecticut River itself has enjoyed a genuine renewal, with campsites and inns spaced along the shore; visitors and residents alike are discovering its beauty.

GUIDANCE An excellent, noncommercial web site, www.ctrivertravel.net, covering the entire stretch of the Connecticut shared by Vermont and New Hampshire is maintained by the **Connecticut River Joint Commissions,** which also publishes the booklet *Connecticut River Heritage Trail.* The handsome railroad station in White River Junction houses a **Welcome Center** (802-281-5050) that's sadly, at this writing, open varying days and hours, along with an evolving transportation museum.

The **Springfield Area Chamber Commerce** (802-885-2779; www.springfield vt.com) answers phone queries year-round (weekdays 8–5) and maintains the 18th-century **Eureka Schoolhouse** (Route 11, near I-91) as a seasonal information booth. **The Windsor–Mount Ascutney Area Chamber of Commerce** (802-674-5910) also answers phone queries; also see www.vacationin vermont.com.

The **Hartford Area Chamber of Commerce** (802-295-7900; 1-800-295-5451; www.hartfordvtchamber.com), 211 North Main Street, White River Junction 05001, covers White River Junction, Quechee, and three other villages in the town of Hartford at the heart of the Upper Valley.

GETTING THERE *By car:* Interstates 91 and 89 converge in the White River Junction–Lebanon area, where they also meet Route 5 north and south on the Vermont side; Route 4, the main east-west highway through central Vermont; and Route 10, the river road on the New Hampshire side. I-91 also joins I-93 just above the northern end of the Upper Valley, offering another quick way home for visitors from points southeast.

By bus: White River Junction is a hub for **Greyhound/Vermont Transit** (802-295-3011; www.vermonttransit.com).

By air: The Lebanon (New Hampshire) Regional Airport (flight schedule: 603-298-8878) is served by **USAirways Express** (1-800-428-4322) from La Guardia in New York.

By train: **Amtrak** (802-295-7160; 1-800-875-7245; www.amtrak.com) stops in White River Junction and Windsor en route to and from New York's Penn Station and Washington, DC. Baggage cars carry bikes. Inquire about connections to St. Albans and Montreal.

GETTING AROUND Several local cab companies connect with planes, buses, and trains. Try **Big Yellow Taxi** (802-281-8294).

WHEN TO GO The Upper Valley, with the exception of Mount Ascutney Ski Resort, is best explored in summer and fall.

MEDICAL EMERGENCY Emergency service is available by calling **911**.

Dartmouth-Hitchcock Medical Center (603-650-5000; www.dhmc.org), 1 Medical Center Drive, off Route 120, between Hanover and Lebanon, is recognized as one of the best teaching hospitals in New England.

Local medical facilities include **Springfield Hospital** (802-885-2151), 25 Ridgewood Road, Springfield, and **Mount Ascutney Hospital** (802-674-6711), County Road, Windsor.

✳ Villages

Springfield. Situated at the confluence of the Connecticut and Black Rivers, Springfield boomed with Vermont's tool industry in the 19th and first half of the 20th century and has suffered as that industry has atrophied. Beyond the defunct factories and the powerful falls, the town's compact downtown shows interesting signs of life. Among the gracious 19th-century mansions in residential neighborhoods terraced above it are the Hartness House (see *Lodging*) and, at 9 Elm Street, the **Springfield Art & Historical Society** (802-885-2415; open May through October, Tuesday through Friday 10–4; Saturday 10–1), with collections of pewter, Bennington pottery, toys and dolls, primitive paintings, and costumes; it also puts on periodic art shows. See *Green Space* for the new Toonerville Trail along the Black River.

Weathersfield Center. On a scenic old north–south road between Springfield and Route 131 stands this nearly secret gem of a hamlet with its brick 1821 Meeting House and Civil War memorial, a particularly sobering reminder of how many young Vermonters served and died (12 boys from just this small village) in that

THE HISTORIC MEETINGHOUSE IN WEATHERSFIELD

Kim Grant

war. The **Weathersfield Historical Society,** housed in the Reverend Dan Foster House (open late June through early October, Thursday through Monday 2–5), displays Civil War memorabilia, archival photos, an old forge, and the last wildcat killed in Weathersfield (1867). It was Weathersfield native William Jarvis who transformed the economy of Vermont—and the rest of northern New England— by smuggling 4,000 sheep out of Spain during his term as U.S. consul in Lisbon. That was in 1810. By 1840 there were upward of 2 million sheep in Vermont.

Windsor. In *Roadside History of Vermont,* Peter Jennison notes that while it is known as the "Birthplace of Vermont" (see Old Constitution House under *To See*), Windsor can also claim to be the midwife of the state's machine tool industry. Windsor resident Lemuel Hedge devised a machine for ruling paper in 1815 and dividing scales in 1827. Asahel Hubbard produced a revolving pump in 1828, and Niconar Kendall designed an "under hammer" rifle, the first use of interchangeable parts, in the 1830s in the picturesque old mill that's now the American Precision Museum. Windsor's mid-19th-century prosperity is reflected in the handsome lines of the columned **Windsor House,** once considered the best public house between Boston and Montreal. The Italianate building across the street was designed in 1850 by Ammi Young as a post office (the oldest federal post office in continuous use in the United States) with an upstairs courthouse that served as Woodrow Wilson's summer White House from 1913 to 1915; the president spent his summers in Cornish, just across the Windsor– Cornish Covered Bridge. Cornish was at the time an artists and writers colony that had evolved around sculptor Augustus Saint-Gaudens. The colony nurtured artist Maxfield Parrish; his painting *Templed Hills* hangs in the Vermont National Bank branch that is next to Windsor House (Parrish left it in perpetua to the bank's tellers for "keeping my account balanced"). It depicts a mountain that resembles Mount Ascutney, towering above water that resembles Lake Runnemede. The lake is now a town-owned conservation area, good for walking and bird-watching, that's sequestered behind the town's mansion row, just north of the bank. South on Main Street, across from the red-and-chrome Windsor diner (Worcester Diner #835), stands the vintage 1798 **Old South Congregational Church.** Designed by Asher Benjamin, the church fortunately retains its classic beauty despite several renovations. Also worth noting: the contemporary St. Francis of Assisi Roman Catholic Church and its panels depicting the Seven Sacraments, donated by noted American painter George Tooker. On the common (off Main Street), St. Paul's, built in 1832, is Vermont's oldest Episcopal church. Townsend Cottage, across the square, is a striking example of 1840s Carpenter Gothic style. North of town a riverside, visitor-geared industrial park features the Simon Pearce glass factory and Harpoon Brewery. South of town 3,144-foot-high Mount Ascutney rises from the river's edge, a state park offering seasonal camping, hiking, a road to the top, and a self-contained ski resort in winter. A nominally priced *Architectural & Historical Walking Tour of Windsor* booklet prepared by Historic Windsor is sold at the Windsor State Craft Gallery.

White River Junction is located at the confluence of the Connecticut and White Rivers and the junction of Interstates 91 and 89. Ironically, the downtown—once a bustling, often raucous railroad hub—is now a bit of a cul-de-sac but well worth finding to shop, to visit the welcome center and the **New England Transportation Museum** housed in the venerable Hotel Coolidge's Amtrak station, or to dine before a performance in the Briggs Opera House. The village periphery now serves the interstates with brand-name motels and fast-food stops. Horace Wells of White River Junction was, incidentally, the first person to use laughing gas as an anesthetic for pulling teeth. White River Junction is actually a village in Hartford, a town that also includes Quechee, Hartford Village, Wilder, and West Hartford.

Chris McKinley

AMTRAK'S VERMONTER PULLS INTO WHITE RIVER JUNCTION.

Hanover, New Hampshire— Dartmouth College. Chartered in 1769, Dartmouth is the ninth oldest and one of the most prestigious colleges in the country, and its handsome buildings frame three sides of an elm-shaded green. The fourth side is lined with visitor-friendly buildings: the large, college-owned Hanover Inn, Hopkins Center entertainment complex, and the Hood Museum of Art. Note the white information kiosk on the green, staffed during summer months. Most visitors find their way into **Baker Memorial Library** to see the set of murals by famous Mexican painter José Clemente Orozco (which some alumni once demanded be removed or covered because of the artist's left-wing politics). When the kiosk is closed, guided tours are offered by the admission office (603-646-2875) in McNutt Hall by student members of Green Key.

Norwich, one of the prettiest towns in Vermont, was settled in 1761 by a group from Marshfield, Connecticut. It has always had close ties to Hanover (just across the bridge) and was itself the original home of Norwich University (founded 1819), which moved to Northfield after the Civil War. The village is an architectural showcase for fine brick and frame Federal homes. Note the Seven Nations House, built in 1832 as a commercial "tenement." Across the way is the Norwich Inn, dating back to 1797 and with a popular brewpub as well as dining room, the hospitable heart of town. Sequestered down by the river (east of I-91), the recently expanded Montshire Museum offers insights into ways the world and universe go 'round as well as into how the river shapes the immediate environment; it also offers trails through its 110 acres. King Arthur Flour's flagship Baker's Store and Baking Education Center on Route 5, south of town, draws devotees from throughout the county.

Thetford has an unusual number of post offices per capita: There are six villages in all. Thetford Center has a friendly general store and handsome brick Methodist church. Thetford Hill is a beauty, the site of Thetford Academy, the Parish Players, and the **Thetford Historical Society** (open August Sundays 2–5) and its Historic Library (open year-round, Monday and Thursday 2–4 and Tuesday 10–noon).

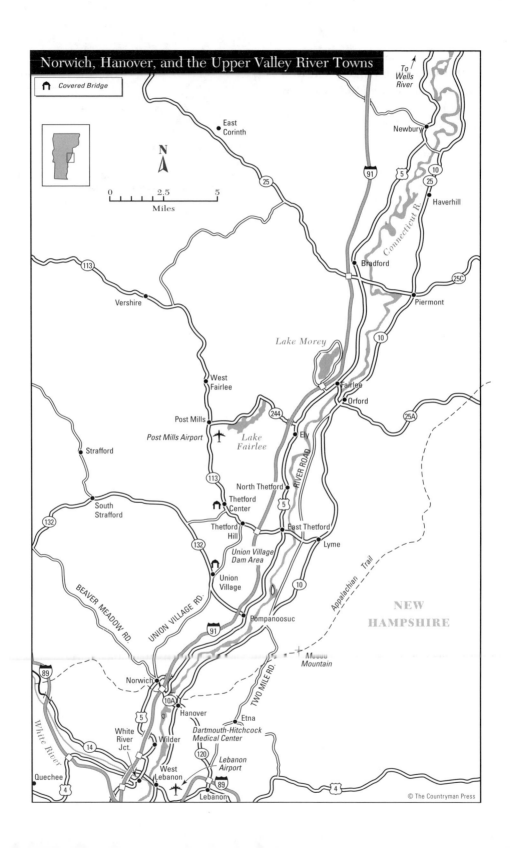

Norwich, Hanover, and the Upper Valley River Towns

Covered Bridge

N

0   2.5   5
Miles

To Wells River

East Corinth

Newbury

Haverhill

Bradford

Vershire

Piermont

Lake Morey

West Fairlee

Fairlee

Orford

Post Mills

Post Mills Airport

Strafford

Lake Fairlee

Ely

RIVER ROAD

North Thetford

Thetford Center

South Strafford

Thetford Hill

East Thetford

Lyme

Union Village Dam Area

Union Village

Appalachian Trail

NEW HAMPSHIRE

BEAVER MEADOW RD.

UNION VILLAGE RD.

Pompanoosuc

Moose Mountain

TWO MILE RD.

Norwich

Hanover

Etna

White River

White River Jct.

Wilder

Dartmouth-Hitchcock Medical Center

Lebanon Airport

Quechee

West Lebanon

Lebanon

© The Countryman Press

Fairlee Village, shelved between the Palisades and a bend in the Connecticut River, is a plain cousin to aristocratic Orford, New Hampshire (well known for its lineup of elegant Federal-era houses), just across the river. But we like it better. Check out Chapman's, a 19th-century pharmacy that has expanded in unusual directions. Summer camps and inns line nearby Lake Morey. Samuel Morey, a resident of Orford and a lumberman in Fairlee, was the inventor of the first steamboat: In 1793, 14 years before Fulton launched his *Clermont*, Morey was puffing up and down the river in a primitive craft barely big enough to hold him and his firewood. The remains of the little steamer are believed to lie at the bottom of Lake Morey, scuttled by its builder when the $100,000 in stock offered him by Robert Fulton turned out to be worthless. Morey also patented an internal combustion engine in 1825. Lake Fairlee, lined with children's camps and with a public swim beach, straddles the town line and is best accessed from Route 244 west of Ely.

Bradford, at the confluence of the Waits River and the Connecticut, is built on terraces of land above the floodplain. Buildings along the Connecticut side of its main street (Route 5) have another level below, and a golf course is sequestered down there behind the downtown. Favorite sons include James Wilson, an ingenious farmer who made America's first geographic globes in the early 1800s. Today the town is a good way stop for lunch and dinner and offers unexpectedly good shopping.

Newbury and Haverhill. The northern reaches of the Upper Valley are defined by these two unusually beautiful towns, both with handsome villages. Haverhill (New Hampshire) actually includes several very different villages. Newbury, Vermont, was known in the 19th century as a mineral spa, but the big old resort hotel has long since vanished.

✳ To See

South to north
MUSEUMS **American Precision Museum** (802-674-5781; www.americnprecision.org), 169 South Main Street, Windsor. Open May 30 through October, daily 10–5; $6 adults, $4 seniors, $18 family. An important, expanding collection of hand and machine tools, assembled in the 1846 Robbins, Kendall & Lawrence Armory, itself a national historic landmark. The firm became world famous in 1851 because of its

THE AMERICAN PRECISION MUSEUM IN WINDSOR

Kim Grant

✎ **Montshire Museum of Science** (802-649-2200; www.montshire.org),
1 Montshire Road, Norwich. Open daily 10–5 except Thanksgiving, Christmas,
and New Year's Day; $7 per adult, $6 per child 3–17. Use of the trails is free.
Few cities have a science museum of this quality. Happily this hands-on science center is on 110 trail-webbed acres beside the Connecticut River. The
name derives from Ver*mont* and New Hamp*shire* and the focus is on demysti-

MONTSHIRE MUSEUM, NORWICH

John Douglas

fying natural phenomena and on the Upper Valley in particular. River exhibits include an elaborate 2.5-acre Science Park: Water bubbles from a 7-foot Barre granite boulder, and from this "headwater" a 250-foot "rill" flows downhill, snaking over a series of terraces, inviting you to manipulate dams and sluices to change its flow and direction (visitors are advised to bring towels). You can also shape fountains, cast shadows to tell time, and push a button to identify the call of birds and insects within actual hearing. Note Ed Kahn's *Wind Wall,* a billboard-sized sheet attached to the museum's tower, composed of thousands of silver flutter disks that shimmer in the breeze, resembling patterns on a pond riffled by wind.

Inside the museum a new, federally funded wing focuses on this stretch of the

Gilbert Fox

THE MONTSHIRE MUSEUM IN NORWICH HAS DOZENS OF FASCINATING EXHIBITS FOR CHILDREN.

Silvio O. Conte National Fish and Wildlife Refuge; exhibits include a giant moose and tanks of gleaming local fish. Still, some of our favorite exhibits are in the original museum: the fog machine up in the tower, the see-through beehive, exhibits illustrating which vegetables and fruits float, and the physics of bubbles. There are also astounding displays on moths, insects, and birds. Most exhibits, even the boa constrictors (at designated times), are "hands on." While there's a corner for toddlers, an outside playground, and many demonstrations geared to youngsters, this is as stimulating a place for adults as for their offspring. The gift shop alone is worth stopping for. Inquire about guided hikes, special events, and exhibits. (See also *Green Space.*)

displays of "the American system" of manufacturing interchangeable parts, especially for what became the renowned Enfield rifle. Special exhibits vary from year to year.

New England Transportation Museum (802-291-9838; www.newengland transportationmuseum.org), Amtrak Station, 100 Railroad Row, White River Junction. Open Tuesday through Saturday 10–3. $2 adult, $1 child. Still evolving, this is a fascinating small museum with exhibits on rail, river, and air history that include dioramas, artwork, and photos as well as railroad memorabilia and models.

Hood Museum of Art (603-646-2808; www.dartmouth.edu/~hood), Dartmouth green, Hanover, New Hampshire. Open Tuesday through Saturday 10–5 and Sunday noon–5; until 9 PM Wednesday. Free. An outstanding collection of 65,000 pieces of art, ranging from Assyrian bas-reliefs donated by missionary graduates in the 1850s to works by Italian masters and American 18th- and 19th-century artists, is displayed in the downstairs galleries. A narrow flight of stairs rises dramatically to the high, skylit Lathrop Gallery, hung with major changing exhibits. Tours are available regularly; call 603-646-1569.

PAUL STARRETT SAMPLE, *BEAVER MEADOW* 1939, AT THE HOOD MUSEUM OF ART, DARTMOUTH COLLEGE. GIFT OF THE ARTIST, CLASS OF 1920, IN MEMORY OF HIS BROTHER, DONALD M. SAMPLE, CLASS OF 1921.

TK

South to north

☙ **Fort at Number Four** (603-826-5700; www.fortat4.com), Route 11, Charlestown, New Hampshire. Open May through October, 10–4; $8 adult, $6 seniors 55 and over, $5 children, under 6 free, $25 per family. Conjuring a little-remembered chapter in New England history, this riverside stockade replicates the fort that stood nearby during the French and Indian Wars in the 1740s. The original fell once but withstood repeated attacks. The complex includes a Great Hall, barns, and furnished living quarters. Costumed interpreters prepare meals, perform chores and crafts. Inquire about special events and reenactments. Check out the superb web site.

The Old Constitution House (802-828-3501; www.historicvermont.org), North Main Street, Windsor. Open late May through early October, Wednesday through Sunday 11–5. $2.50 per adult, free age 14 and under. This is Elijah West's tavern (but not in its original location), where delegates gathered on July 2, 1777, to adopt Vermont's constitution, America's first to prohibit slavery, establish universal voting rights for all males, and authorize a public school system. Excellent first-floor displays trace the history of the Republic of Vermont; upstairs is the town's collection of antiques, prints, documents, tools, and toys. Special exhibits vary each year, and a path out the back door leads to Lake Runnemede.

The Saint-Gaudens National Historic Site (603-675-2175; www.nps.gov/saga), Route 12A, Cornish, New Hampshire. Grounds open daily, dawn to dusk. Buildings open 9–4:30 daily late May through October. $5 adults (good for a week); free under age 17. This glorious property with a view of Mount Ascutney includes the sculptor's summer home and studio, sculpture court, and formal gardens, which he developed and occupied between 1885 and his death in 1907. Augustus Saint-Gaudens (1848–1907) is remembered primarily for public pieces: the Shaw memorial on Boston Common, the statue of Admiral Farragut in New York's Madison Square, the equestrian statue of General William T. Sherman at the Fifth Avenue entrance to Central Park, and the *Standing Lincoln* in Chicago's Lincoln Park. He was also the first sculptor to design an American coin (the $10 and $20 gold pieces of 1907). A new visitors center features a 28-minute film about the artist and his work. Augustus Saint-Gaudens loved the Ravine Trail, a 0.25-mile cart path to Blow-Me-Up Brook, now marked for visitors, and other walks laid out through the woodlands and wetlands of the Blow-Me-Down Natural Area. Saint-Gaudens was the center of the "Cornish Colony," a group of poets, artists, landscape artists, actors, architects, and writers who included Ethel Barrymore, Charles Dana Gibson, Finley Peter Dunne, and Maxfield Parrish; President Woodrow Wilson's wife was drawn into this circle, and the president summered at a nearby home from 1913 to 1915. *Note:* Bring a picnic lunch for Sunday-afternoon chamber music concerts, at 2 PM in July and August.

COVERED BRIDGES The **Windsor–Cornish Covered Bridge** is the longest such span not only in (or partly in) Vermont but also in the United States. Never mind those rumors of a new covered bridge somewhere; this is the real thing, originally constructed in 1866 (admittedly it has been rebuilt). There are also three covered bridges across the Mill Brook (just north and south of Route 44) in Brownsville, and three in Weathersfield: The **Titcomb Bridge** is on Route 106 across from the elementary school; the **Upper Falls Bridge** is on Upper Falls Road (turn south off Route 131 about 0.3 mile west of its junction with Route 106); and the **Salmond Bridge** is on Henry Gould Road (turn north off Route 131, 2.4 miles east of its junction with Route 106). The vintage-1870 **Baltimore Covered Bridge,** originally in North Springfield, has been moved to sit beside the Eureka Schoolhouse on Route 11 in Springfield, just off I-91.

✳ To Do

BALLOONING Post Mills Airport (802-333-9254), West Fairlee. Veteran balloonist Brian Boland offers early-morning and sunset rides. On the summer evening we tried it, the balloon hovered above hidden pockets in the hills, and we saw a herd of what looked like brown-and-white goats that, on closer inspection, proved to be deer. After an hour or so we settled down gently in an East Bradford farmyard and broke out the champagne.

Also see "Woodstock/Quechee Area" for more balloonists and New England's largest balloon festival.

BICYCLING Route I-91 drains a large percentage of traffic from Route 5, but this old highway along the river is still fairly busy. On the New Hampshire side of the river, search out the River Road that runs 8 miles north from Route 12A just north of the Saint-Gaudens site on through Plainfield. Also find the River Road from Route 10 north of Hanover (just north of the Chieftain Motel) through

MOUNT ASCUTNEY RISES BEHIND THE
WINDSOR–CORNISH COVERED BRIDGE.

Robert Kozlow

Lyme, rejoining Route 10 in Orford. Route 10 from Orford to Haverhill is also particularly beautiful, as is Route 5 in Vermont, between Fairlee and Norwich.

For inn-to-inn guided tours in this area, contact **Bike Vermont** (802-457-3553; 1-800-257-2226), and for self-guided tours. **Juniper Hill Inn** in Windsor and **Silver Maple Lodge** in Fairlee (see *Lodging*) cater to bicyclists, offering packages that combine biking and canoeing. **POMG** (1-888-635-BIKE) offers vehicle-supported camping tours.

Note: Amtrak's Vermonter, serving this corridor (see *Getting There*), carries bicycles. It's possible to detrain in Bellows Falls (26 miles south of Windsor), in Windsor, or in White

River Junction and explore this area on two wheels. We suggest, however, consulting some of the above bike-geared resources before you come.

BIKE RENTALS **Ascutney Mountain Resort** (802-484-3511) in Brownsville rents mountain bikes and offers 32 km of trails. **Wilderness Trails** (802-295-7620), Quechee, offers mountain bike rentals and mapped trails.

BIRDING *Connecticut River Birding Trail* (www.birdtrail.org), a pamphlet map/guide highlighting 46 birding sites in the Upper Valley, is free (although donations are appreciated); send a self-addressed stamped envelope (60¢) to Bill Shepard, Project Coordinator, 104 Railroad Row, White River Junction 05001.

BOATING With its placid water and lovely scenery, the Connecticut River through much of the Upper Valley is ideal for easygoing canoeists. Information on primitive campsites along this stretch of the Connecticut River can be found on the **Upper Valley Land Trust's** web site, www.uvlt.org. The **Connecticut River Joint Commissions** (603-826-4800; www.ctrivertravel.net) has published a useful *Boating on the Connecticut River* guide. Canoeing the Connecticut can, admittedly, be a bit of a slog. The headwind is as infamous as the lack of current. So what? Why does canoeing have to be about going great distances?

North Star Canoes (603-542-5802; www.kayak-canoe.com), Route 12A at Balloch's Crossing in Cornish, New Hampshire, just across the river from Windsor. John Hammond will shuttle patrons to put-ins either 3 or 12 miles above the Cornish–Windsor Covered Bridge so that they can paddle downstream toward the river's most famous landmark. Roughly half of North Star's patrons camp, either at **Wilgus State Park** (802-674-5422; see *Green Space*) or at another site in Windsor. This is probably New England's most picturesque livery: The check-in desk in the barn is redolent of bales of hay, and John Hammond may well be out front shoeing horses; the canoes are stacked behind the farmhouse.

Wilderness Trails (802-295-7620), Quechee, offers rentals and guided canoe and kayak trips, as well as shuttle service, for a stretch of the Connecticut north of that serviced by North Star Canoe (see above).

The **Ledyard Canoe Club** (603-643-6709), Hanover, New Hampshire, is billed as the oldest canoe club in America. It's named for a 1773 Dartmouth dropout who felled a pine tree, hollowed it out, and took off downriver (with a book of Ovid's poems), ending up at Hartford, 100 miles and several major waterfalls downstream. Hidden beyond Dartmouth's slick new rowing center, Ledyard is a mellow, friendly, student-run place. The canoeing and kayaking center for the 40 miles above Wilder Dam, it offers kayaking clinics as well as canoe and kayak rentals. No shuttle service.

Fairlee Marine (802-333-9745), Route 5 in Fairlee, offers pontoon, canoe, kayak, and rowboat rentals on the 40-mile stretch of the Connecticut above the Wilder Dam; the river is calm and relatively quiet.

FISHING You can eat the brown and rainbow trout you can catch in the Connecticut River. There's a boat launch at Wilder Dam, another just north of Hanover, and another on the Vermont bank in North Thetford. Guides and classes in fly-tying and fly-fishing are offered by **Lyme Angler** (603-643-1263), a source of fishing gear and tips, 8 South Main Street, Hanover, New Hampshire.
Also see Wilderness Trails in *Boating*.

GOLF **Crown Point Country Club** (802-885-2703), Weathersfield Station Road, Springfield. Eighteen holes, rolling terrain.

Windsor Country Club (802-674-6491); nine holes on Route 5, north of Windsor.

Hanover Country Club (603-646-2000), Rope Ferry Road, off Route 10, Hanover, New Hampshire. A classy, 18-hole course with pro shop and lounge, open May through October.

Lake Morey Inn Resort (802-333-4311; 1-800-423-1211) in Fairlee features an 18-hole golf course on which the Vermont Open has been played for more than 40 years.

Bradford Country Club (802-222-5207); nine holes down by the river.

HANG GLIDING **Mount Ascutney** is one of the prime spots in the country for hang gliding. For lessons, equipment, or a shuttle or flight, check with **Morningside Flight Park** (603-542-4416) in Claremont, New Hampshire.

HORSEBACK RIDING See Kedron Valley Stables in "Woodstock/Quechee Area."

SWIMMING Union Village Dam Area, Thetford (west on Route 132 from Norwich), offers swimming, picnicking, and fishing.

∂ **Storrs Pond Recreation Area** (603-643-2134), Reservoir Road, Hanover, New Hampshire, has a pool, pond, and camping; admission.

∂ **Treasure Island** (802-333-9625), Thetford, on Lake Fairlee, is a pleasant public beach with lifeguards and a tennis court; admission.

The beach at **Mill Pond** in Windsor is town owned, open to the public for a fee. **Stoughton Pond** is between Downers and Amsden, south of Route 131 or north from Route 106, near Springfield Dam Lake. **North Springfield Lake** also offers picnicking and swimming.

✳ Winter Sports

CROSS-COUNTRY SKIING **Lake Morey Inn Resort** (802-333-4800), Fairlee, maintains 12 miles of groomed trails.

Swenson Farm Sawyer Mountain Snowshoe Trails (802-333-4137; www.vtsnowshoetrails.com), Route 5, Fairlee. Bob and Melaine Swenson maintain 4 miles of trails on their Connecticut riverside dairy farm, along with a "moo-seum" filled with collectibles. They also rent and sell Tubbs snowshoes. Trail fee: $9 per person, $22 per family.

See also "Woodstock/Quechee Area."

DOWNHILL SKIING ✔ **Ascutney Mountain Resort** (802-484-7711; snow report and lodging reservations: 1-800-243-0011; www.ascutney.com), Brownsville (I-91, exit 8 or 9). A family-geared, self-contained resort. Current owners Steve and Susan Plausteiner have added major improvements, increasing snowmaking to 95 percent and adding the North Peak area to the mountain, substantially increasing its vertical drop and its expert trails; it's served by a mile-long fast quad chair. Facilities include a 215-room condo hotel, a sports center—with indoor pool and weight and racquetball rooms—a full restaurant, and a base lodge. *Lifts:* One quad, three triples, one double chairlift, one Wonder Carpet. *Slopes and trails:* 56. *Vertical drop:* 1,800 feet. *Snowmaking:* 95 percent. *Nursery/child care:* From 6 weeks. *Rates:* Adults $50 midweek, $54 weekend and holiday; juniors (7–16) and seniors (65–69) $34 midweek, $39 weekend and holiday; Sunday morning adult $46, junior $31. Half day $40. Substantially cheaper if you combine lifts and lodging. Midweek lifts and lodging $75 per person, weekends for 2 nights $125 per adult, $110 junior.

See also "Woodstock/Quechee Area" and "Okemo Valley Region."

✴ Green Space

✔ **Wilgus State Park** (802-674-5422; 802-773-2657), 1.5 miles south of exit 8, I-91, off Route 5, Windsor. Open mid-May through mid-October. This small, quiet campground on the Connecticut River is ideal for canoeists—the 19 lean-tos and tent sites are on the riverbank. Car shuttle service available; playground, picnic tables, hiking trails, canoe rentals.

In Springfield the **Toonerville Trail,** a new 10-foot-wide, paved recreation path good for bicycling and walking, follows the Black River along an old trolley line from the trailhead on Route 11 (behind the Robert Jones Industrial Center) 3 miles to another parking area on Route 5, just north of the Cheshire Bridge across the Connecticut. Just south of this bridge a service road leads to Hoyt's Landing, a recently upgraded put-in on the river, also a scenic picnic spot. At the Eureka Schoolhouse information center on Route 11, ask directions to the Springfield Nature Trail on the northern fringe of town. It winds through 50 acres of fields and woods.

Ascutney State Park (802-674-2060). Open mid-May through mid-

ASCUTNEY MOUNTAIN RESORT

David Brownell

October. Rising out of the valley to an elevation of 3,144 feet, Mount Ascutney is set in more than 2,000 acres of woodland. The 3.8-mile paved road to the summit begins on Route 44A, off Route 5, between Ascutney and Windsor. Of the four hiking trails to the summit, we recommend the 2.9-mile ascent from Weathersfield with an 84-foot waterfall about halfway (the trailhead is on Cascade Falls Road, 3.5 miles north off Route 131). The 3.2-mile Brownsville Trail begins on Route 44 between Windsor and Brownsville; the 2.7-mile Windsor Trail starts on Route 44A in Windsor. Granite was quarried here as early as 1808, and there was a popular summit house. Tent sites, trailer sites, and lean-tos can be reserved. The ski slopes and self-contained Ascutney Mountain Resort are accessible from Route 44 in Brownsville.

&. **Montshire Museum of Science Trails,** Norwich. The museum's 110 acres include a 12-acre promontory between the Connecticut River and the marshy bay at the mouth of Bloody Brook. The 0.25-mile trail leading down through tall white pines to the bay is quite magical. The 1.5-mile Hazen Trail runs all the way to Wilder Village. These trails are hard-packed, accessible to strollers and wheelchairs.

Thetford Hill State Park (802-785-2266). Open mid-May through Labor Day. Just off I-91, exit 14, 1 mile south of Thetford Hill on the Union Village Road. Developed by the Civilian Conservation Corps in the 1930s, 177 acres with a campground (14 tent/trailer sites, two lean-tos, hot showers), hiking and cross-country trails (maintained by Thetford Academy) and swimming in the Union Village Reservoir.

See also Quechee Gorge State Park in "Woodstock/Quechee Area."

✳ Lodging

South to north

RESORTS 🏂 **Ascutney Mountain Resort** (802-484-7711; 1-800-243-0011), Brownsville 05037, includes a 215-room condo hotel with flanking condominiums at the base of the ski area. Accommodations range from standard hotel rooms to three-bedroom suites with kitchen and fireplace and outdoor deck, furnished in reproduction antiques. Facilities include the full-service **Harvest Inn Restaurant** and a sports center, also tennis courts and indoor and outdoor pools, and extensive alpine trails in winter. Summer features tennis programs and children's adventure camps (ages 4–10). Summer and fall, from $75 for a room to $269 for a three-bedroom condo; winter, $75–90 per room to $330–470 three-bedroom condo. Inquire about packages. Five-day midweek packages are $99–139 per person, skiing and lodging included, cheaper for kids.

&. **Lake Morey Resort** (802-333-4311; 1-800-423-1211; www.lake moreyresort.com), Fairlee 05045. On the shore of Lake Morey, this sprawling, lakeside landmark has been reclaimed by members of the Avery family, who initially transformed it into a resort in the 1920s but sold it in the early 1990s. Over the past few years they have virtually gutted and rebuilt it, reducing the number of rooms (there are now 133), redoing bathrooms, phone lines, the works. The formerly '50s-style public spaces have also been totally revamped but the splendid lake view remains key, along with a player-friendly 18-hole golf course. Facilities include indoor and outdoor swimming pools, tennis and racquetball courts, a fitness center, cross-country ski and snowmobile trails in winter, and access to the Dartmouth Skiway. Grounds have also been landscaped. Winter, $87–107 per room, $109–145 per person MAP; summer, $125–195 EP per room, $95–160 MAP per person, including use of sports facilities. Ask about themed weekend packages.

INNS ⌾ ⅙ **Hartness House** (802-885-2115; 1-800-732-4789; www.hart nesshouse.com), 30 Orchard Street, Springfield 05156. In 1903 James Hartness built himself a stone-and-shingle mansion set in 32 acres on a parklike bluff. The inventor (Hartness patented 120 machines), aviator (he held one of the first 100 pilot's licenses in the United States and built Vermont's first airport), astronomer, and governor (1920–22) installed one of the first tracking telescopes in the country at the end of a 240-foot underground corridor connected to the mansion in 1910. It's still in use (inquire about tours), and since 1939 the mansion has been an inn. It now offers 42 old-fashioned guest rooms, 11 in the main house, the remainder in a connecting motel-like annex, each with private bath, phone, and color TV. There's a formal feel to the large lobby, with its traditional check-in desk, and to the pub and dining room (see *Dining Out*). Facilities include a swimming pool and nature trails. $99–175 double includes breakfast. Weddings are a specialty. Inquire about package plans.

The Inn at Weathersfield (802-263-9217; www.weathersfieldinn.com),

1342 Route 106, Weathersfield 05151. Set way back from quiet Route 106, just south of the village of Perkinsville. Dating in part from 1792 but with columns that give it an antebellum facade, this is one of Vermont's most distinctive and romantic inns, known for its fine dining. It's also back from the brink, rescued from bankruptcy by Jane and David Sandelman, who seem to be doing everything right. Each of the 12 guest rooms is different, and while all have phone and private bath, these vary from stall shower to Jacuzzi. Seven have fireplace (some gas, some wood burning). The inn is set in 21 wooded acres; facilities include a pond, and guests are encouraged to bike, canoe, and hike up Mount Ascutney. Traditionally this has also been one of Vermont's outstanding restaurants (see *Dining Out*); judging from reviews, executive chef Scott Myers has put it back on New England's culinary map. $140–210 includes a full breakfast. Inquire about special packages.

⌾ **Juniper Hill Inn** (802-674-5273; 1-800-359-2541; www.juniperhillinn .com), off Route 5 on Juniper Hill Road, Windsor 05089. Set high on a hill above its impressive drive, with a magnificent view of Mount Ascutney and the Connecticut River Valley, this splendid 28-room mansion, built by Maxwell Evarts in 1901, combines Edwardian grandeur with the informal hospitality of innkeepers Rob and Susanne Pearl and their corgis Cuddles and Tucker. Adult guests (and children over 12) can relax by the hearth in the huge main hall, in a second living room (with TV), or in the library with its leather armchairs and unusual hearth. One of Vermont's most romantic getaways, the inn offers no fewer than 11 guest rooms with fireplace (all but the 2 on the third floor are wood burning). All 16 guest rooms have private bath and are furnished with flair and genuinely interesting antiques. We never can decide which we like best, but Room 21 is a beauty (Teddy Roosevelt slept here): canopy bed, wood-burning fireplace, and plenty of places to sit. In Room 4 we like to sit at the desk overlooking Mount Ascutney, and both Rooms 2 and 3 have balconies with this view. Guests gather for meals in the dining room, a deep burgundy (it works) with floor-to-ceiling fireplace. Reserve for candlelight dinners (see *Dining Out*). Inquire about the Yankee Rambler Package, using rental canoes and 18-speed mountain bicycles. On the other hand, we could easily spend a day walking around Lake Runnemede, a hidden conservation area that's great for birding, and by the pool. Rates $105–195 per room, full breakfast included; add $25 for an additional person; add 17.5 percent gratuity on meals and beverages.

🌸 🐾 ♿ **Norwich Inn** (802-649-1143), Box 908, 225 Main Street, Norwich 05055. Originally built as a stage stop by Jasper Murdock in 1797, this is now a very Victorian but cheerful country inn with a total of 23 rooms and four apartments divided among the main building, the Vestry, and a backyard motel, all with private bath, telephone, and cable TV. Innkeepers Sally and Tim Wilson have created attractive public rooms, less formal than the Hanover Inn across the river, a gathering place for Dartmouth parents, faculty, and students. A brewpub, Jasper Murdock's Alehouse, features inn-made brews (see *Eating Out*). The dining rooms are open for breakfast, lunch, and dinner (see *Dining Out*). Rates run from $65 in the off-season in the motel to $149 in high season for a two-bedroom suite in the Vestry. All three meals are served. Dogs are permitted in one twin-bedded room in the motel.

NORWICH INN, NORWICH

Christina Tree

☙ **The Pond House at Shattuck Hill Farm** (802-484-0011; www .pondhouseinn.com), P.O. Box 234, Brownsville 05037. Vermont native David Raymond and Gretel Schuck have created a real gem of a place, an 1830s Cape by the side of a steeply rising back road, with views across fields to mountains. We love the square dining room with its pumpkin pine floors and original six-over-six windows, and we love the spare, tasteful way the three guest rooms are furnished, each with private bath. Breakfast might feature orange French toast, and the dinner menu might include tuna with artichoke hearts or wild mushroom risotto. The 10-acre grounds include a croquet court and gardens as well as the spring-fed swim pond. Horses and polite dogs can be accommodated. In winter there's skating, sledding, and cross-country skiing. Dinner and full breakfast are included in $150 per couple, $200 with dinner (northern Italian). Inquire about Orvis-guided fly-fishing weekends, also about the "puppy getaway weekend."

BED & BREAKFASTS **The Inn at Windsor** (802-674-5670; 802-236-5561), 106 Apothecary Lane, Windsor 05089. Larry Bowser and his wife, Holly Taylor, have restored the vintage-1786 Green Mansion, set above Main Street in downtown Windsor and handy to paths around Lake Runnemede and to Mill Pond. Guests enter through a landscaped garden, are asked to remove their shoes, and are then given freshly laundered slippers. Both guest rooms have antique woodstoves built into the hearth, and there is a working

fireplace in the suite. All three rooms are interestingly, eclectically furnished, as is the gathering space around the original kitchen hearth and a contemporary breakfast room. The old buttery is now a guest party complete with fridge. $125–165 includes a four-course breakfast served when guests desire.

☙ ♫ **Mill Brook Bed & Breakfast** (802-484-7283; www.millbrookbb .com), Box 410, Route 44, Brownsville 05037. Kay Carriere creates extravagant breakfasts for guests at her 1880s farmhouse near Mount Ascutney. She also goes the extra mile to make guests comfortable in her two frilly rooms and three suites, all with private bath and names like Columbine and Raspberry. Fresh-baked goods and hot drinks are always available, and there are no fewer than four common rooms, as well as a hot tub among the trees. Inquire about the swimming hole. Children and some pets (by previous agreement) welcome. $70–140 double.

♫ **Burton Farm Lodge** (802-484-3300; www.bbonline.com/vtburton farm.com), 27 Cross Road, West Windsor 05089-9713. An old farmstead by a large trout pond on a back road near Mount Ascutney. The feel here is that of a homey farm, not your usual B&B. There are two rooms (shared bath). Families are welcome, and children will feel at home immediately. German spoken. $70–80 per couple includes breakfast; $10 per extra person.

🐾 ☙ **Silver Maple Lodge & Cottages** (802-333-4326; 1-800-666-1946; www.silvermaplelodge.com), 520 U.S. Route 5 South, Fairlee 05045. Situated just south of the village on Route 5, Silver Maple was built as a farmhouse in 1855 and has been welcoming travelers for more than 80 years. Now run by Scott and Sharon Wright, it has seven nicely appointed guest rooms in the lodge and eight separate, pine-paneled, shaded cottages. The farmhouse has cheerful sitting rooms with exposed 200-year-old hand-hewn beams in the living room and dining room, where fresh breads appear with other continental breakfast goodies. The newest cottages with kitchenette and working fireplace are real beauties. Play horseshoes, croquet, badminton, or shuffleboard on the lawn, or rent a bike or canoe. Scott will also arrange a ride in a hot-air balloon for you at neighboring Post Mills Airport. Scott grew up on a Tunbridge farm and takes pride in introducing visitors to Vermont. $69–99 per couple. Pets accepted in the cottages.

🍑 **Peach Brook Inn** (802-866-3389), Doe Hill, off Route 5, South Newbury 05051. Ray and Joyce Emery have opened their spacious 1837 home with its splendid view of the Connecticut River. What a special place! Common space includes two nicely furnished parlors with exposed beams and a fireplace, an open kitchen, and a screened porch with a view of Mount Moosilauke across the river. The house is on a country lane in the almost vanished village of South Newbury, once connected to Haverhill, New Hampshire, across the river by a long-gone covered bridge. Plenty of farm animals are within walking distance. There are three comfortable guest rooms; $60–65 with shared bath, $70–75 with private, including full breakfast. No smoking. No children under 10, please; under 18 are $10.

Glenwood (802-866-3396; glenwood@together.net), 4354 Route 5, Newbury 05051. In an early-19th-century house on the fringe of this handsome village, John and Carolyn Keats and their two young daughters offer three comfortable-looking, antiques-furnished guest rooms, two with shared and one with a private bath. Floors are wide planked, there's a working fireplace in the living room, and breakfast is served at the dining room table. $55–75 includes taxes as well as breakfast. An efficiency rental unit (attached but with a separate entrance) with two bedrooms, a living room, and a full kitchen is $550–700 per week.

♿ **The Whipple Tree Bed & Breakfast** (802-429-2076; 1-800-466-4097; www.whipple-tree.com), 487 Stevens Place, Wells River 05081. This is a real find, a contemporary house, designed to be a B&B, perched higher than any other on the Vermont side of the valley, set in no less than 500 acres with spectacular views east to the White Mountains. Bill and Carol Bailey are about as deeply rooted in the area. Bill is descended from General Jacob Bayley, charged during the American Revolution by George Washington to build the famous Bayley-Hazen Road across the Northeast Kingdom. The six spacious guest rooms all have private bath (General Jacob features a gas fireplace and soaking tub), also phone and TV, and the many-windowed common space is immense. Extras include a hot tub, exercise and game room, and meeting space. $140–190; $15 per extra person.

See also **Bailey's Mills B&B** in Reading, described in "Woodstock/Quechee Area."

HOTEL 🐾 ☙ **The Hotel Coolidge**
(802-295-3118; 1-800-622-1124;
www.hotelcoolidge.com), White River
Junction 05001, is one of the last of
the old railroad hotels. All 30
elevator-served guest rooms have private bath, phone, and TV. Some back
rooms are depressingly dark, but others are quite roomy and attractive,
and the family suites (two rooms connected by a bath) are a real bargain.
The hotel sits across from the Amtrak
station and next to the Briggs Opera
House. Local buses to Hanover and
Lebanon stop at the door, and rental
cars can be arranged. Search out the
splendid Peter Michael Gish murals
in the Vermont Room, painted in
1950 in exchange for room and board
while the artist was studying with Paul
Sample at Dartmouth. Owner-
manager David Briggs, a seventh-
generation Vermonter, takes his role
as innkeeper seriously and will
arrange for special needs. $69–79 per
room double. Children free.

HOSTEL 🐾 ☙ **The Hotel Coolidge**
(802-295-3118). A wing of the
Coolidge, described above, is a
Hostelling International facility with
dorm-style beds and access to a self-
service kitchen and laundry. Private
family rooms are also available by
reservation. $19 for HI members, $29
for nonmembers.

**LODGING WORTH CROSSING THE
RIVER FOR** 🐾 **Moose Mountain
Lodge** (603-643-3529; moosemoun
tainlodge.com), P.O. Box 272, Etna,
New Hampshire 03750. Open June
through October, December 26
through mid-March, Wednesday
through Sunday. This is the most
alpine inn in all of New England,
perched high on a steep hill behind
Hanover, just off the Appalachian
Trail with spectacular views to the
west across the Connecticut River to
the Green Mountains. Kay and Peter
Shumway have been here since 1975
and obviously enjoy what they do,
greeting guests like old friends and
preparing memorable meals from the
freshest ingredients. The 11 guest
rooms are small but attractive, with
handmade log beds and five shared
baths. Inside and out, the lodge has
plenty of pine. It was built of stones
and logs cleared from this hill. The
350 acres include a deep pond just
outside the door, ample woods, and
meadows with long views. In winter it
offers 50 miles of cross-country ski
trails. $200 per couple MAP in winter
includes lunch, $90 MAP in summer
and fall; $55 for children 12 and
under MAP.

🐾 🐾 ☙ **Loch Lyme Lodge and Cottages** (603-795-2141; 1-800-423-
2141), Route 10, 70 Orford Road,
Lyme, New Hampshire 03768. The
Main Lodge is open year-round; the
cabins, Memorial Day through mid-
September. There are four rooms in
the inn and 22 brown-shingled cabins
(11 with cooking facilities) spread
along a wooded hillside overlooking a
lake called Post Pond. The big attraction here is a private beach with a
float and a fleet of rowboats, canoes,
and kayaks. Two tennis courts, a baseball field, basketball court, volleyball
net, and recreation cabin are there for
the using, and babysitting is available
for parents who want time off. Breakfast and dinner are served, and a take-
out lunch bar is open for sandwiches
and cones. Loch Lyme was founded
in 1917 and has been owned and
managed by Paul and Judy Barker's
family since the 1940s. No credit

cards. Pets permitted in cabins. From $53 single and $68 double off-season to $110 double in summer (including breakfast). Housekeeping cabins are $625–950 per week; children's rates.

🦌 🏠 ♿ **Piermont Inn** (603-272-4820), 18 Church Street, Piermont, New Hampshire 03779 (across the bridge from Bradford, Vermont). A 1790s stagecoach stop with six rooms, four in the adjacent carriage house (only the two in the inn are open year-round), all with private bath. The two in the main house are outstanding, both carved from the tavern's original ballroom, high-ceilinged and spacious, with writing desks and appropriate antiques. The carriage house rooms are simple but cheery; one is handicapped accessible. Common space includes a living room with fireplace, TV, wing chairs, and a nifty grandfather clock. Charlie and Karen Brown are longtime Piermont residents who enjoy tuning in guests to the many ways of exploring this upper (less touristed) part of the Upper Valley, especially to canoeing the river (they offer a canoe and informal shuttle service). Breakfast is full, and dinner can be arranged. $85–125 in-season, otherwise $65–95. Breakfast is included in winter.

The Gibson House (603-989-3125; www.gibsonhousebb.com), 341 Dartmouth College Highway, Haverhill, New Hampshire 03765. Artist Keita Colton has restored Haverhill's classic 1850 Greek Revival stagecoach stop and offers seven fantasy rooms, lavishly and imaginatively decorated, and breakfasts to match. The house fronts on Route 10, but the sunporch and terraces overlook gardens and the Connecticut River. $120–175 includes a full breakfast.

✳ Where to Eat

South to north

DINING OUT ♫ **Penelope's** (802-885-9186), on the square, Springfield. Open daily for lunch and dinner except Sunday; no lunch on Saturday. Polished woods, stained glass, and greenery, an attractive setting for dining from a large menu. Choices range from beef fillet flambéed in brandy to Rosie's Scrod and baked lasagna. Children's menu. Dinner entrées $10.95–24.95.

Hartness House (802-885-2115), 30 Orchard Street, Springfield. Closed Monday. Open for lunch and dinner weekdays, dinner only on weekends. The dining room in this venerable landmark is a popular special-occasion place for local residents and generally has a good reputation. The dinner menu might include apple fennel and pork sausage wrapped in puff pastry for an appetizer, and prime rib as a main course. A complete dinner with appetizer, entrée, dessert, and a glass of wine is $22.95.

The Inn at Weathersfield (802-263-9217), 1342 Route 106, just south of Perkinsville. Historically this is one of the best restaurants in Vermont, a tradition that seems to be reestablishing itself under new ownership. Executive chef Scott Myers's menu changes constantly but might include venison osso buco braised in port and rosemary with roasted beets and red bliss potatoes, poached Atlantic boneless skate wing with Swiss chard and cranberry potatoes, or coconut and curry quinoa with snap peas, marinated portobellos, basil, and cashews. Entrées $14.50–23.50.

♫ **Windsor Station Restaurant** (802-674-2052), Depot Avenue,

Windsor. Built as a passenger train station (it remains an Amtrak stop), now decorated in natural wood plus velvet and brass. It serves reasonably priced dinner with entrées from chicken Kiev or amandine and veal Madeira to the Station Master filet mignon topped with shrimp, asparagus, and hollandaise sauce. A children's menu is available. Inexpensive to moderate.

Juniper Hill Inn (802-674-5273), Route 5 north of Windsor. Dinner is at 7 PM by reservation Tuesday through Saturday. Innkeeper Susanne Pearl is the chef, offering a four-course prix fixe menu that might include pork tenderloin with prosciutto stuffing and mushroom sauce, or grilled halibut with black bean and corn relish. $35 per person. The wine list is respectable.

Skunk Hollow Tavern (802-436-2139), Hartland Four Corners, off Route 12 north of I-91, exit 9. Dinner Wednesday through Sunday. Reservations suggested. Carlos Ocasio's split-personality restaurant is hidden away in a small village that's easily accessible both from the Connecticut and the Ottauquechee River Valleys. Patrons gather downstairs in the pub to play darts and backgammon and to munch on fish-and-chips, mussels, or pizza; the generally excellent, more formal dining is upstairs in the inn's original parlor. The menu changes every few months, but staples include Chicken Carlos and fish-and-chips. Variables might be red pepper shrimp with Oriental pasta or shiitake chicken; always salad of the day and homemade soups. $7.25–24. Live entertainment Wednesday and Friday nights.

Como Va (802-280-1956), 1 South Main Street, White River Junction.

Open Tuesday through Saturday for lunch and dinner. This appealing trattoria is a popular addition to the Valley. You might begin with carpaccio or mussels simmered with toasted garlic, fennel, sweet tomatoes, and vermouth, and proceed to "pasta your way," combining a choice of pastas with a choice of fillings and sauces ($13.95 adults, $7.95 children). The long list of entrées ranges from classic eggplant Parmesan to herb-roasted lamb chops and rosemary skewered Gulf shrimp. Entrées $13.95–28.95. Regional Italian wines are featured.

Carpenter and Main (802-649-2922; www.carpenterandmain.com), Main Street, Norwich. Open for dinner except Tuesday from 6; reservations a must. Chef-owner Peter Ireland fills the space that was formerly Poule à Dents, but it's been altered substantially to create a livelier, less formal ambience. The menu, too, is less traditional, with vegetarian dishes complementing staples like bouillabaisse and roast pork loin. A fall trio of vegetables, all presented with their tops on, comprised baby pumpkin filled with sage cream and Gruyère, zucchini stuffed with creamy polenta, and sweet onion filled with barley. Try the house pâté for starters. Entrées $18–26.

Norwich Inn (802-649-1143), 225 Main Street, Norwich, popular locally for breakfast, lunch, and dinner, also Sunday brunch. Closed Monday. Although the dining rooms are traditional, they are bright and inviting, far from stuffy. The menu changes every few months, but a dinner menu might include house-cured salmon and potato blinis or escargots and wild mushroom vol-au-vent as appetizers, then a main dish of sautéed fresh

Maine lobster over grilled corn and white bean succotash, or free-form vegetarian lasagna filled with grilled baby carrots, broccolini, and *haricots verts*. Entrées $15.95–24.95.

Peyton Place (603-353-9100; www.peytonplacerestaurant.com), Route 10, Orford, New Hampshire. Open Wednesday through Sunday 5:30–10:30 and for Sunday brunch. Reservations recommended. This is destination dining. A fixture for years in Bradford, this legendary restaurant (named for owners Jim, Heidi, Sophie, and Shamus Peyton) has moved across the river to New Hampshire (it's 0.5 mile down Route 10 from the Fairlee–Orford bridge). It's housed in the vintage 1773 Mann Tavern, the town's restored original tavern, with just five tables but a tavern menu ($6–15.50); there's also a more formal dining room (seven tables). Jim is the chef and known for signature dishes such as lobster and feta salad, served warm with orange vinaigrette. He's also known for his chorizo dumplings and Vietnamese bouillabaisse. Dinner entrées might include rack of lamb with wild mushrooms, vegetarian ravioli handmade to order, and a fresh fish dish, perhaps Caribbean-style tuna with salsa. Ice creams and sorbets are handmade, and desserts usually include chocolate tacos and perhaps warm apple pie with cinnamon ice cream. The wine list is varied and reasonably priced; quality spirits are served. At this writing, patio dining is planned for summer. Entrées $17.50–25.50.

The Perfect Pear Café (802-222-5912; www.theperfectpearcafe.com), the Bradford Mill, Main Street, Bradford. Dinner reservations recommended. Open Tuesday through

Saturday for lunch, Thursday through Saturday for dinner. Chef-owners Eric and Nancy Harting have created a charming bistro serving fresh, sophisticated food. You might begin with pumpkin and walnut ravioli in Gorgonzola cream sauce, then dine on horseradish-crusted sea bass over mashed potatoes garnished with sweet chive oil, or crispy polenta with a portobello and fig glaze over wilted spinach. Nancy makes the desserts from scratch. Try the bread pudding with whiskey sauce. Weather permitting, there's dining on the patio overlooking the Waits River, churning along because the big falls are just across the road. Dinner entrées $11.95–19.95.

Warners Gallery Restaurant (802-429-2120), just off I-91, exit 17, on Route 302, Wells River. Open Tuesday through Thursday 5–8:30 PM, Friday and Saturday 5–9, Sunday 11–8. A dependable (90 percent of the time) all-American family restaurant with some atmosphere. Entrées usually include twin stuffed lobster tails, a fireman's platter, baked stuffed shrimp, and roast prime beef au jus. There's a children's menu, and Sunday brunch (11–2) is billed as "best in the Northeast." Dinner entrées $11.95–22.95. Full liquor license.

Also see **Keepers, Meadows at the Quechee Inn, Parker House Inn,** and **Simon Pearce Restaurant** in "Woodstock/Quechee Area."

EATING OUT *Morning Star Café* (802-885-6987; www.morning-star-café.com), 56 Main Street, Springfield. Open Monday through Friday from 7 AM, until 5 Monday and Tuesday, until 9 Wednesday and Thursday, and until 9:30 Friday; Saturday

8 AM–9:30 PM. An airy storefront with high ceilings, widely spaced tables, periodicals, and the comfortable feel of a big living room; good espresso, chai, and latte, and pastries, plus a full deli with freshly made soups, quiche, salads, sandwiches, and wraps. The dinner menu changes daily; on our last visit it included chicken hibiscus and Cundy's Harbor scallops. There's a wine list.

✒ **McKinley's** (802-885-9186), on the square, Springfield. Same fern-bar atmosphere as Penelope's (see *Dining Out*) but a different menu. A good lunch stop: burgers, taco salad, sandwiches, pastas, and soups.

✒ **Springfield Royal Diner and Precision Valley Corvette Museum** (802-886-1400; www.springfield royaldiner.com), 363 River Street (Route 106). Open Sunday through Thursday 6–9, weekends 6–10. A vintage-1955 diner that stood in Kingston, New York, this chrome classic was moved to its present spot and restored and expanded in 2003 as an adjunct to a showroom full of classic Corvettes, the collection of a local resident who periodically auctions one off to boost the local (depressed) economy. The diner's food is just fine, judging from a cup of potato ham soup and a BLT on wheat toast. Specials included homemade turkey stew and an open-faced roast pork sandwich. Service is fast, and patrons are "honey" and "dear." You don't have to eat to tour the museum, which is free.

✒ **Country Creemee Restaurant,** Downers Corner (junction of Routes 131 and 106), Amsden. Seasonal. Locals will tell you that everything tastes good here; we always get the superlong hot dog to consume at a picnic table under the trees.

Brownsville General Store (802-484-7480), Route 44 just west of the entrance to Ascutney Mountain Resort. A regular general store with busy gas pumps but also with a big red Aga cookstove behind the lunch counter, a clue to the quality of soups and daily specials like chicken and biscuits. Bread is fresh baked, and there's a full deli.

✒ **Dan's Windsor Diner** (802-674-5555), 135 Main Street, Windsor. Open daily 8–8. The new owner is Fred Borcuk, and this spiffed-up 1952 classic Worcester diner retains its rep for good diner food: meat loaf, liver and onions, and macaroni and cheese, along with omelets, burger baskets, pies, and more.

✒ **Shepherd's Pie Restaurant and Deli** (802-674-9390), 131 Main Street, Windsor. Open from 7 AM (Sunday from 8) for breakfast through lunch and dinner until 8 PM; closing Sunday at 3 PM. Every town should have a comfortable gathering spot like Sharon Shepherd's tangerine-walled storefront. The food is fine, judging from a generous chicken quesadilla one summer day and a rather unorthodox but tasty shepherd's pie

SHEPHERD'S PIE RESTAURANT, WINDSOR

Christina Tree

on a chilly autumn evening. Specialties include soups, vegetarian dishes, and "Ralphies" (baked, breaded chicken breast, sliced and rolled into a tortilla with a choice of toppings). The deli is a sandwich source for picnicking on the river, the Mill Pond, or Lake Runnemede.

Yama Restaurant (603-298-5477), 96 Main Street, West Lebanon, New Hampshire (just across the Route 4 bridge from White River Junction; turn right at the light and it's just up on the left in a small shopping center). Open Tuesday through Saturday (until 10 PM) for lunch and dinner; Sunday from 3 PM. The fare is essentially Korean and terrific, if you like a large choice of udon noodle, miso, seaweed, and spicy soups, as well as house specials like "Yukyejang," which turned out to be shredded beef and vegetables in a spicy broth with side dishes of pickled cucumber and sweet but firm baked beans. There are also donburi, tempura, and teriyaki dishes, and a reasonably priced sushi bar (served with miso soup). Wine and beer are served.

Jasper Murdock's Alehouse in the Norwich Inn (802-649-1143), 225 Main Street, Norwich. Open 5:30–9. The house brew comes in many varieties (see *Brews*). The Alehouse is a green-walled, comfortable pub; the bill of fare changes frequently but usually represents some of the best "bar food" in the Valley. The menu might include "Light Fare" like Maine crabcakes and Louisiana oyster po' boys (with homemade French bread), and moderately priced full-fare dishes such as pork schnitzel with apple sauerkraut and cider currant sauce, grilled flank steak with wheatberry and dried fruit sauté, and shepherd's pie.

Alléchante Patisserie and Cafe (802-649-2846), Main and Elm Streets, Norwich. Open Tuesday through Friday 7:30–5:30; until 3 Saturday. Formerly "Alice's," Nicky Barraclough's shop is in a small shopping complex, easy to miss but well known to local residents who drop by for a morning brioche and latte and to check the daily sandwich board. This might include freshly roasted beef with homemade horseradish cream on white sourdough, and imported fresh goat cheese with sliced tomatoes and green olive spread on a baguette. There are also daily baked artisan breads and pastries, plus a full deli with a weekly changing take-out dinner menu. It might include chicken potpies, roast skate with peas and mash and a variety of vegetables, plus a choice of meat and fish. This is also a place to pick up farmstead cheeses. The new name is French for "mouthwatering."

✐ **Fairlee Diner** (802-333-3569), Route 5, Fairlee. Closed Tuesday, otherwise open 5:30–2, until 7 Thursday and 8 Friday. Turn left (north) on Route 5 if you're coming off I-91. This is a classic wooden diner built in the '30s (across the road from where it stands), with wooden booths, worn-shiny wooden stool tops, and good food. The mashed potato doughnuts are special, and both the soup and the pie are dependably good. Daily specials.

Leda's Restaurant & Pizza (802-333-4773), Route 5, Fairlee. Open Wednesday through Sunday for lunch and dinner. This is a friendly standby for Greek specialties like moussaka, gyros, and feta cheese pie along with burgers, pizza, and even rib-eye steak.

Your Place (802-333-9050), Route 5, Fairlee. Open for all three squares but closed Wednesday and Sunday. This is your basic liver and onions, fried clams, and Yankee pot roast kind of place with a full bar.

✄ **Colatina Exit** (802-222-9008), Main Street, Bradford. Open daily 5–10 PM; weekends until 11. Carol Meagher's Vermont trattoria has been here more than 30 years but recently doubled in size and added a wood-fired pizza oven and an expanded to-go. We still like the original dining room best: candles in Chianti bottles, Italian scenes on the walls, checked (green in summer, red in winter) tablecloths, and a few tables in back with a view of the river. The big menu offers plenty of antipasto and insalata choices and traditional Italian dishes like "lasagna classico" and veal parmigiano; also some nice surprises like grilled chicken portofino (with sautéed portobello mushrooms and fresh spinach in a red Marsala marinara sauce) and wood-roasted scallops carbonara (with spinach and smoked bacon). Plenty of pizza choices and calzones. There's also an upstairs pub with river views.

Bliss Village Store and Deli (802-222-4617), Main Street, Bradford. Housed in a former 19th-century hotel, this is a classic general store but with Crock-Pots full of good soup, chili, or stew-fried chicken and a deli with daily specials; tables are in the back—including a booth with the best river view in town.

✄ **The Hungry Bear** (802-222-5288), Route 5 (just off I-91), Bradford, open daily 7 AM–7 PM, until 8 on Saturday, evolved from a hamburger stand into a dependable roadfood stop. At this writing it's upscaling again, but we trust it will still be

known for generous servings and nightly specials.

Newbury Village Store (802-866-5681), 4991 Route 5, Newbury. This is another in the new breed of nouvelle general store that is proliferating around the state. Gary and Maggie Hatch have added comfortable seating near the periodicals and expanded the deli to feature sandwiches named for local landmarks like "The Oxbow" ("basil herb roasted turkey breast with Vermont cheddar, ripe tomatoes, leaf lettuce and the house garlic cream cheese spread on multi grain bread"). There's also a hummus wrap and "the flatlander" ("shaved black pastrami warmed and piled high on rye and pumpernickel swirl bread, topped with swiss cheese and deli mustard"). There are staple groceries, also a selection of wine and Vermont products.

Happy Hours Restaurant (802-757-3466), Route 5, Wells River. Open daily 11:30–8. This solid, pine-paneled family restaurant in the middle of town serves lunch and dinner, fully licensed.

✄ **P&H Truck Stop** (802-429-2141), just off I-91, exit 17, on Route 302, Wells River. Open 24 hours. Dozens of rigs are usually parked outside on one side, and the license plates on cars in the other lot are usually quite amazing. This is a classic truck stop with speedy service, friendly waitresses, and heaping portions at amazing prices.

See also **Skunk Hollow Tavern** under *Dining Out.*

BREWS **Jasper Murdock's Alehouse** in the Norwich Inn (802-649-1143), Main Street, Norwich. Open 5:30–9. Brewmaster Timothy Wilson prides himself on reviving the New

England tradition of inns brewing their own beer (his brews are sold nowhere else). Jasper Murdock's Ales, crafted from English malts, come in four varieties (our favorite is Whistling Pig Red) and have a strong local following.

Harpoon Brewery (1-888-HAR-POON; www.harpoonbrewery.com), south of exit 9, north of Windsor on Route 5. Open Tuesday through Saturday 10–6; tour (and tastings) are usually at 11, 1, and 3. Founded in Boston in 1986 and still Boston based, Harpoon purchased this, the former Catamount Brewery, in 2000. The "visitors center" here consists of a shop that doubles as a "beer garden," selling deli sandwiches and, well, beer.

✳ Entertainment

MUSIC AND THEATER **Hopkins Center for the Arts** (603-646-2422), Dartmouth green, Hanover, New Hampshire. Three theaters, a recital hall, and art galleries feature year-round programs of plays, concerts, and films.

✔ **Northern Stage** (802-296-7000), at the Briggs Opera House, White River Junction. This excellent community theater group offers semi-professional productions year-round. Special children's theater classes and summer arts education classes.

The Parish Players (802-785-4344), based in the Eclipse Grange Hall on Thetford Hill, is the oldest community theater company in the Upper Valley; its September-through-May repertoire includes classic pieces and original works; summer presentations vary.

In the past few seasons, venues have burgeoned for folk, blues, and hard-

to-label, idiosyncratic performers. The **Lebanon Opera House** (603-448-2498), on the green in Lebanon, New Hampshire, is one of the most active. **Opera North** (603-643-1946) stages semiprofessional performances of a very high standard including one major opera, usually at the Lebanon Opera House, every August. Smaller performances are offered at other times of the year in various locations in the Upper Valley.

FILM **Dartmouth Film Society** at the Hopkins Center (603-646-2576), Dartmouth green, Hanover, New Hampshire. Frequent showings of classic, contemporary, and experimental films in two theaters.

The Nugget (603-643-2769), South Main Street, Hanover, New Hampshire. Four first-run films nightly.

✔ **Fairlee Drive-In** (802-333-9192), Route 5, Fairlee. Summer only; check local papers for listings.

MUSIC **The Club Car** (802-674-5551; www.windsorstation.com), next to Windsor Station (see *Dining Out*), opens at 7 PM Friday and Saturday for live jazz and blues.

✳ Selective Shopping

ARTS AND CRAFTS **The Vault** (802-885-7111; www.galleryatthe vault.com), 65 Main Street, Springfield. Located strategically next to the Morning Star Café, this quality crafts store is all about Visual Art Using Local Talent (hence its name) and is definitely worth checking out.

Vermont State Craft Gallery, Windsor (802-674-6729; www.vscg .org), 85 Main Street, Windsor. Open daily 10–6, Sunday 11–5. A stunning retail showcase/gallery for Vermont craftspeople: glass, ceramics, furniture, jewelry, textiles, metal, paper, photography, fine arts, and cards with constantly changing special exhibits.

Cider Hill Farm (802-674-5293), Hunt Road, 2.5 miles west of State Street, Windsor. Sarah Milek's commercial display garden (see *Farms*) is the setting for Gary Milek's studio, displaying his striking Vermont landscapes done in egg tempera, botanically correct floral prints, and stunning cards made from them.

Lampscapes (802-295-8044; www.lampscapes.com), 77 Gates Street, White River Junction. Open Tuesday through Saturday 10–5. Kenneth Blaisdell is a former engineer and a serious landscape artist whose combination studio/shop is one of the more exciting shopping finds in Vermont. The lamps themselves are simple but artistic and the shades are definitely works of art, each one-of-a-kind and ranging from luminescent literal to semi-abstract, truly striking landscapes, priced within reasonable reach.

South Road Pottery (802-222-5798), 3458 South Road, Bradford. Open May through October, daily 10–5; otherwise by appointment. Worth searching out both for its back-road locale and for Bruce Murray's distinctive, functional pottery: butter and condiment dishes, teapots, bowls, mugs, lamps, trays, and more.

BOOKSTORES ✇ The Norwich Bookstore (802-649-1114), Main Street, Norwich. This nifty, bright, very personalized shop in a classic house next to the post office has a knowledgeable staff, a great children's section, and frequent readings and signings by authors and illustrators.

The Dartmouth Bookstore (603-643-3616), 33 South Main Street, Hanover, New Hampshire. A full-service independent bookstore on the campus of Dartmouth College.

Booked Solid (802-222-5826), Main Street, Bradford. Open daily except Sunday. Donna Repsher and Robin Lornitzo have a full house of used and some new books.

FACTORY TOURS AND SHOPS

Simon Pearce Glass (802-674-6280; www.simonpearce.com), Route 5, north of Windsor. Open daily 9–5. Pearce operated his own glassworks in Ireland for a decade and moved here in 1981, acquiring the venerable Downer's Mill in Quechee and harnessing the dam's hydropower for the glass furnace (see "Woodstock/Quechee Area"). He subsequently built this additional, 32,000-square-foot facility down by the Connecticut River. Designed to be visitor-friendly, it includes a catwalk above the factory floor—a fascinating place from which

GLASSBLOWING AT SIMON PEARCE IN WINDSOR

Kim Grant

you can watch glass blown and shaped. Of course there's a big showroom/shop featuring seconds as well as first-quality glass and pottery.

King Arthur Flour Baker's Store (802-649-3361; 1-800-652-3334; ww.kingarthurflour.com), Route 5, Norwich. Open Monday through Saturday 9–6, Sunday 10–4. This home as well as prime outlet for the country's oldest family-owned flour company (since 1790) draws serious bakers, and would-be bakers, from several time zones. The vast post-and-beam store itself is a marvel, its shelves stocked with every conceivable kind of flour and baking ingredient along with a selection of equipment and cookbooks. Bread and pastries are made in the adjacent bakery (with a glass connector allowing visitors to watch the hands and skills of the bakers). Next door is the new Baking Education Center, offering baking classes ranging from beginner to expert, from piecrusts to braided breads and elegant pastries.

Pompanoosuc Mills (802-785-4851; www.pompy.com), Route 5, East Thetford. Open weekdays 9–6, Saturday 9–5, Sunday noon–5. Dwight Sargeant began building furniture in his riverside house, a cottage industry that has evolved into a riverside factory with showrooms throughout New England. Furniture is made to order. Check out the big tent sale Memorial Day weekend.

Copeland Furniture (802-222-5300; www.copelandfurniture.com), 64 Main Street, Bradford. Open Monday through Friday 10–6, Saturday 10–5. Contemporary, cleanly lined, locally made furniture in native hardwoods displayed in the handsome showroom across from Waits Falls. Seconds.

SPECIAL SHOPS Vermont Salvage Exchange (802-295-7616), Railroad Row, White River Junction, for doors, chandeliers, moldings, mantels, old bricks, and other architectural relics.

Ceramica (1-800-270-0900; www .ceramicadirect.com), 94 Main Street, Windsor. This is ostensibly an outlet specializing in Renaissance-inspired majolica that's stunning—also quite expensive.

Dan and Whit's General Store, Main Street, Norwich. Open daily 7 AM–9 PM. Next to the Norwich Inn, a general store among general stores: great bulletin board, groceries, buttons, hardware, clothing, advice.

Chapman's (802-333-9709), Fairlee. Open daily 8–6, until 5 on Sunday. Since 1924 members of the Chapman family have expanded the stock of this old pharmacy to include 10,000 handtied flies, wines, Mexican silver and Indonesian jewelry, used books, and an unusual selection of toys—as well as nightcrawlers and manila envelopes. Check out the antiques in the barn. This time we bought a wooden puzzle and a stove mitt.

Farm-Way, Inc. (1-800-222-9316), Route 25, Bradford. One mile east of I-91, exit 16. Open 8:30–5:30, Friday until 8, closed Sunday. Billed as "complete outfitters for man and beast," this is a phenomenon, a Vermont version of L.L. Bean—which means it's different: Specialties include work boots and rugged clothing that now includes a huge stock of everything from hay to furniture spread through several buildings over 15 acres: tack, pet supplies, syrup, a wide choice of snowshoes (inquire about snowshoe clinics), and probably the state's best choice of jackets. Shoes and boots remain a specialty, from size 4E to 16;

10,000 shoes, boots, clogs, sandals, and sneakers in stock. The emphasis is on American-made.

FARMS Cider Hill Farm (802-674-5293), Hunt Road, 2.5 miles west of State Street, Windsor. Growers of herbs and perennials, creators of herb wreaths, dried-flower arrangements, herbal blends, and apple cider.

Killdeer Farm (802-649-2852) has a farm stand on Route 5 just south of Norwich. Open every day from May through October, with a wide variety of Vermont products, baked goods, and fruit, as well as bedding plants and organic vegetables.

Norwich Farmer's Market, south of Norwich on Route 5. Open Saturday 9–1 from May through October. A real happening, this is the place to see and be seen on summer Saturdays. Local farmers bring produce, wool, baked goods, flowers, and handmade crafts; live music under the gazebo.

Cedar Circle Farm (802-785-4101), East Thetford. Famous for its four varieties of cantaloupes; also good for local peas and strawberries.

Crossroad Farm (802-333-4455), on the crossroad between Routes 113 and 244, Post Mills. Fresh local produce sold at a seasonal stand near the shores of Lake Fairlee.

4 Corners Farm (802-866-3342), just off Route 5, South Newbury. Bob and Kim Gray sell their own produce and flowers. An exceptionally pretty farm, just off but up above the highway.

✳ Special Events

July–August: Sunday-afternoon (2 PM) **lawn concerts** at the Saint-Gaudens National Historic Site (603-675-2175) in Cornish, New Hampshire; free with admission to the grounds. Bring a picnic.

July: On Saturday night at the Old Grange Hall (historical society: 802-824-5294) in Brownsville (West Windsor), **baked bean and salad suppers** have been held since 1935. **Windsor Heritage Days** (weekend following July 4) celebrate Vermont's birthplace as a republic. **Connecticut Valley Fair** (midmonth), Bradford. **Cracker Barrel Bazaar** (third or final weekend), Newbury includes plenty of fiddling (802-866-5521).

August: **North Haverhill (New Hampshire) Fair**—old-style fair with ox and tractor pulls, pig races, and more. **The Quechee Scottish Festival** is big (see "Woodstock/Quechee Area").

September: **Apple Festival** at King Arthur Flour, Norwich. **Octoberfest** at the Harpoon Brewery, Windsor.

October: The annual **Vermont Apple Festival** (802-885-2779), Springfield, is held Columbus Day weekend and includes a crafts show. **Festival Windsor** is an annual autumn celebration.

November: **Annual Wild Game Supper** (Saturday before Thanksgiving) in Bradford (802-222-4721)—hungry visitors pour into the Congregational church for this feast.

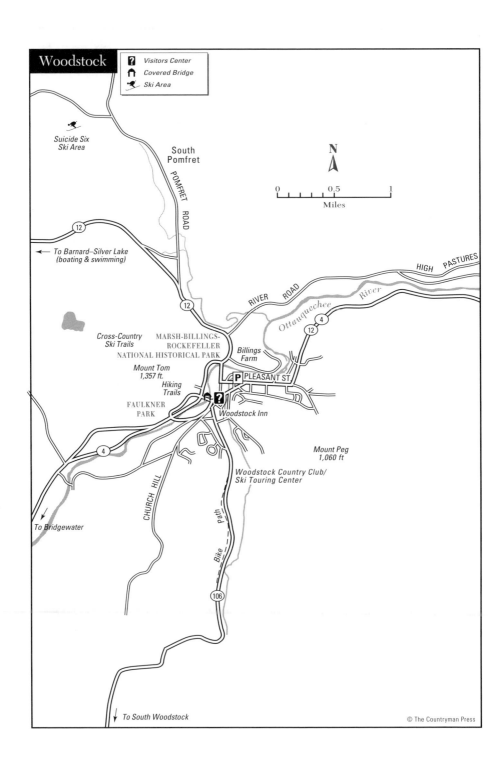

Woodstock

?	Visitors Center
⌂	Covered Bridge
🎿	Ski Area

Suicide Six
Ski Area

South
Pomfret

POMFRET ROAD

N

0   0.5   1
Miles

12

← To Barnard–Silver Lake
(boating & swimming)

HIGH PASTURES

12

RIVER ROAD

Ottauquechee River

4

12

Cross-Country
Ski Trails

MARSH-BILLINGS-
ROCKEFELLER
NATIONAL HISTORICAL PARK

Billings
Farm

Mount Tom
1,357 ft.

Hiking
Trails

P PLEASANT ST

FAULKNER
PARK

Woodstock Inn

4

Mount Peg
1,060 ft

Woodstock Country Club/
Ski Touring Center

CHURCH HILL

Bike Path

To Bridgewater

106

To South Woodstock

© The Countryman Press

WOODSTOCK/QUECHEE AREA

Cradled between Mount Peg and Mount Tom and moated by the Ottauquechee River, Woodstock is repeatedly named among the prettiest towns in America. The story behind its good looks, which include the surrounding landscape as well as historic buildings, is told at the Marsh-Billings-Rockefeller National Historical Park, the country's only national park to focus on the concept of conservation.

The Ottauquechee River flows east through Woodstock along Route 4 toward the Connecticut River, generating electricity as it tumbles over falls beneath the covered bridge at Taftsville and powering Simon Pearce's glass factory a few miles downstream in Quechee Village. Below Quechee it has carved Vermont's "Grand Canyon," 163-foot-deep Quechee Gorge, spanned by Route 4 and by a high, spidery railroad bridge.

The Woodstock Railroad carried passengers and freight the 20 miles east from Woodstock to White River Junction between 1875 and 1933. How to ease current traffic congestion, which includes 18-wheelers headed for Rutland as well as tour buses and tourists in summer and fall and skiers in winter, remains a very real challenge. Route 4 is the shortest way across "Vermont's waist," and an ever-growing stream of vehicles continues to wind up the valley, filing through the middle of Woodstock, around its exquisite green, and on through the village of West Woodstock, following the river west into Bridgewater (past another born-again mill).

Our advice: Get off Route 4. Turn off at Quechee Gorge and walk the canyon rim. Turn off into Quechee Village and follow River Road to Billings Farm. Continue on Route 12 beyond the national park, north to Barnard. Follow Route 106 south from the Woodstock green into horse country. Like most of the world's famously beautiful and heavily touristed areas, especially those that are also home to sophisticated people who could live anywhere, the Ottauquechee River Valley offers visitors plenty to see and do superficially and still more, the more you explore.

GUIDANCE **The Woodstock Area Chamber of Commerce** (802-457-3555; 1-888-496-6378; www.woodstockvt.com), 18 Central Street, Woodstock 05091, keeps an information booth open on the green, June through October (802-457-

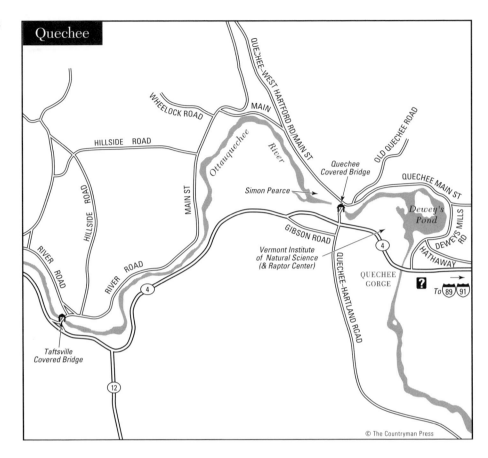

Quechee

1042) and publishes *Window on Woodstock,* a useful free pamphlet guide. Lodging places post available rooms on their web site, and during foliage season the chamber also finds beds in private homes for stranded leaf-peepers. Restrooms are available in the town hall, west of the green.

The Hartford Area Chamber of Commerce (802-295-7900; 1-800-295-5451; www.hartfordvtchamber.com), 211 North Main Street, White River Junction 05001, covers Quechee and four other villages in the town of Hartford. The chamber maintains an information booth on Route 4 at Quechee Gorge, open mid-May through mid-October. Also check out www.easternvermont.com. A year-round Quechee Gorge visitors center is due to open in 2005.

GETTING THERE *By car:* Route 4 west from I-91 and I-89.

By train: **Amtrak** to White River Junction.

By bus: **Vermont Transit** to White River Junction, with connections to and from Rutland via Woodstock; tickets at the Whipple Tree, Central Street, Woodstock.

MEDICAL EMERGENCY Emergency service is available by calling **911.**

PARKING Woodstock's meter wardens are notoriously zealous; red drop boxes in front of the town's two pharmacies are provided to pay fines. The free lot is by the river on Pleasant Street.

WHEN TO COME This area is as genuinely year-round as Vermont gets. Marsh-Billings-Rockefeller National Historical Park and the Billings Farm Museum are open May through mid-October, but Woodstock's early-December Wassail Weekend is its most colorful event, and January through March bring cross-country and alpine skiing.

✳ Villages

Woodstock. In the 1790s, when it became the shire town of Windsor County, Woodstock began attracting influential and prosperous professionals, who, with local merchants and bankers, built the concentration of distinguished Federal houses that surround the elliptical green, forming an architectural showcase that has been meticulously preserved. In the 19th century it produced more than its share of celebrities, including Hiram Powers, the sculptor whose nude *Greek Slave* scandalized the nation in 1847, and Senator Jacob Collamer (1791–1865), President Lincoln's confidant, who declared, "The good people of Woodstock have less incentive than others to yearn for heaven."

Three eminent residents in particular—all of whom lived in the same house but in different eras—helped shape the current Woodstock (see the box on page 240).

"Innkeeping has always been the backbone of Woodstock's economy, most importantly since 1892 when the town's business leaders and bankers decided to build a new hotel grand enough to rival the White Mountain resorts," Peter Jennison writes in *Woodstock's Heritage*. By the turn of the 20th century, in addition to several inns, Woodstock had an elaborate mineral water spa and golf links,

STATELY BUILDINGS ON THE GREEN IN WOODSTOCK

and it had become Vermont's first winter resort, drawing guests from Boston and New York for snowshoeing and skating. In 1934 America's first rope tow was installed here, marking the real advent of downhill skiing.

By the early 1960s, however, the beloved Woodstock Inn was creaky, the town's ski areas had been upstaged, and the hills were sprouting condos. Laurance Rockefeller acquired the two ski areas (upgrading Suicide Six and closing Mount Tom) and had the 18-hole golf course redesigned by Robert Trent Jones Sr. In 1969 he replaced the old inn. Rockefeller also created the Woodstock Foundation, a nonprofit umbrella for such village projects as acquiring and restoring dozens of historic homes, burying power lines, and building a new covered bridge by the green. In 1992 it opened the Billings Farm & Museum. The Marsh-Billings-Rockefeller National Historical Park, which includes the neighboring Rockefeller mansion and the 550 surrounding forested acres on Mount Tom, opened in 1998.

Woodstock itself remains a real town with a lot going on. Events chalked on the "Town Crier" blackboard at the corner of Elm and Central Streets are likely to include a supper at one of the town's several churches (four boast Paul Revere bells), the current film at the theater in town hall, as well as events at the historical society and guided walks or talks at the Vermont Institute of Natural Science (VINS).

Note: The Woodstock Historical Society has published detailed pamphlets and guides available at Dana House (see *Also See*). For a brief history of the town, see Peter Jennison's informative and nominally priced *Woodstock's Heritage.*

Quechee, on Route 4, some 6 miles east of Woodstock, is one of five villages in the township of Hartford. In the mid– and late 19th century life revolved around the J. C. Parker and Co. mill, which produced a soft baby flannel made from "shoddy" (reworked rags). A neighboring mill village surrounded the Deweys Mill, which made baseball uniforms for the Boston Red Sox and the New York Yankees. In the 1950s, however, both mills shut down. In the '60s the Deweys Mill virtually disappeared beneath a flood-control project (see North Hartland Lake under *Green Space*) and 6,000 acres straddling both villages was acquired by the Quechee Lakes Corporation, the largest second-home and condominium development in the state. Thanks in good part to Act 250, Vermont's land-use statute, the end result is unobtrusive. Most homes are sequestered in woods; open space includes two (private) 18-hole golf courses. In Quechee Village the mill is now Simon Pearce's famous glass factory and restaurant, and the former mill owner's mansion is the Parker House Inn. Dramatic Quechee Gorge is visible from Route 4 but is best appreciated if you follow the trail to the bottom. Tourist-geared shops and eateries continue to proliferate along Route 4, but, along back roads, so does village conservation land.

❋ Must See

East to west
Quechee Gorge, Route 4, is one of Vermont's natural wonders, a 3,000-foot-long, 163-foot-deep chasm sculpted 13,000 years ago. Visible from the highway,

it is now encompassed by a state park that includes hiking trails along the rim and down into the gorge. See *Green Space.*

Visitors Center for Billings Farm & Museum and the Marsh-Billings-Rockefeller National Historical Park, Route 12 north of Woodstock Village. Open May through October, daily 10–5. The parking lot and visitors center at Billings Farm serve both the farm and national park with displays on Marsh, Billings, and Rockefeller and a theater showing *A Place in the Land,* Charles Guggenheim's award-winning documentary dramatizing the story of all three men. (There's no admission fee for the restrooms and a gift shop, but a nominal fee is charged to see the film if you aren't visiting the farm or museum.)

⚓ **Billings Farm & Museum** (802-457-2355; www.billingsfarm.org). Open daily May through October and for special events throughout the year. $9 adult, $8 over 65, $7 ages 13–17, $4.50 ages 5–12, $2 ages 3–4. Exhibits demonstrate life on Frederick Billings's model "gentleman's" farm in the 1890s: plowing, seeding, cultivating, harvesting, and storing crops; making cheese and butter; woodcutting and sugaring. The 1890 farm manager's house has been restored. Visitors can also observe what happens on a modern dairy farm with a prizewinning Jersey herd. Look for the sheep and two friendly 2,000-pound workhorses, Ruth and Kate; cows are milked daily at 3 PM. Inquire about special events, like apple days and wool days in fall; Thanksgiving weekend and Christmas weekend celebrations; sleigh rally weekends in January and February; and periodic demonstrations and crafts exhibits, including quilts during the month of August.

Marsh-Billings-Rockefeller National Historical Park (802-457-3368; www.nps.gov/mabi), Route 12 north of Woodstock Village. Mount Tom carriage roads and forest trails (see *Green Space*) are open year-round. Mansion tours are offered late May through October and are limited to a dozen visitors at a time (reservations are advised: $6 adult, $4 seniors). The **Carriage Barn** (late May through October, 10–5; free), an elegant space with dark bead-board walls and the feel of a library, features the exhibit *Celebrating Stewardship—People Taking Care of Places.* It positions Marsh, Billings, and Rockefeller within the time line of America's conservation history. Multimedia displays profile individuals practicing conservation around the world. Visitors are invited to record their own conservation stories on computers. More unusual still for a national park is the reading area with its conference-sized table (crafted from wood harvested on Mount Tom) with relevant books, including children's stories. The Queen Anne mansion is well worth visiting. Notable 19th-century furniture, Tiffany glass, and American art aside, it offers a sense of the amazing indi-

A HALLOWEEN PARADE AT THE BILLINGS FARM & MUSEUM

Billings Farm & Museum

GEORGE PERKINS MARSH (1801–1882), FREDERICK BILLINGS (1823–1890), AND LAURANCE ROCKEFELLER (BORN 1910)

Three men in particular have helped shape Woodstock's landscape. The first, George Perkins Marsh, born and raised here, had damaged his eyesight by age 7 by devouring encyclopedias and books on Greek and Latin. Sent outdoors, he studied the woods, fields, birds, and animals with equal intensity. As a man he noted the effects of logging on the landscape (60 percent of Vermont's virgin forest was harvested in the first half of the 19th century) and the resulting floods and destruction of fisheries. Later, traveling in the Middle East as the U.S. ambassador to Turkey, Marsh noted how once-fertile land had become desert. He wrote: "I fear man has brought the face of the earth to a devastation almost as complete as that of the moon."

Marsh wrote *Man and Nature* at age 63, while U.S. ambassador to Italy. Published in 1864, it is widely recognized as the first book to acknowledge civilization's effect on the environment, and the first to suggest solutions. In contrast to Henry David Thoreau (*Walden* appeared in 1854), Marsh doesn't idealize wilderness. Instead, he attempts to address the interdependence of the environment and society as a whole.

Man and Nature isn't an easy read, but it greatly influenced this country's nascent sciences of forestry and agriculture as well as many of the era's movers and shakers, among them Frederick Billings. Raised in Woodstock, Billings departed at age 25 for San Francisco. That city's first lawyer, he made a fortune registering land claims and speculating in land during the

viduals who lived there. The guided, interpretive tour—about an hour—begins in the former carriage house.

✳ Also See

The Dana House (home of the Woodstock Historical Society, 802-457-1822), Elm Street, Woodstock. Open 10–4 (Sunday noon–4), May through October and certain winter weekends. Admission $5; 40-minute tours on the hour. John Cotton Dana was an eminent early-20th-century librarian and museum director whose innovations made books and art more accessible to the public. Completed in 1807 and occupied for the next 140 years by the Dana family, this historic house has an interesting permanent exhibit portraying the town's economic heritage and an admirable collection of antiques, locally wrought coin silver, portraits, porcelains, fabrics, costumes, and toys. The John Cotton Dana Library is a research and reference center. There is also an exhibit gallery.

The Vermont Institute of Natural Science/Vermont Raptor Center (802-FLY-5000; www.vinsweb.org), Route 4, Quechee. Open daily, year-round, Monday through Saturday 10–4; $8 adults. A beloved institution, VINS has recently gold rush. As a returning son who had "made good," Billings spoke at the 1864 Windsor County Fair, remarking on the rawness of the local landscape, the hills denuded by logging and sheep grazing. In 1869 he bought the old Marsh farm and transformed the vintage-1805 house into a mansion. On Mount Tom he planted more than 100,000 trees, turned a bog into Pogue Pond, and created the carriage roads. Billings's primary home was in New York, and as president of the Northern Pacific Railroad (the reason Billings, Montana, is named for him) he toured the country extensively. He continued, however, to retreat to Woodstock, creating a model dairy farm on his property, a project sustained after his death, through thick and thin, by his wife and two successive generations of Billings women.

In 1934 Frederick Billings's granddaughter Mary French (1910–1997) married Laurance Rockefeller in Woodstock. John D. Rockefeller Jr. had been largely responsible for creating more than 20 state and national parks and historic sites; Laurance inherited his father's commitment to conservation and quickly became an effective advocate of ecotourism. In the 1950s Mary Rockefeller inherited the Billings estate in Woodstock and Laurance bought and replaced the old inn, incorporating the golf course and Suicide Six ski area into one resort. He also created the Woodstock Foundation, a nonprofit umbrella for numerous village projects (see *Villages*) and for collecting local antique farm tools and oral histories, opening the Billings Farm & Museum in 1983. In 1992 the Marsh-Billings-Rockefeller National Historical Park was created. It opened in 1998.

moved to a new home: 47 acres of rolling forestland just west of Quechee Gorge. VINS styles itself as a living museum devoted to birds of prey. Resident raptors include bald eagles, peregrine falcons, snowy owls, hawks, and other birds of prey that have been injured. They are displayed in huge outdoor flight enclosures. There are outdoor interpretive exhibits, nature trails, and a nature shop. Inquire about naturalist-led walks, and flight programs.

A RED-TAILED HAWK MEETS THE PUBLIC THANKS TO VINS.

VINS

⚓ **The Norman Williams Public Library** (802-457-2295), on the Woodstock green. Open daily except Sunday and holidays. A recently renovated Romanesque gem, donated and endowed in 1883 by Dr. Edward H. Williams, general manager of the Pennsylvania Railroad and later head of Baldwin Locomotives. It offers children's story hours, poetry readings, and brown-bag summer concerts on the lawn. Public restrooms.

COVERED BRIDGES There are three in the town of Woodstock—the **Lincoln Bridge** (1865), Route 4, West Woodstock, Vermont's only Pratt-type truss; the **Middle Bridge,** in the center of the village, built in 1969 by Milton Graton, "last of the covered-bridge builders," in the Town lattice style (partially destroyed by vandalism and rebuilt); and the notable red **Taftsville Bridge** (1836), Route 4 east, utilizing multiple king- and queenposts and an unusual mongrel truss. The Taftsville Bridge overlooks a hydroelectric dam, still in use.

SCENIC DRIVES The whole area offers delightful vistas; one of the most scenic shortcuts is the North Road, which leaves Route 12 next to Silver Lake in Barnard and leads to Bethel. Another is Cloudland Road from River Road, and River Road itself, running from Quechee's Main Street to the Billings Farm & Museum in Woodstock.

✳ To Do

BALLOONING Darrek Daoust's Balloons of Vermont (802-291-4887; www.balloonsofvermont), based in Quechee, operates year-round (the two-person basket has a seat) and will launch from your home or inn (conditions permitting); **Balloons Over New England** (1-800-788-5562; www.balloonsover newengland.com) operates seasonally from Quechee, which is also the scene of the **Quechee Hot Air Balloon Festival** on Father's Day weekend in June, New England's premier balloon festival, featuring rides as well as live entertainment and crafts (see *Special Events*).

BICYCLING Bike Vermont (802-457-3553; 1-800-257-2226; www.bikevt.com), Box 207, Woodstock. Vermont's most experienced, most personalized, and altogether best inn-to-inn tour service, offering weekend, 5-, and 7-day trips through much of Vermont. Twenty-one-speed Trek and Cannondale hybrids are available for rent. Tours are also offered to Ireland.

Biscuit Hill Bike and Outdoor Shop (802-457-3377), 490 Woodstock Road (Route 4), West Woodstock. A source of rentals and local bike maps (River Road from Woodstock to Quechee Village is a designated bike trail).

Wilderness Trails (802-295-7620), Clubhouse Road at the Quechee Inn. Bike rentals for the whole family, plus maps.

Woodstock Sports (802-457-1568), 30 Central Street, Woodstock, has mountain and hybrid bike rentals.

BOATING Wilderness Trails (802-295-7620), Clubhouse Road at the Quechee Inn, offers guided canoe and kayak trips; also rentals and shuttle service on the Connecticut, White, and Ottauquechee Rivers, as well as in the Deweys Mills Waterfowl Sanctuary. Inquire about island camping.

Silver Lake State Park (802-234-9451) in Barnard rents rowboats.

FISHING Vermont Fly Fishing School (802-295-7620), the Quechee Inn at Marshland Farm. Marty Banik offers lessons as well as providing tackle and guided fishing on Dewey's Pond and the Connecticut, White, and Ottauquechee Rivers. **Trout on the Fly** (802-685-2180) also offers drift-boat trips and fly-fishing guiding and lessons.

GOLF AND TENNIS Woodstock Country Club (802-457-2114; www.wood stockinn.com), part of the Woodstock Inn and Resort, offers one of Vermont's oldest (1895) and most prestigious 18-hole golf courses, redesigned by Robert Trent Jones Sr. in 1961. There are also 10 tennis and two paddle tennis courts. Facilities include a pro shop, putting green and practice range, lessons, electric carts, restaurant, and lounge.

✧ **Vail Field,** Woodstock. Two public tennis courts and a children's playground.

✧ **Quechee Gorge Mini Golf** (802-296-6669), Route 4, next to Quechee Gorge, 18 holes.

HEALTH & FITNESS CENTER Woodstock Health & Fitness Center (802-457-6656), part of the Woodstock Inn and Resort, Route 106, recently renovated with indoor tennis and racquetball, lap pool, whirlpool, aerobic and state-of-the-art fitness equipment; spa treatments, facials, massage, manicure and pedicure; flexible memberships and day-use options; pro shop.

HORSEBACK RIDING Woodstock has been an equestrian center for generations, especially for the hardy Morgans, which are making a local comeback in South Woodstock.

Kedron Valley Stables (802-457-1480), Route 106, South Woodstock. Generally recognized as one of the best places to ride horseback—if you know how but don't happen to own a horse—in New England. Learn to ride or spiff up your skills in the ring, or take a guided trail ride, a weekend vacation, a 6-day riding clinic (with accommodations at Kendall Homestead), or a 4-day inn-to-inn tour that averages 20 miles a day, 5 hours in the saddle. Over the years Paul and Barbara Kendall have pieced together a network of paths to link appealing inns. They lead riders over hiking and recreation trails, dirt roads, and meadows. Inquire about carriage, wagon, and sleigh rides.

The Green Mountain Horse Association (802-457-1509), Route 106, South Woodstock. Sponsor of the original 100-mile ride, an annual event around Labor Day that draws entrants from all over; shows, trials, and other popular events.

LLAMA TREKKING Woodstock Llama Trekking (802-457-3722; 802-457-5117; www.woodstockllamatreks.com), The Red Cupboard, Route 4, West Woodstock. Mid-May through October, Brian Powell leads patrons on trails up through the woods to a scenic picnic spot.

POLO Quechee Polo Club. Matches are held most Saturday afternoons in July and August on the field near the center of the village.

ROCK CLIMBING ♪ **The Wall** (802-457-2221; www.vermontrocks.com), just east of the intersection of Routes 4 and 12, Quechee. Call for hours and rates. This new indoor rock climbing gym and bouldering cave draws serious local climbers year-round. Equipment rentals and instruction for adults and children; birthday parties a specialty. Also includes an outdoor driving range.

SWIMMING **Silver Lake State Park** (802-234-9451; 802-773-2657), 10 miles north on Route 12 in Barnard, has a nice beach, and there's another smaller one right next to the general store.

♪ **The Woodstock Recreation Center** (802-457-1502), 54 River Street, has two public pools, mostly for youngsters.

Also see *Health & Fitness Center* for an indoor pool.

✳ Winter Sports

CROSS-COUNTRY SKIING AND SNOWSHOEING **Woodstock Ski Touring Center** (802-457-6674; www.woodstockinn.com) utilizes the 30 km trail system on **Mount Tom,** which ranks with some of the best groomed in New England. It's composed largely of 1880s carriage roads climbing gently from the valley floor (700 feet) to the summit (1,250 feet), skirting a small lake, and finally commanding a view of the village below and down the Ottauquechee Valley. The system offers vistas in many directions and a log cabin heated with a woodstove. The center itself, source of tickets, a map, ski and snowshoe rentals (also poles), lockers and lessons, is at the Woodstock Country Club, Route 106 south of the village, part of the Woodstock Inn and Resort, with 10 km of gentle, meadow skiing out the door, connecting with another 20 km of woodland trails on

CROSS-COUNTRY SKIERS IN WOODSTOCK

Woodstock Inn and Resort

Mount Peg as well as 10 km of snowshoe trails. Group and individual lessons; guided, 4-hour picnic tours; rentals; salesroom; lockers; soup and sandwiches; $13.25 per adult, $9 junior; skiers pay half price at the Woodstock Health & Fitness Center.

Wilderness Trails (802-295-7620), Clubhouse Road at the Quechee Inn, has 18 km of track-set trails, including easy loops through the woods and meadows around Quechee Gorge, offering fine views of its waterfalls, also harder trails down into the gorge. Snowshoe rentals are also offered.

DOWNHILL SKIING ♪ **Suicide Six Downhill Ski Area** (802-457-6661; www.woodstockinn.com), South Pomfret, 5 miles north of Woodstock on Pomfret Road. Heir to the first ski tow in the United States, which was cranked up in 1934 but on the other side of this hill. Suicide Six is now part of the Woodstock Inn and Resort complex and has a base lodge finished with native woodwork. Its beginners area has a J-bar ($6 for all day); two double chairlifts climb 655 vertical feet to reach 23 trails ranging from easy to The Show Off and Pomfret Plunge, plus a half-pipe for snowboarders. Lessons, rentals, restaurant. Weekend/holiday lift rates are $48 for adults and $32 for seniors and children; weekdays (with just the big chair running) it's $28 adult, $22 seniors and children. Half-day and single-ride rates; free lifts and rentals midweek (nonholiday) to Woodstock Inn guests.

ICE SKATING **Silver Lake,** by the general store in Barnard. **Union Area,** at Woodstock Union High School, Route 4 West, occasionally has night skating for families. **Woodstock Sports** (802-457-1568), 30 Central Street, Woodstock, offers skate and ski rentals. **Wilderness Trails** (see *Cross-Country Skiing*) in Quechee also rents skates and clears the pond on its property and across the road.

SLEIGH RIDES **Kedron Valley Stables** (802-457-1480; www.kedron.com), Route 106, South Woodstock. Weather permitting, sleigh rides are offered daily.

✳ Green Space

Mount Tom's 1,250-foot summit towers above the village of Woodstock. It's one of Vermont's most walked and walkable mountains. From Mountain Avenue in the village itself **Faulkner Park** (donated by Mrs. Edward Faulkner, one of Woodstock's most thoughtful philanthropists) features a trail patterned on Baden-Baden's "cardiac" walks. A marked, 1.6-mile path zigzags up to the summit (bring a picnic; a bench overlooks the village). The **Marsh-Billings-Rockefeller National Historical Park** encompasses more than 500 acres on the back side of Mount Tom, with 30 miles of footpaths that were originally carriage roads, including a trail and picnic tables at Pogue Pond. Enter on Route 12 at the park (follow signs) or at the trailhead on Prosper Road, just off Route 12. Inquire about frequent seasonal programs offered by the national park (802-457-3368). Also see *Cross-Country Skiing* for winter use.

Mount Peg Trails begin behind the Woodstock Health & Fitness Center on Route 106 (ask directions at the desk). Open May through October. One is roughly 5 miles round trip, a peaceful walk up along easy switchbacks beneath pines with picnic bench at the summit, with views west down the valley to Killington.

Quechee Gorge State Park (802-295-2990; www.vtstateparks.com), off Route 4, Quechee. This 611-acre preserve encompasses the gorge (see *Must See*), and trails from the rim lead gently down (south of Route 4) into the gorge, which should be approached carefully. On a hot day it's tempting to wade into the shallow water at the south end of the gorge—but beware sudden water releases that have been known to sweep swimmers away. Ditto for the rockbound swimming hole at the north end of the gorge under the spillway. Look for picnic tables under the pines on Deweys Mills Road. The campground (open mid-May

POGUE POND IN THE MARSH-BILLINGS-ROCKEFELLER NATIONAL HISTORICAL PARK   Rolf Diamant

through October 15) offers 47 tent/trailer sites, seven lean-tos, and a dump station. This property belonged to a local woolen mill until the 1950s when it was acquired by the U.S. Army Corps of Engineers as part of the Hartland Dam flood-control project.

North Hartland Lake Recreation Area (802-295-2855) is a 1,711-acre preserve created by U.S. Army Corps of Engineers to control the confluence of the Ottauquechee and Connecticut Rivers. It offers a sandy beach, wooded picnic area with grills, and nature trail. Access is poorly marked, so ask directions at the Quechee information booth.

Silver Lake State Park (802-234-9451; January through May: 1-800-299-3071; www.vtstateparks), Route 12, Barnard. Campground open mid-May through Labor Day. On Silver Lake, good for fishing, swimming, and boating (rentals available). The park offers a snack bar and wooded campground with 40 tent/trailer sites and seven lean-tos. Hot showers.

Teagle Landing is Woodstock's vest-pocket park, a magical oasis below the bridge in the middle of town (Central Street). Landscaping and benches invite sitting a spell by the river, a tribute to Frank Teagle (1945–1997), one of Woodstock's most dedicated residents.

Dewey Pond Wildlife Sanctuary, Deweys Mills Road, Quechee. Originally a millpond, this is a beautiful spot with nature trails and a boat launch, good for bird-watching and fishing.

Hurricane Forest, Route 5, White River Junction. This 500-acre town forest harbors a pond and many miles of trails. Ask directions at the Quechee information booth.

Eshqua Bog, off Hartland Hill Road, Woodstock. A 40-acre sanctuary managed by the New England Wild Flower Society and The Nature Conservancy with a white-blazed loop trail circling through 8 acres of wetlands, with orchids blooming in summer. Ask directions locally.

Also see Vermont Institute of Natural Science under *Also See.*

✳ Lodging

RESORTS ⊘ ✍ **The Woodstock Inn and Resort** (802-457-1100; 1-800-448-7900; www.woodstockinn.com), on the green, 05091, is the lineal descendant of the 18th-century Eagle Tavern and the famous "old" Woodstock Inn that flourished between 1893 and 1969, putting the town on the year-round resort map. Today's 142-room, air-conditioned, Colonial-style 1970s edition was created by Laurance S. Rockefeller and has been regularly remodeled and tastefully expanded in recent decades to include a townhouse wing. The comfortably furnished main lobby is dominated by a huge stone fireplace where 5-foot birch logs blaze late fall through spring, the glowing heart of this sociable town.

The main dining room offers fine dining, while the bright, attractive Eagle Café serves all three meals and the appealing Richardson's Tavern is another less formal dining alternative. Common space also includes a library with games and a computer; the grounds feature a landscaped swimming pool. Guests have access to the scenic 18-hole Woodstock Country Club for golf and tennis (it's a cross-country ski center in winter) and to the splendid Health & Fitness Center, plus downhill skiing at the historic Suicide Six area. The creature comforts of these pearly precincts, beautifully appointed and run in most

THE WOODSTOCK INN ON A WINTER'S NIGHT

Woodstock Inn and Resort

respects, make this one of Vermont's premier places to stay and play. Current regular-season rates are $199–299 ($129–248 in spring and November "Value Seasons"); spacious porch and/or fireplace suites in the Tavern Wing are $364–609; and there is a separate cottage, the Justin Morgan House, which has a full kitchen. Children under 14 free when staying in the same room with an adult. MAP available at $66 per person per day. Check out ski and golf packages.

Twin Farms (802-234-9999; 1-800-894-6327; fax: 802-234-9990; www.twinfarms.com), Barnard 05031. Ironically, the shades of Sinclair Lewis, whose novels satirized the materialism of American life in the '20s, and Dorothy Thompson, the acerbic foreign correspondent, hover over this 300-acre, luxurious Shangri-la that used to be their country home. Here and now, an exclusive group of corporate CEOs, heads of government, royalty, and celebrities are welcome to unwind, frolic, and be rich together in sybaritic privacy. Of the four stylish rooms in the main house, Red's is only $950 a day; Dorothy's, $1,100. The 15 cottages range from $1,100 to $2,600, all including Lucullan meals at any hour, open bars, and the use of all recreational amenities, including the former Sonnenberg ski lift, a fully equipped fitness center, Japanese furo, croquet court, pond, and mountain bikes. The common rooms and guest quarters display an extraordinary collection of modern art by David Hockney, Frank Stella, and Roy Lichtenstein, among others. There's a 2-night minimum on weekends, 3 nights over holidays, and a 15 percent service charge. The entire enclave can be yours for $24,000 a day.

⊗ 🐾 ♪ **The Quechee Inn at Marshland Farm** (802-295-3133; 1-800-235-3133; www.quechee inn.com), Quechee Main Street, Quechee 05059. Off by itself on a quiet side road east of Quechee Village, just up from Deweys Mills Pond and Quechee Gorge, this historic farm is a comfortable and attractive inn with 25 guest rooms. Look closely in Room 5 and you'll see the rough-hewn beams of the original Georgian-style house built here by Colonel Joseph Marsh in 1793. With successive centuries and owners it expanded to include a distinctive, two-story, double-porched ell. In 1954 it was actually forced to move to higher ground to escape the rising waters caused by the Hartland Dam. In 1968 it became the first headquarters and accommodations for the Quechee Lakes Corporation; a decade later it was acquired by an energetic couple who established its present looks and reputation, which subsequent owners have preserved.

Rooms vary in size and feel. Three are suites; all have private bath and phone and are furnished with antiques. The brick-floored, raftered lounge with its piano, books, and games opens onto a big, sunny dining room in which breakfast and dinner (see *Dining Out*) are served. The inn is home to the Vermont Fly Fishing School and also offers canoeing and kayaking tours on the Connecticut, White, and Ottauquechee Rivers, along with mountain bike rentals. In winter it maintains 18 km of groomed cross-country ski trails. Guests also enjoy privileges at the nearby Quechee Club with its 18-hole golf course, tennis courts, health center, and pools. Rates range $90–245, depending on room and season. Inquire about packages.

INNS The Jackson House Inn (802-457-2065; 1-800-448-1890; www.jacksonhouse.com), 37 Old Route 4, West Woodstock 05091. This luxuriously appointed and equipped 1890 farmhouse has been expanded to include nine air-conditioned rooms and six single-room suites furnished in period antiques (from several different periods). It's all set amid 5 acres of manicured grounds and gardens, with a spring-fed pond. Rates begin at $195 for the Josephine Bonaparte room on the ground floor, furnished in the French Empire style, and range $290–380 for one of the four new mini suites, three of which have a thermal massage tub for two. One mini suite, the Christine Jackson on the first floor, has a Brazilian mahogany four-poster queen bed, a gas fireplace, and French doors to the brick patio and garden. Rates include a memorable breakfast and a pre-dinner glass of wine and hors d'oeuvres. Your hosts are Carl and Linda Delnegro. Also see *Dining Out.*

⊗ 🐾 ✍ **The Kedron Valley Inn** (802-457-1473; 1-800-836-1193; www.kedronvalleyinn.com), Route 106, South Woodstock 05071. The mellow brick inn has been welcoming visitors since 1828 and served as a stop on the Underground Railroad. The complex now includes the neighboring Tavern Building (built in 1822 as the village store) and a Vermont log motel unit, which sits beside an acre-plus swimming pond with sandy beach. The Kedron Valley Stables (see *Horseback Riding*) are just up the road. The 28 nicely decorated guest rooms, all with private bath,

include 5 suites with Jacuzzi and private deck. While rooms vary, all have canopy or antique oak beds and many have a fireplace or Franklin stove. New owners Jack and Nicole Maiden have cleverly fitted rooms in the log annex with Adirondack-style furnishings; those with fireplace are now some of the most attractive rooms of all. They have also gingered up the Tavern area with comfortable seating, expanded the tavern menu, and extended summer service to the expansive, columned front porch. Room rates are $131–221 double for rooms, $248–297 for suites, B&B. Discounts are available for May and June and midweek, off-peak periods year-round. The inn can host a reception for up to 200 and organizes weddings, using the village church and a horse-drawn carriage or sleigh. Also see *Dining Out.*

✍ **Parker House Inn** (802-295-6077; www.theparkerhouseinn.com), 1792 Main Street, Quechee 05059. An imposing redbrick mansion built in 1857 by Vermont senator Joseph Parker beside his flannel mill on the Ottauquechee River, this inn is best known for food (see *Dining Out*) but is also a comfortable and surprisingly informal place to stay. Chefs Walt and Barbara Forrester are warm hosts. The downstairs parlors are now dining rooms, but there is a small second-floor sitting room with a TV, a sunny downstairs reading nook, a breakfast room, and a riverside porch. The seven guest rooms all have private bath. Four on the second floor are high-ceilinged and antiques furnished, while three on the third are less formal. Ours had a pullout couch and was plenty large enough for a family. $135–165 includes a full breakfast.

In Woodstock 05091

Note: Parking can be tough, hence the advantage of the many in-town B&Bs described below. All face major thoroughfares, however; you might want to request back- or side-facing rooms.

The Charleston House (802-457-3843; 1-888-475-3800; www .charlestonhouse.com), 21 Pleasant Street. This luxurious, recently expanded Federal brick town house (vintage 1835) in the middle of the village is especially appealing, with period furniture in nine guest rooms, all with private bath and air-conditioning, several with fireplace and Jacuzzi. Rates are $115–225 and include full breakfast in the dining room or continental breakfast bed-side. Your genial hosts are Willa and Dixi Nohl (Dixi for many years managed Burke Mountain ski area in the Northeast Kingdom).

Canterbury House (802-457-3077; 1-800-390-3077; www.thecanterbury house.com), 43 Pleasant Street. Bob and Sue Frost's village Victorian has seven air-conditioned rooms with private bath (our favorites are the original second-floor bedrooms in the front) and air-conditioning. Guests meet around the hearth in the large, gracious living room. From $120 for a back room overlooking the parking lot to $165 for the Monk's Tale, which has a fireplace and cable TV. Full breakfast.

Ardmore Inn (802-457-3887; 1-800-497-9652; www.ardmoreinn.com), 23 Pleasant Street. A meticulously restored 1850 Greek Revival that's been Victorianized and offers five spacious rooms, each with private marble bath. Innkeepers Cary and Charlotte Hollingsworth are still fresh from Pasadena (California) and enthusiastic about their new home. The rooms we like best here are Tully, with its tall four-poster and eyebrow windows, and Maggie's Room, a back room that's the smallest and cheapest but features a tall, carved oak double bed and morning light. Guests breakfast around the formal dining room table and relax in the attractive parlor or on the large, wicker-filled, screened veranda. $110–175 includes breakfast and afternoon tea.

The 1830 Shire Town Inn (802-457-1830; 1-866-286-1830; www.1830shiretowninn.com), 31 South Street. Down Route 106 from the Woodstock Inn but still within walking distance of the green. Arlene Gibson is a natural host, and her 1830 home has three comfortable rooms with private bath. Our favorite is the downstairs, very private Woodstock Room, set into the rocks with a leafy view. The common rooms feature wide-pine floors, hand-hewn beams, a fireplace, and good art. $75–135 includes a hearty country breakfast.

⌁ **The Woodstocker** (802-457-3896; 1-866-662-1439; www.woodstockervt .com), 61 River Street (corner of Route 4). The arrangement of rooms in this rambling wooden addition to a classic 1830s Cape is explained by its former life as an apartment house. Tom and Nancy Blackford offer two suites with living room, kitchen, and deck (great for families) and seven more spacious rooms with private bath, most with air-conditioning. $145–195 double with big buffet breakfast.

The Village Inn of Woodstock (802-457-1255; 1-800-722-4571;

www.villageinnofwoodstock.com),
41 Pleasant Street, is a romantic pink
Victorian manse with fireplaces, oak
wainscoting, and pressed-tin ceilings.
David and Evelyn Brey offer seven
comfortable rooms with private bath.
$105–240 in high season, $85–155 in
low with full breakfast.

Just beyond town

☙ **Winslow House** (802-457-1820;
www.thewinslowhousevt.com), 429
Woodstock Road (Route 4), West
Woodstock 05091. A mile west of the
village, Tod and Jennifer Minotti have
fitted their five bright, spacious guest
rooms with every possible comfort:
bedside lights, cable TV, air-
conditioning, individually controlled
heat, phone, and refrigerator as well
as private bath. Three are suites with
sitting rooms. This is a Georgian
farmhouse with common rooms tastefully furnished in comfortable
antiques. It backs on the town playing
fields and a path along the Ottauquechee. $100–140 double, more dur-
ing foliage. Free pet boarding in a
heated barn out back.

Century House (802-457-2857;
www.centuryhousewoodstock.com),
471 Woodstock Road (Route 4), West
Woodstock 05091. This is, in fact, a
century-old house. Anne Foye has
just refurbished it and welcomes
guests (especially writers) to the two
comfortable west-wing rooms with
shared bath or the Vermont Suite, two
connected rooms with a bath, fridge,
and microwave.

Out of town

Note: The countryside around Woodstock is some of the most beautiful
and hospitable in Vermont.

Shephard's Hill Farm (802-457-
3087; etathume@sover.net), P.O. Box
34, Taftsville 05073. High on a hill
above the Tafstville General Store,
Ellen Terie raises sheep, a breed
developed in Idaho that's good for
both wool and high-quality meat. This
is a new, beautifully designed house,
spacious and airy with a large, open
kitchen and spacious two-story living
room, tastefully furnished in antiques
and wonderful "stuff" collected over
many years and many interests, with
mountaintops to die for in every
direction. Ellen, herself an artist as
well as a psychoanalyst, has covered
the walls with a large, varied art collection. The two guest rooms (both
queens, the larger one with mountain
views) are on their own second-floor
wing and share a bath and well-
appointed sitting room. $110–150
(less for longer "farmstays" in which
guests are invited to share in chores)
includes a full breakfast. Dinner can
be arranged.

🐾 ✎ **Top Acres Farm** (802-457-2135;
topacresfarm@aol.com), 3615
Fletcher Hill Road, South Woodstock
05071. This is a fabulous find for
couples or families wishing to get
away for a week or so. While Milton
and Pat Fullerton accept guests for a

TOP ACRES FARM B&B IN
SOUTH WOODSTOCK

Christina Tree

night or two, you won't want to leave this 1850s gabled white-clapboard, hilltop farmhouse that's been in the family—and known for the quality of its maple syrup—for four generations. There are two apartments, both with a fully equipped kitchen, laundry facilities, TV, and VCR. The first-floor, one-bedroom apartment has its own deck; its second-floor counterpart has three bedrooms, a large living room, and a dining room. Fridges are stocked for your first morning's breakfast. From $95; $125 for the upstairs apartment.

⌀ **Inn at Chelsea Farm** (802-234-9888; www.innatchelseafarm.com), P.O. Box 127, Route 12, Barnard 05031. Some places just click the moment you walk in, and for us this classic white Cape, set back from Route 12 and surrounded by fields, was one of those places. Inside spaces flow from the living room with its fireplace and are filled with quiet light and nicely decorated; the art is original and good. The three guest rooms, each named for a season (there's no "winter"), are also bright and comfortable without being fussy, and fitted with fine linens and down comforters. A large ground-floor suite has a cherry four-poster, a sofa, armchairs, a coffee table, and TV if requested. Host Emmy Fox spent much of her life managing a prestigious Bermuda inn, and hospitality comes naturally. Children are welcome, there are pet sheep in the field. Inquire about fly-fishing. Silver Lake State Park and its beach are just up the road. $115–130 per couple includes a full breakfast.

The Fan House (802-234-9096; the fanhouse.com), P.O. Box 294, Route 12 north, Barnard 05031. This distinguished, 1840s clapboard house is

filled with light, decorated with heirloom tapestries and antique furnishings to create the feel of an Italian farmhouse. The three artfully furnished guest rooms have private bath and are appointed with high-thread-count linens and Turkish bath sheets. Silver Lake and the Barnard General Store are within walking distance. $110–180 includes a full breakfast.

🍴 ⌀ **Deer Brook Inn** (802-672-3713; www.deerbrookinn.com), 535 Woodstock Road (Route 4), Woodstock 05091. Five miles west of Woodstock and 10 miles east of Killington's Skyeship Gondola, George DeFina and David Kanal have added some great decorating touches to this restored 1820 farmhouse, set back in fields across the road from the Ottauquechee River. The floors are wide honey-colored pine, and each of the five rooms has a full bath and climate-controlled heat and air-conditioning. A ground-floor two-room suite with a sitting room is good for families. Our favorite of the four second-floor rooms is Room 1, with its skylight above the bed and in the bathroom. This is one of the few places around to charge single rates ($75–110) as well as double ($95–130). The full breakfast is served either at a common or an individual table in the light-filled dining room.

Applebutter Inn (802-457-4158; 1-800-486-1734), P.O. Box 395, Happy Valley Road, Taftsville 05073. This is gem of a B&B, a rare melding of an exceptionally beautiful house with taste and warmth. A former Jersey farm, off the main drag, the house is a graceful 1850s Federal, with pillars and gables, and a bright, spacious dining area/library. There is also an elegantly comfortable yellow living room with a fireplace, and the house is furnished throughout with 19th-century antiques; wide-pine floors show between Oriental rugs. The six guest rooms, each named for a different variety of apple, all have private bath. They vary in size from the Granny Smith Room with skylights, a four-poster king, and a sitting area (with a day/trundle bed) down to the Baldwin Room with a double bed and hall bath. Your hosts are Barbara Berry and Michael Pacht. $95–185 per couple (with an additional $25 for each additional person) includes a full breakfast and afternoon tea.

❧ **Bailey's Mills Bed & Breakfast** (802-484-7809; 1-800-639-3437; www.baileysmills.com), RR 1, Box 117, Reading 05062. As happens so often in Vermont, surprises lurk at the end of a back road, especially in the case of this venerable guest house, a few miles west of Route 106. With a two-story porch and fluted columns, Bailey's Mills resembles a southern antebellum mansion. The 17-room brick home includes 11 fireplaces, two beehive ovens, a dance hall, and an 1829 general store, all part of an ambitious manufacturing complex established by Levi Bailey (1766–1850) and operated by his family for a century. Today Barbara Thaeder offers several comfortable rooms, two with working fireplace, each with a cozy sitting area and private bath, tastefully furnished with antiques. A spacious solarium makes Mom's Room an especially appealing suite. The library with its Rumford fireplace has a large collection of fascinating books and is furnished, as is the dining room, with family antiques and "old stuff." Paths lead off across the meadows into the woods and to a

swim pond. Barbara is an avid conservationist, a member of Green Hotels of Vermont. $90–155 with breakfast; slightly higher in foliage season and over some holidays; special rates for "Rent the Inn" extended stays and packages. (Ask about the adjacent Spite Cemetery.) Justly popular Keepers restaurant (see *Dining Out*) is minutes away.

⌘ ♿ **Maple Leaf Inn** (802-234-5342; 1-800-516-2753; www.mapleleafinn.com), P.O. Box 273, Route 12, Barnard 05031. Gary and Janet Robison opened up this sparkling new place in a faithfully reproduced turn-of-the-20th-century Victorian farmhouse, designed specifically as a B&B. Stenciling, stitchery, and Janet's handmade quilts decorate the seven air-conditioned guest rooms, each with a capacious private bath, king-sized bed, sitting area, telephone, and TV/VCR. Most guest rooms have wood-burning fireplace and whirlpool bath. The parlor, library, and dining room are bright and inviting. Rates are $130–230 with full breakfast. The Country Garden Room on the main floor has easy access for anyone who needs special assistance, and a whirlpool bath.

Greystone Bed & Breakfast (802-484-7200; 1-888-473-9222), Route 106, Hammondsville 05062, 11 miles south of Woodstock. This is an 1830s house, faced with stone quarried from a ledge across the road. Connie Miller offers two bedrooms with private bath (one can be a family suite) on the second floor and a suite with a king or twin beds, sitting room, and private bath on the third; $85 for the bedrooms, $115 for two in the suite; lower midweek. Rates include a full breakfast. An enthusiastic rider, Connie is active in the nearby Green Mountain Horse Association. Keepers restaurant (see *Dining Out*) is next door.

Herrin House Inn (802-296-7512; 1-800-616-4415; www.herrinhouse inn.com), P.O. Box 312, Quechee–Hartland Road, Quechee 05059. This is a totally renovated farmhouse, spiffy inside and out, with four luxurious guest rooms, handsome common space, and an "enchanted cottage." It's sited on 20 acres with a pond for fishing and ice skating. Guests enjoy access to golf, pools, and other facilities at the Quechee Club. $120–235 depending on room, season, and day of the week.

MOTELS 🐾 🎿 **Pond Ridge** (802-457-1667), Route 4, West Woodstock 05091. Set way back from Route 4, 1.5 miles west of Woodstock and in 6.5 landscaped acres with a picnic/barbecue area bordering the Ottauquechee River (swimming, fishing), this is a real find. Christine and David Coates offer 14 units fitted with two double beds or one queen as well as air-conditioning, cable TV, and coffee machines, also six apartments with full kitchens, great for families. Rooms are $49–99 (more in foliage); a two-bedroom apartment is $125–158. Children 6 and under are free; a cot is $10.

🐾 **The Shire Motel** (802-457-2211; www.shiremotel.com), 46 Pleasant Street, Woodstock 05091. Location, location. This two-story, independently owned 33-unit motel is within walking distance of downtown, and while it fronts on Pleasant Street (Route 4), it backs on the river (request a room in back). A separate, new building with six upscale rooms is also in back; another recently refurbished building houses three more

high-end rooms. All rooms are very clean and comfortable with phone and computer hook-up, furnished with two queens, two doubles, or a king. From as low as $68 to $178, depending on room and season.

Also see **Farmbrook Motel** in "Killington/Plymouth Area."

OTHER LODGING 🎿 **Quechee Lakes Resort** (www.quecheelakes.com) offers several hundred rental units, ranging from small condos to six-bedroom houses, all with access to resort facilities, which include the golf courses and clubhouse with its indoor pool and squash courts. Several local realtors specialize in these rentals, including **Quechee Associates** (802-295-1999; 1-800-639-5110; www.quecheeassociates.com), **Quechee Lakes Rentals** (802-295-1970; www.pbpub.com/quecheelakes), and **Care-free Quechee** (802-295-9500; www.carefreevermont.com).

🎿 **Kendall Homestead** (802-457-2734), Route 106, South Woodstock 05071. This fine old family house on a knoll close to the Kedron Valley Stables (see *Horseback Riding*) has three bedrooms and baths, plus sitting rooms and kitchen and laundry facilities. Good spot for families or groups of horseback riders; available by the day, weekend, week, or month; inquire for flexible rates.

Note: For camping at the area's two state parks, see *Green Space*.

✳ Where to Eat

DINING OUT **The Prince and the Pauper** (802-457-1818; www.prince andpauper.com), 24 Elm Street, Woodstock. Open daily for dinner (reservations advised). Nouvelle and Continental cuisine in a candlelit, elegantly rustic setting. Owner-chef Chris Balcer has, over more than 20 years, created and upheld consistently superior standards. A recent sampling of the $41 prix fixe dinner included, among a choice of half a dozen starters, the chef's own pâté of pork, veal, and chicken livers with sun-dried cherries and pistachios. We then had a choice of half a dozen entrées, including Cantonese roast duckling, and medallions of veal sautéed with roasted tomatoes, porcini mushroom, and Marsala, finished with sweet butter and served with artichoke bread pudding. Patrons tend to linger in the premium wine bar, where you can also dine from a bistro menu that includes Maine crabcakes and a choice of hearth-baked pizzas (bistro entrées $13–20). One of the state's best; "worth every calorie and dollar," we said in the first edition of this book, and we have had no reason to change our minds.

Simon Pearce Restaurant (802-295-1470; www.simonpearce.com), The Mill, Quechee. Open for lunch (11:30–2:45) and dinner (6–9; reservations advised) daily. This is a cheerful, upbeat, contemporary place for consistently superior food, served on its own pottery and glass, overlooking the waterfall. Despite its high profile as a tourist stop (with a store that remains open through the dinner hours), it gets raves from locals for the wine list and service as well as the food. The patio is open in summer, and the Ballymaloe brown bread alone is worth a visit. Lunch entrées could be spinach and cheddar cheese in puff pastry or beef and Guinness stew; at dinner you might begin with Sullivan Harbor farm-smoked salmon, a crispy potato cake, and lemon crème fraîche, then dine on crisp roast duckling

served with vegetable fried rice and mango chutney. Dinner entrées range from $19 for spinach and roasted garlic ravioli to $28 for New York sirloin.

The Woodstock Inn and Resort (802-457-1100; www.woodstockinn .com), on the green, Woodstock. Open for dinner and Sunday brunch. The large, cheerfully contemporary main dining room, with its alcoves and semicircular bay, is an especially attractive setting for the sumptuous Sunday brunch buffet ($24.95) and executive chef Daniel Jackson's truly superior dinners. Entrées might include a bouillabaisse of sea scallops, mussels, and Gulf shrimp in saffron-tomato broth, or pine nut crusted rack of lamb with truffled white beans, slow-roasted tomatoes, and toasted cumin jus. Entrées $25–30. Lighter fare and breakfast and lunch are served in the less expensive Eagle Café and in Richardson's Tavern.

THE DINING ROOM AT SIMON PEARCE OVERLOOKS THE OTTAUQUECHEE RIVER.

Kim Grant

The Jackson House Restaurant (802-457-2065), Route 4 west, Woodstock. Open Wednesday through Monday. Sophisticated cuisine in surroundings of understated (but sometimes noisy) simplicity. Graham Elliot Bowles is the newest chef at this highly touted and priced restaurant. Patrons can choose from a three-course prix fixe menu ($55) that might begin with a warm peekytoe crabcake and feature sautéed wild Pacific salmon, ending with cardamom-ginger crème brûlée. The 11-course "Chef's Degustation" and a similar vegetarian menu are each $95.

The Meadows at the Quechee Inn at Marshland Farm (802-295-3133; 1-800-235-3133; www.quecheeinn .com), Clubhouse Road, Quechee. Open nightly, this country-elegant dining room is just enough off the beaten track to be a discovery, the quiet setting for dependably good food. You might dine on crispy Long Island duck with a passion fruit apricot demiglaze, or on roasted Australian rack of lamb. Entrées $21–28; a "supper menu" features lighter dishes ranging from classic bouillabaisse to wine and shallot marinated beef tips served with a Boursin potato pancake ($12–17).

The Barnard Inn (802-234-9961; www.barnardrestaurant.com), 10 miles north of Woodstock on Route 12, Barnard. Open Tuesday through Saturday from 5, dinner 6–9. Reservations advised. Chef owners Ruth Schimmelpfennig and Will Dodson operate this 1796 brick house with its nicely appointed formal rooms. A three-course $40 prix fixe menu includes a choice of soups, salads, and appetizers such as mussels steamed in saffron and orange white wine fumé, or applewood-smoked salmon with horseradish crème fraîche. Entrées might include roast lamb with wild mushrooms and rosemary-roasted potatoes, or pork loin with roasted garlic mashed potatoes and apple-pear chutney. Desserts are $8 extra and usually include Ruth's crème brûlée. In the less formal Max's Tavern, the menu might range from pasta primavera with prosciutto ($13) to roasted lamb top round with "fixins" ($18). A large selection of wines and beers is available by the glass.

✿ **The Kedron Valley Inn** (802-457-1473; www.kedronvalleyinn), Route 106, 5 miles south of Woodstock. Open for dinner (reservations suggested). While the innkeepers here have changed, chef Jim Allen continues to win applause for stylish "nouvelle Vermont" cuisine. This is one of Vermont's oldest inns, and the large, low-beamed dining room is country elegant. Appetizers might include a seafood terrine and grilled Andouille sausage. A wide choice of entrées ranges from raviolis stuffed with an array of vegetables and cheeses to oven-roasted pork tenderloin brushed with maple syrup and served with Vermont apple chutney. Entrées $21–27. The newly expanded Tavern also offers a full and popular menu. It might include chicken Marsala and grilled salmon as well as burgers and BBQ. There's also a children's menu; children's drinks and "cocktails" are served. The award-winning wine list is a point of pride.

🍸 **Wild Grass** (802-457-1917), Gallery Place, Route 4, Woodstock. Open for dinner Tuesday through Saturday. This appealing restaurant fills a niche in town, offering a dining-out ambience and menu at affordable prices. New chef Christopher Brewer's menu includes old favorites like crispy sage leaves with dipping sauces, grilled Jamaican jerk chicken, and crispy roast ducking. Tempting starters include a roasted garlic plate with Vermont chèvre and grilled croustades, and several interesting salads. Dine on veal piccata, grilled salmon, or a vegetable ragout with asparagus, leeks, artichokes, red onions, and dried tomatoes. Full liquor license. Entrées $10.75–16.75.

Mangowood Cafe (802-457-3312), 530 Woodstock Road (Route 4), West Woodstock. Open Tuesday through Saturday 6–9:30. Chef-owner Teresa Tan, who grew up in Malaysia and is a graduate of the Cordon Bleu, has teamed up with chef James "Shadow" Henahan (executive chef for 10 years at Simon Pearce), and the happy results are creative, Asian-inspired dishes. Tan and her partner Amy Martsolf have transformed the former dining room of the Lincoln Inn into a relaxing, softly lit setting in which patrons try new taste combinations such as pan-seared duck breast with a chile-lime sauce, served with lotus seed macadamia spring rolls. Fish dishes are a specialty—say, sesame-seared sashimi-grade yellow tuna served with noodle cakes, wasabi, and pickled ginger. Don't pass up the maple ginger crème brûlée. Warning: We tried the nightly special, a Mongolian lamb shank slow-braised in aromatic herbs and spices and served with pumpkin custard rice. It was delicious but too much food. Entrées $19–26. Full liquor license.

Parker House Inn (802-295-6077; www.theparkerhouseinn.com), 1792 Main Street, Quechee. Open for dinner daily 5:30–9; reservations, please. Innkeepers Barbara (the pastry chef)

and Walt (a Culinary Institute of America graduate) Forrester offer simply good American food in the elegant front rooms of their classic brick Victorian mill owner's mansion. In summer tables are set on the outdoor terrace overlooking the Ottauquechee River. It's an à la carte menu with a nightly choice of half a dozen entrées that might include chicken piccata, or rotisserie-roasted pork finished in a chimichurri sauce. Entrées $16–24.

✎ **Keepers** (802-484-9090), Route 106 at Baileys Mill Road, Reading. Open Tuesday through Saturday 5–9, until 9:30 Friday and Saturday. The former Hammondsville Store is now one of the most popular restaurants around. Totally rebuilt, it comprises three connecting rooms, painted a warm green, with finished wood floors, good-sized pedestal tables, and hardy wooden office chairs. The feel is Shaker and the food is fresh, simply presented on white ironstone, and outstanding. Choose from several salads as well as starters, then dine on the likes of sea scallops in green curry with jasmine rice and crushed peanuts or an herb-rubbed half chicken with mashed potatoes, Swiss chard, and sherry caper sauce. Desserts might include ginger crème brûlée and an old-fashioned Bavarian layer cake. Entrées $14–19.50, but there's also always a "blackboard sandwich" ($7.50) and "Stump's burger" ($7) or a hearty mussel chowder ($10). Beer and wine. The downside: No reservations for fewer than six people.

Also see **Norwich Inn, Carpenter and Main,** and **Skunk Hollow Tavern** in "Upper Valley River Towns," and **The Corners Inn and Restaurant** in "Killington/Plymouth Area."

EATING OUT **Bentley's Restaurant** (802-457-3232), Elm Street, Woodstock. Open daily for lunch and dinner. The original restaurant here, an oasis of Victoriana and plants, has been expanded to include a café/ice cream parlor. A lifesaver in the middle of town, good for everything from brawny hamburgers and croissant sandwiches to veal Marsala and Jack Daniels steak. Frequent live entertainment.

☙ **FireStones** (802-295-1600), Route 4, Waterman Place, Quechee. Open daily for lunch and dinner and Sunday brunch. Live piano music Friday and Saturday evenings. Bill Decklebaum and David Creech, proprietors of Bentley's (see above), also help oper-

BENTLEY'S RESTAURANT IN WOODSTOCK
Kim Grant

ate this rustic, lodgelike restaurant, with a big wood-fired oven as its centerpiece, featuring made-to-order flatbreads, fire-roasted shrimp marinated in Long Trail Ale, fire-roasted chicken, and steaks. You'll also find pastas, soups, sandwiches, and salads; BBQ baby back ribs and good daily specials; and a friendly barman. Children's menu; outdoor deck.

Pane e Salute Italian Bakery (802-457-4882), 61 Central Street, Woodstock. Open for lunch noon–2:30, for Sunday brunch 10–2, and Friday and Saturday for dinner (reservations recommended)—but hours vary with the season, so check. This small café/bakery has acquired a passionate following. Classic peasant soups (mostly vegetarian), panini (premade bar sandwiches), and a wide choice of pastas, salads, and daily specials are offered at lunch. Sunday brunch plates include baked omelet with zucchini, tomato, and parmigiano, and rosemary-roasted chicken. The dinner menu includes a pasta course as well as entrées. Beer and wine, and of course espresso, cappuccino, and café latte, are served. Breads are also sold.

☙ **New England Steak House** (802-457-4022), Route 4 east (in the Sunset Farm Barn), Woodstock. Open daily for dinner from 5:30. A natty, informal, relatively inexpensive restaurant specializing in beef and seafood, also a salad bar. Families are welcome; children's menu.

☙ **Farina Family Diner and Restaurant** (802-295-8955), Quechee Gorge Village. Open year-round from 7 AM for all three meals; closed Tuesday. A genuine 1946 Worcester Diner #787 that once stood in Holyoke, Massachusetts, then was moved here in 1991 and expanded to include a rear dining room. Booths up front, tables in the back, fresh-brewed coffee, and an all-American menu. Children's menu. Gum-cracking waitresses, roast chicken and meat loaf, pies and other good comfort food.

Woodstock Country Club (802-457-6672), Route 106 south, Woodstock. Open in summer for lunch 11:30–3. This is a Woodstock insider's meeting spot for lunch but open to the public, especially appealing on sunny days when you can dine on the deck. Designer sandwiches and salads, burgers, a good grilled Reuben.

Sakura Island (802-296-7600), 6962 Woodstock Road (Route 4), Quechee. Open daily for lunch and dinner. The "chef's specialties" are a familiar Asian fusion mix—General Tso's chicken, BBQ spare ribs, Buddha's delight, and the like. Sushi and sashmi are the specialties of this house, and they get good reviews.

Woodstock Coffee & Tea (802-457-9268), 43 Central Street, Woodstock. Open Monday through Saturday 7–6, Sunday 9–5. Judging from its popularity, this comfortably furnished café fills a real need in the village. A variety of coffee roasts and blends as well as signature drinks, hot and cold, are offered. Breakfast sandwiches and exceptional corn muffins. Fruit smoothies are also featured, along with teas and fresh, locally made pastries, and "quick bites" for breakfast and lunch. Be brave: Try "The Zombie."

Umpleby's, "makers of fine baked goods" (802-672-1300), The Mill, Route 4, Bridgewater. Open 7:30–5:30; closed Monday. Charles Umpleby specializes in breads (try the crazy wheat) but also bakes genuine European-style croissants and raspberry brioche for breakfast, delectable leek and onion tarts, sausage rolls, and individual quiches to go with homemade soups, served up by wife Carolyn. If it's not mealtime, check out the homemade ice cream.

⊘ Mountain Creamery (802-457-1715), Central Street, Woodstock, serves breakfast daily 7–11:30, lunch until 3, pastry and espresso until 6. This is the local meeting place but less friendly to visitors than it used to be. Soups, sandwiches, salads, daily specials, and their own handmade ice cream as well as apple pie. Pies and cakes are also for sale.

Ott Dog Snack Bar (802-295-1088), Route 4, Quechee Gorge. Open mid-May through mid-October. Family owned with the motto "Not fast food. Good food fast." Fresh soups and five different kinds of hot dogs are the specialties.

Barnard General Store (234-9688), Route 12, Barnard Village. A classic general store (established 1832) but with a 1950s lunch counter good for ice cream, soups, and sandwiches as well as pizza all day. Handy to Silver Lake.

BARNARD GENERAL STORE

Kim Grant

South Woodstock Country Store (802-457-3050), Route 106, South Woodstock. Open Monday through Friday 6–6, Saturday 7–6, Sunday 8–5. The only general store we know that has its own chef. Under new owner Dan Noble, the front of the store stacks staples and local specialties like the fabulous Woodstock Water Buffalo yogurt made in South Woodstock (the water buffalo are around the corner up on Churchill Road). Stop by for homemade muffins, omelets, or breakfast sandwiches; soups, sandwiches, and pizzas at lunch. Check the menu for dinner take-homes like eggplant parmigiana.

PICNICS On a beautiful summer or fall day the best place to lunch is outside. In Woodstock itself there's Teagle's Landing, right on Central Street by the river, and Faulkner Park on Monument Avenue. See *Green Space* for other ideas.

The Village Butcher (802-457-2756), 18 Elm Street, Woodstock, a superb butcher and a deli with specials to go, along with its top-flight meats, wines, and baked goods, plus homemade fudge.

Woodstock Farmers' Market (802-457-3658), Route 4 west, has a thoughtful deli case, plus soups and an outstanding selection of sandwiches, fresh fish, free-range chicken, local produce, meals to go, and Baba à Louis bread and cookies.

❋ Entertainment

Pentangle Council on the Arts (802-457-3981; www.pentangle arts.org), Town Hall Theater, 31 The Green, Woodstock. First-run films are shown Friday through Monday evenings at 7:30 in the Town Hall Theater. Live presentations at town hall and at the Woodstock Union High School include a variety of musical and other live entertainment. Check the Town Crier blackboard at the corner of Elm and Central Streets for current happenings.

❋ Selective Shopping

ANTIQUES SHOPS The Woodstock area is mecca for antiques buffs. There are two big group galleries. **Quechee Gorge Village Antique Mall** (802-295-1550), Route 4, east of Quechee Gorge, open daily, is one of New England's largest antiques collectives, with some 450 dealers represented. The **Antiques Collaborative** (802-296-5858), Waterman Place, Route 4 at the blinking light in Quechee, is also open daily (10–5) and shows representative stock from some 150 upscale dealers: period furniture usually in good condition, silver, Oriental rugs, and more.

Among more the more than dozen individual dealers: **Wigren & Barlow** (802-457-2453; www.wigrenandbar low.com), 29 Pleasant Street, is Woodstock's most elegant antiques shop, with a large selection of fine country and formal furniture, decorative accessories, and garden appointments (open daily 10–5); **Church Street Antiques** (802-457-2628), west of the green in Woodstock, has a wide variety, furniture (usually including antique high chairs), mirrors, Quimper and majolica ware (open Wednesday through Saturday 10–5, Sunday 1–5); at **American Classics** (802-457-4337), 71 Central Street, Woodstock, carefully selected, upscale folk art and antiques fill several second-floor rooms (open June through October, daily 10–5 except Wednesday); **Pleasant Street Books** (802-457-4050), 48 Pleasant Street, Woodstock, carries 10,000 selected titles in all fields (open daily 11–5 in summer and fall, by appointment off-season); **Fraser's Antiques** (802-457-3437), Happy Valley Road, just off Route 4 in Taftsville, has a good stock of early American furniture and accessories; **Who Is Sylvia?** (802-457-1110), 26 Central Street, in the old village firehouse, houses two floors of great vintage clothing and accessories for men as well as women; **Mill Brook Antiques** (802-484-5942), Route 106, Reading (11 miles south of Woodstock), has a shop and barn full of early American furniture, primitives, stoneware, china, quilts, and more (open year-round, but call ahead).

ART GALLERIES Galleries come and go in Woodstock. Present offerings in Woodstock include: **Woodstock Folk Art** (802-457-2012), 8 Elm Street, specializing in contemporary carvings, prints, and antiquities. **Stephen Huneck Studio** (802-457-3206), 49 Central Street, offers the celebrated St. Johnsbury woodcarver's fanciful animals of all kinds adorning furniture, wall reliefs, jewelry, and other witty, uncommon pieces. **Gallery on the Green** (802-457-4956), corner of Elm Street, features original art, limited-edition prints, photography, and occasionally sculpture, from New England artists. **Polonaise Art Gallery** (802-457-5180), 15 Central Street, features contemporary and traditional styles in paintings and sculpture. **Robert O. Caulfield Art Gallery** (802-457-1472), 11 The Green, is the artist's studio; realistic oil and watercolor landscapes and street scenes.

ARTISANS **Charles Shackleton Furniture** and **Miranda Thomas Pottery** (802-672-5175; 1-800-245-9901; www.shackletonthomas.com), The Mill, Route 4, Bridgewater, and at 23 Elm Street, Woodstock. Open daily 10–5:30 at both places; inquire about mill tours. This couple met at art school in England and again at Simon Pearce Glass. Charles was an apprentice glassblower before he switched to furniture making; Miranda founded the pottery studio there, and the showroom carried both their work. But no longer. They have since acquired the western third of the Bridgewater Mill, and Charles works with more than two dozen fellow crafters to produce exquisite furniture. It's made to order, but models are displayed (along with seconds at the mill), complemented by Miranda's

THE CLEAR LAKE FURNITURE GALLERY IN WOODSTOCK

Kim Grant

Charles Shackleton Furniture/Miranda Thomas Pottery

CHARLES SHACKLETON FURNITURE AND MIRANDA THOMAS POTTERY ARE BASED AT THE MILL AT BRIDGEWATER CORNERS.

MILLS The Bridgewater Mill, also known as "The Old Inn Marketplace" and "The Mill," Route 4, Bridgewater. The core of this vast, yellow wooden mill dates back to the 1820s, when it worked cotton, switching to wool in the 1840s, supplying woolen uniforms and blankets for the troops in several wars. In the 1970s when it closed, the building was saved by a local bootstrap effort and became a hive of small shops. It has had its ups and downs since, but current occupants are a rich mix. By far the most famous are **Charles Shackleton Furniture** and **Miranda Thomas Pottery** (see *Artisans*), whose shop and workspace are accessible from the west entrance. **F. H. Gillingham & Sons** (802-672-3332) has a branch here, and there are also some 20 local vendors. The Mill's upper floors are partially filled with offices and artists' studios, launching pads for enterprises like **David Crandall's** (802-672-5475) custom-styled 18-karat gold jewelry. Crandall began on the second floor but has since moved to prime first-floor space beside Shackleton/Thomas at the west entrance.

distinctive pottery, hand thrown and carved with traditional designs, such as rabbits, fish, and trees. Her pottery is housed in a former worker's cottage in the mill's parking lot.

Clear Lake Furniture Gallery (802-457-2822; www.clearlakefurni

ture.com), 24 Elm Street, Woodstock. Open Monday through Saturday 10–5; Sunday hours vary. Handcrafted in a workshop in Ludlow, this line of furnishings is well worth checking out—but don't expect to walk way with a table or dresser. Rather, it will

The central, oldest part of The Mill is a wonderfully mixed bag. Down in the basement, occupying space that was used not so long ago to incubate the Long Trail Brewery (now housed in a spiffy brewery just up Route 4; see "Killington/Plymouth Area"), is the **Hillbilly Flea Market** (802-672-1331; open Thursday through Sunday 10–5). Obviously based on the "one man's junk is another man's treasure" theory, this treasure trove has upscaled a couple of notches in as many years and now specializes in very usable furniture. On the first floor, beyond the village post office, is the **Sun of the Heart Bookstore** (802-672-5151, open daily 10–6). The mill's oldest tenant, it's a genuinely bright spot at its heart, an independent shop reflecting owner Akanakha Perkins's interest in many New Age subjects. Also well worth checking is **Northern Ski Works Outlet** (802-672-3636; www.northernski.com), an outlet for retail shops by that name in Ludlow and Killington. The aromas of baking, suffusing much of the first floor, emanate from **Umpleby's** (802-672-1300), a small café tucked in a back corner overlooking the Ottauquechee River (see *Eating Out*).

Simon Pearce Glass (802-295-2711; www.simonpearce.com), The Mill, 1760 Main Street, Quechee. The brick mill by the falls in the Ottauquechee was the 19th-century home of J. C. Parker and Co., producing "shoddy": wool reworked from soft rags. Parker was known for fine baby flannel. It closed for a spell, then served as offices for Quechee Lakes Resort. In 1981 Simon Pearce opened it as a glass factory, harnessing the dam's hydropower for his glass furnace. Pearce had already been making his original glass for a decade in Ireland, and here he quickly established a reputation for his distinctive production pieces: tableware, vases, lamps, candlesticks, and more. Visitors can watch glass being blown and can shop for individual pieces from the retail shop, along with Simon Pearce pottery. The shop (802-295-2711) is open 9–9 daily; pottery throwing can be viewed daily 9–4, glassblowing 9–9. The Simon Pearce Restaurant (see *Dining Out*), overlooking the falls, is justifiably one of Vermont's most popular. Simon Pearce now also operates a large, visitor-friendly glass and pottery factory in nearby Windsor (see "Upper Valley River Towns") as well as in Maryland and Pennsylvania. His glass and pottery are sold in over 300 stores throughout the country.

Woodstock Clayworks (802-672-5005), Route 4 west (5 miles west of Woodstock, 2 miles east of Bridgewater), open May through October. Barbara Thompson Knutson's work is both whimsical and functional and includes birdbaths, planters and vases, teapots and mugs. The gallery itself is set in a garden, well worth visiting. We treasure her simple clay centerpiece that holds both flowers and candles. be specially designed for you in your choice of woods.

FossilGlass (802-457-4102), 75 Central Street, Woodstock. Christina Salusti's distinctive glassware is sold in top shops around the country, but Woodstock is home. This new store showcases the full spectrum of her work and serves as an outlet. Hand-spun plates, bowls, and platters are unusually shaped and frequently partially colored; the surfaces suggest fossil imprints.

Peter Bramhall (802-672-5141), Bridgewater Center. The back-road studio of this unique glassblower may be visited by appointment.

Woodstock Potters (802-457-1298), Mechanic Street, Woodstock, has a studio/workshop for stoneware and hand-painted porcelains, plus gold and silver jewelry.

BOOKSTORES The Yankee Bookshop (802-457-2411), Central Street, Woodstock, carries an unusually large stock of hardbound and paperback books for adults and children, plus cards; it features the work of local authors and publishers. **Shiretown Books** (802-457-2996; www.shiretownbooks.com), 9 Central Street, Woodstock, is an intimate, very personalized shop that has a carefully selected stock of books for adults and children. Also see Sun of the Heart Bookstore in the box on page 263.

SPECIAL SHOPS

In Woodstock Village
F. H. Gillingham & Sons (802-457-2100; 1-800-344-6668), Elm Street, owned and run by the same family since 1886, is something of an institution, retaining a lot of its old-fashioned general store flavor. You'll find plain and fancy groceries, wine,

housewares, and hardware for home, garden, and farm. Mail-order catalog.

✿ **Woodstock Pharmacy** (802-457-1306), Central Street. Open daily 8–6 and Sunday morning until 1. Another Woodstock institution that has branched out well beyond the basics, especially good for stationery and (downstairs) for children's toys and books.

Unicorn (802-457-2480), 15 Central Street, is a treasure trove of unusual gifts, cards, games, toys, and unclassifiable finds.

The Vermont Workshop (802-457-1400), 73 Central Street, features a wide selection of gifts and crafts, furniture, rugs, and lamps.

Arjuna (802-457-3350), 20 Central Street, is a small cornucopia of unusual collectibles and items from around the world, plus funky jewelry.

The Whipple Tree (802-457-1325), 7 Central Street, has yarns, knitting, sewing, and art supplies (and Vermont Transit bus tickets).

Also see FossilGlass under *Artisans*, and check out *Antiques Shops*.

In and near Quechee
Fat Hat Factory (802-296-6646), at the corner of Route 4 and Clubhouse Road, Quechee, offers "spirited hats and carefree clothing," most of it made right here: skirts, pants, and sweaters as well as hats.

New England Specialties Shoppe (802-295-6163), Route 4, Quechee. The Laros's store, east of the gorge, has an especially large and carefully selected stock of Vermont products, from cheese, syrup, and preserves to sweatshirts and toys. In the same complex look for **Ottauquechee Valley Winery** (802-295-9463), sequestered behind the Mesa Home Factory Store. It's a relatively new off-shoot of North River Winery in Jacksonville, producing half a dozen fruit wines from pears and apples, rhubarb, and a blend of blueberries and apples.

♂ Quechee Gorge Village (802-295-1550; 1-800-438-5565; www.quecheegorge.com), Route 4 at Quechee Gorge. The most elaborate of several Route 4 shopping complexes, it includes the Antiques Center (see *Antiques Shops*) and Farina Family Diner (see *Eating Out*), also an arts and crafts center, general store, and Christmas Loft.

Vermont Toy & Train Museum and Gift Shop at Quechee Gorge (802-295-1550; 1-800-438-5565; www.quecheegorge.com), Route 4, 1 mile east of Quechee Gorge. Open year-round, an antique merry-go-ground, a 2-foot-gauge railroad, interactive games, and a gift shop.

Talbot's Herb & Perennial Farm (802-436-2085), Hartland–Quechee Road, 3 miles south of the Route 4 blinker. Open early April through October, daily 9–5 except Monday. Patty and David Talbot have been a popular source of local herbs, perennials, and annuals since 1971.

Taftsville Country Store (802-457-1135), Route 4 east, Taftsville. Refurbished and restocked, this 1840 landmark carries carefully chosen Vermont gifts as well as a good selection of cheeses, maple products, jams, jellies, smoked ham, and bacon, plus staples, wine, and books.

Sugarbush Farm (802-457-1757; 1-800-281-1757), RR 1, Box 568, Woodstock, but located in Pomfret: Take Route 4 to Taftsville, cross the covered bridge, go up the hill, turn

left onto Hillside Road, then follow signs. *Warning:* It's steep. Beware in mud season, but it's well worth the effort: Sample seven Vermont cheeses, all packaged here along with gift boxes, geared to sending products to far corners of the world. In-season you can watch maple sugaring, walk the maple and nature trail, meditate in the Luce family's small woodland chapel, or visit with their farm animals.

Scotland by the Yard (802-295-5351), Route 4, 3 miles east of Woodstock, imports tartans and tweeds, kilts, capes, coats, sweaters, skirts, canes, books, records, oatcakes, and shortbreads.

The Fool on the Hill (802-457-3641; www.thefoolonthehill.com), Route 4 west of Quechee Gorge. Open daily 9–5, later in fall. Closed January through mud season. Ed and Debbie Kerwin's unabashed tourist trap sells pottery, gifts, and Vermont specialty foods. Memorial Day through October, it features corn roasting on an open flame.

✳ Special Events

Note: Check the **Town Crier blackboard** at the corner of Elm and Central Streets in Woodstock for the week's happenings.

Washington's birthday: A week of **Winter Carnival** events sponsored by the Woodstock Recreation Center (802-457-1502)—concerts, Fisk Trophy Race, sleigh rides, square dance, torchlight ski parade.

May: **Plowing Match** (first weekend) between dozens of teamsters and draft horses and oxen at Billings Farm & Museum, also the scene of **Sheep Shearing.** In downtown Woodstock the **Memorial Day Parade** is worth a trip to see.

First Sunday of June: **Covered Bridge Quechee/Woodstock Half Marathon.**

Father's Day weekend: **Quechee Hot Air Balloon Festival** (802-295-7900)—a gathering of more than two dozen balloons with ascensions, flights, races, crafts show, entertainment.

July 4: **An Old Fashioned 4th** at Billings Farm & Museum includes a noon reading of the Declaration of Independence, 19th-century-style debates, games, and wagon rides.

August: **Quechee Scottish Festival** (third Saturday)—pipe bands, sheep-dog trials, Highland dancing, more than 50 clans. **Billings Farm Quilt Show** (all month). Also at the farm: **Antique Tractor Parade** (first Sunday) and **Children's Day** (last Saturday).

Mid-October: Quechee **antiques and crafts festivals. Apple & Crafts Fair** (Columbus Day weekend), Woodstock—more than 100 juried craftspeople and specialty food producers.

Second weekend of December: **Christmas Wassail Weekend** includes a grand parade of carriages around the Woodstock green, Yule log lighting, concerts.

Central Vermont 3

KILLINGTON/PLYMOUTH AREA

THE WHITE RIVER VALLEYS

SUGARBUSH/MAD RIVER VALLEY

BARRE/MONTPELIER AREA

Kim Grant

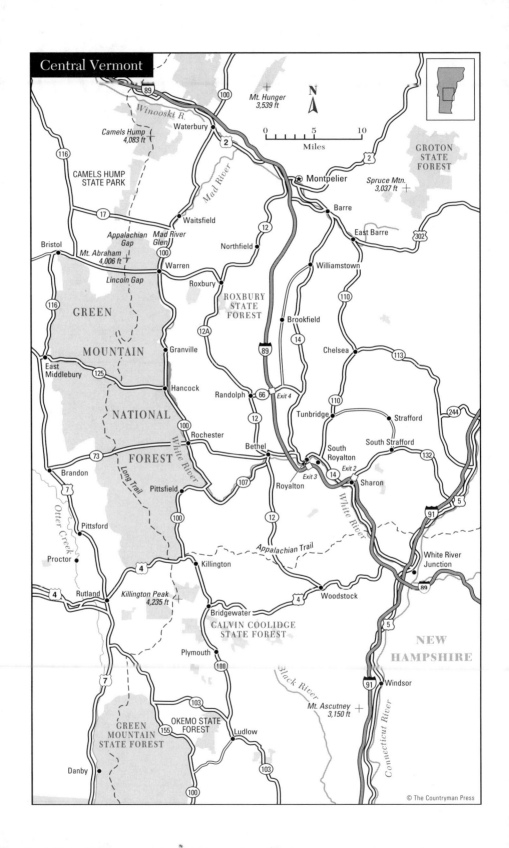

© The Countryman Press

KILLINGTON/PLYMOUTH AREA

Killington is the largest ski resort with the longest ski season in the East. It boasts seven mountains and the most extensive snowmaking system in the world. It's said that some 18,000 visitors can bed down within 20 miles.

Killington Peak, the second highest summit in the state, is flanked by other mountains and faces another majestic range across Sherburne Pass. Although the road through this upland village has been heavily traveled since the settling of Rutland (11 miles to the west) and Woodstock (20 miles to the east), there was never much of anything here. In 1924 an elaborate, rustic-style inn was built at the junction of Route 4, the Appalachian Trail, and the new Long Trail. A winter annex across the road was added in 1938, when Pico (now part of Killington) installed one of the country's first T-bars. But the logging village of Sherburne Center (now the town of Killington) was practically a ghost town in 1957 when Killington began.

Condominiums cluster at higher elevations while lodges, inns, and motels are strung along the 5-mile length of Killington Road and west along Route 4 as it slopes ever downward through Mendon to Rutland. Ski lodges are also salted along Route 100 north to the pleasant old town of Pittsfield, and in the village of Chittenden, sequestered up a back road from Route 4, near a mountain-backed reservoir. In summer this is exceptional hiking and mountain biking country. The K1 Express Gondola, to the summit of Killington Peak, carries bikes. What Killington terms "Endless Adventures" include major golf and tennis programs and plenty of family-geared activities. Summer also brings theater and ballet, a series of musical, horsey, and other events, and—because this is still primarily a winter resort area—substantial savings on summer accommodations.

Southeast of Killington, down Route 100 and a few miles up Route 100A, stands the village of Plymouth Notch, looking much the way it did on August 3, 1923, when Calvin Coolidge was sworn in by his father as the 30th president of the United States in his kerosene-lit home. Now the President Calvin Coolidge State Historic Site, it's arguably the only Vermont village in which the story of its remarkable residents as well as its buildings has been preserved.

GUIDANCE **Killington Lodging Bureau** (1-800-621-6867), Route 4, located in the Shops at the Shack. Open daily 8 AM–9 PM mid-November through May, the

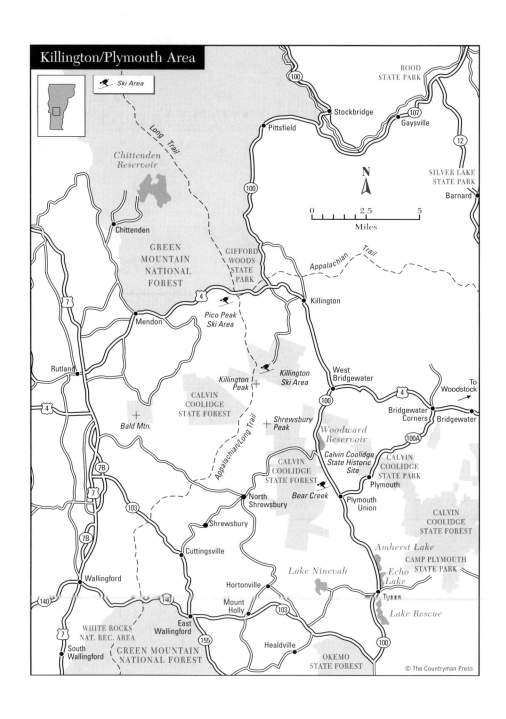

Killington/Plymouth Area

Ski Area

ROOD STATE PARK

Stockbridge

Gaysville

107

Pittsfield

100

12

Chittenden Reservoir

N

SILVER LAKE STATE PARK

Barnard

0   2.5   5

Miles

Chittenden

100

GREEN MOUNTAIN NATIONAL FOREST

GIFFORD WOODS STATE PARK

Appalachian Trail

Long Trail

7

4

Killington

Mendon

Pico Peak Ski Area

Rutland

Killington Peak

Killington Ski Area

West Bridgewater

To Woodstock

4

CALVIN COOLIDGE STATE FOREST

100

Bridgewater Corners

Bridgewater

Bald Mtn.

Shrewsbury Peak

Woodward Reservoir

100A

Appalachian/Long Trail

7B

CALVIN COOLIDGE STATE FOREST

Calvin Coolidge State Historic Site

CALVIN COOLIDGE STATE PARK

7

103

North Shrewsbury

Bear Creek

Plymouth

Plymouth Union

CALVIN COOLIDGE STATE FOREST

7B

Shrewsbury

Amherst Lake

CAMP PLYMOUTH STATE PARK

Cuttingsville

Lake Ninevah

Echo Lake

Wallingford

Hortonville

Tyson

Lake Rescue

140

140

Mount Holly

103

WHITE ROCKS NAT. REC. AREA

East Wallingford

155

Healdville

100

South Wallingford

GREEN MOUNTAIN NATIONAL FOREST

OKEMO STATE FOREST

© The Countryman Press

bureau keeps a tally on vacancies and makes reservations. A wide variety of 2- to 5-day ski packages is available; for summer packages, phone 1-877-4K-TIMES. The web site for all information related to the area is www.killington.com.

Killington Chamber of Commerce (802-773-4181; 1-800-337-1928; www.killingtonchamber.com) is a source of year-round information about the area.

GETTING THERE *By rail:* **Amtrak's** Ethan Allen Express (1-800-USA-RAIL) from New York City stops in Rutland.

By bus: **Vermont Transit** stops en route from Rutland to White River Junction at Killington Depot, Route 4 near Killington Road. Most inns will pick up guests.

By plane: Rutland Airport is served by **Commutair,** operated by Continental Airlines from Boston. For direct service from New York, see "Burlington Region."

GETTING AROUND **Killington Limousine** and van shuttle (802-770-3977; 802-353-TAXI) and **Gramps Shuttle** (802-236-6600).

WHEN TO GO In theory Killington's ski season begins mid-October and runs through May, but the full trail system rarely opens before Christmas, and by Easter it's pretty much all over with. Given its size and high profile, Killington attracts more ski-weekers than other New England areas, enough for a lively midweek atmosphere but still leaving ample room on the slopes (not always true during February weekends and school vacations). July through foliage season is pleasant: plenty to do and a wide choice of places to stay at off-season prices.

MEDICAL EMERGENCY Emergency service is available by calling **911.**

Rutland Regional Medical Center (802-775-7111), 160 Allen Street, Rutland.

Killington Medical Clinic (802-422-6125; Killington Courtesy phone: ext. 625), adjacent to Rams Head Lodge, provides emergency medical services to the resort area.

KILLINGTON PEAK On a clear day the view from the summit of the state's second highest mountain (4,235 feet) encompasses five states. It sweeps northwest to the Adirondacks, east to the White Mountains, and north along the spine of the Green Mountains. It's the spot on which the Reverend Samuel Peters in 1763 is said to have christened all that he could see "Verd monts." The K1 Express Gondola (daily Memorial Day through Labor Day, then daily mid-September through Columbus Day; 802-422-6200) hoists visitors up from the Killington Base Lodge to the Peak Restaurant (open with a cafeteria menu for lunch and for special dinners in foliage season) just below the summit, and a nature trail leads to the peak. No matter how hot it is down on Route 4, chances are you will need a jacket on top. Bring a picnic and stay a while. This is one of those special places.

THE CALVIN COOLIDGE STATE HISTORIC SITE

Vermont Division for Historic Preservation

CALVIN COOLIDGE AND PLYMOUTH NOTCH Calvin Coolidge (1872–1933) is best remembered for his dry wit and thrift, his integrity and common sense, all famously Vermont virtues. The village of Plymouth Notch—in which Coolidge was born, assumed the presidency, briefly governed the country (in the summer of 1924), and is buried—is said to be the best-preserved presidential birthplace in the nation. It may also be the best-preserved Vermont village, offering an in-depth sense of the people who lived there.

In the spirit of Coolidge himself, the village remains low-key: no 1920s costumed interpreters, no multimedia displays. The cheese factory built by the president's father, John Coolidge, showcases the history of Vermont cheesemaking and produces its own granular curd cheese. The square-steepled Union Christian Church, with its acoustically superb interior, is the setting for frequent concerts and lectures. The general store sells pickles, afghans, and some Vermont specialty foods like dilled carrots and Moxie—reportedly Coolidge's favorite drink (it was, after all, Prohibition).

"Colonel" John Coolidge became storekeeper here in 1868, and his son Calvin was born on the Fourth of July, 1872, in the modest attached house. The family moved across the street to the larger "Coolidge Homestead" when he was 4 years old, and it was there, because he happened to be home helping with the haying, that Vice President Calvin Coolidge learned of President Warren Harding's unexpected death. At 2:47 AM on August 3, 1923, he was sworn in, by his father, as 30th president of the United States.

"I didn't know I couldn't" was the reply Coolidge Sr. gave when reporters asked how he knew he could administer the presidential oath of office. "Colonel John" was a former state senator, a notary public, and the village sheriff as well as shopkeeper. His terse response typifies the dry wit for which his son would later became known.

It should come as no surprise that in this classic Vermont village you encounter a classic Vermont family. The Coolidges were hardworking (up before dawn for chores), self-sufficient (you see an intricate quilt that was stitched by Cal at age 10 and a graceful carriage built by his father), and closely linked to the land. Coolidge is buried with seven generations of his family in the small grave-yard across the road from the village. Village residents numbered 29 during Coolidge's presidency, and a high percentage of these formed the Old-Time Dance Orchestra, which played in the dance hall above the general store. This same room served as the office of the Summer White House for a dozen days in 1924. At the time Calvin and his wife, Grace, were grieving the death of their son Calvin Jr., a promising 16-year-old who had died due to a complication from an infected blister he acquired while playing tennis at the White House.

Plymouth resident Ruth ("Midge") Aldrich opened several tourist cabins (prefab jobs brought up from Boston) to accommodate the Secret Service and a Top of the Notch Tea Room to serve a steady stream of the Coolidge-curious. Plymouth Notch, however, never hit the big time as a tourist attraction, perhaps because, while he continued to visit "The Notch," President Coolidge himself retired to private life not here but in his adopted home, Northampton, Massachusetts. After graduating from nearby Amherst College, Coolidge had opened a law practice in Northampton, and it was there that he met his wife (fellow Vermonter Grace Anna Goodhue, who was teaching there at the Clarke School for the Deaf) and served as mayor. He represented Northampton in the Massachusetts Legislature before becoming governor of the Bay State, and he died in Northampton.

It was Aurora Pierce, the family housekeeper, who fiercely preserved the Coolidge Homestead, adamantly opposing even minor changes, like plumbing and electricity. Not until Aurora's death in 1956 did Vermont's Historic Sites Commission assume management of the house and its contents (which Grace Coolidge had deeded to them). The state had already purchased the 1840s village tavern that had also been Calvin's mother's home, turning it into a lunchroom and information center.

The President Calvin Coolidge State Historic Site presently encompasses 25 buildings, the majority of the village. Twelve buildings, including the cheese factory, the 1840s church, the general store and its upstairs hall (restored to look just as it did as the office of the Summer White House), and the hand-hewn Wilder Barn (housing farm implements and horse-drawn vehicles), are open to the public. A stone-faced visitors center (with changing exhibits) has been added, power lines have been buried (electricity actually didn't reach Plymouth until after Calvin's death), and roads have been paved. Otherwise the village looks about as it did in the 1920s, sitting quietly at the foot of East Mountain. It's set in 560 acres presently owned by the Vermont Division for Historic Preservation, surrounded by the 500-acre Coolidge State Park, in turn abutting the 18,000-acre Calvin Coolidge State Forest. The President Coolidge State Historic Site

Vermont Division for Historic Preservation

PRESIDENT CALVIN COOLIDGE

(802-672-3773; www.historicvermont.org/coolidge) is open late May through mid-October, daily 9:30–5. Admission $6.50 per adult, children 14 and under free. During the off-season the Aldrich House, which doubles as an office and exhibit space, is open weekdays (no charge)—but call ahead.

✳ To Do

AERIAL RIDES The **Killington K1 Express** runs from Killington Base Lodge to the top of Killington Peak (see the box on page 271). During foliage season (mid-September to Columbus Day), the **Killington Skyeship Express,** a speedy, eight-passenger gondola, runs from Route 4 to an elevation of 3,800 feet. Both cost the same, and for both the phone is 802-422-6200.

BICYCLING Killington Mountain Bike Center (802-422-6232; 1-877-4K-TIMES). The Killington K1 Express Gondola operates Memorial Day through Columbus Day hoisting bicyclists and their bikes to Killington Peak, accessing 45 miles of marked trails; $8 for a trail pass, $20 for a ride on the gondola. During foliage season the Skyeship (see above) is also available. Guided tours, instruction, bike rentals and packages.

True Wheels (802-422-3234; www.truewheels.com), top of the Killington Road, also rents mountain bikes. The only place on the mountain for bike repair, and a great source of info for local trail and road riding.

CANOEING AND KAYAKING **Chittenden Reservoir** is a sublime place to canoe or kayak, an expansive 674 acres and backed by mountains. Boat access is at the end of Chittenden Dam Road. **Woodford Reservoir** on Route 100 south is another beautiful spot to paddle.

Kayak King (802-422-2070; www.kayakking.8m.com) in Killington offers kayak rentals on Kent Pond.

FISHING Licenses are available from the Killington town clerk, River Road, and also from sporting goods stores and state park rangers. Landlocked salmon and trout can be had in Chittenden Reservoir; trout are the catch in Mendon Brook. There also is fishing in Kent and Colton Ponds, and the White, Tweed, and Ottauquechee Rivers. Woodward Reservoir on Route 100 south and Echo Lake in Tyson (accessible from Plymouth Camp State Park) are also good fishing.

Stream & Brook Fly-Fishing at the Cortina Inn (802-773-3333; www.stream brook.com) offers beginners programs and guided trips.

FOR FAMILIES ✔ **Killington/Pico Adventure Center** (802-422-6200; www .killington.com) is physically divided between the base areas of Pico, down on Route 4, and of Killington itself. Open Memorial Day through late June on weekends, then daily through Labor Day, 10–5. An Adventure Center Pass covers everything; passes are also available for single activities.

✔ *At Pico:* **The Alpine Slide.** Patrons ride a triple chairlift up and then slide down a total of 3,410 feet; the slide begins halfway up the mountain with a sweeping view of the valley to the west. Lunch and snacks are served at a snack bar. "Endless Activities" here also include miniature golf (19 holes) and chairlift rides.

CHITTENDEN RESERVOIR

Christina Tree

✔ *At Killington:* Water slides, outdoor climbing wall, skateboard and in-line skate park, as well as mountain biking and a hiking center.

GOLF **Killington Resort** (802-422-6700; www.killington.com), Killington Road, Killington, has its own 18-hole, 6,326-yard, par-72 course designed by Geoffrey Cornish. Weekend clinics and golf packages. PGA professional instruction, rental clubs. The **Mountain Golf School** (1-800-343-0762), at the Killington Resort, features 2-day weekend and 3-day midweek instructional programs.

Green Mountain National Golf Course (802-422-GOLF; www.gmngc.com), Barrows–Towne Road and Route 100, Killington. This highly rated 18-hole course opened in 1996 and includes a clubhouse, three practice teeing areas, four target greens, and an 8,000-square-foot putting green.

Also see White River Golf Club in The "White River Valleys"— affordable and good for families.

HEALTH SPAS/FITNESS Cortina Health Club (802-773-3333; www.cortina inn.com), Cortina Inn, Route 4, Killington. Heated indoor pool, whirlpool, exercise room, saunas, massage, facials, exercise classes.

Pico Sports Center (802-747-0564), Route 4, Killington. A 75-foot Olympic lap pool, aerobics area, fitness and cardiovascular room, Jacuzzi, saunas, tanning, massage, fitness evaluations.

The Spa at the Woods (802-422-3139; www.spaatthewoods.com), Killington Road, Killington. Built as the heart of a deluxe condo complex but open to drop-ins, an unusually attractive, full-service spa with pool, Jacuzzi, and a full massage and body treatment menu.

Mountain Green Health Club (802-422-3113; www.mtgreen.com), center of Killington Village. Located in the Mountain Green complex, a club with a 54-foot indoor lap pool, Jacuzzi, aerobics classes, steam rooms, sauna, massage.

New Life Hiking Spa (1-800-228-4676; www.newlifehikingspa.com), based at the Inn of the Six Mountains (see *Lodging*). Mid-May through October. Since 1978 Jimmy LeSage has been refining and fine-tuning fitness programs (2 to 11 days and longer) that combine sensible eating and moderate exercise. The daily regimen begins with a prebreakfast walk and includes body conditioning, yoga, and hiking (all levels). Meals are varied, and the focus is on increasing energy and stamina (a good solo vacation).

HIKING Deer Leap Trail, off Route 4 behind the Inn at Long Trail, is the most popular short hike: a 45-minute one-way trek up a winding, moderately steep path that yields a panoramic view from the top of a 2,490-foot cliff. You can continue along the Long Trail to Chittenden Reservoir (spot a car) or branch east at the Maine Junction on the Appalachian Trail. Consult hiking guides for details. This trail also connects with Gifford Woods State Park (see *Green Space*).

THE VISITORS CENTER AT THE CALVIN COOLIDGE STATE HISTORIC SITE

Kim Grant

Bald Mountain. This 3-mile, 3-hour round-trip hike is in Aiken State Forest, off Stratton Road from Route 4 in Mendon. The blue-blazed circle trail begins opposite the entrance to **Tamarack Notch Camp.**

Fox Creek Inn (see *Lodging*) shuttles hikers to the Long Trail as part of the Country Inns Along the Trail program (www.inntoinn.com).

Killington Hiking Center (802-422-6200) at Killington base lodge. Pick up a hiking map to the mountain and its lifts. Inquire about "Hike and Stay" packages.

HORSEBACK RIDING **Mountain Top Stables** (802-483-2311; www.mountain topinn.com) offers an equestrian program from Memorial Day through Columbus Day geared to every level from beginner to experienced riders, both English and Western. Jumping, dressage, and cross-country instruction is also offered, along with the basics of driving the two resident Percherons. Group and private instruction, sleigh rides.

Hawk Center (802-672-3811; www.resort.com), at Salt Ash, Route 100, in Plymouth, offers lessons, trail rides, and hayrides in summer.

ROCK CLIMBING **Green Mountain Rock Climbing Center** (802-773-EDGE; vermontclimbing.com). Based in Rutland and at the Killington Snowshed Lodge, offering lessons and climbs for all abilities, from age 4 up. Inquire about winter ice climbing.

TENNIS **Killington School for Tennis at the Cortina Inn** (802-773-3331), Route 4, Killington. Weekend and 5-day, midweek packages are available Memorial Day through early September, using nine outdoor courts and the Village at Killington. It also features a Junior Tennis Academy.

Summit Lodge (802-422-3535), Killington Road, Killington. Six outdoor courts are available to the public.

Public courts are also maintained by the towns of Chittenden and Killington.

✳ Winter Sports

CROSS-COUNTRY SKIING AND SNOWSHOEING **Mountain Meadows Ski Touring Center** (802-775-7077; 1-800-221-0598; www.xcskiing.net), Thundering Brook Road off Route 4, Killington. One of Vermont's oldest and most serious touring centers, set high (1,500–1,800 feet) on the rolling acreage of the Mountain Meadows Lodge; 57 km groomed for skating and classic stride, plus 500 acres of backcountry terrain; some snowmaking, instruction, rentals, also telemark lessons and rentals. Tours of the backcountry available.

Mountain Top Ski Touring Center (802-483-6089; www.mountaintopinn .com), **Mountain Top Road** Chittenden. Eighty kilometers of groomed trails begin at Mountain Top Inn, an ideal location at 1,495–2,165 feet, with sweeping views of Chittenden Mountain and Reservoir; rentals and lessons, limited snowmaking.

Hawk Inn & Mountain Resort (802-672-3811; www.hawkresort.com), Route 100 south, Plymouth, offers rentals, lessons, and groomed trails meandering along a brook.

Killington Snowshoe Tours (1-800-767-7031; www.killingtonsnowshoetours). Based at Beattie's Trailside Lodge on Route 100 north, Katy Landwehr offers rentals and daily tours ranging from introductory lessons on the neighboring golf course to guided tours up and down Killington and Pico.

DOWNHILL SKIING/SNOWBOARDING ✍ **Killington Resort** (switchboard: 802-422-3333; information: 802-422-6200; www.killington.com), Killington. With seven parking lots, seven base lodges, six interconnected mountains—plus Pico—and an entirely separate novice area, Killington is unquestionably big. When it was purchased by the American Skiing Company in 1996, it was dubbed the Beast of the East. Thanks to its four entry points and far-flung network of lifts and trails, the crowds are neatly dispersed throughout the area. The virtually self-contained Rams Head Family Mountain features a family center for rentals, skier development program registration, child care, food court emporium, and Snow Play Park. *Lifts:* 31, including 12 quads (6 high-speed) plus the Skyeship and K1 Express Gondolas, 4 doubles, 6 triples, 8 surface lifts (52,973 rides per hour). *Trails and slopes:* 200. *Vertical drop:* 3,050 feet. *Snowmaking:* 752 acres of terrain with 1,850 snowguns. *Snowboarding:* Half-pipe with 12-foot walls, five terrain parks. *Facilities:* Six cafeterias, five ski rental shops, one mountaintop restaurant, four lounges. *For children:* Comprehensive Perfect Kids ski and snowboard coaching program based at the Family Center. Children 12 and under ski and ride free when accompanied by an adult with a 5-day pass; kids 5 and under ski free with an adult. *Special programs:* School for Ski Professionals, for Snowboard Professionals, Women's Snowboard Clinics, early-December Ski Raceweek and Snowboard Freeriding and Carving Camp, Women's Turn, Mogul

KILLINGTON RESORT

Rob Bossi

Clinic Weekends. *Rates:* 1-day—adult $67, young adult $54, junior $43. Multiday rates and interchangeable tickets (with other ASC resorts) can bring adult tickets down to $52 per day, less if you buy online at least 14 days in advance or combine with lodging.

Bear Creek Mountain Club (802-672-4242; www.bearcreekclub.com). The chairlift operates Thursday through Sunday and during holiday weeks in-season at the former Round Top ski area. A 1,300-foot vertical drop, a chairlift, a recently expanded clubhouse, and limited ticket sales are the draw at this evolving semiprivate resort. Nonmembers are welcome by reservation: $75 per adult, $50 junior, $30 on Sunday morning. Inquire about lifetime memberships.

DOGSLEDDING **Arctic Paws** (802-775-1010), based at Mountain Meadows in Killington. Jim and Sue Gail offer hour-long dogsled mushing on and around Kent Pond.

SLEIGH RIDES **Cortina Inn** (802-773-3333), Route 4 east, Mendon. Wednesday, Saturday, and some holidays. Sleigh rides are also offered at **Mountain Top Resort** (802-483-2311) and as part of ski weeks at Killington (802-422-6200).

SNOWMOBILING **Vermont Snowmobile Tours** (1-800-286-6360; www.ver montsnowmobile tours.com), junction of Routes 4 and 105 south, West Bridgewater. One and 2-hour tours, plus full-day and moonlight tours, with access to hundreds of miles of groomed trails; rental helmets, clothing, and boots. This is also a source of info about local clubs.

Killington Snowmobile Tours (802-422-2121), based at Killington, offers snowmobile tours plus tours to Killington Peak for Wednesday-night dinner.

❈ Green Space

Note: For more information about both of the following, see www.vtstateparks.com.

Calvin Coolidge State Forest. This 18,000-acre preserve, which actually includes Killington Peak, is scattered through seven local towns and divided by Route 100 into two districts. The recreational center is **Coolidge State Park** (summer: 802-672-3612; winter: 802-885-8891; 1-800-299-3071), Route 100A east of Plymouth Notch. Open mid-May through mid-October, these 500 acres include a campground (60 campsites including 35 lean-tos, a dump station, picnic area, and restrooms with hot showers), picnic shelter, and hiking and snowmobile trails. In another part of the forest Camp Plymouth State Park, off Route 100 in Tyson, served as a Civilian Conservation Corps (CCC) camp in 1933 and offers a beach on Echo Lake (picnic area, food concession). Inquire about gold panning and trails into the abandoned village of Plymouth Five Corners. North of the turnoff for Route 100A, the steep CCC Road (marked for Meadowsweet Farm) climbs away from Route 100 into the western swatch of the forest, with beautiful views back down the valley. It's unfortunate (but sensible) that this road is closed in winter because it harbors some of the area's snowiest cross-country trails, accessible only by going the long way around through Shrewsbury (see *Scenic Drive* in "Okemo Valley Region").

Gifford Woods State Park (summer: 802-775-5354; winter: 802-885-8891; 1-800-299-3071), 0.5 mile north of Route 4 on Route 100, Killington. The campground (27 tent/trailer and 21 lean-to sites, hot showers) is patronized by hikers on the Appalachian Trail, which runs through the park. Across the road is the Gifford Woods Natural Area, a 7-acre stand of virgin hardwoods (sugar maple, yellow birch, basswood, white ash, and hemlock). Trails lead up to Deer Leap Mountain and to the lovely waterfalls where Kent Brook enters Kent Pond. In winter cross-country trails connect with Mountain Meadows.

☀ Lodging

Note: Killington's Skyeship Gondola on Route 4 also puts the inns of Plymouth to the southeast within easy reach, and lodging in both Woodstock (see "Woodstock/Quechee Area") and Ludlow (see "Okemo Valley Region") is within 14 miles. See *Guidance* for central reservations numbers.

RESORTS ✍ **The Killington Grand Resort Hotel & Conference Center** (1-888-64-GRAND; www.killingtonresortvillage.com), 228 East Mountain Road, Killington 05751. At the base of the lifts, this 200-room, vintage-1997 facility offers standard hotel rooms, also studios and one-, two-, and three-bedroom suites (with kitchen). It's immense, with endless corridors and Vermont's biggest meeting space (the Grand Ballroom)—ergo conventions. The rooms are, however, irreproachably comfortable. Amenities include an outdoor heated pool, health club, on-site daycare, Ovations Restaurant (see *Dining Out*), and a café. It's close not only to the base lodge, but in summer to the golf course. Summer rates are $150 for a hotel room, in winter $266; a one-bedroom suite (four people) goes for $227 in summer, $400 in winter. Better values year-round if combined with a sports package.

🐾 ✍ ♿ **Hawk Inn and Mountain Resort** (802-672-3811; 1-800-685-4295; www.hawkresort.com), Route 100, Plymouth 05056. Set on 1,200 acres and owned by longtime residents Brenda and Jack Geishecker, this ranks among Vermont's most luxurious resorts. Lodging options include freestanding "mountain villas" salted away on hillsides with splendid views, also the townhouse-style Ledges Villas high above the Black River Valley and the 50-room Hawk Inn and River Tavern. Situated halfway between Killington and Okemo (theoretically 10 minutes from each) and 3 miles from the trails at Bear Creek Mountain Club, the resort is well positioned for alpine skiers and offers its own extensive cross-country trail network as well as a heated outdoor pool, a spa, and ice skating and sleigh rides. In summer there's tennis, horseback riding, swimming, mountain biking, and fly-fishing, as well as canoeing, kayaking, sailing, and rowing on Lake Amherst. The heart of the inn itself is a 19th-century farmhouse, and rooms are in modern wings. Each is decorated differently. Some have whirlpool bath; all are equipped with down comforters, feather beds, and large-screen TV. The spa has a large indoor/outdoor pool, massage and spa therapy services, and a salon. In winter rates are $250–450 per couple in the inn, $320–750 in the Ledges Villas, and $360–950 in the freestanding mountain villas; in summer/fall $250–395 in the inn, $320–650 in the Ledges Villas, and $360–820 in Mountain Villas. Inn rates include full breakfast. See *Dining Out* for the River Tavern. Lunch is served poolside during summer.

⊕ 🐾 🐾 ♿ **Cortina Inn and Resort** (802-773-3333; 1-800-451-6108; www.cortinainn.com), Killington 05751. This modern luxury lodge on Route 4 is designed for the average American family out to pamper themselves. In summer there's serious tennis (www.killingtontennis.com) with pros using eight courts, also the Stream & Brook Fly-Fishing School (lessons and guide service) and golf programs utilizing eight local golf courses. The grounds include an extensive nature and a touring trail system connecting with both the Mountain Meadows and Mountain Top trail networks in winter. Year-round there's the fitness center with whirlpools, saunas, exercise machines, and indoor pool; massage and spa therapies are offered. Afternoon tea is served in the two-story lobby, which has a round hearth in the center and exhibit space for local sculpture and art in the gallery. There are 89 air-conditioned rooms, all with private bath and individually decorated, and seven suites, some with fireplace and whirlpool bath (Room 215 is immense), some suites with lofts, and five rooms that are wheelchair accessible. Common space includes a game room, art gallery, and library. $119–159 per couple B&B low seasons; $139–199 B&B high seasons. Children $8 in the same room with parent (breakfast included). Pets find a pet treat waiting on arrival. The Cortina dining rooms are Zola's Grille and casual Theodore's Tavern (see *Dining Out* and *Eating Out*). Inquire about tennis, golf, and ski packages.

CILLY GENERAL STORE AT THE CALVIN COOLIDGE STATE HISTORIC SITE

Christina Tree

⊕ 🐾 **Mountain Meadows Lodge** (802-775-1010; 1-800-370-4567; www.mtmeadowslodge.com), Thundering Brook Road, Killington 05751. The main building is an 1856 barn, nicely converted into a classic lodge with an informal dining room, spacious living room with a lake view, and game room. Now run by Michele and Mark Werle, the inn is geared to families year-round, catering to people who like the outdoors in warm-weather months and as well as in winter. You might want to inquire, however, about whether there's a weekend wedding. This is a hospitable, thoroughly relaxing kind of lodge. There are 20 guest rooms, many of them great for families, all with private bath. A sauna and outdoor Jacuzzi are among the amenities. In summer there is a swimming pool and 100-acre Kent Pond, which abuts the property and is good for fishing and canoeing as well as swimming; the town tennis courts are just down the road. In winter this is a major ski touring center (see *Cross-Country Skiing and Snowshoeing*); dogsled mushing is also an option. Year-round residents include a miniature potbellied pig, a pony, sheep, chickens, and a rooster. The lake is stocked with trout and bass. Low seasons $85–100 per couple B&B; high season $100–300 for a family room.

⊙ ☃ ☙ **Mountain Top Inn** (802-483-2311; 1-800-445-2100; www .mountaintopinn.com), Mountain Top Road, Chittenden 05737. Set high on rolling acres overlooking Chittenden Reservoir, this self-contained resort has recently acquired new owners and a total makeover. The resort has long been known as one of the few places to offer horseback riding and for its cross-country skiing (both are open to the public; see *To Do*). Now the equestrian program has been expanded and each of the 33 rooms in the main inn has been redecorated (TVs hidden in armoires) and "themed"— Stags Run, for instance, features a huge rough-hewn log bed. Many now have pampering plumbing, including whirlpool tubs. Request a room with a lake view. There are also three cottages and several private "resort chalets" available for larger groups. In addition to riding, summer activities include swimming in both the lake and a heated pool, tennis, lawn games, canoeing and kayaking, claybird shooting, and fly-fishing. Rooms in the inn are $155–345 (no meals; add 15 percent service) during summer and winter seasons. Breakfast is $14, MAP $65, and AP $80. Pets are $25 per night (they receive a dog bed, bowls, and a welcome treat) plus a $200 security deposit. Inquire about the many packages.

INNS ☘ ☙ **The October Country Inn** (802-672-3412; 1-800-648-8421; www.octobercountryinn.com), junction of Routes 4 and 100A, Bridgewater Corners 05035. Handy to

Killington and Woodstock (8 miles) as well as most of the things to do and see in this chapter, yet sequestered up a back road with hiking trails that lead past the swimming pool to the top of a hill for a sweeping, peaceful view. This old farmhouse has a large, comfortable living room with inviting places to sit around the hearth and at the big round table in the dining room—not to be confused with the other cheery dining room in which guests gather around long tables for memorable meals, which can be Greek, Mexican, Asian, French, or, occasionally, American. Innkeepers Edie and Chuck Janisse offer candlelit dinners featuring homemade bread, cakes, homegrown vegetables and herbs, and wine. Breakfasts are equally ambitious, geared to fuel bikers in summer and skiers in winter. The 10 guest rooms (8 with private bath) vary in size; most have queen-sized beds, and all are carefully decorated. $115–195 includes dinner and/or breakfast for two. Open most of the year.

♿ **Fox Creek Inn** (802-483-6213; 1-800-707-0017; www.foxcreekinn .com), 49 Chittenden Dam Road, Chittenden 05737. This is backwoods luxury in a superb house built by the inventor William Barstow, who retired here after selling his various holdings for $40 million right before the 1929 stock market crash. Ann and Alex Volz offer nine carefully furnished guest rooms, all with private bath, most with Jacuzzi, and a couple with gas fireplace. The Honeymoon Suite, also good for a family of four, has two fireplaces and a two-person Jacuzzi. Guests gather around the big stone fireplace in the paneled den, in the comfortable living room, and at the cozy bar. Candlelight dinners are a point of pride. There is swimming, canoeing, and fishing in the Chittenden Reservoir just down the road, and in winter you can cross-country ski. Rates are $160–295 B&B, $190–325 MAP ($249–409 during foliage season).

🦌 ♿ **The Vermont Inn** (802-775-0708; 1-800-541-7795; www.vermont inn.com), Killington 05751. Set above Route 4 with a view of Killington and Pico, this is a 19th-century farmhouse with a homey feel to its public rooms—the living room with woodstove, the pub/lounge with fireplace, a game room, and an upstairs reading room, a welcome nook in the evening when the dining room is open to the public (see *Dining Out*). Summer facilities include a pool, a tennis court, and lawn games. The sauna and hot tub are available year-round. Innkeepers Megan and Greg Smith offer 18 guest rooms, ranging from smallish to spacious, all bright with brass and antique or canopy bedstead and private bath. Five have a fireplace, one with a Jacuzzi and one, wheelchair accessible. $115–155 per couple MAP in summer, $125–250 MAP in fall; 2-day winter weekends, $360–570 MAP. Less for midweek and longer stays. Inquire about golf, fishing, and other packages.

🐾 **Red Clover Inn** (802-775-2290; 1-800-752-0571; www.redclover inn.com), Box 7450, Woodward Road, Mendon 05701. This is a handsome 1840s landmark set in 13 acres. Several of the 14 rooms have all the bells and whistles: cathedral ceiling, a whirlpool from which you can operate (via remote control) the gas fireplace, TV, VCR, and more. All rooms are attractive, each different, with plenty of light. Our favorite is Tuscany, with a queen bed, skylights, and a double soaking tub. Common space is ample, and the dining rooms are public. Facilities include a landscaped pool and small pond. $145–290 per couple B&B, $60 higher in foliage season. Pets permitted in the carriage house at $20 extra per day.

Casa Bella Inn & Restaurant (802-746-8943; 1-877-746-8943; www.casa bellainn.com), P.O. Box 685, Pittsfield 05762. Located 8 miles north of Killington in the center of the village on a handsome green, this double-porched old inn has been welcoming guests since 1835. Innkeeper Susan Cacozza is from Britain and her husband, Franco, is a chef from Tuscany. The restaurant is important here and open to the public (see *Dining Out*), but the feel is very much that of a village country inn in the center of this classic Vermont town that's removed from, but still handy to Killington. The eight guest rooms, all with private bath, are $90–145.

∞ **Salt Ash Inn** (802-672-3748; 1-800-SALT-ASH; www.saltashinn .com), Route 100, Plymouth 05056. Built as an inn in the 1830s, presently owned by Jonathan Petrie and Jordan Phillips, this is a special place. A pub in the former general store retains the original grocery counter and wooden post office boxes (where Calvin Coolidge picked up his mail), and a circular hearth serves the purpose of the old potbellied stove. The 17 rooms are divided among three buildings (we prefer the 9 in the main house); all have private bath, TV, and hair dryer. Facilities include a heated outdoor pool, a hot tub, and DSL access. The entire place can be rented by groups of up to 50. $95–235 B&B,

depending on the room (they range from economy to deluxe with fire-place), the season, and the day of the week; less for weekdays and longer stays; group discounts. Ski-season weekends are 2-day packages.

LODGES ✒ **The Inn of the Six Mountains** (802-422-4302; 1-800-228-4676; www.sixmountains.com), Killington Road, Killington 05751. A 103-room, four-story, Adirondack-style hotel with gabled ceilings, sky-lights, balconies, and a two-story lobby with a fieldstone fireplace. Common spaces include a second-floor sitting room and a third-floor library. There is also a spa with lap pool, Jacuzzis, and exercise room, plus a dining room. In summer $138–188 (for a suite) per couple, fall $199–249, winter $149–309, depending on the day and week. In winter $281 per person for 2 days includes skiing, lodging, and breakfast. Children are free with two adults but $17 if over 12. Inquire about Jimmy LeSage's New Life Hiking Spa (www.newlife hikingspa.com), a program based here early May through October.

🐾 **The Inn at Long Trail** (802-775-7181; 1-800-325-2540; www.innat longtrail.com), Route 4, Killington 05751. Closed in shoulder seasons. This is the first building in New Eng-land specifically built to serve as a ski lodge. It began in 1938 as an annex to a splendid summer inn that has since burned. Designed to resemble the inside of the forest as much as pos-sible, the interior incorporates parts of trees and boulders and is a casual place. The inn caters to through-hikers on the Appalachian and Long Trails and outdoors people of all sorts. The 22-foot-long bar is made from a

single log, and a protruding toe of the backyard cliff can be seen in both the pub and the dining room. The 14 rooms are small but cheery (2 are family suites); there are 5 two-room suites with fireplace. The hot tub is used only in winter. Dinner is served varying nights in the restaurant, but you can usually count on McGrath's Irish Pub (see *Eating Out*). Summer rates are $68–98 per room B&B; in winter, from $119 B&B; nonholiday weekends, $340–448 per couple. MAP costs more at peak times. Gra-tuity is 10 percent. Pets by advance arrangement.

✒ **Cascades Lodge** (802-422-3731; 1-800-345-0113; www.cascades lodge.com), 58 Old Mill Road, Killington 05751. The MacKenzie family's neat, contemporary, 46-room hostelry is practically next to the Killington base lodge. Some rooms have balconies, and there's an indoor pool, sundeck, whirlpool, sauna, lounge, and highly rated restaurant (see *Dining Out*). Rates $99–139 in summer, $139–219 in fall and on win-ter weekends, less midweek in winter, more for suites, 9 percent gratuity. Children stay free in summer and fall.

🐾 ✒ **Butternut on the Mountain** (802-422-2000; 1-800-524-7654; www.butternutlodge.com), Box 306, Killington Road, Killington 05751. Open year-round except May and June. A family-owned motor lodge with 18 large standard rooms with color TV and phone. Facilities include an indoor heated pool, whirlpool, fireside library and lounge, game room, laundry facilities, and Mrs. Brady's restaurant (see *Eating Out*). $56–200 per room with continental breakfast, 15 percent service charge; ski packages available. Pets accepted in summer and fall by previous arrangement.

MOTEL ♨ ✍ **Farmbrook Motel** (802-672-3621; www.farmbrook motel.com), Route 100A, Plymouth 05056. An unusually attractive 12-unit motel attached to a handsome early-19th-century house, 3 miles from Coolidge's birthplace, handy to Killington; in summer the beautifully landscaped, brookside grounds have outdoor fireplaces and picnic tables. Some rooms sleep five; two kitchenettes. Rates $55–95 per couple; children under 12, free.

CONDOMINIUMS **The Killington Lodging Bureau** (in ski season: 1-800-621-6867; otherwise: 1-877-458-4637; www.killingtonresort village.com) serves hundreds of mountain properties, among them **Killington Resort Villages**—700 condo units, including the Killington Grand—and **Sunrise Mountain Village,** high on the mountain. In summer Killington Resort Villages becomes a mini resort in its own right, nicely landscaped and filled with a mix of mountain bikers, families, golfers, retirees, and family reunions. Amenities include pools and whirlpools for each condo cluster. In winter you can walk to the lifts, and while some units are slope-side, other are a schlep from the shuttle to the base lodge. Still, you're right at the nerve center of Killington's vast lift and trail network. Winter rates range upward from $232 per person for 5-day, 5-night packages. In summer packages start at $41 and in fall at $51 per person per day. **Pico Resort Hotel** on Route 4 in Killington abuts the Pico base lodge. The 152 units are well done: one-bedroom suites in the

Village Square; two-, three-, and four-bedroom units in the village, with phone and marble-faced fireplace. The sports center here has a 75-foot indoor pool, Nautilus equipment, aerobics room, Jacuzzi, saunas, and lounge. Same prices as Killington Resort Village.

Also see **Tupper Farm Lodge** and **Hawk North** in "The White River Valleys."

CAMPGROUNDS See *Green Space* for information on camping in Calvin Coolidge and Gifford Woods State Parks.

✳ Where to Eat

DINING OUT **Hemingway's** (802-422-3886; www.hemingwaysrestau rant.com), Route 4, Sherburne Flats, east of Killington. Closed Monday and Tuesday. Between Linda's eye for detail in the decor and service and Ted's concern for freshness, preparation, and presentation, the Fondulas have created one of the most highly rated dining experiences in New England. Chandeliers, fresh flowers, and floor-length table linens grace the peach-colored, vaulted main room, while a less formal atmosphere prevails in the garden room and stone-walled wine cellar. It's billed as "regional, classic cuisine." You might begin with a Vermont quail with polenta cake and white bean vinaigrette, or roasted eggplant and red pepper soup with olive and Parmesan toast, then dine on sea bass with lobster, toasted coucous, spinach, and shallots, topped off with mascarpone spice cake with apple cider and currants. The four-course prix fixe menu is $55–65, but inquire about midweek specials; wine-tasting menu $87. A totally vegan menu is available with advance notice.

The Corners Inn and Restaurant (802-672-9968), Route 4, Bridgewater Corners. Open for dinner Wednesday through Sunday. Reservations suggested. Known for the unusual ways he uses fresh, local ingredients, chef-owner Brad Pirkey has created an informal, standout small restaurant in an 1890 farmhouse. In winter request a table near the fireplace, and in summer, on the terrace. There's also a friendly bar. Specials on a summer night included beef Wellington and lobster spring rolls, and the menu ranged from homemade pastas with sweet Italian sausage, prosciutto, mushrooms, garlic, and roasted red peppers to veal with wild mushrooms and artichoke hearts. Entrées $15.95–18.95. All entrées come with daily homemade cheese spread and fresh-baked bread.

🦞 ♫ **The Countryman's Pleasure** (802-773-7141), just off Route 4, Mendon. Open 5–9 daily. Chef-owner Hans Entinger is known for top-drawer Austrian-German specialties: veal schnitzel cordon bleu, sauerbraten, goulash, and so on. Seafood is also a specialty. The attractive dining rooms occupy the first floor of a charming house. There's a long wine list, and beers as well as international coffees and nonalcoholic wines and beers are served. The atmosphere is cozy, informal. Early-bird specials (before 6 PM) are under $14. Otherwise entrées are $15.95–29.95. Children's menu.

🦞 ♫ ♿ **The Vermont Inn** (802-775-0708; 1-800-541-7795), Route 4, Killington. Open for dinner nightly. Chef Stephen Hatch has captured first place three times in the Killington-Champagne Dine Around Contest. It's a pleasant inn dining room with a fireplace and a varied menu that changes nightly. Entrées might range from eggplant Parmesan and Vermont roast turkey to rack of lamb. There's a children's menu and, in summer only, early-bird specials are available until 6:30. Otherwise entrées are $12.95–21.50.

Zola's Grille at the Cortina Inn (802-773-3333), Route 4, Killington. Open daily for dinner. This is a spacious, nicely decorated dining room. You might begin with grilled shrimp wrapped in prosciutto, then dine on scallops atop spinach and creamed oysters with buckwheat blinis. Entrées $17.95–21.50. The Sunday buffet brunch is a winner at $14.95.

♿ **The River Tavern** (802-672-3811) at Hawk Inn and Resort, Route 100, Plymouth. Open for breakfast daily, lunch and dinner in high seasons. Dinner reservations recommended. The restaurant itself is country elegant, with windowed walls framing the landscape. A summer à la carte menu might feature Batten Kill trout and pork tenderloin that's been marinated in maple and soy. Entrées $19–24.

🦞 **Choices Restaurant** (802-422-4030), Glazebrook Center, Killington Road, Killington. Open Wednesday through Sunday for dinner; Sunday brunch 11–2:30. This combination bistro/brasserie/pub has a huge menu of savory appetizers, salads, soups, raw bar, sandwiches, and pastas, not to mention entrées ranging from curried vegetables with couscous to filet mignon with portobello mushrooms and double-cream blue cheese. Chef-owner Claude Blays is a 1975 graduate of the Culinary Institute of America. Entrées $12.50–22.

❦ **Birch Ridge Inn** (802-422-4293; www.birchridge.com), Killington Road and Butler Road, Killington. Open for dinner Wednesday through Sunday and nightly during holiday weeks. Hidden away up off Killington Road, this oddly shaped inn (essentially two interconnected A-frames) features a dining room and lounge with some ambience. The menu is ambitious, with dishes such as mushroom strudel wrapped in flaky pasty with creamed leeks, or sesame-rimmed rare tuna with wakame salad and coconut-scented jasmine rice. Entrées $19.95–25.50. Lounge and full liquor license.

The Mountain Top Inn and Resort (802-483-2311; www.mountain topinn.com), Mountain Top Road, Chittenden. Open for dinner by reservation to nonguests. The inn dining room is large and formal, with views down to the reservoir. It's an à la carte menu with starters like crab and lobster gateau, a choice of salads, and entrées like pepper-crusted grouper with crab, lobster, and collard green topping, "ravioli ala campagna" (handmade with Vermont chèvre and fresh mushrooms), and rack of lamb. Entrées $23–36. The **Highlands Tavern,** also at the inn, is open daily for lunch: $11–23).

❦ ♪ **Cascades Lodge Restaurant** (802-422-3731), top of Killington Road at Killington Village. Open daily in-season, featuring big breakfasts. Locally known as a good dinner bet with plenty of choices and a dinner menu ranging from eggplant marinara to roast duck with raspberry sauce; fabulous desserts like chocolate mousse à la orange. Pub menu, kids' menu, and nightly specials. Entrées $11.95–18.95.

♪ ♿ **Ovations Restaurant at the Killington Grand Resort** (802-422-6111), 228 East Mountain Road, Killington, is open daily 11–9:30. This is a family-geared hotel dining room with soups and salads served all day and dinner selections ranging from burgers and pasta to steak *au poivre.* Entrées $14–22.

Casa Bella Inn (802-746-8943), Route 100, Pittsfield. Franco Cacozza is the chef-owner of this pleasant restaurant in the former Pittsfield Inn, a classic old stage stop in the classic village 8 miles north of Killington. The menu is traditional, too, and authentic. Try the linguine *al pecatore* (sautéed with shrimp, squid, and clams in a light tomato sauce) or the saltimbocca *alla romana* (veal scaloppine topped with ham, cheese, and sage) and a selection of Italian wines and homemade desserts. Entrées $12.50–20.75.

The Garlic (802-422-5055), midway up Killington Road. Open daily for dinner from 4 PM, happy hour at 3. A cozy, informal setting for hearty Italian, with a choice of pasta dishes and entrées featuring the namesake ingredient. From $13.50 for "The Puttanesca" (linguine with the house sauce) to $24.95 for garlic-marinated char-grilled rack of lamb.

EATING OUT ♪ **Grist Mill** (802-422-3970), Killington Road on the Summit Lodge grounds. Open for lunch and dinner, Sunday brunch; also for breakfast on weekends and holidays. The building is designed to look like a gristmill that has always stood on Summit Pond (there's a 90-year-old waterwheel). The inside is airy and pleasing, dominated by a huge stone hearth. The dinner menu ranges from steaks and veal dishes through grilled swordfish to vegetable stir-fry. There's a children's menu and blackboard specials. Full liquor license.

McGrath's Irish Pub and the Inn at Long Trail (802-775-7181), Route 4, Killington. The pub is open nightly; the restaurant, during high season. The 22-foot-long bar is made from a single log, and a protruding toe of the backyard cliff can be seen in both the pub and the dining room. The first place to serve Guinness on tap in Vermont, the pub boasts Vermont's largest selection of Irish whiskey and features Irish country and folk music in the pub on weekends. The house specialties are Guinness stew and shepherd's pie.

Casey's Caboose (802-422-3795), Killington Road, Killington. Open daily from 3 PM; lunch is served Saturday, Sunday, and in holiday weeks. The building incorporates a circa-1900 snowplow car and a great caboose to house the coveted tables, but you really can't lose: The atmosphere throughout rates high on our short list of family dining spots. Free buffalo wings during happy hour. Burgers and salads all day and a great children's menu.

Ppeppers Bar & Grill (802-422-3177), in the Killington Mall, Killington, open daily 7 AM–11 PM, is a popular spot for breakfast, lunch, dinner, and take-out food. On a weekday in summer this was the only place open and it was great: a cool and colorful inside with a central U-shaped counter/bar and booths around the walls, also patio tables. At breakfast omelets are a specialty; there's always a homemade soup of the day plus vegetarian specials, wraps, and burgers at lunch. Dinner specialties

include citrus-marinated mahimahi, pastas, and BBQ ribs. Full liquor license. A great kids' menu.

Charity's 1887 Saloon-Restaurant (802-422-3800), midway up Killington Road, Killington. Open daily for dinner. Happy hour (free wings), 3–6. Tiffany shades, 1880s saloon decor, and wooden booths—this is the place for French onion soup, a Reuben, or vegetarian casserole at lunch; steak is a good dinner choice. Informal, satisfying.

Peppino's Ristorante Italiano (802-422-3293), near the foot of Killington Road, Killington. Open nightly in summer and ski season. A traditional, reasonably priced Italian restaurant with predictable menu and decor, reliable.

Mountain Meadows Lodge (802-775-1010), Thundering Brook Road, Killington. Open to the public by reservation on weekends during ski season. This pleasant, family-geared lodge (see *Lodging*) offers reasonably priced buffets and a children's menu.

Back Behind Saloon (802-422-9907), junction of Routes 4 and 100 south, West Bridgewater. Open from 4 in the tavern, at 5 for dinner nightly during ski season and summer, less in the off-season. A zany atmosphere (look for the red caboose and antique Mobil gas pump), barnboard, stained glass, a big hearth. Specialties like venison and saloon roast duck augment basic American fare: steaks and chicken, generous portions. Entrées on the high side ($13.95–22.50). Children's menu.

Theodore's Tavern (802-773-3331), Cortina Inn, Route 4, Killington. A good bet for casual dining and après-ski.

Sugar & Spice (802-773-7832), Route 4, Mendon. Open 7–2 daily. A pancake restaurant housed in a large replica of a classic sugarhouse and surrounded by a 50-acre sugarbush. Besides dining on a variety of pancake, egg, and omelet dishes, along with soups and sandwiches, you can watch both maple candy and cheese being made several days a week. Gift shop.

♪ ♿ **Mrs. Brady's** (802-422-2020), Killington Road at Butternut on the Mountain. Open seasonally, so check. The atmosphere is casual and colorful, and the menu features a salad bar, steak, and seafood; includes a great American burger platter and gobbler (turkey on a grinder with stuffing and gravy), as well as baked stuffed lobster. There are also pasta, veal, and steak dishes; stir-fries; plus pizza and a children's menu.

See also "Rutland and the Lower Champlain Valley." Rutland is an exceptionally good "eating-out" town.

PIZZA **Outback Pizza** (802-422-9885), Killington Road, Killington. Open from 3 in spring and winter, from 5 in summer and fall. Features wood-fired stone-baked pizza with prime ingredients.

Pizza Jerks (802-422-4111, Killington Road). Open from 11 AM. A local favorite, part of a virtual café with Internet access.

✳ Entertainment

MUSIC The **Killington Music Festival** (802-773-4003), a series of mostly chamber music concerts in Snowshed Lodge and at a scattering of other local sites; weekends in July and August.

APRÈS-SKI **The Wobbly Barn** (802-422-3392), Killington Road, Killington. A steak house (dinner 5–11) with plenty of music, dancing, blues, rock 'n' roll. Ski season only.

The Nightspot (802-422-9885), Killington Road, Killington. Dancing nightly to a DJ. Free ski tuning and happy-hour hors d'oeuvres nightly.

McGrath's Irish Pub at the Inn at Long Trail (802-775-7181), Route 4, Killington. Live Irish music on weekends to go with the Gaelic atmosphere and Guinness on tap. It's a great pub with a 22-foot-long bar made from a single log and a boulder protruding from the back wall.

Pickle Barrel (802-422-3035), Killington Road, Killington. "Some of the finest rock 'n' roll bands in the East."

✳ Selective Shopping

Bill's Country Store (802-773-9313), at the junction of Routes 4 and 100, Killington, stocks a broad spectrum of Vermont products, including cheese, maple goodies, deerskin gloves, and woodwork.

The Shops at the Shack and **The Ski Shack** (802-773-3600), Route 4 at Killington Road, Killington. Open daily 9–5:30. This place has just about everything in the way of sports clothes and equipment for adults and kids, much at discount prices; boutique name-brand shops include Nordica, The North Face, Children's Shop, and Nike.

Long Trail Brewing Company (802-672-5011; www.longtrail.com), Route 4 west at Bridgewater Corners, produces Long Trail Ale as well as Pollenator, India Pale Ale, Stout, Blackberry, Wheat, and Harvest.

Tastings and pub fare, daily noon–5.

See also the box on pages 262 to 263 for the Marketplace at **Bridgewater Mill** in "Woodstock/Quechee Area."

✳ Special Events

January–March: Frequent **alpine ski and snowboard events** at Killington and Pico.

Memorial Day weekend: **Rage Weekend** with **Killington Triathlon:** ski/snowboard, mountain bike, cross-country run.

July 4: **Calvin Coolidge Birthday Memorial,** Plymouth.

July–August: **Killington Music Festival** (802-773-4003).

August: **Killington Renaissance Festival.**

Columbus Day weekend: **Sheep and Wool Festival. Brew Fest,** Killington.

THE WHITE RIVER VALLEYS

V anishing Vermont" could be the subtitle for this chapter. As I-89 sweeps up through central Vermont in a grand 52-mile arc—from White River Junction to Montpelier—it yields a series of panoramas. Motorists see the high wall of the Green Mountains beyond the Braintree Range on the west and catch glimpses of an occasional valley village. What they don't see is one of Vermont's best-kept secrets: the classic old villages, abrupt valleys, and hill farms along the White River and its three branches.

The White River rises high in the Green Mountains above Granville Gulf and rushes down through Hancock, widening and slowing among farms in Rochester, keeping company with Route 100 until Stockbridge, where its course dictates a dogleg in the highway. Turning sharply east and carving a narrow valley for Route 107 (the Gaysville reach is an especially challenging one for kayakers during spring freshets), the river reaches Bethel and begins to parallel Route 14 and I-89. As it courses through the Royaltons and Sharon on its way to the Connecticut River, tubing and fishing possibilities increase with the input of the three northern branches.

Each of these streams, rising some 20 miles north of the main stem of the river, has carved its own valley. The First Branch, shadowed by Route 110, threads six covered bridges, lush farmland, and the unselfconsciously beautiful villages of Chelsea and Tunbridge. The Second Branch begins above the picturesque village of Brookfield, known for its floating bridge, and flows south along Route 14. The Third Branch rises in Roxbury, conveniently near a fish hatchery, and flows south through a lonely valley (along Route 12A) to Randolph, one of the few I-89 exits and an Amtrak stop as well as the only commercial center of any size in this entire area.

Beautiful as these valleys are, the high east–west roads that connect them, climbing up over the hills and down into the next valley, are more rewarding still. To begin exploring this back-roaded and unresortified heart of Vermont, you might exit in Sharon and climb through the Straffords to Tunbridge and north to Chelsea, west to Brookfield, then south to Randolph, on down Route 12, and west over Rochester Mountain. See *Scenic Drives* for tours that can pleasantly fill many days.

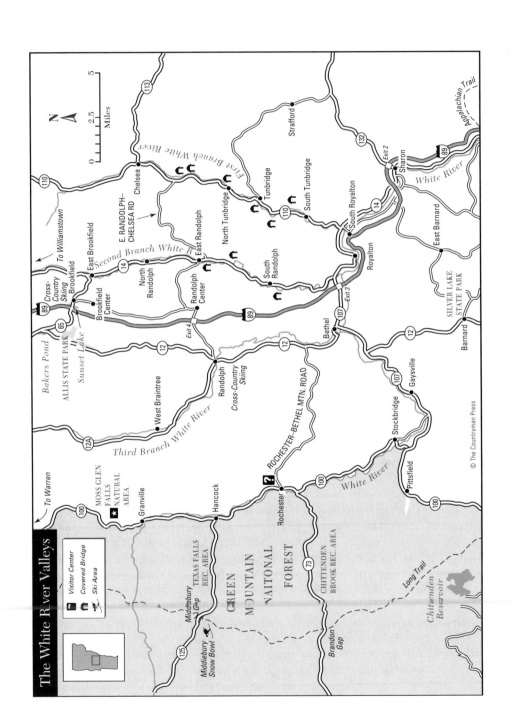

The White River Valleys

Legend:
- ? Visitor Center
- ⌐ Covered Bridge
- Ski Area

N

0   2.5   5
Miles

To Warren

To Williamstown

To Williamstown

113

110

Chelsea

E. RANDOLPH–
CHELSEA RD

First Branch White River

Strafford

132

Exit 2

Sharon

White River

Appalachian Trail

89

East Brookfield

Second Branch White R.

14

East Randolph

North Tunbridge

Tunbridge

South Tunbridge

110

South Royalton

14

East Barnard

SILVER LAKE
STATE PARK

Brookfield

Cross-
Country
Skiing

89

65

Bakers Pond

ALLIS STATE PARK

Sunset Lake

Brookfield
Center

North
Randolph

Randolph
Center

South Randolph

South
Randolph

Royalton

89

Exit 3

107

Bethel

Barnard

12

Exit 4

12

West Braintree

Randolph

Cross-Country
Skiing

12

ROCHESTER–BETHEL MTN. ROAD

107

Gaysville

Stockbridge

12A

Third Branch White River

100

Granville

MOSS GLEN
FALLS
NATURAL
AREA

Hancock

Rochester

?

100

White River

Pittsfield

100

© The Countryman Press

125

Middlebury Gap

Middlebury
Snow Bowl

TEXAS FALLS
REC. AREA

GREEN
MOUNTAIN
NATIONAL
FOREST

73

CHITTENDEN
BROOK REC. AREA

Brandon Gap

Long Trail

Chittenden
Reservoir

GUIDANCE Randolph Area Chamber of Commerce (802-728-9027; 1-877-772-6365; www.randolphvt.com), 31 Route 66, Randolph 05060. Phone answered and office open year-round, weekdays 8:30–4; information center maintained Memorial Day through mid-October at State Plaza just off I-89, exit 4 (next to the Mobil station).

Green Mountain National Forest Ranger District Office and Visitors Center (802-767-4261), Route 100 in Rochester. Open 8–4 daily (except Sunday) Memorial Day through Columbus Day, weekdays off-season. A magnificent new center (restrooms) with detailed information on hiking, biking, picnicking, bird-watching, camping, and other recreation in this part of the GMNF.

Eastern Vermont Gateway (1-888-848-4199), the state's marketing organization for this region, publishes a magazine and maintains a web site, www.eastern riververmont.com.

The Herald of Randolph (802-728-3232), Box 309, Randolph, a weekly published on Thursday, carries local news and events for Orange and northern Windsor Counties.

GETTING THERE *By bus:* **Vermont Transit** buses stop just off I-89 at White River Junction and Randolph.

By train: **Amtrak's** Vermonter (1-800-USA-RAIL). Randolph and White River Junction (see "Upper Valley River Towns") are stops for trains from Washington, DC, New York City, and Springfield and Amherst, Massachusetts, with connecting bus service to Montreal; the baggage car has bike racks.

By car: This area covers a wide, hilly swath of Vermont. I-89 runs diagonally across it but with only three exits (Sharon, Bethel, and Randolph). Towns are connected by beautiful old east–west ridge roads as well as north–south valley roads. See *Scenic Drives* for suggested routes.

GETTING AROUND *Taxi:* **JT's Taxi & Courier** (802-728-6209) is based in Randolph.

Car rental: **Especially Imports** (802-728-4455), Route 66, Randolph, can arrange to meet you at the train.

WHEN TO GO Brookfield and Rochester offer winter cross-country skiing, and Tunbridge draws Vermonters for the Vermont History Expo in June and the World's Fair in September. March brings sugaring; in May there's kayaking and in summer, tubing along the lower reaches of the White River. Given its scattering of appealing places to stay and its farms and back-roads scenery, this is a rewarding getaway area anytime except mud season (April and early May).

MEDICAL EMERGENCY Emergency service is available by calling **911**.

Gifford Medical Center (802-728-4441), 44 South Main Street, Randolph.

✳ Villages

Sharon Village. An old commercial center at the junction of the river road (Route 14) and the high road (to Strafford), this remains a cluster of services just off I-89. The columned Sharon Trading Post is a classic general store with a serious meat department, also selling local maple products. The **Sharon Historical Society,** also at this crossroads, is open summer Sundays (1–3) and in early August on Old Home Day, a lively event at which guests over 70 can eat free at the chicken pie supper.

South Royalton Village. On a bend in the river and off Route 14, this classic railroad village frames an outsized green with an elevated, recently rebuilt bandstand and a Civil War cannon. A granite arch recalls the 1780 raid on Royalton by more than 300 Native Americans commanded by an English lieutenant. The railroad hotel, an 1887 brick Queen Anne–style commercial block, the train depot, and many of the clapboard buildings within eyeshot have all received a new lease on life thanks to the presence of Vermont's first and only law school. Founded in 1972 and headquartered in a tower-topped old school building, Vermont Law School now draws students from around the country. In the village of **Royalton,** north on Route 14, most buildings predate the Civil War.

Tunbridge. Some 20,000 people jam into this village of 400 for 4 days each September. They come for the **Tunbridge World's Fair,** said to have originated in 1761 when the town received its charter from George III to hold two fairs each year. In fact, the fair dates from 1867. Sited in a grassy, natural bowl by a bend in the river, it has everything an agricultural fair should have: a midway, livestock displays and contests, a Floral Hall, collections of old-time relics, dancing, sulky racing, a fiddlers contest, horse pulls, a grandstand, and more. Known as the "Drunkards Reunion" during a prolonged era when it was claimed that anyone found sober after 3 PM was expelled as a nuisance, it's now billed as a family event. The fairgrounds are also the site of the annual June Vermont History Expo, showcasing Vermont historical societies from around the state. Tunbridge boasts four covered bridges (see our map), a fishing hole, and a photogenic brick Methodist church (in South Tunbridge).

Strafford. If it were any nearer a highway this quietly spectacular village would be mobbed with tourists but, happily, it's 15 miles northwest of I-91, 9 miles north of I-89, and not on the way to anywhere except Tunbridge. Coming *from* Tunbridge, the road climbs steeply through woods and fields, finally cresting and beginning its downhill run through beautifully restored farms with ponds out back (pools would be too garish), stables, and other signs of wealth not evident on the western side of the mountain. Aristocratic homes—which include the Gothic Revival **Justin Morrill Homestead** (see sidebar, page 296)—cluster near the common, at the head of which stands the churchlike white-clapboard Town House, built in 1799, so classic it's a staple of New England photo books.

Chelsea. Chelsea has been hailed as one of the few remaining bastions of "Vermont character." It is a town with not one but two picturesque commons and an unusual survival rate of dairy farms and maple producers. Noteworthy buildings include a steepled church, the Orange County Courthouse, a brick library, its own bank (since 1822), and many Federal-era homes, one now the outstanding Shire Inn. An amazing number of services—post office, restaurants, barber, and fish and wildlife office—are compressed into a small space. The commercial heart of town revolves around twin 1818 brick buildings that both house general stores, one of which (Will's) is known for its ice cream.

Brookfield. "Pond Village," as it's known, easily ranks among the most picturesque four-corners in all New England. It boasts the state's oldest continuously operating library (established in 1791) and Sunset Lake, traversed by a recently rebuilt floating bridge, buoyed by barrels (the lake is too deep to support a pillared span). During summer much of its traffic stops midway to fish, and on the last Saturday in January it's a coveted viewing point for one of New England's last ice-harvest festivals. At the center of the village is Green Trails Inn, with extensive cross-country trails. Ariel's Restaurant, overlooking the pond, draws diners from a 50-mile radius. Allis State Park, a few miles west, offers camping, picnicking, and a sweeping view. The **Marvin Newton House,** Ridge Road in Brookfield Center, is an eight-room home built in 1835, now housing local historical exhibits (open Sundays in July and August, 2–5; $2; 802-276-3959).

Christina Tree

TWIN GENERAL STORES DISTIN-
GUISH CHELSEA VILLAGE.

Bethel. At the confluence of the White River and its Third Branch as well as of Routes 107 and 12, this was once a major source of white granite used to face such buildings as Washington, DC's, Union Station. An eight-sided former school, now a community center, stands on Route 14 in West Bethel.

Randolph (population: 4,800). Randolph Center (east on Route 66 from I-89 exit 4) is clearly the oldest of the five Randolphs. It's a lineup of brick and clapboard Federal-era mansions along a main street that was cut unusually wide with the idea that this might be the state capital. Instead, it is now a quiet village in which life centers on Floyd's General Store and the nearby complex of Vermont Technical College, grown from the grammar school built here in 1806. According to a historical marker, musician and schoolmaster Justin Morgan brought a young stallion from Massachusetts to his home here in 1789 (Justin Morgan the man lies buried in the nearby cemetery; the grave of Justin Morgan the horse is marked by a simple stone off Route 110 in Chelsea). Randolph remains a horsey community, but with the arrival of the railroad in the mid–19th century, population shifted from the center down to the valley, 3 miles west (now the other side of I-89). It's here that Amtrak now stops, at the station on Main Street, steps from the **Chandler Center for the Arts,** a lively town-owned performance center. The **Randolph Historical Society Museum** (802-728-6677), upstairs in the police station, exhibits memorabilia, with the emphasis on railroading; three rooms are furnished in circa-1900 style. (Open May through October, first Sunday 2–4, also July 4 and by appointment. $1 per adult.) Don't pass up the old-fashioned Ben Franklin's, recently rebuilt after a major fire and an exceptionally

JUSTIN MORRILL HOMESTEAD (802-828-3015; www.historicvermont.org), Route 132, Strafford Village. Open Memorial Day through Columbus Day, Wednesday through Sunday 11–5; tours on the hour. Justin Morrill never went to college but is remembered as the congressman who sponsored the Land Grant Colleges Acts (one in 1862 and another in 1890) that created more than 76 present institutions, currently enrolling some 2.9 million students. Many have evolved into state universities. The son of a Strafford blacksmith, Morrill made enough money as a country storekeeper (which he parlayed into a chain of stores) to retire at age 38 and enter politics on an antislavery and temperance platform. He served in Congress for 44 years (1855–98), never finding much time to spend in his striking, 17-room Gothic Revival mansion because he kept getting reelected. A man who was instrumental in the design and construction of the Washington Monument and the Library of Congress, Justin Morrill helped design his own house and (now restored) gardens and orchard. The icehouse and carriage barn are fitted with interpretive panels about Morrill and the many national events in which he played a role. Inside and out, this is a fascinating house, well maintained by the Vermont Division for Historic Preservation. Inquire about frequent events including the annual croquet tournament, the 19th-century apple festival, and Sunday-afternoon programs (2 PM) such as painting, landscape gardening, village walks, and more.

JUSTIN MORRILL HOMESTEAD IN STRAFFORD

well-stocked representative of that vanishing breed. The **Independence Day parade** here is one of the biggest around.

Rochester straddles Route 100 in a quiet valley between the Green Mountains and the Braintree Range. It has a large village green, a reclusive summer population, and a surprising spread of lodging options, from luxurious hideaways to a working farm. The village itself is tiny but full of surprises, with a real choice of places to eat. The approach over Rochester Mountain provides panoramic views and a delightful alternation of field and forest. North of the village on Route 100 the magnificent new **Green Mountain National Forest Visitors Center** orients sportsmen, picnickers, and hikers to the largely uninhabited western portion of the town that lies within the GMNF. The Bingo area, in particular, offers swimming holes, abandoned town roads, cellar holes, and Civil War–era cemeteries. Rochester is also a center for mountain biking and for cross-country skiing. The **Rochester Historical Society** is housed over the library (802-767-4759). Summer brings **Chamber Music Society** programs at the Federated Church and Sunday-evening concerts on the green.

✳ To See

Floating Bridge at Sunset Lake, Brookfield Village. First built in 1820 and replaced six times since, this is the only heavily used bridge of its kind in the country. It's quite picturesque. On our last visit it was sagging badly.

Joseph Smith Memorial and Birthplace (802-763-7742; www.placesto visitlds.org), Dairy Hill Road, South Royalton. Open year-round during daylight hours; seasonal guided tours late May through mid-October, Wednesday through Sunday 9–7; check for off-season hours. A marker on Route 14 (1 mile southeast of the village) points you up a steep, 2-mile hill to a complex maintained by the Church of Jesus Christ of the Latter-day Saints. The property itself begins with a steep hill of maples leading to a hilltop visitors center with paintings, sculpture, exhibits, and a film housed in two buildings. A 38.5-foot-high shaft, cut from Barre granite in 1908, marks the site of the farm on which the founder of the Church of Jesus Christ of Latter-day Saints was born in 1805 and lived until he was 10. Each foot on the shaft marks a year in the life of the prophet, who was murdered by a mob in Carthage, Illinois, in 1844. The 360 well-maintained acres include picnic tables.

THE JOSEPH SMITH MEMORIAL AND BIRTH-PLACE NEAR SOUTH ROYALTON
Christina Tree

COVERED BRIDGES There are five covered bridges in Tunbridge: the **Cilley Bridge,** south of the junction of Route 110 with Strafford Road and built in 1883; the **Howe Bridge** (1879), east off Route 110 in South Tunbridge; and in North Tunbridge, the 1845 **Flint Bridge** and 1902 **Larkin Bridge,** both east of Route 110. The **Mill Bridge** (1883), crushed by ice in the winter of 1999, has been rebuilt. In Randolph two multiple kingpost bridges, both built in 1904, are just off Route 14 between East Randolph and South Randolph. In Chelsea there is the **Moxley** or **Guy Bridge,** an 1886 queenpost, east off Route 110.

SCENIC DRIVES **The Quickie Tour:** Sharon to South Royalton via Strafford and Tunbridge (22 miles). Take I-89 to exit 2, Sharon, good for gas and food, and climb Route 132 to Strafford, site of the Justin Morrill Homestead and the Town House. Continue up and over the hills and down into Tunbridge. If time permits turn north on Route 110 for 5 miles and past three covered bridges (see above) to Chelsea, a good place to stay. Otherwise turn south on Route 110 for the 5 scenic miles back (past one covered bridge) to Route 14 at South Royalton and pick up I-89 again at exit 3 in Royalton, or turn back down Route 14 to Sharon. En route you pass the turnoff for the Joseph Smith Memorial.

Royalton to Randolph via Granville Gulf (117 miles). Take I-89 to exit 3, just west of Eaton's Sugar House. The low road west (Route 107) follows the White River to Route 100, but the high road over **Rochester Mountain** saves 11 miles and is beautiful besides. At the junction in Bethel take Route 12 north a little more than 2 miles and turn left onto Camp Brook Road. At the height-of-land the view is a panorama of the Green Mountains ahead. Keep to the main road (the one with the line down the middle) until a T, and turn left (it's marked) for the descent into Rochester. Turn north on Route 100 and, 4 miles up, note the Hancock Hotel and the turnoff for Middlebury Gap, Route 125 (see below). Continuing north on Route 100, the mountain walls close in as you near **Granville Gulf** and **Moss Glen Falls.** Turn off Route 100 into **Warren Village** (see "Sugarbush/Mad River Valley") and follow signs 2 miles to East Warren, where you turn onto the **Roxbury Gap Road.** Be sure to pull out near the top for a look back down the valley. It's a popular soaring center, and you may see a glider or hawks riding the thermal waves. Continue downhill to Route 12A and turn south, following the railroad tracks and the Third Branch of the White River past the turnoff for Braintree Hill to Randolph and back to I-89, exit 4.

Randolph Center, Brookfield, Chelsea (27 miles). Take I-89 to exit 4 and turn east into Randolph Center, then north along a glorious ridge road (marked TO BROOKFIELD) to Brookfield with its famous floating bridge across Sunset Lake, leading to Allis State Park. Even addicted as we are to shortcuts, we recommend passing up the gravel road from East Brookfield to Chelsea, go around through East Randolph (6 miles south on Route 14, then turn onto the road marked for Chelsea; it's 6 more miles). Chelsea is a good place to stay and from which to explore the Barre–Montpelier area. Otherwise return on Route 110 and Route 14 to I-89, passing six covered bridges.

Middlebury Gap. Robert Frost Memorial Drive is too glorious a stretch of road to pass by. From Route 100 in Hancock turn onto Route 125 west and take the short detour into **Texas Falls** (see the box on page 300). Route 125 continues to climb through Middlebury Gap (the Long Trail crosses at an altitude of 2,149 feet). Then it's on through the Green Mountain National Forest until the rambling yellow, wooden Bread Loaf Inn and its annexes unexpectedly appear, banked in hydrangeas. Owned by Middlebury College, this 1860s hotel is nationally known for its summer literary programs. Note the turnoff just west for the **Robert Frost Cabin.** A dirt road leads to the Homer Noble farm; a short way past the farm is the cabin in which Robert Frost spent 23 summers. Continue to the Robert Frost Wayside (see "Addison County and Environs"). Return the way you came or continue to Middlebury and return to Route 100 via Brandon Gap (Route 73), Appalachian Gap (Route 17), or Lincoln Gap (see "Sugarbush/Mad River Valley").

✳ To Do

BIKING In Randolph the **Three Stallion Inn** offers its own network of trails and rents bikes.

Green Mountain Bikes (802-767-4464; 1-800-767-7882; www.greenmountainbikes.com), Route 100 in the village of Rochester. Doon Hinderyckx is a fount of information about local trails in and beyond the national forest. He offers guided tours and rents and sells mountain and cross bikes.

Also check with the Green Mountain National Forest Visitors Center (see *Guidance*) and see this chapter's *Scenic Drives*.

BOATING AND TUBING While most of the White River is navigable in high water (May through July), the 20-mile stretch from Rochester to Bethel is especially popular with canoeists, tubers, and kayakers. A good place to put in is at the cement bridge just south of Rochester. **Vermont River Adventures** (802-234-6361; www.tubevermont.com), based at White River Valley Camping, Route 107 in Gaysville, rents kayaks, tubes, and life jackets.

Tubing: Tubing on the White River is so popular that you can rent tubes at a number of places along the stretch from Gaysville to South Royalton. Try the **Gaysville Trading Company** (802-234-9118) on Route 107, and the **Stockbridge General Store** (802-234-9118).

FARMS TO VISIT ✐ **Neighborly Farms of Vermont** (802-728-4700; 1-888-212-6898; www.neighborlyfarms.com), North Randolph Road, Randolph Center. Rob and Linda Dimmick and their three children run an organic dairy and make organic cheeses that they sell at the farm and through area stores. Visitors are welcome to see the cows and watch cheesemaking (call ahead).

Vermont Technical College maintains a demonstration farm in Randolph Center (802-728-3395). Visitors can tour the sugarhouse, apple orchard (pick your own in-season), and dairy barn.

Maple Ridge Sheep Farm (802-728-3081; www.mrsf.com) in Braintree, said to be the oldest and largest Shetland sheep farm in the country, produces fleece, machine-washable sheepskin, yarn, knit and woven items, meat. Call first.

✐ **Marge's B&B at Round Robin Farm** (802-763-7025), RR 1, Box 52, Fay Brook Road, Strafford 05072. This is a 350-acre working dairy farm with one of

TEXAS FALLS, Hancock. On Route 125 west of Route 100, a sign points to the road to the falls. It's 0.25 mile. The falls are an exceptional series of shoots and pools, rimmed by interesting rock formations and spanned by footbridges. Swimming is not permitted, but a short, steep (be careful) trail leads down to the falls. A quarter mile farther up the road is a picnic area with grills and outhouses.

TEXAS FALLS

Kim Grant

Vermont's famous 10-sided round barns (built in 1917). It's been in the family for six generations. The 60 head of cows are milked between 5 and 7 PM; visitors welcome. There's also a sugarhouse and a B&B (see *Lodging*).

FISHING Trout abound at the junction of the Tweed and White Rivers, downstream of Bethel, above Randolph, and below Royalton. Fly-fishing enthusiasts find the Bethel area good for large rainbow and brown trout, while below Royalton there are bass, spring walleye, and trout.

Trout on the Fly (802-685-2100; www.troutonthefly.com). Brookfield-based husband-and-wife team Brad Yoder and Tamara Hutzler specialize in the White River and its tributaries, fly-fishing for all varieties of bass and trout. They offer lessons and float trips. Catch-and-release. Prices are high, but so is service—and guided trips include a gourmet streamside lunch.

Fishing licenses are available at **Tracy's Midway,** a convenience store and gas station on North Main Street in Sharon.

Bakers Pond on Route 12 in Brookfield has a parking area and boat launch, good for trout fishing. There is a boat access on **Rood Pond** in Williamstown and a canoe access on **Sunset Lake** in Brookfield, also stocked with trout. The floating bridge is a popular fishing spot.

White River National Fish Hatchery, Gaysville (Bethel), Routes 12/107 west of Bethel Village, raises imprint salmon for the Connecticut River restoration program.

Roxbury State Fish Hatchery, Route 12A in Roxbury, raises brookies and Atlantic salmon, over 350,000 fish per year. It abuts the Third Branch of the White River, and the fishing downstream can be amazing.

GOLF **Montague Golf Club** (802-728-3806), Randolph. One of the oldest courses in Vermont, 18 holes. The Second Branch of the White River winds through it. Light fare is served in the clubhouse; lessons offered. *Note:* A driving range maintained by the Three Stallion Inn is just west on Route 66.

The White River Golf Club (802-767-GOLF), Route 100, Rochester. Nine holes, clubhouse with a restaurant serving lunch (dinner by arrangement). Open May through October. Affordable, great for families, a historic and beautiful course. Next to it is a driving range (802-767-3211).

HIKING The **Green Mountain National Forest** (see *Guidance*) harbors numerous trails. On Route 100 itself in Granville Gulf there are two short nature trails. At Moss Glen Falls, the 0.5-mile loop on the west side of the road is more rugged than the 1-mile loop on the east side.

In **Allis State Park,** Brookfield (off Route 12; see *Green Space*), a 2.5-mile trail circles down through meadows and back up through woods. A trail leads from the picnic area to a fire tower with one of the best views in central Vermont (on a clear day, from Killington–Pico to Mount Mansfield to Ascutney). The Bear Hill Nature Trail is another reason for finding this special place.

LLAMA HIKING Heart of Vermont Llama Hikes (802-889-9611), Fernwood Llama Farm, Spring Road, Tunbridge. Memorial Day through Columbus Day: Picnic hikes, moonrise hikes, half- and full-day hikes offered through the rural countryside. Fiber and fiber products also sold.

PICNICKING Brookfield Gulf, Route 12 west of Brookfield. Picnic facility, nature trail.

Braintree Hill, Braintree Hill Road (off Route 12A just west of downtown Randolph). A great picnic spot with an early cemetery and sweeping views to the White Mountains. The handsome Braintree Meeting House here is open by appointment and on Old Home Day (first Sunday in August).

Bingo Brook in Rochester off Route 73 in the national forest. Picnic sites with grills by a mountain stream, good for fishing and swimming.

Also see Allis State Park in *Green Space*, Texas Falls in *To See*, and the Robert Frost Wayside in *Scenic Drives*.

SWIMMING Ask locally about various swimming holes in the First, Second, and Third Branches and the main stem of the White River. In Randolph Center there is a human-made beach, bathhouse, and picnic area. There is also a pool at the recreational park in Randolph.

❋ Winter Sports

CROSS-COUNTRY SKIING AND SNOWSHOEING Green Mountain Ski Touring Club (802-728-9122; 1-800-424-5575; www.3stallioninn.com), Three Stallion Inn, off Route 66, Randolph. Thirty-five kilometers of groomed and tracked trails weave through woods and meadows; instruction and rentals available; marked from Route 66. Ski and snowshoe rentals; biweekly snowshoe tours.

Nordic Adventures (802-767-3272; www.vt-nordicadventures.com), Route 100, Rochester Village. Dean Mendell offers a full line of cross-country equipment and snowshoes, lessons, and guided tours.

Green Mountain National Forest (see *Guidance*) maintains trails in Rochester on Liberty Hill and at Chittenden Brook.

Also see Green Trails Inn under *Lodging*.

❋ Green Space

Allis State Park (802-276-3175), Brookfield. Open May 30 through September 15. A camping area with 22 sites, 4 with lean-tos (no hook-ups), each on a wooded loop road separate from the picnic area, in which you can choose tables on a windy hilltop or under a pavilion. A hiking trail (see *To Do*) commands a fine view of the valley northward.

Green Mountain National Forest (GMNF). Among the highlights of the Rochester district of the GMNF are the Long Trail and the Texas Falls Recreation Area (see *To See*). A good short hike is from Brandon Gap north 0.6 mile to the cliffs of Mount Horrid, where there are views to the east. Because of the abundance of other things to do in this area, be sure to drop in the new GMNF Visitors Center 2 miles north of the Rochester green on Route 100 (802-767-4261).

✳ Lodging

INNS 🍃 🐾 **The Shire Inn** (802-685-3031; 1-800-441-6908; www.shire inn.com), Chelsea 05038. This is precisely the kind of Vermont country inn that everyone fantasizes about: a classic 1832 Federal-era brick mansion furnished with antiques, rooms with canopy beds and working fireplaces (all private bath), set right on the green of a handsome-yet-workaday village. It's the kind of place that could easily be too stiff and self-conscious, but thanks to Jay and Karen Keller, you'll feel right at home from the moment you enter the sunny parlor with its elegant hearth and canary in the window. Be sure to arrive in good time for dinner, a five-course candlelight event that might begin with a three-layer vegetable terrine followed by a pear sorbet, then chicken Wellington, veal Sicilian, or a vegetable ravioli with basil sauce, followed by a salad and irresistible dessert (wine is served). Upstairs Jay has laid a fire that's waiting when you fall into that canopy bed. The breakfast selection might include apple pancakes, herb-cheese omelets, and spinach quiche. The Kellers are delighted to tune in guests to the possibilities of things to see and do; bicycles and cross-country skis (snowmobile trails web the area) are provided. You might, however, want to just find yourself a corner of the flower garden. The six rooms are $120–165 B&B, $195–235 including dinner plus 15 percent service. No smoking. Children under 7 inappropriate.

⊙ **Green Trails Inn** (802-276-3412; 1-800-243-3412; www.green trailsinn.com), Brookfield 05036. It all began with Jessie Fiske, a Brookfield native who became one of the first women professors at Rutgers University in New Jersey. She rented rooms to her students and associates, who spent summers horseback riding and "botanizing" with Miss Fiske. The present inn consists of 13 rooms (9 with private bath) and one suite, some in the 1790s Guest House (one room retains its 18th-century stenciling), more in the inn, which offers a large hearth and a sunny dining room. The horses are gone, but the trails are still good for walking and cross-country skiing (33 km are marked and groomed). The inn sits just across from the floating bridge and a small beach on SunsetLake, which invites canoeing and fishing. Nina Gaby and Craig Smith are your friendly hosts. Jessie Fiske's old riding ring up on the hillside is now a frequent site for weddings for up to 250 people. Rates are $90 per couple (shared bath) to $160 for the two-room suite with a fireplace or Jacuzzi, breakfast included; MAP available. *Note:* Ariel's Restaurant (see *Dining Out*) is across the street.

⊙ **Three Stallion Inn** (802-728-5575; 1-800-424-5575; www.3stallion inn.com), Lower Stock Farm Road, off Route 66, Randolph 05060. Geared to sports-minded guests, especially cross-country skiers, mountain bikers, and golfers, also to weddings and small groups. This stone farmhouse is set on 1,300 acres of pasture and woodland, with some 35 miles of tracked trails, part of an old estate—the Green Mountain Stock Farm. The lively Morgan's Pub (see *Eating Out*) and the inn's restaurant (see *Dining Out*) are set off from the rest of the inn. Facilities include a fitness room, a whirlpool and sauna, two tennis courts, and an outdoor lap pool. The adjoining Montague Golf Club is 18 holes, and the inn also maintains a driving range. There's swimming and brown trout in the Third Branch of the White River, which runs through the property, and a trout pond invites catch-and-release. The 15 guest rooms include 3 family suites and range from $80 (shared bath) to $170 double for a room with private bath. Continental breakfast included; MAP and group packages available. Inquire about weddings and special packages.

⚘ ✿ **Tupper Farm Lodge** (802-767-4243; www.tupperfarmlodge.com), 4609 Route 100, Rochester 05767. An 1820s farmhouse on Route 100, known for its friendly atmosphere and good cooking. Roger and Ann Verme have been welcoming guests since 1971. They accommodate 30 in 10 rooms, most with private bath. They cater to skiers and bicyclists with bountiful breakfasts and candlelit dinners. The swimming hole is across the road in the White River. $47–54 per person MAP, $70 per couple. B&B rate available in summer only; ski-week and children's rates.

The Huntington House Inn (802-767-91400; huntingtonhouseinn@earthlink.net), 16 Huntington Place, Rochester 05767. At the back of Rochester's large green, this small, appealing inn has been a dining destination for many years. It's recently acquired new owners and a total makeover. When we stopped by on a sleepy summer day we saw three tastefully furnished guest rooms with private bath, air-conditioning, and TV but no innkeeper. The chef (see *Dining Out*) showed us around. $95–135 includes breakfast.

BED & BREAKFASTS ⚘ **Cooper-Webber House** (802-767-4742), Route 100 (Box 436), Rochester 05767. Ron and Sandy Brown have skillfully restored this magnificent vintage-1830s Federal house in the center of Rochester Village. Enter through the screened patio furnished with rocking chairs into a big country kitchen. Beyond: comfortable, uncluttered common spaces with fireplaces. Three guest rooms are unfussily furnished with early-19th-century-style (but comfortable) four-poster beds and handmade quilts. One room with a private bath, two with shared. Also a suite. An upstairs library with a wood-stove is stocked with irresistible books. $70–75 includes a full breakfast.

Brookfield Guest House (802-276-3146; www.brookfieldbandb.com), Pond Village, Brookfield 05036. Former Bostonians George and Connie Karal offer a sophisticated B&B with a large veranda in the middle of this special village, steps from Sunset Lake and its floating bridge. The two suites are beauties, especially the ground-floor green room with private bath, sleeping three. Upstairs, two rooms share a bath. $95–225 per couple includes a full breakfast. No children under 10, please.

⚘ **The New Homestead** (802-767-4751), Rochester 05767. Don't be put off by the funky exterior of this old house in the village. Inside it's clean and comfortable, with an eclectic mix of art and attractive quilts: five rooms, three with private bath, two with shared. $55 per room, $50 single year-round includes a sumptuous breakfast of homegrown eggs, jams, spuds, and homemade bread. Your hosts are Sandy Haas and David Marmor.

🐾 **Inn at Johnnycake Flats** (802-485-8961; www.johnnycakeflats.com), 47 Carrie Howe Road, Roxbury (visible from Route 12A) 05669. Off the beaten track, but handy to Sugarbush, geared to guests with an interest in nature. Hosts Debra and Jim Rogler have traveled in New Zealand, Australia, and throughout the States and enjoy tuning guests into their surroundings, beginning with the 16 surrounding acres with sheep and two frog ponds. The house was an early-1800s stage stop, and the living room fireplace is made from handmade bricks. There are three guest rooms furnished with antiques and Debra's quilts. Choose from double, queen, or twin beds; a two-bunk room can work for children. $105–125 (for the room with private bath and a little library), a country breakfast included. Guests are welcome to use the innkeepers' snowshoes, cross-country skis, and bicycles.

🐾 **Greenhurst Inn** (802-234-9474; 1-800-510-2553), 88 North Road, Bethel 05032, a Victorian mansion on the western fringe of Bethel, across Route 107 from the river. There are 13 guest rooms, 7 with private bath (the most cheerful on the third floor); these include a spacious tower room ($90) and the Victorian Suite, tucked under the eaves with a skylight. Long-time innkeeper Lyle Wolfe has a library of more than 4,000 books. $50–95 double per room; $100 for Victoria's Suite, with a sitting room

and private bath; breakfast included. Dogs accepted.

FARMS ∞ 🐾 🐾 🐾 **Harvey's Mountain View Inn** (802-767-4273), Rochester 05767. High above the valley in the North Hollow area, this spot offers spectacular mountain views. While it's no longer the working farm it was for six generations of Harveys (it's been in the family since 1809), Don welcomes guests as his family has since 1960. The 10 rooms (2 with private bath) are clean and comfortable, suited for family reunions, small groups, and weddings. There's also a two-bedroom housekeeping cottage (pets permitted) and a heated pool. Open year-round. $65–70 per person based on double occupancy, $75 single, includes a hearty breakfast *and* dinner.

🐾 🐾 **Marge's B&B at Round Robin Farm** (802-763-7025), RR 1, Box 52, Fay Brook Road, Strafford 05072. This is a 350-acre working dairy farm with one of Vermont's famous 10-sided round barns (built in 1917). It's been in the family for six generations.

ROUND ROBIN FARM IN STRAFFORD
Christina Tree

🐾 🖈 **Liberty Hill Farm** (802-767-3926; www.libertyhillfarm.com), 511 Liberty Hill Road, Rochester 05767. This is the real thing: a working, 150-head dairy farm set in a broad meadow, backed by mountains. Its 1890s red barn with cupola is one of the most photographed and painted in Vermont (Woody Jackson has printed it on silk screens that, we're told, sell by the thousands in Japan). There's a capacious white-clapboard 1825 farmhouse and, best of all, there is farmwife-host par excellence Beth Kennett. Beth's own family's farming history dates back to the 17th century in Maine, and "farmer" Bob Kennett's roots run deep into New Hampshire soil. Both families were horrified when Beth and Bob moved "west" to this 109-acre spread in this magnificent Vermont valley. Their own sons are now grown, but visitors of all ages are treated to a sense of how much fun (and work if they so desire) living on a farm can be.

Meals are served family-style, and Beth makes everything from scratch. The dinner we sampled on a summer evening at 6 (BYOB) was as delicious as it was prodigious: incredibly moist sliced turkey, a zucchini casserole, cucumber salad, a garden salad with tomatoes, pumpkin muffins, mashed potatoes, fresh-picked sweet corn, a choice of homemade dressings and stuffings—all set in the middle of a table seating eight adults and at least as many children. The kids disappeared after the main course, and adults lingered over blueberry pie with homemade (from the farm's own milk) raspberry ice cream.

There's plenty of common space, including a parlor with woodstove, but in summer everyone seems to congregate on the porch. There are seven guest rooms (five with double beds, one with two single beds, and a room with five single beds) and four shared baths; families can spread into two rooms sharing a sitting room and bath. In summer you can hear the gurgle of the White River (good for trout fishing as well as swimming), and in winter you can ski or snowshoe up into the woods and off into the village across the meadows. $75 per adult, $35 per child under 12, MAP.

LIBERTY HILL FARM

Kim Grant

What's offered is the homey, clean, and cheerful farmhouse with its Mission-style dining room and sitting room with a TV/VCR, or rooms therein (two rooms with double bed and two with twins, shared bath), plus a fridge with the fixings for making your own breakfast in the big country kitchen. Marge Robinson lives within call in the adjacent house. Cross-country ski or walk woods and meadows. No smoking and no pets, please. A double room is $35 per person per night. Inquire about the price for the whole house. Snowmobile trails run right through the property.

Placidia Farm Bed & Breakfast (802-728-9883; www.placidia.com), Randolph 05060. This is an apartment in a hand-hewn log home (deck, kitchen, bedroom, and living room) on a large farm with its own pond. A full breakfast in Viola Frost-Latinen's plant-filled sunporch is included. $100 per couple; $45 each additional person. Not appropriate for children under age 13.

SECOND HOMES AND COTTAGES

🕊 **Hawk North, Vermont's Mountain Hideaway** (1-800-832-8007; www.vthideaway.com), Box 529, Route 100, Pittsfield 05762. Hawk homes are nicely designed vacation houses, hidden away in the woods on sites scattered around Rochester and Stockbridge. No longer related to Hawk Mountain Resort, Hawk North maintains a check-in office at the junction of Routes 100 and 107. Each of the 10 homes is individually owned, and decor varies, but all offer a spacious living/dining room and deck, full kitchen, and two to four bedrooms. Some have sauna and/or hot tub. Rates fluctuate widely with the season: $240–475 per night for two to four bedrooms.

🐾 **Birch Meadow Farm** (802-276-3156; www.bbhost.com/birch meadow), 597 Birch Meadow Drive, Brookfield 05036 (East Street off Route 65 south). This is Mary and Matt Comerford's woodsy hideaway, with three modern, air-conditioned log cabins equipped for housekeeping. There are TVs and woodstoves, plus a B&B suite in the main house, which sits high on a hill with splendid views and a swim pond. $99–120 per couple, $15 each additional adult, $5 per child. Rates include the initial morning's breakfast in the cabins.

CAMPGROUNDS **Lake Champagne Campground** (802-728-5298), P.O. Box C, Randolph 05061. Open Memorial Day weekend through mid-October. A 150-acre property with fields, a 3-acre swim lake, hot showers, mountain views, and facilities for tents through full-sized RVs.

Limehurst Lake Campground (802-433-6662), 4101 Route 14, Williamstown 05679. This family-geared campground offers 76 sites with full hook-ups for RVs, a separate area for lean-tos and tents, modern restrooms, hot showers, a water slide, a sandy swim beach, boat rentals and fishing (no license required), and a game room.

Chittenden Brook Campground in the Green Mountain National Forest (802-767-4261), 5.3 miles west of Rochester on Route 73. The 17 campsites are fitted with picnic tables and grills; there are hand-operated water pumps and vault toilets. The surrounding forest provides good fishing, hiking, and birding. No trailers over 18 feet. No hook-ups or showers.

Note: Primitive camping is permitted almost everywhere in the Green Mountain National Forest.

Allis State Park (summer: 802-276-3175; winter: 802-885-8891; reservations: 1-800-299-3071). Open mid-May through Labor Day. Named for Wallace Allis, who deeded his Bear Mountain Farm to the state as a campground and recreational area. Sited on the summit of Bear Mountain, it includes a picnic area and trail to the fire tower, also 18 tent and 8 lean-to sites, each with a picnic table and fireplace. Hot showers but no hook-ups.

✴ Where to Eat

DINING OUT ✑ **Ariel's Restaurant & Pond Village Pub** (802-276-3939), Brookfield. Reservations requested. Open Friday and Saturday with a full menu; Wednesday, Thursday, and Sunday with a pub menu. Overlooking Sunset Lake in the middle of "Pond Village," this restaurant is known as one of the best places to eat in Vermont. Lee and Richard are chef-owners who specialize in Mediterranean and Pacific Rim dishes, unusual combinations of ingredients and spices. On an October day you might begin with a crabcake in Kataify pastry, then dine on seared sea scallops with celeriac and potato puree, chiogia beets, and chive butter sauce, or pumpkin ravioli with butter and sage, topped off with a lemon napoleon with raspberry coulis. Entrées $19.50–26. In the Pub entrées are far less and children are welcome.

Stone Soup Restaurant (802-765-4301), on the green, Strafford. Open for dinner Thursday through Sunday 6–9. Reservations strongly suggested.

There is no sign for this elegantly rustic restaurant that has acquired a strong following over the past two decades. You step from Strafford's handsome green into a cheery tavern room with a large hearth. The candlelit, low-beamed dining rooms are beyond. On our last visit, the blackboard menu included eggplant soup, osso buco, and garlic and lime chicken. Note the attractive herb garden. Personal checks, but no credit cards. Entrées $18.95–25.95.

♿ **Three Stallion Inn** (802-728-5575), off Route 66 (just off I-89), Randolph. Open for dinner Tuesday through Saturday, weekends in winter. This is a large, pleasant dining room with a menu that might include roast pork tenderloin stuffed with apples, pistachios, and sage, or free-range Vermont veal scaloppine with lobster sauce. Entrées $13.50–18.50. Also see Morgan's Pub under *Eating Out.*

🍲 **Huntington House Inn Restaurant & Tavern** (802-767-9140), 16 Huntington Place, Rochester. Open Wednesday through Sunday for dinner; lunch on weekends. Reopened after a total remake, this attractive dining room is dimly lit, the setting for meals that might begin with a savory Vermont cheese custard. The dinner menu we saw included crispy aioli-baked fillet of haddock, and grilled duck breast with risotto potato pancakes and orange horseradish jam. Entrées $15–27. The pub offers sandwiches, salads, and dinners priced $8–14.

Fox Stand Inn (802-763-8437), Route 14, Royalton. Dinner, Tuesday through Saturday. Open from 5 for drinks, from 6 for dinner. Homegrown beef and farm produce served in a landmark 1818 stagecoach inn. Local residents vouch for it; patio dining in summer. The full multicourse dinner menu is $22 prix fixe, while lighter tavern menu entrées run $3–12.

∞ **The Inn at Idlewood** (802-763-5236), Route 132, Sharon. Open Friday and Saturday by reservation year-round. Chef-owners Alex Bird and Marcy Marceau have both studied in France and are known as caterers but have established a huge reputation for their small dining rooms. "We don't turn tables," Alex stresses. "You are here for the evening." The ever-changing menu is a five-course dinner with a choice of entrées. One May night it included pan-seared Cavendish quail in mahogany glaze, and roast sea bass on a bed of fennel and roasted pepper. The choice of three desserts included chocolate walnut brandy torte. The prix fixe is $50 and there's a long wine list, a mix of Californian and French. There are also several attractive rooms and a new wedding barn and deck. Weddings are definitely the house specialty.

EATING OUT Roadfood, listed geographically south to north, off I-89.

I-89, exit 2
Dixie's Country Kitchen (802-763-8721), Route 14 in Sharon on the way to South Royalton. Open for lunch and dinner. Good roadfood, seafood, steak, and $6.95 specials.

Chelsea Station (802-763-8685) on the green, South Royalton. Booths, a counter, breakfast from 6 AM, a friendly atmosphere, and a basic menu.

I-89, exit 3
Eaton's Sugar House, Inc. (802-763-8809; 1-888-VT-MAPLE). Lo-

cated at the junction of Routes 14 and 107 in Royalton, just off I-89. Open daily 7–3. A good old-fashioned family-owned restaurant featuring pancakes and local syrup, sandwiches, burgers, and reasonably priced daily specials. Try the turkey club made with fresh-carved turkey on homemade bread. Vermont maple syrup, cheese, and other products are also sold (see *Selective Shopping*).

Route 110 in Chelsea
Dixie's II, Chelsea. In the middle of the village, housed in a classic old brick bank building. This cheerful spot with a potbellied stove and blackboard menu is open 6:30–2 Sunday through Thursday; Friday and Saturday it's open for dinner, too. Daily specials.

The Pines, Chelsea Village. Open from 3 PM. A friendly rural pub with a pool table, the local gathering spot and the food is fine.

Route 12 north of Bethel
Onion Flats (802-234-5169) north of

DIXIE'S II RESTAURANT IN CHELSEA
Christina Tree

Bethel. Roadfood, good cones, and onion rings.

I-89, exit 4 in Randolph
Debbie's Corner Café (802-728-6062), 2 Merchants Row. Open for breakfast and lunch, known for omelets and specialty sandwiches.

Morgan's Pub at the Three Stallion Inn (800-424-5575), off Route 66 (just off I-89). This is a popular local gathering place with a tavern menu that usually includes char-grilled Black Angus burgers and grilled chicken sandwiches.

Randolph Village Pizza (728-9677), 1 South Main Street. Open daily 11 AM–9 PM, until 10 in summer and on weekends year-round. A wide variety of better-than-average pizzas and calzones; also salads, grinders, and pasta.

Along Route 100
Rochester Café & Country Store (802-767-4302), Route 100, Rochester Village. Open at 7 for breakfast until 11:30, lunch until 4. Good fries and burgers.

Kristina's Kitchen (802-767-4258), 30 North Main Street (Route 100), Rochester. Open Monday and Thursday 8–5; Wednesday, Friday, and Saturday 8–8; Sunday 9–3. Closed Tuesday. Just north of the general store and gas pumps, this 12-table café is part of the appealing complex that includes Seasoned Booksellers and a branch of Raiments & Adornments and features pottery by Judy Jensen (see *Selective Shopping* for all three) across the road. Good in the morning for espresso, fresh-made breads and muffins, and at lunch for soups, salads, and sandwiches. Dinner might feature pastas, fresh seafood, always vegetarian choices; beer and wine served.

Old Hancock Hotel (802-767-4976), Hancock, at Route 125. Open weekdays 7–9, until 8 in winter. A 19th-century village hotel known for its breads, muffins, and pies, good roadfood. Pick up a sandwich to take to nearby Texas Falls (see *To See*).

OLD HANCOCK HOTEL

Kim Grant

✳ Entertainment
The Playhouse Movie Theatre, Main Street, Randolph, is the oldest movie house in the state. Shows first-run flicks.

Randall Drive-In Movie Theatre, Route 12 in Bethel, operates in summer only.

✳ Selective Shopping

CHRISTMAS TREES Redrock Farm
(802-685-2282; 866-685-4343;
www.Christmastrees.net), 2 Redrock
Lane (off Jenkins Brook Road, which
is off Route 110), Chelsea. Call before
coming, but you can pretty much
drop by any day of the year and pick
out a balsam fir or white spruce (up to
7 feet) and it will be FedExed to
you—anywhere in the contiguous 48
states—at Christmas. Trees are
$20–40 plus shipping; wreaths, too.
Picking your tree is more difficult
than you might think, given the thousands to choose from, but Richard
and Stephanie Rockwood don't rush
you. Once tagged with your name,
your tree continues to stand during
those 6 weeks in which most northern
trees are making their way to market.
Whether you live in California,
Florida, or Boston, what you get is a
freshly cut tree. You can order rather
than select it, but that's missing half
the fun. Fishermen are welcome to
test their skills on the pond, and anyone can paddle the boat.

CRAFTS Judy Jensen Clay Studio
(802-767-3271), Route 100 back
behind the Rochester Café. Open
daily. Jensen's work ranges from tiny
vases to large urns, tile to chess sets,
sculpture, handmade cards, and
plenty of highly decorative functional
ware. She also displays work in fiber,
wood, glass, iron, and paper.

**MUSIC BOXES Porter Music Box
Museum & Gift Shop** (802-728-
9694; 1-800-811-7087; www.porter
mbx.com), Route 66 between I-89
and downtown Randolph. Open May
through December (call for hours).
Small admission. The former home

**CHANDLER MUSIC HALL Chan-
dler Center for the Arts** (802-728-
9133), Main Street, Randolph. A
fine, acoustically outstanding
music hall built in 1907 and
restored to mint condition. It's now
open year-round for musical and
theatrical performances: chamber
music, blues, jazz, opera,
folksingers, the Vermont symphony,
and Mud Season Talent Show.

and office of Dwight and Mary Porter
and the Porter Music Box Company.
A large collection of music boxes is
displayed, and both boxes and recordings are sold.

SUGARHOUSES These maple producers sell syrup year-round and welcome visitors into their sugar shacks
during March production period.
Silloway Farms (802-728-5253; 802-
728-5503), Boudro Road, Randolph
Center, welcomes up to 20 visitors at
a time.

JUDY JENSEN AT HER ROCHESTER CLAY
STUDIO AND CRAFTS SHOP
Christina Tree

MICHAEL EGAN AT WORK

Kim Grant

MICHAEL EGAN'S *BLUE IN GREEN CANE VASE*

Michael Egan

Plush Quartz Art Glass (802-767-4547), Route 100, Granville. Open Tuesday through Sunday 9–5. Don't pass up this roadside studio and gallery. Vermont native Michael Egan shapes Venetian-style freehand blown glass into spectacular vases, pitchers, and a variety of housewares as well as art glass.

Vermont Technical College Farm (802-728-3395; 802-728-3391), Randolph, Route 66 east off I-89, invites visitors to tour sugaring operations.

North Hollow Farm (802-767-4255), Route 100, Rochester. Maple syrup, gift baskets.

Eaton's Sugar House, Inc. (802-763-8809), junction of Routes 14 and 107, just off I-89, exit 3. Open daily 7–3. An old-fashioned, family-run, maple-focused complex in which you can watch maple candies being made and find a wide selection of maple treats, in addition to Vermont cheese and other products. A good place to get Christmas greens. See also *Eating Out*.

SPECIAL STORES **The Bowl Mill** (802-767-4711; outside Vermont: 1-800-828-1005), Route 100, Granville. Open 9–5 daily, year-round. Tours offered 9–2:30 weekdays. Decorative wooden bowls have been made here since 1857, with present machinery dating from the 1880s. Good for woodenware, toys, crafts, cards, books, baskets, maple products, specialty foods.

Raiments & Adornments (802-765-4335), Route 132, South Strafford Village. Open Thursday through Saturday 11–5, Sunday 1–5. This mix of top-quality designer and vintage clothing is well worth a stop. Check out the branch store at 30 Main Street in Rochester Village (open Sunday through Tuesday 8–5, Wednesday through Saturday 8–8).

Cover to Cover Books (802-728-5509), 27 North Main Street, Randolph. A friendly, full-service store, also cards, gifts. Inquire about author signings.

Old Schoolhouse Books (802-763-2434), 106 Chelsea Street, on the green, South Royalton. An interesting selection of old and new books.

Seasoned Booksellers (802-767-4258; www.seasonedbooks.com), 30 North Main Street, Rochester. Librarian Sandy Lincoln specializes in sustainable lifestyles, wilderness tales, and renewable energies.

The Brick Store and Specialty Shop (802-234-5378), Main Street, Bethel. Clearly an old-time country store with a 1930s soda fountain, an outlet for locally made Vermont Castings stoves, also selling Vermont handcrafted items, souvenirs, cards, gifts and more.

South Royalton Market (802-763-2400), on the village green, South Royalton. Open daily.

The Raptor Academy (802-767-3552), Route 100, Rochester. Noted bird carver Floyd Scholz operates a small store exhibiting his work and selling carving supplies. Inquire about the series of workshops that regularly draw students from around the country.

✷ Special Events

Last Saturday of January: **Brookfield Ice Harvest Festival**—ice cutting, ice sculpting, hot food, sledding, skating, skiing.

February: **Strafford Winter Carnival.**

March: **Open sugarhouses.**

Mid-June: **Vermont History Expo,** a 2-day gathering of Vermont historical societies from throughout the state, bringing their exhibits to fill the Tunbridge Fairgrounds—historic reenactments and demonstrations, music, grandstand, and many varied events.

HARVESTING ICE AT THE FLOATING BRIDGE IN BROOKFIELD   VDT

July: **July 4 parade** in Strafford, a bigger one in Randolph (usually over 5,000 spectators), with food and crafts. **Family Farm Festival,** Randolph Center. **Chandler Players** perform at Chandler Center for the Arts, Randolph. **Chelsea Flea Market**—150 dealers cover both greens.

July–August: **Randolph Gazebo Series** (802-728-3010)—Tuesday-evening music. **Summer music school**—workshops at the Mountain School, Vershire. **Huntington Farm Show**, Strafford. **Brookfield Blues Festival** (August), off Route 65 in Brookfield. The **South Royalton Town Band,** in business for more than a century, gives free concerts on the green Thursday evenings. **Sharon Old Home Day.**

September: **New World Festival** (Sunday before Labor Day) at the Chandler Music Hall in Randolph features Celtic music, in addition to food and crafts. **White River Valley Festival**, Bethel. **Tunbridge World's Fair** (www.tunbridgefair.com), Tunbridge, 4 days midmonth, ongoing for more than 130 years in a superb setting, definitely one of the country's most colorful agricultural fairs with horse and oxen pulling, contra dancing, sheepdog trials, livestock and produce judging, horse racing, amusement rides, pig races, pond rides, and more.

Columbus Day weekend: **Lord's Acre Supper**—sale and auction, Barrett Hall, Strafford.

November: **Annual Hunters' Supper,** Barrett Hall, Strafford.

SUGARBUSH/MAD RIVER VALLEY

There were farms and lumber mills in this magnificent valley before Mad River Glen began attracting skiers in 1948, but the unique look and lifestyle of this community has been shaped by three ski areas, just as truly as the earlier villages grew around mills and commons. Its present character has been evolving since the '60s, when Sugarbush and then Glen Ellen (the two have since merged) triggered an influx of ski-struck urbanites who formed polo and foxhunt groups, built an airport, and opened and patronized a gliding school, specialty shops, and fine restaurants. Young architects eager to test new theories of solar heating and cluster housing designed New England's first trailside homes, first bottom-of-the-lift village and condominiums. Most of these settling skiers have remained, their numbers now augmented by their grown children and second-home owners who have come to retire. It's a well-heeled, active, ecological- and community-minded group.

Physically just 4 miles apart, philosophically Sugarbush and Mad River Glen seemed at opposite poles of the ski world in the '90s. By then it was painfully clear that northern New England's natural snow is too fickle a base for the big business that skiing had become, and that to make snow you need water. The two ski areas faced this challenge in their own ways. Mad River Glen, the "ski it if you can" mountain, kept its demands modest, operating the nation's oldest lift, and becoming the country's first cooperatively owned ski area (divided among upward of 2,000 shareholders). It also remains the only area in the East that bars snowboarders, featuring telemarking and animal tracking instead.

Water for making snow was, however, essential for the survival of Sugarbush, a major ski resort and the Valley's workhorse. Luckily, in 1995 it was bought by the Maine-based American Ski Company (ASC) and acquired a 63-million-gallon snowmaking pond (to store water siphoned from the Mad River during peak flows) and other needed infrastructure improvements. ASC's proposal to build one of its signature "grand" hotels at the base of Lincoln Peak was, however, defeated, and the multiresort operator seemed to lose interest. Happily, this three-peak resort is now owned by a partnership composed of longtime residents and Valley skiers, who have been involved with both of its resorts and have an understanding of how the two complement each other. At this writing the big news in the Valley is the ongoing construction of The

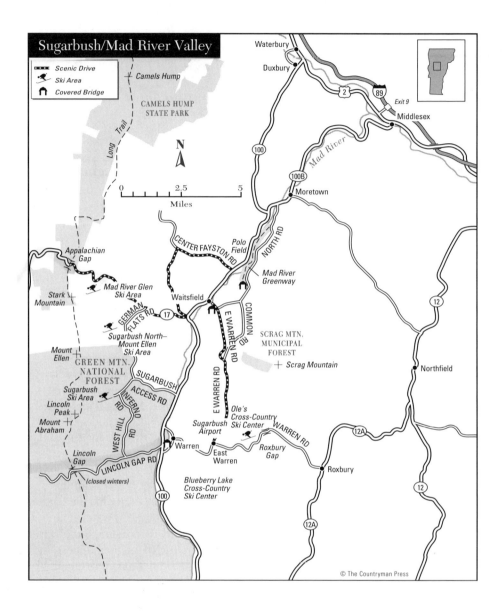

Sugarbush/Mad River Valley

Legend:
- ▪▪▪ Scenic Drive
- 🎿 Ski Area
- ⌂ Covered Bridge

⊥ Camels Hump

CAMELS HUMP
STATE PARK

Long Trail

N

0   2.5   5
Miles

Waterbury
Duxbury
2
89
Exit 9
Middlesex

100

Mad River

100B
Moretown

CENTER FAYSTON RD
Polo Field
NORTH RD

Appalachian Gap

Mad River Greenway

Stark Mountain
Mad River Glen Ski Area
Waitsfield
12

GERMAN FLATS RD
17
COMMON RD
E WARREN RD

Sugarbush North–Mount Ellen Ski Area

Mount Ellen
GREEN MTN. NATIONAL FOREST

SCRAG MTN. MUNICIPAL FOREST
⊥ Scrag Mountain
Northfield

SUGARBUSH ACCESS RD

Sugarbush Ski Area
Lincoln Peak
Mount Abraham

INFERNO RD
WEST HILL RD

E WARREN RD

Ole's Cross-Country Ski Center
Sugarbush Airport
WARREN RD
12A

Lincoln Gap

Warren
East Warren
Roxbury Gap
Roxbury

LINCOLN GAP RD
(closed winters)

Blueberry Lake Cross-Country Ski Center

100

12A

12

© The Countryman Press

Lodge, a 140-unit condo hotel designed by local architect David Sellers to complement the original 1960s ski village at the base of Lincoln Peak (centerpiece of Sugarbush Resort).

Not so long ago the very question of what to call this valley (Mad River? Sugarbush?) would have sparked a debate, but residents now agree: It's the Mad River Valley, named for the river down its center. Seven miles wide, it is magnificent, with meadows stretching to the Roxbury Range on the east. In summer and fall there is hiking on the Long Trail over some of the highest peaks in the Green Mountains, soaring in gliders above the valley, mountain biking on ski trails and high woods roads, horseback riding, fishing and swimming in the Mad River itself, not to mention outstanding golf, tennis, and polo.

With direct links to the Champlain Valley via the scenic roads through Appalachian and Lincoln Gaps on the west, this is a logical lodging and dining hub from which to explore some of Vermont's most magnificent and varied landscapes, especially during foliage season. Dining and shopping are as good as you'll find at any resort area in the East. Several thousand visitors can bed down here on any given night, but it's far from obvious where.

Visitors tend to drive right through on Route 100 (the Valley spine), seeing nothing more than the clump of roadside shops in Waitsfield, missing Warren Village (6 miles south, just off Route 100) entirely. "The Valley" (as it's known locally) lacks the high-profile image enjoyed by rival Green Mountain resorts to north and south—which is fine by residents and regulars.

GUIDANCE Sugarbush Chamber of Commerce (802-496-3409; lodging: 1-800-82-VISIT; www.madrivervalley.com), Box 173, Waitsfield 05673. A walk-in visitors center in the General Wait House, Route 100, Waitsfield, is open year-round 9–5 weekdays, Saturday 9–1. During crunch times, vacancies are posted after 5 PM in the lobby by the courtesy phone (available 24 hours). Request the helpful, free guide.

Green Mountain National Forest Ranger District Office and Visitors Center (802-767-4261), Route 100 in Rochester. Open 8–4. While this magnificent new information center is 25 miles south of Warren, it's worth knowing it's there (see "White River Valleys") as a resource for exploring much of the area immediately west and south of the Valley.

GETTING THERE *By bus and train:* Waterbury, 12 miles north of Waitsfield, is the nearest **Vermont Transit** and **Amtrak** stop.

By air: **Burlington International Airport** is 45 miles away; see in "Burlington Region" for carriers.

By car: Valley residents will tell you that the quickest route from points south is I-89 to Randolph and 15 miles up Route 12A to Roxbury, then 8 miles over the Roxbury Gap to Warren. This is also the most scenic way (the valley view from the top of the gap is spectacular), but be forewarned that this high road can be treacherous in winter. In snow, play it safe and take I-89 to Middlesex, exit 9, then Route 100B the 13 miles south to Waitsfield.

ALONG ROXBURY GAP ROAD

Kim Grant

GETTING AROUND During ski season the **Mad Bus** fleet circles among condos at the top of the access road and restaurants and nightspots. These are free 26-passenger buses that link the Valley floor to all three mountain base areas, running daily and until 1:30 AM on Saturday night.

C&L Taxi (802-496-4056) and **Morf Transit** (802-864-5588; 1-800-696-7433) offer local and long-distance service.

Note: Waitsfield–Champlain Valley Telecom offers free local calls on some pay phones (but not all, so check) scattered around the Valley. Wireless Internet service is widely available in local lodgings.

WHEN TO GO Christmas week through February is high season, high volume, especially in a snowy season when Mad River Glen is wide open. Midweek during this same period is cheaper and far quieter. Ditto for March when the human-made snow base at Sugarbush is deep and weekend crowds have eased. By mid-April it's all over, and forget May and June, but come for the Warren Fourth of July parade and the many events that follow. As noted above, thanks to the gap roads (see *Scenic Drives*), this is an ideal hub for foliage. After the leaves fall it's dead until mid-December.

MEDICAL EMERGENCY Emergency service is available by calling **911.**
Ambulance (802-496-3600). **Mad River Valley Health Center** (802-496-3838), Route 100, Waitsfield. **Mad River Internal Medicine** (802-496-2202).

✳ Villages

Note: The Mad River Valley includes Moretown (population: 653) to the north and Fayston (population: 1,040), an elusive town without a center that produced potatoes in the 1860s and was an important lumbering presence into the early 20th century. It's home to Mount Ellen and Mad River Glen ski areas and to inns along Route 17 and the German Flats Road.

NEAR WARREN

Kim Grant

Warren Village. The village center of the long-established farm town of Warren (population: 1,680) is a compact clapboard cluster of town hall, steepled church, and bandstand, with a double-porched general store by a waterfall across from an inn. At first glance the village doesn't look much different from the way it did in the 1950s when Route 100 passed through its center, but the effect of Sugarbush, the ski resort that's way up an access road at the other end of town, has been total. The Pitcher

Sugarbush Resorts/David Brownell

THE SLOPES OF MOUNT ELLEN RISE BEHIND THE WAITSFIELD FEDERATED CHURCH.

Inn's self-consciously plain face masks an elegant restaurant and some of the most elaborate (and expensive) themed rooms in Vermont; the Warren Store (once a stagecoach inn itself) stocks a mix of gourmet food and upscale clothing and gifts. Arts, antiques, crafts, and a full-service spa are within an easy walk, and a covered bridge spans the Mad River. The village is the setting for one of Vermont's most colorful July 4 parades.

Waitsfield. The most populous (around 1,500) of the Valley's towns and its commercial center with two small, tasteful shopping malls flanking Route 100 on land that was farmed until the 1960s. The old village center is 0.5 mile up Route 100, a gathering of 19th-century buildings, including a library and church, on and around Bridge Street (it's a covered bridge). Much larger and denser than it first looks, the village offers a sophisticated mix of boutiques and services, a movie house with a wine bar, and several first-rate restaurants. Changing historical exhibits are displayed in the General Wait House. Benjamin Wait, you learn, had been a member of Vermont's famed Rogers' Rangers and weathered dozens of French and Indian Wars battles, as well as serving in the Revolution before founding the town at age 53 in 1789. He later was pitted against his fellow settlers on the question of where to put the common. He wanted it just about where the commercial center is today (the original common has been left high and dry out on Joslin Hill Road). Largely denuded of its woods during its era as a logging and sheep-farming community, the town is now mostly wooded and home to more people than ever.

✳ To Do

In winter the Valley's magnets are its alpine and cross-country ski areas, but in summer there are no chairlifts, no slides, no factory outlets, just an unusual number of activities to pursue. Check the following list!

BICYCLING The Valley's wide variety of terrain, from smooth dirt roads to technical singletrack, lends itself to mountain biking. For rentals and service, check

Clearwater Sports (802-496-2708), **Inverness Ski Shop** (802-496-3343), and **Stark Mountain Bike Works** (802-496-4800), all on Route 100 in Waitsfield. The routes listed under *Scenic Drives* are also popular bike routes. Rentals and tours available.

Mad River Greenway. A 3-mile trail follows the Mad River from a parking area on Trembly Road (turn off Route 100 north of Waitsfield at the sign for the Mad River Inn).

CANOEING AND KAYAKING *✐* **Clearwater Sports** (802-496-2708), Route 100, Waitsfield. Barry Bender offers learn-to-canoe and -kayak programs, full-moon canoe cruises on Waterbury Reservoir, camping excursions, also a children's day program (ages 9–13) and a 5-day wilderness camp program for 9- to 13-year-olds.

Vermont Pack & Paddle Outfitters (802-496-9006), Route 100, Waitsfield, offers kayaking and canoeing tours.

FARMS TO VISIT **Mountain Valley Farm** (802-496-9255; www.vermontexperi ence.com), 1719 Common Road, Waitsfield 05673. Set high on an open shoulder of the valley with a classic, steepled red barn, the farm welcomes visitors for wagon and sleigh rides, weddings, birthday parties, or simply to visit the barnyard animals and walk or cross-country ski. Inquire about the guest suite.

Three Shepherds Cheese (802-496-3998), 42 Roxbury Gap Road. Open yearround. Half a dozen kinds of cheeses are made and aged here, sold at the East Warren Schoolhouse along with books and local produce. **Rootswork** (802-496-2474; rootswork@madriver.com)—a nonprofit organization devoted to promoting and nurturing local agriculture—is also based here.

FISHING Numerous streams offer good fly-fishing. The chamber of commerce (see *Guidance*) keeps a list of half a dozen guide services. Vermont fishing licenses are required and can be bought at **Kenyon's Variety Store,** Route 100, Waitsfield.

Vermont Pack & Paddle Outfitters (802-496-9009), Route 100, Waitsfield, offers guided fly-fishing and ultralight fishing tours. **Fly Fish Vermont** (802-253-3964). John Bob Shannon offers 4-hour instructional stream tours.

FITNESS CENTERS **Sugarbush Health & Racquet Club** (802-583-6700; www.sugarbush.com), Sugarbush Village, Warren. An outstanding complex with indoor and outdoor pools, indoor and outdoor Jacuzzis, whirlpool, sauna steam room, exercise room, indoor squash, tennis and racquetball courts, massage room, aerobics studio, 11-station Nautilus, and a full range of cardiovascular equipment. The **Valley Rock Gym** (802-583-6754), part of this complex, features an indoor climbing wall, open 3–9 PM.

The Bridges Family Resort and Tennis Club (802-583-2922; 1-800-453-2922; www.bridgesresort.com), Sugarbush Access Road, Warren. A year-round health and tennis club with indoor and outdoor tennis, heated pools, fitness center, hot tub, and sauna.

GOLF Sugarbush Golf Course (802-583-6725), Warren, at the Sugarbush Inn. An 18-hole, Robert Trent Jones Sr. course, PGA rate 42, par 72; cart and club rental, lessons, practice range, café. Inquire about golf/lodging packages.

HIKING *Walks & Rambles in Vermont's Mad River Valley,* available at the chamber of commerce (see *Guidance*), unlocks the area's many superb hiking secrets.

The **Long Trail** runs along the ridge of the Green Mountains here and is easily accessible from three places: the two gap roads and the Sugarbush Bravo chairlift (weekends only). From the Lincoln Gap Road (the gap itself is 4.7 miles west of Route 100) you can hike a short way south to Sunset Ledge for a view of the Champlain Valley and Adirondacks. The more popular hike, however, is north from the gap (be advised to start early; parking is limited) to the Battell Shelter and on to Mount Abraham (5 miles round-trip), a 4,052-foot summit with spectacular views west, south as far as Killington Peak, and north as far as Belvidere Mountain. From Mount Abraham north to Lincoln Peak (accessible by the Sugarbush Resort chairlift) and on to Mount Ellen (4,135 feet) is largely above tree line; 3,600-foot General Stark Mountain to the north is best accessed (still a steep 2.6-mile hike) from Route 17 at Appalachian Gap. For details about the two shelters, contact the **Green Mountain Club** (802-244-7037; www.green mountainclub.org). Mill Brook Inn's Joan Gorman also recommends beginning 2.1 miles up Tucker Hill Road at the small parking area (on the left) at the CAMEL'S HUMP STATE FOREST sign. Follow the blue blazes through the stand of pines known as "the Enchanted Forest" to the top of Dana Hill Road (approximately 1 hour round-trip, good for skiing and snowshoeing).

Mad River Glen (802-496-3551; www.madriverglen.com) offers a full schedule of guided backcountry trips and bird-watching tours.

HORSEBACK RIDING Vermont Icelandic Horse Farm (802-496-7141; www.icelandichorses.com), North Fayston Road, Waitsfield. Year-round. These strong, pony-sized mounts were brought to Iceland by the Vikings, but are still relatively rare. Karen Winhold uses them for 1- and 2-hour, half- and full-day trail rides and (seasonal) inn-to-inn treks from her stable in Waitsfield Common. The horses have an unusually smooth gait (faster than a walk, gentler than a trot). Skijoring is offered in winter.

Dana Hill Stable (802-496-6251), Route 17, Fayston. Clinics, extensive coaching weeks.

MINI GOLF ✿ **Lots-O-Balls** (802-244-5874), Route 100, in Duxbury, between Waitsfield and Waterbury. Open in-season from 11 AM, a great 19-hole miniature golf course.

POLO Sugarbush Polo Club (802-496-8938). The oldest and most active polo club in Vermont holds matches Thursday, Saturday, and Sunday during summer months and a USPA-sanctioned tournament on July 4. Lessons available. Polo fields are in Waitsfield Village near the Health Center and at the junction of the East Warren and Roxbury Gap Roads. Public welcome.

GAP DRIVES Appalachian Gap. Even if you aren't continuing down the other side, be sure to drive up Route 17 past tho Mad Rivor Glcn bacc orca to its high point (there's parking at the trailhead for the Long Trail) and look down across the Champlain Valley, across the lake, to the Adirondacks in the distance. This is a great sunset ride.

Lincoln Gap is the steepest of Vermont's east–west gap roads (nothing allowed in tow, good brakes required, closed in winter), and the most spectacular. It begins on Route 100 just below Warren Village and climbs for 3 miles, seemingly straight up to the top of the 2,424-foot-high Lincoln Gap, where there's a pullout, a trailhead for the Long Trail. Next come magnificent vistas south, across farm fields (this stretch of road is unpaved in wide places and paved when it narrows). The village of Lincoln, clustered around a good general store, is about as quiet as Vermont gets. Continue through West Lincoln and down to Bartlett Falls in Rocky Dale (see "Addison County and Environs").

For the **ultimate foliage loop** drive west over the Appalachian Gap (Route 17) 16 miles from Waitsfield to Route 116, then 2 miles south on Route 116 to the Lincoln Gap Road and head back east 14 miles to Warren.

SCENIC DRIVES East Warren Road. If you miss this road, you miss the heart of the Valley. From Bridge Street in Waitsfield Village, cross the covered bridge, bear right onto East Warren Road, and continue the 6 miles to East Warren. The views are of the Green Mountains set back across open farmland. For an overview of the Valley, take the Roxbury Gap Road up to the pullout (be careful, because there aren't many places to turn around). From East Warren, loop back the 2 miles through Warren Village to Route 100.

BRAGG HILL ROAD

Kim Grant

Bragg Hill Road. The views from this peerless old farm road are magnificent: down across pastures and the narrow valley cut by the Mill Brook to Mount Ellen. Begin at Bragg Hill Road (off Route 100 just north of the Route 17 junction) and drive uphill, continue as it turns to dirt, and follow it around (bearing left); it turns into Number 9 Road and rejoins Route 17.

Granville Gulf. (see map on page 292 in "White River Valley.") Drive Route 100 south from Warren and the Valley quickly disappears, replaced by a dark, narrow, and twisty pass, part of the Granville Gulf State Reservation.

At the height-of-land, the Mad River begins its north-flowing course toward the Gulf of St. Lawrence and the White River rises, flowing south to eventually empty into Long Island Sound. A few miles south **Moss Glen Falls** spills down a steep cliff by the road. To turn this 20-mile drive into a day trip, continue to Hancock and across the Middlebury Gap to Middlebury, back across Appalachian or Lincoln Gap (see the box on page 322) to the Mad River Valley.

SOARING **Sugarbush-Warren Airport** (802-496-2290; 1-800-881-SOAR), Warren. Respected as one of the East's prime spots for riding thermal and ridge waves. Glider lessons, rides, food; open daily May through October. Solo and private lessons, rides, vacations available for all ages. Come just to see who's gliding in and out; lunch at the Diner Soar Deli.

SPAS **Alta Day Spa** (802-495-2582; www.altadayspa.com), 242 Main Street, Warren Village. Long established in the Valley, more recently moved to its present location in a house across from the Pitcher Inn, with which it shares ownership and patrons. A full menu of spa services is offered, from massage to aromatherapy to facials and salon services.

MadRiver Massage (802-496-5638; www.madrivermassage.com), Starch House overlooking the Mill Brook, Route 100, Waitsfield (just north of the Route 17 junction). Open daily 10–5, Sunday seasonally. A full range of massage, also shiatsu, reflexology, Reiki, and "stress-diffuser," plus body and bath products.

SUMMER DAY CAMPS ✺ **Sugarbush Resort** (802-583-2381), the **Bridges Family Resort and Tennis Club** (802-583-2922; 1-800-453-2922) in Warren, **Clearwater Sports** (802-496-2708) in Waitsfield, and the **Sunrise Montessori School** (802-496-5435) in Waitsfield all offer summer day camps. For ages 13 and up there's even a weeklong **Junior Soaring Camp** (802-492-2708) at the Sugarbush Airport (see *Soaring*). **Mad River Glen** also offers nature-geared day camps in summer.

SWIMMING South of Warren Village, the Mad River becomes a series of dramatic falls and whirlpools cascading through a gorge. The most secluded swimming hole is by the **Bobbin Mill** (the first right off Route 100 after Lincoln Gap Road, heading south); park by the gravel pit and follow the path through the pines to a series of pools, all icy cold. Ask locally about **Warren Falls** and the best spot for skinny-dipping. The **Lareau Farm swimming hole** (now a town park) in the Mad River, south of Waitsfield on Route 100, is best for kids. **Blueberry Lake** in Warren is now owned by the Green Mountain National Forest; the **Ward Fishing Access area** on Route 100B in Moretown is another good bet. **Bristol Falls** is just about 10 miles from Warren via the Lincoln Gap Road. The **Sugarbush Sports Center** features a large, L-shaped outdoor pool with adjacent changing facilities, café, bar, and Jacuzzi; the **Bridges Family Resort and Tennis Club** offers indoor and outdoor pools and swimming lessons. Many inns also have outdoor pools. Inquire about the Punch Bowl (clothing optional).

TENNIS The Bridges Family Resort and Tennis Club (802-583-2922; 1-800-453-2922), Sugarbush Access Road, Warren, offers indoor and outdoor courts and year-round tennis clinics for both adults and juniors.

WALKING AND RUNNING The Mad River Path Association (802-583-8181) maintains several ever-evolving recreation paths in the Valley, namely: the **Warren Path,** beginning near Brooks Field at Warren Elementary School (Brook Road, Warren); the **Millbrook Path** in Fayston, running along the hill through the woods (blue blazes) between Millbrook Inn and Tucker Hill Lodge, on up across German Flats Road to the Inn at Mad River Barn; the **Mad River Greenway** (see *Bicycling*); and the **Village Path,** which begins at Fiddlers' Green and heads south to the Irasville Cemetery and beyond. See also *Hiking* and *Scenic Drives.*

✳ Winter Sports

CROSS-COUNTRY, TELEMARK SKIING, AND SNOWSHOEING Ole's Cross-Country Center (802-496-3430; 1-877-863-3001; www.olesxc.com), at the airport, Warren. Fifty km of machine-tracked trails radiate out across the meadows and into the woods with elevations ranging from 1,120 to 1,640 feet. This is a hidden treasure at the heart of the valley—with views of the mountains on both sides. Rentals and instruction. Breakfast and lunch served weekends 10–3, otherwise soups and sandwiches 9–5 at the Diner Soar Deli.

Blueberry Lake Cross-Country Ski Center (802-496-6687), Plunkton Road, Warren. On the scenic, east side of the Valley, a total of 60 km of secluded trails.

Clearwater Sports (802-496-2708), Route 100, Waitsfield, offers rentals, along with custom and group tours, backcountry skis, and "skins" for attempting local stretches of the Catamount Trail (below).

Local trails: **Puddledock** in Granville Gulf State Reservation on Route 100, south of Warren, has 3.5 miles of ungroomed trails marked with red metal triangles; a map is available at the registration box.

Check out the *Mad River Valley Snowshoe Trails* map/guide published by Map Adventures (www.mapadventures.com), detailing 15 tours and identifying local animal tracks.

Catamount Trail (www.catamount trail.org). Check the guidebook (see "What's Where") and web site for stretches of the trail in the Valley. The most popular begins at The Battleground (see *Lodging*) on Route 17 and climbs steadily uphill to the Beaver Ponds in the Phenn Basin Wilderness area.

CROSS-COUNTRY ON THE SUGARBUSH GOLF COURSE

©Dennis Curran

Stark Mountain by Snowshoe (Mad River Glen: 802-496-3551; www.madriver glen.com), Warren. Half a dozen trails ranging in length from a short spur to 2.2 miles are marked, and Mad River's resident naturalist Sean Lawson offers a full program of guided **tracking treks,** including 2-hour **Nighttime Nature Rambles** every Friday and Saturday during ski season. A nature center is presently being rehabbed and expanded. **Telemarking** is also a longtime specialty at **Mad River Glen.** Inquire about rentals, lesson and lift packages, and special events.

SEAN LAWSON LEADS UNUSUAL TRACKING TREKS AND NATURE RAMBLES.

DOWNHILL SKIING ❧ **Sugarbush** (information: 802-583-6300; ski report: 802-583-SNOW; www.sugarbush.com; lodging reservations: 1-800-53-SUGAR). Two separate trail systems on two major peaks—3,975-foot Lincoln Peak at Sugarbush South and 4,135-foot Mount Ellen at Sugarbush North—originally two different ski areas—were linked in 1995 by a 2-mile (9½-minute) quad chair traversing the undeveloped Slide Brook Basin that separates them. Snowmaking coverage, long adequate at Mount Ellen, was also tripled to cover substantially more terrain at Lincoln Peak. Sugarbush skiers will tell you how fortunate their resort was to be sidelined during the era in which a large percentage of New England's best ski trails were smoothed, widened, and generally homogenized. In particular they are thankful that the Castle Rock trails, recognized throughout the country as some of the meanest, most natural, and most interesting expert terrain at any major American ski resort, survive. *Lifts:* 17—7 quads, 3 triples, 4 doubles, and 3 surface. Lifts operate 9—4, 8:30—4 weekends and holidays. *Trails:* 115; 20 acres of patrolled tree skiing; 468 skiable acres. *Vertical drop:* 2,650 feet.

SUGARBUSH SUMMIT

Snowmaking: 285.5 acres overall. *Facilities:* Cafeterias, lounges, ski shops, rentals, restaurants, sports center, condominiums. *Ski school:* Sugarbush Ski and Snowboarding School clinics, special teen program; women's clinics, guided backcountry skiing. *Snowboarding:* Rentals, lessons, terrain parks. *For children:* Nursery from infancy; special morning and afternoon programs for older kids.

"STEEP" SKIING AT SUGARBUSH

Rates: In 2003–04, $48–61 adults, $39–41 juniors and seniors; cheaper with lodging packages. Inquire about the "Sugar Card," available online, free. Skiers wear it like a season pass (you need a photo ID), and it's good for substantial discounts for skiing; there's also no need to go to the ticket booth, and it's good for all on-mountain purchases (it goes directly to your credit card). The ski school, headed by Olympian Warren Miller and extreme skier John Egan, features learning by doing.

♪ **Mad River Glen** (802-496-3551; in-state snow reports: 1-800-696-2001; outstanding web site. www.madriver glen.com). In 1995 one of New England's oldest major ski areas (the first to offer slope-side lodging) became the first to be owned cooperatively by its skiers, retaining its enviable reputation as one of the most challenging yet friendliest places to ski. Its vertical drop puts it in the big league, but the number of lifts and trails remains consciously limited. The Sunnyside Double Chair was replaced in 1998, the first capital improvement since 1982, and access to the summit of Stark Mountain (3,836 feet) is via the vintage-1948 single chair (the only one left in the country). All trails funnel into the central base lodge area, the better for families—many of whom are now third-generation Mad River skiers—to meet. Many trails are off the ski map. A favored place for tele-marking, it's the only place in New England in which snowboarding is out-lawed—and the only one with a serious snowshoe trail system and full program of snowshoeing/nature treks. On a good snow day it's the region's best ski buy. *Lifts:* Four chairs, including the single, plus the Callie's Corner Handle Tow. *Trails and slopes:* 20 expert, 10 intermediate, 14 novice, a total of 800 skiable acres. *Vertical drop:* 2,000 feet. *Snowmaking:* 15 percent, which includes top to bottom on the Practice Slope, also other high-volume, low-elevation areas. *Facilities:* Base lodge, cafeteria, and pub; also the newly rehabbed Birdcage, halfway up the mountain, serving sandwiches, drinks; ski shop, rentals, ski school. *For children:* Cricket Club Nursery for 6 weeks–6 years; programs for ages 3–17 include Junior Racing and Junior Mogul programs. *Rates:* $45 adults, $33 juniors (14 and under) and seniors (65–69), $38/$26 half-day, multiday rates. Under 6 and over 70 ski free.

ICE SKATING **Sugarbush Inn** (802-583-6100; 1-800-537-8427) in Warren offers skating on flooded tennis courts. **The Skatium** at Mad River Green Shopping Center in Waitsfield (lighted) offers rentals, also available from neighboring **Inverness Ski Shop** (802-496-3343); free day and night skating on the groomed hockey rink at Brooks Recreation Field off Brook Road in Warren.

SKIJORING Inquire about this sport (also about winter horseback riding) at **Vermont Icelandic Horse Farm** (802-496-7141) in Waitsfield (see *Horseback Riding*).

SLEIGH RIDES **Mountain Valley Farm** (802-496-9255) in Waitsfield offers sleigh rides, as does **Mad River Carriage Co.** (802-496-2104) off East Warren Road in Waitsfield.

SNOWMOBILING Eighty miles of local trails are maintained by the Mad River Ridge Runners; snowmobile registration can be purchased at **Kenyon's Store,** Route 100, Waitsfield. No rentals.

✱ Lodging

Note: The Sugarbush-based (1-800-53-SUGAR) reservation service is open 9–5 daily, 8–8 during high ski season, serving roughly half the Valley's condos and 21 inns and B&Bs.

Note also: Many lodging places in the Valley charge an extra 4 percent community fee in addition to the usual 9 percent state tax, so you may want to ask. Most also request a 2-night minimum stay on winter and other popular weekends.

RESORTS **Sugarbush Inn** (802-583-6100; 1-800-537-8427; www.sugarbush.com), Warren 05674. The centerpiece of this complex is the fairly formal, 42-room Sugarbush Inn, owned by the same company that owns the mountain. There's a 24-hour front desk, room phones, air-conditioning, a library and sitting room, and an outdoor pool. $80–190 per couple, breakfast included, service extra.

The Bridges Family Resort and Tennis Club (802-583-2922; 1-800-453-2922), Sugarbush Access Road, Warren 05674. A self-contained resort just down the access road from the Sugarbush main lifts and base lodge. Facilities include indoor tennis, squash, an indoor pool, saunas, Jacuzzi and exercise room, and 100 condo-style units ranging from one to three bedrooms, each with fireplace,

THE PITCHER INN IN WARREN

Kim Grant

sundeck, TV, and phone, some with washer/dryer. $145–600, cheaper the longer you stay; inquire about ski and tennis packages.

INNS The inns listed below serve dinner as a matter of course; B&Bs may serve dinner on occasion.

Pitcher Inn (802-496-6350; 1-888-TO-PITCH; www.pitcherinn.com), Warren 05674. Designed by architect David Sellers to look like it's been sitting here in the middle of Warren Village for a century, the white-clapboard inn just opened in the 1997–98 winter season, replacing a building that had burned. Inside, however, the inn offers some extraordinary spaces, notably a cozy small library with books and a hearth, far from the large, elegant dining room that's open to the public (see *Dining Out*); there's also an attractive pub with a hearth. Each guest room was designed by a different architect to convey a different aspect of local history. The Lodge, for instance, suggests a Masonic lodge (once a major social force in the Valley), with a ceiling painted midnight blue and delicately studded with stars, and obelisk-shaped posts on the king-sized bed. From a bedside switch in the Mountain Room, you can make the sun rise and set over the mountains painted on the facing wall. Bathrooms are splendid. The Alta spa across the road, under the same ownership, offers massage, facials, and a variety of sap therapies. Two of the 11 rooms are suites. $330–600 includes breakfast in the inn, $660 in the suites.

❦ ☸ Millbrook Inn & Restaurant (802-496-2405; 1-800-477-2809; www.millbrookinn.com), Route 17, Waitsfield 05673. Open year-round except April, May, and late October to Thanksgiving. This 19th-century farmhouse is a gem. You enter through the warming room, actually heated by a woodstove in winter. The living rooms invite you to sit down. The heart of the ground floor, however, is the dining room, well known locally as one of the best places to dine in the Valley (see *Dining Out*). Each of the seven guest rooms is different enough to deserve its own name, but all have stenciled walls, bureaus, antique beds with firm, queen- or king-sized mattresses, and private bath. Our favorite is the Shell Room with a wedding-ring-patterned quilt on the antique bed with its shell-shaped inlaid headboard and a picture of Thom's grandparents on the wall. A ski lodge since 1948, Millbrook has become a true country inn since Joan and Thom Gorman took over in 1979. They are constantly redecorating and landscaping the garden (breakfast is served on the patio, weather permitting), sustaining their enthusiasm with spectacularly adventurous, low-budget travels (Mount Kilimanjaro, South Africa, the Milford Track, Patagonia, and more). In winter $130–150 per couple MAP; in summer $130 MAP, $90 B&B. The two-bedroom house on the wooded hillside across the brook rents for $300 a day in winter (minimum 3 days), less for a week, negotiable price in summer. Children age 6 and older are welcome. Pets by prior approval. Wireless DSL access.

∞ **West Hill House** (802-496-7162; 1-800-898-1427; www.westhillhouse .com), 1496 West Hill Road, Warren 05674. A gabled farmhouse off in a far corner of the golf course but convenient both to Sugarbush lifts and to the village of Warren. Dotty Kyle, an irrepressible chef, and Eric Brattstrom, a former contractor who can't stop himself from improving and expanding the place, offer eight guest rooms, including two suites, all with private bath with either a Jacuzzi tub and shower or steam bath/tub/shower combo and all with gas fireplace. The four-poster suite, up its own spiral staircase, has all the bells and whistles: fireplace, four-poster canopy queen-sized bed, study with daybed, and bath with Jacuzzi and fireplace. Guests gather around the dining room table for multicourse breakfasts (with, perhaps, a vegetable soufflé), also for candelight dinners (on request). The house offers an unusual amount of common space: a living room, library with fireplace, and sunroom with views to the mountains and spectacular gardens. Step out the front door to cross-country ski or play golf, out the back into 9 wooded acres. $125–190. Check out the outstanding web site and inquire about family reunions and weddings.

∞ **1824 House Inn** (802-496-7555; 1-800-426-3986; www.1824house .com), 2150 Main Street (Route 100), Waitsfield 05673. North of the village, the gabled house is a beauty, decorated with an eye to room colors, Oriental rugs, and well-chosen antiques, in addition to comfort. The eight guest rooms vary, but all have private bath and feather bed. There are gracious drawing and dining rooms with fireplaces. The 15-acre property invites walking and cross-country skiing. There's also a good swimming hole in the Mad River just across the road, and the 1870s post-and-beam barn can shelter wedding receptions. The new owners are John Lumbra and Karl Lein. Lumbra, a professional chef, delights in whipping up four-course meals (see *Dining Out*), and Klein most recently remodeled homes. $99–153 per room includes a full breakfast and afternoon tea. Two-day minimum on weekends, 3 on winter holidays.

The Waitsfield Inn (1-800-758-2801; 1-800-758-3801; www.waits fieldinn.com), P.O. Box 969, Route 100, Waitsfield 05673. Innkeepers Ronda and Mike Kelley seem equal to the task of managing this middle-of-the-village inn, an 1825 parsonage with a "great room"—offering plenty of space to relax in front of the hearth—in the (former) attached carriage and horse barn. The dining rooms (open to the public) are well away from the several comfortable spaces reserved for guests. The 14 guest rooms (all with private bath) vary from cozy doubles to family rooms with lofts. Appropriate for children age 6 and older. $105–160 includes a full breakfast. Lunch and brunch are also served.

⊚ ❦ ✦ **Inn at Mad River Barn** (802-496-3310; www.madriver barn.com), 2849 Mill Brook Road, Waitsfield 05673. Betsy Pratt, former owner of Mad River Glen Ski Area, preserves the special atmosphere of this classic 1940s ski lodge, with its massive stone fireplace and deep leather chairs, and a dining room filled with mismatched oak tables and original 1930s art. The food (breakfast only in summer, dinner too in winter) is fine, as are the pine-walled guest rooms, all with private bath (those in the annex come with small kitchenette). In summer the appeal of the place is enhanced by the pool, secluded in a grove of birches, and by the deck overlooking landscaped gardens,

a setting for weddings and receptions. In winter a trail connects with Mad River Glen. $70–110 per room includes breakfast. Dinner is $15 extra; special children's rates. Add 8 percent service charge in winter.

Tucker Hill Lodge (phone/fax: 802-496-3983; 1-800-543-7841; www .tuckerhill.com), Marble Hill Road, Waitsfield 05673. A classic 1940s ski lodge with a fieldstone hearth in the living room. Innkeeper David Jackson has newly renovated all 18 rooms. All have private bath, phone, TV, and data port. $59–169 per double room, including continental breakfast.

BED & BREAKFASTS ⊚ **The Inn at Round Barn Farm** (802-496-2276; www.innattheroundbarn.com), East Warren Road, Waitsfield 05673. Named for its remarkable round (12-sided) barn built in 1910, now a cultural and reception center with a lap pool and greenhouse on its ground floor, this old farmhouse is one of New England's most elegant bed & breakfasts. Innkeeper Anne Marie DeFreest offers 12 antiques-furnished rooms, 7 with gas fireplace, several with steam shower and/or Jacuzzi, all overlooking the meadows and mountains. Guests who come in winter are asked to leave their shoes at the door and don slippers to protect the hardwood floors. Common space includes a sun-filled breakfast room, a stone terrace, a book-lined library, and a lower-level game room with pool table, organ, TV, VCR, and a fridge stocked with complimentary soda and juices. From $130 midweek for a double room with a regular shower to $265 on weekends in high season for a room with marble fireplace, canopy king bed, and Jacuzzi. Prices include gourmet breakfast and afternoon edibles. A series of workshops ranging from cooking classes to watercolor and photography are offered mid-April through mid-August. Weddings are a specialty of the barn, which also serves as a venue for summer concerts (see *Entertainment*). In winter the inn maintains extensive snowshoe trails (snowshoes are complimentary to guests). Appropriate for children 15 and older.

∞ ♪ **The Lareau Farm Country Inn** (802-496-4949; 1-800-833-0766; www.lareaufarminn.com), Route 100, Waitsfield 05673. Guests feel right at home, checking in via the kitchen and settling into the two sitting rooms (one with a fireplace). The broad, columned back porch overlooks an expansive spread of lawn that stretches down to a great (10-foot-deep) swimming hole and backs into a steep wooded hill. This is a 150-year-old farmhouse set in a wide meadow along the Mad River, a total of 67 acres with trails to walk or ski. Susan Easley, a warm host, offers 12 guest rooms and a suite with Jacuzzi, all nicely furnished with antique beds, quilts, and rockers. $90–135 for a double room with private bath, $80 with shared bath, includes a full breakfast (2-night minimum on weekends). $135–165 for the suite. Children are welcome "with well-behaved parents," and families occupy rooms along an ell off the main house. Weddings are a specialty; dinner on weekends is served in the American Flatbread Kitchen (see *Eating Out*) in the adjoining barn.

♞ ♪ **Mountain View Inn** (802-496-2426; www.mountainview.com), 1912 Mill Brook Road (Route 17), Waitsfield 05673. This very Vermont house is bigger than it looks, with seven nicely decorated guest rooms (private baths). It's been geared to guests since it became one of the Valley's first ski lodges in 1948. Since 1978, under ownership by Fred and Suzy Spencer, the year-round feel has been that of an unusually hospitable small country inn. Rooms are furnished with antiques (our favorite is the 1840s "rolling pin" tigerseye maple bed) and bright quilts. Guests gather around the wood-burning stove in the living room and at the long, 299-year-old harvest table for breakfast. Handy to Mount Ellen, Mad River Glen, and the Mill Brook Path. $110–140 per couple B&B.

The Featherbed Inn (802-496-7151; www.featherbedinn.com), Route 100, Waitsfield 05673. Clive and Tracey Coutts devoted 3 years to restoring this early-19th-century farmhouse before hanging out their shingle. The two-room Beatrice Suite has a pencil-post canopy bed and wet bar; the Ilse Suite offers a cathedral ceiling and a queen-sized sleigh bed; all the rooms have a feather bed. There are also eight more traditional rooms. Common spaces are tasteful and inviting, from the living room with its woodstove and grand piano to the den with TV. Set back from Route 100, the house overlooks lawn and fields. Rates include a full breakfast: $85–165.

Deer Meadow Inn (802-496-2850; 1-888-459-9183; www.deermeadow inn.com), P.O. Box 242, Warren 05674. Off by itself in the middle of the valley near the airport (the hub for cross-country trails in winter). A traditional Vermont house set in 35 acres with three attractive, antiques-furnished guest rooms, all with private bath, phone, and TV. Two spring-fed ponds on the property are good for swimming and fishing (trout and bass). $135–150 includes a full breakfast.

Beaver Pond Farm (1-800-685-8285; beaverpondfarminn.com), 1225 Golf Course Road, Warren 05674. Nancy and Bob Baron spent 6 months renovating this gracious house before reopening it for the 2003–04 ski season. Overlooking a beaver pond and the rolling expanse of the Sugarbush Golf Course, they offer five rooms, all with private bath and fine linens and down comforters, also spa robes to ease your way to the outside hot tub. Breakfast is an event, and the 24-hour wet bar includes complementary coffee and tea, honor-system wine and beer. $115–175.

The Mad River Inn (802-496-7900; 1-800-832-8278; www.mad riverinn.com), P.O. Box 75, off Route 100, Waitsfield 05673. A house with turn-of-the-20th-century detailing, like fine woodwork and large picture windows with lace etchings in the living room. The seven guest rooms and one suite are furnished with an eye to Victorian fabric, color, and antiques. The house overlooks a gazebo, meadow, and the Mad River, and it's handy to a good swimming hole. Facilities include an outdoor Jacuzzi and a downstairs game room and BYOB bar. Rates from $95 for the smallest room with a private but hall bath to $150 for the largest with private bath on a weekend; a three-course breakfast and afternoon tea are included. Children 5 years and older are welcome.

The Sugartree Inn (802-583-3211; 1-800-666-8907; www.sugartree.com), Sugarbush Access Road, Warren 05674. This is a modern ski lodge, but Frank and Kathy Partsch have done their utmost to create a country-inn atmosphere. The nine rooms have quilts, canopy and brass beds, and private bath; a large oak-furnished suite has a gas fireplace. Guests gather by the fireplace in the living room, and breakfast is served in the adjoining dining room. Breakfast specials include chocolate chip pancakes. $99–195 per couple B&B.

Weathertop Lodge (802-496-4909; 1-800-800-3625; www.weathertop lodge.com), 755 Mill Brook Road, Waitsfield 05673. The atmosphere is that of a ski lodge rather than a country inn, but it's appealing any time of year. The common room has a field-stone fireplace, stereo, piano, cable TV, video games, and VCR. There's also a fitness center with an array of exercise machines and a hot tub and sauna. The nine rooms are large, with two queen beds and a full bath. Mike and Lisa Lang are the new innkeepers. $95–139 per room.

Caravan Bed & Breakfast (802-496-7420; caravanbandb.com), 746 Route 100, Moretown 05660. This is the former Honeysuckle Inn, an 1820s farmhouse that rambles back from the road, surrounded by 2 acres of gardens and fields beyond. Penny Percival and Jon Sutton offer five brightly decorated guest rooms and an attractive living room with a cheerful hearth and comfortable seating, good books, and games. Breakfast is full and healthy, using local ingredients as much as possible. $75–90 in summer, $90–105 in foliage and ski seasons, includes afternoon baked goods as well.

Yellow Farmhouse Inn (802-496-4263; 1-800-400-5169; www.yellow

farmhouseinn.com), P.O. Box 345, 550 Old County Road, Waitsfield 05673. The newest inn in the valley, this 1850s farmhouse sits off above meadows, minutes from the middle of Waitsfield. Dennis and Victoria Alberts have totally renovated this old house, creating an uncluttered, inviting breakfast room and open beamed living room. There are seven guest rooms and a suite (all private baths); several rooms have gas or electric Vermont Castings stoves, some whirlpool tubs, all uncluttered but comfortable. Guests receive a pot of coffee at their door and sit down to a three-course breakfast. $95–255 (the high end is for a suite).

MOTEL 🌺 ✍ **Wait Farm Motor Inn** (802-496-2033; 1-800-887-2828), Waitsfield 05673. Paul and Michelle Lavoie's eight motel units, four with kitchenette, as well as two double rooms in the main house, constitute this friendly family business. $50–84 per couple.

CONDOMINIUMS The Valley harbors more than 400 rental condominium units, many clustered around Sugarbush (Lincoln Peak), more scattered along the access road, and some squirreled away in the woods. No one reservation service represents them all.

Sugarbush Village Condominiums (802-583-3333; 1-800-537-8427). The resort manages a total of 250 condominium units in the rental pool, ranging from suites to four-bedroom mountain homes. Winter rates: $300 for a slope-side two-bedroom condominium, from $200 if not slope-side; from $70 per night, $420 per week for a one-bedroom condo in summer.

Sugarbush Resort Condos (802-583-6100; 1-800-537-8427; fax: 802-583-3209). A total of 200 units, most walk-to-the-slopes, with health club access. From $90 for a one-bedroom, $165–550 for two-bedroom, up to $700 for a four-bedroom unit. Less off-season.

✍ **The Battleground** (802-496-2288; 1-800-248-2102), Route 17, Fayston 05673. An unusually attractive cluster of 26 town houses, each designed to face the brook or a piece of greenery, backing into each other and thus preserving most of the 60 acres for walking or ski touring (the area's 60 km network of trails is accessible). In summer there's a pool, tennis and paddle tennis courts, and a play area for children. Mad River Glen is just up Route 17. Rates (2-night minimum) for two-, three-, and four-bedroom units are $170–500.

🐾 🏠 ✍ **Powderhound Lodge** (802-496-5100; 1-800-548-4022; fax: 802-496-5163; www.powderhound inn.com), P.O. Box 369 (Route 100), Warren 05674. The old roadside farmstead now serves as reception and dining rooms—with a ski-season pub—for the 44 condo-style apartments clustered in back. Each of these consists of two rooms, one with two beds and another lounging/dining space with two more daybeds and a TV; token cooking facilities. It's all nicely designed and maintained, nothing fancy but a good deal for families and couples who like the privacy of their own space with an option to mix with fellow guests. Summer facilities include a swimming pool; there's a hot tub for year-round use, plus a winter shuttle to the mountain. $84–169 in winter, with many 2- and 3-day (also midweek) ski packages; $84–99 in summer plus 3 percent service. Pets are $5 per night.

✳ Where to Eat

DINING OUT *Note:* The Valley restaurants are unusual in both quality and longevity. Most have been around for quite some time and, like most culinary landmarks, have their good and bad days.

Pitcher Inn (802-496-6350), Warren Village. Open for dinner. The elegant inn dining room features an à la carte menu to match, orchestrated by chef Sue Schickler. You might begin with sorrel soup with smoked salmon crouton and dine on grilled black bass with Thai green curry, coconut basmati rice, and green Romano beans, or a grilled vegetable napoleon with mozzarella, pesto, and browned butter vinaigrette. Entrées $24–34. The choice of wines by the glass is large, and the wine list itself is long and widely priced.

Chez Henri (802-583-2600), Sugarbush Village. Open only during ski season for lunch, brunch, and dinner. (Check in the off-season.) A genuine bistro. In 1963 Henri Borel relinquished his position as food controller for Air France to open this snug, inviting café with a fireplace, marble bar (imported from a Barre soda fountain), and terrace for dining out front in summer. Dinner entrées usually include roast duck with a fruit and pepper sauce and bouillabaisse, but most items change frequently so that longtime patrons can always find something new. Come early to get one of the coveted booths in the bar. Entrées $15–26.

🍲 Millbrook Inn & Restaurant (802-496-2405), Route 17, Waitsfield. Open for dinner except April, May, and late October through mid-

December. For more than 20 years Thom Gorman has been the chef and Joan Gorman the pastry chef, hostess, and waitress in their attractive dining room, a double parlor with hearth and French doors opening on a garden. (The couple reenergize during the months they close by hiking, backpacking, kayaking, and camping in the world's far corners.) They offer an eclectic, changing menu that might range from eggplant Parmesan to scampi and always includes a fish of the day and an "innkeeper's choice," along with a few Indian dishes, a legacy of Thom's Peace Corps days. We recommend the badami rogan josh, a wonderfully spiced (local) lamb dish. All dinners include Joan's anadama bread, as well as salad and starch—but save room for one of her freshly made pies, cakes, or ice creams. The wine list is varied and reasonably priced, influenced by the Gormans' ongoing discoveries in Argentina, South Africa, and Australia. Beer is also served. Entrées $10.50–17.95.

The Spotted Cow (802-496-5151), Bridge Street Marketplace, Waitsfield. Open for lunch and dinner daily except Monday in summer; in winter for dinner only. Reserve for dinner. This is Jay Young's latest project (Bermuda born and bred, Young owned the Sugarbush Inn for many years, then Jay's in the Mad River Green). Small and stylish, this is an in spot. The Bermuda fish chowder we sampled for lunch was superb. Dinner might be grilled breast of duckling with forest mushrooms, dried cherries and port, applejack maple and pork sausage stuffing, saffron, basmati rice, and *haricots verts*. Entrées $18.95–26.95.

The Common Man Restaurant
(802-583-2800; www.common
manrestaurant.com), German Flats
Road, Warren. Dinner only, closed
Monday off-season. Reservations suggested. A mid-19th-century barn hung
with chandeliers and warmed by an
open hearth, this is a Vermont dining
landmark, still owned by Michael
Ware who opened it in 1972 during
the glitziest of Sugarbush eras. It has
burned down, been rebuilt, and continues to earn good reviews. The
menu changes weekly, but many signature dishes don't. Appetizers might
include puff pastry with tenderloin
tips in peppercorn cream sauce;
entrées might range from penne pasta
with grape tomatoes, Gorgonzola, and
cream to a ragout of Vermont venison
with mushrooms and red wine.
There's always a homemade pasta
choice. Desserts are tempting and the
wine list, extensive. Entrées
$14–26.50.

🦞 **The Warren House Restaurant
& Rupert's Bar** (802-583-2421),
2585 Sugarbush Access Road, Warren. Open for dinner daily from 5:30.
Formerly Sam Rupert's, this attractive
place still offers an inviting, low-key
bar and "modern American cuisine"—
entrées like herb-crusted pan-seared
Atlantic salmon over a mustard-dill
aioli, and balsamic-braised New
Zealand lamb shank. Entrées
$11.95–19.95.

1824 House Inn (802-496-7555;
1-800-426-3986; www.1824house
.com), 2150 Main Street (Route 100),
Waitsfield 05673. Dinner by reservation. North of the village, a 19th-
century farmhouse with elegant dining rooms is the setting for four-
course dinners prepared by chef-
owner John Lumbra. The several

choices for each course might include
lobster ravioli with chive oil and
cream sauce, then butternut squash
and apple soup; filet mignon stuffed
with blue cheese and wrapped in
bacon; topped off by crème brûlée.
$40 prix fixe.

🌿 **Bass Restaurant** (802-583-3100),
Sugarbush Access Road, Warren.
Open nightly for dinner. The new
owners of this attractive, glass-walled
landmark with its round hearth are
Ed and Nancy Sirlin. Their à la carte
menu might include harvest vegetable stuffed trout with lobster
cream sauce and crisp oven-roasted
duck with maple sweet potatoes.
$12.50–19.

EATING OUT 🦞 🌿 **Easy Street Café**
(802-496-7234), Route 100, 0.5 mile
south of the junction of Routes 100
and 17 (next to the Catholic church).
Open daily for breakfast and lunch
8–4 and dinner (except Monday)
5:30–9:30. A great addition to the Valley! The kitchen is wide open, and the
aromas are irresistible. On the damp
day we stopped there was a choice of
freshly made soups and chilis, sandwiches on freshly baked bread, and
freshly made pastries, along with self-
serve coffees and teas. The dinner
menu is surprisingly varied: You
might begin with roasted littlenecks
with cob-smoked bacon or vegetable
tempura, then dine on vegetable timballo with grilled portobello, shellfish
in Thai-style curried broth with
noodles, scallions, mushrooms, and
sprouts, or on rosemary-marinated
rack of lamb. You could also simply
have a crispy fish wrap with a
mesclun, scallion, shredded lettuce,
and tomato salad. Kids 12 and under
can have a hamburger or grilled

cheese with fries. This is also a source of take-out meals. The adjacent Purple Moon Pub (see *Après-Ski*) also features comfortable seating and good food as well as live music on weekends.

♠ ♂ **The Den** (802-496-8880), just north of the junction of Routes 100 and 17 in Waitsfield. Open daily for lunch and dinner until 10:30, sandwiches until 11. The cheerful, pubby heart of the Valley; booths, stained glass, a summer patio. The menu is large and always includes a homemade soup, a wide choice of burgers, and a salad bar; dinner entrées might include a grilled half duckling and jerk pork as well as house steak. A wide selection of beers.

American Flatbread Kitchen (802-496-8856), at the Lareau Farm Country Inn, Route 100, Waitsfield. Open Friday and Saturday 5:30–9:30, year-round (more or less). George Schenk's distinctive pizza is baked in a primitive, wood-fired oven heated to 800 degrees; the results are distributed to stores from Florida to Chicago. On weekends the kitchen becomes an informal dining space featuring flatbread (toppings include cheese and herb, sun-dried tomato, homemade sausage with mushroom) and exceptional salads whose dressing boasts homemade fruit vinegar. Also specials such as grilled vegetables with garlic-herb sauce and oven-roasted chicken. Dine in or take out. Beer served. Each night Schenk writes a dedication, always food for thought.

♂ **Jay's** (802-496-8282), Mad River Green Shopping Center, Route 100, Waitsfield. Open for breakfast, lunch, dinner, and Sunday brunch. A family restaurant, bright and spacious, with an immense menu. Dinner might be chicken pesto, pasta pillows filled with broccoli and Vermont cheddar in a curry cream sauce, or Jay's Giant Burger. Children's menu, pizzas; full liquor license.

♠ ♂ **Hyde-Away Inn** (802-496-2322), Route 17, Waitsfield. Tavern open from 4, dining room 5:30–9:30 (9 midweek). An informal, affordable restaurant with plenty of appetizers and soups, sandwiches, and burgers. The dinner menu might include crabcakes served with homemade roasted red pepper aioli, Vermont maple chicken with garlic mashed potatoes, and vegetable pasta. All entrées come with salad and homemade bread. Seasonal outdoor deck dining. Children's menu and toy area.

♠ **Rositas Mexican Restaurant** (802-583-3858; www.rositasmexican food.com), Sugarbush Access Road, across from the Bridges, Warren. Open from 5 PM except Wednesday off-season. Reputedly better than its predecessor (Miguel's Stowe-Away), featuring salads, monster burritos, carne asada, and shrimp in tequila plus homemade desserts. Juan Gorilla's cantina and sports bar with a 61-inch screen HDTV is downstairs.

♂ **Michael's Good to Go** (802-496-3832), Village Square Shopping Center (a few doors down from Mehuron's Market), Waitsfield. Open daily except Sunday 4 PM–closing. Michael Flannagan, one of the Valley's favorite chefs, has a loyal following that has followed him from one enterprise to the next. This latest venture is geared to condo dwellers and local residents with a menu ranging from Asian fusion to Vermont turkey potpie and Baja-style fish tacos plus the likes of a cheesy cheese pizza for kids.

🍴 **Egan's Big World Pub and Grill**
(802-496-5557), Madbush Falls
Motel, Route 100, Waitsfield (near
the Sugarbush Access Road). Open
for lunch Wednesday through Saturday, dinner nightly. Named for local
extreme skier John Egan (who skis
the world), this is a hangout for hard-
core skiers and boarders. The atmosphere is casual—a brewpub with
booths and a slightly more formal dining area: good burgers, pastas, salads,
a great marinated eggplant sandwich,
and (winter only) a dynamite Hungar-
ian goulash. Egan's Extreme Ale is the
house brew.

Valley Pizzeria (802-496-9200),
4752 Main Street (Route 100), Waitsfield. Open 11–9:30, Sunday 4–9:30.
New York–style pizza (not too thick or
too thin) with a wide variety of toppings, hand tossed and baked in a
stone oven. Eat in or take out; burgers and salads also served. Try the
Greek pizza. No beer or wine.

Warren Store (802-496-3864), Warren Village. Open daily 8–7, Sunday
until 6. Year-round the bakery produces French and health breads, plus
croissants and great deli food and
sandwiches; in summer a deck overlooks the small waterfall.

Three Mountain Cafe, Mad River
Green Shopping Center, Waitsfield.
The café and espresso bar features
croissants, pastries, and chocolate
truffles to go with the coffee.

Sweet Pea Natural Foods (802-496-
7763), Village Square shopping center, Route 100, Waitsfield. Back
behind Tempest books, a source of
vegetarian soups and sandwiches as
well as body care products, organic
produce, healthy drinks, and more.

✳ Entertainment

The Eclipse Theater (802-496-
7787; 1-888-212-1142; www.eclipse
theater.com), Route 100 (look for the
entrance just north of the shopping
centers), Waitsfield. Showing independent and mainstream films weekdays but featuring a Saturday Concert
Series with well-known artists (check
the web site; you can order online).
There's usually a Saturday dinner/
movie special, a Sunday brunch/mati-
nee, and live music in the Starlight
Lounge (beer and wine) Thursday
through Sunday, a coffeehouse atmosphere, frequent jazz. Check the
week's listings.

Green Mountain Cultural Center
(802-496-7722) at the Joslyn Round
Barn, Waitsfield. This concert and
exhibit space in a classic round barn is
the setting for a series of summer
concerts, along with workshops and a
major foliage-season art exhibit. The
Valley Players (802-583-1674;
www.valleyplayers.com), a community
theater company, produces three or
four plays a year in its own theater
just north of Waitsfield Village, Route
100. The **Phantom Theater** (802-
496-5997 in summer), a local group
with New York City theater community members, presents original
plays and improvisational performances for children and adults at Edge-
comb Barn in Warren. Also note **Mad
River Chorale** performances in June
and December (check with the chamber of commerce: 802-496-7907).

APRÈS-SKI The Blue Tooth (802-
583-2656), Sugarbush Access Road,
Warren. A ski-season "mountain
saloon"; open from 3 PM in ski
season for après-ski snacks and
drinks, moderately priced dinners,

live entertainment, dancing. **The Hyde-Away** (802-496-2322) is the hot spot near Mad River Glen (Route 17). **The Purple Moon** (802-496-3400; www.purplemoonpub.com), Route 100 south of the Route 17 junction, features a fireplace, a mahogany bar, couches, and atypical late-night pub food like Vermont goat cheese fondue; live music Saturday nights. At the other end of the spectrum is the **Mad Mountain Tavern** (802-496-2562; www.madmountain-tavern.com), junction of Routes 100 and 17, featuring weekend winter ski-season music and dancing.

✳ Selective Shopping

ANTIQUES Warren Antiques (802-496-4025), Warren Village. Open daily 10–5 May through October, then by appointment. Victoriana, furniture, ephemera.

ART GALLERIES Artisans Gallery (802-496-6256), Bridge Street, Waitsfield. Open daily 10–5. A highly selective collection of furniture, baskets, canes, rugs, glass, decoys, ornaments, photography, and much more. The fine-art and furniture galleries are in the rear.

⊚ **The Bundy Fine Arts Center** (802-496-5055), Bundy Road (off Route 100), Waitsfield. Phone to check hours. An interesting building that offers a mix of good art, in addition to a sculpture garden around and beyond a reflecting pond. A popular site for weddings.

Parade Gallery (802-496-5445) in Warren Village offers an affordable selection of prints and original art.

Black Newt Ironworks Sculpture Studio (802-496-5843), Route 100, Waitsfield Village. A converted town barn and former blacksmith shop is studio space for John Matusz, who sculpts in steel and stone.

Bridge Street Bakery (802-496-0077), Bridge Street, Waitsfield. Artist owned, a café most notable for its local paintings, prints, and photography (all for sale).

CRAFTS SHOPS AND GALLERIES
Cabin Fever Quilts (802-496-2287), the Old Church, Waitsfield. Closed Tuesday, otherwise open 10–5. Machine-sewn, hand-tied quilts come in a range of sizes and patterns, priced $175–400; also pillows, gifts, and quilt fabrics.

Waitsfield Pottery (802-496-7155), Route 100 across from Bridge Street. Ulrike Tesmer makes functional, hand-thrown stoneware pieces, well worth a stop.

WARREN VILLAGE POTTERY

Kim Grant

Warren Village Pottery & Crafts (802-496-4162), corner of Fuller Hill and Main Street, Warren Village. Usually open daily 10–5. The functional stoneware is made on the premises; also a selection of crafts and candles.

Luminosity Stained Glass Studio (802-496-2231), the Old Church, Route 100, Waitsfield. This is a very special shop. Since 1975 Barry Friedman has been fashioning Tiffany lamp shades and a variety of designs in leaded and stained glass; the shop also carries some interesting jewelry. Items are priced from $15 for great necklaces to $15,000 for an exquisite lamp.

Mad River Glass Gallery (802-496-9388), 4237 Main Street (Route 100), Waitsfield Village. Melanie and Dave Leppia's handsome gallery displays original designs in blown and cast glass.

Bradley House in Warren Village showcases work by an amazing variety of local craftspeople. It's a trove of hand-loomed rugs, woven baskets, quilts and pillows, wooden bowls, metalwork, furniture, fabric art, pottery, handblown glass, and more. Open daily.

Labyrinth Gifts (802-496-2259), Village Square Shopping Center, Waitsfield. Formerly Tulip Tee Crafts. Priscilla Case is perpetuating this store's reputation for handcrafted jewelry, unusual pottery, blown glass, and fine prints, but she has added kites, puzzles and wooden toys, shower clothes, and gifts and Vermont souvenirs.

The outstanding **Plush Quartz Art Glass** studio is in Granville, south of Warren on Route 100; see "The White River Valleys."

SPECIAL SHOPS Warren Store and More, Warren Village. Staples, wines, and the deli and bakery are downstairs (see *Eating Out*); upstairs is one of Vermont's best-kept secrets, an eclectic selection of clothing, jewelry, and gifts. We treasure everything we have bought here, from earrings to a winter coat.

All Things Bright and Beautiful (802-496-3397), Bridge Street, Waitsfield. You'll find an incredible number of stuffed animals and unusual toys on two floors of this old village house.

The Store (802-496-4465), Route 100, Waitsfield. Since its 1965 opening, this exceptional shop has grown tenfold, now filling two floors of an 1834 former Methodist meetinghouse with superb early American, French, and English antiques, cookware, tabletop gifts, collectibles, lifestyle books, Vermont gourmet products, and children's toys and books from around the world.

Tempest Book Shop (802-496-2022), Village Square, Waitsfield. This family-run bookstore is a trove of titles in most categories, including children's books. We like their motto: "A house without books is like a room without windows" (Horace Mann). CDs, cassettes, posters, and more than 10,000 books in stock.

Alpine Options (1-888-888-9131). Locations: at Sugarbush Resort, on the access road, and at Mad River Glen. Open daily, Fridays until 11 during ski season. Ski and snowboard rentals, demos and repair, best quality and all-around service according to the locals.

SUGARHOUSES Eastman Long & Sons (802-496-3448), Tucker Hill

Road, Waitsfield. "Sonny" Long sets 6,000 taps high on 100 wooded acres that have been in his family for generations. He maintains that the higher the elevation, the better the syrup, and he welcomes visitors to his roadside sugarhouse during sugaring season. On summer weekends, he sells from his van at the junction of Routes 100 and 17.

Palmer's Maple Products (802-496-3675), East Warren Road, Waitsfield. Delbert and Sharlia Palmer sell syrup from their farm on this scenic road.

✻ Special Events

Note: Check with the chamber of commerce (see *Guidance*) and its web site (www.madrivervalley.org) for weekly listings of special events.

March: Annual **New England Telemark Festival,** Mad River Glen.

April: **Vermont Adventure Games,** featuring the **Sugarbush Triathlon**—canoe, kayak, bicycle, cross-country ski races (more than 600 competitors), Sugarbush.

July 4: Outstanding **parade,** Warren Village.

July–August: Summer productions by the **Valley Players** and by the **Phantom Theater** (see *Entertainment*). **Green Mountain Polo Tournament,** Warren.

August: **Vermont Festival of the Arts** throughout the Valley. **Mad River Valley Century Ride** (third Saturday; www.mrvcenturyride .com)—a 100-mile ride through central Vermont based at the Hyde-Away Inn/Restaurant (see *Eating Out*).

August–October: **Farmer's Market,** Saturdays 9:30–2 at the junction of Routes 17 and 100. Crafts and food as well as produce.

Labor Day weekend: 2-day **crafts exhibits. Green Mountain Stage Race** (www.gmsr.org).

Early October: **Soaring Encampment** throughout the Valley. **Sugarbush Antique Car Show.**

December: **Christmas celebrations** throughout the Valley.

BARRE/MONTPELIER AREA

Any attempt to understand the character of Vermont entails a visit to Montpelier: a stroll through the Vermont Historical Society Museum and into the ornate but informal State House built of Vermont granite and marble. Good food and pleasant shopping are nearby on State and Main Streets.

An exit on I-89, Montpelier is also at the hub of old roads radiating off into the hills, including Route 2, which runs all the way to Bangor, Maine, and Route 302 to Portland, which begins here as central Vermont's big commercial strip, "the Barre–Montpelier Road."

Billed as "the granite capital of the world," Barre continues to quarry, cut, and sculpt its high-quality gray granite, now used primarily for tombstones. The big attraction is the Rock of Ages Quarry in Graniteville, southeast of town, but Barre's Main Street has plenty to offer and its two cemeteries showcase the work—ranging from quirky to spectacular—of generations of Barre sculptors. The newly opened Vermont History Center (headquarters for the Vermont Historical Society), the recently restored old Labor Hall, and the Barre Opera House, one of Vermont's most beautiful and liveliest theaters, are all right downtown.

Southwest of Montpelier is the proud old town of Northfield, home of Norwich University and of no fewer than five covered bridges. East Barre and East Montpelier are both rural villages. Head either northeast on Route 2 or southeast or Route 302 to quickly find yourself in little-touristed farm country and forest.

GUIDANCE **A Vermont Information Center** (802-828-5981), 134 State Street, Montpelier, is open 10–6 weekdays. Housed in a red-clapboard house across the street from the capitol, it has knowledgeable, friendly staff and a restroom.

In downtown **Barre** the Old Pinsly Depot, just off Main Street, is now a combination welcome center and showcase for the evolving Granite Museum (802-476-4605). Open Monday through Friday 10–4, Saturday 10–1. It offers restrooms, area information, and exhibits.

Central Vermont Chamber of Commerce (1-877-887-3678; www.central-vt.com) publishes a helpful booklet guide to the area and keeps track of member

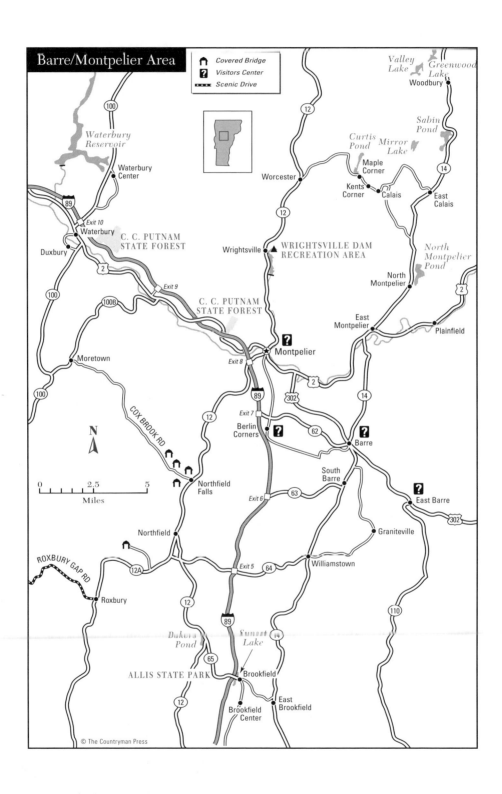

Barre/Montpelier Area

Covered Bridge
Visitors Center
Scenic Drive

Valley Lake
Greenwood Lake
Woodbury

Waterbury Reservoir

100

Waterbury Center

Sabin Pond

12

Curtis Pond
Mirror Lake

Maple Corner

14

Worcester

Kents Corner
Calais
East Calais

89

Exit 10
Waterbury

C. C. PUTNAM STATE FOREST

12

Wrightsville
WRIGHTSVILLE DAM RECREATION AREA

North Montpelier Pond

Duxbury

2

Exit 9

North Montpelier

100

C. C. PUTNAM STATE FOREST

2

100B

East Montpelier
Plainfield

Moretown

Montpelier

Exit 8

100

2

Exit 7

302

14

COX BROOK RD

12

Berlin Corners

62

Barre

N

South Barre

0   2.5   5
Miles

Northfield Falls

63

Graniteville

East Barre

302

Northfield

Exit 6

ROXBURY GAP RD

12A

Exit 5

64

Williamstown

Roxbury

12

110

89

Dakota Pond

Sunset Lake

14

65

ALLIS STATE PARK

Brookfield

12

Brookfield Center

East Brookfield

© The Countryman Press

vacancies during foliage season. Its walk-in info center is at 33 Stewart Road, Berlin Corners. (Off I-89 exit 7, take your first left; it's 0.5 mile on your left at the first four-corners.) Open weekdays 9–5.

GETTING THERE *By bus:* **Vermont Transit** (1-800-451-3292) from Boston to Montreal, connecting with New York and Connecticut service, stops in Montpelier at a disgraceful trailer off State Street.

By train: **Amtrak** (1-800-USA-RAIL; www.amtrak.com) stops in Montpelier Junction, a mile west of town on the other side of I-89.

By car: For **Montpelier** take I-89, exit 8. At the second traffic light, make a left, crossing the river on Bailey Avenue. At the light, turn right onto State Street. The red-clapboard building that houses the information center (see *Guidance*) is on your right, a good place to park. The capitol and Vermont Historical Society are a short way up across the street.

To reach **Barre** take I-89 to exit 7 and follow signs for Route 62, a divided highway to Main Street.

WHEN TO GO This is a rare corner of Vermont that varies little from season to season. Come January through April to see the Vermont Legislature in action.

MEDICAL EMERGENCY Emergency service is available by calling **911.**

Central Vermont Medical Center (802-229-9121) is in Berlin off Route 62; exit 7 off I-89.

✳ Towns

Montpelier. The smallest and possibly the most livable of the nation's state capitals, Montpelier is a town of fewer than 9,000 people, with band concerts on summer Wednesdays, high school playing fields just a few blocks from the capitol. The gold dome of the State House itself is appropriately crowned by a green hill rising steeply behind it. A path leads right up that hill into **Hubbard Park,** more than 110 leafy acres with windy roads, good for biking and jogging. The Stone Cutters Way down along the Winooski River is also a pleasant

IN MONTPELIER

Kim Grant

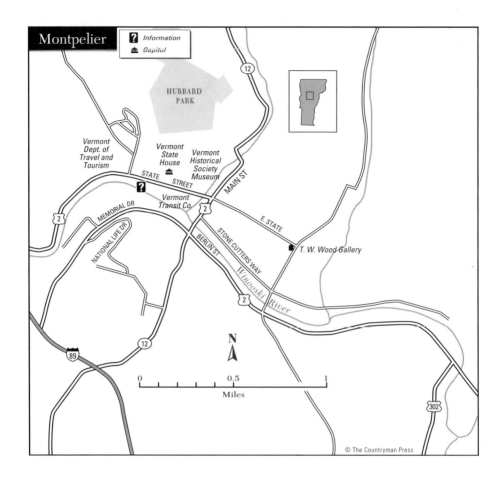

bike or jog. The State House, the Vermont Historical Society Museum, and the T. W. Wood Art Gallery are all must-see sights. Montpelier, moreover, is home base for the **New England Culinary Institute (NECI),** currently enrolling some 650 students and staffing three of the town's outstanding restaurants.

Precisely why this narrow floodplain of the Winooski was selected as Vermont's statehouse site in 1805 is uncertain, as is why it was named for a small city in the Languedoc region of France. The fact is, however, that Vermont's first legislators picked a town noted for its unusual number of whiskey distilleries and named it for a town best known for its wine and brandy. It's also true that Montpelier is unusually accessible, by roads both old and new, from every corner of central and northern Vermont.

Barre. This is a city of 9,300 people, surrounded by a town of 7,600. Motorists caught in Main Street's perpetual traffic may ponder the facades of the commercial buildings. Most date from 1880–1910, during which the community's population jumped from 2,000 to 12,000, swollen by stonecutters and craftsmen from Scotland, Eastern Europe, Italy, and French Canada, not to mention England,

Scandinavia, Spain, Germany, and the Middle East. This volatile mix of largely underpaid workers who elected a socialist mayor were not afraid to strike for their rights or to shelter victims of strikes elsewhere. In the World War I era, many famous anarchists and socialists spoke here. The **Old Labor Hall** (vintage 1900) on Granite Street (off North Main), the focal point of this struggle, has been restored and can be rented or toured (phone: 802-476-0567). The quarries continue to employ some 2,000 people to produce one-third of the country's memorial stones—for which **Hope Cemetery** and **Elmwood Cemetery** serve as museums. A formal **Vermont Granite Museum** (www.granitemuseum.com) is taking shape in a former granite shed on the Barre–Montpelier Road; in the meantime there are exhibits to see in the downtown visitors center in the former depot.

The quarries themselves are southeast of town, primarily in Graniteville, where Millstone Hill has been chipped and chiseled since 1812, when the bedrock was turned into millstones, door stoops, and posts. In the 1830s huge slabs were hauled by oxen to build the State House, but it was only after the Civil War that the railway and a series of inventions enabled Barre to make its mark. The memorial stone business escalated after 1888, when the branch railroad finally linked the quarries to finishing sheds in the valley and to outlets beyond. All but one of the major quarries are owned by Rock of Ages. This company has long made its operations a showcase for visitors, who can view the unforgettable, surrealistic landscape of the quarries themselves, hear the roar of the drills, and watch ant-sized men chip away at the giant pits.

Northfield (population: 5,790). This town's mid-19th-century commercial blocks suggest the prosperity that it enjoyed while native son Charles Paine served as governor. Paine actually railroaded the Vermont Central through his hometown instead of the more logical Barre. The old depot, now a bank, stands at one end of the handsome common. Today the town's pride is Norwich University, a private, coed college of 1,000 cadets, which bills itself as "the oldest private military college in the United States." In the Norwich University Museum in White Memorial Chapel, you learn that this institution sent more than 300 officers into the Civil War. It wasn't until 1867, however, that the college moved to Northfield from its original site in Norwich. More Northfield memorabilia as well as changing exhibits can be seen in the **Northfield Historical Society Museum** housed in the Old Red Brick Schoolhouse, Stagecoach Road (open March through December, Sunday through Wednesday 1–3).

✳ To See

In Montpelier
✍ **The Vermont Historical Society Museum** (802-828-2291; www.vermont history.org), 109 State Street, Montpelier. Open Tuesday through Saturday year-round 10–4; Sunday from May through October only, noon–4; closed Monday. $5 adult; $3 children 6–17, students with ID cards, and seniors. This outstanding state museum, maintained by the Vermont Historical Society on the ground floor of the replica of the Pavilion Hotel (which occupied this site between 1870 and 1966), has recently reopened after a total renovation. *Freedom & Unity: One*

Vermont State House (802-828-2228), State Street, Montpelier. Open Monday through Friday 8:45–4:15, closed holidays. Friends of the Vermont State House offers tours Monday through Friday 10–3:30, Saturday 11–2:30, July through mid-October, otherwise open for self-guided tours. Visitors are welcome to watch the legislature in action, January through mid-April.

In 1805, when Montpelier was chosen as the "permanent seat of the legislature for holding all their sessions," it was on the condition that the town give land for the capitol and get it built by 1808. The resulting three-story building was nine-sided, with a cupola, and warmed by a two-story stove. Legislators sat on plank seats at pine desks that were said to have been "whittled out of use" by the representatives' jackknives. The whole building had to be demolished in 1836 and was replaced by a granite Grecian temple designed by the Federal-era architect Ammi Young. After it was virtually destroyed by fire, it was rebuilt along the same but larger lines and completed in 1857.

While several chambers are quite opulent, there is noticeable informality in the way the 150 state representatives and senators talk with their constituents while standing in the Hall of Flags or seated on the black walnut sofas (which cost $60 apiece in 1859) at either end. The statue of Ethan Allen on the steps is Danby marble, and the handsome black-and-white floor of the lobby was quar-

ried on Isle La Motte. The lobby is lined with portraits of Vermont-born heroes including Admiral George Dewey, Admiral Charles Clark (like Dewey, a hero of the Spanish-American War), and Calvin Coolidge, 30th president of the United States. Note especially the enormous oil painting by Julian Scott, *The Battle of Cedar Creek, 1864*. The cannon on the front steps was captured from the Hessians at the battle of Bennington in 1777. The Roman lady atop the gold-leafed dome is Ceres, goddess of agriculture.

THE GOLD DOME OF THE VERMONT STATE HOUSE   Kim Grant

Ideal Many Stories, the new permanent exhibition, tells the story of Vermonters from the year 1600 to the present time. ("Freedom in Unity" is the state motto.) Beginning with Vermont's geological history, it then dramatizes Abenaki Indian life; draws visitors into Bennington's Catamount Tavern to explore the state's beginnings; and explores life in the 19th century through interactive exhibits and re-created buildings: a general store, creamery, marble shed, train station, and more. The story includes tourism (1900–1940s), World War II, the changing landscapes of the late 19th century, and a "hall of voices."

Christina Tree

THE VERMONT HISTORICAL
SOCIETY MUSEUM IN MONTPELIER

T. W. Wood Art Gallery and Arts Center (802-828-8743) at Vermont College (now a part of Norwich University), College Street (corner of East State Street), Montpelier, open Tuesday through Sunday noon–4. The gallery displays Civil War–era art by local artist Thomas Waterman Wood and mounts excellent shows on contemporary Vermont artists and craftspeople. Token admission.

In Barre
Rock of Ages Visitors Center (802-476-3119; www.rockofages.com), 560 Main Street, Graniteville. The easiest way to get there, even from Montpelier, is via I-89 exit 6 to Route 63. At the light go straight and follow signs. From the observation deck of the Manufacturing Division (open year-round, except holidays and associated days, Monday through Friday 8–3:30), you'll see the granite being polished and sculpted by master sculptors. The adjacent new visitors center is open May through October, Monday through Saturday 8:30–5 and Sunday noon–5 (closed July 4), with many displays and interactive exhibits. From June through mid-October there's also a narrated shuttle tour to a working, 50-acre, 600-foot-deep quarry farther up the hill.

SCULPTOR AT THE ROCK OF AGES

Vermont History Center (802-479-8500; www.vermonthistory.org), 60 Washington Street, Barre. Open weekday office hours. Housed in the splendid Spaulding School, designed in 1891 by Lambert Packard—the architect of St. Johnsbury's Fairbanks Museum—the Vermont Historical Society headquarters includes a gallery with changing exhibits.

Hope Cemetery, Route 14 just north of downtown Barre. If you're coming in off I-89 on Route 62, continue straight ahead up Maple Street (Route 14); if on North Main Street (Route 302), turn up Maple. The impressive main gates are a way up on your left; you can drive in. The 6,000 memorials here range from classic tableaux to a half-scale racing car, all sculpted by stonecutters for themselves and their families and among the most elaborate to be found anywhere in the world. **Elmwood Cemetery,** at the opposite end of downtown (Route 302 turns into Washington Street as it heads east; take Hill Street at the first Y and it's right there), also has many striking memorials. Tours of Barre cemeteries can be arranged through the Old Labor Hall (802-476-0567).

COVERED BRIDGES

In Northfield
Off Route 12 in Northfield Falls (turn at the general store) stand three covered bridges: the **Station Bridge,** spanning 100 feet, and the **Newell Bridge** are within sight of each other; farther along Cox Brook Road is the **Upper Bridge,** with a span of 42 feet. Another bridge is just south off Route 12 on Slaughter House Road.

SCENIC DRIVES Roxbury to Warren. The road through Roxbury Gap, while not recommended in winter, is spectacular in summer and fall, commanding a breathtaking view of the Green Mountains from the crest of the Roxbury Range. Do not resist the urge to stop, get out, and enjoy this panorama. Ask locally about the hiking trail that follows the ridgeline from the road's highest point.

Northfield to Moretown. The Cox Brook Road (marked on our map) connects Northfield Falls with the village of Moretown. It's dirt part of the way, offering views in both directions near the crest and passing through three covered bridges at the Northfield Falls end. In Northfield Turkey Hill Road begins across from Depot Square and climbs up to panoramic views.

VERMONT'S COAT OF ARMS
Vermont History Center

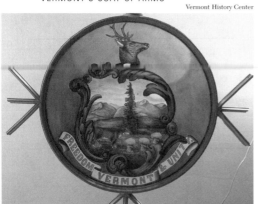

✳ To Do

BIKING Check out the Central Vermont Chamber of Commerce web site (www.central-vt.com) for suggested routes through this area. **Onion River Sports** (802-229-9409; www.onionriver.com), 20 Langdon Street, Montpelier, is the source of local bike maps and rentals (mountain bikes and hybrids).

BOATING AND FISHING Wrightsville Dam, just north of Montpelier; **North Montpelier Pond,** with a fishing access off Route 14; and **Curtis Pond** and **Mirror Lake** in Calais (pronounced *Callus*). **Nelson Pond** and **Sabin Pond** in Woodbury are both accessible from Route 14, as are **Valley Lake** and **Greenwood Lake** (good for bass and pike). The **Stevens Branch** south of Barre offers brook trout.

✍ **East Roxbury Fish Hatchery,** 2 miles south of Roxbury on Route 12A. This is a state hatchery in which salmon species are raised; children are allowed to feed the fish.

Reel Vermont (802-223-1869; www.reelvt.com), at the waterfall on Curtis Pond in Calais, offers canoe and kayak rentals and guided fishing trips.

GOLF Montpelier Elks Country Club (802-223-7457), Country Club Road, Montpelier, nine holes. **Barre Country Club** (802-476-7658), Plainfield Road, Barre, 18 holes. **Northfield Country Club** (485-4515), Roxbury Road, Northfield, nine holes.

HIKING/WALKING *Guidance:* **The Green Mountain Club** (802-244-7037), RR 1, Box 650, Route 100, Waterbury Center 05677. Encourages general inquiries and trail description updates (see *Hiking and Walking* in "What's Where").

Spruce Mountain, Plainfield. An unusually undeveloped state holding of 500 acres, rich in bird life. The trail begins in Jones State Forest, 4.2 miles south of the village; the 3-hour hike is described in *50 Hikes in Vermont* (Backcountry Guides) and in *Day Hiker's Guide to Vermont* (Green Mountain Club).

Worcester Range, north of Montpelier. There are several popular hikes described in the books listed under Spruce Mountain (above), notably **Elmore Mountain** in Elmore State Park (a 3-mile trek yielding a panorama of lakes, farms, and rolling hills; see "Stowe and Waterbury"), **Mount Worcester** (approached from the village of Worcester), and **Mount Hunger.**

Groton State Forest, east of Montpelier. This 25,000-acre forest offers an extensive year-round trail system. See "St. Johnsbury, Craftsbury, and Burke Mountain."

Hubbard Park and **North Branch River Park** in Montpelier are both accessible from the Vermont Institute of Natural Science (VINS) North Branch Nature Center (802-229-6206; www.vinsweb.org), 713 Elm Street (Route 12 north). Hubbard Park, also accessible from the State House, is 200 acres webbed with trails and a stone observation tower; North Branch offers gentle trails along this branch of the Winooski as well as more challenging, higher-altitude trails. Both parks are used for cross-country skiing and snowshoeing. The nature center offers a full program of birding and other events.

HORSEBACK RIDING Autumn Harvest Inn (802-433-1355), Williamstown (2 miles off I-89, exit 5). Trail rides.

SWIMMING Wrightsville Dam Recreation Area, Route 12 north; also numerous swimming holes in the Kents Corner area.

CROSS-COUNTRY SKIING Morse Farm Ski Touring Center (802-223-2740; 1-800-242-2740; www.morsefarm.com), 1168 County Road, Montpelier (3 miles from downtown). Open 9–4 daily, 8–4 Sunday and holidays. At an elevation of 1,200 feet, the farm offers a series of loops ranging from 0.7 to 3.9 km. Rentals, lessons, and a warming hut with snacks, soups, and hot drinks by the woodstove. Separate snowshoe trails. $9.50 for up to 4 hours, $12 all day, less for snowshoers. **Onion River Sports** (802-229-9409; www.onionriversports.com), 20 Langdon Street, Montpelier, rents cross-country skis and snowshoes.

Note: For more on winter sports, see "Sugarbush/Mad River Valley."

✳ Lodging

In Montpelier 05602
The Inn at Montpelier (802-223-2727; www.innatmontpelier.com), 147 Main Street. Two stately, adjacent Federal houses have been renovated and luxuriously furnished. Amenities include central air-conditioning, downstairs guest pantries for coffee and tea at any hour, in-room cable TV, and phone. A marvelous Colonial Revival veranda wraps around the brick Lamb-Langdon house. Of the 19 rooms, the deluxe chambers with fireplace ($172–194) are the handsomest rooms in town. The smaller king-, queen-, and twin-bedded rooms ($109–136, more in foliage season) are also lovely; all come with private bath and continental breakfast. Your hosts are Rita and Rick Rizza.

Capitol Plaza (802-223-5252; 1-800-274-5252; www.capitolplaza.com), 100 State Street. The former landmark tavern, a four-story downtown hotel with room service, a two-tiered café, and **J. Morgans,** a steak house featuring Sunday brunch, jazz nights, and weekend entertainment as well as conference and reception facilities. The 53 rooms vary from the standard motel models to individually decorated "colonial guest rooms" to one-bedroom suites. From $104 for a standard double to $189 for a suite (higher in foliage season).

✎ **Betsy's Bed & Breakfast** (802-229-0466; www.betsysbnb.com), 74 East State Street. Betsy and Jon Anderson are warm, helpful hosts who offer 12 attractive rooms and suites in adjacent Queen Anne and Victorian houses and a carriage house in a quiet hillside neighborhood, a short walk from the middle of town. Rooms have private bath, cable TV, air-conditioning, and phone (with voice mail and data ports); five suites have full kitchen. $65–85 in low season, $85–105 in high ($10 more in foliage season), includes a generous breakfast. Discounts for 3 nights or more.

Comfort Inn at Maplewood (802-229-2222; 1-800-228-5150), RR 4, Box 2110 (take exit 7 off I 80 for 0.2 mile). This handsome and relatively new motor inn has 89 rooms, 18 two-room suites with kitchenette, and a VIP suite with kitchenette and whirlpool. Rates from $90 double, $130 for suites in summer (more during foliage season), with continental breakfast.

Beyond

🕊 **The Northfield Inn** (802-485-8558; www.thenorthfieldinn.com), 228 Highland Avenue, Northfield 05663. Aglaia Stalb has renovated a grand old 1902 hillside mansion, nicely landscaped with a gazebo overlooking the town. Aglaia is a motherly, hospitable host who worries that her guests are well fed and oriented to her handsome town and its scenic surroundings (which include five covered bridges). There are 12 big, old-fashioned guest rooms, 9 with private bath (several combine into family suites), furnished with antiques, brass or carved-wood beds, and European feather bedding. It's delightfully easy to get lost in this rambling old house with its scattered common spaces, including a library, parlor, game room, and comfy third-floor TV room (in which we watched a memorable Red Sox loss to the Yankees). $95–179 (for a suite), including a three-course breakfast and snacks throughout the day.

🕊 🐾 ♿ **The Autumn Harvest Inn & Restaurant** (802-433-1355; www.autumnharvestinn.com), Clark Road, Williamstown 05679, Route 64 east from exit 5 off I-89. This century-old hilltop farm has splendid views and 46 acres now geared to raising and boarding horses (trail rides are available to guests); in winter trails are used by cross-country skiers and snowmobilers (they connect to VAST trails). Carolyn White offers 18 plain but bright and cheerful guest rooms with private bath and TV, including one that's handicapped equipped and two semisuites, one with a fireplace. There's a big fireplace in the living room, and two dining rooms are open to the public (see *Dining Out*).

Guests enjoy the swimming pond, two night-lit tennis courts, and sleigh rides. Rates $99–159 EP in summer, $69–139 in winter.

🕊 **Maplecroft Bed & Breakfast** (802-476-0760; www.maplecroftvermont.com), 70 Washington Street, Barre 05641. Convenient for anyone researching Vermont history or genealogy next door at the new Vermont History Center (originally a rather grand high school), this striking Victorian house is on Route 302 just above downtown and the small city park. Built by a granite sculptor in 1887, it is now home to local librarians Paul Heler, who also happens to be a magician, and Marianne Kotch. They offer four guest rooms, all with private bath and with beds featuring quilts made by Marianne (quilters, librarians, and magicians get a 10 percent discount). Needless to say there are plenty of good books around, as well as comfortable seating to read in the living room with its gas fireplace. $80 includes a continental breakfast with homemade jams and scones or popovers.

🕊 **Marshfield Inn & Motel** (802-426-3383), 5630 Route 2, Marshfield. Open April through November. John and Jean Krajewski's big Victorian, flat-roofed farmhouse is set back and above Route 2 and forms the centerpiece of this friendly complex. Lodging is in the 10 neighboring motel units with queen or two double beds. A nominally priced breakfast (there's a full menu) is served in the main house. Halfway between Montpelier and St. Johnsbury, it's a good hub from which to explore in many directions, and there's a path back through the extensive property. $60 double in summer, $90 in foliage season.

✓ **Hollister Hill Farm B&B** (802-454-7725; www.hollisterhillfarm.com), 2193 Hollister Hill Road, Marshfield 05658. Technically in Marshfield but less than 2 miles uphill from Plainfield Village, this is a splendid 1820s farmhouse set in 204 acres with three guest rooms, all with private bath. Bob and Lee Light fled New Jersey for Vermont in 1972 and milked cows for 25 years, eventually replacing them with beefalo, pigs, chickens, and turkeys, all of which they sell from the farm store in the barn, along with honey from their hives and their own maple syrup. One guest room has a red cedar sauna; the other two have fireplace (one can be a family suite by adding an adjoining room). In winter guests are invited to bring cross-country skis, and they will find snowshoes here; VAST trails also run through the property. $90–100 includes a full, homegrown and -hatched as well as -homemade breakfast.

Pie-in-the-Sky Farm Bed & Breakfast and Retreat (802-426-3777; www.pieinsky.com), Dwinell Road, Marshfield 05658. This rambling Civil War–era farmhouse was home for a time to the Pie-in-Sky commune; it's since been a dairy farm and home for Jay Moore and Judy Sargent for many years. Three upstairs rooms can be rented as a suite, with or without living room and kitchen facilities, or as individual double and single rooms. There's common space, a guest kitchen with fridge and snacks, a sunroom with hot tub, and 120 acres with a beaver pond and a barn (the cows are gone, and guest horses are welcome), as well as access to VAST trails on the property. Groton State Forest with hiking trails and swimming is nearby. From $85 (for a double) to $150 (for the full six-room apartment).

✓ **Country Cottage B&B** (802-426-3655), 3314 Route 232, Marshfield 05658. Dan and Judy Lloyd, who used to run the Creamery Inn in Cabot, now own and operate this establishment in Marshfield near Groton State Forest. They have two guest rooms with private bath. Children welcome, but no pets, please. Rates range $75–85, including full breakfast.

✳ Where to Eat

DINING OUT **Chef's Table** (802-229-9202), 118 Main Street, Montpelier. Open Monday through Friday for lunch, Saturday for dinner only. Reservations requested for dinner. This is the Montpelier-based New England Culinary Institute's upscale restaurant. Lunch on duck confit with handmade fettuccine, or a warm blue crab leek tartlet. The dinner menu might include starters like pistachio-dusted pork porterhouse and lemon thyme braised osso buco. Entrées $15–22.

🍴 **Sarducci's** (802-223-0229), 3 Main Street, Montpelier. Open Monday through Saturday 11:30 AM–midnight; Sunday 4–midnight. Reserve. Above-average Italian dishes blossom in this very popular, spacious, columned, yellow-walled restaurant with an open wood-fired oven. Request a table overlooking the river. Many daily specials, antipasti, customized pizzas, salads, and 18 pasta choices, including shrimp with angelhair, tomatoes, and garlic. At dinner we can recommend the saltimbocca (sautéed veal with prosciutto and fresh sage in a portobello mushroom sauce, served with risotto). Entrées come with a "mista salad" and are surprisingly reasonable, given both the quality and atmosphere: $10.95–15.95.

Conoscenti (802-262-3500), 52 State Street, Montpelier. Open Monday through Thursday 5–10, Friday until 11. Billed as creative cosmopolitan cuisine with Italian roots, chef-owner Dale Conoscenti's trendy trattoria features gleaming wood, white tablecloths, and family portraits on the walls. Everything is made from scratch (even the ice cream) and, while the menu changes frequently, it might include hand-rolled gnocchi, timballo (Italian potpie), and lobster ravioli with layers of wilted spinach, lobster, squash puree, and a drizzle of truffle oil. Entrées $19.95 (for spaghetti and meatballs) to $29.95 for grilled Black Angus rib eye.

The Autumn Harvest Inn & Restaurant (802-433-1355), Route 64, Williamstown. The superb views from the main dining room and wraparound porch complement dinners here Tuesday through Saturday. Begin with baked stuffed mushrooms or crabcakes with honey mustard sauce, and follow with honey Dijon chicken or duck with cranberry Armagnac glaze. $11.75–17.50.

Sean and Nora's (802-476-SEAN), 276 North Main Street, Barre. Monday through Thursday 11:15–9, Friday and Saturday 11:15–11, Sunday 4–8:30. This newcomer to Barre is about "food from America's neighborhoods," which includes staples like turkey, house-smoked Memphis ribs, and North End three-cheese manicotti. Dinner entrées $10.95–16.95.

Also see **Ariel's Restaurant** in Brookfield in "The White River Valleys."

In Montpelier
The Main Street Bar and Grill (802-223-3188), 118 Main Street. Open for breakfast, lunch, and dinner daily, as well as Sunday brunch. Montpelier-based New England Culinary Institute's signature eatery, a multilevel restaurant and pub with seasonal outdoor seating and a viewing window into the kitchen. Lunch on poached pear and Stilton salad with ginger bisque, or sausage and mussel stew. At dinner begin with a warm beef short rib terrine, and then choose between New England leg of venison and pan-seared rainbow trout. Entrées average $16.

The Mountain Café (802-223-0888), 7 Langdon Street. Open Monday through Saturday for lunch 11–3, dinner Saturday night until 9, Sunday brunch 10–3. Tucked away at the end of Langdon (off Main), this is some of the best food to be found in central Vermont. Don't be discouraged if you have to wait a few minutes in line to place your order. Grab a menu and study the many possibilities. An avocado salad with goat cheese, walnuts, ripe tomatoes, shredded red cabbage, carrots, and beef on greens, served with fabulous bread, was one of the best lunches we have had—a sentiment echoed by folks at the adjoining table who had ordered entirely different things, one a soba noodle dish and the other a fresh salmon panini. The most expensive lunch item is $6.95. Choose from many smoothies and teas.

✷ **Julio's** (802-229-9348), 54 State Street. Open Monday through Saturday for lunch and dinner, opening at 4 on Sunday. A colorful Mexican restaurant that doesn't pretend to be the ultimate in authenticity but fills the bill as a pleasant downtown eatery, good for a grilled eggplant sandwich as well as a taco salad, for a hearty bowl of mussels or goat cheese enchiladas. There's a kids' menu and sidewalk dining, weather permitting. Fully licensed.

La Brioche Bakery & Cafe (802-229-0443), 89 Main Street. Open daily, 6:30 AM–7 PM weekdays, Saturday 8–5:30, Sunday 8–5. The source of pastries and bread for all New England Culinary Institute Montpelier restaurants. Eat in the dining room or on the patio or take out breakfast and sandwiches.

Coffee Corner, corner of Main and State. Open 6–3. A great little diner that's been here forever and specializes in fresh produce, fresh-baked bread, booths, and fast, friendly service.

Hunger Mountain Food Co-op (802-223-8004), 623 Stone Cutters Way. Open 8–7:30. Hidden away in a corner of this supermarket-style cooperative is an expanded deli with many vegetarian choices and a very attractive glass-sided café area overlooking the river.

Capitol Grounds (802-223-8411), 45 State Street. An inviting coffeehouse filled with the aroma of roasting coffees and comfortable corners in which to sip them. Inquire about jazz, country, and blues nights.

On the Barre–Montpelier Road
❧ Wayside Restaurant and Bakery (802-223-6611), Barre–Montpelier Road (Route 302). Open daily 6:30 AM–9:30 PM. Vermont's ultimate family restaurant, featuring "home cooking away from home." Breakfast on corned beef hash and eggs (that comes with homefries and toast), sausage gravy on a biscuit, or baked oatmeal. Lunch on the soup of the

day and maple cream pie, dine on pork liver and bacon or rib-eye steak. The children's menu is $2.95. Brian and Karen Zecchinelli offer over 200 menu items to choose from, plus at least four daily specials, and they're fully licensed.

In Barre
Del's (802-476-6684), 248 North Main Street. Open Monday through Saturday for lunch and dinner, Sunday from 4 PM. Sited across from the courthouse, this is a justly popular local gathering spot with a colorful decor and a suspiciously wide selection: pastas, Mexican dishes, pizza, subs. No complaints, however, about a great taco salad and fast, friendly service at lunch. Patrons vouch for the pasta. Pizza and subs are also available all evening.

All Fired Up (802-476-2036), 9 Depot Square. Just off Main Street. Open daily 11–9. Not much atmosphere but good pizza, baked in an imported Italian wood oven. Also soups like Tuscan sausage and rice; "sandwich tarts" like sausage, caramelized onion, and mozzarella; and fresh ravioli.

The Farmer's Diner (802-476-6292), 240 North Main. Open Sunday through Wednesday 7–3; Thursday through Saturday until 8. A diner with a difference. The menu is basic soups and sandwiches, meat loaf and roast beef with gravy, with breakfast served all day, but the difference is where it comes from: Roughly two-thirds of everything on the menu is from area farms, and as much as possible is organic. Owner Tod Murphy has established a small meat-processing plant at which he also smokes and cures ham and bacon (from locally raised pigs), and he has developed his own system for collecting milk, produce, and more. Murphy hopes to establish a nationwide franchise of similar diners serving locally grown and processed fare. The menu, incidentally, includes a vegetarian Reuben, as well as scrambled tofu with home fries and veggie links.

In Plainfield
River Run Restaurant (802-454-1246; www.riverrunsoul.com), 53 Main Street (off Route 2). Open Wednesday through Sunday 7–3, Friday and Saturday 5–9. Jimmy and Maya Kennedy dish up soul food to crave for: biscuits and sausage, grits and jalapeños as well as pancakes for breakfast, fried catfish and BBQ ribs, jambalaya and meat loaf for lunch, and some BBQ at dinner along with "fancy southern" items like roast duck, pork tenderloin, and pan-seared scallops and shrimp. BYOB. Sunday brunch is big.

In Marshfield
Rainbow Sweets (802-426-3531), Route 2. Closed Tuesday, otherwise open weekdays 9–6, Friday and Saturday 9–9, Sunday 9–3. Bill Tecosky and Patricia Halloran's colorful café has been a destination in its own right for going on 30 years. Stop by in the morning for a plain brioche and espresso or lunch a little later on a brioche filled with warm spinach and walnuts; dine on Moroccan-style shredded chicken in phyllo or real pizza. Come anytime for a St. Honore (a profiterole filled with custard, dipped in caramel with cream on puff pastry) or to pick up some butter cookies.

In Northfield
Pioneer Restaurant (802-485-5142), Route 12A. No pretense here, just a local restaurant serving baked haddock, fried steak, pasta with meatballs. Lots of food. Full liquor license.

Depot Square Pizzeria (802-485-5500), Depot Square. Open Tuesday through Thursday 11:30–8:30, Friday and Saturday until 11. Sunday hours vary with the season. A pleasant little restaurant with bentwood chairs, flowers on the tables, and a menu that includes reasonably priced Italian specialties as well as pizza.

✳ Entertainment

THEATER **Barre Opera House** (802-476-8188), corner of Prospect and Main Streets, Barre. Built in 1899, after fire destroyed its predecessor, this elegant, acoustically outstanding, recently restored 650-seat theater occupies the second and third floors of the city hall. The Barre Players, a community theater, perform spring through fall, and this is also a venue for year-round music, dance, and other theater productions.

Lost Nation Theater Company (802-229-0492; www.lostnationt heater.org), Montpelier City Hall Arts Center, 128 Elm Street, Montpelier. First-rate productions of contemporary plays, classics, and original works year-round by a professional troupe. The Summer Theater Series features five different shows, June through October, 5 nights a week.

FILM **Savoy** (802-229-0509), 26 Main Street, Montpelier, presents art and alternative films with two daily showings, occasional speakers, and special events.

The Capitol (802-229-0343), 93 State Street, Montpelier, and **The Paramount** (802-479-9621), 241 North Main Street, Barre, are both classic old movie houses showing first-run feature films.

✳ Selective Shopping

ARTS STUDIOS AND GALLERIES

The Artisans' Hand (802-229-9492; www.artisanshand.com), 229 Main Street at City Center, Montpelier. Open Monday through Saturday 10–5:30, Friday until 8, Sunday noon–4. An exceptional variety of quality Vermont craftwork by a cooperative of some 125 artisans in many media.

River Street Potters (802-224-7000). Some 20 individual potters share this studio producing stoneware and porcelain, whimsical and functional.

SPA (Studio Place Arts) (802-479-7069; www.studioplace.com), 201 North Main Street, Barre. This arts center offering classes for both adults and children maintains the Studio Place Arts Gallery.

Thistle Hill Pottery (802-223-8926; www.thistlehillpottery.com), Powder Horn Glen Road, in the hills north of Montpelier. Jennifer Boyd sells her handmade functional stone pottery: dinnerware, vases, lamps, and more; bargains, seconds. Her studio is near Morse Farm.

Black Thorn Forge (802-426-3369), 3821 Route 2, Marshfield (between Plainfield and Marshfield). Working in a red barn, Steve Bronstein makes functional and sculptural ironwork.

Tait Studio Pottery (802-426-3153), 1696 Route 2 (across from Rainbow Sweets), Marshfield. Open Wednesday through Friday 1–5, weekends 10–5. The attractive store features Trevor Tait's colorful stoneware.

Also see www.vermontcrafts.com. This area is particularly rich in studios that open to visitors over the Memorial Day weekend and may or may not be accessible on a regular basis. Worth checking.

BOOKSTORES ✐ **Bear Pond Books**
(802-229-0774), 77 Main Street, Montpelier. Open daily, until 9 on weekends. One of the state's most inviting bookstores, heavy on literature, art, and children's books; author readings.

Rivendell Books (802-223-3928), 100 Main Street, Montpelier. Primarily used with some new books, remainders, bargain-priced best sellers.

Barre Books (802-476-3114), 158 North Main Street, Barre. Open until 6, Friday until 9, a good array of general books.

Capitol Stationers (802-223-2393), 54 Main Street, Montpelier, includes new books, with a strong Vermont and New England section.

The Country Bookshop (802-454-0187; www.thecountrybookshop.com), 35 Mill Street (off Route 2 at the blinker), Plainfield. Open daily 10–5, Friday 10–7. Some 30,000 books, plus postcards and paper ephemera; Ben Koenig's specialties include folk music, folklore, and books on bells.

The Northfield Bookstore (802-458-4588), 67 Depot Square, Northfield. Open Tuesday through Friday 9–5:30, Saturday 9–3, Sunday 10–2. "Affable books and knowledgeable service" is the mission statement for this pleasant store stocking primarily used books with some best sellers, also cards, records, a children's section, and comfortable seating. Coffee, too.

FARMS **Morse Farm Maple Sugarworks**
(802-223-2740; www.morse farm.com), 1168 County Road (the

western extension of Main Street), Montpelier. Open year-round, daily except holidays. The farm has been in the same family for seven generations. The shop features its own syrup and maple products, including a "maple creemee" cone, and Vermont crafts and products. Come watch sugaring off in March. Sugar-on-snow. Also see *Cross-Country Skiing.*

Bragg Farm Sugarhouse & Gift Store (802-223-5757; 1-800-376-5757), Route 14, East Montpelier. Open daily, November through April 8:30–6, May through October 8:30–8. This is a fifth-generation farm, and syrup is still collected the traditional way (in 2,500 buckets) and boiled over wood fires. The shop carries a variety of maple and other Vermont crafts and specialty foods and includes a maple ice cream parlor.

Danforth's Sugarhouse (802-229-9536), Route 2, East Montpelier. Open year-round, Tuesday, Wednesday, and Friday 8–5, Saturday 8–noon. A fourth-generation sugaring operation and maple product gift shop.

Grandview Winery (802-456-7012; www.grandviewwinery.com), East Calais. Open late May through November with tastings at the Cold Hollow Cider Mill in Waterbury year-round. Off Route 14 south of the village, the tasting room at the farm is set in gardens, hung with works by Vermont artists. The wine is extensive, from rhubarb, dandelion, and blueberry to French grape blends; hard cider, too.

✿ **Knight's Spider Web Farm** (802-433-5568; www.spiderwebfarm.com), off Route 14 on Spider Web Road, Williamstown Village. Open daily 9–6; January through March by appointment. The weirdest farm you ever will see: Artists Will and Terry Knight began by preserving, painting, and mounting spiderwebs from their own barn, and now grow spiders that you can watch as they weave their webs and then buy the results, mounted on wood; gifts and pine accessories.

Also see Hollister Hill Farm under *Lodging.*

SPECIAL SHOPS Marshfield Village Store (802-426-3306), Route 2, Marshfield. This classic, pillared, double-porched general store has formed the center of Marshfield since 1852. It's presently run by three generations of the Bernek family and dedicated to the "If we don't have it, you don't need it" credo; also Vermont products (will ship) and great directions.

ANTIQUES East Barre Antique Mall (802-479-5190), 133 Mill Street, East Barre. Open daily 10–5. Closed Monday. In the middle of this one-street village sandwiched between Routes 302 and 110 is this big unlikely former department store, and it houses central Vermont's largest group shop: 350 dealers represented on three floors with plenty of furniture as well as dishes and glassware, one whole room of kitchenware. A former innkeeper, Bob Somaini prides himself on the tidiness and cleanliness as well as the size and depth of the store. He also prides himself on the spread he puts out for customers during his huge Super Bowl Sale (Super Bowl weekend).

Onion River Sports (802-229-9409), 20 Langdon Street, Montpelier. An outstanding sporting goods store specializing in camping, cross-country, and biking gear, with cross-country and bike rentals.

Woodbury Mountain Toys (802-223-4272), 24 Main Street, Montpelier. This independent specialty toy store carries major lines and some locally made items, many hard-to-find items.

Buch Spieler Music (802-229-0449; www.bsmusic.com), 27 Langdon Street, Montpelier. Open Monday through Thursday 10–6, Friday until 8, Saturday until 5, Sunday 11–4. An independent music store specializing in all kinds of music from around the word for all kinds of people, since 1973.

Green Mountain Hooked Rugs (802-223-1333; www.greenmountain hookedrugs.com), 146 Main Street, Montpelier. Open Wednesday through Sunday noon–5. Owned and operated by fourth- and fifth-generation rug makers. There are rugs for sale, but this is about rug-making supplies and classes.

✳ Special Events

Memorial Day weekend: **Open Studios weekend** throughout Vermont (www.vermontcrafts.com).

Early June: **Vermont Dairy Celebration,** State House lawn in Montpelier.

June–August: **Montpelier City Band Concerts,** State House lawn Wednesday at 4 PM.

July: **Montpelier's Independence Day Celebration,** sponsored by the **Onion River Arts Council** (802-229-9408) on the State House lawn, features performances and a giant fireworks display. **Barre Homecoming Days** (last weekend)—music, fireworks, street dance, art exhibit. **Vermont Quilt Festival,** a 3-day event on July's third full weekend, at Norwich University in Northfield (www.vqf.org)—New England's largest annual quilt event.

Labor Day weekend: In Northfield, a pageant, parade of floats, and Norwich cadets.

September: **Old Time Fiddlers' Contest,** Barre Auditorium, one of new England's oldest contests. The **Barre Granite Festival** (weekend after Labor Day) at the evolving Granite Museum (see *Guidance*) is the scene of rock splitting and cutting, a chicken barbecue, and more.

Early October: **Vermont Apple Celebration,** State House lawn, Montpelier.

Late October: **Festival of Vermont Crafts,** Montpelier High School (call Central Vermont Chamber of Commerce, 802-229-5711).

November: **Greater Barre Crafts Fair.**

December 31: **First Night** celebrations, Montpelier.

Lake Champlain Valley

Kim Grant

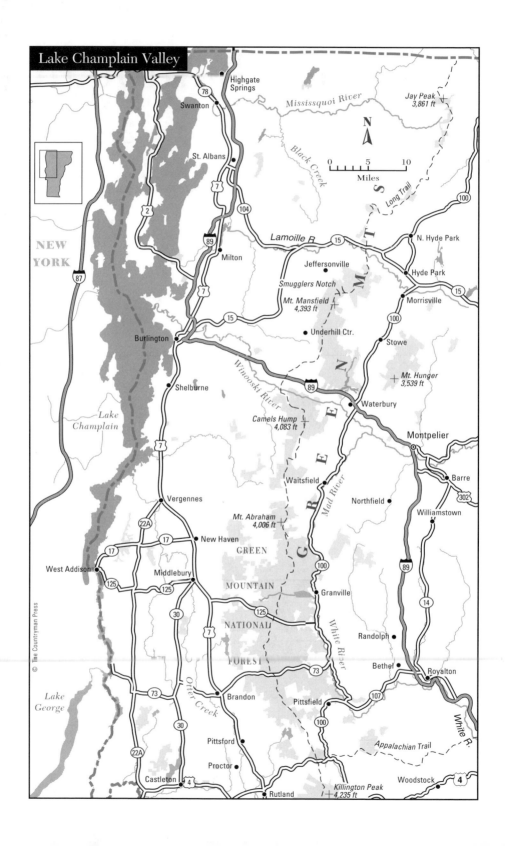

Lake Champlain Valley

RUTLAND AND THE LOWER CHAMPLAIN VALLEY

Rutland, now Vermont's fourth largest city, has been bypassed in recent years by the population growth in Chittenden County. However, the city remains more than just a convenient commercial adjunct to the Killington-Pico ski resorts. Stolid, early-Victorian mansions and streets crisscrossed with railroad tracks testify to its 19th-century prosperity—when Rutland was known as "the marble city"—and it has retained its industrial base.

Today city fathers are trying hard to reconstitute the downtown core, buoyed by the return of railroad passenger service. The daily *Rutland Herald,* the oldest newspaper in the state, continues to win frequent journalism awards, including a Pulitzer Prize in 2001.

The long-established shops along Merchants Row and Center Street have held their own in recent years and number upward of 100 within just a few square blocks; they include some genuinely interesting newcomers. This is, moreover, a good restaurant town.

Rutland is the business and shopping center for the Lower Champlain Valley, a broad, gently rolling corridor between New York State and the Green Mountains. In contrast to the rest of Vermont, this valley is actually broad enough to require two major north–south routes. Route 7 is the busier highway. It hugs the Green Mountains and, with the exception of the heavily trafficked strip around Rutland, is a scenic ride. Route 30 on the west is a far quieter way through farm country and by two major lakes, Lake Bomoseen and Lake St. Catherine, both popular summer meccas.

Route 4 is the major east–west road, a four-lane highway from Fair Haven, at the New York line, to Rutland, where it angles north through the middle of town before turning east again, heading uphill to Killington. Route 140 from Wallingford to Poultney is the other old east–west road here, a quiet enough byway through Middletown Springs, where the old mineral waters form the core of a pleasant park.

GUIDANCE **The Rutland Region Chamber of Commerce** (802-773-2747; 1-800-756-8880; www.rutlandvermont.com), 256 North Main Street, Rutland 05701; visitors center (802-775-0831) at the junction of Routes 7 and 4, open late May through mid-October. The chamber supplies an illustrated *Visitor's Guide.*

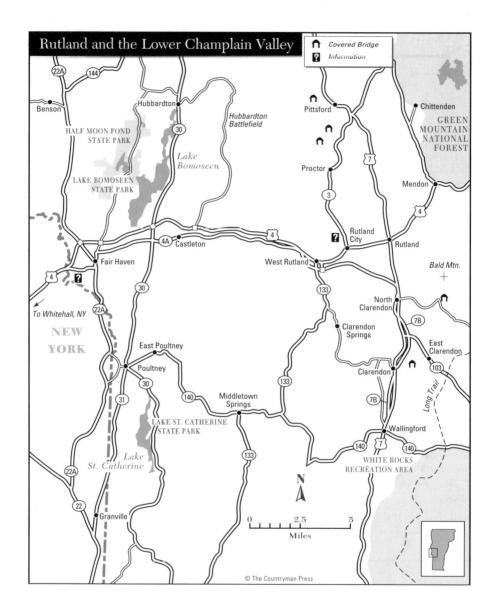

Rutland and the Lower Champlain Valley

Covered Bridge
Information

Benson
Hubbardton
Hubbardton Battlefield
Pittsford
Chittenden
GREEN MOUNTAIN NATIONAL FOREST
HALF MOON POND STATE PARK
30
Lake Bomoseen
Proctor
Mendon
LAKE BOMOSEEN STATE PARK
3
7
4A Castleton
4
Rutland City
Rutland
Fair Haven
West Rutland
Bald Mtn.
To Whitehall, NY
30
133
North Clarendon
7B
NEW YORK
East Poultney
Clarendon Springs
East Clarendon
103
Poultney
133
Clarendon
Long Trail
31
30
140
Middletown Springs
7B
LAKE ST. CATHERINE STATE PARK
133
Wallingford
Lake St. Catherine
140
7
140
22A
WHITE ROCKS RECREATION AREA
N
22
Granville
0   2.5   5
Miles

© The Countryman Press

The Fair Haven Welcome Center (802-265-4763) on Route 4 near the New York line is open every day 7 AM–9 PM.

Crossroads of Vermont (1-800-756-8880; www.vermontcrossroads.com) is the regional marketing organization.

Area chambers of commerce: **Poultney** (802-287-2010; www.poultney.com); **Brandon** (802-247-6401; www.brandon.org); **Killington** (802-773-4181; www.killingtonchamber.com).

GETTING THERE *By train:* **Amtrak** (1-800-USA-RAIL). Daily service to and from New York City on the Ethan Allen Express.

By air: **USAirways Express/Colgan Air** (1-800-272-5488; www.colganair.com). USAirways Express small planes offer daily connecting service to Boston's Logan International Airport.

By car: Routes 7 and 4; Route 103 from Bellows Falls.

By bus: **Vermont Transit,** from Albany, Boston, and other points.

GETTING AROUND *By bus:* **Marble Valley Regional Transit District** (802-773-3244), operator of "The Bus," connecting Killington, Castleton, the Rutland airport, and other points in the area.

MEDICAL EMERGENCY Emergency service is available by calling **911.**

Rutland Regional Medical Center Fast Track Emergency Service (802-747-3601), 160 Allen Street.

✳ Villages

Fair Haven, located where Routes 4, 4A, and 22A intersect, is at the core of Vermont's slate industry. One of its earliest developers in the 1780s was the controversial Matthew Lyon, who started an ironworks and published a newspaper called *The Scourge of Aristocracy,* in which he lambasted the Federalists. Elected to Congress in 1796, Lyon had scuffles on the floor of the House and criticized President Adams so vehemently that he was arrested and jailed under the Alien and Sedition Act. Lyon's case caused such a national uproar that this patently unconstitutional censorship law was soon rescinded. Lyon was reelected to Congress while still in jail and took his seat in time to cast the tie-breaking vote that made Thomas Jefferson president instead of Aaron Burr.

Around the spacious green are three Victorian mansions (two faced with marble) built by descendants of Ira Allen, founder of the University of Vermont.

Poultney, on Route 30, the home of Green Mountain College, also has significant journalistic associations: Horace Greeley, founder of the *New York Tribune,* lived at the venerable Eagle Tavern in East Poultney while he was learning the printing trade at the East Poultney *National Spectator* in the 1820s (and organizing a local temperance society). Working with him was George Jones, who helped found the *New York Times* in 1851.

East Poultney is a picturesque village worth detouring to see. The fine white Baptist church, built in 1805, is the centerpiece, standing on a small green surrounded by late-18th- and early-19th-century houses. The general store is also a classic and a source of good deli sandwiches. Its picnic benches are within earshot of the Poultney River, here a fast-flowing stream.

Castleton, at Routes 4A and 30, has triple historical significance: Ethan Allen and Seth Warner planned the capture of Ticonderoga here; on a nearby hill in Hubbardton, Colonel Warner's scrubby militiamen made a valiant rear-guard stand while halting the British invasion force on July 7, 1777, the only Revolutionary War battle actually fought on Vermont soil; and the town itself is a showcase of Greek Revival houses. One offshoot of the conspiratorial meeting in Remington's Tavern in 1775 was the exploit of the blacksmith Samuel Beach—

Vermont's own Paul Revere—who reputedly ran some 60 miles in 24 hours to recruit more men from the countryside for the raid on Ticonderoga.

After the Revolution, Castleton grew rapidly. Thomas Royal Dake, who arrived in about 1807, left his hallmark of design and workmanship on the pillared houses that line Main Street, including the **Ransom-Rehlen mansion,** with its 17 Ionic columns; and Dake's masterpiece, the Congregational Meeting House, now the **Federated Church,** with the lovely pulpit that Dake completed with his own funds. These heirloom houses are open for tours during Castleton's Colonial Days, usually held in late July. Between 1850 and 1870 the West Castleton Railroad and Slate Company was the largest marble plant in the country. During these years a large Welsh community grew up in the area. The town is also the site of Castleton College, part of the Vermont State College system, which has an active arts center.

Benson, west of Route 22A, 8 miles north of Fair Haven, is one of those tiny proverbial villages "that time forgot" except as a scenic photo op, but which in recent years has developed a creative personality with its artisans and special shops.

✳ To See

MUSEUMS Chaffee Center for the Visual Arts (802-775-0356; www.chaf feeartcenter.org), 16 South Main Street, Rutland. Closed Tuesday, otherwise open 10–5, noon–4 Sunday. One of the state's outstanding art galleries, representing 250 Vermont artists, in a former private house listed on the National Register of Historic Places. It has permanent and periodic exhibits and a youth gallery for school displays. Traditional and contemporary paintings, sculpture, crafts, graphics, and photography are included. Donation expected.

Vermont Marble Exhibit (802-459-2300; 1-800-427-1396; www.vermont-marble.com), Route 3 from West Rutland, Proctor. Open mid-May through mid-October, daily 9–5. Admission charge. The first commercial marble deposit was discovered and quarried in Vermont in 1784. The Vermont Marble Company, formed in 1870 when Redfield Proctor merged several quarries, has mined one of the state's principal resources. Marble from Proctor and Danby was used for the U.S. Supreme Court building, the Lincoln Memorial, and the Beinecke Library at Yale, among many other notable edifices. Proctor himself served as governor, U.S. senator, and secretary of war. Several other members of the Proctor family and chief executives of the company also filled the governor's chair, forming a political dynasty that lasted nearly a century. The company, run by the Swiss-based Pleuss-Staufer Industries since 1976, was closed down in 1991, but nearly 100,000 people still visit the marble exhibit every year, making it one of the biggest tourist attractions in New England. Featured are a special geological display, a film dramatizing the origins and uses of marble, a gallery of bas-reliefs of American presidents, a gift shop, **Dorothea's Cafe,** replicas of the *Pietà* and the *Last Supper,* a sculptor in residence, and a factory viewing site from which to watch the various stages of transformation from rough-cut blocks to polished slabs. The museum recently completed a walkway leading to the old Sutherland Falls Quarry.

Slate Valley Museum (518-642-1417; www.slatevalleymuseum.org), 17 Water Street, Granville, NY 12832. Open year-round, Tuesday, Thursday, and Friday 1–5, Saturday 10–4. Admission $2.50 per person; children 12 and under are free. Just across the New York border in the heart of the slate industry's historic base, on a site where immigrant quarry workers once lived in tenements, this 19th-century Dutch barn reflects the many colors and shapes of slate. It includes a quarry shanty, tools, a mural, paintings, photographs, family artifacts, and a gift shop.

The New England Maple Museum (802-483-9414; www.maplemuseum.com), Route 7 north of Pittsford. Open June through mid-October, daily 9–5. $2.50 admission; group rates. The museum has an attractive display of the history, production, and consumption of maple syrup, once called "sweet water," and its by-products. You can view the Danforth Collection of antique equipment, murals, and a 10-minute slide show, and there is a tasting area and gift shop. Mail-order service.

Norman Rockwell Museum (802-773-6095; www.normanrockwellvt.com), Route 4 east, Rutland. Open June through November, daily 9–5. Admission $4. The chronological displays of Rockwell's magazine covers, many ads, posters, portraits, and other published illustrations make this an interesting documentary of changing American graphic styles. Audiovisual self-guided tour. Gift shop.

CENTER STREET IN DOWNTOWN RUTLAND

Kim Grant

Rutland Historical Society (802-775-2006), 96 Center Street, Rutland. The distinctive, 1860 Nickwackett Fire Station serves as the society's home, open for public use Monday 6–9 PM, Saturday 1–4 PM, and by appointment.

The Carving Studio and Sculpture Center (802-438-2097; www.carving studio.org), P.O. Box 495, 636 Marble Street, West Rutland 05777. Open June through August, Monday, Wednesday, and Friday 10 AM–1 PM. The center offers 2-, 5-, and 7-day workshops in most sculpture disciplines. Participants and visitors alike are inspired by artists in residence, exhibitions, and the location among historic marble quarries in the Green Mountains. The Company Store offers gifts, tours, and refreshments.

HISTORIC SITES **The Hubbardton Battlefield** (802-759-2412; www.his toricvermont.org) is on Monument Road in East Hubbardton, 7 miles north of the posted Route 4 exit. A small, hilltop visitors center is open late May through early October, Wednesday through Sunday 9:30–5. Admission $2. Battle buffs won't want to miss the diorama and audiovisual display of this 1777 skirmish, detailing how a small force of Green Mountain Boys led by Colonel Seth Warner, together with a Massachusetts militia and a New Hampshire regiment, managed to defeat a far larger British contingent led by General Burgoyne.

Paul P. Harris Memorial, Route 7 south of Rutland, Wallingford. Paul Harris (1868–1947), who founded Rotary International while he was working in Chicago, went to school here in the small brick building on Main Street, where the local club still meets.

Wilson Castle (802-773-3284), Route 3 from West Rutland toward Proctor. This 32-room, 19th-century stone "château" on a 115-acre estate is furnished with elaborate European and Oriental pieces, stained glass, and a variety of wood paneling. Guided tours are given June through mid-October, daily 9–5. Admission $7.

COVERED BRIDGES There are six in the area: the 1836 **Kingsley** or **Mill River Bridge,** East Street, off Airport Road, East Clarendon; the 1880 **Brown Bridge,** off Cold River Road, Shrewsbury; the 1840 **Depot Bridge,** off Route 7 north, Pittsford; the 1849 **Cooley Bridge,** Elm Street, Pittsford; the 1843 **Gorham** or **Goodnough Bridge,** Gorham Bridge Road, off Route 3, Pittsford; and the 1830 **Twin Bridge,** East Pittsford Road, off Route 7 north, Rutland.

FISH HATCHERY **Pittsford National Fish Hatchery** (802-483-6618), Furnace Road, Pittsford. Open 8–4 daily. The Fish and Wildlife Service raises landlocked salmon and lake trout here.

✳ To Do

BIKING There's a lot of great bike riding in this area. The roads west and south of Rutland are little traveled and very scenic. Also, there are snack bars sprinkled throughout the area, which always helps. Rentals and route advice are available from the **Great Outdoors Trading Company** (802-775-9989) and from the **Sports Peddler** (802-775-0101) at 158 North Main Street, both in Rutland.

BOATING Boats can be rented from **Lake Bomoseen Marina** (802-265-4611; www.lakebomoseenmarina.com) and from **Duda Water Sports** (802-265-3432), also on Lake Bomoseen.

FISHING **Green Mountain Fishing Guide Service** (802-446-3375), 593 Route 140, Tinmouth. Fishing expeditions guided by Rod Start, a Vermonter with 25 years of fishing experience.

GOLF **The Rutland Country Club** (802-773-2354), a mile north of the business section on North Grove Street, Rutland. An 18-hole golf course on rolling terrain; restaurant.

Proctor-Pittsford Country Club (802-483-9379), Corn Hill Road, Pittsford. 18 holes, lounge, and restaurant.

Lake St. Catherine Country Club (802-287-4060), Route 30, south of Poultney. 18 holes, lounge, and restaurant.

The Prospect Bay Country Club (802-468-5581) in Castleton offers nine holes.

Stonehedge Golf (802-773-2666), Route 103 west, North Clarendon, is a nine-hole, par-3 public course.

Also see "Killington/Plymouth Area."

HIKING **White Rocks Recreation Area,** Route 140 off Route 7 in Wallingford. Follow signs from the White Rocks Picnic Area. The big feature here is a 2,600-foot, conical white peak surrounded by quartzite boulders that retain ice and snow into summer. We advise picking up a hiking guidebook (see *Hiking and Walking* in "What's Where") before starting out.

Delaware Hudson Rail Trail, Poultney–Castleton. A rail-trail enjoyed by hikers, walkers, bikers, equestrians, and cross-country skiers. A guide is available from the Department of Forest and Parks in Pittsford.

Helen W. Buckner Memorial Preserve (802-229-4425), West Haven. Hiking trails and nature exploration in this Nature Conservancy tract.

HORSEBACK RIDING ♬ **Pond Hill Ranch** (802-468-2449), Pond Hill Road, Castleton, offers trail rides and hayrides.

Also see Mountain Top Stables in "Killington/Plymouth Area."

HUNTING **Tinmouth Hunting Preserve** (802-446-2337), East Road, Wallingford, has 800 acres of varied cover where individual and group pheasant, partridge, and quail shoots can be arranged from September through March (except on Sunday). Five sporting-clay shooting areas have been added.

RODEOS **Pond Hill Ranch** (802-468-2449), Castleton. Saturday-night rodeos all summer long and into fall. Go into Castleton and follow the signs to Pond Hill.

SWIMMING **Elfin Lake Beach,** off Route 140 west, 2 miles southeast of Wallingford.

See also *Green Space.*

SKIING See "Killington/Plymouth Area."

SLEIGH RIDES **Cortina Inn** (802-773-3333), Route 4 east, Mendon. Wednesday, Saturday, and some holidays.

Pond Hill Ranch (802-468-2449), Castleton. One- to 3-hour rides.

FITNESS CENTERS **The Gymnasium** (802-773-5333), 30 Merchants Row, Rutland. A complete wellness and cardiovascular center, open Monday through Friday 6 AM–9 PM, Saturday and Sunday 7–7.

Green Mountain Rock Climbing Center (802-773-3343; www.vermontclimb ing.com), Route 4, Rutland. Open Monday through Friday noon–9, weekends 10–8. Adults $17, 12 and under $11. Anybody from age 2 on up can learn to rock climb on rock walls in this climate-controlled indoor setting. Prices include equipment and all-day use of the center; first-time belay lessons ($10) are available.

Vermont Sport & Fitness Center (802-775-9916), 40 Curtis Avenue, Rutland. Outdoor pool, indoor/outdoor tennis, racquetball, cardio equipment.

Vermont Martial Arts Academy (802-773-1373), 114 West Street, Rutland.

Mountain Yoga (802-773-5045), 135 Main Street, Rutland.

Fair Haven Fitness (802-265-3470), 8 Main Street, Fair Haven.

✳ Green Space

Lake Bomoseen, just north of Castleton, is a popular local summer colony. The lake gained notoriety in the 1930s because of Alexander Woollcott's summer retreat on Neshobe Island. The portly "Town Crier" entertained such cronies as Harpo Marx, who was known to repel curious interlopers by capering along the shore naked and painted blue.

Lake Bomoseen State Park (802-265-4242; 802-483-2314), Route 4 west of Rutland, exit 3, 5 miles north on Town Road. Its 60 campsites and five lean-tos are set in a lovely wildlife refuge; beach, picnic area, nature program, trails, boat ramp, and rentals.

Half Moon Pond State Park (802-273-3848; 802-483-2314), Fair Haven, off Route 4 west of Rutland, exit 4, 7.5 miles north on Route 30, 2 miles west on Town Road, 1.5 miles south on Town Road. Wooded campsites around a secluded pond; rental canoes; hikes to **High Pond,** a remote body of water in the hills.

Lake St. Catherine State Park (802-287-9185; 802-483-2314), 9.5 miles south of Poultney on Route 30. Fifty-two campsites, sandy beaches, fishing, boat rentals, nature trails.

✳ Lodging

INN ♬ **The Victorian Inn at Wallingford** (802-446-2099; www.thevictorianinn.com), P.O. Box 338, 9 North Main Street, Route 7, Wallingford 05773. This fine, restored historic village mansion has six very comfortable guest rooms with private bath, and the atmosphere is family-friendly, thanks to the upbeat proprietors, Constantine and Soo Schonbachler. There's a cozy, publike bar and three dining rooms that are both formal and casual, fine settings for superior food (see *Dining Out*). Room rates $120–140 ($20 foliage supplement) with full breakfast.

SUITES **The Victorian** (802-287-5505; www.victoriansuites.com), 2541 Vermont Route 31, Poultney 05764. Cathy and Bruce Ferguson have restored this 1890 Victorian and turned it into one- and two-bedroom rental suites, complete with equipped kitchen and sitting room. One-bedroom suites rent for $70 in midweek and $110 on weekends and holidays; two-bedroom suites go for $95 and $130, respectively. No credit cards.

BED & BREAKFASTS **The Inn at Rutland** (802-773-0575; 1-800-808-0575; www.innatrutland.com), 70 North Main Street, Rutland 05071. This is a large, 1890s town house on Route 7 just north of the center of town, now owned by Leslie and Steven Brenner. All 11 distinctive guest rooms have phone, private bath, and antiques, plus color TV. The differences are in size and position. We suggest a room in the back, away from Route 7. The woodwork in the dining room is exceptional, and the fireplaced living room is attractive. Rates of $90–205 include a full breakfast.

The Phelps House (802-775-4480; 1-800-775-4620; www.thephelps house.com), 19 North Street, Rutland 05071. Eight bedrooms, plus a private apartment that sleeps eight; playroom and tennis court. Betty Phelps's wonderfully primitive murals are worth the visit to what has been called "the first Frank Lloyd Wright house built in Vermont." $65–85.

Baker's Bed & Breakfast (802-775-4835; 1-888-778-4835), 80 Campbell Road, Rutland 05071 (off Dorr Drive, south of the business district), is a spacious 1826 redbrick house with an inviting veranda and a swimming pool. Steve and Leslie Baker offer three large bedrooms with private bath. There's a living room, a library, and a dining room for brunchlike breakfasts, included in the $125 rate.

∞ **I. B. Munson House** (802-446-2860; 1-888-519-3771; www.ibmun son.com), 37 South Main Street, Wallingford 05773, run by Lisa and Charles McClafferty, is furnished with classic Victorian antiques and period decor, including claw-footed bathtubs. There are seven guest rooms, all with private bath, two with working fireplace. Rates range from $130–215 per room in high season to $120–165 in low, including full gourmet breakfast. Ask about children and pets when you call.

Maplewood Inn (802-265-8039; 1-800-253-7729; www.maplewood inn.net), Route 22A south, Fair Haven 05743. Lisa and Don Osborne's historic 1843 Greek Revival farmhouse (on the National Register of Historic Places), set in fields, is decorated in period style with common rooms that ramble on and on.

There is a breakfast room with hot-beverage bar, and a parlor with complimentary liqueurs. The Blue Room, Rose Room, and Oak Suite are especially attractive. Four of the five rooms have a fireplace, and all have private bath, cable TV, and air-conditioning. Rates are $99–150 ($119–170 during foliage and holiday season), including a continental-plus breakfast buffet.

Memory Lane (802-468-5394), 503 Main Street, Castleton 05735. Antique furniture, toys, dolls, and china fill this Federal-style house, originally the home of the cofounder of the medical school at Castleton College. Now Barbara and Thomas Ettori offer two guest rooms with private bath, at $55–100.

Fair Haven Inn Bed & Breakfast (802-265-9706), 18 Main Street, Fair Haven 05743. Linda Lemnotis runs this town house with a wraparound veranda, three bedrooms with private bath, cable TV in the den, fax and copier service, a wet bar (BYOB), and a sitting room with fireplace. Rates $100–150.

Priscilla's Victorian Inn (802-235-2299), 52 South Street, Middletown Springs 05757. Priscilla Lane's inn has vintage gingerbread charm, six large Victorian rooms with private bath, a game room, and English gardens. $95 per room, double occupancy.

White Rocks Inn (802-446-2077), 1774 Route 7, Wallingford 05773. Malcolm and Rita Swogger's elegantly furnished farmhouse and its spectacular, landmark barn are on the National Register of Historic Places. The five guest rooms, each with private bath, have either king, queen, or double canopy beds and can be had for $100–180 double occupancy, including full breakfast. The Milk House Cottage (with a whirlpool bath, living room, and full kitchen) is EP or B&B by the day or by the week. Children over 12 are welcome in the house, of any age in the cottage.

See also Maple Crest Farm and Buckmaster Inn in "Okemo Valley Region."

MOTELS

In Rutland 05071

Mendon Mountain Orchards (802-775-5477; www.mendonorchards.com), 16 Route 4, Mendon, isn't really a motel but rather a series of pleasant, old-fashioned cabins, surrounded by orchards, with a pool and a shop for homemade goodies, apples in-season, cider, and flowers. $45–60 for a double.

Holiday Inn (802-775-1911; 1-800-HOLIDAY), Routes 7 and 4 south, includes **Paynter's Restaurant,** an indoor pool, sauna and exercise room, and **Centre Stage** lounge. $99–299 double. Rutland also has a **Best Western** (1-800-528-1234), a **Ramada Limited** (1-888-818-3297), a **Red Roof Inn** (1-800-RED-ROOF), a **Travel Inn** (1-866-775-4348), a **Comfort Inn** (1-800-228-5150), and an **Econo Lodge** (1-800-4-CHOICE).

CAMPGROUNDS See *Green Space* for information on campgrounds in Lake Bomoseen State Park, Half Moon Pond State Park, and Lake St. Catherine State Park.

✴ Where to Eat

DINING OUT See also "Killington/Plymouth Area."

Royal's 121 Hearthside (802-775-0856), 37 North Main Street (junction of Routes 4 and 7), Rutland. Open daily 11–3 and 5–9:30, Sunday noon–9. The legendary Ernie Royal is no longer alive, but his spirit lives on. Mesquite and hearthside grill specialties: prime rib, chops, seafood, and lobsters. Dinner entrées range $17.95–26.95.

Little Harry's (802-747-4848), 121 West Street, Rutland. Open daily 5–10. This offspring of the popular Harry's Cafe in Mount Holly occupies the old space of 121 West. Owner Harrison Pearce calls his venture the "general store of ethnic eating." Besides pad Thai, a "signature" noodle dish, Little Harry's offers such fare as lamb chops, trout, Greek salads, and lively Spanish dishes plus burritos and steak sandwiches from what Pearce calls a "user-friendly" menu. Moderate.

The Victorian Inn at Wallingford (802-446-2099), 9 North Main Street, Route 7, Wallingford, serves dinner Tuesday through Saturday and a bountiful Sunday brunch buffet laid out in the kitchen. Closed in November until Thanksgiving. Swiss-born chef-owner Constantine Schonbachler's really exceptional Continental specialties have won a strong local following. Dinner might be sautéed calf's liver with Madeira sauce, grilled chicken with caramelized shallots, or roast rack of lamb with port wine sauce. Dinner for two with wine comes to about $90.

The Fair Haven Inn (802-265-4907; 1-800-325-7074), 5 Adams Street, Fair Haven. In a spacious, neo-Colonial setting, the Lemnotis family serves American-Mediterranean fare Monday through Saturday for lunch 11:30–2 ($3.95–9.95). Dinner is served Monday through Saturday 5–9

and Sunday noon–8, and includes veal Florentine ($16.95), moussaka ($10.95), and jumbo shrimp à la Grecque ($17.95). Other specials include spanakopita and seafood souvlakia.

EATING OUT The Palms (802-773-2367), 36 Strongs Avenue, Rutland. Italian cooking is a specialty in Rutland because of all the Italians who came to work in the marble quarries. The Palms offers cooking by the fourth generation of the Sabatoso family, who prepare such specialties as baked lasagna, veal à la Palms, and steak Delmonico.

South Station (802-775-1736), at the Trolley Barn, 170 South Main Street, Rutland. Open daily for lunch and dinner, specializing in prime rib of beef and such munchies as fried potato skins, zucchini sticks, stuffed mushrooms, chicken wings, hearty soups, salads, burgers, and teriyaki beef or chicken. Dinner prices range from $8.95 for burgers to $24.95 for certain specials.

Three Tomatoes (802-747-7747), 88 Merchants Row, Rutland, has the same northern Italian flair as its siblings in Burlington and in Lebanon, New Hampshire—wood-fired pizzas and all. Open for dinner nightly from 5 PM. Shrimp sautéed with tomato, Greek olives, basil, garlic, crushed red chiles, and white wine, tossed with linguine, is but one sample dish. Entrées $10.95–14.95.

🍲 **Back Home Again** (802-775-9800), 23 Center Street, Rutland, serves sandwiches, salads, soups, and wraps, homemade breads, muffins, and wonderful desserts. They also prepare fresh juices, special smoothies, fancy coffees, and a drink called maté. Open Monday through Thursday 8–9, Friday 8–3, closed weekends.

☙ **The Sirloin Saloon** (802-773-7900), 200 South Main Street (Route 7 south), Rutland. One in a Vermont mini chain (there are three), this colorful restaurant (lots of glasswork, art, and gleaming brass) is a good bet for family dinners. The menu runs from ground sirloin to prime rib to seafood cooked over the wood-fired grill. Entrées $11–19.

Panda Pavilion (802-775-6682; 802-775-6794), Route 4 east, by Home Depot, Rutland. Open 11:30–9:30 Monday through Saturday, 1–10 Sunday for dinner only. Highly praised Szechuan-Hunan-Mandarin cuisine, like Double Happiness Chicken. Take-out service.

Birdseye Diner (802-468-5817), Main Street, Castleton. This restored 1940s Silk City diner, open all day, is a justifiably popular spot for college students and local residents alike. Complete dinners begin at $7.95.

LakeShore Pub & Grill (802-273-3000), Route 30, on Lake Bomoseen. This locally popular place features live music on summer weekend evenings.

Wheel Inn (802-537-2755), Lake Street at Stage Road, Benson. Open daily 6 AM–9 PM, this family-friendly place has a loyal following largely because of its very reasonable prices. Menu offerings range from meat loaf to broiled scallops, none of which is more than $14, including salads and sides.

Tokyo House, (802-786-8080), 106 West Street, Rutland. Open for lunch 11–3, dinner 4:30–10. Owner Ming Li is known for sushi, sashimi, and bento boxes. Eat in or take out; beer and wine.

Clem & Company (802-747-3340), 51 Wales Street, Rutland. Breakfast is served all day, every day, until closing at 1:30 PM. There are also great soups, salads, and sandwiches for lunch. A fast, friendly local eatery.

Seward Family Restaurant (802-773-2738), 224 North Main Street, Rutland. The Sewards have run a dairy business in the area since forever, and Seward's ice cream is among the best. Besides ice cream, the restaurant offers solid home cooking and a large gift shop of Vermont products.

Also see Costantino's Italian Imports in *Selective Shopping*.

COFFEEHOUSE/WINE BAR Coffee Exchange (802-775-3337), 101–103 Merchants Row, Rutland. Open Monday through Friday from 7 AM, Saturday from 8 AM; on Friday the place doesn't close down until 10 PM. "Jazz, java, and jabber" is the theme of this upbeat coffee bar and sophisticated wine room at a key downtown intersection. Patrons sip and nosh on exotic beverages and pastries at outdoor tables in summer—perhaps macadamia cream coffee and orange-poppyseed scones. Salads, soups, and sandwiches at lunch.

✳ Entertainment

Paramount Theatre (802-775-0570; www.paramountvt.org), 30 Center Street, Rutland. After years of a concerted community effort, this lovely old theater has been brought back to life with dance, music, drama, even magic and juggling acts. Call for tickets and schedules of events.

Crossroads Art Council (802-775-5413), 39 East Center Street, Rutland, sponsors a series of concerts, theater and ballet performances, and an arts education program.

See also LakeShore Pub & Grill under *Eating Out*.

Movieplex 9 (802-775-5500), downtown Rutland Plaza, and **Westway 1-2-3-4** (802-438-2888), Route 4 in West Rutland, show first-run flicks.

✳ Selective Shopping

BOOKSTORES **Charles E. Tuttle Company** (802-773-8930), Main Street, Rutland, facing the park, has one of the largest stocks of used and rare books in New England. Charles Tuttle began his publishing company in Tokyo right after World War II and built it into a major supplier of beautifully produced books on Oriental art and other Asian subjects.

The Book King (802-773-9232), Merchants Row, Rutland, is a bright, well-stocked store for new adult and children's books, paperbacks, and cards.

✐ **Annie's Book Stop** (802-775-6993), Trolley Square, 120 South Main Street, Rutland. Annie's has a large selection of new books and pre-read paperbacks; specializes in children's books and books on tape, plus educational puzzles and games.

The Bookshed (802-537-2010), at the corner of Lake and Stage Roads, Benson, is a used- and antiquarian-book store with thousands of volumes just where you wouldn't expect to find it—in the tiny village of Benson.

SPECIAL SHOPS **Great Outdoors Trading Company** (802-775-6531), Woodstock Avenue, Rutland, is a vast, complete sporting goods store, with a bike shop, gun shop, archery center, and fly-rod department, among others.

The Seward Vermont Dairy Deli Shop (802-773-2738), 224 North Main Street (Route 7), Rutland. One corner of this vast restaurant (see *Eating Out*) showcases the cheddar cheeses produced by Cabot and Crowley (Seward family members no longer make their own cheese). One specialty is sharp cheddar, aged more than 9 months. Maple syrup and creamed honey are also available. The ice cream is the showstopper, however.

Costantino's Italian Imports (802-747-0777), 10 Terrill Street, Rutland. Former antiques dealer Dan Costantino has renovated the former Bartlett's Studio building to create a shop that features shelves of imported Italian meats, cheeses, pasta, and olive oil. In the back a deli offers Italian sandwiches and pasta salads.

Vermont Canvas Products (802-773-7311), 179 Woodstock Avenue, Route 4 east, Rutland, makes customized luggage and handbags. Open daily except Sunday.

Truly Unique (802-773-7742), Route 4 east, Rutland, has an uncommon collection of country antiques, Vermont products, and gifts.

Rocking Horse Country Store (802-773-7882), Route 4 east, Rutland, combines Vermont food products (including its own homemade wine jelly), gifts, antiques, and collectibles.

Fred's Dollhouse and Miniature Center (802-483-6362), 3224 Route 7 north, Pittsford. Open Monday through Saturday 9:30–5, Sunday 11–5, and by appointment. This is where you can get dollhouses and miniature furnishings, accessories, scaled lumber, hardware, electrical systems, and wallpaper, plus doll-house and furniture kits.

Hand Made in Vermont (802-446-2400; www.handmadeinvermont.com), 205 South Main Street, Wallingford. Open June through November 1, Thursday through Monday 11–6; from November 2 through May, the store is open 11–6 on weekends only. Housed in America's first pitchfork mill, this gallery store showcases the work of Vermont artists and craftspeople, including glass, pottery, furniture, and jewelry.

Farrow Gallery & Studio (802-468-5683), Old Yellow Church, Main Street, Castleton, shows Patrick Farrow's limited-edition, award-winning bronze sculptures, along with the work of other Vermont artists.

Peter Huntoon Studio (802-235-2328; www.peterhuntoon.com), 17 Studio Lane, Middletown Springs. Open by appointment. Huntoon is one of Vermont's premier watercolorists, who also teaches and conducts workshops at his studio. His work is available for viewing and for sale.

✳ Special Events

Late February: **Great Benson Fishing Derby,** sponsored by the Fair Haven Rotary Club—many prizes in several categories, including best ice shanty. Tickets for the derby: P.O. Box 131, Bomoseen 05732.

Mid-July: **SolarFest** (802-235-2866; www.solarfest.org) has become an annual solar-powered music festival and sustainable future fair in Poultney.

August: **Castleton Colonial Days,** Castleton (see *Villages*).

Early August: **Art in the Park Summer Arts Festival,** Rutland, sponsored by the Chaffee Center (802-775-0356), in Main Street Park, junction of Routes 7 and 4 east.

Early September: **Vermont State Fair** (802-775-5200)—midway, exhibits, races, demolition derby, and tractor pulls animate the old fairgrounds on Route 7 south, Rutland.

Mid-September: **Rutland Region Ethnic Festival** (802-483-6939), downtown Rutland.

Mid-October: **Art in the Park Fall Foliage Festival,** Rutland, sponsored by the Chaffee Center (802-775-0356).

October 31: Rutland had one of the nation's first **Halloween parades,** and it's still one of the best.

December 31: Rutland's **First Night** celebration.

ADDISON COUNTY AND ENVIRONS

INCLUDING MIDDLEBURY, VERGENNES, BRANDON, AND BRISTOL

Addison County packs as much contrasting scenery within its borders as any county in the country. On the east it includes the high wall of the Green Mountains, laced with hiking trails and pierced by four of the state's highest, most dramatic "gaps" (passes). The mountains drop abruptly through widely scattered hill towns—Lincoln, Ripton, and Goshen—into a 30-mile-wide, farm-filled valley, Vermont's largest concentration of dairy farms and orchards. Lake Champlain is far narrower here than up around Burlington, and the Adirondacks in New York seem higher and nearer, forming an improbable but spectacular backdrop to cows, water, red barns, and apple trees.

This stretch of the Champlain Valley is particularly popular with bicyclists, not only because it's the flattest piece of Vermont, but also because its quiet old farm roads wind through orchards to discoveries like the "Fort Ti Ferry" ("serving people and their vehicles since Mozart was three months old") and "the world's smallest bank" in Orwell.

Middlebury, the hub of Addison County, is among New England's most sophisticated towns, the home of one of its most prestigious private colleges and many interesting shops.

We hope that this book will lure visitors to explore the entire valley: the easily accessible scenery along Route 7 as well as the Lake Champlain shoreline, notched at regular intervals with quiet and accessible bays, and the Green Mountain forest roads, with their occasional but spectacular lake and valley views.

GUIDANCE **Addison County Chamber of Commerce** (802-388-7951; 1-800-SEE-VERMONT; www.midvermont.com), 2 Court Street, Middlebury 05753, in the Painter House, offers information about every corner of its domain, from Vergennes and Bristol in the north to Orwell in the south. Open Monday through Friday 9–5. This unusually large walk-in information center publishes a map/guide, stocks brochures, and refers visitors to a wide variety of lodgings,

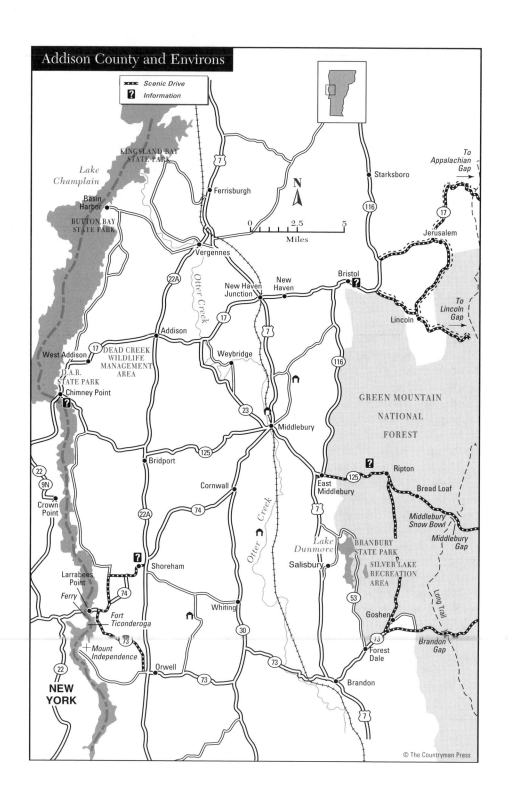

Addison County and Environs

- ▪▪▪▪ Scenic Drive
- ❓ Information

Lake Champlain

KINGSLAND BAY STATE PARK

Ferrisburgh

7

Basin Harbor

BUTTON BAY STATE PARK

Vergennes

22A

Otter Creek

New Haven Junction

New Haven

17

7

Starksboro

116

To Appalachian Gap →

17

Jerusalem

To Lincoln Gap →

Bristol ❓

Lincoln

116

West Addison

17

DEAD CREEK WILDLIFE MANAGEMENT AREA

Addison

Weybridge

D.A.R. STATE PARK

Chimney Point ❓

23

Middlebury

GREEN MOUNTAIN

NATIONAL

FOREST

22

9N

Crown Point

125

Bridport

Cornwall

22A

74

Shoreham ❓

Larrabees Point

Ferry

74

Fort Ticonderoga

Mount Independence

22

Orwell

73

NEW YORK

Whiting

30

73

Otter Creek

❓ Ripton

125

Bread Loaf

East Middlebury

7

Lake Dunmore

BRANBURY STATE PARK

SILVER LAKE RECREATION AREA

Salisbury

53

Middlebury Snow Bowl

Middlebury Gap

Long Trail

Goshen

73

Forest Dale

Brandon Gap

Brandon

7

N

0   2.5   5
Miles

© The Countryman Press

from inns and bed & breakfasts to seasonal cottages on Lake Dunmore. During foliage season it is unusually resourceful in finding lodging for all comers.

Vergennes Chamber of Commerce (802-877-0080), P.O. Box 335, Vergennes 05491, has an information booth on the common.

Brandon Area Chamber of Commerce (802-247-6401), P.O. Box 267, Brandon 05735; visitors booth on Park Street with brochures and information in front of the library across from the Brandon Inn. There's an informative self-guided walking tour guide to the town's rich architectural heritage.

Moosalamoo, from the Abenaki word possibly meaning "the moose departs," is a dandy map and guide, with site signage, to the trails and other natural features of some 20,000 acres of Green Mountain National Forest, published and distributed by the Moosalamoo Partnership, available at chambers of commerce, the Catamount Trail Association, other outdoor recreation organizations, and several inns. Or call 802-247-6735; 1-800-448-0707.

GETTING THERE *By bus:* **Vermont Transit** (802-864-6811; 1-800-451-3292) stops in Brandon and Vergennes as well as Middlebury. This is the Burlington-to-Albany run, so New Yorkers and Bostonians must change in Rutland.

By car: The major north–south highway is Route 7, but we advise anyone from Boston to approach through the Middlebury Gap (see *Scenic Drives*). From the west you can take the toll bridge at Chimney Point year-round or the seasonal ferries described below.

By ferry: **Lake Champlain Ferry** (802-864-9804) from Essex, New York, to Charlotte operates spring through fall, takes 20 minutes, and puts you just above Vergennes.

Fort Ticonderoga Ferry (802-897-7999), Larrabees Point to Fort Ticonderoga. Memorial Day weekend through June, 8–6 daily; July through Labor Day 8 AM–9 PM, then 8–6 through the last Sunday in October. Cars $6 one-way, $10 round-trip.

MEDICAL EMERGENCY Emergency service is available by calling **911.**

✳ Villages

Middlebury (population: 8,000) is the county seat and hub of Addison County. It's also the home of prestigious Middlebury College and one of Vermont's handsomest, liveliest, most welcoming communities. Inns and restaurants serve visitors as well as potential students and their parents, and in recent years it has become a great place to shop. Middlebury College (founded in 1800 and now one of the nation's most sought-after private colleges) owes much to the energy and vision of Gamaliel Painter, a surveyor who settled here before the Revolution. Painter accompanied Ethan Allen on the Fort Ticonderoga raid and returned to Middlebury to become the town's principal landowner, sheriff, judge, and assemblyman. The fine mansion on Court Street, presently housing the information center, belonged to Painter. Another benefactor was Joseph Battell, who owned thousands of acres of forest and mountain land that he left to the college and the state when he died in 1915. He was the proprietor of the famous old summit house, the Bread Loaf Inn, now the nucleus of the summer Bread Loaf School of English and the Bread Loaf Writers Conference. Battell also owned a weekly newspaper in which he fulminated against the invasion of motorcars. Emma Hart Willard, who pioneered in the education of women, was another Middlebury luminary.

The town's proudest buildings—the courthouse, the Middlebury Inn, the Battell House, and the fine Congregational church—are grouped, along with compact business blocks, around the common. It's a short walk down Main Street to the churning Otter Creek falls, a centerpiece for dozens of shops that have proliferated in the old mills and marbleworks on both banks of the river, connected by a footbridge. With the Vermont State Craft Center as its anchor store, this is now one of Vermont's most interesting places to shop.

Brandon. A peaceful town of some 4,000 inhabitants and an often underrated appeal, Brandon has an unusual array of 19th-century houses in an eclectic and intriguing mix of Federal and Victorian styles. Sited in Rutland County (it's just over the southern border of Addison County) between Otter Creek and the Neshobe River, it was the home of Thomas Davenport, who invented and patented an electric motor in 1838, and the birthplace of Stephen A. Douglas (1813–1861), the "Little Giant" of the famous debates with Abraham Lincoln in 1858, when Douglas was a senator from Illinois. Brandon's hospitality to travelers is growing with the addition of some interesting new places to stay.

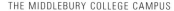

THE MIDDLEBURY COLLEGE CAMPUS
Leight Johnson

Bristol. Billing itself as the "Gateway to the Green Mountains," Bristol is nestled at the foot of Lincoln Gap, at the junctions of north–south Route 116 (less heavily trafficked than Route 7) and east–west Route 17. Its broad Main Street is lined with a delightful mix of stores and restaurants, housed in a 19th-century building that leads to a square green, complete with fountain, park benches, and old cannon. The local site to see is the **Lord's Prayer Rock** (on the south side of Route 17 entering Bristol from the east), a flat rock inscribed with the Lord's Prayer. A physician named Joseph C. Greene

commissioned the inscription in 1891, presumably because he was still thankful
for having reached this point safely when, as a youth, he was hauling logs over
steep roads.

Vergennes, midway between Middlebury and Burlington, has long claimed to
be the smallest city (2,300 residents) in the United States. Although 5 miles
inland, its history and its present activities are linked closely to Lake Champlain.
Otter Creek winds from the city to the lake, and the road leads to Basin Harbor,
site of the area's premier resort and the Lake Champlain Maritime Museum. We
recommend the lake road south from Basin Harbor, by Button Bay State Park
and the D.A.R. State Park to Chimney Point. The ruins of the 18th-century fort
at Crown Point in New York are just across the Lake Champlain Bridge.

Vergennes's site on an impressive falls and its handsome, early-19th-century
commercial buildings suggest an unusual history. This is, in fact, one of the oldest, as well as the smallest, cities in the country. It was founded by Donald
McIntosh in 1764 and later named by Ethan Allen for Charles Gravier, comte de
Vergennes, the French minister of foreign affairs who was a strong supporter of
the American Revolutionary cause.

In 1811–12 Thomas Macdonough used the Otter Creek Basin just below the
falls to build—in record time—three ships, including the 734-ton, 26-gun
Saratoga. He also equipped nine gunboats, using them all to defeat the British
fleet in Lake Champlain off Plattsburgh in 1814.

Shoreham is known for its many orchards. Shoreham Village is a beauty, with a
classic Congregational church (1846), a Masonic temple (built in 1852 as the
Universalist church), and the graceful St. Genevieve Catholic Church (1873), as
well as the old inn and general store. Follow Route 74 southwest from the village
through the orchards; or continue straight on Witherell Road where 74 jogs
south, then turn south (left) onto Smith Street along the lake. Either way, you
get to Larrabees Point, the site of Teachout's Store, built in 1836 from stones
taken from Fort Ticonderoga just across the lake. The excursion boat M/V *Carillon* now departs from this spot; next door the small, car-carrying "Fort Ti" cable
ferry makes the crossing to the fort itself in 6 minutes flat. It has held the franchise from the Vermont and New York legislatures since 1799, but records indicate the service was initiated by Lord Jeffery Amherst in 1757 for use by his
soldiers in the campaigns against the French. Continue south on Route 73 to the
turnoff for Mount Independence.

Orwell. Best known for Mount Independence, the small village at the center of
this orchard and dairying community circles a long, sloping green with a brick
Congregational church (1843) on a rise by the white-clapboard town hall (built
in 1810 as the Baptist church). It all overlooks a brief line of shops with the
First National Bank of Orwell, billed as "the world's smallest bank," in the middle. Chartered in 1863 (but known as the Farmers Bank for many years, before
Lincoln granted it the country's 212th official charter), the bank remains a real
center of town, with notices of upcoming events tacked to the authentic old
teller's cages. The other village nerve center is **Buxton's Store,** the genuine
article.

JOSEPH BATTELL BRIDGE The bridge that Joseph Battell built in downtown Middlebury is but one element of an enormous and enduring legacy of mountaintops and mortar that this eccentric bachelor left to the state of Vermont as a whole and to Middlebury College in particular.

Battell was born in 1839 to a wealthy and influential Vermont family. He attended Middlebury College, but ill health kept him from finishing his degree. Instead, he went off to travel the world; upon his return he bought land in the mountain town of Ripton, where he ran an inn, mainly for his friends. Today that land and those buildings house two of the college's most highly regarded summer programs: the Bread Loaf School of English and the Bread Loaf Writers Conference. In addition to being publisher of the *Middlebury Register,* a local newspaper, Battell was also an author. One of his oddest efforts was a book titled *Ellen, or, The Whisperings of an Old Pine,* a dense tome that is seldom read but much wondered about.

Battell was a man who loved mountains and woods and hated cars, so much so that he refused to allow cars on the road that ran up to his Ripton inn. Yet it was because of Battell that the stone bridge spanning Otter Creek in downtown Middlebury is still, a century later, a key to the transportation infrastructure in Addison County. The original wooden bridge that carried traffic across the creek burned down a century ago. Middlebury's town fathers, in a fit of economy, decided to build an iron bridge on the site, but Battell was opposed, arguing that a stone bridge would last significantly longer than an iron one. So determined was he that he is said to have paid the difference out of his own pocket.

A pioneering conservationist, Battell used to send his hired man into the woods, armed with blank deeds and instructions to buy as much acreage as he could from any farmer or logger he came across. Over time he acquired about 35,000 acres, including Camels Hump, which he donated to the state of Vermont for use as a state park. His landholdings also reached over Bread Loaf Mountain from East Middlebury to Hancock, Granville, and Rochester, along Route 100, and followed the spine of the Green Mountains from Mount

✳ To See

MUSEUMS Middlebury College Center for the Arts (802-443-6433), Route 30, Middlebury. Open Tuesday through Friday 10–5, weekends noon–5. The college's small but distinguished permanent collection of paintings and small sculptures plus changing exhibits are displayed in galleries within the multi-tiered arts center, which also includes a café and several performance areas.

Ellen south to Brandon Gap. When he died in 1915, most of this land was bequeathed to Middlebury College, which has sold off much of it over the years, keeping only a few hundred acres.

Battell is also the father of the University of Vermont's Morgan Horse Farm. He began breeding Morgans on his farm in the latter 1800s, an interest that would prove instrumental in saving America's first breed of horse from extinction. He hired architect Clinton Smith to build the beautiful white farm buildings that still stand in Weybridge. With typical Battell intensity, he spent years tracing out the pedigrees published in the first volume of the *Morgan Horse Register* in 1894. Then in 1906 he gave his farm and his Morgan horses to the U.S. government. It remains a working horse farm to this day, supplying stock to Morgan breeders across the country.

THE BATTELL BRIDGE IN DOWNTOWN MIDDLEBURY

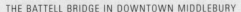

Leight Johnson

The Henry Sheldon Museum (802-388-2117), Park Street, Middlebury. Open year-round, Monday through Friday 10–5, also Saturday late May through October. Guided and self-guided tours. $4 per adult, $3.50 for seniors, and $2 for children 6–18. This 1829 marble merchant's house has no fewer than six black marble mantels and holds an intimate collection of furnishings, tools, household articles, clothes, books, games, and other artifacts portraying Vermont folkways, all displayed in period rooms. A modern research ell has been added, with a gallery for changing exhibits. There are also frequent special events.

The **Vermont Folklife Center** (802-388-4964), 3 Court Street, Middlebury (in Masonic Hall). This growing organization (founded in 1984) collects and presents the traditional arts and folkways of Vermont, primarily through taped interviews. It mounts changing exhibits and sells its publications.

Lake Champlain Maritime Museum (802-475-2022), Basin Harbor, Panton, at the entrance to the Basin Harbor Club off Panton Road west of Vergennes. Open daily 10–5 from May 1 through mid-October; $10 adults, $8 seniors, $5 for children 6–17. This museum has been evolving steadily over the decades. It began with the gift of a local schoolhouse constructed from native limestone in 1808, moved stone by stone (2,000 of them) and reconstructed to house exhibits. The museum's 10 buildings, spread over 3 acres, now house dozens of small craft built around the lake over a period of 150 years, and exhibits on a number of chapters in the lake's story, including the saga of the hundreds of wrecks still beneath the surface. Attempts to raise them, you learn, began in the 1930s but have been abandoned because divers and historians have accepted the obvious: Wood that's been submerged in fresh water quickly disintegrates when exposed to air. Instead, the state of Vermont has created five underwater parks; inquire about guided scuba tours, lectures, and field trips, and demonstrations and courses in boatbuilding. A working replica of Benedict Arnold's 54-foot gunboat, *Philadelphia,* built on the spot, is also on view. The bookstore carries a good selection of maritime-related books, prints, clothing, and gifts.

THE GUNBOAT REPLICA *PHILADELPHIA* UNDER SAIL ON LAKE CHAMPLAIN
Lake Champlain Maritime Museum

HISTORIC HOMES Rokeby Museum (802-877-3406), 3 miles north of Vergennes on Route 7 in Ferrisburgh. Open for guided tours May through October, Thursday through Sunday at 11, 12:30, and 2, and by appointment year-round. $6 adults, $4 students and seniors. Exhibits evoke the lives of four generations of a Quaker family whose members included pioneers, farmers, and Rowland E. Robinson, the 19th-century author, illustrator, and naturalist. Rokeby was an important stop on the Underground Railway for freedom-seeking slaves before the Civil War.

The John Strong D.A.R. Mansion (802-759-2309), Route 17, west of 22A, West Addison, open Memorial Day through Labor Day, weekends 9–5. $3 per adult, $2 seniors and students. This is one of several substantial houses and buildings made of stone taken from the ruins of Fort Crown Point and skidded across frozen Lake Champlain by oxen. General Strong, an early settler and Green Mountain Boy, built his (third) residence here in 1796 with brick from his own clay pits on the "Salt Lick" where he first hunted deer. Furnishings reflect five generations of the family.

HISTORIC SITES **Mount Independence State Historic Site** (802-948-2000), 8 miles west of Orwell on the shore of Lake Champlain, marked from the junction of Route 73 off Route 22A. Grounds open year-round; museum open Memorial Day through Columbus Day, Wednesday through Sunday 9:30–5:30. Opened in 1996, a boat-shaped visitors center exhibits archaeological artifacts and tells the story of the thousands of men who weathered a brutal winter on this fortified peninsula in 1776–77, facing Fort Ticonderoga across a narrow strip of lake. Eventually they defeated the British at Saratoga, one of the most decisive victories of the Revolution. Four marked trails begin at the information center and wander down to the lake through 400 wooded acres.

Fort Ticonderoga (518-585-2821), Ticonderoga, New York. Open mid-May through mid-October daily. $12 per adult, $6 children 7–12. The 18th-century stone fort has been restored and includes a museum displaying weapons and uniforms. It was built by the French (who named it Fort Carillon), captured by the English general Jeffery Amherst, and held by the British until 1775, when Ethan Allen and his Green Mountain Boys took the fort by surprise, capturing the guns that eventually helped free Boston. The fort is easily accessible from Larrabees Point on the Vermont shore.

Crown Point State Historic Site (518-597-3666), Crown Point, New York. Open mid-May through October, Wednesday through Saturday 10–5, Sunday 1–5. Free. Just across the Lake Champlain Bridge from Chimney Point, West Addison, Vermont. Fifteen miles north of Fort Ticonderoga, Crown Point was once a far larger, more important fortification, and in 1775 it was the source of 29 pieces of cannon captured by the colonists and hauled off to Boston. The complex includes 18th-century ruins and a visitors center.

Chimney Point State Historic Site (802-759-2412), at the Vermont end of the Lake Champlain Bridge, Route 125. Open Memorial Day through Columbus Day, Wednesday through Sunday 9:30–5:30. An 18th-century tavern houses a well-mounted display on Native American and French colonial heritage.

GARDENS **Pinewood Gardens** (802-247-3388), Route 7 south, Brandon. Excellent perennials and annuals for sale, plus display gardens. Open Easter through Christmas.

Rocky Dale Gardens (802-453-2782), 62 Rocky Dale Road, Bristol. Open daily 9–6 except Tuesday. Extensive displays on 3 acres with dramatic rock outcroppings, plus a retail nursery.

Pine Tree Gardens (802-453-2587), 140 North Street, Bristol. Open late April through October, Monday through Friday 9–6, Saturday 8–5, Sunday 9–4. Greenhouses, display gardens, and a retail nursery.

FARMS AND ORCHARDS ✺ **The UVM Morgan Horse Farm** (802-388-2011), 74 Battell Drive, Weybridge, open May through October, daily 9–4. Go through downtown Middlebury, heading west on Route 125, then turn right onto Route 23 (Weybridge Street) and follow signs. Admission. The first "Morgan" was born in the late 1790s and is recognized as the sire of an entire breed of Vermont horse. Colonel Joseph Battell began breeding Morgans on this farm in the 1870s and is credited with saving the breed (America's first developed breed of horse) from extinction. The farm is now a breeding and training center operated by the University of Vermont. Guided tours of the stables and paddocks are available, along with an audiovisual presentation about the Morgan horse and farm.

✺ **Yankee Kingdom Orchard** (802-759-2387), Lake Street, West Addison. Overlooking Lake Champlain, pick-your-own apples, strawberries, and pumpkins; also a petting zoo, children's play area, wagon rides, cider pressing. The Yankee Kingdom Festival in early September is a great event for kids.

✺ **Wooly Hill Farm** (802-758-2284), 2695 Rattlin' Bridge Road, Bridport. An organic sheep and alpaca farm with a yarn shop, spinning supplies, and gifts. Barn tours are offered Tuesday through Saturday 10–noon, but call ahead. Also in Bridport is **Champlain Valley Alpacas** (802-758-3276), 326 Fiddlers Lane, which can be seen by appointment Monday through Saturday 8–5. Farther south in Brandon, Deb and Ed Bratton raise alpacas at **Maple View Farm** (802-247-5412) and invite tourists to see their animals.

THE UVM MORGAN HORSE FARM IN WEYBRIDGE

Kim Grant

COVERED BRIDGES The **Pulp Mill Covered Bridge,** between Middlebury and Weybridge, spanning Otter Creek near the Morgan Horse Farm, is the oldest in the state (1808–20) and the last two-lane span still in use.

Halpin Bridge (1824), Middlebury, 2 miles east of Route 7, off Halpin Road, is Vermont's highest bridge above the streambed.

Station Bridge, across Otter Creek in Cornwall (2 miles east of Route 30 on Swamp Road), is a 136-foot Town lattice bridge built in 1836.

Shoreham Covered Railroad Bridge, East Shoreham off the Whiting–Shoreham Road (turn south onto Shoreham Depot Road); the bridge is marked on area maps. A Howe bridge built in 1897 by the Rutland Railroad, spanning the Lemon Fair River. A designated state historic site.

Spade Farm Covered Bridge, located along Route 7 in Ferrisburgh, is now on the property of the Artisans Guild and Starry Night Café. It was built in 1824 and moved 3 miles to its present location in 1959.

SCENIC DRIVES **Middlebury Gap.** This is our favorite approach to Addison County from the southeast, and this stretch of Route 125 is more dramatic driving east to west. Begin in Hancock and stop at Texas Falls (see our map on page 292). The road quickly crests at its junction with the Long Trail, near the Middlebury Snow Bowl. Then it's all downhill through the woods until the huge, wooden Bread Loaf Inn (now part of Middlebury College) improbably appears. The Robert Frost Wayside Picnic Area and the Interpretive Trail are a short way beyond. We also like to stop in the small, 19th-century cemetery a bit farther down, where a wind chime strikes softly in a row of maples. The picturesque hill town of Ripton is just below, and as the road continues to plunge into the valley, you glimpse the Adirondacks in the distance.

Brandon Gap. Route 73 is a high road over Goshen Mountain and through Brandon Gap. At the height-of-land, several wooded hiking trails are posted, and a rest area has been sited to catch the full majesty of Mount Horrid's Great Cliff. The road then rushes downhill with Brandon Brook, joining Route 100 and the White River below Rochester.

Note: A well-surfaced woods road (Goshen Road) runs south from Ripton through the national forest, past the turnoffs for Silver Lake and past Blueberry Hill to Route 73 in the Brandon Gap.

Appalachian Gap. East from Bristol, Route 17 climbs steadily for 4 miles (past the Jerusalem General Store), eases off for a couple of miles, and then zigzags steeply to crest at more than 3,000 feet, yielding some spectacular views before dropping into the Mad River Valley. It's even more spectacular heading west.

Lincoln/Appalachian Gap Loop. From Bristol, follow Routes 17/116 to the turnoff for Lincoln 2 miles east of Bristol, past Bartlett Falls (be sure to stop) to Lincoln and out the Downingsville Road to Jerusalem, back down on Route 116 to Route 17.

Lincoln Gap. Follow Routes 17/116 east from Bristol, as above, but from Lincoln continue on the narrow Gap Road, unpaved in sections. Again there are beautiful views, and you are quickly down in Warren. *Note:* Unsuitable for trailers and RVs. Closed in winter.

Along Lake Champlain. See *Villages* for Shoreham and Orwell.

✳ To Do

APPLE PICKING September and early October is apple time in Addison County, where you are welcome to pick your own (PYO). The orchards are particularly thick in and around Shoreham: **Atwood Orchard** (802-897-5592) on Barnum Hill, 0.5 mile from its stand on Route 22A (3 miles south of Shoreham Village), offers PYO apples and sells honey, syrup, and apple pies; also a picnic area and views of Lake Champlain. **Douglas Orchards** (802-897-5043), 1 mile west of the village on Route 74, has PYO apples, cherries, berries, and pumpkins, as well as a cider mill, a retail store, and hand-knit felt hats designed by Betty Douglas. **Champlain Orchards** (802-897-2777), farther west on Route 74, offers PYO fruits, cider-mill tours, and weekend concerts in the orchard during apple season.

BICYCLING It's no coincidence that the country's first bicycle touring company was founded in this area. According to Bruce Burgess, a pioneer tour leader, there just isn't a more rewarding place to bike anywhere than this swath of the Champlain Valley, with its relatively flat terrain and mountain views, its wealth of back roads leading through covered bridges, connecting historic sites and comfortable inns with ample swimming holes, ice cream, and antiquing stops en route. Burgess shares a word of warning: Beware deceptively quiet but narrow, truck-trafficked roads like Route 22A and Route 30.

Bike Vermont (1-800-257-2226), based in Woodstock, gets good reviews for guided, small-group inn-to-inn tours in this area.

Vermont Bicycle Touring (VBT) (802-453-4811), Box 711, Bristol, the state's oldest bike tour company, offers guided group inn-to-inn tours.

The Bike Center (802-388-6666), 74 Main Street, Middlebury, is a source for a variety of rental bikes.

Country Inns Along the Trail (1-800-838-3301), Van Cortland Road, Brandon 05733. Bike tours usually begin and end at Churchill House Inn, which has a fleet of bikes for rent at $15 per day, including helmet. Other inns are on the itinerary. A brochure is available from the Churchill House.

Mountain Biking at Blueberry Hill (802-247-6735), Goshen. An extensive network of ski trails and woods roads that is well suited to mountain biking; rentals, lessons.

BIRDING **Otter Creek**, near Lake Champlain in Vergennes, and the **Dead Creek Wildlife Management Area** in Addison (off Route 17) are particularly rich in bird life, especially during migration seasons. See also "What's Where."

BOATING **Carillon Cruises** (802-897-5331), a 60-foot, 49-passenger replica of a 1920s Thousand Islands luxury motor yacht, operates daily Father's Day through Labor Day. Geared to groups in spring and fall but walk-ons accepted (call ahead), from Teachout's Lakehouse Store and Wharf at Larrabees Point. The 1½-hour cruise, beginning at 11 AM, and 1 and 3 PM, goes up to Hand's Cove, then across to Fort Ticonderoga (you can debark and catch a later boat), and on to Mount Independence and Mount Defiance, while the captain tells you what was happening along the route in the 1770s.

Kim Grant

THE M/V *CARILLON* EXCURSION BOAT ON LAKE CHAMPLAIN

Boat rentals are available from **Vermont Houseboat Vacations** (802-948-2375), Route 73A, Orwell; **Buoy 39 Marina** (802-948-2411), Route 73A, Orwell; **Waterhouses** (802-252-4433), West Shore Road, Lake Dunmore (rents rowboats, canoes, motorboats, sailboats); **Champlain Bridge Marina** (802-759-2049), West Addison (boat access, pump-out station for boats less than 35 feet); **Chipman Point Marina & Campground** (802-948-2288), Route 73A (dockage for 60 boats, grocery store, pump-out station, game room, swimming, boat rentals); and **Lake Dunmore Kampersville** (802-352-4501), in Salisbury, which also rents rowboats, canoes, sailboats, and motor bugs.

FACTORY TOURS **Otter Creek Brewing** (1-800-473-0727), 85 Exchange Street, Middlebury. Open daily for free guided tours. Free samples, retail sales of its Copper Ale, Stovepipe Porter, and lagers.

FISHING **Otter Creek** is a warm-water stream good for smallmouth bass and northern pike. The cooler **Neshobe River,** especially in Forest Dale, is better for trout, and rainbows can be found in the **Middlebury River** just below Ripton. The **New Haven River** between Lincoln and Bristol and south of New Haven Mills also offers good trout fishing.

FITNESS CENTERS **Vermont Sun** (802-388-6888), 88 Exchange Street, Middlebury, is a spacious indoor sports and fitness center with training equipment, an Olympic-sized pool, and racquetball courts. Open daily for members; guests by the day or week.
Middlebury Fitness (802-388-3744), Wilson Road off Route 7 south, Middlebury, features state-of-the-art equipment. Guests by the day or by the week.

GOLF **Ralph Myhre Golf Course** (802-388-3771), Route 30 just south of the Middlebury campus, is owned and operated by the college; 18 holes.
The Basin Harbor Club (802-475-2311), Vergennes, 18 holes.
Neshobe Golf Club (802-247-3611), Town Farm Road (just off Route 73), Brandon. Open April through October. A full-service club; 18 holes.

HIKING **The Green Mountain National Forest District Office** (802-388-4362), Route 7, Middlebury, offers a pamphlet guide to 28 day hikes.

Country Inns Along the Trail (1-800-838-3301). A dozen other inns collaborate with Churchill House (1-877-248-7444) to provide lodging along an 80-mile stretch of the Long Trail and some of its side trails, including the section over Mount Mansfield.

Middlebury Area Land Trust (802-388-1007) publishes *Trails Around Middlebury,* a map/guide to 14 miles of trails.

HORSEBACK RIDING **Mazza Horse Service** (802-758-9240), Hemenway Road, Bridport. Trail-riding, lessons.

Firefly B&B (802-453-2223), Bristol. Open May through October for riding. Set off a back road high in the mountains, an expanded chalet with just three guest rooms (private bath). Beginning in spring 2004, Firefly will be working with a local operation to offer trail rides over dirt roads and woods trails.

SWIMMING **Middlebury Gorge,** East Middlebury, off Route 125 just above the Waybury Inn, where the road suddenly steepens beyond the bridge. Paths lead down to the river.

Bartlett Falls, Bristol. Near the beginning of the Lincoln Gap Road (off Route 116 in Rocky Dale) there's a pull-off for this popular swimming hole. A bronze plaque explains that the land is a gift from Irving Wesley Sr., in memory of his son who died at 19 fighting a 1943 forest fire in British Columbia. It's a beautiful spot by a stream with shallow falls dropping into pools. Swimming shoes are a good idea.

See also *Green Space.*

✳ Winter Sports

CROSS-COUNTRY SKIING **Carroll and Jane Rikert Ski Touring Center** at the Bread Loaf Campus of Middlebury College (802-388-2759), Route 125, Ripton, 12 miles from the main campus, is owned and operated by Middlebury College. It has more than 42 km of groomed trails in the area of the Robert Frost Farm and the college ski bowl. Elevations range from 975 to 1,500 feet. Rentals, accessories, repairs.

Blueberry Hill Inn (802-247-6735), Goshen, has 50 km of tracked and groomed trails plus another 20 km of outlying trails on elevations of 1,400–3,100 feet. This is a surefire cross-country mecca during even marginal seasons. The ski center has retail and rental equipment, waxing, and repairs.

DOWNHILL SKIING **Middlebury College Snow Bowl** (802-388-4356), 13 miles east of Middlebury on Route 125, at Bread Loaf. A throwback to a less commercial era of skiing: well-maintained, winding trails with a library in the base lodge! Two double chairs, one triple, a total of 15 trails; 40 percent covered by snowmaking. It also offers a ski school, rentals, cafeteria. Closed December 25. Adults $35 weekends, $26 weekdays.

✳ Green Space

Note: Public preserves are clustered on the eastern and western fringes of the valley.

On or near Lake Champlain

Button Bay State Park (802-475-2377; 802-483-2314), on Panton Road just below Basin Harbor. Named for the unusual, buttonlike clay bank formations, with a splendid view across the lake to the Adirondacks; 72 campsites, picnic areas, swimming, fishing, nature museum, and trails. Rocky Point juts into Lake Champlain like the prow of a ship.

Kingsland Bay State Park (802-877-3445), Ferrisburgh. Marked from Route 7. Facilities include a picnic area on Lake Champlain, also tennis courts and hiking trails. This is a particularly lovely overlook of Kingsland Bay with lawns that roll down to the lakeside shaded by old maples. Weddings and summer get-togethers are very popular here.

Dead Creek Wildlife Management Area (802-759-2397), 7 miles east of the D.A.R. State Park on Route 17, is a 2,800-acre, semiwilderness tract. Except for certain refuges, it is open to the public. The information booth isn't always staffed, because the supervisor is generally in the field, but a self-guided tour folder is available.

D.A.R. State Park (802-759-2354; 802-483-2314), 8 miles west of Addison on Route 17, has a campground with 71 sites and a picnic area. Steps lead down to a smooth shale beach for swimming.

In or near the Green Mountain National Forest

Lake Dunmore, in Salisbury between Brandon and Middlebury on Route 53 off Route 7, is a tranquil, 1,000-acre lake that has licked its once infamous mosquito problem. It is lined with summer cottages at the foot of Mount Moosalamoo and along its hiking trails. On the east shore road is **Branbury State Park** (802-247-5925), with a sandy beach, boating, snack bar, picnic grove, museum nature trail, and hiking to the Falls of Lana. The trail begins just south of the Branbury Park entrance, and it's just 0.5 mile to the picnic area and falls. From Route 53 it's 1.6 miles past these falls up to **Silver Lake,** a mountain lake that was the site of religious camp meetings in the 1880s; a large hotel (actually constructed as a seminary) occupied the site of the present picnic area and stood until around 1940, when it was destroyed by fire. About 1 mile long, it is now part of the Green Mountain National Forest, accessible only by foot and mountain bike (0.6 mile via the Goshen Trail from the second parking lot on Forest Road 27, off Goshen Road). There are 31 primitive campsites and a nature trail around the lake; swimming is permitted.

"Robert Frost Country" in the Green Mountain National Forest is a title officially bestowed in 1983 on a wooded piece of the town of Ripton because it's here, in a log cabin, that the poet summered for 39 years. This section of Route 125, between the old Bread Loaf Inn (part of the Middlebury College campus) and the village, has been designated the Robert Frost Memorial Highway; there is also a Robert Frost Interpretive Trail and a Robert Frost Wayside picnic area near the road leading to the farm and cabin. The picnic area has grills and drinking water, and it's shaded by red pines that were pruned by Frost himself. Just east of the wayside, a dirt road leads to the Homer Noble Farm, which Frost bought in 1939. Park in the lot provided and walk past the farm to Frost's cabin (it's not open to the public). The Robert Frost Interpretive Trail, a bit west on the opposite side of Route 125, is an easy walk, just 0.75 mile. It begins with a bridge across Beaver Pond (we actually saw a beaver here one time) and winds through woods and meadow, by seven Frost poems mounted along the way. This trail is also popular with cross-country skiers and snowshoers, and with July and August blueberry pickers.

Texas Falls, in Hancock, is easily accessible from the marked road, 3 miles east of the Middlebury Gap. It's a short drive to the parking area, and the succession of falls is just across the road, visible from a series of paths and bridges. There's also a picnic area.

✳ Lodging

Mid VT for All Seasons Area Guide, Mid VT Map (1-800-733-8376; www.midvermont.com). This comprehensive guide to area lodging is available by calling the 800 number or visiting the web site.

INNS ⊙ ♂ ♿ **Swift House Inn** (802-388-9925; fax: 802-388-9927), 25 Stewart Lane, Middlebury 05753. Formerly the family estate of the legendary philanthropist Jessica Stewart Swift, who lived to be over 100, the

SWIFT HOUSE INN

Kim Grant

Swift House is now under the ownership of Jim and Katrina Kappel. Antiques, elaborately carved marble fireplaces, formal gardens with more than 20 rosebushes, and other gracious amenities add to the charm of this 1814 mansion. Common space in the inn itself includes a cozy pub as well as two attractive living rooms. A continental breakfast is served in the cherry-paneled main dining room, in the library, or on the sunporch. There are 10 guest rooms in the main house, 5 in the gatehouse, and 6 in the renovated 1886 carriage house. One room is wheelchair accessible, as is the dining room. Rates per room are $110–245 in high season, $90–225 in low season. Some suites have fireplace, sitting area, whirlpool tub, and cable TV. The dining room, closed for a couple of years, reopened in the summer of 2003 (see *Dining Out*).

⊙ ☃ ♿ **Lilac Inn** (802-247-5463; 1-800-221-0720; www.lilacinn.com), 53 Park Street, Brandon 05733. One of New England's most romantic inns, this grand old mansion has been totally restored. Built with an imposing five-arched facade in 1909 by a Brandon-born financier, the mansion,

RESORT 🏨 ♂ ♿ **Basin Harbor Club** (802-475-2311; 1-800-622-4000, www.basin harbor.com), Box 7, Vergennes 05491, located on Lake Champlain 5 miles west of town, off Panton Road. Open mid-May through mid-October. This is Vermont's premier family-run resort. The 700-acre retreat offers 136 rooms, most in cottages scattered along the shore. Since 1886, when they began taking in summer boarders, members of the Beach family have assiduously kept up with the times. Over the years a large swimming pool, an 18-hole golf course, and even an airstrip have been added. Still, the handsome old farmhouse has been preserved. In summer Dutchman's-pipe climbs as it always has around the porch pillars, and three grand old maples shade the lawn, which slopes to the extensive flower gardens and the round harbor beyond. There are 18 rooms in the inn, 13 more in the attractive stone Harbor Homestead. The 77 cottages, geared to families (and well-behaved pets), vary in rate depending on size and location. All have phone, fridge, and wet bar; many have fireplace. Eight cottages are handicapped accessible, with ramps and bathrooms, as are all public areas. The lakeside units are worth the little extra, with views of the lake and the Adirondacks so extraordinary that it's difficult to tear yourself away from the window or deck, especially at sunset.

Basin Harbor manages to please both children and elderly couples. Youngsters can take advantage of the beach, elaborate playground, and lively, supervised (complimentary) children's program available 9:30 AM–1:30 PM for ages 3–15, and younger children can also dine together and play until 9 PM. For those 10–15, there are golf and tennis clinics, movies, mixers, and video games in the Red Mill, the resort's informal restaurant off by the airstrip. Those who like to dress for dinner have ample opportunity; at the main restaurant, men and boys over 12 must wear jackets and ties. The food is fine (see *Dining Out*). Daily rates per couple $120–350 B&B; with a full American plan (the only plan available from June 13 through September 1), $216–447 per couple; add 15 percent gratuity. Daily rate extra for children 3 and older, depending on age. There are also golf, tennis, and fall foliage packages; inquire about kayaking, horticultural workshops, and birding and nature treks.

now owned by Shelly and Doug Sawyer, has some splendid common spaces (a glassed-in ballroom is the scene of chamber concerts and wedding receptions) and a wide entrance hallway with a grand staircase. There is also a formal garden with a gazebo and cobbled patio, a small living room with a fireplace and floor-to-ceiling bookcases, and a bar with comfortable seating. The nine ample guest rooms all have luxurious bathrooms with deep, claw-footed tubs; each is furnished in antiques and has a hidden TV. The bridal suite has a pewter canopy bed, whirlpool bath, fireplace, and dressing area. There is one handicapped-accessible room. Weddings are a specialty. Rates include a full breakfast, served in the oak-paneled dining room, where dinner is also served Thursday through Saturday. $225–325 in high season, otherwise $135–225. Inquire about MAP, winter weekends featuring music or dramatic readings, and the cottage for four. Children must be over 12, and pets require prior approval.

⊕ 🐾 🐾 ✿ ♿ **Blueberry Hill Inn** (802-247-6735; 802-247-6535; 1-800-448-0707; www.blueberryhillinn.com), Goshen 05733, on Forest Road 32 in Ripton. Over the past three decades Tony Clark has turned this blue 1820 farmhouse on a high, remote back road into one of New England's most famous country inns. The big lures are fine food, hiking and mountain biking, and, in winter, cross-country skiing. But there is more to it: a sure

touch. The 12 rooms—some with loft, all with full bath—have their share of antiques. The common rooms are sunny and inviting with geraniums blooming in the greenhouse off the kitchen and a stone fireplace in the dining room. Guests are encouraged to mingle, from morning coffee to evening hors d'oeuvres and dinner. This inn has long been known for its food, and current chefs more than deserve the reputation, producing elaborate, creative dinners featuring fresh, local ingredients. The cross-country ski center, with 75 km of groomed trails, tends to be snowy, thanks to its elevation, if there is any snow in Vermont. MAP rates per person: $100–160, depending on the season. There are four rooms that can accommodate a family group, with special rates for children 12 and under in same room with parent. BYOB. No smoking.

🐾 **The Middlebury Inn** (802-388-4961; 1-800-842-4666; www.middle buryinn.com), 14 Courthouse Square, Middlebury 05753, has been the town's imposing chief hostelry since 1827. The Emanuel family has completely renovated the 75 guest and public rooms. Rooms in the main house are on two floors (there's a 1926 Otis elevator) and are furnished in reproduction antiques. They have private bath, cable TV, air conditioner/heater, and direct-dial phone. There are also 20 motel units with inn-style furnishings, and the adjacent Porter Mansion, full of handsome architectural details, has 10 Victorian rooms. The common rooms include a vast, comfortable lobby with a formal check-in desk and portraits of the Battell family and Robert Frost. Elegant afternoon tea and light dinners

THE BLUEBERRY HILL INN IN GOSHEN

Kim Grant

are available in the pubby Morgan Tavern; dinner and buffet breakfast are served in the pillared, Wedgwood blue, formal dining room (see *Dining Out*). Lunch is served in the Rose Room and on the front porch in summer and early fall. Thoughtful touches include readable books on shelves near guest rooms and umbrellas next to the door for guests to use. Continental breakfast is included in rates that run $90–400 double, including afternoon tea. Inquire about packages. Pets are welcome in the motel units for a small daily fee, and arrangements for babysitting can be made.

The Shoreham Inn (802-897-5081; out-of-state: 1-800-255-5081), Route 74 west, Shoreham 05770. This friendly, comfortable place is a great antidote if you've overdosed on Laura Ashley wallpaper and mints on the lacy coverlets of antique beds. Rooms are whimsically decorated, some with daybeds for families, and plenty of singles for the many bicyclists and hikers who frequent the inn. There are 10 guest rooms, 9 with private bath. The many-windowed inn, which dates from 1790, sits in the middle of a small village, surrounded by apple country and not far from Larrabees Point, Mount Independence, Fort Ticonderoga, New York, and the college town of Middlebury. The common rooms are filled with pictures, plants, and, frequently, the aroma of coffee, soup, or other things cooking and baking in the kitchen. $75 single with full breakfast, $105 double.

Churchill House Inn (802-247-3078; 1-877-248-7444; www.churchill houseinn.com), 3128 Forest Dale Road (Route 73), Brandon 05733. Located west of the Brandon Gap on Route 73, this old farmhouse, run by Richard Daybell, has nine guest rooms furnished in 19th-century style. There are zesty dinners and breakfasts, and canoeing, hiking, bicycling, snowshoeing, and cross-country ski expeditions are offered. MAP rates are $180–220 per room plus 15 percent gratuity; $25 less per person for breakfast only; inquire about 3- and 5-day packages.

Waybury Inn (802-388-4015; 1-800-348-1810; www.wayburyinn .com), Route 125, East Middlebury 05740. A historic, 14-room village inn, open all year. The Waybury was a favorite of Robert Frost's when he lived up the hill in Ripton. There's no pool, but a swimmin' hole under the nearby bridge can be used to cool off in the heat of the summer, while you can warm up in the Pub the rest of the year. Dinner and Sunday brunch are served year-round. The rates are $110–215 double, including a full breakfast. Two-night minimum stay on busy weekends and holidays.

Chipman Inn (802-388-2390; 1-800-890-2390; www.chipmaninn.com), P.O. Box 115, Route 125, Ripton 05766. On the way to or from Bread Loaf and the Middlebury College Snow Bowl, this inn sits in the center of the tiny village of Ripton, which consists of a schoolhouse, community meetinghouse, church, and general store. It's also within striking distance of Robert Frost's house and cabin and the Robert Frost Trail. This is an attractive 1828 house with eight guest rooms of varying sizes (we suggest requesting one at the back of the house), all with private bath. Guests gather in the lounge/bar and around a very large old hearth or settle into the sunny sitting room near the woodstove.

Innkeepers Joyce Henderson and Bill Pierce encourage breakfast guests to sit together at long tables. Rates are $90–160 per couple in high season, $80–135 in low season, with full breakfast. Children 12 and older.

⊙ ✍ **The Inn at Baldwin Creek** (802-453-2432; www.innatbaldwin creek.com), 1868 North Route 116, Bristol 05443. Open year-round. A classic Vermont farmhouse inn set on 25 acres including a perennial garden with paths down to Baldwin Creek. Mary's Restaurant, attached to the inn, is a favorite regional dining spot (see *Dining Out*). Four guest rooms with private bath include a two-room suite, which works well for families. Weddings and catered events for up to 200 people. Heated outdoor swimming pool. Innkeeper Linda Harmon and chef Doug Mack have been in business for 20 years and counting. $135–185 per room in summer, $95–145 in winter, including full breakfast and afternoon tea.

🐾 ✍ **The Brandon Inn** (802-247-5766; www.historicbrandoninn.com), 20 Park Street, Brandon 05733. A large brick landmark overlooking the village green, this inn dates from 1892 and is on the National Register of Historic Places. Innkeepers Sarah and Louis Pattis have scaled down the number of guest rooms from 46 to 37, refurbishing them nicely. Number 217, a two-room suite, is especially attractive ($155 MAP). Low-season rates are $125–185 per room; in high season, $165–280. Children under 12 are free in their parent's room (except for meals), and are welcome. There are TV rooms upstairs as well as large living rooms downstairs, and some of the 19th-century furniture and a good deal of the atmosphere survive. The

inn's 5 landscaped acres include a swimming pool (with Jacuzzi) and a stretch of the Neshobe River, good for trout fishing. An 18-hole golf course is just up the way. Buses from New York, Boston, and Montreal still stop, as stages once did, at the front door.

BED & BREAKFASTS

In and around Middlebury 05753

&. **The Inn on the Green** (802-388-7512; 1-888-244-7512), 71 South Pleasant Street. A recent addition to the downtown hospitality scene, this very attractive 1803 Federal town house has two impressive, colorfully decorated suites in the main house, plus eight other spacious rooms, each with private bath, phone, and cable TV. There's also a more contemporary carriage house, same amenities. Rates $98–240.

🐾 **Fairhill** (802-388-3044), 724 East Munger Street, 4 miles east of Middlebury, on 75 acres of woodland, marsh, and meadows. Russell and Fleur Laslocky's 1825 center-chimney Cape has three guest rooms, one with a four-poster double bed and private bath. The breakfast area is in an 18th-century granary. Rates $80–100.

In and around East Middlebury 05740

⊙ **By the Way B&B** (802-388-6291), 407 East Main Street. Barbara Simoes, who has taken over from her mother, Nancy, provides two spacious guest rooms with private bath and air-conditioning, as well as a guest house. Rates are $95–190 per room with full breakfast; the wraparound veranda is appealing, and an in-ground swimming pool is set in the orchard. Children 8 and older.

∞ **Wild Wind B&B** (802-453-4557; www.wildwindvermont.com), 430 Orchard Road, Lincoln 05443. A shingle-style home at the base of Mount Abraham, Wild Wind offers truly remarkable panoramic views of mountains and valleys all around. The two rooms—French and Victorian— are done in full style. It's open Memorial Day through October, 2-night minimum stays, no children under 15. $225.

In and around Vergennes 05491

The Strong House Inn (802-877-3337; www.stronghouseinn.com), 94 West Main Street (Route 22A). This is a real beauty, built in the 1830s by Samuel Paddock Strong in the graceful Federal style, with fine workmanship such as curly maple railings on the freestanding main staircase. Mary and Hugh Bargiel offer 14 guest rooms, all with private bath, cable TV, and telephone. The rooms are in the main house as well as in Rabbit Ridge Country House, which is a new building on the grounds. Rates are $80–275 (more during foliage and holiday seasons), including full breakfast and afternoon refreshments. Inquire about quilting and crafting weekends.

Emerson Guest House (802-877-3293; emersonhouse.com), 82 Main Street. Six bright and airy guest rooms in this Victorian town house are named for New England writers and poets. $65–150 with full breakfast.

& **Whitford House** (802-758-2704; 1-800-746-2704; www.whitfordhouse inn.com), 912 Grandey Road, Addison 05491. On Grandey Road between Nortontown and Townline Roads off Route 22A (ask directions!). Sited east of the lake in rich farmland, it's set among flower gardens on 2 acres of mowed lawns with spectacular views of the Adirondacks from the outdoor deck. Tranquillity and warm hospitality are the hallmarks of Bruce and Barbara Carson's 18th-century farmhouse, with two upstairs bedrooms (king or twin beds) and private baths. A spacious first-floor bedroom has a four-poster double bed and private bath. The Great Room, with its fireplace made from local Panton stone, is a perfect place for relaxing. There is also a cottage with a large bedroom (king-sized bed), sitting room with sofa bed, and full bath. $110–225 in low season (plus $25 for each additional guest); $135–250 in high season. Price includes afternoon refreshments, full breakfast, and loan of the Carsons' canoe and bicycles. Breakfasts are events in themselves, and visiting chefs prepare memorable five-course, prix fixe dinners when reservations are made.

Heatherstone B&B (802-759-3180; www.visitheatherstone.com), 3324 Jersey Street South, Addison 05491. If it's views you want, this is the place. Set out in the farmland of Addison County, this three-bedroom stone house has spectacular views of the Adirondacks. Breakfast is served at 8:30 in the Great Room. Other amenities include a sauna and hot tub. $115–250 with breakfast.

✔ **Barsen House Inn** (802-759-2646; 1-888-819-6103; www.barsen houseinn.com), 53 TriTown Road, Addison 05491. Daphne and Peter Jensen offer a two-bedroom private wing with living room, TV, and private bath. Kids will find plenty to do here: gathering eggs, picking berries, catching frogs, or roasting marshmallows in the fire pit. There's also swimming and boating access nearby.

Rates $75–170 with continental breakfast.

South and west of Middlebury
Quiet Valley Bed & Breakfast
(802-897-7887), 1467 Quiet Valley Road, Shoreham 05770. A new house built along traditional lines with wide pine floors to maximize the light and views across the Lemon Fair River to the hills. Bruce Lustgarten burns only applewood in the large, shallow, Rumford-style fireplace in the living room, and Jane enjoys preparing "healthy" breakfasts for guests. The three guest rooms with four-poster bed and fireplace have private or shared bath. Rates $85–125.

🐾 **Buckswood Bed & Breakfast**
(802-948-2054), 633 Route 73E, Orwell 05760. Open year-round. Linda and Bob Martin offer two guest rooms (private baths) and ample common space in their 1814 home, located in a pleasant country setting just east of Orwell Village. Dinner by reservation. Rates of $60–70 per couple include breakfast. Polite pets accepted.

In and around Brandon 05733
Old Mill Inn (802-247-8002; 1-800-599-0341), 79 Stone Mill Dam Road (Route 73 east). Owned by Ed and Cindy Thomas, this is an attractive farmhouse set above the Neshobe River, adjoining the 18-hole Neshobe Golf Club. Guests enter through a sunny breakfast room and find two large living rooms with wing chairs, a piano, TV, and Cindy's artwork. The four guest rooms have private bath, stenciling, and carefully chosen antiques. Three dogs and a barn cat share the premises. Guests can take advantage of the swimming hole in the neighboring rushing stream.

$85–95 per couple includes a full country breakfast.

The Inn on Park Street (802-247-3843; 1-800-394-7239; www.theinn onparkstreet.com), 69 Park Street. Park Street is as close as Brandon comes to a la-di-da address, what with all its fancy Victorian homes, many of which are on the National Historic Register. Tracey and Thomas Heaney offer five guest rooms, each with its own style but all with private bath and lots of antiques. They do robes and slippers here, and you can ask for a rose-petal turndown for special occasions. Rates with full breakfast: $115–195. The Heaneys also do dinner packages: a minimum of six courses for $45 per person, by reservation.

Rosebelle's Victorian Inn (802-247-0098; www.rosebelles.com), 31 Franklin Street, P.O. Box 370, Route 7. This nicely restored, mansard-roofed house has a high-ceilinged living room with fireplace and TV and a large dining room—the setting for afternoon tea and full breakfasts. Guests with small musical instruments are especially welcome. Hostess Ginette Milot speaks French. The five guest rooms all have private bath, and two rooms can be joined to form a suite for four. $95–125 per double in high season, $85–110 in low. Children over 10 must have a separate room. Two-night minimum stays are required on holiday weekends and during foliage season.

The Gazebo Inn (802-247-3235; 1-888-858-3235), 25 Grove Street (Route 7). This is another attractive in-town, circa-1865 classic house, with a wood-burning stove in the sitting room. It's decorated with folk art and antiques and has four comfortable guest rooms, private baths. Antiques shop on premises; families welcome. Rates include a full breakfast at $90–120 per couple.

Judith's Garden (802-247-4707), 423 Goshen–Ripton Road, Goshen 05733. Locally noted for its lovely perennial gardens in a mountainous setting, with easy trail access for hikers, walkers, and cross-country skiers who want to take advantage of the Moosalamoo region. Proprietors Judith Irven and Dick Conrad serve smoked salmon and dill quiche, among other breakfast dishes. The gazebo in the garden is a particularly nice summer spot. This restored 1830s farmhouse has three attractive bedrooms with private bath; $90–105 per room includes breakfast.

🐾 **Salisbury Village Bed & Breakfast** (802-352-6006), P.O. Box 214, Salisbury 05769. Not far from Lake Dunmore, this restored farmhouse has four guest rooms, two with private and two with shared bath ($65–75), and welcomes polite pets at $10 per night—even providing daycare for them.

🐾 ✎ **Birdcage B&B Inn** (802-247-4634; 1-866-247-4634; www.bird cagevermont.com), P.O. Box 391, Wheeler Road. Princess Jirina Obolensky welcomes guests to her Victorian home on 40 acres. There's a private hiking or cross-country skiing trail and a sauna to relax in afterward. The three rooms with private bath rent for $85–205 with full breakfast.

Other choices in the Brandon area include **12 Franklin Street B&B** (802-247-6672; www.12franklin street.com) and the **Wyndmere House B&B** (802-247-5006).

🐾 **Crystal Palace Victorian B&B** (802-453-4131; 1-888-674-4131), 48 North Street. This impressive 1897 mansion with a turret provides six guest rooms; $85–130 with full breakfast. Dogs are welcome.

Bristol Coach House B&B (802-453-2236), 23 West Street. Patricia Highley's home from the early 1800s overlooks the village green. The three rooms have shared bath and rent for $65–75, including continental breakfast.

See also Firefly B&B under *Horseback Riding.*

COTTAGES **Lake Dunmore.** Some cottagers hope that the lake will remain off the beaten track; however, it's being "discovered." Here are some good bets:

✎ **Lake Dunmore's Sunset Lodge** (802-352-4290; off-season: 515-249-5888; www.sunsetlodgevermont.com), 425 West Shore Road, Salisbury 05769. Nineteen housekeeping cottages with easy access to swimming, fishing, and boating. $500–700 weekly from May through October.

North Cove Cottages (in summer: 802-352-4236; in winter: 617-354-0124), P.O. Box 76, Salisbury 05769. Nine housekeeping cottages, sandy beach, free rowboats; $53–85 per night (2-night minimum), $322–504 per week.

Note: The Addison County Chamber of Commerce (802-388-7951) has a list of rental cottages on both Lake Dunmore and Lake Champlain.

MOTELS **Courtyard by Marriott** (1-866-211-4607; www.middlebury courtyard.com), 309 Court Street

(Route 7 south), Middlebury 05753. A brand new Courtyard just south of Middlebury Village is done in New England style with a wraparound porch. There are 89 rooms, a hot breakfast buffet, indoor pool, and exercise room. $89–275, including breakfast.

Lagasse's Country Cottages (802-247-6644; 1-800-759-6537), 1246 Franklin Street (Route 7 south), Brandon 05733. Open year-round. Located on Route 7, 1 mile south of Brandon, this is a shady campus of 20 cozy one- and two-room cottages of the kind so familiar in premotel motoring days. Most of the cottages have fireplace and cable TV, and there's a stocked trout pond, swimming pool, miniature golf across the highway, and a steak house next door (see *Eating Out*). Rates for two: $65–75.

FARM VACATION **Cream Hill Farm** (802-897-2101), P.O. Box 205, Shoreham 05770. Rene and Paul Saenger welcome families to their 1,100-acre diversified farm, with beef cattle. This is very much a working farm (meaning it smells like a farm, and its owners may be preoccupied with farm chores). The 1830s renovated farmhouse has two large guest rooms, one with private bath. Call for rates.

CAMPGROUNDS See *Green Space*.

✳ Where to Eat

DINING OUT **The Storm Café** (802-388-1063), 3 Mill Street, Middlebury. This intimate, casual spot by the river is considered by many to serve the most imaginative food in town, if not in the state. Dinner is available 5–9 Tuesday through Saturday. Entrées range $14–22 and include barbecued pork loin, baked herb polenta, and a fish special of the day.

Swift House Inn (802-388-9925), 25 Stewart Lane, Middlebury. Dinner at this very popular downtown inn (see *Lodging*) is served 6–9 Thursday through Monday. Among the specialties are the rustic Tuscan barlotti bean zuppa ($5), the artichoke beignets ($9), and the foraged mushroom cassoulet ($10). And then you'll have to choose an entrée . . .

Fire & Ice Restaurant (802-388-7166; 1-800-367-7166), 26 Seymour Street, Middlebury. Open 11:30–9:30 daily except Monday. "Good Food & Legal Vice," it says of itself; excellent lunch and dinner plus Sunday brunch in an informal stained-glass and mahogany setting that has recently been enlarged. A local favorite since 1974, specializing in steaks ($14.95–20.95), prime rib ($14.95–19.95), and chicken dishes like a fresh boneless breast sautéed in a champagne and mushroom cream sauce ($14.95). The name was inspired by a Robert Frost poem.

Roland's Place (802-453-6309), Route 7, New Haven. A grand old tower-topped mansion, this 1796 house is the setting for dinner and Sunday brunch year-round, lunches for groups of 10 or more by reservation. Owner-chef Roland Gaujac has a Provençal background but specializes in foods fresh off the nearby farms. His menu often includes local trout, venison, or emu as well as more conventional fare, all very well prepared. (Guest rooms available at $75–105.)

Basin Harbor Club (802-475-2311), Basin Harbor, off Panton Road, 5 miles west of Vergennes. If you don't stay at Basin Harbor, there's all the more reason to drive out for lunch or dinner, to see the lakeside setting and savor the atmosphere. The food is fine, too. The menu and dining room are both large. The menu changes frequently, but at dinner (reserve) you might begin with Green Mountain smoked trout, then enjoy seared breast of ginger-soy-marinated duck. The prix fixe is $36 plus 15 percent service charge. The wine list is extensive and excellent. Jacket and tie required. More casual dining is available in the **Red Mill,** which is on the grounds.

Tully and Marie's (802-388-4182; tullyandmaries.com), 5 Bakery Lane, Middlebury, open daily 11:30 AM–midnight; Sunday brunch. Closed Tuesday in winter. You have the sense of being wined and dined on a small, three-decker art deco ship beached on the bank of Otter Creek. Recent menu offerings included salad of Vermont organic baby greens with fresh strawberries, Gorgonzola, toasted pecans, and black cherry vinaigrette; rare pan-blackened Ahi tuna with wasabi aioli, orange sesame glass noodles, and baby greens; and Mayan-style achiote-spiced chicken fajitas with poblano chiles, caramelized onions, jicama, and mango, served with margarita slaw. Entrées run in the $10–15 range.

Mister Up's (802-388-6724), on the Bakery Lane plaza, Middlebury, open daily lunch–midnight; Sunday brunch buffet 11–2. Dine outdoors on the riverside deck or in the brick-walled, stained-glass, oak-and-greenery setting inside. The menu is equally colorful, ranging from the Ultimate Salad Bar and Bread Board to grilled steaks, seafood, and pasta dishes: $13–20.

The Middlebury Inn (802-388-4961; 802-388-4666), 14 Courthouse Square, Middlebury, serves breakfast and dinner in the Wedgwood blue Founders Room. Lunch is served in the Rose Room and on the front porch in summer and early fall, and light dinner is served in the Morgan Tavern. A popular appetizer here is fried Cabot cheese (deep-fried Vermont cheddar served with apple-maple sauce for dipping). The moderately priced menu includes fresh seafood, Angus steaks, and a rotating market special each evening. Dinner includes hot popovers.

Christophe's on the Green (802-877-3413), 5 North Green Street, Vergennes. Open for dinner Tuesday through Saturday from early May through October. Reservations suggested. Housed in the old hotel in the middle of town, a first-class French restaurant. You might begin with Cornish hen baked in phyllo, then dine on braised rabbit with mushrooms and tomatoes, served with a garlic flan and *pommes gauffrettes,* and finish with espresso crème caramel served with cardamom cream. All appetizers are $6, entrées $17.50, desserts $5.50. The prix fixe for three courses is $25.

Mary's Restaurant at Baldwin Creek (802-453-2432; 1-888-424-2432), at the junction of Routes 116 and 17, Bristol. Open year-round Wednesday through Sunday for dinner 5:30–9:30, with breakfast served daily for guests at the inn. Highly and widely regarded, chef Doug Mack has made a name for this restaurant on the banks of Baldwin Creek by serving a variety of seasonal and local specialties including local rabbit, venison, and free-roam chicken, forest mushroom pie, a vegetarian Angel on Earth, and the ever-wonderful cream of garlic soup. There are also a number of special Wednesday Farmhouse Dinners and cooking classes. Entrées $18–25; there is a bistro menu that runs $8–12.

The Dog Team Tavern (802-388-7651), a jog off Route 7, 4 miles north of Middlebury. Open for dinner daily. Gift shop. Opened in the 1930s by Sir Wilfred Grenfell (1865–1940), the British medical missionary who established hospitals, orphanages, schools, and cooperative stores in Labrador and near the Arctic Circle. Moderately priced, traditional New England fare (sticky buns, relish trays, et al.). Fried chicken dinners are $12.95, ham steak is $14.95, and prime rib is $18.95. The Dog Team has had the same menu for years now, and it keeps people coming back for more.

The Brandon Inn (802-247-5766), 20 Park Street, Brandon. Open for dinner daily except Tuesday and Wednesday. Austrian-trained owner-chef Louis Pattis and David Bofhinger make moderately priced dinner something of an event, with appetizers like crabcakes with a mango-habanero fruit sauce and entrées like roast duck served with wild blueberry ginger sauce.

Bobcat Café (802-453-3311), Main Street, Bristol. A friendly local eatery operated by veteran chef Robert Fuller. The food is substantial and well prepared, with small plates and large plates ranging $8–30. The Black Angus burgers are excellent, as is the highly popular Misty Knoll chicken dish. The enormous wooden bar was scavenged from a warehouse across the lake, and there aren't many empty bar stools. Open 7 nights from 5 PM on.

Black Sheep Bistro (802-877-3288), 253 Main Street, Vergennes. Open summer and early fall, Monday

through Saturday 5–9:30 PM, this intimate place has earned favorable reviews with chef Michel Mahé's innovative French dishes. Small plates are $5, large plates are $15; it simplifies the math. Limited seating; no credit cards.

EATING OUT ✒ **Rosie's Restaurant** (802-388-7052), 1 mile south of Middlebury on Route 7, is open daily (6 AM–9 PM in winter, until 10 May through November) and serves a lot of good, inexpensive food. This family mecca expands every eight months or so to accommodate its fans. There's a friendly counter and three large, cheerful dining rooms. We lunched on a superb beef and barley soup and turkey salad on wheat. Dinner choices run from fish-and-chips to Smitty's top sirloin, and there are always stir-fries.

Noonie's Deli (802-388-0014), 2 Maple Street (in the Marble Works), Middlebury. Open Monday through Saturday 9–9, Sunday 11–9. Good soups, the best sandwiches in Addison County (a half sandwich is plenty)— on homemade bread, you design it. Eat in or take out.

Squirrel's Nest Restaurant (802-453-6309), Route 116, Bristol. Open daily for breakfast, lunch, and dinner; Sunday brunch. Good family dining. Creemees and take-out year-round.

Amigo's (802-388-3624), on the green, Middlebury, serves Mexican specials from light snacks to full dinners, weekdays from 11:30, Sunday from 4.

Patricia's Restaurant (aka Sally's Place) (802-247-3223), Center Street, Brandon. Open daily from 11 for lunch and dinner; 1–8 Sunday, when there's a senior citizen discount on complete dinners. Traditional fare like grilled pork chops, fried haddock, and Italian dishes ranging from cheese ravioli to spaghetti with hot sausage.

Bristol Bakery & Café (802-453-3280), 16 Main Street, Bristol. Open daily from 5 AM, except Sunday when it opens at 6. This inviting storefront is filled with the aroma of coffee and breads. Design your own sandwich or stop for a muffin and espresso and take home a loaf of sourdough bread; there are also blackboard luncheon specials.

Eat Good Food (802-877-2772), 221 Main Street, Vergennes. A welcome addition to the culinary scene in Vergennes, this is primarily a gourmet take-out, but there are also tables for eating in. A good choice for lunch, dinner, or picnics, it's open Monday through Friday 9 AM–7 PM, Saturday and Sunday 9–6.

Cubbers (802-453-2400), Main Street, Bristol. A local favorite for red- and white-sauce pizza. Eat in or take out.

American Flatbread (802-388-3300; www.americanflatbread.com), 137 Maple Street, at the Marble Works, Middlebury. The company started in the Mad River Valley but has spread like a well-turned pizza crust. The all-natural pizza is made with organic flour and toppings and baked in a wood-fired oven. Serving Friday and Saturday evenings 5–9:30 year-round, with outdoor seating when possible. They'll do take-out, but only if they're not too busy, so call ahead.

Lagasse's Steak House (802-247-6644; 1-800-579-6537), 1246 Franklin Street, Brandon. Grilled chicken, pork chops, filet mignon, prime rib, and New York sirloin ($13.95–18.95) come with soup, salad and bread bar, and a choice of starch. There's a kids' menu, some seafood dishes, and it's open all year.

MICROBREWERY **Otter Creek Brewing** (1-800-473-0727), 793 Exchange Street, Middlebury. Open Monday through Saturday 10–6. Free guided tours at 1, 3, and 5 PM. Ales and other beers can be sampled in the Tasting Room.

✳ Entertainment

Middlebury College Center for the Arts (802-388-3711, ext. SHOW). The theater and concert hall in this dramatic new building on the college campus (Route 30) offer a full series of concerts, recitals, plays, dance companies, and film and video programs.

Vergennes Opera House (802-877-6737; www.vergennesoperahouse .com), Main Street, Vergennes. A renovated, century-old theater that once rang with the sounds of vaudeville now offers a spicy variety of music and theater in addition to "Friday Flicks"—silent movies on the first Friday of each month.

✳ Selective Shopping

ART GALLERIES **Woody Jackson's Holy Cow** (802-388-6737), Main Street, Middlebury. Woody himself, a Middlebury graduate whose Holstein products have become almost more of a symbol of Vermont than the maple tree, is usually on the premises. His black-and-white Holstein cows, immortalized on Ben & Jerry's ice cream cartons, decorate T-shirts, aprons, coffee mugs, boxer shorts, and more.

✒ **Norton's Gallery** (802-948-2552), Route 73 in Shoreham. The small red gallery overlooking Lake Champlain houses an amazing menagerie of dogs, rabbits, birds, and fish, along with flowers and vegetables—all sculpted from wood in unexpected sizes, unquestionably works of art and a visual delight for children and adults alike.

Prescott Galleries (802-453-4776), 47 East River Road, Lincoln. Reed Prescott III exhibits his oil paintings, many of which feature the Addison County landscape. Open May through December, Tuesday, Friday, and Saturday 10–5 or by appointment.

ANTIQUES SHOPS Middlebury Antique Center (802-388-6229; in Vermont: 1-800-339-6229), Route 7 at the junction of Route 116 in East Middlebury. A fascinating variety of furniture and furnishings representing 50 dealers.

Brookside Antiques (802-948-2727), Route 22A, Orwell. This historic Greek Revival home used to be an inn but now features fine 18th- and 19th-century furniture and country collectibles.

BOOKSTORES Vermont Book Shop (802-388-2061), 38 Main Street, Middlebury, was opened in 1947 by Robert Dike Blair, who retired several years ago as one of New England's best-known booksellers and the publisher of Vermont Books, an imprint for the poems of Walter Hard. John and Laura Scott are the proprietors these days. Robert Frost was a frequent customer for more than two decades, and the store now specializes in autographed Frost poetry collections. It has a special section set aside for Vermont authors right up front.

Deerleap Books (802-453-4062), Main Street, Bristol. Open daily except Monday. A small, friendly, and carefully stocked bookstore that entices you to browse and to buy. Author readings are held.

Otter Creek Used Books (802-388-3241), Main Street, Middlebury, is a book browser's delight: 25,000 very general titles.

✒ **Monroe Street Books** (802-388-1622), 7 Monroe Street, Middlebury. Open 10–6 Memorial Day through October, but it's a good idea to call. Dick and Flanzy Chodkowski have some 20,000 titles; specialties include children's books and cartoon, comic, and graphic art.

Bulwagga Books & Gallery (802-623-6800), corner of Route 30 and Shoreham Road at the Whiting Post Office. More than 10,000 titles plus an art gallery, handcrafted furniture, and a reading room with mountain views and coffee.

In the Alley Books (802-388-2743), in the alley across from the Frog Hollow Craft Center, Middlebury. Specialties are naturalist writings, poetry, peace studies, leftist U.S. history, feminist writings, Eastern religions, Native Americans, homesteading, and natural food cookbooks. Also used CDs and vintage vinyl LPs. Open Tuesday through Saturday afternoons and some Wednesday and Thursday evenings.

CRAFTS SHOPS The Vermont State Craft Center at Frog Hollow (802-388-3177), Middlebury. Open spring through fall, Monday through Saturday 9:30–5, as well as Sunday afternoon. This nonprofit shop combines the natural beauty of Otter Creek falls, just outside its windows, with a dazzling array of the best art and crafts work in Vermont. More than 200 Vermont artisans are represented, and you can come away with anything from a 50¢ postcard to a magnificent handcrafted $14,000 harpsichord. A feast for the eyes, it's also a serious shopping source with an outstanding selection of pottery, woven clothing, wall hangings, jewelry, and woodwork, among other things.

Warren Kimble Gallery and Gift Shops (802-247-3026), 62 Country Club Road, Brandon. Open May through October, weekdays 9–5, weekends 10–4. Folk artist Warren Kimble has made quite a name for himself nationally with his stylized animals and rural Vermont scenes, which appear on everything from aprons to lamps to furniture. This gallery/gift shop complex is where it all began.

Sweet Cecily (802-388-3353), Main Street, Middlebury. Nancy Dunn, former Frog Hollow gallery director, has assembled her own selection of ceramics, folk art, hooked rugs, and other items from 100 craftspeople, including Mexican and Amish artisans.

Danforth Pewterers (802-388-0098), 211 Maple Street, Middlebury, is best known for its distinctive pewter buttons, found in stores throughout New England. Fred and Judi Danforth actually continue a family tradition begun by Revolutionary War hero Thomas Danforth II. They also make pewter jewelry, oil lamps, and tableware. The retail shop in the Marble Works offers demonstrations of pewter making as well as a full line of products. Open June through December, Monday through Saturday 10–5, Sunday 11–4.

Robert Compton Potter (802-453-3778; www.RobertComptonPottery.com), Route 116, Bristol. As of 2003 Compton was in the process of building a three-chambered kiln that he has been designing for the past 4 years. There will be over 10,000 bricks and 22 arches incorporated in this Roman/Gothic structure, intended to serve as a work of art as much as it does a unique tool for firing pots in an ancient manner common to Japanese-style kilns. To see images of the kiln, go to the web site and click on "New Noborigama Pictures."

Lincoln Pottery (802-453-2073), 220 West River Road, Lincoln. Judith Bryant creates wheel-thrown stoneware. Her studio and showroom are located in an old dairy barn. Open daily noon–5.

SPECIAL SHOPS **Wood Ware** (802-388-6297), Route 7 south of Middlebury, is the home of good values in furniture, beds, lamps, solid butternut door harps, and dozens of other items. Interesting gift items as well. Open daily except Sunday in winter.

THE FROG HOLLOW SHOPS IN MIDDLEBURY

Kim Grant

Kennedy Brothers Marketplace
(802-877-2975), 11 North Main Street
(Route 22A), Vergennes, no longer
produces its own oak and pine
woodenware, but a Factory Marketplace serves as cooperative space for
many woodworkers and craftspeople.
Open daily 9:30–5:30.

Maple Landmark Woodcraft (1-
800-421-4223; www.maplelandmark
.com), 1297 Exchange Street, Middlebury, manufactures games and gift-
ware, including the well-known
"Name Trains" and "Montgomery
Schoolhouse" lines. Weekdays 9–5,
Saturday 9–4.

Vermont HoneyLights (802-453-
3952; 1-800-322-2660), 9 Main Street,
Bristol. Unusual assortments of hand-
poured and rolled beeswax candles
are produced in this small building.
These are not the same candles you
see in every gift store between here
and Los Angeles. Worth a look.

Beau Ties Ltd. (802-388-0108;
1-800-488-8437; www.beautiesltd
.com), 69 Industrial Avenue, Middlebury. Tour the facility to see hand-
crafters making bow ties from every
fabric imaginable. The retail store feature the current catalog choices plus
vintage ties, accessories, and gifts.
The store is open weekdays 10–4:30.

✳ Special Events

Late February: **Middlebury College
Winter Carnival** (802-388-4356)—
ice show, concerts, snow sculpture.

Mid-March: **The Pig Race** winds up
with a fine pork barbecue. Information from Blueberry Hill Inn, Goshen
(see *Cross-Country Skiing*).

Memorial Day weekend: Middlebury's
Memorial Day parade is a popular

annual event featuring lots of school
marching bands, Scouts, Little Lea-
guers, politicians, floats, and fire
trucks. It starts at 9 AM (not sharp),
but you can catch the same parade
2 hours later in **Vergennes** if you
prefer to sleep in.

Early June: **Annual Ladies Car
Rally** (802-877-6737). This is a special—and very popular—fund-raiser
for the Vergennes Opera House. If
you happen to have a wonderful
antique car (the driver must be
female, but the navigator needn't),
you could call ahead to register. If
not, come catch the finish of the rally
with festivities on the Vergennes
green.

July 4: Bristol hosts one of the most
colorful **Independence Day
parades** around. Brandon's parade is
the day before.

Early July: A 6-day **Festival on the
Green,** Middlebury, features individual performers and groups such as the
Bread & Puppet Theater as well as a
potpourri of music from folk to jazz to
exotic international talent. No charge
for admission.

Early August: **Addison County
Field Days** (802-545-2257), New
Haven. Livestock and produce fair,
horse pull, tractor pull, lumberjacks,
demolition derby, and other events.
There's also a **Taste of Vermont** dinner one night that requires reservations, but the food is worth the small
effort.

Mid-December: **Holiday Open
House at the Henry Sheldon
Museum** (802-388-2117), Park
Street, Middlebury. Come take a look
at Christmas as it used to be with
holiday traditions, activities, and decorations.

BURLINGTON REGION

Superbly sited on a slope overlooking Lake Champlain and the Adirondack Mountains, Burlington is Vermont's financial, educational, medical, and cultural center. While its fringes continue to spread over recent farmland (the core population hovers around 40,000, but the metro count is now more than 150,000), its heart beats ever faster. Few American cities this size offer as lively a downtown, as many interesting shops and affordable, varied restaurants, or as easy an access to boats, bike paths, and ski trails.

"Downtown Vermont" may sound like a contradiction, but that's just what Burlington is. Vermont is known for mountains, white-steepled churches, and cows, for rural beauty and right-spirited residents. Its only real city is backed by and overlooks mountains, has more steeples than high-rises, and offers plenty of green space (more about the cows later). Burlington actually pushes the possibilities of the sophisticated, urban good life—the ecological, healthy, responsible good life, that is.

The community was chartered in 1763, four years after the French were evicted from the Champlain Valley. Ethan Allen, his three brothers, and a cousin were awarded large grants of choice lots along the Onion (now Winooski) River. In 1791 Ira Allen secured the legislative charter for the University of Vermont (UVM), from which the first class, of four, was graduated in 1804. UVM now enrolls more than 9,000; it is now just the largest of the city's four colleges.

Ethan and Ira would have little trouble finding their way around the city today. Main streets run much as they did in the 1780s—from the waterfront uphill past shops to the school Ira founded and on to Winooski Falls, site of Ira's own grist- and sawmills.

Along the waterfront, Federal-style commercial buildings house shops, businesses, and restaurants. The ferry terminal and neighboring Union Station, built during the city's late-19th-century boom period as a lumbering port—when the lakeside trains connected with myriad steamers and barges—are now the summer venue for excursion trains, ferries, and cruise boats. The neo-Victorian Burlington Boathouse is everyone's window on Lake Champlain, a place to rent a row- or sailboat, to sit sipping a morning coffee or sunset aperitif, or to lunch or dine on the water. The adjacent Waterfront Park and promenade are linked

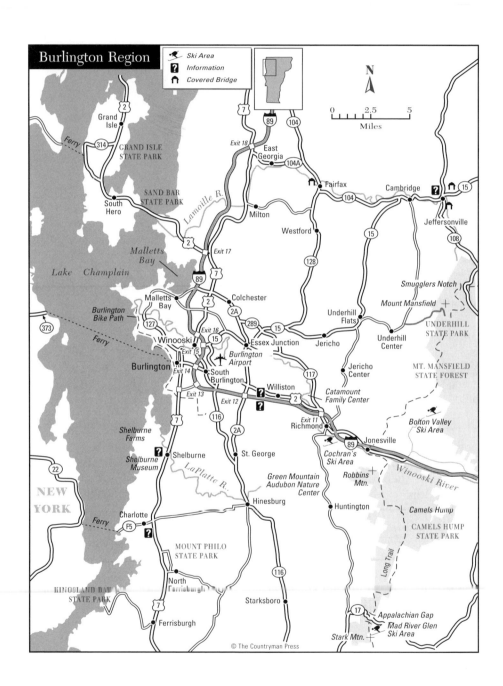

Burlington Region

Ski Area
Information
Covered Bridge

N

0   2.5   5
Miles

Grand Isle
Ferry
GRAND ISLE STATE PARK
Exit 18
East Georgia
104A
Fairfax
Cambridge
15
SAND BAR STATE PARK
South Hero
Milton
Westford
15
Jeffersonville
108
Lamoille R.
Exit 17
128
Smugglers Notch
Malletts Bay
89
7
Mount Mansfield
UNDERHILL STATE PARK
Lake Champlain
Malletts Bay
Colchester
2A
289
15
Underhill Flats
Burlington Bike Path
127
Underhill Center
MT. MANSFIELD STATE FOREST
373
Ferry
Winooski
Exit 16
15
Essex Junction
Jericho
Exit 15
Burlington Airport
South Burlington
Williston
117
Jericho Center
Burlington
Exit 14
Exit 13
Exit 12
2
Catamount Family Center
Exit 11
Richmond
Bolton Valley Ski Area
7
116
2A
Cochran's Ski Area
89
Jonesville
Winooski River
Shelburne Farms
St. George
Green Mountain Audubon Nature Center
Robbins Mtn.
Shelburne Museum
Shelburne
LaPlatte R.
Camels Hump
NEW YORK
22
Hinesburg
Huntington
CAMELS HUMP STATE PARK
Charlotte
Ferry
F5
MOUNT PHILO STATE PARK
Long Trail
KINGSLAND BAY STATE PARK
North Ferrisburgh
116
7
Starksboro
17
Appalachian Gap
Mad River Glen Ski Area
Ferrisburgh
Stark Mtn.

© The Countryman Press

by bike paths to a series of other lakeside parks (bike and in-line skate rentals abound), which include swimmable beaches.

Halfway up the hill, the graceful Unitarian Church, designed in 1815 by Peter Banner, stands at the head of Church Street—now a bricked, traffic-free marketplace for four long blocks, a promenade that's become a 21st-century-style common, the place everyone comes to graze.

Theater and music are constants, but Burlington is best when winter winds soften to cool breezes. The city celebrates summer with an exuberance literally trumpeted from the rooftops in its opening salvo to summer: the Discover Jazz Festival. The weeklong celebration includes some 200 performances. Stars perform at the Flynn Center for the Performing Arts, but jazz venues include buses, trolleys and ferries, street corners, parks, rooftops, and restaurants. This festival is followed by the Mozart Festival (also in varied venues) and a variety of music, both indoor and out, all summer.

Burlington in the 1950s and '60s was a different place. Docks and waterside railyards had become privately owned wastelands, littered with rusting debris. The few public beaches were closed due to pollution, and the solution was seen as "urban renewal." In the '70s some 300 homes and 40 small businesses were demolished, and large luxury condo/retail development was planned. Then in 1981, Burlington elected as mayor Bernie Sanders, who had campaigned on the slogan, "The Waterfront Is Not for Sale."

The present waterfront includes several new parks, such as Oakledge (formerly a General Electric property), just south of downtown, and Leddy (site of a former rendering plant) in the North End, and the waterside green space is linked by an 8-mile recreational path that now extends across the Winooski River into Colchester and someday soon will extend across Lake Champlain to the Champlain Islands on the bed of the old Rutland Railroad.

Downtown lodging options are mysteriously limited. Still, it is possible to walk from one high-rise hotel and several pleasant B&Bs to sights and water excursions, dining and shopping. Of course it's also appealing to bed down in the real countryside that's still within minutes of the city, so we have included B&Bs in nearby Jericho, Williston, Richmond, and Shelburne.

A couple of decades ago the Shelburne Museum, 6 miles south of the city, was the big sight-to-see in the area, although in recent years this "collection of collections" has been upstaged by Burlington itself. The museum's treasures range from a vintage Champlain Lake steamer to outstanding art and folk art, and at neighboring Shelburne Farms, New England's most fabulous estate, there are plenty of prizewinning cows (and cheese), miles of lakeside walks, and a mansion in which you should dine, sleep, or at least breakfast.

GUIDANCE **The Lake Champlain Regional Chamber of Commerce** (802-863-3489; 1-877-686-5253; www.vermont.org), 60 Main Street, Burlington 05401. Request brochure guides. Open Monday through Friday 8:30–5 year-round, also weekends 10–2 Memorial Day through Labor Day. Not the most obvious place for an information center (it's housed in the former motor vehicles building, halfway between Church Street and the waterfront), this one is

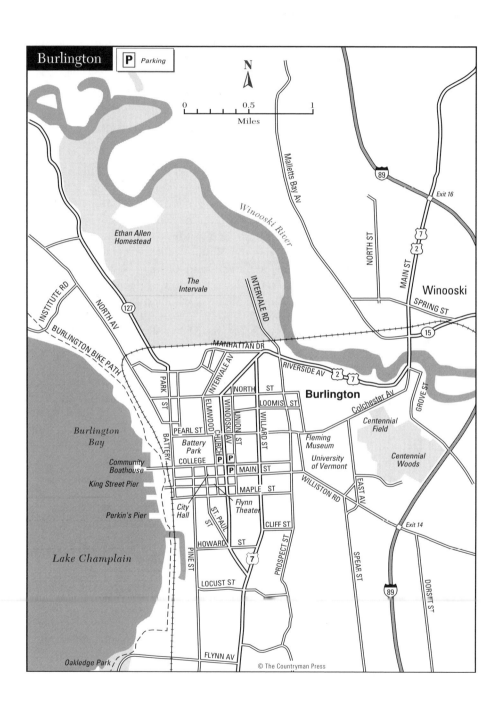

Burlington   🅿 Parking

N

0   0.5   1
Miles

Winooski River

89

Exit 16

Ethan Allen
Homestead

NORTH ST

MAIN ST

7
2

Winooski

SPRING ST

INSTITUTE RD

NORTH AV

127

The
Intervale

INTERVALE RD

BURLINGTON BIKE PATH

MANHATTAN DR

15

RIVERSIDE AV

2
7

Burlington

Colchester Av

GROVE ST

PARK ST

INTERVALE AV

NORTH   ST

ELMWOOD

WINOOSKI

UNION ST

LOOMIS   ST

WILLARD ST

Centennial
Field

Burlington
Bay

PEARL ST

CHURCH

AV

Battery
Park

COLLEGE

🅿
🅿

Fleming
Museum

University
of Vermont

EAST AV

Centennial
Woods

Community
Boathouse

BATTERY ST

🅿 MAIN   ST

King Street Pier

MAPLE   ST

Perkin's Pier

City
Hall

ST. PAUL

Flynn
Theater

CLIFF ST

WILLISTON RD

PINE ST

ST

PROSPECT ST

SPEAR ST

Exit 14

Lake Champlain

HOWARD

7

89

DORSET ST

LOCUST ST

Oakledge Park

FLYNN AV

© The Countryman Press

augmented by a staffed information booth at the airport. This is also the regional marketing organization.

Newspapers: The daily *Burlington Free Press.* For current entertainment happenings, pick up *Seven Days,* a fat, free weekly published Wednesday and available in most shops and cafés.

GETTING THERE

Note: Burlington is Vermont's single most car-free destination, accessible by bus from Boston and Montreal and by train from New York City and Montreal, blessed with good local public transport and little need to use it.

By air: **Burlington International Airport** (802-863-2874) is just 3 miles from downtown, served by American, Continental Express, United Airlines, USAirways, and Delta Connection. **JetBlue and Northwest** are the two new airlines serving Burlington, and JetBlue has led the way in discounting ticket prices, so there are good deals to be had (www.jetblue.com). Half a dozen auto rental firms are at the airport.

By bus: **Vermont Transit Company** (in New York and New England: 1-800-451-3292; within Vermont: 1-800-642-3133; from Canada: 1-800-552-8737), headquartered in Burlington, offers service to Albany, Boston, New York City, Montreal, Portland, and many points between. Buses depart from 345 Pine Street, south of the downtown area; plenty of parking.

By car: I-89, Routes 7 and 2.

By ferry: **The Lake Champlain Transportation Company** (802-864-9804; www.ferries.com), King Street Dock, Burlington. Descended from the world's oldest steamboat company, LCTC offers three local car-ferry services. Between mid-May and mid-October the car ferries make the 75-minute crossing between Burlington and Port Kent, New York. April through early January they also ply between Charlotte, just south of Burlington, and Essex, New York. Year-round service is offered on the 15-minute run between Grand Isle (see "The Northwest Corner") and Plattsburgh, New York.

By train: **Amtrak** (1-800-USA-RAIL; in Canada: 1-800-4-AMTRAK). The Vermonter (Washington to St. Albans via New York and Springfield, Massachusetts) stops at Essex Junction, 5 miles north of Burlington. (The station is served by two cab companies and by Burlington CCTA buses; see *Getting Around.*) Faster, more scenic service from New York City is available via the Adirondack to Port Kent, New York, connecting with the ferry to Burlington, connecting with the free trolley up Main Street.

GETTING AROUND *By bus:* **Chittenden County Transportation Authority**
(802-864-0211). CCTA bus routes radiate from the corner of Cherry and Church Streets (hub of the Church Street Marketplace), serving the Shelburne Museum, the airport, the ferry, and the Champlain Mill in Winooski as well as all the colleges and shopping areas. The fare is $1, and transfers are free. The CCTA also operates the College Street Shuttle, a free trolley on wheels circling the waterfront, Church Street, and UVM.

By trolley: A free, year-round trolley runs up and down the length of College Street, from the medical complex and UVM at the top of the hill to Union Station and the ferry dock on the lake. Stops are marked, and it's timed to meet the Champlain Valley Flyer.

MEDICAL EMERGENCY Emergency service is available by calling **911.**

Fletcher Allen Health Care (802-847-2434) on the UVM campus, Colchester Avenue, Burlington, has a 24-hour emergency room.

✳ Nearby Villages

Jericho. Northeast of Burlington, Jericho is best known for the **Old Red Mill** (Jericho Historical Society: 802-899-3225), on Route 15 at Jericho Corners (open Monday through Saturday 10–5, Sunday 1–5, except January through March when it's open only Wednesday, Saturday, and Sunday). This tower-topped, 1800s red mill set above a gorge is one of the most photographed buildings in Vermont and appropriately houses prints and mementos relating to one of the state's most famous photographers, Wilson A. "Snowflake" Bentley. A Jericho farmer who was the first person in the world to photograph individual snowflakes, Bentley collected more than 5,000 microphotos. A basement museum also tells the story of the many mills that once lined six sets of falls. Sales from the crafts store benefit the preservation of the building, which is owned by the Jericho Historical Society. A 20-acre park behind the mill, along the river, offers picnic tables and hiking trails. Ask directions to nearby Jericho Center, with its oval village common and **Desso's General Store** (802-899-3313), which occupies a gray, wooden building that's architecturally difficult to describe. It's just a genuine, old-fashioned general store. Lil and Gerry Desso carry the usual fresh, frozen, and canned produce, plus socks, mittens, gloves, boots, and so on. The syrup and beans (which, we can attest, bake up nicely) are local.

Richmond. East of Burlington on Route 2 (I-89, exit 11) and the Winooski River, Richmond was badly damaged in the flood of 1927 but still has a brief, architecturally interesting downtown. Turn down Bridge Street and drive by the old Blue Seal grain store (now a restaurant; see *Dining Out*) and the library (a former church) to the **Old Round Church.** This 16-sided building, one of the most unusual in the state, was constructed in 1812–13 as a community meetinghouse to serve five denominations (open daily July 4 through Labor Day 10–4, also weekends in spring and fall).

Shelburne. Beyond the commercial strip that's Shelburne Road (Route 7 south from Burlington) lie two of Vermont's greatest treasures, both the legacy of 19th-century railroad heirs William Seward and Lila Vanderbilt Webb. In the 1880s the couple hired Frederick Law Olmsted to landscape their 4,000-acre lakeside model farm, and in 1946 their daughter-in-law founded a major museum of Americana. Today 1,400 acres of the estate—Shelburne Farms—survive as a combination inn and demonstration farm, complementing the exhibits in no fewer than 37 buildings in the nearby Shelburne Museum. Inevitably shops and attractions continue to multiply along Route 7; the latest, the Vermont Teddy Bear Company Factory and Museum, threatens to draw more visitors than either

Shelburne Farms or the Shelburne Museum. (See *To See* for details about all three.)

Winooski is just across the 32-foot Winooski Falls from Burlington. Ira Allen was the first to harness the water that subsequently powered several mammoth, brick, 19th-century mills, attracting the workers from Ireland, Canada, and Eastern Europe who settled in the cottages that line its streets. The falls, with its art deco bridge, and the common, framed by the vintage-1867 Winooski Block and the handsome Champlain Mill (now a shopping/dining complex), still form the center of town. St. Michael's College with its Playhouse (presenting a variety of stage performances) and art gallery (802-654-2535) is just up Allen Street (Route 15).

❋ To See

MUSEUMS AND ATTRACTIONS ✍ ♿ **Shelburne Museum** (802-985-3344; www.shelburnemuseum.org), Route 7, Shelburne (6 miles south of Burlington), is open late May through late October, daily 10–5, with daily tours of selected buildings 1–4 PM through early December. $17.50 adults, $7 youths (6–14). Family cap: $45. Tickets are good for 2 consecutive days. This fascinating "collection of collections" features American folk art but also includes paintings by Rembrandt, Degas, Monet, and Manet. More than three dozen buildings, many of them historic transplants from around New England, each house a different collection. They are set in 45 landscaped acres that include flower and herb gardens, an apple orchard, and more than 90 varieties of lilacs (the annual Lilac Festival is usually Memorial Day weekend).

An adequate description of the collections (more than 80,000 objects) would fill a separate chapter. Highlights include a 1915 steam locomotive and a vintage-

AFTER THE WEDDING (1942) BY GRANDMA MOSES

Shelburne Museum

THE CAROUSEL AT THE SHEL-
BURNE MUSEUM

Kim Grant

1890 private Palace Car; the side-wheeler *Ticonderoga,* in her basin near the Colchester Reef Lighthouse; the amazing folk art in the Stagecoach Inn (weather vanes, cigar-store figures, trade signs, and figureheads); the American paintings (Fitz Hugh Lane, Winslow Homer, and many other lesser-known but superb 19th-century New England painters); the Webb Memorial Building, with its elegant rooms (originally in a New York penthouse) hung with impressionist paintings (including a portrait of the museum's founder, Electra Havemeyer Webb, by Mary Cassatt); and the heirloom quilts (the collection includes some 900 American quilts). There are also the Horseshoe Barn's marvelous carriages; the Castleton Slate Jail; Shaker Shed; Dorset House and its decoys, Audubon game bird prints, and fowling pieces; a general store; an up-and-down sawmill; an old-fashioned carousel; and much more. The ticket is good for 2 days because you may well want to allow time to absorb it all.

Acquisitions continue, but this is still substantially the collection of one woman, gathered at a time when few people were interested in Americana. Electra Havemeyer was 18 in 1910 when she bought her first cigar-store figure. Three years later she married James Watson Webb, of Shelburne (son of the wealthy couple who had built Shelburne Farms; see below). Over the next 30 years she raised five children, traveled widely, and managed homes on Long Island and in Manhattan and a 50,000-acre "camp" in the Adirondacks, as well as the Shelburne estate. Gradually she filled all her holdings (even her indoor tennis court) with her collections, founding the museum in 1947 when her husband retired to Shelburne. Both died in 1960, but their vision for the museum was fulfilled by their son, the late J. Watson Webb Jr.

The **Owl Cottage Family Activity Center** gives kids some hands-on time; a number of displays, such as a model circus parade, are also geared to children. There's a museum shop and cafeteria, picnic areas, and electric trams for the disabled or just footsore. The visitors center is a rare round barn. Inquire about gallery talks, classes in traditional crafts, and frequent special events.

✍ **Shelburne Farms** (802-985-8686; www.shelburnefarms.org), marked from Route 7, Shelburne. The Farm Store and Visitors Center (802-985-8442), with an exceptional introductory film, are open daily year-round, 9–5 (10–5 in the off-season). Mid-May through mid-October, general admission for the walking trails, children's farmyard, and cheesemaking operation on the 1,400-acre lakeside property costs $6 adults, $4 children 3–14; full 1½-hour wagon tours are offered five times daily mid-May through mid-October. Guided tours cost $9 for adults, $7 for children. November through April, no charge for the walking trails.

Inquire about inn and garden tours, Breeding Barn tours, and special events.

Much of this grand 1880s lakeside estate is now a nonprofit experimental farm and educational and cultural center. Comprising 3,800 acres at its zenith, this "duchy" was landscaped by Frederick Law Olmsted (who also designed Central Park) and pioneer forester Gifford Pinchot. It was designed for William Seward Webb and Lila Vanderbilt Webb (it was their daughter-in-law Electra Havemeyer Webb who founded Shelburne Museum). It included, and still does, a model farm with magnificent Norman-style barn buildings and a 110-room brick summer "cottage" on a bluff overlooking Lake Champlain.

The mansion is now the Inn at Shelburne Farms (open late May through mid-October; see *Lodging* and *Dining Out*). The immense, five-story, 416-foot **Farm Barn** (housing pigs, chickens, and other farm animals) is now a place for children to collect eggs, learn to milk a cow, or enjoy a hayride. It also houses the cheesemaking facility; the **Coach Barn,** once occupied by locally bred Hackneys, now houses changing art exhibits and frequent workshops. The most recent addition to the holdings is the massive **Breeding Barn,** where the Hackneys were bred. The farm's prizewinning cheddar cheese, made from its own herd of Brown Swiss cows, is sold, along with other Vermont products, in the Farm Store. A walking trail winds from the visitors center about 1 mile to the top of Lone Tree Hill for sweeping views of Lake Champlain and the Adirondacks. Inquire about naturalist-led bird walks and special events.

Tip: The Inn at Shelburne Farms is open to the public by reservation for breakfast as well as dinner. (No admission fee.) Enjoy the most elegant breakfast in the area, and then stroll the lakeside perennial, herb, and rose gardens.

Burlington waterfront. As noted in the chapter introduction, Burlington's waterfront revival is both dramatic and accessible to the public. The handsome (vintage-1915) **Union Station** at the base of Main Street is now public space

THE NORMAN-STYLE BARN AT SHELBURNE FARMS

Kim Grant

(changing art exhibits), and the King Street Dock remains home to the **Lake Champlain Transportation Company** (LCTC), established in 1826. At the base of College Street at the College Street Pier, the (1991) **Community Boathouse** echoes the design of the Lake Champlain Yacht Club built on this site in 1889. The new jewel of the waterfront is **ECHO at the Leahy Center for Lake Champlain** (802-864-1848; www.echovermont.org), 1 College Street, operated by the Champlain Basin Science Program. ECHO, which stands for "ecology, culture, history, and opportunity," is both a world-class lake aquarium and a science center. This is a must-see for the whole family. ECHO is open to the public year-round, daily 10–5; Thursday to 8 PM. Closed only Thanksgiving, Christmas Eve, and Christmas Day. Admission is $9 for adults, $8 for seniors and students, $6 for children 3–17. The **Burlington Bike Path** links these sites with the nearby **Waterfront Park** to the north (it includes a promenade and picnic shelter) and with **Perkin's Pier** (parking, boat launch, and picnic area) just to the south and to several more beaches and parks in both directions. Not surprisingly, shops and restaurants have proliferated along neighboring Battery Street; **Battery Park** is the setting for free summer concerts Thursday and Sunday and for frequent special events.

Church Street Marketplace. The city's shopping and dining hub, the Church Street Marketplace extends four car-free blocks, from the graceful Unitarian Church, designed in 1815 by Peter Banner, to City Hall at the corner of Main Street. A fanciful fountain plays at its head, and the bricked promenade is spotted with benches and boulders from different parts of the state. The marketplace buildings themselves, a mix of 19th-century and art deco styles, house more than 100 shops and an ever-increasing number of restaurants. Walk through one storefront and you are in the **Burlington Town Center,** a multilevel (stepped into the hillside), multishop complex resembling many in Montreal but few in New England. Unlike Boston's Quincy Market, Church Street is a public thoroughfare, geared as much to residents as to tourists.

SUNSET AT PERKIN'S PIER IN BURLINGTON

Kim Grant

Robert Hull Fleming Museum (802-656-0750; www.uvm.edu), Colchester Avenue, on the University of Vermont campus. Open September through April, weekdays 9–4, Saturday and Sunday 1–5; closed Monday May through August and holiday weekends year-round. Limited parking. $3 per adult; over 54 and under 18, $2. Varied collections of art, natural history, archaeology, and geology. Holdings include ancient primitive art from several cultures and continents, a collection of American portraits and landscapes (from the 18th century to contemporary works), and frequent special exhibits, plus a gift shop. The building was designed by the renowned firm of McKim, Mead and White, which also designed UVM's Ira Allen Chapel (1927) and Burlington's City Hall.

Fire House Center for the Arts (802-865-7165), 135 Church Street, Burlington, next to City Hall. Open Wednesday through Sunday noon–6, but noon–8 on Friday. A nonprofit community space showcasing work by top Vermont artists. Inquire about First Friday Art Trolley Tours, a free tour of local art galleries the first Friday of every month, April through November (5–7 PM).

The Ethan Allen Homestead (802-865-4556; www.ethanallenhomestead.org), off Route 127 just north of the downtown Burlington waterfront (take the North Avenue Beaches exit off Route 127, the Northern Connector). Open all year, daily from May through October and weekends during the off-season. Vermont's godfather is memorialized here in the timber farmhouse in which he lived out the last years of his turbulent life; he died in 1789. The visitors center offers interesting descriptive and multimedia exhibits, and the setting is a working garden and an extensive park with some 4 miles of walking trails along the Winooski River. $5 per adult, $4 seniors, $2.50 ages 5–17; under 5 free; family rate $14.

Heritage Winooski Mill Museum (802-655-9477), Champlain Mill, Winooski. Monday through Saturday 10–9, Sunday noon–5. No admission charge. Gallery and hall exhibits on life and work in the mills at Winooski Falls circa 1835 through 1956.

THE ETHAN ALLEN HOMESTEAD

Kim Grant

FOR FAMILIES ✤ **Vermont Teddy Bear Company Factory and Museum** (802-985-3001; 1-800-829-BEAR), 6655 Shelburne Road, Route 7 at the south end of Shelburne Village. Open daily 9–6, Sunday 10–5. A phenomenon in its own right, the huge, fanciful new birthplace of well over 100,000 teddy bears a year now includes a museum depicting teddy bear history; visitors are also invited to make their own teddy bear ($19–24) and to take the highly entertaining tour ($2 adults, free for children under 12.). There is, of course, a huge teddy bear store.

✤ **National Museum of the Morgan Horse** (802-985-8665), Route 7 at Bostwick Road, Shelburne. Open Monday through Friday 9–4, Saturday 10–2. A small museum depicts the history of the Morgan horse in America. Token admission.

✳ **To Do**

BICYCLING The **Burlington Bike Path** runs for 8 miles along the waterfront, connecting eight different parks, beginning with Oakledge Park in the south. A ferry will shuttle you across the Winooski River to the continuation of the path in Colchester and on up to the Champlain Islands. Fun side trips include Ethan Allen Park, the Ethan Allen Homestead, Intervale Community Farms, and the Salmon Hole Fishing Area off Riverside Avenue. **Rental bikes** (including tandems, trailers, and trail-a-bikes) and in-line skate rentals are available from the **SkiRack** (802-658-3313), 85 Main Street. This path is used for walking, running, and in-line skating as well as biking. Note that CCTA buses and trolleys have bicycle racks. For serious bicyclists, we recommend the *Burlington Vermont Hiking and Biking Map*, published by Map Adventures (802-253-7489) in Stowe, which details several Burlington area loops and longer tours on both sides of Lake Champlain, using ferries. Mountain bikers should check out the **Catamount Family Center** (802-879-6001), Governor Chittenden Road, Williston: a 40 km trail system, also rentals and food in the 1796 house built by Vermont's first governor as well as the two-guest-room **Catamount's B&B** (802-878-2180) nearby at 592 Governor Chittenden Road. There is also the **Essex Transportation Trail,** a 3-mile rail-trail from the Essex Police Station to Route 15 (Lang Farm); the **Shelburne Recreation Trail,** from Bay Road through Shelburne Bay Park to Harbor Road; the unpaved **Intervale Bikepath,** from Gardener's Supply on Intervale Avenue to the Ethan Allen Homestead; and **Causeway Park** in Colchester, a packed gravel trail that follows an old railroad bed out into Lake Champlain. **Bolton Valley** (see *Winter Sports*) also offers mountain biking on its cross-country and alpine trails.

BOATING *Note:* The regular LCTC 75-minute ferry crossing from Burlington to Port Kent, New York, is a great ride and a bargain.

BURLINGTON'S CHURCH STREET MARKETPLACE
Kim Grant

Burlington Community Boathouse (802-865-3377), foot of College Street, Burlington. Rowboats, Rhodes and Laser sailboat rentals, captained day sails, sailing lessons, fishing charters, June through October. **Winds of Ireland** (802-863-5090), based here, offers day and sunset sails, bareboat charters, and instruction.

Spirit of Ethan Allen III (802-862-8300). Seasonal, daily scenic cruises as well as dinner cruises aboard a triple-deck, 500-passenger excursion boat, departing from the Burlington Community Boathouse (see above) mid-May through mid-October. Narrated sightseeing, plus sunset cruises, dinner, murder mystery, and variety show cruises. Specialty cruises include a lobster fest, a night of Big Band music, and a luau on the lake. Sightseeing cruise fare: $9.95–12.95 adult, $3.95 ages 3–11.

Lake Champlain Cruises (802-864-9669; www.ferries.com/cruise), King Street Dock, Burlington. The *Adirondack*, the *Champlain*, and now a third cruise boat, the *Northern Lights*, regularly sail the waters of Lake Champlain, offering brunch, lunch, dinner, scenic, and entertainment cruises of all sorts. The caterer runs two local seafood restaurants. The supper club and special entertainment cruises cost about $35 per person, less for the daytime outings.

✒ **Lake Champlain Community Sailing Center** (802-864-2499; www.lccsc .org), located along the Burlington Bike Path, is a nonprofit, public access sailing center with a host of learn-to-sail and learn-to-canoe programs for kids, adults, and families, as well as rentals. Keelboat rentals cost $50 per hour ($310 for 8 hours) on weekends, less on weekdays. LCCSC also offers adaptive programs for the disabled.

Also note: Day sails and local marinas are listed with the Lake Champlain Regional Chamber of Commerce (see *Guidance*).

DIVING **Lake Champlain Historic Underwater Preserves** (802-457-2022). The Vermont Division for Historic Preservation maintains five shipwrecks, identified by Coast Guard–approved buoys, at various points on Lake Champlain; all are open to scuba divers. The *Horse Ferry*, the *Coal Barge*, and the *General Butler* are off Burlington. The *Phoenix* and the *Diamond Island Stone Boat* are in Colchester and Vergennes, respectively. **Waterfront Diving** (802-865-2771), 214 Battery Street, Burlington, provides equipment rentals, instruction in snorkeling, underwater archaeology, video, and scuba, and charters to historic preserved shipwrecks.

See also *Boating*.

FISHING **Champ Charters** (802-864-3792), Burlington, offers charter boats. Check out **Schirmer's Fly Shop** (802-863-6105), 34 Mills Avenue, South Burlington, specializing in Ed Schirmer's own flies, instruction, tackle, and accessories. The **Salmon Hole fishing area** off Riverside Avenue, just beyond Tortilla Flats Mexican Restaurant, is a popular local spot.

GOLF **Vermont National Country Club** (802-864-7770), Dorset Street, South Burlington, 18 holes; **Marble Island Resort** (802-864-6800), Marble Island Road, Malletts Bay, Colchester, 9 holes; **Rocky Ridge Golf Club** (802-482-2191), St. George (5 miles south on Route 2A from exit 12 off I-89), 18 holes; **Kwiniaska** (802-985-3672), Spear Street, Shelburne,

FOR BIRDERS ✒ **The Birds of Vermont Museum** (802-434-2167), adjacent to the Green Mountain Audubon Center at 900 Sherman Hollow Road, Richmond. Open May through October, daily 10–4; by appointment in winter. Carvings of more than 200 species of birds by Robert Spear Jr.; also nature trails, recorded birdsongs. Small admission fee.

18 holes; **Williston Golf Course** (802-878-3747), Williston, 18 holes; **Essex Country Club** (802-879-3232), Old Stage Road, Essex Junction, 18 holes; **Cedar Knoll Country Club** (802-482-3186), Hinesburg, 27 holes; **Links at the Lang Farm** (802-878-0298), 39 Essex Way, Essex, 18 holes.

HIKING See Camels Hump State Park under *Green Space*.

HORSEBACK RIDING **Georgia Stables** (802-524-3395; 802-893-7268), Beebe Hill Road, Georgia. Trail riding for all abilities.

KAYAKING **Champlain Kayak Club** (www.ckayak.com) and the **Lake Champlain Maritime Museum** (www.lcmm.org) are both excellent sources of information.

True North Kayak Tours (802-860-1910). Jane and David Yagoda offer instruction and guided tours from a variety of locations on Lake Champlain. Inquire about multiday paddles through the Champlain Islands with B&B lodging.

Mountain Lake Expeditions (802-777-7646). The proprietor is Franz Rosenberger.

Tide Line (802-863-6174). Tours operated by Jamie Mittendorf.

PaddleWays (802-238-0674; www.paddleways.com). Burlington-based Kevin and Michele Rose offer 3-hour tours, instructional classes, full-day and multiday tours on Lake Champlain.

Umiak Outfitters (802-865-6777; www.umiak.com). Based in Stowe, Umiak offers guided kayaking on Lake Champlain and rentals at its waterfront location on Burlington's North Beach.

Kayak and canoe rentals also are available from the **Alpine Shop** (802-862-2174) on Williston Road in South Burlington, **Canoe Imports** (802-651-8760) on Dorset Street, the **Ski Rack** (1-800-882-4530) in downtown Burlington, the **Small Boat Exchange** (802-864-5437), also downtown, and **Perkin's Pier** (802-864-4858) right on the waterfront.

SPECTATOR SPORTS ✍ **The Vermont Expos** (802-655-4200), Burlington's minor-league baseball team, play at Centennial Field (off Colchester Avenue) all summer. You can park at UVM and take a shuttle bus to the game. The season is mid-June through September 1, tickets are cheap, the park is lovely, the concession food is pretty good, and there's a giant Day-Glo dancing Champ mascot for the kids. All in all, a great time—and the baseball isn't bad. The Expos operate a souvenir store in the Champlain Mill (802-655-9477), Winooski.

SWIMMING **North Beach Park** (802-862-0942), off North Avenue at Institute Road, Burlington (turn at the high school), provides tent and trailer sites plus swimming from a long, sandy beach, mid-May through October; vehicle charge. (Just before the park is the entrance to Rock Point, where the Episcopal Diocese of Vermont maintains Bishop Hopkins' Hall School, the bishop's residence, a conference center, and an outdoor chapel.)

Other beaches: **Leddy Park,** also off North Avenue; **Oakledge Park,** off Route 7 south of the city, at the end of Flynn Avenue; **Red Rocks Park,** South Burlington's public beach on Queen City Park Road.

✳ Winter Sports

CROSS-COUNTRY SKIING *Northern Vermont Adventure Skiing,* a weatherproof map ($6.95) detailing cross-country trails throughout the region, is available at local outlets and from Map Adventures (802-253-7489), 846 Cottage Club Road, Stowe 05672.

Bolton Valley (802-434-3444), Bolton. Ranging in elevation from 1,600 to 3,200 feet, this 50 km network is Vermont's highest cross-country system, with snow that usually lasts well into April. A total of 45 km are machine groomed, meaning tracked for the most part, rolled elsewhere. There is a wide and gently sloping 3.6-mile Broadway and a few short trails for beginners, but most of the terrain is backwoods, much of it splendidly high wilderness country. You can take an alpine lift to the peak of Ricker Mountain and ski Old Turnpike, then keep going on cross-country trails for a total of 7 miles. There are rentals in the cross-country center, and experienced skiers are welcome to stay in the area's high huts by reservation. Telemarking is a specialty here, along with guided tours. Trail fee.

The legendary 12-mile **Bolton-to-Trapp trail** originates here (this is by far the preferred direction to ski it), but requires spotting a car at the other end or on Moscow Road. Inquire about the exciting new telemark/backcountry trail beginning at the top of Bolton's Wilderness Chair and meandering down into Little River State Park in Waterbury–Stowe. Again, a car needs to be spotted at the other end.

✎ **Catamount Family Center** (802-879-6001), 421 Governor Chittenden Road, Williston. The 40 km of trails—30 of them machine tracked, 2 km lit—are on rolling terrain, geared to all abilities. Guided tours, rentals, instruction, warming hut. Trail fee.

Note: See *Green Space* for more about local parks with trails that lend themselves to cross-country skiing.

DOWNHILL SKIING **Bolton Valley** (802-434-3444; 1-877-926-5866), Bolton. This substantial ski mountain has the highest base elevation in the East. It has changed hands frequently in recent years but now seems firmly financed by a consortium of local businesspeople. Its base facilities were renovated in 1999. The 50 ski trails and slopes (seven lifts, including one quad and four double chairs) here are on 3,680-foot Bolton Mountain, which towers above its neighbors in a lonely stretch of country 20 miles east of Burlington, 20 miles west of Montpelier. Set atop a 4-mile access road that is, in turn, a long way up Route 2 from anything else, it offers a genuinely self-contained resort atmosphere guaranteed to make you want to stay put for a week. Half-day and night-skiing prices also available.

✎ **Cochran Ski Area** (802-434-2479), Cochran Road, Richmond. A small, family-owned and -oriented ski area run by a family of former Olympic skiers.

Note: See also Smugglers' Notch Resort in "North of the Notch and the Lamoille Valley," "Stowe and Waterbury," and "Sugarbush/Mad River Valley." Five major alpine areas are within easy striking distance of Burlington.

ICE SKATING Leddy Arena (802-864-0123), Leddy Park, Burlington. Rentals. Skating from **Waterfront Park** on Lake Champlain is also a special rite of winter; flags indicate ice safety.

SLEIGH RIDES Shelburne Farms (802-985-8442) offers rides in 12- to 15-passenger sleighs. For a description of the setting, see *Museums and Attractions.*

✳ Green Space

Burlington Parks and Recreation (802-865-7247). Request a copy of the Burlington *Bike Paths & Parks* map or pick it up at the chamber of commerce. Burlington's lakeside parks are superb. **Oakledge Park** (take Flynn Avenue off Pine Street or Route 7) offers swimming and picnicking (parking fee, but you can bike or walk in). **Red Rocks Park** just south, occupying the peninsula that divides Burlington from South Burlington (take Queen City Parkway off Route 7), offers walking trails (no bikes allowed) as well as a beach. **Ethan Allen Park** (North Avenue) is a 67-acre preserve, once part of Ethan's farm (it's near the Homestead) and webbed with trails that climb to the Pinnacle and to a stone tower built on Indian Rock in 1905 (open Memorial Day through Labor Day, Wednesday through Sunday noon–8); both high points offer panoramic views of Lake Champlain.

Winooski Valley Park District (802-863-5744) consists of more than two dozen well-run parks, including beaches, boat launches, tennis courts, and an extensive riverside bike path. **The Intervale** (entrance on Riverside Avenue) along the Winooski River offers walking as well as bike trails and includes Intervale Community Farms (802-660-3508), Gardener's Supply (retail and catalog outlet), and a seasonal organic farm stand. Also along the Winooski: a children's discovery garden and walking trails in the 67-acre park around the Ethan Allen Homestead (park headquarters), at **Macrea Farm Park,** and **Half Moon Cove Park. Delta Park** at the mouth of the Winooski River is a magical place with a sandy trail traversing woods to a wetland observation platform. **Centennial Woods** offers nature trails; access is from East Avenue.

Bayside Park (802-655-0811), Colchester. The site of a 1920s resort, the park now offers sports facilities, a beach, and walking trails. In winter this is also a popular spot for ice fishing, sailboarding, and ice skating.

For **Sand Bar State Park** and other green space to the north, see "The Islands" in "The Northwest Corner."

To the east

Underhill State Park (802-899-3022), within the Mount Mansfield State Forest, offers camping (mid-May through mid-October), a Civilian Conservation Corps log picnic pavilion, and four trails to the summit ridge of Mount Mansfield. It's accessed from the Pleasant Valley Road west of Underhill Center.

The Green Mountain Audubon Nature Center (802-434-3068), Huntington. (Turn right at Round Church in Richmond; go 5 miles south to Sherman Hollow Road.) Trails wind through 230 acres of representative habitats (beaver ponds, orchards, and woodlands). Interpretive classes are given. Groups are welcome to watch (and help in) the wood-fired sugaring conducted each year. Open all year, but call ahead to confirm.

Camels Hump State Park. Vermont's most distinctive and third highest mountain (4,083 feet) is best accessed from Huntington via East Street, then East Street to Camels Hump Road. Request a free map and permission for primitive camping (at lower elevations) from the Vermont State Parks in Waterbury (802-241-3655; 1-800-VERMONT; www.vtstateparks.com). The **Green Mountain Club** (802-244-7037) on Route 100 in Waterbury Center also has maps and maintains shelters, lodging, and the Hump Brook Tenting Area. Camping facilities are available in nearby Little River State Park. The name "Camel's Rump" was used on Ira Allen's map in 1798, but by 1830 it was known as "Camel's Hump." *Note:* All trails and roads within the park are closed during mud season.

To the south

LaPlatte River Marsh Natural Area, Shelburne; parking on Bay Road. Managed by The Nature Conservancy of Vermont, this 211-acre preserve at the mouth of the LaPlatte River is rich in bird life. It is traversed by an easy trail (45 minutes round-trip).

Shelburne Bay Park, Shelburne. (Park on Bay Road, across from the entrance to the Shelburne Farms visitors center.) The Shelburne Recreation Department maintains a blue-blazed trail along the bay through mixed woods.

Shelburne Farms. Five miles of easy trails on 1,400 acres landscaped by Frederick Law Olmsted.

H. Lawrence Achilles Natural Area, Shelburne, access off Pond Road. A short hiking trail leads to Shelburne Pond.

Mount Philo State Park (802-425-2390; 802-372-5060), Charlotte. A small mountaintop picnic area and campground, with spectacular views of the valley, lake, and Adirondacks. A short but steep ascent off Route 7 (not recommended for trailers or large RVs); 15 campsites; $1 per adult admission.

Kingsland Bay State Park (802-877-3445), Ferrisburgh. West from Route 7 on Little Chicago Road, about 1.5 miles north onto Slang Road, 3 miles to Lake Champlain. Picnic areas, tennis courts, on 130 acres.

✳ Lodging

In Burlington 05401

HOTELS ⟁ **Wyndham Burlington** (802-658-6500; 1-800-WYNDHAM), 60 Battery Street. Formerly the Radisson-Burlington, this 256-room hotel has been given a $3 million face-lift, and floors six and seven have been converted to a "Club Level" with robes, slippers, and a private concierge service. There are now 15 meeting/ event rooms ranging from small to large, a lobby bar, and the **Oak Street Café.** This hotel has the best lake views in town. Rates $109–169. Six rooms are handicapped accessible.

🐾 ✎ ⟁ **The Sheraton-Burlington** (802-865-6600; 1-800-677-6576;

www.sheratonburlington.com), 870 Williston Road. With 309 rooms, this is Vermont's largest hotel and the city's convention and trade center. It's set on campuslike grounds in South Burlington at the top of the hill behind the UVM campus and the medical center, near the I-89 (exit 14W)–Route 2 interchange with easy bus access to downtown. $79–229 per room, depending on season. Small pets permitted.

BED & BREAKFASTS Willard Street Inn (802-651-8710; 1-800-577-8712; www.willardstreetinn.com), 349 South Willard Street. The classiest place to stay in Burlington, a brick mansion built grandly in the 1880s up on the Hill (adjoining the UVM and Champlain College campuses). It offers 14 guest rooms, all with private bath. Guests enter a cherry-paneled foyer and are drawn to the many-windowed, flower-filled solarium with a woodstove, where breakfast is served. There is also a spacious living room with a grand piano and hearth, and a dining room. Guest rooms are decorated individually and range in size and detailing from the master bedroom to former maids' rooms, but all are tastefully done and equipped with phone, TV, and air-conditioning. Top dollar is for a canopy bed, lake view, and private bath (but lake views can also be enjoyed for far less). $115–215 includes a full breakfast.

Lang House (802-652-2500; 1-877-919-9799; www.langhouse.com), 360 Main Street. New innkeeper Kim Borsavage offers nine rooms with private bath in a restored 1881 Eastlake Victorian, done in period furnishings and antiques. Everything is close by, and a chef prepares breakfast. $130–195, breakfast included.

Howard Street Guest House (802-864-4668), 153 Howard Street. Available by the night year-round. A beautiful space in a detached carriage barn: a sunny, open living room, dining area, and minimal kitchen with skylights, all furnished with flair, including a queen bed and a pullout sofa. Andrea Gray's house is in a quiet residential area, within easy walking distance of the waterfront and Church Street Marketplace. Good for a romantic getaway or a businessperson requiring space to spread out. $140 for the room. Discounts for stays of more than 3 days.

Burlington Redstone (802-862-0508; www.burlingtonredstone.com), 497 South Willard Street. A long but possible walk from downtown, nearer to UVM, this handsome mansion was built in 1906 of local redstone. Helen and George Long offers two guest rooms with shared bath and one with private, along with gracious common spaces, including an invitingly landscaped garden. No children under 13, please. $99–135 includes a full breakfast. Ask about the Carriage House for extended stays.

Beyond Burlington

RESORT ✈ **Bolton Valley Resort** (phone/fax: 802-434-3444), Bolton Valley 05477. A mountaintop cluster of condominiums, lodge, restaurants, shops, and a sports center set on 5,000 wooded acres. In winter Bolton Valley is a ski resort; in summer the focus is on tennis, mountain biking, and golf, with formal programs for children. An outdoor pool, an extensive network of hiking trails, and a nearby 18-hole golf course are also part of the summer picture. Facilities include the150-room slope-side hotel (some rooms have a fireplace and kitchenette) and more than 120 one- to four-bedroom condominium units. The sports center houses an exercise room, pool, tennis courts, and game room. Rates for the hotel rooms range $89–319; for a condominium unit, $149–649.

INNS Inn at Shelburne Farms (802-985-8498; www.shelburnefarms.org), Shelburne 05482. Open mid-May through mid-October. Guests are treated to a peerless taste of Edwardian grandeur. The 45-room, Queen Anne–style mansion was built by William Seward and Lila Vanderbilt Webb on a bluff overlooking Lake Champlain. Completed in 1899, the house is the centerpiece of a 1,400-acre estate (see *Museums and Attractions*).

Perhaps because its transition from mansion to inn in 1987 entailed a $1.6 million restoration but no sale (the Webb family has turned the estate into a nonprofit environmental education organization), there is a rare sense of a time as well as place here. Turn-of-the-20th-century furnishings predominate (most are original), and you feel like an invited rather than a paying guest. You can play billiards in the richly paneled game room, leaf through one of the 6,000 leather-bound books, or play the piano in the library. Common space includes the Main Hall, a magnificent room divided into sitting areas with fireplaces and dominated by a very grand staircase. There's also an elegant tearoom (tea is served daily) and the Marble Room, a formal dining room with silk damask wall coverings, a marble floor, and long windows overlooking the formal gardens and lake. Don't miss the third-floor playroom, with its dollhouses.

Guest rooms vary in size and elegance, from the second-floor master bedroom to servants' quarters, which means room prices also vary. The Green Room, in which we slept, was painstakingly but far from fussily decorated; its wallpaper was specially made to echo the mauve-and-green fabric in a splashy '20s screen. With its alcove desk, freestanding old mirror, fresh flowers, luxurious turn-of-the-20th-century bath, and water view, there was a sense of comfort and space. Guests have access to tennis, boating, a swimming beach, and walking trails. Rates for the 24 luxurious, individualized bedrooms (17 with private bath) run $110–380, including a 15 percent service charge. There is a 2-night minimum stay on weekends. Breakfast and dinner are extra, and memorable. No smoking.

♿ **The Inn at Essex** (802-878-1100; 1-800-727-4295), 70 Essex Way (Route 15 east), Essex Junction 05452. There are innlike common spaces, and the 120 rooms and suites are decorated with country-chic wallpapers and fabrics; 30 have working fireplace, and 2 have Jacuzzi. The large, neo-Colonial complex is set in landscaped gardens in a commercial, suburban area handy to IBM, 10 miles northeast of downtown Burlington. Facilities include a conference center and an outdoor heated swimming pool. A free shuttle to the airport is also offered. $179–499 includes continental breakfast. Inquire about special packages. Butler's, the inn's formal restaurant (see *Dining Out*), and the more casual café are both staffed by students from the New England Culinary Institute.

BED & BREAKFASTS Willow Pond Farm (802-985-8505), 133 Cheesefactory Lane, Shelburne 05482. Open early spring through late fall. If we had special sections for birders and gardeners, Sawyer and Zita Lee's elegant home would top both lists. Zita inherited the 200-acre farm, and in 1990 the couple designed and built this exceptional retirement house, a blending of old lines and modern spaces. Windows let in the view of rose and perennial gardens, with their many bird feeders, and the small pond. The living/dining room overlooks the gardens and ponds and conveys an unusual sense of light and space. A full breakfast and the Lees' special cappuccino blend are served at the formal, oval table in the dining area or out on the terrace. The upstairs master bedroom overlooks the Adirondacks, and there is a sleeping loft for kids. The two smaller rooms are also furnished in fine antiques, Oriental carpets, and handmade quilts on the king- and queensized beds. All have private bath. $90–130 with breakfast. There is a 2-night minimum.

&. **Heart of the Village Inn** (802-985-2800; 1-877-808-8134; www.heartofthevillage.com), 5347 Shelburne Road, P.O. Box 953, Shelburne 05482-0953. A handsome 1880s home next to the town green and library (1816) and across from town hall. The two living rooms, dining room, and five guest rooms are all carefully, comfortably decorated. All have air conditioning and in-room connections for phone and cable TV, as well as private bath; the carriage barn houses the four most deluxe rooms, a honeymoon suite with a whirlpool bath, and one room with wheelchair access. Rates are $115–225, with breakfast and afternoon refreshments included.

☖ **Homeplace B&B** (802-899-4694), P.O. Box 96, Old Pump Road (off Route 15), Jericho 05465. The sprawling house is set in a 100-acre wood with hiking paths. Guests can meet horses, sheep, ducks, chickens, cats, dogs, and a donkey. The guest area is separated from the family quarters and includes a large library and living room. Four rooms, two with private bath and two with shared (twin or double beds). $65–75 single, $75–85 double, full breakfast included. Pets possible for a small fee.

&. **Sinclair Inn Bed & Breakfast** (802-899-2234; 1-800-433-4658), 389 Route 15, Jericho 05465. This fully restored 1890 Queen Anne "painted lady" is located in a village setting within easy driving distance of Burlington. All six rooms have private bath and air-conditioning, and one is fully handicapped accessible. Sally Gilbert-Smith is your hostess. $80–150 per couple includes a full breakfast. Children over 12 welcome.

Hidden Gardens B&B (802-482-2118; www.thehiddengardens.com), 693 Lewis Creek Road, Hinesburg. This contemporary post-and-beam house in the country is surrounded by 26 acres of woods and extensive gardens but is easily accessible to the sights in the Burlington area. The two comfortable guest rooms, one a double and one a king, have a shared bath and rent for $75–85. There are two friendly dogs on the premises.

Cobb Brook Farm Weekend B&B (802-434-3574), 151 Charlie Smith Road, Huntington. Sandra Moore's weekend bed & breakfast backs up to Camels Hump State Park. The three guest rooms rent for $65–75 per night.

The Richmond Victorian Inn (802-434-4410; 1-888-242-3362), 191 East

Main Street, P.O. Box 652, Richmond 05477. On Route 2 in the village of Richmond (2 miles off I-89), this exceptionally clean and classy house has six comfortable guest rooms, all with private bath, all individually decorated with antiques and equipped with good reading lights. Children over 12, please. Gail Clark will pick up Long Trail hikers. Rates $85–125 for a double including full breakfast.

🐾 🦴 **Maple Grove Farm B&B** (802-878-4875; maplebnb@aol.com), 3715 Oak Hill Road, Williston 05495. Open year-round. Ginger and David Isham are the fourth generation of the Isham family to operate this 120-acre farm, one of the last four in this historic town just east of Burlington. While they have sold their dairy herd, the Ishams still raise cattle, and the vintage-1852 Gothic Revival farmhouse retains its surrounding fields and sugarhouse. Guests are comfortably bedded in two rooms vacated by the family's six grown children. One room has a double bed, and the other has a queen. Baths are shared, breakfast is full, and children are welcome. Common space includes a big living room and a den with piano. $50–75; discounts for more than 3 nights.

🦴 🦴 **Black Bear Inn** (802-434-2126; 1-800-395-6335; www.blkbearinn .com), 4010 Bolton Access Road, Bolton 05477. Built in the '60s as a ski lodge, now very much a hilltop country inn known for its fine food. Chef-owner Ken Richardson is a Culinary Institute of America grad (see *Dining Out*). The 25 rooms all have private bath and country decor and range from standard to luxurious (hot tubs and gas fireplaces). Richardson has weathered the changing fortunes at Bolton Valley Resort, with which he

shares this hilltop, and continues to offer access to the resort's many facilities. This is also a favorite place for groups (one family group has been coming for 30 years), at which time the dining room is closed. A standard room is $99 for two with breakfast in spring and summer, $150 for two with breakfast and dinner. Better rooms have premium fees. Pets are invited to stay at the Bone & Biscuit Inn.

🦴 **Elliot House** (802-985-1412; 1-800-860-4405), 5779 Dorset Street, Shelburne 05482. This 1865 Greek Revival farmhouse adjoins conservation land with a view west to the Adirondacks. Anne and George Voland offer three bedrooms, all with private bath; there's also a sitting room with piano. Guests are welcome to walk the meadows; sheep, chickens, and ducks are in residence. Rates $80–100 per room with full breakfast.

⊙ 🦴 🦴 ♿ **The Millhouse B&B** (802-453-2008; www.millhousebb .com), 394 State Prison Hollow Road, Starksboro 05487 (just off Route 116, south of Hinesburg). Open mid-May through mid-October. While it's 25 miles from Burlington, this gem of a bed & breakfast run by Pat and Ron Messer isn't really in any other region (as defined by our chapters), either. The house retains its graceful 1831 lines and sits just above a rushing brook, near enough so that the sound of the water is constant. The sleeping arrangements include the upstairs master bedroom (shared bath) and two suites, one with three bedrooms (a large twin bedroom and two small single rooms) and another composed of two double bedrooms plus private baths. The house (on the National Register of Historic Places) is tastefully, comfortably decorated with plenty of common space, including a great back porch. The downstairs suite is handicapped accessible. Rates, including a breakfast and afternoon snack, are $40–45 per person, and children are $20 extra. Inquire about the studio cottage on the falls (where pets are allowed).

By the Old Mill Stream (802-482-3613; www.bythestream.com), 84 Richmond Road, Hinesburg 05461. This is a pleasant place: an 1860s rambling farmhouse with wide, wooden floorboards and tin ceilings. There are three upstairs guest rooms, two with private bath, and a double living room and dining room; grounds include gardens that border a waterfall (it powered the mill for Isaiah Dow, who built the house). $70–130 includes a full breakfast.

✔ 🐾 **Windekind Farm** (802-434-4455; www.windekindfarms.com), 1425 Bert White Road, Huntington 05462. Hidden away in an upland valley that's seen little development since its was farmed out around 1900, this is a beautifully restored farmhouse with lodging. Close to Camel's Hump State Park and the Catamount Trail and an extensive network of cross-country and snowshoeing trails. Includes a fully equipped apartment in the neighboring "studio," ideal for two adults and two children. Mark and Marijke Smith welcome guests in the farmhouse itself and host weddings and tented receptions on their ample lawn. $225–250 per weekend, $525–626 per week.

MOTOR INNS 🐾 ✔ ♿ **Hawthorn Suites** (802-860-1212; 1-800-527-1133; www.harthotels.com), 401 Dorset Street (just off Route 2), South Burlington 05403. Opened in 1998 by Chuck and Ralph DesLauriers, with an open timbered lobby, featuring suites with separate living rooms (containing foldout couches) and bedrooms: 73 one-bedroom suites and 6 two-bedroom. Facilities include an indoor pool, a spa/Jacuzzi, and fitness machines. While it's located in the heart of South Burlington's strip malls, it's just minutes from downtown Burlington. $99–280 (depending on length of stay) includes a breakfast buffet.

🐾 ✔ ♿ **The Wilson Inn** (802-879-1515; 1-800-521-2334; www.wilson inn.com), 10 Kellogg Road, Essex Junction 05452. The 42 units all include a bedroom, living room, and full kitchen. Handy to IBM rather than Burlington (10 miles away), it can work for families as well as businesspeople. Amenities include a free breakfast buffet, a grocery shopping service, and access to the neighboring fitness center. Some handicapped-accessible units available. Suites range from $65 for a studio to $239 for a penthouse with fireplace and Jacuzzi; discounts for longer stays. The **Eclipse Grill,** a pleasant surprise, serves dinner 4–10 Tuesday through Saturday, offering seafood cioppino ($17.95) and potato-crusted salmon ($16.95).

✔ ♿ **Marriott Courtyard** (802-879-0100; 1-800-321-2211), 177 Hurricane Lane, Williston 05495. At exit 12 off I 80, this Marriott Courtyard is a known quantity with a laundry, in-room refrigerators and work desks, HBO, a whirlpool, and an exercise room. Both rooms and suites are available. Rates begin at $119 for a room with two double beds.

🐾 ✔ **Hampton Inn** (802-655-6177; 1-800-HAMPTON), 42 Lower Mountain View Drive (Route 7 north), Colchester 05446, exit 16 off I-89. North of Burlington, the inn offers 188 well-furnished rooms, indoor pool, Jacuzzi, fitness facilities, free airport shuttle, and continental breakfast. Standard room rates begin at $119.

✳ Where to Eat

Note: Burlington offers the best choice of restaurants and cafés between Boston and Montreal, but the best are not all downtown.

DINING OUT Inn at Shelburne Farms (802-985-8498; www.shelburnefarms.org), Shelburne. Open for dinner by reservation from mid-May through late October. This turn-of-the-20th-century manor offers imaginative cuisine in a magnificent setting: walls covered in fin de siècle silk damask from Spain, a black-and-white marble floor, and a stunning sunset view of Lake Champlain and the Adirondacks. You might begin with chilled Amish peach and sparkling wine soup and dine on naturally raised beef tenderloin with sweet corn and Swiss chard polenta ($29) or pan-roasted chicken with a ragout of beets, fingerling potato, fava beans, *haricots verts*, and roasted pepper tapenade ($21). Dessert might be a chocolate truffle cake with peppermint ice cream, mixed berry napoleon with sweet mascarpone cream, or Vermont-made cheeses with poached figs and crostini. Smokers can have coffee served on the terrace. Breakfast, open to the public by reservation, is also an event: granola pancakes, brioche French toast, eggplant and cheddar frittata, or poached eggs with herbed hollandaise and home fries.

Café Shelburne (802-985-3939), Route 7, Shelburne. Open for dinner

daily except Monday. Located across the road from the Shelburne Museum, this chef-owned and -operated authentically French bistro serves consistently fabulous fare. Lobster over homemade fettuccine and a hunter's plate that includes quail, rabbit, and venison are stars in an overall excellent menu. The desserts are sinful. This is unquestionably one of the best restaurants in the state. Entrées are in the $20–25 range.

Pauline's Café & Restaurant (802-862-1081), 1834 Shelburne Road (Route 7 south). Open daily for lunch, brunch, and dinner, also Sunday brunch. It is worth braving the strip development traffic. In the elegant simplicity of the downstairs café or the more formal upstairs dining rooms, subtle cuisine featuring wild and local ingredients (mushrooms, cattail shoots, sea beans, fresh black and white truffles, for example) is artfully presented in sensible portions. Entrées might be pork loin scaloppine with apricot, sherry, and herb sauce; loin of Vermont rabbit with artichoke hearts and mushrooms; or veal tenderloin with wild mushrooms. Café: moderate. Upstairs: expensive.

Butler's (802-878-1100), the Inn at Essex, Route 15, Essex Junction.

A SIDEWALK CAFÉ ON CHURCH STREET

Kim Grant

Open for dinner nightly. In the deft hands of the New England Culinary Institute, the cuisine in this elegantly formal, green-walled room with high-backed, upholstered chairs is a visual as well as gustatory treat. Dinner might start with asparagus leek soup ($3.75) and Chef Jacques's rich country pâté ($5.75); proceed to grilled breast of duck with fig chutney ($16), crisp-skin salmon with fennel risotto ($17), or grilled rack of lamb with polenta and broccoli rabe ($21). Elaborate desserts might include a caramelized phyllo napoleon with cranberry compote.

Smokejacks (802-658-1119), 156 Church Street, Burlington. Open daily for lunch and dinner. The decor is understated, almost stark in contrast to what even the menu describes as "bold food." Culinary Institute of America–trained Leslie Myers and Don Kelp obviously strive to be creative. Chances are we will never again have the opportunity to lunch on black bean turkey chili soup with sour cream, corn, and pumpkin seeds. We're glad we did! Dinner entrées like balsamic-grilled Cavendish quail and "paella" (including a crispy duck leg as well as the usual seafood and sausage). Request a cheese plate and a glass of wine (the wine selection is long and interesting); also great martinis. Moderate to expensive.

Blue Seal Restaurant (802-434-5040), Bridge Street, Richmond. Open Tuesday through Saturday 5:30–9:30. Reservations suggested. Housed in a vintage-1854 feed store, chef-owner Debra Weinstein's casual restaurant may not look—or charge—the part, but it's right up there with the Burlington area's finest. The menu is American food with south-

western flavors. You might begin with the vegetarian soup of the day or a warm spinach salad with nuggets of bacon and goat cheese ($5–7.50), then dine on pan-roasted salmon with roasted garlic mashed potatoes, herb oil, and salsa, or marinated portobello mushrooms with grilled new potatoes, sautéed spinach, and goat cheese. A favorite dessert is double-layered devil's food cake with coffee swirl ice cream. Entrées $10.50–16.

Black Bear Inn (802-434-2920), at the Bolton Valley Resort, off Route 2 in Bolton. Reservations requested. Chef-owner Ken Richardson is a Culinary Institute of America graduate who has turned his hilltop lodge into a dining destination for Burlington residents. The menu, which changes nightly, is limited to five entrées, so you might want to call to check, and to reserve. You might begin with escargots sautéed with roasted garlic and red wine (or a cream of carrot and red pepper soup), then dine on a center-cut rib pork chop with wild rice and cranberry relish or a confit of duck with broccoli rabe, sausage, and sage. Entrées run $12.95–17.95.

Opaline (802-660-8875), 1 Lawson Lane, Burlington. This French restaurant has only a few tables, so reservations are a must. The food is expensive but very good. Heed the warning in the parking lot and get a sticker from the maître d' or you will get towed, an unpleasant finish to an otherwise excellent dining experience.

Iron Wolf (802-865-4462), 86 St. Paul Street, Burlington. Dinner is served Tuesday through Saturday from 5:30 PM. Reservations recommended. Diners have been known to wax poetic about the juicy fillet of beef. They cannot say enough about chef Claus Bockwoldt's fillet of pork with its port wine and veal stock reduction, or his butter-soft lamb and white beans. Entrées $13–21.50. Wine store open from 11 AM to closing.

Waiting Room (802-862-3455), 156 St. Paul Street, Burlington. Open Tuesday through Saturday 5:30 PM– 2 AM; Sunday brunch. Reservations accepted. The Waiting Room brought metropolitan flavor to the Burlington after-hours scene when it opened in August 2001. On most nights there's music provided either by a DJ or a live group. The performances comple- ment a sophisticated dinner menu served until midnight along with an extensive wine selection and well- stocked bar. Live music starts at 10:30 every night except Sunday, when it starts at 10 AM. You might dine on lamb shanks osso buco with white beans ($19) or bouillabaisse with monk- fish, mussels, clams, and shrimp ($21).

Starry Night Café (802-877-6316), 5359 Route 7, Ferrisburgh. Dinner seatings are 5–9:30 daily except Tues- day. Entrées range from grilled mahimahi in a smoked tomato and mussel beurre blanc ($20), to a goat cheese ravioli with spinach, tomato, and basil sauce ($15). Desserts are all $5.50. Call ahead, because it's a full 25-minute drive south of Burlington.

EATING OUT *Note:* Thanks to Burlington's huge student population, many of the following restaurants offer "dining-out" quality at "eating- out" prices.

In Burlington
Sweetwater's (802-864-9800), 120 Church Street (corner of College Street). Open Monday through Satur- day 11:30 AM–1:30 AM, Sunday 10:30 AM–1 AM. Housed in a former and splendidly restored 1920s bank building, this is a deservedly popular spot. One of the house specialties is bison. You might lunch on a bison burger, a salmon sandwich, or a choice of daily specials; dine on wood- grilled chicken served with sun-dried tomatoes and shiitake mushrooms. The square bar is one of Burlington's prime rendezvous spots. Moderate.

Trattoria Delia (802-864-5253), 152 St. Paul Street. Open daily 5–10. A dimly lit, nicely decorated space with a helpful, knowledgeable wait staff, tempting antipasti and primi pastas, a wide choice of entrées (ranging from chicken to wild boar), nightly specials, and regional Italian wines. Entrées range from $13 for spaghetti *con von- gole* (with fresh clams) to $26 for *filetto al barbera d'alba* (filet mignon with white truffle butter). Reservations.

Daily Planet (802-862-9647), 15 Center Street. Open daily. The light bar menu is served 4–5 PM and again 9:30–11 PM; dinner is 5–9:30 . The atmosphere is light and casual with a solarium and airy dining room, both filled with small tables. The All Nat- ural Planet Burger ($6.95) is a cus- tomer favorite, and the vegetarian offerings are numerous, including wild mushroom pasta ($12.50) and eggplant manicotti ($11.95).

NECI Commons (802-862-6324), 25 Church Street. Open daily for light breakfast, lunch, dinner, and take-out. This three-story building at the upper end of Church Street is filled with New England Culinary Institute students both learning and putting what they've learned into practice. The space includes several dining rooms, varying in tone, all hip and inviting. Generally excellent and innovative cuisine.

Sakura (802-863-1988), 2 Church Street. Lunch Monday through Saturday, dinner daily. Vermont's first (but no longer its only) Japanese restaurant is a resounding success. At lunch its soothing ambience is an oasis of calm and an appropriate setting for savoring sushi and sashimi dishes or simply deep-fried salmon served with a tangy sauce. Vegetarians will appreciate dishes like avocado, bean curd, boiled spinach, vegetable tempura, and hijiki (cooked seaweed). Lone diners appreciate the seats lining the long sushi bar.

Three Tomatoes (802-660-9533), 83 Church Street, in the cellar of the old Howard Opera House at the marketplace. A fine, busy place with an excellent northern Italian menu, plus top-drawer, wood-fired pizzas. You might lunch on the pasta of the day, or dine on fusilli sautéed with wood-smoked chicken, sweet peas, mushrooms, plum tomatoes, black pepper, rosemary, and light cream. Outdoor tables in summer. Italian mineral water and wines featured. Moderate.

Five Spice Café (802-864-4045), 175 Church Street. Open Monday through Saturday for lunch (11:30–3) and dinner (5–9:30), Sunday 11–2 for dim sum brunch. Dim sum offerings are $1.75–3.75 for a small plate or steamer. The dishes are from a variety of Asian countries—Thailand, Vietnam, Indonesia, and India, as well as China—and the spices are as hot as you care to take them. The atmosphere is appealing. Try the ginger-tangerine cheesecake.

Parima Restaurant (802-864-7917), 185 Pearl Street. Open for lunch and dinner. Polished wood and brass and ornate glass lamps are the unlikely but pleasing decor for a wide selection of classic Thai dishes.

Halvorson's Upstreet Cafe (802-658-0278), 16 Church Street. Open for lunch, dinner, and brunch. An old landmark that's expanded its basic all-American menu and added beer and wine to meet the changing nature of the street. In summer check out its hidden courtyard; inquire about Thursday-night jazz.

Red Square Bar and Grill (802-859-8909), 136 Church Street. Open afternoons for people-watching and for dinner. Jack O'Brien's attractive space features a copper bar, local art, music 6 nights a week, and is best known for its Sunday gospel brunch: $13.95 includes the music.

Stone Soup (802-862-7616), 211 College Street. Open Monday through Friday 7–7, Saturday 8–5, closed Sunday. A hugely popular storefront café specializing in vegetarian dishes, great soups, salads, and breads. Inexpensive.

Cobblestone Deli & Market (802-865-3354), 152 Battery Street. Open daily, weekdays 7–7, Saturday 8–6, Sunday 8–5. No view (wrong side of Battery Street) but a pleasant café with a good deli: soups, sandwiches, coffees, wines, and microbrews. Pick up a sandwich to take on the bike path or to picnic by the lake.

Leunig's Bistro (802-863-3759), Church and College Streets. Open daily for breakfast, lunch, and dinner. In classic bistro style, Leunig's has dark wood, gleaming coffee machines, streetside tables, and status as the hub of Church Street. Frequent live entertainment.

Henry's Diner (802-862-9010), 155 Bank Street, is a long-established, authentic diner around the corner from the Church Street Marketplace. Here you can get the meat loaf and thick gravy you've been hankering for. Closed Monday.

Nectar's (802-658-4771), 188 Main Street. A basic eatery for breakfast and lunch but famed for its french fries with gravy and its owner's association with the musical group Phish. Because it has a cabaret license (nightly music), it's the only restaurant in town that allows smoking.

Bove's Cafe (802-864-6651), 68 Pearl Street. Open Tuesday through Sunday for lunch and dinner. An old favorite with booths and a row of tables between; traditional Italian menu, full bar. Inexpensive.

The Vermont Pub and Brewery (802-865-0500), 144 College Street. Open daily 11:30 AM–1 AM. Housed in a modern building but with an old beer-hall atmosphere (tile floor, huge bar, brass), specializing in ales and lagers brewed on the premises. The menu includes Cornish pasties, cock-a-leekie pie, bratwurst, and fish-and-chips.

India House (802-862-7800), 207 Colchester Avenue. Lunch and dinner Tuesday through Saturday; Sunday brunch. This warm and hospitable restaurant serves traditional curries, tandoori chicken, and the like, plus puffy poori bread.

Single Pebble (802-865-5200), 133 Bank Street. This is the Burlington branch of the restaurant that opened in Barre several years ago to great acclaim. Chef Steve Bogart has trained in China, and his food is as good as you'll find this side of the Yangtze River. Give the mock eel a try.

🐌 **Penny Cluse Cafe** (802-651-8834), 169 Cherry Street. Innovative, healthy, hearty breakfasts and lunches. Famous for black beans, polenta, great biscuits. This is one of the best values in Burlington.

🎵 **The Hot Dog Lady.** Lois Bodoky has her imitators, but she was the first and she's still the most reasonably priced and all-around best. Look for her cart at noon every day at the Church Street Marketplace: $1 hot dog with kraut.

On the waterfront

The Ice House (802-864-1800), 171 Battery Street. Open for lunch and dinner daily, Sunday brunch, with seasonal open-air decks overlooking the ferry slip and marina. This was a pioneer of the city's upscale restaurant scene, a 19th-century icehouse with massive walls and timbers. American regional dishes feature seafood and Vermont lamb. We recommend the shrimp pico (shrimp and crabmeat stuffing in puff pastry with lobster cream sauce; $18.50). You might lunch on sautéed chicken with garlic, herbs, and white wine in a tomato cream sauce on tortellini ($6.95). Save room for hot cheesecake.

🎵 **Shanty on the Shore** (802-864-0238), 181 Battery Street. Open daily 11–11. Handy to the ferry with great lake views from inside as well as out; good for burgers and sandwiches as well as seafood platters, even escargots. A children's menu and choice of exotic drinks also offered.

Breakwater Cafe & Grill (802-864-9804), King Street Dock. Part of the LCTC ferry complex, an informal dockside space serving sandwiches, fried baskets, soups, and salads all day and evening in summer; inquire about frequent live music.

Whitecaps (802-862-1240), at the Boathouse. Open Memorial Day through Labor Day, 7:30 AM–sunset. A relaxing, casual spot; small menu; bar; moderate prices.

In Winooski

Papa Frank's (802-655-2433), 13 West Center Street. Open Monday through Friday 11–10, Saturday 4–10. A red-sauce Italian neighborhood restaurant that caters to families as well as students. Good for pizza, calzones, but also classic dishes. The vegetables are fresh, and garlic bread comes with your order. A bit tricky to find if you're driving because of one-way streets, but it's just a couple of blocks from the Champlain Mill.

Sneakers (802-655-9081), 36 Main Street, serves a great breakfast and lunch Monday through Friday, dinner Monday through Saturday, weekend brunch. Locals consider this the best breakfast in the area; options include eggs Benedict and freshly squeezed orange juice. The dinner special may be seafood or lamb. Inquire about live music on weekends.

Waterworks (802-655-2044), the Champlain Mill. Open for lunch, dinner, and Sunday brunch. Occupying the prime space in the turn-of-the-20th-century mill, overlooking the dam spillway and rapids of the Winooski River. You can dine outside in a greenhouse area or savor the view through the mill's long windows. The large menu ranges from sandwiches to Wiener schnitzel, steak, stir-fries, and nightly specials.

In Colchester

♪ Colchester Reef Lighthouse (802-655-0200), 8 Mountain View Drive, adjacent to the Hampton Inn just off I-89, exit 16. Lunch, dinner, and Sunday brunch. Nowhere near the water, but a bustling, cheerful, steak-and-seafood place, with the biggest salad bar around; good for families (kids' menu). Full bar.

Libby's Blue Line Diner (802-655-0343), 1 Roosevelt Avenue, Route 77, Colchester, with its tile floor and marble counters, attracts itinerant diner buffs and area fans for breakfast, lunch, and dinner daily. Try the banana bread French toast.

Williston Road to Richmond

Daily Bread Bakery Café (802-434-3148), Richmond Center. Open daily 8–4. People leave I-89 south (turn right at the Cumberland Farms and look for the aqua sign at the end of a parking lot on your left) just to drop by for breakfast, lunch, or Saturday and Sunday brunch, or even for a slice or two of maple bread.

Al's French Frys (802-862-9203), 1251 Williston Road, South Burlington. Really, that's how it's spelled. Open daily 10:30 AM–midnight. Burlington's own (amazingly fast) fast-food joint, spanking clean and small-town friendly with first-class fries, burgers, dogs, and shakes. Handy enough to I-89, exit 14E, to work well as roadfood.

On Shelburne Road (Route 7 south)

♪ Perry's Fish House (802-862-1300), 1080 Shelburne Road. Open Monday through Saturday 5–10, Sunday 4–10. A big, bustling, landlocked pier with an extensive menu of moderately priced, first-rate seafood that attracts large numbers of locals. Specialties include batter-fried clams. Children's menu.

Harrington's (802-985-2000), Shelburne. Across from the Shelburne

Museum, a good bet if you can snag one of the few tables and don't mind the Styrofoam at the excellent deli here. Specialties include the "World's Best Ham Sandwich" (Harrington's is known for its corn-smoked ham); also smoked turkey, quiche, homemade soups, sausage chili made with Harrington's own pork sausages, and chocolate mousse.

In Hinesburg
♪ **Good Times Café,** Route 116, Hinesburg, where the road takes a sharp left. Lunch and dinner Tuesday through Sunday 11–9. Music on Wednesday night. The homemade pizza here is great ($8.50 and up), as are the soups, salads, and daily dinner specials. This is a find.

CAFFEINE/SNACKS

In Burlington
Dobra Tea (802-951-2424), 86 Church Street, Burlington. Open 11–10 weekdays, noon–10 weekends. "Dobra" means "good" in Czech, and this is the first U.S. member of a Czech chain of tea houses offering 60 flavors from 10 countries and serving them as they would be in their native venue. Savor Ilati, a rich, black tea from Nepal served in square ceramic cups; or Tung Ting from Taiwan, served in small shallow cups. Each pot is freshly brewed at the precise temperature and for the time required.

Mirabelle's (802-658-3074), 198 Main Street. A delightful bakery/eatery featuring special teas, espresso, pastries, sandwiches, and light fare. Look for the waterfront offshoot.

Muddy Waters (802-658-0466), 184 Main Street, just up from Church Street. Excellent coffee, homemade

desserts, vegan specials, smoothies, beer and wine by the glass, brick walls, sofas, lots of reading material and earnest conversation.

Uncommon Grounds (802-865-6227), 42 Church Street. They roast their own here, and also sell tea and pastries. A good people-watching spot.

Speeder and Earl's. A small counter and café tables at 104 Church Street, a zany shop at 412 Pine Street, same complex as the Fresh Market, featuring their own blends and assorted pastries.

Ben & Jerry's (802-862-9620), 36 Church Street. This isn't the original location, but the world's legendary ice cream makers did get their start in the neighborhood.

✳ Entertainment

Note: For current arts and entertainment in Burlington, call the **Burlington City Arts line** at 802-865-7166, or check *Seven Days*, a free weekly publication that's available everywhere around town.

MUSIC Vermont Mozart Festival performances (802-862-7352), 110 Main Street, Burlington 05401. Summer concerts in various settings—on ferries, at the Shelburne Museum and/or Shelburne Farms, at the Basin Harbor Club, in churches. Winter chamber series.

Vermont Symphony Orchestra (802-864-5741), 77 College Street, Burlington. One of the country's first statewide philharmonics presents a five-concert Chittenden County series at the Flynn Center; outdoor summer pops at Shelburne Farms and elsewhere.

St. Michael's College concerts (802-655-2000), in Winooski, feature jazz, pop, and classical productions.

Burlington Oratorio Society (802-864-0471). A volunteer, 50-voice choir presents several concerts a year.

The Discover Jazz Festival (Flynn box office: 802-86-FLYNN; www.discoverjazz.com), Burlington, 10 days in early June, a jazz extravaganza that fills city parks, clubs, restaurants, ferries.

Battery Park Summer Concert Series, Burlington, Thursday and Sunday nights.

THEATER **Flynn Center for the Performing Arts** (802-86-FLYNN), 153 Main Street, Burlington. The city's prime stage for music and live performance is a refurbished art deco movie house, now home to plays, musical comedies, jazz concerts, and lectures, in addition to movies. It now has a gallery and several smaller performances spaces as well.

Royall Tyler Theater (802-656-2095), at the University of Vermont, Burlington, stages an eclectic, top-notch seasonal repertory of classic and contemporary plays.

St. Michael's College Theater Department (802-654-2000), Winooski, presents two major productions, fall and spring; also an excellent summer playhouse series (802-654-2281).

Lane Series (802-656-4455) sponsors major musical and theatrical performances around Burlington fall through spring.

DRIVE-IN *♫* **Sunset Drive-In** (802-862-1800), Route 127 off North Avenue, Colchester. It's for real: three screens, a snack bar, and a kiddie playground.

MUSICAL VENUES For jazz, blues, rock, and dance clubs, check out these nightspots, all in Burlington: **Nectar's** (802-658-4771), 188 Main Street, and above it, **Club Metronome** (802-865-4563). **135 Pearl Street** (802-863-2343) is the area's gay and lesbian rallying point; dance floor and cabaret theater downstairs, bar and dining room up. **Red Square Bar and Grill** (802-859-8909) offers frequent nightly music and a Sunday gospel brunch. **Rira** (802-860-9401), an Irish bar at 123 Church Street, has traditional Irish music on Wednesday night, and the **Thai Bar at Parima** (802-864-7917) has music Thursday through Saturday starting at 10 PM. The **Waiting Room** (802-862-3455) offers music for the non-hard-rock crowd. **Higher Ground** (802-654-8888), 1 Main Street, Winooski (next to the Champlain Spectrum Mall), offers live music.

✳ Selective Shopping

DOWNTOWN MARKETPLACES **The Church Street Marketplace.** Nearly 100 stores, restaurants, and services line several blocks of Church Street, nicely paved, landscaped, closed to traffic, and enlivened by seasonal arts and crafts shows, weekend festivals, and wandering entertainers (and street people).

Pine Street area. A small yet delectable cluster of businesses on Pine Street between Marble Avenue and Howard Street, just south of the Vermont Transit terminal. Parking is never a problem. Highlights include the Fresh Market, the Burlington Futon Co., Speeder and Earl's Coffee, and Beverly's Cafe; a number of smaller craft businesses are behind Speeder and Earl's.

Burlington Town Center. This vast indoor agora, mostly underground, has 80 stores stocking just about everything, linked to a parking garage and Filene's. Several food stalls for grazers.

ART GALLERIES **Fire House Art Gallery,** 135 Church Street, Burlington. Pick up a copy of the *First Friday Art Trolley Tours* pamphlet guide. The trolley runs only first Fridays, but the map is a good gallery locator any day. On our own tour we were most impressed with the **Doll-Anstadt Gallery** (802-864-3661), 91 College Street. Ruby Anstadt offers a mix of striking paintings (changing shows) and decorative art.

Furchgott & Sourdiffe Gallery (802-985-3848), 86 Falls Road, Shelburne. A tasteful gallery in an old farmhouse, offering local art.

Also check out the **Exquisite Corpse Artiste,** 47 Maple Street (802-864-8040), just off Battery Street.

ANTIQUES SHOPS **Ethan Allen Antique Shop** (802-863-3764), Williston Road, Route 2 east of Burlington, has a large stock of early American and country furniture and accessories. Open daily; Sunday by appointment.

Architectural Salvage Warehouse (802-658-5011), 53 Main Street, Burlington, offers artifacts from old houses and buildings.

Burlington Centre for Antiques (802-985-4911), 3093 Shelburne Road, south of Burlington. Open daily year-round. Two large floors offer quality antiques in every size and shape from more than 70 dealers.

Route 7 Antiques (802-859-0917), 388 Shelburne Road in the south end of town. Open Tuesday through Sunday. An intimate collection of elderly and antique items, reasonably priced.

Champlain Valley Antique Center (802-985-8116), 4067 Shelburne Road, Shelburne, offers the wares of 25 dealers. Also try **Upstairs Antiques** (802-859-8966), on Flynn Avenue in Burlington.

BOOKSTORES

In Burlington
The small **Everyday Book Shop** (802-862-5191) at 194 College Street is the lone surviving independent bookstore in the downtown area. **Waldenbooks'** branch (802-658-6019) is in the Burlington Town Center on the lower level. **Barnes & Noble** (802-864-8001), 102 Dorset Street, is a two-story book department store in South Burlington, and **Borders Books** (802-865-2711) is at 29 Church Street. **Bygone Books** (802-862-4397) sells some of its inventory of antiquarian books at **Whistlestop Antique**s on Flynn Avenue and on its web site but no longer has a retail outlet.

Elsewhere
🐷 **Flying Pig Children's Books** (802-425-2600) is at 86 Ferry Road just off Route 7 in Charlotte. **The Book Rack and Children's Pages** (802-872-2627), another great spot for kids, is located in the Essex Outlet Center in Essex.

CRAFTS SHOPS

In Burlington
Frog Hollow on the Marketplace (802-863-6458), 86 Church Street, is a branch of the Vermont State Craft Center of Middlebury, a showcase for fine things crafted in the state, from

furniture and art glass to handwoven scarves.

Designers Circle (802-864-4238), 52 Church Street, features beautifully crafted jewelry. **Bennington Potters North** (1-800-205-8033), 127 College Street, sells kitchenware, home furnishings, glass, and woodenware, and Bennington pottery at "factory prices." **Church and Maple Glass Studio** (802-863-3880), 225 Church Street. Closed Sunday. Bud Shriner, a former emergency room physician, bought the old Yellow Cab garage several years ago and has transformed it into a glassblowing studio with a reasonably priced array of crafted glass.

FARM Vermont Wildflower Farm (802-425-3500), Route 7, Charlotte (5 miles south of the Shelburne Museum). Open May through October, daily 10–5. A multimedia show; 6 acres of wildflowers in test fields and woodland settings; flowers and trees labeled along paths; a large gift shop; and "the largest wildflower seed center in the East." Nominal admission.

FOOD AND DRINK Lake Champlain Chocolates (802-864-1807), 750 Pine Street, Burlington. Open 7 days. The home of the American Truffle, and other expensive candy, discounts some of its premium chocolates. Tours are possible with reservations.

Snowflake Chocolates, Route 15, Jericho Corners. Bob and Martha Pollak's handcrafted chocolates are so good. Try the dark, liqueur-laced truffles.

Fresh Market (802-863-3968; 1-800-447-1205), 400 Pine Street, Burlington. Formerly the Cheese Outlet, this market still specializes in cheeses from Vermont as well as from around

the world. Also most other Vermont products, and a source of sandwiches, baked goods, wines, deli meats, fresh produce, and exotic deli items.

Magic Hat Brewing Company (802-658-BREW), 5 Bartlett Bay Road, South Burlington (turn off Route 7 at the Jiffy Lube). A microbrewery offering free tours and samples, Wednesday through Saturday; also a retail store.

Note: The **Saturday Farmer's Market** in City Hall Park (8:30–2:30 summer through fall) is good for baked goods, clothes, and art as well as fruits and veggies.

SPORTS STORES Burton Snowboards (802-862-4500), 80 Industrial Parkway (near Oakledge Park), Burlington. Open Monday through Friday 8–6, Saturday noon–5. The factory's retail and factory outlet for Vermont's name-brand snow- and skateboards and gear. Also check out the downtown Burlington store (802-863-0539) at 145 Cherry Street.

The Outdoor Gear Exchange (802-860-0190), 191 Bank Street, Burlington. Used and new outdoor sporting equipment: cross-country skiing, snowshoeing, rock climbing, hiking, and backpacking gear. It's rock climbing central.

The Downhill Edge and Ski Rack (802-862-2282), 65–85 Main Street, Burlington. This combined store features high-performance sailboards, gives lessons, and offers rentals at Leddy Beach and the Marble Island Resort. It's also a major source of cycling, running, in-line skate, and ski gear and wear, as well as rentals.

Climb High (802-985-5055), 2438 Shelburne Road, Shelburne. Hiking, biking, rock climbing, cross-country skiing—you name it, this store has the gear for it, plus quick and reasonable repairs. The best part is that you don't have to drive into downtown Burlington.

VINTAGE CLOTHING AND FURNISH-INGS **Old Gold** (802-864-7786), 180 Main Street, is a fun and funky store. **Battery Street Jeans** (802-865-6223), 182 Battery Street, offers more grungy but cool clothing. **Recycle North** (appliances, furniture, books) and **Garment Gallery** (clothing and jewelry) are similar shops at 266 Pine Street. All are in Burlington.

MORE SPECIAL STORES

In Burlington
Peace and Justice Store (802-863-8326), 21 Church Street, run by the city's active Peace and Justice Coalition, a source of alternative publications and third-world-crafted items—jewelry, cards, clothing—all purchased from wholesalers committed to nonexploitation and social justice. The bulletin board is also worth checking.

Gardener's Supply (802-660-3505), 128 Intervale Road (there's also an outlet at Taft's Corners in Williston). One of the largest catalog seed and garden suppliers in New England, with a retail store and nursery adjacent to demonstration gardens along the Winooski River in Burlington's Intervale.

Apple Mountain (802-658-0500), 30 Church Street, is a Vermont products gift and food shop; on the touristy side, but fun.

In the Charlotte–Shelburne area
Dakin Farm (802-425-3971), Route 7, Ferrisburgh (and the Champlain Mill, Winooski), is one of the principal purveyors of cob-smoked hams and bacon. This roadside store also stocks a variety of other Vermont food products and gifts.

Shelburne Farm Store and Visitors Center (802-985-8442), open daily year-round 9–5 (10–5 in the off-season; see a full description of what this place is about under *Museums and Attractions*). The store features the prizewinning cheddar cheeses made from the milk of the estate's own Brown Swiss herd. A variety of Vermont products is also stocked.

Harrington's, Route 7, across from the Shelburne Museum, Shelburne, has been known for years for its delectable (and expensive) corncob-smoked hams, bacon, turkey, pork chops, and other goodies. The shop also displays an array of cheeses, maple products, griddlecake mixes, jams, fruit butters, relishes, baked goods, wines, and coffees. Harrington's headquarters (Route 2, Richmond) include a smaller store.

The Shelburne Country Store, Route 7, Shelburne, encloses several gift galleries under the same roof—a sweets shop, foods, lamp shades.

✐ **The Vermont Teddy Bear Factory Store** (802-985-3001; 1-800-829-BEAR), 6655 Shelburne Road (Route 7), Shelburne (see *For Families*), is immense.

In Winooski
The Champlain Mill (802-655-9477), 1 Main Street, a creatively converted woolen mill, holds 30 smart shops, a well-stocked bookshop, plus two good restaurants, a bakery, and a deli; also several interesting clothing stores.

Blackthorne Forge (802-655-7676), 94 West Canal Street. Assorted traditional fixtures, plus unusual sculptured clocks.

Also in Greater Burlington

University Mall (802-863-1066), Dorset and Williston Streets (I-89, exit 14E), South Burlington. Your basic shopping mall with 70 stores; Ames, Sears, and JCPenney are the anchors. The **Essex Outlet Fair** (802-657-2777), Routes 15 and 289 in Essex, includes Polo Ralph Lauren, Jones New York, Levi's, Jockey, and Bali, plus a new cinema complex.

✳ Special Events

February: **Burlington Winter Festival,** at Waterfront Park—dogsled rides, snow and ice sculptures (802-864-0123).

Saturday before Lent: **Magic Hat Mardi Gras**—a parade and block party at the Church Street Marketplace.

March: **Vermont Flower Show** at the Sheraton in South Burlington—3 days of color and fragrance mark the end of winter.

May: **Lilac Sunday** at Shelburne Museum (802-985-3346)—a festival of 19th-century food and games when the museum's many lilac bushes are in peak bloom.

Early June: **Arts Alive,** a showcase of Vermont artists. **Vintage auto rally** at the Shelburne Museum (802-985-3346). **Discover Jazz Festival**—for 9 days, the entire city of Burlington becomes a stage for more than 200 musicians (see *Entertainment*). **Lake Champlain International Fishing Derby**—for details about registration and prizes, check with the chamber of commerce.

Late June: **Green Mountain Chew Chew,** Burlington—a 3-day food festival featuring more than 50 restaurants; continuous family entertainment. **Showcase of Agriculture** at the American Morgan Horse Association (802-985-4944), adjacent to the Shelburne Museum.

Early July: Gala **Independence Day celebrations** on the Burlington waterfront—fireworks over the lake with live bands in Battery Park, children's entertainment, a parade of boats, and blessing of the fleet.

Mid-July–mid-August: **Vermont Mozart Festival** performances in various locations, including Lake Champlain ferries (see *Entertainment*).

Mid-August: **The Shelburne Craft Fair** at Shelburne Farms features dozens of exhibitors.

Late August: **Champlain Valley Exposition,** Essex Junction Fairgrounds—a big, busy, traditional county fair with livestock and produce exhibits, trotting races, midway, rides, spun-sugar candy—the works.

Mid-September: **Annual Harvest Festival,** Shelburne Farms (802-985-8686). **Fools-A-Float**—a parade of land and sea craft, downtown Burlington. **Art Hop**—open-studio weekend in Burlington.

Early October: **Marketfest** celebrates Burlington's cultural diversity.

Early December: **Christmas Weekend** at the Shelburne Museum, a 19th-century festival; call 802-985-3344 for dates and details.

December 31: **First Night** (802-863-6005), the end-of-the-year gala—parades, fireworks, music, mimes, and other performances that transform downtown Burlington into a happy "happening."

THE NORTHWEST CORNER

Interstate 89 is the quickest but not the most rewarding route from Burlington to the Canadian border. At the very least, motorists should detour for a meal in St. Albans and a sense of the farm country around Swanton. We strongly recommend allowing a few extra hours—or days—for the route up through the Champlain Islands, Vermont's Martha's Vineyard but as yet unspoiled.

THE ISLANDS

The cows and silos, hay fields and mountain views couldn't be more Vermont. But what about those beaches and sailboats? They're part of the picture, too, in this land chain composed of the Alburg peninsula and three islands—Isle La Motte, North Hero, and South Hero.

The Champlain Islands straggle 30 miles south from the Canadian border. Thin and flat, they offer some of the most spectacular views in New England: east to the highest of the Green Mountains and west to the Adirondacks. They also divide the northern reach of the largest lake in the East into two long, skinny arms, freckled with smaller outer islands. It's a waterscape well known to fishermen and sailors.

This is Grand Isle County, Vermont's smallest, with a small but steadily growing year-round population. It was homesteaded by Ebenezer Allen in 1783 and has been a quiet summer retreat since the 1870s.

In the 19th century visitors arrived by lake steamer to stay at farms. Around the turn of the 20th-century a railway spawned several hotels, and with the advent of automobiles and Prohibition, Route 2—the high road down the spine of the islands—became one of the most popular roads to Montreal, a status it maintained until I-89 opened in the 1960s.

Happily, the 1960s, as well as the '70s, '80s, and '90s, like the interstate, seem to have passed these islands by. The selection of North Hero as summer home of the Royal Lipizzan Stallions in the 1990s is the biggest thing that's happened here since Theodore Roosevelt's visit in 1901. (It was here at Lieutenant Governor Nelson Fisk's estate that Vice President Theodore Roosevelt, who was attending a Vermont Fish and Game League banquet, learned that President William McKinley, also a visitor here in 1897, had been shot in Buffalo, New York.)

Isle La Motte is the smallest and quietest of the islands, and it's crossed and

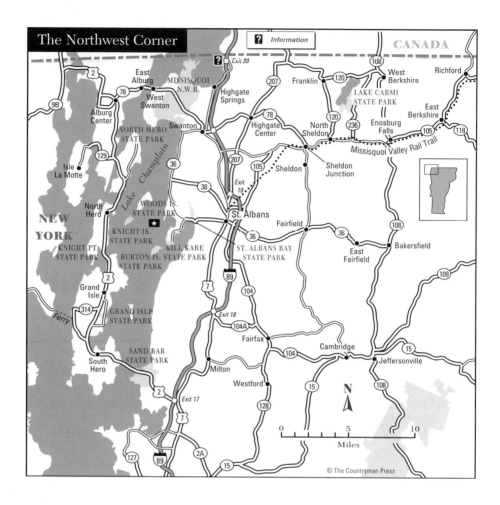

circled by narrow roads beloved by bicyclists. St. Anne's Shrine near the northern tip marks the site of a 17th-century French fort, and a rocky, tree-topped hump in the middle of a cow pasture at the southern end of the island is said to be the oldest coral reef in the world. Other evidence of the island's geological distinction can be seen in its stone houses, as well as in the marble facades of New York's Radio City Music Hall and the U.S. Capitol building. A quarry for the unique black Isle La Motte limestone marble is once again being worked after years of closure.

The rural, laid-back beauty of these islands is fragile. Their waterside farms and orchards are threatened, not by tourism, but by quiet, steady suburbanization. Burlington is just south of Grand Isle, and Montreal is just 60 miles north.

Viewed primarily as a summer destination, this is a great place to visit in September and October when its many orchards are being harvested and bicycling is at its best. Roads are little trafficked, mysteriously overlooked by mainstream leaf-peepers.

GUIDANCE **Champlain Islands Chamber of Commerce** (802-372-5683; info@champlainislands.com; www.champlainislands.com), P.O. Box 213, North Hero 05474, next door to the Hero's Welcome General Store, maintains a year-round office and publishes a list of accommodations, restaurants, marinas, camp-grounds, and trailer parks.

GETTING THERE *By car:* From New York State and Montreal, Route 2 from Rouses Point, and from Vermont, Route 78 from Swanton (an exit off I-89). From Vermont on the south, I-89 exit 17 to Route 2, which runs the length of the islands.

By ferry: **Lake Champlain Transportation Company** (802-864-9804) offers year-round, 15-minute ferry crossings between Gordon's Landing, Grand Isle, and Cumberland Head, New York.

MEDICAL EMERGENCY Emergency service is available by calling **911.**

Marine emergencies: Call 802-372-5590.

✳ Must See

St. Anne's Shrine (802-928-3362), Isle La Motte, Route 129. An open-sided Victorian chapel on the shore marks the site of Vermont's first French settlement in 1666. There are daily outdoor Masses in summer and Sunday services as long as weather permits. The shrine is a pleasant and peaceful place with a public beach, a cafeteria, and a picnic area in a large pine grove, presumably descended from what Samuel de Champlain described as "the most beautiful pines as I have ever seen" near this spot. Champlain himself is honored here with a massive granite statue, which was carved in Vermont's Pavilion at Montreal's 1967 Expo. The complex is maintained by the Edmundites, the order that runs St. Michael's College in Colchester.

ST. ANNE'S SHRINE ON ISLE LA MOTTE   VDT

✳ Also See

Hyde Log Cabin, Route 2, Grand Isle. Open July through Labor Day, Wednesday through Sunday 11–5. Admission $1. Built by Jedediah Hyde in 1783, the cabin was restored by the Vermont Board of Historic Sites in 1956 and leased to the Grand Isle Historical Society, which has furnished it with appealing 18th-century artifacts—furniture, kitchenware, toys, tools, and fabrics.

Isle La Motte Historical Society. Open July through August, Saturday 2–4. This old stone school building and blacksmith shop is on Route 129, 4 miles south of the bridge. Displays include a sculpture of local stone that's been partially polished, graphically illustrating that the stone used in many local buildings is marble. The nearby Chazian Reef, said to be the oldest coral reef in the world, is 450 million years old. Coral rock can harden into limestone that, over millennia, can turn to marble.

The Fisk Quarry Preserve, Isle La Motte. The reef actually comprises 1,000 acres underlying the entire southern third of Isle La Motte. The one reef site that currently can be visited by the public is at the Fisk Quarry Preserve, which adjoins Fisk Farm (see *Lodging*). Owned by the Isle La Motte Reef Preservation Trust, the preserve offers a pedestrian footpath with public viewing area where ancient reef-building organisms can be seen in the quarry walls. Parking is 600 feet to the south of the path. The Preservation Trust asks the public to park only in the designated area, and not alongside the road.

Fish Culture Station (802-372-3171), Bell Hill Road, Grand Isle. Just beyond the Plattsburgh, New York, ferry on Route 314, look for the large hatchery (it's precisely 2 miles up Route 314 from Route 2), open 8–4 daily. Fish are brought to the facility as freshly spawned eggs (up to 2.2 million eggs at any one time), incubated, then transferred to a series of tanks; well worth checking out.

✳ To Do

BICYCLING With its flat roads (little trafficked once you are off Route 2) and splendid views, the islands are popular biking country. Isle La Motte is especially well suited to bicycling. There are five interpretive theme loops that roam through the gently rolling terrain, easily followed with the help of a map available at the chamber of commerce. Still in the planning stage is a rail-trail that links South Hero with Colchester by following the railbed of the old Rutland Railroad. The trip takes you on a magnificent journey across Lake Champlain. Lake views don't get any better than this, and it's flat to boot. The chambers of commerce have maps to guide you. The trial run in August 2001 was a smashing success.

Rental bikes: Check with **Hero's Welcome General Store** (802-372-4161), North Hero Village, and **Bike Shed Rentals** (802-928-3440), Isle La Motte, West Shore Road, 1 mile south of St. Anne's Shrine. Open daily July through August, weekends in June, September, and October. Both Ruthcliffe Lodge and Terry Lodge (see *Lodging*) offer bikes to their guests.

FISK FARM RUIN ON ISLE LA MOTTE

Christina Tree

Mountain Lake Expeditions (802-777-7646) has instituted a very helpful delivery service that deposits bicycles, kayaks, or canoes right at your front door.

BIRDING Located on one of the major flyways, the islands are particularly rich in bird life: Herons, eagles, ospreys, cormorants, among others, migrate through the area. Prime birding sites include the South Hero Swamp and Mud Creek in Alburg and the Sand Bar Wildlife Refuge across from Sand Bar State Park. See also Knight's Island Sate Park under *Green Space.*

BOATING Rental boats are available in North Hero from **Anchor Island Marina** (802-372-5131), **Charlie's Northland Lodge** (802-372-8822), and **Hero's Welcome** (802-372-4161; kayaks and canoes only). In South Hero, **Apple Tree Bay** (802-372-3922) offers canoes, sailboats, and pontoon boats. **Tudhope Sailing Center and Marina** (802-372-5320), at the bridge in Grand Isle, also offers sailboats, powerboats, boat slips, sailing instruction, and charters. **Mountain Lake Expeditions** (see *Bicycling*) will bring kayaks and canoes right to your door.

BOAT EXCURSIONS **Driftwood Tours** (802-373-0022), North Hero, offers several daytime, sunset, and moonlight cruises in a boat that seats a maximum of six passengers. Captain Holly Poulin offers nature and fishing tours and also does dinner cruises in conjunction with the North Hero House. The trips take 2 hours and leave from the North Hero House Pier.

Ferry Cruise (802-864-9804), Route 314, Grand Isle. If you don't get out on the water any other way, be sure to take the 15-minute ferry to Plattsburgh, New York, and back.

FISHING Lake Champlain is considered one of the finest freshwater fisheries in America. With the right bait and a little luck, you can catch trout, salmon, smelt, walleye, bass, pike, muskellunge, and perch. Don't expect area fishermen to give away their favorite spots, but you can find hints, maps, equipment, bait, and advice from local fishing pundit Charlie North at **Charlie's Northland** in North Hero.

GOLF **Alburg Country Club** (802-796-3586), Route 129, 3 miles west of South Alburg; 18 holes, gentle, shady terrain, snack bar.

Barcomb Hill Country Club at Apple Tree Bay (802-372-5398), Route 2, South Hero. Open May until late October. A par-3 executive golf course. Rental carts and clubs.

Wilcox Golf Course (802-372-8343), Grand Isle, offers nine lakeside holes, golf carts, pro shop, rentals.

✔ **Beaver Creek Mini Golf** (802-372-5811), Route 2, North Hero. Open Memorial Day through Labor Day. An 18-hole miniature golf course.

✳ Green Space

✔ **Alburg Dunes State Park** (802-796-4170), Alburg. Recently opened, features a shallow sandy beach, excellent for swimming with young ones, rare flora and fauna; limited day use only. Call for directions or ask locally.

✑ **North Hero State Park** (802-372-8727) has 99 wooded tent or trailer sites and 18 lean-to sites arranged in three loops, each with a restroom and hot showers (no hook-ups); mostly in lowland forests with access to open fields, a beach, boat launch, boat rentals, and picnic and children's play areas.

Grand Isle State Park (802-372-4300) has 155 campsites, including 33 lean-tos (no hook-ups) on 226 acres, with a beach, a nature trail, and a recreation building.

Knight's Island State Park by way of Burton Island State Park (802-524-6353). The *Island Runner* (802-524-6353), a ferry operated by the state, crosses the water to Knight's Island every couple of hours between Memorial Day and Labor Day. There's even an optional gear delivery service. The camping at Knight's Island is primitive (there are no facilities) and even clothing is optional! To maximize privacy, campsites are hidden from public view. Not to be missed is the brochure-guided "Walk of Change" that explores island ecology.

✑ **Knight Point State Park** (802-372-8389), located on the southern tip of North Hero, is the best place to swim, especially if you have small children. A former farm facing The Gut, a quiet, almost landlocked bay, its grounds include a fine brick house and a nature trail that loops around the point, through maple and oak groves. From the sandy beach you can watch sailboats and yachts pass through the drawbridge between the islands. Canoes and rowboats are available for rental in the park.

Sand Bar State Park (802-372-8240) fills to capacity on sunny weekends in summer, but this oasis with its sandy beach and adjacent waterfowl area is a fine place to relax on weekdays.

See also *Green Space* in "St. Albans and Swanton" for the Missisquoi National Wildlife Refuge.

✳ Lodging

Note: See *Green Space* for information on campgrounds in North Hero and Grand Isle State Parks. Families who don't camp tend to rent cottages for a week or more. The chamber of commerce can furnish details about numerous old-fashioned lakeside cottage clusters.

INNS AND BED & BREAKFASTS 🌾

Thomas Mott B&B (802-796-4402; 1-800-348-0843), 63 Blue Rock Road, Alburg 05440. This 1838 English country cottage with a splendid view of the Green Mountains is a real find. Hosts Lee and Linda Mickey keep a fridge full of complimentary Ben & Jerry's ice cream pops. There are three bedrooms, each with private bath, and a suite with two bedrooms and shared bath. Guests are welcome to use the canoes and the swimming/fishing dock. Cross-country skiers and snowmobilers are at home here in winter (local rentals available), with 40 miles of dedicated trails adjacent. More daring guests can try skydiving or paragliding from the Franklin County Airport in Swanton. $90–105.

♿ **North Hero House** (802-372-4732; 1-888-525-3644; www.northhero house.com), Route 2, North Hero 05474. Open year-round. This century-old summer hotel has become a popular spot for boaters, bikers, and travelers of all sorts. All the rooms—9 upstairs and 17 more across Route 2—have private bath, and many baths now have Jacuzzi. The inn offers a comfortable sitting area, an inviting pub, a small library, and a large public dining room beyond (see *Dining Out*). Facilities include a long, grassy dock at which Champlain steamers once moored; canoes, kayaks, power- and pedal boats are available. Our favorite (alas, the most expensive) rooms are in the three buildings that face, even extend out over the lake—Homestead, Southwind, and Cove House—so that you fall asleep to lapping water. In summer $95–255 per couple B&B, $16 per child. Prices fall off a bit in winter (October 24 through May 15). The many specialty weekends include murder mysteries and musical events. Check the web site.

Fisk Farm (802-928-3364), 44 West Shore Road, Isle La Motte 05463. Owner Linda Fitch offers two lovely guest cottages. The former Ice House, built of wood and stone next to the main house, is a beauty, a place we would like to reserve for a special occasion, but only in warm weather (it has a fireplace but no other heating). There is a rustic Shore Cottage, said to have been built as a playhouse in North Hero and brought across the ice. The ruins of a gray stone mansion have been preserved in the front garden, the scene of Sunday teas, and the horse and carriage barn has been preserved as an art gallery. The mansion burned in 1924, but thanks to Fitch, who has dedicated the last few years to restoring the property, it's an exceptionally tranquil place that offers a window into not only the history of Vermont but also the world (see The Fisk Quarry Preserve under *Also See*).

Rates begin at $85 for the Shore Cottage and $100 for the Ice House (both of which have their own kitchens) but vary according to the length of time reserved and the season. Guests may help themselves to the herb garden.

♪ **Ruthcliffe Lodge & Restaurant** (802-928-3200; 1-800-769-8162; www.ruthcliffe.com), 1002 Quarry Road, Isle La Motte 05463, open Mother's Day through Columbus Day. Way out at the end of Old Quarry Road, this lakeside compound includes a small motel and lodge with a total of six rooms and three suites, all with private bath and many featuring lakeside panoramas. Mark and Kathy Infante are warm hosts, and the food is well known and highly rated (see *Dining Out*); three meals a day are served. There's a 40-foot water's-edge patio for dining, as well as the cozy dining room in the lodge. Swimming and fishing are out the front door; rental boats and bikes are available. Rates range from $99 for a double room with a half bath to $139 for a two-room adjoining unit with a bath and a half, including a full country breakfast.

The Ransom Bay Inn (1-800-729-3393), 4 Center Bay Road, Alburg 05440. A stone house built beautifully in the 1790s, originally a stagecoach stop, set back from Route 2 within walking distance of a small beach. Plenty of common space: an open-beamed living room area opening onto a patio and a more formal parlor, two large airy and two smaller guest rooms, all nicely furnished and with private bath. $75–85 double, year-round, includes full breakfast. Dinner is served to guests with advance notice ($18).

LAKE CHAMPLAIN VALLEY

Paradise Bay Bed & Breakfast (802-372-5393), 50 Light House Road, South Hero 05486. This is a very gracious new house in a secluded setting with plenty of deck space overlooking the lake. The two large, nicely furnished guest rooms share a bath in a separate wing. $89–125 per couple.

☙ **Charlie's Northland Lodge** (802-372-8822; 802-372-3829), 3829 Route 2, North Hero 05474, open all year, built by Charlie's grandparents early in the 19th century. Two guest rooms, furnished in country antiques, share a bath, a private entrance, and a guest parlor. $85 double includes continental breakfast. It's part of a nifty little complex that includes a sporting and gift shop, boat and motor rentals, fishing licenses, bait, and tackle. Housekeeping cottages available.

Terry Lodge (802-928-3264), 2925 West Shore Road, Isle La Motte 05463. Open May 15 through October 15. A friendly, family kind of place in a superb location: on a quiet road not far from St. Anne's Shrine, across a narrow road from the lake with a fine lakeside deck and swim raft. Most of the seven rooms in the lodge itself have lake views. Breakfast and dinner (family-style) are served. There's also a four-unit motel ($95–125), a housekeeping cottage ($500 per week), and a housekeeping apartment ($475 per week) in the rear. Bike rentals and golf are available nearby. Lodge rooms are $80 with breakfast, $115 per couple MAP. Request one of the front rooms with a lake view.

☙ **Allenholm Orchards Bed & Breakfast** (802-372-5566; 1-888-721-5666; www.allenholm.com), 150 South Street, South Hero 05486. Pam and Ray Allen offer a guest suite—a bedroom furnished in family antiques,

OVERLOOKING LAKE CHAMPLAIN IN NORTH HERO

Kim Grant

including a queen-sized canopy bed, and a large living room with a TV, VCR, board games, and full-sized pool table, plus a full private bath, patio, rose garden, and private airport. A country breakfast is served upstairs in the dining room or, if preferred, on your patio. The suite is on the lower level of the Allens' modern home; it opens onto more than 100 acres of apples, billed as Vermont's oldest commercial orchard. Established in the 1870s, it's now owned and operated by the sixth generation of Allens. $90 per couple for the bedroom, $150 for the entire suite.

Ferry Watch Inn (802-372-3935), 121 West Shore Road, Grand Isle 05458. This wonderfully restored lakefront home, originally built in 1800, overlooks the broad lake with spectacular views of the Adirondacks and the most wonderful sunsets. Janet and Troy Wert offer three guest rooms (two with shared bath; one with private bath) with antique double beds renowned for their comfort. The property is within walking distance of a nine-hole golf course. $95 per room with shared bath or $115 with private bath includes full country breakfast.

Crescent Bay Farm (802-372-4807; www.crescentbaybb.com), South Hero 05486. This restored 1820s farmhouse is a working farm with three guest rooms, two with private bath. The room with the shared bath is $85 per night; $105 with private bath. Breakfast is included.

✾ Heron's Way B&B (802-372-8352; www.heronsway.com), 424 Route 2, South Hero 05486. With a private sandy beach and dockage. The king bedroom with private bath and balcony overlooking the lake rents for

$115 per night. Rooms with queen or twin beds and shared bath are $95 per night. Pets are accepted for a $50 charge.

OTHER LODGING ✾ ⬥ Shore Acres Inn and Restaurant (802-372-8722; www.shoreacres.com), 237 Shore Acres Drive, North Hero 05474. Motel rooms open May through early October. This pleasant motel commands one of the most spectacular views of any lodging place in Vermont. Set in sweeping, peaceful, beautifully groomed grounds, 19 comfortable rooms face the lake and the Green Mountains. There's a bar/lounge; breakfast and dinner are served (see *Dining Out*). There are also four guest rooms in the garden house, away from the lake. Susan and Mike Tranby have worked hard to make this an exceptionally friendly as well as comfortable place. Amenities include lawn chairs, two clay tennis courts, a driving range, lawn games, and 0.5 mile of private shore for swimming. All rooms have either a queen, king, two twins, or two doubles, TV, and ceiling fan or air conditioner when lake breezes fail. $90–160 per room.

Wilcox Cove Cottages & Golf Course (in summer: 802-372-8343; in winter: 802-879-7807), Route 314, mailing address: 3 Camp Court, Grand Isle 05458. Open June through mid-September. This homey, lakeside cottage colony and nine-hole public golf course, less than a mile from the ferry, is a real find (adults preferred). Each of the eight cottages has a living room, dining area, fully equipped kitchen, one bedroom with twin beds, bathroom with shower, and one or two screened porches. They are completely furnished except for sheets, pillowcases, and bath and kitchen towels, and can be rented for about $400 a week including green fees. Occupancy is limited to two people unless arrangements are made in advance.

✳ Where to Eat

DINING OUT Sand Bar Inn at Apple Island Resort (802-372-6911), Route 2, South Hero. A fine-dining restaurant with a casual atmosphere right on the lake, this place is not what you would expect when seen from Route 2. Among the offerings are a duck breast in blackberry sauce served with ginger polenta and duck confit ($17), several fish and shellfish dishes, and grilled pesto lamb chops ($19). Reservations are suggested. In-season the restaurant is open daily 5–9. The chef also does private parties.

Shore Acres (802-372-8722), Route 2, North Hero. Reservations for dinner are a must much of the time. Also open for breakfast May through October and for lunch in July and August; dinner is served weekends until New Year's as well. The dining room's large windows command a sweeping view of the lake, with Mount Mansfield and its flanking peaks in the distance. It's a very attractive room with a large fieldstone hearth. You might begin with coconut-beer-battered shrimp ($5.25) or grilled homemade polenta ($3.95), then dine on Apple Island chicken or roast rack of lamb. Entrées ($12.95–21.95) come with home-baked bread, a salad, and seasonal vegetables. The chocolate pie is famous.

Ruthcliffe Lodge (802-928-3200), Old Quarry Road, Isle La Motte.

Open mid-May through Columbus Day for dinner, July and August for lunch. Overnight moorings available for dinner guests. Be sure to reserve for dinner before you drive out to this rustic building, way off the main drag and overlooking the lake. Dine in the pine-paneled dining room or outside on the deck. Owner-chef Mark Infante specializes in Italian dishes like chicken Marsala and veal Sorrentina, but the menu might also include shrimp scampi Ruthcliffe ($19.95) or a chicken penne pignoli ($17.95). Entrée prices include soup, salad, and vegetables.

North Hero House (802-372-8237), Route 2, North Hero. Open year-round, this historic old inn is known as a good bet for dinner. Dining on the glassed-in porch is popular, and the main dining room is adjacent to a solarium that's used for private parties. Selections on the fall dinner menu might include roast Atlantic salmon wrapped in crisp rice paper ($18), a farmer's market grilled vegetable strudel with Israeli couscous ($16), or grilled pork tenderloin with Hawaiian pineapple, port, and dried cherry demiglaze ($18). The pub, recently renovated in a marine motif, has its own menu for casual fare.

WEDDING RECEPTIONS ⚭ Grand Isle Lake House, East Shore Road, Grand Isle. For details and reservations, contact Bev Watson at 802-865-2522. Built on Robinson's Point as the Island Villa Hotel in 1903, this is a classic mansard-roofed 25-room summer hotel with a wraparound porch, set in 55 acres of lawn that sweep to the lake. From 1957 until 1993 it was a summer girls camp run by the Sisters of Mercy. Since 1997 it has been owned by the Preservation Trust of Vermont, which has restored the upstairs rooms beautifully, as it has the lobby, kitchen, and dining rooms. It is currently available as a site for conferences and wedding receptions (80 can sit down in the dining room and another 125 guests on the porch; tents on the lawn can accommodate 250 guests).

EATING OUT **Hero's Welcome** (802-372-4161), Route 2, North Hero Village. Open daily year-round, an upscale general store with a good deli, a bakery, and a café. "Heroic" sandwiches—think Thomas Jefferson and Gentleman Johnny Burgoyne—and freshly made soups.

North Hero Marina (802-372-5953), Pelot's Point Road, North Hero. You eat on the porch, no more than 10 people at a time, and the pool next door invites you in to pass the time between courses. The eating arrangements make it very seasonal. The house specialty is fish of all sorts.

Margo's Café and Bakery (802-372-6112), Route 2, Grand Isle. Behind this simple facade lies a cozy, popular bakery-café serving continental breakfast and light lunches indoors, outdoors, or to go, and featuring the work of local artists. Margo recently added a dinner menu, BYOB, which might be sole stuffed with asparagus, carrots, and scallions in a lemon verbena sauce for $11.95, or prosciutto purses in white wine and purple basil sauce for $12.50.

Northern Comfort Dining (802-796-4114), Route 2, Alburg. Breakfast and lunch are served daily 7 AM–2 PM (it opens at 8 in the off-season). Breakfast is well-prepared waffles, eggs Benedict, and such, but for

lunch you might want to try the Ostrich Country Grand made with ostrich meat bought a few miles down the road at the local ostrich farm. No kidding.

Grand Isle Ferry Dock Snack Bar, South Hero. Breakfast 7–11 AM; open until 8 PM on Friday, otherwise until 6. Don't miss the french fries or the homemade bread that Chuck and Ruth Hager make for sandwiches. Check out the orange and peach julep. Tables inside and picnic tables outside.

Links on the Lake (802-796-3586), Route 129, Alburg. Good food and reasonable prices in a pretty setting at the Alburg Country Club. The seafood pasta sells for $14.95, while the house special, Hungarian goulash, is $11.95.

Sun Burger's Snack Bar along Route 2 in Grand Isle is a grand place to stop for ice cream or the eponymous burgers.

Saber's Saloon, Route 2, Alburg. A new and favorite local family restaurant and lounge. The saloon is housed in a nondescript gray building north of town. It's open Wednesday through Sunday 4–8 PM, and the parking lot is full on weekend nights.

Note: See also Fisk Farm under *Lodging* and inquire about Tea Garden Art Shows with music on summer Sundays, 1–5.

✳ Entertainment

Royal Lipizzan Stallions (802-372-5683), mid-July through August, performing Thursday through Sunday at the Herrmann Farm, Route 2, North Hero. Tickets through the chamber of commerce. Visitors welcome every day. These are elegant and unusually strong white horses bred in the 16th century for battle and show, known for their intricate maneuvers, many executed while in midair. Only a few hundred representatives of the breed survive. Colonel Herrmann's family have been training Lipizzans since 1618, when their ancestors received some as a gift from Hapsburg Austrian Emperor Ferdinand II. The Herrmanns winter in Florida and come to North Hero for 6 weeks each summer.

Music at Snow Farm Vineyard (802-372-9463), West Shore Road, South Hero. If you fancy meeting the locals, a popular event is the Thursday summer music series beginning at 6:30 PM on the vineyard's lawn. The music ranges, over the course of the season, from classical to rock. It's free, and all you need to bring is a picnic and a chair. You can buy your wine on site.

✱ Selective Shopping

ANTIQUES Pick up a current copy of the pamphlet guide *Antique the Champlain Islands* at Hero's Welcome General Store. The usual count is half a dozen shops, but they are all seasonal and tend to close as one thing, open as another. Standbys include the **Alburg Country Store,** Main Street (Route 2), middle of Alburg Village, the **Back Chamber Antiques Store,** North Hero Village, and **Simply Country,** south of the village. Also check with **Alburg Auction House,** Lake Street, Alburg, open Saturday 2–6 and 7–midnight.

CRAFTS **McGuire Family Furniture Makers** (802-796-4337), 44 South Main Street (Route 2), Alburg. Open year-round, but call. Two generations of this talented family are involved in the day-to-day production of stunning furniture in spare, heirloom early American designs: beds, tables, grandfather clocks, dressers—anything you want designed, and some surprisingly affordable. The showroom is in a very attractive wood-shingled house in the village of Alburg.

Island Craft Shop, located behind the chamber of commerce and open daily mid-May through mid-October. Works of local and area artisans.

ORCHARDS ✿ **Allenholm Farm** (802-372-5566), 111 South Street, South Hero. Open July through December 24, 9–5. A sixth-generation, 100-acre apple orchard with a farmstead selling Vermont cheese, honey and maple syrup, jams and jellies, and Papa Ray's famous homemade pies. There's also a petting paddock with rabbits, goats, horses, and donkeys. See also *Special Events* (the Allens are the power behind the October Apple Fest).

Hall's Orchard (802-928-3418; 802-928-3226), Spaulding Road, Isle La Motte. The 1820s brick house sits across from the orchard that has been in the same family since the house was built. The apples we bought here on a crisp October morning are the best we can remember finding anywhere.

Hackett's Orchard (802-372-4848), 86 South Street, South Hero. Perennials, and syrup in spring; small fruits and fresh-picked vegetables in summer; apples, cider, and pumpkins in fall. The farm stand has a family picnic and play area. Fresh cider doughnuts are a specialty, as are the homemade fruit pies.

SPECIAL STORES **Hero's Welcome General Store** (1-800-372-HERO; fax: 802-372-3205), P.O. Box 202, Route 2, North Hero. Former Pier 1 CEO Bob Camp and his wife, Bev, have transformed this 19th-century landmark into a bright, smart, multi-level emporium: café and bakery, gift shop, art gallery, grocery, Vermont gourmet food products, sports clothes, wine shop, and bookstore, retaining its flavor as a community gathering spot. They offer canoe and bike rentals as well as lake cruises, and have plans for other features and services.

Charlie's Northland Sporting and Gift Shop. A serious fishing-gear source, but also assorted sportswear and gifts.

WINERY **Snow Farm Vineyard** (802-372-9463), 190 West Shore Road (follow signs from Route 2 or Route 314), South Hero. Open Memorial Day through October, 10–4:30. Vineyard tours are offered daily at 11 and 2. This pioneering Lake Champlain vineyard is the fruition of several years' hard work by lawyers Molly and Harrison Lebowitz. Visitors enter a barnlike building that is the winery/showroom with a tasting counter. There they learn that this is still a relatively new operation (opened in 1997). Initially it is processing and bottling wine from grapes grown in New York's Finger Lakes, gradually mixing these with the harvest from vines on Snow Farm's 10 acres. The farm's Blanc de Noirs was

awarded a bronze medal at the 1998 Eastern International Wine Competition. (See also *Entertainment.*)

✳ Special Events

Note: Check with the chamber of commerce about weekly events. See Fisk Farm under *Lodging;* inquire about Tea Garden Art Shows with music, summer Sundays.

June: **Taste of the Islands: Food & Wine** (second weekend), South Hero —local food purveyors show off their culinary creations, accompanied by Snow Farm Vineyard wines. **Celebrate Champlain! Islands Festival** (third weekend), Grand Isle—classes and demos on sailboarding, kayaking, sailing, and canoeing; music and BBQ.

July 4: **Parades** and **barbecues** in South Hero and Alburg.

Mid-July–August: **Lipizzan Stallions** (see *Entertainment*).

August: **Grand Isle County Art Show & Sale** (first weekend). **Northumbrian Pipers Convention Community Dance and Concert** (last weekend), North Hero Town Hall.

Early September: **Teddy Roosevelt Toast,** Isle La Motte, at the Fisk Farm—a presentation pays tribute to a person or group that has furthered TR's mission with respect to our natural resources and cultural heritage.

Columbus Day weekend: **Apple Fest**—crafts fair, a "press-off," plenty of food and fun.

Once an important railroad center and still the Franklin County seat, St. Albans (population: 8,082), on Route 7, is showing signs of revitalization. Its firm place in the history books was assured on October 19, 1864, when 22 armed Confederate soldiers, who had infiltrated the town in mufti, held up the three banks, stole horses, and escaped back to Canada with $201,000, making this the northernmost engagement of the Civil War. One of the raiders was wounded and eventually died, as did Elinus J. Morrison, a visiting builder who was shot by the bandits. The surviving Confederates were arrested in Montreal, tried, but never extradited; their leader, Lieutenant Bennett H. Young, rose to the rank of general. When he visited Montreal again in 1911, a group of St. Albans dignitaries paid him a courtesy call at the Ritz-Carlton!

Swanton was settled by the French about 1700 and later named for a British captain in the French and Indian Wars. It is now (population: 4,622) is growing again after a long period of relative stagnation. During World War I the long-abandoned Robin Hood–Remington Arms plant produced millions of rounds of ammunition for the Allied armies. At one end of the village green dwell a pair of royal swans. This park is the focus for the Swanton Summer Festival.

GUIDANCE Franklin County Regional Chamber of Commerce (802-524-2444; www.stalbanschamber.com), 2 North Main Street, St. Albans 05478, provides brochures and general information.

The Swanton Chamber of Commerce (802-868-7200), Swanton 05488, has an information booth at the north end of the village green. Open occasionally.

MEDICAL EMERGENCY Emergency service is available by calling **911.**

Northwestern Medical Center (802-524-5911; 1-800-696-0321), St. Albans.

✳ To See and Do

Franklin County Historical Society (802-527-7933), facing Taylor Park, open June through September, Tuesday through Saturday 1–4, or by appointment. This museum was established by the St. Albans Historical Society in 1971 in a three-story brick schoolhouse erected in 1861. The Beaumont Room has been fitted up as a fascinating, old-time country doctor's office. Another room has period costumes, while a third houses Central Vermont Railroad memorabilia. Upstairs are farm tools, a maple sugaring exhibit, and other artifacts of the region. Admission is $3 for adults.

Chester A. Arthur Birthplace, North Fairfield. A replica of the little house where the 21st (and usually underrated) president was born can be found 10 miles east on Route 36 to Fairfield (open June through mid-October, Wednesday through Sunday and holidays, 9:30–5:30). In the visitors center, exhibits examine the controversy over the actual site of Arthur's birth, which had an impact on the question of his eligibility to serve as president. Arthur's conduct as president in light of his reputation as a leading New York State political boss is also examined.

Abenaki Tribal Museum and Cultural Center (802-868-2559), 100 Grand Avenue, Swanton. Open 9–4 Monday through Friday (it's a good idea to call ahead), the center offers two interesting exhibits about Abenaki life, including fur trade and transportation, in times past. There are some great old photos.

West Swanton Orchards and Cider Mill (802-868-9100), 32 Church Road, Swanton. Open 10–5 daily. A family-owned orchard with 11 varieties of apples, a cider mill, and a gift shop featuring Vermont products and homemade baked goods. Take a walk on the nature trail that winds through the 62 acres of trees.

GOLF Champlain Country Club (802-524-9895), Route 7, 3 miles north of St. Albans. Nine holes, some terraced. Snack bar.

Richford Country Club (802-848-3527), 84 Intervale Avenue, Richford. Nine holes, established 1930.

Enosburg Falls Country Club (802-527-2296), Routes 105 and 108, Enosburg Falls. 18 holes.

BIKING Missisquoi Valley Rail Trail (802-524-5958), 140 South Main Street, St. Albans. The Northwest Regional Planning Commission supervises this 26.5-mile-long trail, converted from the abandoned Central Vermont Railroad bed into a path for cross-country skiing, bike riding, hiking, snowmobiling, dog-sledding, snowshoeing, and just plain strolling, but not for ATVs or dirt bikes. It leads from St. Albans to Sheldon Junction, from there to Enosburg Falls, and winds up in Richford. You can stop along the trail at **The Abbey** restaurant for lunch (or breakfast if you're a real early bird). A free map/guide shows trailside facilities.

Porter's Bike Shop (802-868-7417), Grand Avenue, Swanton, is a find for out-of-luck bicyclists. Mr. Porter—or at least we assumed it was Mr. Porter—houses an impressive array of bike parts in his small shop, and he's a handy man to have around when something on the bike gets broken.

CANOEING AND FISHING Raven Ridge Canoe Rental and Guide Service (802-527-4616; 1-888-527-4616), Enosburg. Chas Salmon and Olga Lermontov provide fishing guides for bass, trout, northern pike, and walleye. They rent kayaks and canoes (with life jackets) and shuttle you to and from the river. They also take families and groups on wildlife-viewing and photographic expeditions.

❋ Green Space

St. Albans Bay State Park, 4 miles west on Route 36, is a good place for picnics, but the water is too shallow and weedy for decent swimming.

MUSEUMS AND PUBLIC BUILDINGS FLANK THE TOWN GREEN IN ST. ALBANS.
Kim Grant

Kamp Kill Kare State Park (802-524-6021), once a fashionable summer hotel site and then, for years, a famous boys summer camp; on Point Road off Route 36, St. Albans Bay. It can be crowded on weekends, but it's usually blissfully quiet other days; swim beach, playgrounds, boat rentals, access to Burton Island.

Burton Island State Park (802-524-6353), a lovely, 350-acre island reached from Kill Kare by park boat or by your own. Facilities include 42 campsites, including 22 lean-tos, and a 100-slip marina with electrical hook-ups and 20 moorings. Campers' gear is transported to campsites by park vehicle. Fishing off this beautiful haven is usually excellent. Also accessible for day use; swim beach, food concession, hiking trails, boat rentals.

Lake Carmi State Park (802-527-8383), exit 19 off I-89, 2 miles on Route 104; 1.5 miles north on Route 105; 3 miles north on Route 108, in Enosburg Falls. Set in rolling farmlands, the 482-acre park has 178 wooded campsites, including 35 lean-tos and some on the beach of this sizable lake; nature trails; boat ramp and rentals.

Woods Island State Park (802-879-6565), 2 miles north of Burton Island. Primitive camping on an island of 125 acres. Five widely spaced campsites with no facilities; fires are not allowed. The island is unstaffed, although there are daily ranger patrols; reservations for campsites must be made through Burton Island State Park (see above). There is no public transportation to the island; the best boat access is from Kill Kare.

The Missisquoi National Wildlife Refuge (802-868-4781), on the river's delta, lies 2 miles west of Swanton on Route 78 to East Alburg and the islands. Habitats are about equally divided among brushland, timberland, and marsh, through which wind Black Creek and Maquam Creek Trails, adding up to about 1.5 miles or a 2-hour ramble; both are appropriately marked for the flora and fauna represented. It's open most of the time, but call ahead to confirm.

✱ Lodging

RESORT ✿ ♿ **The Tyler Place Family Resort** (802-868-4000), Box 901, Route 7, Highgate Springs 05460. Open late May through mid-September. One of the country's oldest and most popular family resorts continues to thrive on 165 acres of woods, meadows, and a mile of undeveloped lakeshore. At the height of the season it's rather like a jolly, crowded cruise ship with a lively crew; faithful partisans have been returning year after year for three generations of the Tyler family's management. They provide just about every conceivable form of recreation for adults and children 2–17 years of age, with separate programs and dining for each group (special arrangements for infants). The children's recreation centers are exceptional.

There are heated indoor and outdoor swimming and wading pools, six tennis courts, and equipment for kayaking, fishing, and sailboarding. Accommodations vary: You'll find the contemporary inn, plus 27 fireplaced cottages, a farm, and a guest house, for a total of 58 cottages and family suites. Each unit has two or more bedrooms, air-conditioning, and a pantry or kitchen unit. The inn has a spacious dining room with good food, and a big lounge with bar. Rates are per adult; $89–277 for most of the season, with some packages available at either end of the season.

FARM VACATION 🐾 🍃 Berkson Farms (802-933-2522), 1205 West Berkshire Road (Route 108 north), Enosburg Falls 05450. A mile north of the village, this 600-acre working dairy farm welcomes families year-round. The renovated, nicely maintained, 130-year-old farmhouse, managed by Sam and Lisa Hogaboom, can accommodate 8 to 10 people in four bedrooms, one of which has a private bath. There's a spacious living room and a library as well as a comfy family and game room with TV and VCR. But the main attractions, especially for kids, are the cows, ducks, sheep, and goats, along with sugaring in-season. Cross-country skiing can be enjoyed, along with hayrides and local swimming holes, and there's golf at the nearby 18-hole Enosburg Falls Country Club. Rates are $55–65 per couple, including a full breakfast. Well-behaved pets accepted.

BED & BREAKFASTS Country Essence B&B (802-868-4247; www.countryessence.com), RD 2, Box 95, Swanton 05488, 1.5 miles north of the village on Route 7. Armand and Cheryl Messier provide two pretty rooms with private bath, reached by a private staircase entrance in their 1850s homestead on 12 groomed acres. There's an in-ground swimming pool. $65 per room double occupancy with country breakfast. French is spoken.

Bayview B&B (802-524-5609), 860 Hathaway Point Road, St. Albans 05478. Located on Hathaway Point

amid the colony of bayside cottages, this simple remodeled farmhouse with a nice screened-in porch has three rooms with shared bath at $50–65 per room. Continental breakfast. Weekly rates.

Wagner Road B&B (802-849-6030; 1-800-842-6030), 92 Fairfield Street, St. Albans 05478 (on Wagner Road, off Route 104, near Silver Lake). Gail and Ned Shulman's 1806 Cape Cod, located on 103 acres in Fairfax, has doubles at $55–75 with full breakfast; swimming pool in summer, cross-country trails in winter.

The Old Mill River Place (802-524-7211), Georgia Shore Road, St. Albans 05478, is a classic five-bay brick Federal built in 1799 as a wedding present for Sarah Allen Evarts, Ethan Allen's niece, occupied by the Neville and Bright families since 1926. There are three antiques-furnished rooms with shared bath: Evarts has a lake view; Wheeler has twin cannonball low-post beds; Percival features a queen-sized four-poster and fireplace. $60–65 per double, including afternoon tea and generous country breakfast.

🔗 🍷 🐾 🍃 **Buck Hollow Farm** (802-849-2400; 1-800-849-7985; www.buckhollow.com), 2150 Buck Hollow Road, Fairfax 05454, off Route 104, occupies a renovated 1790s carriage house on 400 spectacular acres. Brad Schwartz has decorated each of the four rooms (with two shared baths) with antiques, queen-sized four-poster, and TV. Guests are encouraged to use the four-person outdoor hot tub and the heated pool; and children have a play area and can ride the pony. Rates range $63–103 per room, including full country breakfast.

Tetreault's Hillside View Farm (802-827-4480), 143 South Road, Fairfield 05455, is a warm, hospitable home in a quiet village. There's a fireplace in the family room, lots of antique furniture, and braided rugs. French spoken. $50–60 per double.

Parent Farmhouse B&B (802-524-4201; 1-888-603-7135), 854 Pattee Hill Road, Georgia 05468. Lucy and Roger Parent offer three rooms with shared bath at the rate of $85 for a double, $55 for a single. The farmhouse is near Lake Champlain with plenty of walking and biking opportunities.

OTHER LODGING **Comfort Inn & Suites** (802-524-3300; 1-800-228-5150; www.vtcomfortinn.com), 167 Fairfax Road, Route 104, at exit 19 off I-89, St. Albans 05478. This new branch of the well-known chain has 63 guest rooms and 17 suites, complimentary continental breakfast, indoor pool, and fitness room, at $59–99 with special rates for families, seniors, and business groups.

The Cadillac Motel (802-524-2191), 213 South Main Street, St. Albans 05478, is a pleasant cluster of 54 units surrounding a swimming pool, with mini golf, badminton, and a coffee shop in summer. $60–80 double.

&. **Econo Lodge** (802-524-5956; 1-800-55-ECONO; www.econolodge.com), 287 South Main Street, St. Albans 05478, has a AAA rating and the look of a B&B. Rooms range $85–115 per night, and "senior-friendly" rooms are available.

CAMPGROUNDS See Burton Island State Park, Lake Carmi State Park, and Woods Island State Park under *Green Space.*

Homestead Campground (802-524-2356), exit 18 off I-89 in Georgia, offers 160 shaded campsites with water and electric hook-ups, laundry facilities, hot showers, cabin and camper rentals, a playground, and two swimming pools. The season is May 1 through October 15.

✻ Where to Eat

Jeff's Maine Seafood (802-524-6135), 65 North Main Street, St. Albans, obviously began as a fish shop and deli and has expanded into an attractive restaurant with specialties like pecan-crusted salmon ($16) and a New York strip steak with wild mushrooms ($18). Open for lunch and dinner Monday through Saturday. This is one of the top chowder houses in the state.

The Old Foundry Restaurant (802-524-9665), 3 Federal Street, St. Albans. Housed in one of the city's few 1840s buildings to have escaped the town's big 1895 fire, this is a great setting for traditional fare, like charbroiled rib steak and filet mignon (both $14.95), fried seafood, and charbroiled salmon fillet ($13.95).

Chow!Bella (802-524-1405), 28 North Main Street, St. Albans. An intimate wine bar with an eclectic menu, especially vegetarian dishes and fish. The atmosphere is welcoming and hospitable. Open for lunch and dinner daily except Sunday.

Simple Pleasures Cafe (802-527-0669), 84 North Main Street, St. Albans. Cappuccino, sandwiches, baked goods.

McGuel's Irish Burro (802-527-1276), 1820 Lake Street, St. Albans. The owners are Irish, and the food is Mexican. Prices are very reasonable:

Combo platters run $8–11. Fajitas are a house specialty. The restaurant is open 11:30 AM to 8 or 10 PM, depending on the day. The same menu is available in the pub.

Foothills Bakery (802-849-6601), 1123 Main Street, Fairfax. This bakery, housed in the old post office and much beloved by a local clientele, serves freshly baked muffins, scones, Danishes, cinnamon buns, and frittata early on, then sandwiches on fat slices of homemade bread. Open 6–6 except on Friday, when it closes at 4 PM.

Chester's in the Square (802-827-3974), Route 36, Fairfield. Chester's is named for Chester Arthur. Home-baked ham and turkey sandwiches, cream of celery soup, shepherd's pie, chowders, cookies, and all the comfort food you could ever want. Closed Sunday.

Uncle Sam's Restaurant (802-527-7340), 51 South Main Street, St. Albans. A bright, casual place serving breakfast all day, plus lunch and dinner.

My-T-Fine Creamery Restaurant (802-868-4616), 73 First Street, Swanton. Open daily for home-style breakfast, lunch, and dinner.

The Pines Restaurant (802-868-4819), Route 7, Swanton. A good place for family fare.

✳ Selective Shopping

Better Planet (802-524-6835), 44 North Main Street, St. Albans, is a bright place for books, toys, games, puzzles, hobby kits, and art supplies.

Richford Antique and Craft Center (802-848-3836), 66 Main Street, Richford. Open daily 10–5. Twenty rooms filled with antiques, crafts, and collectibles.

✳ Special Events

Early– mid-April: **Maple Sugar Festival,** St. Albans—for 3 days the town turns into a nearly nonstop "sugarin' off" party, courtesy of the local maple producers, augmented by arts and crafts and antiques shows and other events.

Last week of July: **Swanton Summer Festival**—parades, band concerts, square dancing, arts and crafts shows.

Mid-September: **Civil War Days** (802-524-2444), St. Albans. A lively weekend of encampments at Taylor Park, a tour of an Underground Railroad home, echoes of the 1864 Confederate Raid, parade, barbecue, music, and a crafts show.

STOWE AND WATERBURY

NORTH OF THE NOTCH AND THE
LAMOILLE VALLEY

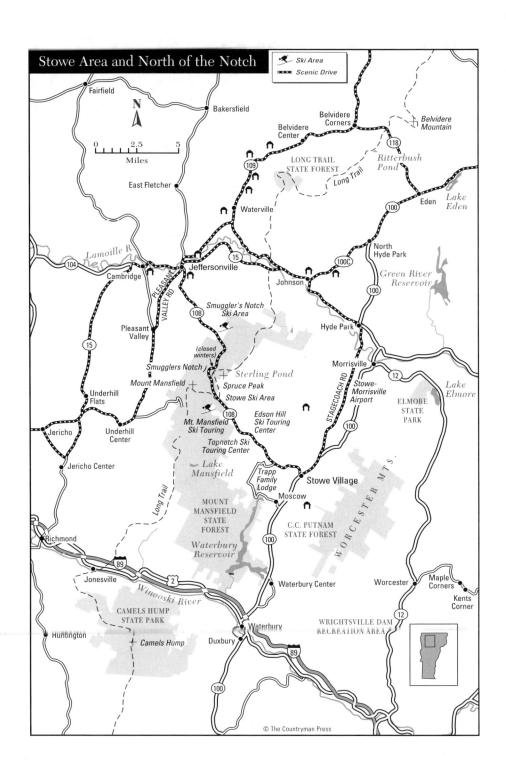

Stowe Area and North of the Notch

Ski Area
Scenic Drive

N

0   2.5   5
Miles

Fairfield
Bakersfield
Belvidere Corners
Belvidere Mountain
Belvidere Center
118
Long Trail
LONG TRAIL STATE FOREST
109
Ritterbush Pond
East Fletcher
100
Eden
Lake Eden
Waterville
Lamoille R.
104
15
North Hyde Park
Cambridge
Jeffersonville
100C
Green River Reservoir
Johnson
100
PLEASANT VALLEY RD
108
Smuggler's Notch Ski Area
Hyde Park
Pleasant Valley
15
(closed winters)
Sterling Pond
Morrisville
12
Lake Elmore
Smugglers Notch
Spruce Peak
Stowe-Morrisville Airport
ELMORE STATE PARK
Underhill Flats
Mount Mansfield
Stowe Ski Area
108
Edson Hill Ski Touring Center
100
STAGECOACH RD
Jericho
Underhill Center
Mt. Mansfield Ski Touring
Topnotch Ski Touring Center
Jericho Center
Lake Mansfield
Trapp Family Lodge
Stowe Village
WORCESTER MTS.
Long Trail
Moscow
MOUNT MANSFIELD STATE FOREST
C.C. PUTNAM STATE FOREST
100
Richmond
89
Waterbury Reservoir
Jonesville
2
Winooski River
Waterbury Center
Worcester
Maple Corners
Kents Corner
CAMELS HUMP STATE PARK
12
Huntington
Camels Hump
Duxbury
Waterbury
WRIGHTSVILLE DAM RECREATION AREA
89
100

© The Countryman Press

STOWE AND WATERBURY

Known as the "ski capital of the East," Stowe is the state's premier summer resort as well. A 200-year-old village that looks like a classic Vermont village should look, it's set against the massive backdrop of Mount Mansfield, which looks just like Vermont's highest mountain should look.

By the mid–19th century, men were already taxing their imaginations and funds to entice visitors up onto the heights of Mount Mansfield—which bears an uncanny resemblance to the upturned profile of a rather jowly man. In 1858 an inn was built under the Nose, a project that entailed constructing a 100-yard log trestle above a chasm and several miles of corduroy road made from hemlock. In Stowe Village at that time, a hotel, the Mansfield House, accommodated 600 guests.

Swedish families moved into Stowe in 1912 and began using their skis to get around. Then, in 1914, the Dartmouth College librarian skied down the Toll Road. Serious skiing, however, didn't begin until 1933, when the Civilian Conservation Corps cut a 4-mile-plus trail for just that purpose. The following year the town formed its own Mount Mansfield Ski Club, setting up basic lodging near the bottom of the ski trail in a former logging camp. By 1937 a rope tow had been rigged from the camp to the top of the trail, powered by a Cadillac engine. Lift tickets cost 50¢ per day, $5 per season.

While its name keeps changing, the Stowe Resort Company is still the same outfit formed in 1951 from the various small concerns that had evolved in the 1930s and '40s to serve skiers, and it's still owned by the same insurance company. The good news is continuity and an immense sense of pride and history. Sometimes slow to respond to the demands of this quickly changing industry, the company has become much more aggressive over the past decade with its building and expansion plans.

What the "Mountain Company" does, it always does first-class. Just as it was a Cadillac engine (not the Ford used elsewhere) that first hauled Stowe skiers, the eight-passenger gondola, installed in 1991, is one of the world's fastest, and the Cliff House in the summit Octagon offers lunch complete with a view. On the other hand, a small '50s base lodge, expanded and renovated a couple of times, still serves the mountain's primary trail network—although not for long.

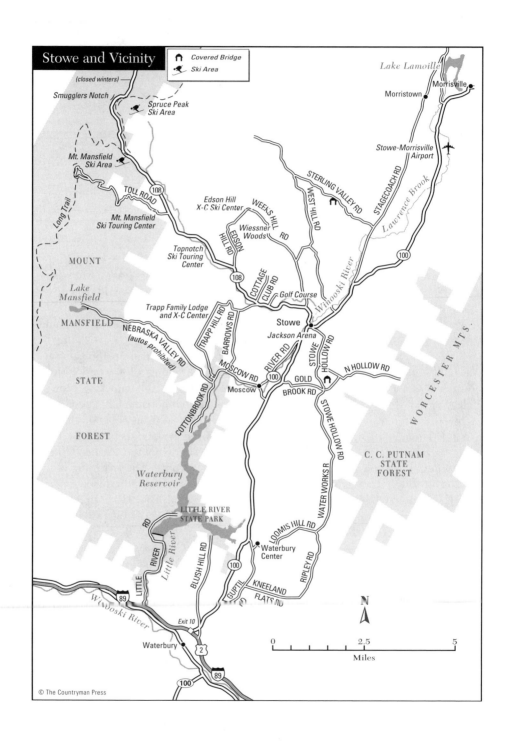

Stowe and Vicinity

⌂	Covered Bridge
⛷	Ski Area

Lake Lamoille

(closed winters)

Smugglers Notch

Spruce Peak Ski Area

Morristown

Morrisville

Mt. Mansfield Ski Area

Stowe-Morrisville Airport

Long Trail

TOLL ROAD

108

STERLING VALLEY RD

WEST HILL RD

STAGECOACH RD

Lawrence Brook

Edson Hill X-C Ski Center

WEEKS HILL RD

100

Mt. Mansfield Ski Touring Center

Wiessner Woods

EDSON HILL RD

MOUNT

Topnotch Ski Touring Center

108

COTTAGE CLUB RD

Golf Course

Winooski River

Lake Mansfield

Trapp Family Lodge and X-C Center

TRAPP HILL RD

BARROWS RD

Stowe

Jackson Arena

MANSFIELD

NEBRASKA VALLEY RD (autos prohibited)

MOSCOW RD

RIVER RD

100

GOLD BROOK RD

STOWE HOLLOW RD

N HOLLOW RD

Moscow

WORCESTER MTS.

STATE

COTTONBROOK RD

STOWE HOLLOW RD

C. C. PUTNAM STATE FOREST

FOREST

Waterbury Reservoir

WATER WORKS R

LITTLE RIVER STATE PARK

RD

Little River

LOOMIS HILL RD

BLUSH HILL RD

Waterbury Center

RIPLEY RD

100

GUPTIL

KNEELAND FLATS RD

N

89

Windooski River

Exit 10

LITTLE RIVER RD

Waterbury

2

0   2.5   5

Miles

100

89

© The Countryman Press

The Mountain Company in recent years has been focusing on its most basic need: water. In the '90s it became painfully clear that natural snow in northern New England is too fickle a base for the huge business that skiing has become. Ski operators and skiers alike are not about to invest big bucks unless they can depend on snow, and to make snow you need water.

Stowe has won approval for its Master Plan, which includes a village of 400 housing units at the base of Spruce Peak, along with a new Spruce base lodge, an 18-hole golf course, and a lift that will ferry skiers between Mansfield and Spruce across Route 108 without removing their skis. Also in the works are plans to expand the Mansfield base lodge, add two new lifts, and enlarge the Inn at the Mountain. The plan calls for all this to be accomplished over the next decade.

In the meantime the quality of alpine skiing and snowboarding at Stowe remains high. The cross-country ski network of more than 150 km is outstanding, not only in its extent but also in its quality, thanks in good part to its elevation: Many trails meander off the high walls of the cul-de-sac in which the resort nestles, and you can usually count on snow on many miles of trail through April.

Stowe actually now attracts more visitors in summer and fall than it does in winter. From June through mid-October it offers a superb golf course, tennis courts, theater, an alpine slide, and gondola rides to the top of the mountain, as well as hiking, biking, fishing, and special events every week of summer and fall. Year-round it boasts more than 2,200 rooms, accommodating a total of 7,500 visitors on any given night. There are also more than 50 restaurants and 100 or so shops.

What's most amazing about Stowe is the way it has managed to keep its commercial side low-key and tasteful, a sideshow to the natural beauty of the place. Even in nonskiing months, most visitors are lured from their cars and onto their feet and bicycles, thanks to the 5.5-mile Stowe Recreation Path, which parallels the Mountain Road from the village (albeit at a more forgiving grade) to Mount Mansfield, through cornfields, wildflowers, and raspberry patches.

In warm-weather months Stowe is also an excellent pivot from which to explore northern Vermont: 30 miles from Burlington, just over the Notch from the little-touristed Lamoille - Valley, and a short drive from both Montpelier and Barre on the one hand and the Northeast Kingdom on the other. Lodging options range from funky to fabulous, including a number of self-contained resorts as well as inns, lodges, motels, and condominiums. The Stowe Area

A CHURCH IN STOWE

Kim Grant

Association has been in business since 1936, matching visitors with lodgings they can afford and enjoy.

Most Stowe-bound visitors know Waterbury, 10 miles down Route 100, simply as an I-89 exit; they know the strip just to the north as the home of Ben & Jerry's ice cream factory, one of the state's most popular attractions. The old town itself lies along a southward bend in the Winooski River, and several interesting shops and restaurants are housed in the brief downtown between the traffic light and the railroad station. Waterbury Reservoir, accessible from Waterbury Center, is the obvious place in this area to swim and paddle a canoe or kayak.

GUIDANCE **The Stowe Area Association** (802-253-7321; for toll-free reservations: 1-800-247-8693; Box 1320, Stowe 05672; www.gostowe.com). Open daily November through March, 9–8; the rest of the year 9–5. This service, housed in its own building in the middle of Stowe Village, provides information on more than 60 local lodging places and will make reservations; it also publishes seasonal guides listing most things in the area and is a walk-in source of advice about what's going on. The **Stowe-Smuggler's Notch Region Marketing Organization** is another good source of information (1-877-247-8693; www.stowe smugglers.com).

GETTING THERE *By bus:* **Vermont Transit/Greyhound** stops in Waterbury with connections from Boston, New York, and points south.

By train: **Amtrak** from Washington, DC, New York City, and Springfield, Massachusetts, stops in Waterbury.

By plane: The **Stowe-Morrisville Airport,** 7 miles north, provides private plane services and charters. **Burlington International Airport,** 34 miles away, is served by major carriers (see "Burlington Region").

By taxi: **Peg's Pickup/Stowe Taxi** (1-800-370-9490).

By car: From most points, I-89 exit 10, and 15 minutes north on Route 100.

GETTING AROUND During winter season the **Stowe Trolley** (802-253-7585) circles the 7 miles between the village and the mountain every 30 minutes, 7:30 AM–10 PM. Pick up a schedule. Trolley tokens are $1, and 1-week passes cost $10. Tuesday and Thursday shopping runs to Morrisville are also offered; in summer trolley tours run every day, leaving the town office at 11 AM and lasting 75 minutes.

MEDICAL EMERGENCY Emergency service is available by calling **911.**

Copley Hospital (802-888-4231), Morrisville.

✳ To See

Mount Mansfield, the highest point in Vermont—4,395 feet (it gained 2 feet when it was remeasured in 1998) at the Chin—yields a truly spectacular view, accessible primarily in summer, unless you can clamber up to the summit from the Cliff House restaurant at the top of the gondola over ice and snow. In summer there are two easy ways up: the Toll Road and an eight-passenger gondola.

The Toll Road (802-253-3000) begins 7 miles up Route 108 from the village of Stowe; look for the sign on the left just before the Inn at the Mountain. Open late May through mid-October, weather permitting, 10–5. $16 per car in 2003 and raised annually. Motorcycles are no longer permitted; bikes and hikers are free. First laid in the mid–19th century, this steep, winding road led to a hotel that served the public until 1957. (It was demolished in the mid-1960s.) The road also serves as a ski trail in winter. It terminates at the Mount Mansfield Summit Station, just below the Nose (4,062 feet). A 0.5-mile Tundra Trail follows the Long Trail (red-and-white blazes on the rocks) north to Drift Rock (the trek should take 20 minutes); another mile along the trail brings you to the summit of Mount Mansfield (round-trip: 2 hours).

The gondola (802-253-7311) at Stowe operates mid-June through mid-October, weather permitting, 10–5; $12 per adult; $7 per junior (6–12); $10.50 for seniors (65 and older); $31 for a family of four round-trip. The eight-passenger gondola runs from Midway Lodge to the Cliff House (see *Dining Out*); a half hour's trek brings you up to the Chin. However you get there, the view from the summit (the Chin) is spectacular on a clear day: west across 20 miles of farmland to Lake Champlain; east to the Worcester Range across the Stowe Valley; north to Jay Peak (35 miles distant) across the Lamoille Valley; and south, back along the Green Mountains, to Camels Hump. Mount Washington is visible to the east, Whiteface to the west. Be sure to catch the 5 PM gondola unless you fancy a long walk down.

Stowe Village. A classic, early-19th-century Vermont village with a spired white meetinghouse at one end of Main Street and a brick stagecoach inn at the other, Stowe offers a satisfying variety of stores and restaurants all within an easy stroll. The former wooden high school (one block up School Street from Main) is now the **Helen Day Art Center** (802-253-8358), open in summer daily noon–5 except Monday, closed Sunday too in winter. The changing art exhibits are frequently well worth checking out ($3 per adult, $1 seniors, and 50¢ students). The mid-19th-century Bloody Brook Schoolhouse next door is open on request in summer months.

Smugglers Notch is the high (elevation: 2,162 feet), extremely winding and narrow stretch of Route 108 just north of Mount Mansfield, with 1,000-foot cliffs towering on either side. The first carriage road through this pass wasn't opened until 1894, but the name reflects its heavy use as a route to smuggle cattle down from Canada during the War of 1812. One of two formally designated State Scenic Roads in Vermont, Smugglers Notch is known for rock formations: Smugglers Head, Elephant Head, the Hunter and His Dog, the Big Spring, Smugglers Cave, and the Natural Refrigerator. The Notch is closed in winter, inviting cross-country skiing and snowshoeing. See also *To See* in "North of the Notch and the Lamoille Valley."

Vermont Ski Museum (802-253-9911, www.vermontskimuseum.org), Old Town Hall, 1 South Main Street, Stowe. See the actual lifts that carried the first skiers up the Vermont mountains and the ski equipment they used to come down. Discover how dozens of tiny ski areas grew into the handful of mega resorts that dominate the industry today. Watch old ski movies and vintage ski footage on a giant plasma screen. Closed Tuesday except during holidays. Admission by donation.

Ben & Jerry's Ice Cream Factory Tours (802-882-1260), Route 100 (take exit 10 off I-89), Waterbury. No American ice cream has a story, let alone a taste, to match that of the totally Vermont-made sweet and creamy stuff concocted by high school buddies Ben Cohen and Jerry Greenfield, who have sold the company to Unilever. More than two decades ago they began churning out Dastardly Mash and Heath Bar Crunch in a Burlington garage; they have now outgrown this seemingly mammoth plant, which has outstripped the Shelburne Museum as Vermont's number one attraction. A half-hour tour of the plant is offered all year, daily 10–5. The gift store, selling an amazing number of things relating to cows and Vermont, is open 10–6, as is the Scoop Shop. The tour includes a multimedia show, a look (from an observation platform) at the production room, and a free sample of one of the many "euphoric flavors." The grounds include picnic facilities and some sample black-and-white cows. $2 adults, children free.

COVERED BRIDGES The **Gold Brook Bridge** in Stowe Hollow, also known as Emily's Bridge because Emily is said to have taken her life from it (in different ways and for different reasons in the different stories) and reportedly returns to haunt it on occasion. There is another picturesque bridge across the Sterling Brook, off the Stagecoach Road, north of the village.

SCENIC DRIVES Not only is Stowe pleasantly situated for touring in all directions, but it is also organized to offer visitors well-researched printed tours. Pick up a copy of *Roads and Tours* from the **Stowe Area Association** (see *Guidance*). Don't fail to drive Smugglers Notch.

AT THE BEN & JERRY'S ICE CREAM FACTORY IN WATERBURY

Kim Grant

AIR RIDES For **hot-air ballooning,** inquire at Stoweflake Mountain Resort and Spa (802-253-7355). Whitcomb Aviation, based at the Stowe-Morrisville State Airport (802-888-7845), offers **glider rides,** instruction, and rentals.

ALPINE SLIDE **Stowe's alpine slide** (802-253-3500) is accessed from the Spruce Peak Base Lodge, Mountain Road, Stowe. Open late June through early September, 10–5, then on weekends through Columbus Day. $11 per adult, $8 per junior or senior; discounts for five-ride packages.

BIKING The equipage here is a mountain bike, and the rental sources are the **Mountain Sports & Bike Shop** (802-253-7919), **AJ's Ski & Sports** (802-253-4593; 1-800-226-6257), **Pinnacle Ski & Sports** (802-253-7222; 1-800-458-9996), **Stowe Action Outfitters** (802-253-7975), and **Topnotch Resort** (802-253-8585), all on the Mountain Road (Route 108) in Stowe. Neophytes usually head for the 5.5-mile **Stowe Recreation Path** (see *Hiking and Walking*); next there's a 10-mile loop through part of the Mount Mansfield State Forest and into the Cottonbrook Basin. The **Mountain Sports & Bike Shop** and the **Inn at Turner Mill** (802-253-2062), both along the Mountain Road, offer mountain biking tours. Pick up a copy of the *Mt. Mansfield/Stowe Area Biking Map/Guide* published by Map Adventures in Stowe (802-253-7489); it maps and describes 32 local mountain bike trail and road rides.

BOATING Canoes can be rented from **AJ's Ski & Sports** (802-253-4593), **Stowe Action Outfitters** (802-253-7975), and **Umiak Outfitters** (802-253-2317), Stowe. Umiak also offers kayak rentals, lessons, and guided trips on the Winooski and Lamoille Rivers, on Lake Champlain, and throughout the state.

CAMPING **Little River Camping Areas** (802-244-7103; off-season reservations: 1-800-658-6934), Waterbury 05676. Six miles north of Waterbury on the Waterbury Reservoir: 64 campsites, including 6 lean-tos, swimming, hiking, rental boats, snowmobile trails in Little River State Park.

See also *Green Space* for information on camping in Smugglers Notch and Elmore State Park.

CARRIAGE RIDES **Edson Hill Manor, Golden Eagle Resort,** and **Stowehof Inn** in Stowe all offer carriage rides. **Charlie Horse Sleigh Rides at Topnotch** (802-253-2215) in Stowe offers carriage and wagon rides, as does the **Trapp Family Lodge** (802-353-5813).

CYCLISTS ON THE STOWE RECREATION PATH

©Dennis Curran

FISHING The Little River in Stowe is a favorite for brook trout, along with Sterling Pond on top of Spruce Peak and Sterling Brook. Contact **Reel Vermont** (802-223-1869), geared to guiding everyone (families included) from neophytes to pros. **Catamount Fishing Adventures** (802-253-8500), run by Willy Dietrich, is located in Stowe. It offers year-round guide service, including ice fishing. **Fly Fish Vermont** (802-253-3964; www.flyrodshop.com) is another Stowe resource.

GOLF **Stowe Country Club** (802-253-4893), an 18-hole course with a 40-acre driving range, putting green, restaurant, bar, pro shop, lessons; inquire about the Stowe Golf School. **Stoweflake Mountain Resort and Spa** (802-253-7355), adjacent to the Stowe Country Club, also offers instruction. The **Farm Resort** (802-888-3525), Route 100, 6 miles north of Stowe in Morrisville, offers nine holes and a driving range. The **Players Club** (802-253-2800) is a year-round golf and indoor training facility.

Blush Hill Country Club (802-244-8974), a nine-hole course in Waterbury, has marvelous views.

Country Club of Vermont (802-244-1800), Waterbury. This 18-hole course gets rave reviews.

HEALTH SPAS **The Spa at Topnotch** (802-253-8585) and **Golden Eagle Resort Motor Inn** (802-253-4811) are both available for day visits. **Trapp Family Lodge** (802-253-8511) offers massage services. The **Stowe Gym** (802-253-2176) on the Mountain Road has state-of-the-art machines, aerobics and Spinning classes, and more. In fall 2003 the **Stoweflake Spa & Sports Club** (802-253-7355) unveiled a large new facility that includes a hair-and-nail salon, treatment and fitness rooms galore, whirlpools, saunas, steam rooms, and lots of staff to pamper you. The **Swimming Hole** (802-253-9229) on Weeks Hill Road has a lap pool and fitness center, aqua aerobics, personal training, swimming instruction, a children's pool, and a water slide.

HIKING AND WALKING **Green Mountain Club (GMC)** (802-244-7037; www.greenmountainclub.org), a few miles south of Stowe Village on Route 100 in Waterbury Center, maintains a Hiker's Center stocked with hiking maps, guides, and gear. Inquire about workshops and special events.

Stowe Recreation Path is a 5.5-mile paved path that begins in Stowe Village behind the Community Church, winds up through cornfields, wildflowers, and raspberry patches, and parallels Mountain Road (but at a more forgiving pitch). It's open to walkers, joggers, bicyclists, and more. Note the **Quiet Path** along the Mayo River, a mile loop off the main path (it begins across from the Golden Eagle) reserved for walkers (no mountain bikers or in-line skaters).

Mount Mansfield. See the introduction to this section and *To See* for a general description of Vermont's highest mountain. For walkers (as opposed to hikers), it's best to take the Toll Road or gondola up and follow the Tundra Trail. Serious hikers should at least purchase the weatherproof map of the Mount Mansfield region and can profit from the *Long Trail Guide,* both published by the Green

Mountain Club. A naturalist is on hand May through November along the heavily traveled, 2.5-mile section of the Long Trail between the Forehead and the Chin; the Green Mountain Club maintains Butler Lodge, 0.5 mile south of the Forehead, and Taft Lodge, below the Chin, as shelters for hikers.

Smugglers Notch. The Long Trail North, clearly marked, provides an easy, mile-plus hike to Sterling Pond, a beautiful spot at 3,000 feet, and fish-stocked, too. The Elephant's Head can be reached from the state picnic area on Route 108; a 2-mile trail leads to this landmark—from which you can also continue on to Sterling Pond and thence out to Route 108 only a couple of miles above the picnic area. No one should drive through Smugglers Notch without stopping to see the Smugglers Cave and to clamber around on the rocks.

Other local hikes are detailed in *Day Hiker's Guide to Vermont,* which is published by the Green Mountain Club and available from the Stowe Area Association: **Stowe Pinnacle** is a popular 2.8-mile climb; **Mount Hunger** (4 miles) is the highest peak in the Worcester Range; **Taft Lodge** (3.4 miles) is steep but takes you to the oldest lodge on the Long Trail; **Belvidere Mountain** in Eden is a 3½-hour trek yielding good views in all directions; **Ritterbush Pond** and **Devil's Gulch,** also in Eden, are about 2½ hours round-trip; and **Elmore Mountain** in Elmore State Park is a 2- to 3-hour hike with spectacular views.

Camels Hump, from Waterbury. See "Burlington Region" for details. This trail is also detailed in *50 Hikes in Vermont* (Backcountry Publications). One trail starts from Crouching Lion Farm in Duxbury; it's a 6½-hour round-trip hike to the unspoiled summit of Vermont's third highest mountain. Pick up a map at the GMC Hiker's Center (see above).

Little River Trail System, Mount Mansfield State Forest, Waterbury. There are seven beautiful trails through the Ricker Basin and Cotton Brook area, once a settlement for 50 families who left behind cellar holes, stone fences, cemeteries, lilacs, and apple trees. Accessible from both Stowe and Waterbury. Pick up the self-guiding booklet from the Vermont State Department of Forests, Parks and Recreation in Waterbury (802-241-3678).

See also "Barre/Montpelier Area" for hiking in the Worcester Range.

Note: The *Northern Vermont Hiking Trails Map/Guide* published by Map Adventures (802-253-7489) in Stowe is worth picking up.

HORSEBACK RIDING Topnotch Stables (802-253-8585), Mountain Road, Stowe, offers trail rides and carriage lessons. **Edson Hill Manor Stables** (802-253-8954), Stowe, gives private lessons, trail rides. Also **Stowehof Inn** (802-253-9722), the **Mountain View Equestrian Center** (802-253-9901), and **Peterson Brook Farm** (802-253-9052), all in Stowe. **Windy Willows Farm** (802-635-7300) offers what the owner calls "Wicked Good View!" trail rides all year long.

IN-LINE SKATING Stowe-in-Line Skate Park (802-253-3000) at the base of Spruce Peak features a speed oval, a half-pipe, freestyle ramps, and a timed downhill slalom course. Rentals available.

ROCK CLIMBING Check with **Umiak Outfitters** (802-253-2317) in Stowe for instruction and ropes course.

SWIMMING Waterbury Reservoir, the obvious local beach, was closed for repairs in 2003 but scheduled to reopen in 2005. **Forest Pool** on Notchbrook Road, **Sterling Falls,** and the swimming holes in **Ranch Valley** are all worth checking; ask locally for directions. Many lodging places also have their own pools that nonguests may use for a fee.

TENNIS The Racquet Club at Topnotch (802-253-9308), Stowe. Four indoor and 11 outdoor courts, pro shop, instruction, videotape, 8 AM–11 PM.

Stowe Mountain Resort Tennis Courts (802-253-7311), six well-maintained clay courts adjacent to the Inn at the Mountain, 8–6, available by the hour (dress: whites required).

Free public courts can be found at the town recreation area off School Street. A number of inns have courts available to the public; inquire at the Stowe Area Association (802-253-7321).

❊ Winter Sports

CROSS-COUNTRY SKIING A 150 km network of trails that connects ski centers in this area adds up to some of the best ski touring in New England. Given the high elevation of much of this terrain, the trails tend to have snow when few other areas do, and on windy, icy days, cross-country can be better in Stowe than downhill. All four touring centers (in Stowe) honor the others' trail tickets (if you ski, not drive, from one to the next).

Trapp Family Lodge Cross-Country Ski Center (802-253-8511). Located on the Trapp Hill Road, off by itself in the upper reaches of the valley, this is one of the oldest and most beautiful commercial trail systems—40 km of set trails and a total of 85 km of trails at elevations of 1,100–3,000 feet. The basic route here is up and up to a cabin in the woods, a source of homemade soups and chili. Start early enough in the day and you can continue along ridge trails or connect with the Mount Mansfield system. Lessons, equipment rental and sales, and outstanding pastries are all available, as well as guided tours.

Stowe Mountain Resort Cross-Country Center (802-253-3688), Mountain Road. Located near the Inn at the Mountain, this center offers 35 km of set trails, plus 45 km of backcountry trails, at elevations of 1,200–2,800 feet. Trail fees are $14 adults, $7 for juniors and seniors. It's possible to take the Toll House lift partway up the Toll Road and ski down (a good place to practice telemarking). You can also take the quad close enough to the summit to enable you to climb to the very top (via the Toll Road) for a spectacular view out across Lake Champlain; the descent via the Toll Road is relatively easy. Another beautiful trail circles Sterling Pond high in the saddle between Spruce and Madonna Mountains (accessible via chairlift). Connecting trails link this system with the Trapp Family Lodge trails (see above) along some of Stowe's oldest ski trails, such as Ranch Camp and Steeple, dating to the 1920s, now backcountry trails winding along the curved inner face of the mountain.

Edson Hill Ski Touring Center (802-253-7371), Edson Hill Road. Relatively uncrowded on the uplands north of the Mountain Road, the area offers 30 miles of set trails, 25 more on outlying trails at elevations between 1,200 and 2,150 feet; instruction, rental, sales, full lunches, and guided tours available.

Topnotch Touring Center (802-253-8585), Mountain Road, Stowe. Novice to expert, a total of 20 km of groomed trails; instruction, equipment rental, café, and restaurant available, also changing rooms.

Backcountry tours are offered by the **Stowe Mountain Resort** (802-253-3688) and **Trapp Family Lodge** (802-253-8511).

Remember: Backcountry skiing is best done with a guide if you don't know the area.

DOWNHILL SKIING ✍ **Stowe Mountain Resort** (1-800-253-4SKI; www.stowe .com for information, snow reports, and slope-side lodging). See the chapter introduction for the history and proposed future of the ski resort. The oldest section of the Mount Mansfield Base Lodge looks exactly as it did in the 1950s and continues to serve the mountain's primary trail network: the legendary expert Front Four trails that plunge down the mountain's face, and half a dozen intermediate trails that snake down its more forgiving slopes. A quad (wear a neck warmer and/or face mask) goes up to the 1940s-era Octagon. With the exception of Starr and Goat, which are too steep to cover or groom, most trails here are coated with artificial as well as natural snow, and conditions are usually fine. It's an easy traverse from this side of the mountain to the trails served by the gondola up to the Cliff House, from which long, ego-building runs like Perry Merrill sweep to the valley floor. Stowe regulars ski Mount Mansfield in the morning, switching after lunch to south-facing Spruce Peak across Route 108. Spruce Peak, with its Children's Adventure Center (connected by free shuttles every 20 minutes), serves as home to the ski school and children's programs, and several lifts access extensive novice trails. *Lifts:* Eight-passenger gondola, one high-speed quad chairlift, seven double and triple chairlifts, two surface. *Trails:* 48, also glade skiing; 25 percent expert, 59 percent intermediate, 16 percent beginner. *Vertical drop:* 2,360 feet on Mount Mansfield, 1,550 feet on Spruce Peak. *Snowmaking:* Covers 73 percent of the terrain trails served by 9 of the 11 lifts. *Facilities:* Eight restaurants, including those in the Inn at the Mountain, three base lodges, plus the Octagon Web Cafe (you can send free e-mail postcards) and the Cliff House at the top of the busiest lifts; cafeterias, rentals, ski shops, shuttle bus. *Ski school:* 200 instructors; a lift especially designed for beginners at Spruce Peak, where novices learn to make the transition from easy to intermediate trails. *Night skiing:* More than 20 acres on Mount Mansfield are lighted Thursday through Saturday nights 5–9. *For children:* Daycare from 6 weeks in Cubs Infant Daycare. The Children's Learning Center offers daycare or a combo of care and lessons at Spruce Peak. *Rates:* $58 per adult midweek and weekend; $38 per child under 13 and seniors 65 and older; 5 and under free. Add $2 to the ticket price for holidays.

(*Note:* For downhill skiing at **Smugglers' Notch,** see "North of the Notch"; it is possible to ski back and forth between the two areas when the Spruce Chair is operating.)

ICE CLIMBING The **Inn at Turner Mill** (802-253-2062) offers information about ice climbing expeditions, and the owner himself is an avid climber. Smugglers Notch itself is favored by ice climbers.

ICE SKATING Ice skating is available at the Olympic-sized **Jackson Arena** (802-253-4402) in the village. Call for public skating times. There's also skating on the pond at **Commodores Inn** (802-253-7131). The town of Waterbury has a large new skating arena called the **Ice Center** (802-244-4040).

SLEIGH RIDES In Stowe sleigh rides are found at **Stoweflake Resort** (802-253-7355), **Stowehof Inn** (802-253-9722), **Edson Hill Manor** (802-253-7371, not Tuesday or Thursday), **Trapp Family Lodge** (802-253-5813), **Mountain View Equestrian** (802-253-9901), and **Charlie Horse Sleigh Rides** (802-253-2215).

SNOWBOARD RENTALS **Misty Mountain Snowboards** (802-253-3040), top of the Mountain Road, Stowe. They advertise "the fastest snowboard rentals in town."

SNOWMOBILING **Stowe Snowmobile Tours** (802-253-6221) offers rentals and tours of the Mount Mansfield State Forest, and is also a source of information about local trails. **Smugglers' Notch Snowmobile Tours** (1-800-347-8266), based at Sterling Ridge Inn, on the other side of the Notch in Jeffersonville, also offers guided trips from the Stowe side.

SNOWSHOEING Tubbs, New England's leading snowshoe manufacturer, is located in Stowe but at this writing offers no retail store or visitors outreach program. On the other hand, **Umiak Outdoor Outfitters** (802-253-2317) offers guided moonlit snowshoe tours, fondue dinner tours, and even a package tour at the Ben & Jerry's Factory in Waterbury so you can snowshoe before you eat the ice cream. **Trapp Family Lodge Cross-Country Ski Center** has designated more than 15 km of its trails as snowshoe-only. The **Stowe Mountain Resort Cross-Country Center** has cut 5 km of dedicated trails and permits snowshoers on all 80 km of its cross-country trails. **Topnotch at Stowe Resort** has also designated some snowshoe-recommended routes, and permits snowshoes on all 20 km of its trails.

The obvious place to go is, of course, up the unplowed stretch of Route 108 into Smugglers Notch, and the more adventurous can also access more than 40 miles of hiking terrain on and around Mount Mansfield, but it's best to check with the **Green Mountain Club** (see *Hiking and Walking*), which also sponsors a mid-February Snowshoe Festival. Local rental sources are plentiful. Pick up a copy of *Northern Vermont Adventure Skiing*, a weatherproof map/guide detailing trails throughout the region. It's available at Umiak and other local stores in Stowe.

✳ Green Space

For fees and reservation rules, see *Campgrounds* in "What's Where."

Mount Mansfield State Forest. The largest state forest in Vermont—27,436 acres—much of which lies on the other (western) flank of the mountain. The 10-mile Cottonbrook Trail starts at Cottonbrook Road off Nebraska Valley Road in Stowe. Follow the blazes.

Smugglers Notch State Park (802-253-4014), Stowe 05672; 10 miles up Mountain Road (Route 108) from Stowe Village, open mid-May through mid-October. Thirty-eight campsites, including 14 lean-tos. A few miles beyond the camping area, just beyond the highest point on this high, winding road—open only late May through November, weather permitting—is a turnoff with parking, toilet, and an information center.

Elmore State Park (802-888-2982), Lake Elmore 05657. Open mid-May through mid-October, 14 miles north of Stowe on Route 100, then east to Morrisville, south 5 miles on Route 12; 709 acres with a beach, bathhouse, rental boats, 64 sites for tents and trailers including 5 lean-tos, picnicking, hiking trail up Elmore Mountain.

Wiessner Woods. An 80-acre preserve with nature trails maintained by the Stowe Land Trust. The entrance is on Edson Hill Road, the next right after the entrance to Stowehof Inn.

✳ Lodging

Most accommodations are found either in Stowe Village or along—or just off—the 7.2-mile Mountain Road (Route 108), which connects the village with the ski slopes. Unless otherwise noted, all are in Stowe 05672.

RESORTS ✎ ₺ **The Trapp Family Lodge** (802-253-8511; 1-800-826-7000; www.trappfamily.com), 700 Trapp Hill Road, is an alpine-modern version of the fabled Austrian schloss once owned by the family of *Sound of Music* fame. Johannes von Trapp lives nearby and remains involved in the property's day-to-day operations. The 73-room lodge with its 17-room luxury wing offers ample common space: a charming greenhouse sitting room, three common rooms with fireplaces, and a library, cocktail lounge, large dining room, and conference facilities. Twenty more rooms are in the motel-style Lower Lodge, and 100 guest house time-share units (inquire about vacancies) are ranged in tiers on the slope below, commanding sweeping views of the Worcester Range. The inn's 2,700 acres are webbed with cross-country ski trails, also good for splendid walks. There are tennis courts and a spring-fed pool as well as an indoor pool, a sauna, and a workout room in the Sports Center. Come in late March (when the sugarhouse is operating and the sun is warm but there is still snow on the high and wooded trails) or in early December (when there is sometimes snow), and you can pay half as much as you would in foliage season. A 2- or 3-day minimum is mandatory in peak periods like foliage and Christmas. Inquire about family packages (children 16 and under stay free), and about nature walks, snowshoeing, sleigh rides, and children's, exercise, and cross-country ski programs. $250–495 in summer; $270–495 in fall, excluding the Columbus Day weekend. For Columbus Day, Thanksgiving, and Christmas, the rates run $495–670 and include a five-course dinner and full breakfast.

❧ **The Stowe Inn** (802-253-4030; 1-800-546-4030; www.stoweinn.com), 123 Mountain Road. This inn has changed hands several times in recent years, but the new owners, Jed and Annika Lipsky, have set about renovating and refurbishing the place with a sense of purpose and good taste. The 17th-century landmark building overlooks Stowe's Little River. It offers 18 comfortable bedrooms with private bath as well as bright, spacious common areas with fireplaces in the main building and another 20 rooms in the Carriage House, which is more in the motel style. The dining room, leased to a well-respected local chef, opened in late 2003. Rates in summer and winter range from $68 for a double room in the Carriage House midweek to $148 for a deluxe room in the main inn on the weekend. All rates include continental breakfast.

⌒ 🐾 ✍ ♿ **Edson Hill Manor** (802-253-7371; 1-800-621-0284; www.stowevt.com), 1500 Edson Hill Road. Set on 225 cultivated acres on a high slope, the manor was built in the 1940s with brick from the old Sherwood Hotel of Burlington. Most of the living room beams were hewn for Ira and Ethan Allen's barn, which stood in North Burlington for more than a century. In the inn itself the nine guest rooms are each very individual, most with wood-burning fireplaces and hand-painted mural in the bath. The honeymoon suite with a view over the gardens is Room 3, and

Room 5 has gables, a canopy bed, and the same view. Four carriage houses, each with three or four units, are ranged in tiers behind the main house; these have knotty-pine walls, wing chairs and reproduction antiques, fireplaces, books, and a spacious, in-the-woods feel. Under the ownership of William O'Neil and family, the small dining room has acquired an enviable reputation (see *Dining Out*). Living rooms are furnished in antiques, hung with exceptional art. Facilities include a stable and trails for horseback riding, outdoor pool, stocked trout pond, and 40 km of cross-country trails. Rates are $139–199 per couple B&B or $40 more with dinner; multiday packages available.

⌒ 🐾 ♿ **Green Mountain Inn** (802-253-7301; 1-800-253-7302; www.greenmountaininn.com), 18 South Main Street. The brick-and-clapboard face of this landmark dates back to 1833, when it was built as a private home. In the 1850s it became a hotel, and it last changed ownership in 1982, when it was acquired by a Canadian, Marvin Gameroff, who has since tastefully renovated the rooms in the inn itself, outfitting them with country furniture especially made for the inn, adding niceties like salt-glaze stoneware lamps and appealing art. The 105 antiques-filled rooms and suites, all with private bath, air-conditioning, cable TV, and telephone, are located in the Main Inn, Annex, Clubhouse, Mill House, Depot Building, Sanborn House, and, most recently, the Mansfield House with special amenities such as fireside double Jacuzzi, DVD player with surround sound, marble bath, and original artwork. The dining options: a formal Main Street Dining Room, and the downstairs Whip Bar & Grill, which offers a poolside patio in summer and a fire in colder months (see *Eating Out*). Afternoon tea and cookies are served in the living room. $125–415 per room in winter and summer (2-night minimum stay on weekends); less in the off-season. The suites and efficiencies are more. Guests enjoy complimentary use of Athletic Club facilities, located just the other side of the pool.

∞ ♪ **Inn at the Mountain and Condominiums** (802-253-3656; 1-800-253-4754; www.stowe.com), 5781 Mountain Road. The Mount Mansfield Company's luxurious 32-room lodge, as well as a number of town houses and truly luxurious one-, two-, and three-bedroom Mountain Club condominiums, are currently the closest lodging to the lifts. Facilities include **H. H. Bingham's** restaurant, clay tennis courts, swimming pools, and the **Toll House Health Spa.** From $99–329 EP per room or suite in low season to $229–559 in high season. Some condos sleep up to eight people comfortably (children under 12 stay free). Less through numerous packages.

∞ **Stowehof Inn** (802-253-9722; 1-800-932-7136; www.stowehofinn .com), 2 miles off Route 108 on the road to Edson Hill. The Stowehof specializes in weddings, and the innkeepers have created a fantasy world from the moment you step through its sod-roofed porte cochère, supported by two maple trees. No two of the 46 guest rooms are alike (some suites, a few fireplaced demisuites with optional kitchenette). The public rooms are quixotically furnished with mementos like the divining rod that

located the water source for the building. Windows everywhere let in the view. Facilities include a taproom, a dining room known for nouvelle French dishes (see *Dining Out*), tennis courts, a putting range, a pool with a view, a sauna, and cross-country ski trails connecting with the larger network. On the adjacent working farm, guests can see cattle and ride horses. Rates start at $110 in winter midweek and climb to $445 for the best rooms on a holiday weekend, with minimum stays required. Dinner plans are available for an extra $35 per person. Some lodging packages include breakfast and some don't, so ask.

∞ 🐾 ♪ ও **Topnotch Resort** (802-253-8585; 1-800-451-8686; www.top notch-resort.com), 4000 Mountain Road. Uncommonly comfortable rooms, luxurious areas for lounging, the convivial **Buttertub Bistro,** and the stately, glass-sided, highly rated main dining room at **Maxwell's.** The health-and-fitness spa offers a program as well as superb facilities, including an indoor pool with a waterfall. Contemporary sculpture surrounds the outdoor swimming pool. A red barn down across the Mountain Road serves as a cross-country ski center in winter (50 km of groomed trails connect with other trail systems in Stowe); you'll also find a riding stable, indoor and outdoor tennis courts, and a handy skating rink. Rates begin at $175 and run to $630 for a double room or suite in low season, $235–730 in high. Rates include use of the pool and Jacuzzi; the exercise program is extra. A MAP plan is offered; inquire about spa packages. Pets welcome.

♪ ও **Golden Eagle Resort Motor Inn** (802-253-4811; 1-800-626-1010),

511 Mountain Road. The 12-unit motel that Herb and Ann Hillman bought in 1963 has evolved through two generations into an amazing 60-acre complex with 76 rooms, 11 efficiencies, four condos, one guest house, and two apartments. Family geared as well as owned, it offers a lot for children. In summer there's a formal hiking and crafts program on selected days for 3- to 12-year-olds, and on certain nights, year-round, there are movies with popcorn. Amenities include a playground as well as an attractive health spa with indoor pool, large whirlpool, sauna, universal exercise equipment, massage service, and exercise classes. There are also outdoor heated pools (swimming lessons are offered); a clay tennis court; fish-stocked ponds; shuffleboard, badminton, lawn games, and game rooms; and a coffee shop and restaurants. Throughout, you have the sense of a well-run resort. A 50-acre wildlife area with walking trails adjoins the property. Breakfast is included in $99–209 per room; fully handicapped-accessible rooms; also shuttle service to the Amtrak station.

Stoweflake Mountain Resort & Spa (802-253-7355; 1-800-253-2232; www.stoweflake.com), Mountain Road. The small ski lodge that the Behra family opened more than 30 years ago has mushroomed into a full-facility 94-room resort (including 40 new luxury suites) and 36 town houses. There are bright, comfortable, inn-style rooms in the original lodge and many nicely furnished motel rooms (besides its own motel wing, the resort includes the former Nordic Motor Inn). All rooms have cable TV, phone, and private bath;

common space includes a library and lobby with fireplaces and sitting area, along with a large living room with a sunken fireplace. The Spa & Sports Club includes a Cybex circuit, racquetball/squash court, indoor pool, Jacuzzi, sauna, and steam and massage rooms. There are also tennis courts, badminton, volleyball, croquet, horseshoes, and a professional putting green and driving ranges. The links at the Stowe Country Club adjoin the property. Dining options include **Winfield's Bistro** and the pubby **Charlie B's**. $150–280 per room or suite; $320–850 for townhouse units; MAP rates and many packages.

INNS AND BED & BREAKFASTS

The Gables Inn (802-253-7730; 1-800-GABLES-1; www.gablesinn.com), 1457 Mountain Road. Randy Stern and Annette Monachelli are warm, personable hosts who have created one of Stowe's most relaxing and welcoming inns. Common rooms include a comfortable living room with fireplace, a plant-filled solarium, and a downstairs game room/lounge (BYOB). There's a swimming pool on the landscaped grounds, which angle off from Mountain Road, across from an open stretch of the Stowe Recreation Path. The hot tub is right outside the door, the better to hop into in winter. Each of the 18 rooms (all with private bath) in the main house is different. Four in the Carriage House (handicapped accessible) feature whirlpool and fireplace; the two Riverview suites in the neighboring house across the brook have a fridge, microwave, and coffeemaker, as well as a fireplace and double Jacuzzi. The famously good breakfasts are also open to the public and generally considered the best in town (see *Eating Out*). Rates are $80–235 B&B in high season, $78–165 in low season.

Stone Hill Inn (802-253-6282), 89 Houston Farm Road (off Route 108), Stowe 05672. A luxury bed & breakfast run by Amy and Hap Jordan. Nine guest rooms all have two-person Jacuzzi, comfy king-sized beds, and gas fireplace. Hap cooks breakfast, which is taken in a sunny room overlooking woods and fields. $250–375 per room, depending on the season.

Three Bears at the Fountain (802-253-7671; 1-800-898-9634; www .three-bearsbandb.com), Route 100 north. Suzanne and Stephen Vazzano run this wonderful old farmhouse and converted barn as a bed & breakfast. Notice the fountain out front. Rates $100–200 per room.

𝄞 **Fiddler's Green Inn** (802-253-8124; 1-800-882-5346; www.Fiddlers GreenInn.com), 4859 Mountain Road, 5 miles from the village toward the mountain. Less than a mile from the lifts, this pleasant yellow 1820s farmhouse can sleep no more than 18 guests (making it great for small groups) in seven comfortable guest rooms tucked under the eaves. Guests gather around the fieldstone hearth in the living room and at the long table off the sunny kitchen. BYOB. Hammocking or hiking and skiing, depending on the season, are close by. In summer and winter longtime owners Bud and Carol McKeon cater to bicyclists and cross-country skiers. Room rates are $60–125 B&B; dinner possible on request. Families welcome.

🐾 𝄞 **The Inn at Turner Mill** (802-253-2062; 1-800-992-0016), 56 Turner Mill Lane. Sequestered in the pines by Notch Brook, off Mountain Road just a mile from the lifts, this complex was splendidly built in the 1930s by an eccentric woman doctor. Its 10 wooded acres include a mountain stream and "refreshing" swimming hole; there's also an outdoor pool. The family-geared efficiencies and apartments, which must be rented for a minimum of a week at a time, are nicely decorated, with cable TV, some with hearth, access to sauna, Jacuzzi, and cross-country trails. Greg and Mitzi Speer are friendly hosts who can find a babysitter and help with transfers from Burlington or Waterbury. Snowshoe rentals are available, and guests get half a day free. When it was built, this was as high as a car could drive up the Mountain Road, and the Civilian Conservation Corps ski trails (now cross-country ski trails) are within easy striking distance. Weekly rates range $500–900 per room, and the rooms sleep from two to four people. No meals.

🐾 𝄞 **Ski Inn** (802-253-4050), 5037 Mountain Road. Harriette Heyer has been welcoming guests to Stowe's oldest ski lodge—one of the handiest places to the lifts—since Pearl Harbor Day, and she specializes in solo travelers. Designed as a ski lodge, the inn is set back from the Mountain Road amid hemlocks and evergreens. The 10 guest rooms are bright and meticulously clean, each with both a double and a single bed; shared and private baths. There is a pine-paneled BYOB bar and attractive sitting and dining rooms. Stowe's cross-country network can be accessed from the back door. $55–65 per person MAP (dinners are hearty) in winter; $55–65 per room with continental breakfast in summer.

∞ 🐾 **Brass Lantern Inn** (802-253-2229; 1-800-729-2980; www.brass lanterninn.com), 717 Maple Street

(Route 100), is a welcoming B&B at the northern edge of the village. Your host is Andy Aldrich, a Vermonter raised on a Richmond dairy farm, who was named Vermont B&B Innkeeper of the Year for 2001. His work as a homebuilder is evident in this nicely renovated 1800s building, with its planked floors and comfortable common rooms. The nine stenciled and papered guest rooms are furnished with antiques and hand-stitched quilts; all have private bath, and six have whirlpool tub and gas-burning fireplace. A small pub and porch are for guests only. Guests enjoy gym privileges at the Stowe Gym. Breakfast is a serious affair, maybe sourdough French toast, apple crêpes, or broccoli and mushroom quiche. $85–135 in low season, $95–165 in regular, and $115–225 per couple in high season. Small weddings are a specialty. Pets are possible at a separate two-bedroom rental cottage owned by the inn (though not in the inn itself).

🍴 **Auberge de Stowe** (802-253-7787; 1-800-387-8789; www .aubergedestowe.com), 692 South Main Street. This 18th-century brick farmhouse and converted carriage house (it was the Bittersweet Inn) is a find. Shawn and Chantal Kerivan offer eight rooms, including one suite, six with private bath. The house is right on Route 100 along the river, but there is a view and a sense of space in the back. Amenities include a comfortable living room, a game room with BYOB bar, a good-sized swimming pool, a large lawn, and a hot tub. Rates, which are less than $100 per room, include a substantial continental breakfast with homemade pastries. The owners speak both German and French.

&. **Ten Acres Lodge** (802-253-7638; 1-800-327-7357), 14 Barrows Road. This 1840s red-clapboard inn has a luxurious feel and a reputation for fine dining. We recommend the suites with fireplace, sitting area, and a balcony in Hill House Suite, a newish complex up behind the old inn. Many of the rooms have been completely refurbished. The two cottages, one with two and the other with three bedrooms, and with kitchen and fireplace, are also exceptional. The grounds include a pool, tennis court, and hot tub. Doubles are $115–440.

Ye Olde England Inn (802-253-7558; 1-800-477-3771; www.eng landinn.com), 433 Mountain Road. Anglophiles can revel in the English accent, decor, and menu. The rooms are unabashedly luxurious, from the 17 Laura Ashley–style rooms in the inn to the 2 two-bedroom English "cottages" beside the swimming pool (each with fireplace, Jacuzzi, and kitchen). There are 10 suites on a rise behind the inn, each with a four-poster bed, Jacuzzi, deck, and lounge with a fireplace, wet bar, fridge, and microwave. A full English breakfast and tea are included in $99–395 rates, except in the cottages. Mr. Pickwick's Pub & Restaurant serves lunch and dinner (see *Eating Out*). The extravagant breakfasts are served in **Copperfield's,** the inn's other dining room.

Foxfire Inn (802-253-4887; www .foxfire.com), 1606 Pucker Street (Route 100) north of Stowe Village. This early-19th-century farmhouse is set on 70 wooded hillside acres. The five guest rooms have wide-board floors (several have exposed beams) and are furnished with antiques, each with private bath. Downstairs there is plenty of space for guests away from the large, public dining room, well respected for its Italian fare (see *Dining Out*). $130 per double room in high season, $80 in low season, includes a full breakfast served in the garden room.

☉ ☀ ✎ ⟁ **Commodores Inn** (802-253-7131; 1-800-44-STOWE; www.commodoresinn.com), P.O. Box 970, Route 100 south. Carrie Nourjian runs this establishment with 72 large rooms, all with private bath (request one in the back, overlooking the lake). There's a living room with a fireplace; also two Jacuzzis and saunas and an outdoor pool. The **Stowe Yacht Club Steakhouse and Sport Lounge** (a popular watering hole and spot for an evening burger) overlooks a 3-acre lake on which model sailboat races are regularly held. $78–162 per person in winter; less in summer and multidays year-round. Breakfast is included.

In Waterbury 05676
The Inn at Blush Hill (802-244-7529; 1-800-736-7522; www.blush hill.com), 784 Blush Hill Road, off Route 100, hidden away on 5 hilltop acres with spectacular views across the valley and reservoir (good for boating and swimming). All five rooms have private bath; one has a fireplace, another has a 15-foot-wide view of the mountains, and a third, a Jacuzzi bath. The handsome, wine-red, gabled Cape dates to 1790, and the living room has that nice snug feel (there's a vintage-1840 hearth and an oak armoire that opens into an entertainment center). Country breakfasts are served on an old farmhand's table in the sunny, many-windowed kitchen. Your hostess is Pam Gosselin. $85–160 per couple includes a full breakfast and evening refreshments.

☉ ☀ ✎ **The Old Stagecoach Inn** (802-244-5056; 1-800-262-2206; www.oldstagecoach.com), 18 North Main Street. A classic stagecoach inn built in 1826 with a triple-tiered porch but substantially altered in the 1880s, when a millionaire from Ohio added oak woodwork, ornate fireplaces, and stained glass. Renovated in 1987, the inn is run by John and Jack Barwick. There are eight guest rooms and three efficiency suites, all tastefully furnished but varying widely—from a queen-bedded room with a sitting area, fireplace, and private bath to small rooms with a shared bath. Two efficiency suites are studios; the other has two bedrooms and a sitting area. Many of the rooms are large enough to accommodate families. Coco, the African gray parrot, sits by the fireplace in the living room adjoining the library, with its fully licensed bar. Regular-season rates are $60–120 per room; foliage-season and winter holidays $70–180. A full breakfast, including a selection of hot dishes, is included. Pets allowed in some rooms.

☉ ☀ ✎ **Grünberg Haus** (802-244-7726; 1-800-800-7760; www.grunberg haus.com), 94 Pine Street, Route 100 south of Waterbury. This secluded, Tyrolean-style chalet has 14 guest rooms, 8 with private bath, and two cabins (open Memorial Day through October) where pets are allowed. Innkeepers Jeff and Linda Connor serve a full breakfast of homemade breads and baked goods, a fresh fruit creation, and a main dish such as ricotta-stuffed French toast. Facilities include a garden deck with a warm-weather Jacuzzi and self-serve pub and game room. Hiking and snowshoe trails behind the inn feed into a

20 km cross-country trail system. The dark-wood-beamed common rooms include a large fieldstone fireplace. In winter the inn offers discounts at Stowe, Sugarbush, Bolton, and Mad River Glen (all within easy striking distance) and keeps four sets of snowshoes on hand. Rates are $70–155 in low season, $110–205 in high. Children must be over age 5. Dog in residence.

Thatcher Brook Inn (802-244-5911; 1-800-292-5911; www.thatcher brook.com), exit 10 off I-89, then take Route 100 north. Twenty-one guest rooms in this restored Victorian country inn, once the home of a lumber baron, all have private bath, and many have a whirlpool and/or fireplace.

WATERBURY'S THATCHER BROOK INN

Kim Grant

Bailey's Fireside Tavern offers a cozy fireplace and a pub menu, but there's also the fine-dining **Restaurant at Thatcher Brook Inn,** which has an excellent reputation.

In Waterbury Center 05677

& **The Black Locust Inn** (802-244-7490; 1-800-366-5592; www.black locustinn.com), 5088 Waterbury–Stowe Road (Route 100). This is an 1832 three-gabled home with six rooms that have private bath, polished wood floors, and stained-glass transoms. One king-bedded room is handicapped accessible. Len, Nancy, and Valerie Vignola (assisted by golden retriever Lady) get great reviews for hospitality. $119–235 includes three-course breakfasts and afternoon appetizers.

May Farm B&B (802-244-7306; 1-800-729-9093; www.mayfarm.com), 4706 Waterbury–Stowe Road, Waterbury Center. The farm, built in 1790, offers down comforters, stained glass, and a hot tub under the stars. Breakfast is served in three courses, and if that doesn't hold you, there's a late-afternoon beverage service with hors d'oeuvres. Rates $60–125.

MOTELS

In Stowe 05672

Arbor Inn (802-253-4772; 1-800-543-1293; www.arborinnstowe.com), 3214 Mountain Road. This is the former home of Olympian Billy Kidd. The owners offer 12 rooms and suites, all with private bath, recently renovated and furnished in antiques, equipped with TV and a small fridge. Two rooms have fully equipped kitchen; four have a fireplace, and two come with two-person whirlpool tub. Common space includes a game room, pool table, and outdoor pool and Jacuzzi. Amenities include two fieldstone fireplaces, spectacular views of Mount Mansfield, and English gardens in summer. $65–299 per room with full breakfast.

& ⚘ **Alpenrose** (802-253-7277; 1-800-962-7002), 2619 Mountain Road. A pleasant, small motel with just five rooms, four of which are efficiencies with kitchenettes; direct access to a cross-country network and the Stowe Recreation Path. $60–80 per room in winter, $55–65 in low season, no meals included.

In Waterbury 05676

⚘ ⚬ **Best Western Waterbury-Stowe** (802-244-7822; 1-800-621-7822), 45 Blush Hill Road, exit 10 north, I-89. There are 83 rooms with private bath and a restaurant for casual dining. Amenities include a large indoor pool and a full-sized fitness center with high-end weight and aerobic equipment, hot tub, and sauna. Positioned just off the interstate, this is a popular way stop with family-geared rates and access to Sugarbush as well as Stowe. $160–200 per couple in high season, $80–150 in low; many family-sized rooms; continental breakfast is included.

CONDOMINIUMS Stowe Country Rentals (802-253-8132; 1-800-639-1990; www.stowecountryrentals.com) handles condos and houses. **Country Village Rentals** (802-253-8777; 1-800-320-8777; www.cvrandr.com) specializes in upscale homes, both old and new. **All Seasons Rentals** (802-253-7353; 1-800-54-STOWE; www.stowerentals.com), **Blue Heron Rentals** (802-253-7791; 1-800-42-HERON; www.blueheronrentals.com), and **Rentals at Stowe** (802-

253-9786; 1-800-848-9120, ext. 624; www.rentalsatstowe.com) also rent homes and condos.

The Village Green at Stowe (802-253-9705; 1-800-451-3297), 1003 Cape Cod Road, Stowe 05672. Seven nicely designed buildings set on 40 acres (surrounded by the Stowe Country Club links) contain 73 two- and three-bedroom town houses, all brightly furnished. A recreation building has a heated indoor pool, Jacuzzi, sauna, game and changing rooms; also an outdoor pool and two tennis courts. Winter rates excluding holidays begin at $280–375 per night for a two-bedroom unit with a minimum of 2 nights; less for additional nights. $235–310 per night in summer, more for three-bedroom units; weekly rates.

🐾 **Notch Brook Condominiums** (802-253-4882; 1-800-253-4882), 1229 Notch Brook Road, Stowe 05672. In the shadow of Spruce Peak with a spectacular view of Mount Mansfield, an unusually well-built (though no one seems to know why Vermont architect Robert Burley designed them with flat roofs) complex of 36 rooms and 35 condominiums ranging from doubles through three-bedroom town houses. Most rooms are available by the day and week. Amenities include saunas, tennis, an outdoor pool that's heated for winter use, and complimentary continental breakfast. $80–325 per unit in winter, less in summer; more in peak holiday periods.

1836 Cabins (802-244-8533), Box 128, Waterbury Center 05677, are tucked into a pine forest whose logging roads become cross-country ski trails in winter. Completely furnished one- and two-bedroom units with kitchen, TV; telephone on request. Rates $99 for two, standard; $139 for deluxe (gas fireplaces); more over holidays.

DORMS ⚑ **Round Hearth at Stowe** (802-253-7223), 39 Edson Hill Road, Stowe 05672. A dormitory-style operation, complete with chaperones and all sorts of amenities for teen groups, such as DJ dances on Saturday night, outdoor hot tubs, and large-screen TVs. Merry and Grady Vigneau do everything from winter ski trips to summer sports camps and basket-making workshops. They also own and operate the **Red Fox Alpine Lodge at Smugglers Notch.** Call for group rates.

CAMPGROUNDS See *Green Space* for information on campgrounds in Smugglers Notch.

✳ Where to Eat

DINING OUT Blue Moon Cafe (802-253-7006), 35 School Street, Stowe. Open for dinner daily. A very small, candlelit bistro with a huge reputation. Owner Jim Barton serves "contemporary American" dishes. The menu changes weekly, but you might begin with tequila-cured salmon with blue corn cake and chipotle mango crème fraîche ($8.25) or venison carpaccio ($10.25), then dine on banana leaf steamed halibut with Thai coconut curry ($19.50) or roast duck with dried cherries, port wine, and wild rice ($22). Dinner for two with wine is about $90.

Edson Hill Manor (802-253-7371), 1500 Edson Hill Road, Stowe. Open for dinner nightly in-season; reservations required. The small, gracious dining room at this low-key resort has

soared to the top of local restaurant ratings. The menu changes daily. The appetizer menu ($9–11) might feature smoked duck French toast and Cajun paella. Entrées ($19–24) might be bacon-roasted Chilean sea bass, seared rare tuna loin, or roast rack of New Zealand lamb.

Mes Amis (802-253-8669), 311 Mountain Road, Stowe. With Ile de France now gone, Mes Amis is the premier French restaurant in Stowe. The food is French bistro-style and very well done. There are a number of small rooms, which creates an intimate dining atmosphere. You might begin with oysters on the half shell and move on to duck breast, salmon encrusted in sweet potato, or an excellent rabbit stew. Entrées $18–25.

Red Basil (802-253-4478), Mountain Road, Stowe. The hot new Thai restaurant in town. Appetizers include fried crab wontons and Thai ravioli (both $5.95); house specials are pattaya ($19.95), which is seafood in green curry sauce, or a dish called swimming ($19.95), which is soft-shell crab and duck with tamarind sauce and red curry sauce. They also make a mean martini.

Foxfire Inn and Italian Restaurant (802-253-4887), Route 100, north of Stowe Village. Dinner nightly. Favored by local residents for a predictably good night out. The setting is a 1850s country farmhouse, and the menu is large. You might begin with rolled eggplant (baked with ricotta and prosciutto, mozzarella, and Romano cheese) ($6.50), then dine on veal saltimbocca ($18.95) or chicken stuffed with Gorgonzola cheese, pancetta, and figs sautéed in a creamy Marsala wine sauce ($16.50).

Emily's at Stowehof Inn (802-253-9722), 2 miles off Route 108, Stowe. American nouvelle cuisine in a dramatic dining room. Appetizers range $8–15 and include lobster and smoked salmon terrine, a trio of dumplings, and antelope carpaccio. The entrées run $17–30, including prime filet mignon, prosciutto-wrapped quail, and seared diver scallops. Inquire about sleigh-ride and dinner packages in winter. **Coslin's Pub** offers less formal fare, complimentary appetizers during ski season, and live jazz on Friday night.

Trapp Family Dining Room (802-253-8511), Trapp Hill Road, Stowe. Austrian chef Juergen Spagolla offers noteworthy formal dining with a three-course ($36) and five-course ($42) prix fixe menu; always includes Austrian specialties, like Wiener schnitzel with spaetzle, but also varied fare, like fresh sea scallops sautéed in a Riesling cream sauce and roasted stuffed quails with pear schnapps served with braised red cabbage. Lighter meals are served in the lounge and in the Austrian Tea Room, which specializes in tortes, strudels, and wursts.

Trattoria La Festa (802-253-8480), 4080 Mountain Road, Stowe. Dinner served daily except Sunday (open on long weekends). On the upper reaches of the Mountain Road with terrace dining in summer, a pleasant dining room that's owned by three experienced chefs, two of them brothers born and raised in Aprilia, a small coastal town not far from Rome. True to the nature of an Italian trattoria, the food is varied. Reliably delicious antipasti, such as carpaccio di carne (thin slices of filet mignon with onions, capers, extra-virgin olive oil;

$8.50); specialty pastas like penne Michelangelo (penne sautéed with fresh vegetables and grilled shrimp in a garlic wine sauce; $14.50); and four-course, family-style dinners can be preordered.

EATING OUT

In Stowe
Cliff House (802-253-3665), in the Octagon at Mount Mansfield's summit. Dinner is a thing of the past, but lunch is served 11–3 each day. It's impossible to beat the view, and where else would you go out to lunch via gondola? You might begin with a cup of Atlantic lobster bisque ($5.95) or baked Brie in pastry ($8.95). Winter warmers include a lamb stew ($12.95) or shepherd's pie ($11.95).

Gracie's Restaurant (802-253-8741), Main Street, Carlson Building, Stowe Village. Open 11:30 AM–midnight, this richly paneled pub with booths, a hearth, and heavily dog-themed decor is a great place to eat when you pull into town late. We have enjoyed dining alone on one of Gracie's outstanding burgers at the bar, and on the nightly special (shrimp jambalaya or Gracie's scampi) with friends. At lunch we recommend Gracie's famous chicken sandwich served with bacon, mayo, and guacamole ($7.95) or the vegetable flatbread ($6.95). Gracie, who was owners Paul and Sue Archdeacon's dog (his picture hangs at the bottom of the stairs), was a fixture at the Shed all those years Paul worked there as bartender.

♂ **McCarthy's Restaurant** (802-253-8626), Mountain Road next to the Stowe Cinema. Open 6:30–3 daily. The local gathering place: quick, cheerful service, an open black-and-white-checked tile kitchen, oilcloths

on the tables, wood skis on the walls, and deep wooden booths. Daily specials for breakfast and lunch, plus a big breakfast menu and a wide selection of soups and sandwiches on homemade breads. Kids' menu, boxed lunches to go. Great all around.

✍ **Restaurant Swisspot** (802-253-4622), Stowe Village. An old reliable, open nightly for lunch and dinner. Soups, quiche, and fondue are lovingly prepared. For lunch, there are tempting burgers with Swiss cheese, and a wide variety of sandwiches. Fondues are a specialty of the house; try the Swiss cheese fondue ($25 for two) or beef fondue bourguignon for two ($33). Other options range from Wiener schnitzel ($16) to pesto shrimp ($15). Children's menu. Try the Matterhorn sundae with hot Tobler sauce ($4).

✍ **The Gables Inn** (802-253-7730; 1-800-GABLES-1), 1457 Mountain Road. Breakfast served 8–10:30 daily, Sunday and holiday brunch until 12:30. Breakfast is an event, served on the enclosed front porch and in the cheerful dining room. The daily blackboard breakfast specials might include French toast stuffed with cream cheese, walnuts, and molasses ($6.50); a Vermont cheddar cheese omelet with mushrooms, peppers, onions, and garden herbs ($5.75); or kippers with onions ($5).

✍ **The Shed** (802-253-4364), Mountain Road, open daily for lunch and dinner, also Sunday buffet brunch and a late-night menu (10–midnight). Ken Strong's old landmark pub has expanded over the years into a complex that includes a microbrewery as well as a large, greenhouse-style dining room. The varied menu includes salads, tacos, baked onion soup, zucchini

boats, barbecued ribs, seafood strudel, and, of course, Shed burgers. Children's menu.

Whip Bar & Grill (802-253-7301), Main Street at the Green Mountain Inn. Open daily 11:30–9:30; Sunday brunch is a specialty. For charm and good food at palatable prices, the Whip is difficult to beat. The antique buggy whips, brass dumbwaiter, and vintage photos recall the tavern's status. It boasts Stowe's first liquor license, from 1833. In summer there's patio dining and a view of lawns and the pool; in winter the focus is on a roaring hearth. There is a blackboard menu, always a choice of grilled meats or fish, a raw bar, and specials ranging from pan-blackened fish to Montreal smoked meat with hot mustard. Dinner specials include grilled sea scallops with a honey lemon thyme glaze and maple-marinated pork chops served with apple-rhubarb chutney.

✍ **Miguel's Stowe-Away Lodge and Restaurant** (802-253-7574), 3148 Mountain Road. This snug old farmhouse, the original Miguel's, is a reliably good bet featuring innovative Mexican fare like *carnitas de cordero* (marinated lamb served with rice and beans), as well as the usual Tex-Mex "especiales" and a gringo and full children's menu. This is the place for margaritas.

Mr. Pickwick's Pub & Restaurant at Ye Olde England Inn (802-253-7558), 433 Mountain Road. Open for lunch, dinner, and Sunday brunch. "A Dickens of a place" offers bangers and mash ($14.95) or steak-and-kidney pie ($15.95). Ostrich steak served with sweet potato spaetzle ($22.95) and Vermont pheasant breast with lobster-truffle smashed potatoes

($22.95) are among the exotic dinner entrées. There is a vast collection of beers, single-malt whiskeys, vintage ports, and a martini bar.

Moscow Tea House (802-253-2955), Moscow. Open year-round, Thursday through Saturday noon–5. Call ahead for reservations. Homemade pastries and savories are served with herbal and regular teas on the veranda and in the combination tearoom/gift shop with dried herbs and flowers hanging from the rafters.

Dutch Pancake Cafe (802-253-5330), 900 Mountain Road at the Grey Fox Inn. Open daily 7:30–11 AM, for brunch until 12:30 PM on winter weekends and holidays, and for dinner 5:30–8:30 PM. There are about as many types of pancakes (more than 80) served here as you could think of, and then some, ranging from peaches and cream to shredded potato leek with cheese ($5.25–9.75). Dinner could be flatbread pizzas, hearty sandwiches, or . . . pancakes.

🍴 Depot Street Malt Shoppe (802-253-4269), Depot Street, Stowe Village. A consciously '50s decor with a reasonably priced menu to match, a great lunch stop with old-style fountain treats like malted frappes, egg creams, and banana splits.

In Waterbury

Michael's on the Hill (802-244-7476), Route 100 between Waterbury and Stowe. Michael's is the new kid in town, and already this is a local favorite. You might dine on skillet chicken with buttermilk Vidalia onion rings and wilted greens ($15.95) or a whole lobster with leeks and corn ($28.95). In general, entrée prices run $15–30, with the menu adapted frequently to seasonal foods. Piano

music is offered on Friday and Saturday nights. Dinner 5–9; closed Tuesday.

Mist Grill (802-244-2233), 95 Stowe Street. Open daily. Baked goods and coffee 6:30 AM–4 PM; breakfast 7–10:30; lunch 11–2:30; daily dinner 5:30–9; Sunday dinner 5–8. Housed in a vintage-1807 mill, this wonderful, scenic restaurant offers good atmosphere and better food. Lunch features soups, salads, grilled panini, sandwiches, burgers, and cold cuts. Excellent bistro fare is served from 5:30 on, and reasonably priced Sunday-night suppers are family-style, a choice of four entrées—maybe roast chicken, beef Burgundy, polenta lasagna, and seafood risotto.

Arvad's (802-244-8973), 3 South Main Street. Open daily 11:30–11:30. A great way stop (just off I-89, exit 10) with attractive brick-walls-and-hanging-plants decor, varied lunch and dinner menus, a full bar. Dine on pasta primavera ($12) or chicken, beef, pork, or shrimp stir-fry ($13). Nightly specials; try the Cabot fries (made with the local cheddar).

✳ Entertainment

Stowe Cinema (802-253-4678), at the Stowe Center, Route 108. Standard seats as well as a bar viewing area for first-run films.

The Lamoille County Players (802-888-4507) stage plays at the Hyde Park Opera House, Hyde Park.

Stowe Theater Guild (802-253-3961), staged upstairs at the Akeley Memorial Building in Stowe Village, offers a series of summer musicals and Broadway favorites.

Stowe Performing Arts (802-253-7792) presents a series of three summer Sunday-evening concerts followed by three **Vermont Mozart Festival** concerts held in the natural amphitheater of the Trapp Family Meadow. Patrons are invited to bring a preconcert picnic. The setting is spectacular, with the sun sinking over Nebraska Notch.

APRÈS-SKI There are reputedly 50 bars in Stowe. Along the Mountain Road, look for après-ski action at the **Matterhorn** (802-253 2800), with live music every weekend during ski season. **Charlie B's,** at Stoweflake, is also usually lively, as is **Mr. Pickwick's Pub,** source of one of Vermont's largest selections of beers (the better to wash down its steak-and-kidney pie).

✳ Selective Shopping

ARTISANS **Stowe Craft Gallery, Shimmering Glass & Design Center** (802-253-4693), Mountain Road, Stowe. Outstanding crafts from throughout the country including contemporary crafts, jewelry, and wearables. The interior design showroom features lighting, rugs, hardware, and furniture.

Little River Hotglass Studio & Gallery (802-253-0889), 593 Moscow Road, Moscow. We are kicking ourselves for not stocking up on the lovely, reasonably priced glass Christmas balls that Michael Trimpol creates in this small and very attractive studio just off Route 100. The specialty is exquisite colored glass creations: weights, bowls, balls, and perfume bottles. Open to the public Thursday through Sunday.

Ziemke Glass Blowing Studio (802-244-6126), Route 100, Waterbury Center. Showroom open daily

10–6. Glass is usually blown Thursday through Sunday.

Stowe Gems (802-253-7000), in the village near the Helen Day Art Center. Barry Tricker polishes and sets exquisite stones, including tanzanite, tourmaline, Tahitian pearls, and freshwater pearls.

Samara's Cards & Gifts (802-253-8318), Red Barn Shops, Mountain Road, Stowe. An exceptional selection of work by Vermont artisans: quilts, soft sculpture, jewelry, wooden toys, batik, stained glass, and more.

Vermont Clay Studio (802-244-1126), Route 100, Waterbury, open daily 10–6. Pottery sold, made, and taught.

Vermont Rug Makers (802-253-6288), Stowe Village. A branch of the Johnson store: distinctive, locally handwoven rugs and hangings, also a stock of imported Turkish and Oriental rugs.

Moriarty Hat & Sweater Shop (802-253-4052), Stowe. Many long years ago, Mrs. Moriarty began knitting caps for Stowe skiers, and her distinctive style caught on. It is now widely imitated, but the originals remain a Stowe tradition.

FOOD AND DRINK **Cabot Annex Store** (802-244-6334), 2653 Waterbury–Stowe Road (Route 100), Waterbury, 1.4 miles north of Ben & Jerry's, in the same complex as Lake Champlain Chocolates (see below). Open daily, year-round. While the prizewinning cheese isn't made here, this is its major showcase, displaying a full line of dairy products (plenty of samples), along with other Vermont specialty foods and crafts. Also in the annex store are **Lake Champlain**

Chocolates (802-241-4150), the chocolate maker that started out in Burlington, and the **Vermont Teddy Bear Co.,** makers of those gift bears. Open 9–6 daily.

Cold Hollow Cider Mill (802-244-8771; 1-800-3-APPLES), Route 100, Waterbury, is one of New England's largest producers of fresh apple cider; visitors can watch it being pressed and sample the varieties. The retail stores in this big red barn complex stock every conceivable kind of apple jelly, butters, sauces, natural fruit preserves, honey, pancake mixes, pickles, and mustards, plus Vermont books and other gifts. Open daily 8–6, year-round.

OTHER Bear Pond Books (802-253-8236), Depot Building, Stowe Village. Open daily. An excellent full-service bookstore; calendars, cassettes, and cards, too.

Brick House Book Shop (802-888-4300), Stagecoach Road, Morristown Corners. Open daily except Monday. Proprietor Alexandra Heller has amassed 70,000 old books, fiction and nonfiction, hardcover and paperback. She also offers a search and mail service.

Shaw's General Store (802-253-4040), 54 Main Street, Stowe Village. Established in 1895 and still a family business, a source of shoelaces and cheap socks as well as expensive ski togs and Vermont souvenirs.

Lackey's Variety Store (802-253-7624), Main Street, Stowe Village, open 8:30–8:30 daily. An 1840s building that has housed many enterprises and is now "just a variety store," according to Frank Lackey, its owner of more than 48 years. An anomaly in this resort village, it still stocks nail clippers, india ink, shoe polish, scissors, not to mention patent medicine and magazines. The walls are hung with posters for 1930s ocean liners and long-vanished local movie houses and lined with antique bottles, boxes, and other fascinating ephemera.

Stafford's Country Store and Pharmacy (802-253-7361), Main Street, Stowe Village. The village's full-service pharmacy (parking in the rear), also a selection of European music boxes, toys, books, and Vermont products.

Stowe Street Emporium (802-244-5321), 23 Stowe Street, Waterbury. A large, eclectic selection of clothing and gifts.

Fly Rod Shop (802-253-3964), 954 South Main Street, Stowe, carries a full line of name-brand fishing gear. Bob Shannon also offer full- and half-day instructional tours.

Straw Corner Mercantile (802-253-3700), Mountain Road, Stowe. Folk art, Americana gifts, and decorative accessories. Shaker boxes, Nantucket baskets, cards, calendars, boxes, and earthenware.

Misty Meadows Herb and Perennial Farm (802-253-8247), 785 Stagecoach Road, Stowe. Open mid-May through fall, 9–5 daily. Display gardens feature herbs and perennials in a farm setting; also potpourri, everlasting wreaths, seasonings, and herbs.

Nebraska Knoll Sugar Farm (802-253-4655), 256 Falls Brook Lane, Stowe. The sugarhouse is open in-season, and syrup and maple cream are available year-round. We advise calling before, especially in winter when the steep back road (especially if you come via Trapp's) is four-wheel-drive only (we chickened out three-fourths of the way there).

See also the Johnson Woolen Mills in "North of the Notch and the Lamoille Valley"; the short and scenic drive there is certainly worth the effort.

✳ Special Events

Mid-January: **Winter Carnival** is one of the oldest and most gala village winter carnivals in the country—a week of snow sculptures, sled-dog races, ski races, public feeds.

Last weekend of February: **Stowe Derby,** the country's oldest downhill/cross-country race—a 10-mile race from the summit of Mount Mansfield to Stowe Village, which usually attracts about 300 entrants.

Easter: **Easter parade** at Spruce Peak; **Easter egg hunt.**

May: Lamoille County Players present **musicals** at the Hyde Park Opera House.

Late June: **Stowe Flower Festival.**

July 4: **Parades, fireworks, Stowe Marathon,** the world's shortest marathon; separate festivities in the village of Moscow, too small for its own band, so they parade to the music of radios.

Mid-July: **Stoweflake Hot-Air Bal-loon Festival,** Stowe Country Club. **International Food and Wine Festival,** Stoweflake Resort Field.

Late July: **Stowe Performing Arts Summer Festival,** a week of concerts ranging from chamber to symphony music, including bands and choral groups, presented in a number of places. **Lamoille County Field Days,** a weekend agricultural fair in Morrisville—tractor pulling, crafts, children's rides.

Early August: Annual **antique and classic car show,** 3 days.

Late August: Lamoille County Players stage a **musical** in the Hyde Park Opera House.

Second weekend of October: **Stowe Foliage Art & Craft Festival** (802-253-7321), Stowe Events Field. Three days of juried art and fine crafts from 160 exhibitors, wine tasting, music, magicians, and a special "off the grid" section.

Pre-Halloween: **Lantern Tours.** Carry a candlelit lantern while taking a "ghost walk" through Stowe, hearing tales of the village's resident ghosts. Tuesday through Thursday and Saturday nights at 8, September 13 through November 1. Walks begin at the visitors center on Main Street (802-244-1173).

NORTH OF THE NOTCH AND THE LAMOILLE VALLEY

Vermont's most dramatic road winds up and up from Stowe through narrow, 2,162-foot-high Smugglers Notch, then down and around cliffs and boulders. Just as it straightens and drops through woodland, motorists are startled by the apparition of a condominium town rising out of nowhere (Smugglers' Notch Resort, a self-contained, family-geared village that accommodates some 2,000 people). However, as Route 108 continues to descend and finally levels into Jeffersonville on the valley floor, it's clear that this is a totally different place from the tourist-trod turf south of the Notch. This is the Lamoille Valley.

Smugglers Notch, as well as the village of Jeffersonville, is in Cambridge, one of several towns worth exploring along the Lamoille River. Jeffersonville has been a gathering place for artists since the 1930s, and Johnson, 9 miles west along Route 15, is also now an arts center. It's easy to see why artists like this luminous landscape: open, gently rolling farm country. The Lamoille River itself is beloved by fishermen and canoeists, and bicyclists enthuse about the little-trafficked roads.

While Smugglers Notch is the more dramatic approach, the prime access to the Lamoille Valley region is Route 100, the main road north from Stowe, which joins Route 15 (the major east–west road) at Morrisville, the commercial center for north-central Vermont. Just west on Route 15 is Hyde Park, the picturesque county seat, famed for its year-round theater.

North of the Lamoille Valley is the even less-trafficked Missisquoi River Valley, and between the two lies some beautiful, very Vermont country.

GUIDANCE Stowe–Smugglers Notch Regional Marketing Organization (1-877-247-8693; www.stowesmugglers.org), Morrisville, is a source of information for the entire region.

Lamoille Valley Chamber of Commerce (802-888-7607), P.O. Box 445, 43 Portland Street, Morrisville 05661. The office in the Tegu Building in Morrisville is open year-round. A summer information booth is at the junction of Routes 15 and 100 at the Morrisville Mobil station; open May through October.

GETTING THERE *By air:* See "Burlington Region." Given 48 hours' notice, Smugglers' Notch Resort arranges transfers for guests.

By train: **Amtrak** stops at Essex Junction (1-800-872-7245).

By car: When the Notch is closed in winter, the route from Stowe via Morrisville is 26 miles, but in summer via Route 108 it's 18 miles from Stowe.

MEDICAL EMERGENCY Emergency service is available by calling **911**.

✳ To See

Smugglers Notch. During the War of 1812, Vermonters hid cattle and other supplies in the Notch prior to smuggling them into Canada to feed the British army—which was fighting the U.S. Army at the time. A path through the high pass has existed since Native American days, but it wasn't until 1910 that the present road was built, which, with its 18 percent grade, is as steep as many ski trails and more winding than most. Realizing that drivers are too engrossed with the challenge of the road to admire the wild and wonderful scenery, the state's Forests and Parks Department has thoughtfully provided a turnoff just beyond the height-of-land. An information booth here is staffed in warm-weather months; this is a restful spot by a mountain brook where you can picnic, even grill hot dogs. The Big Spring is here, and you can ask about hiking distances to the other local landmarks: the Elephant Head, King Rock, the Hunter and His Dog (an outstanding rock formation), Singing Bird, the Smugglers Cave, Smugglers Face, and the natural reservoir. See the "Stowe and Waterbury" chapter for details about the easy trail to Sterling Pond and about the trail to the Elephant Head.

NAVIGATING SMUGGLERS NOTCH

Kim Grant

COVERED BRIDGES *In and around Jeffersonville:* Look for the **Scott Bridge** on Canyon Road across the Brewster River near the old mill that's now Kelly's Restaurant; the 84-foot-long bridge is 0.1 mile down the road. To find the **Poland Bridge** (1887) from the junction of Routes 108 and 15, drive north and turn onto Route 109, angling off on the road along the river; the bridge is in 0.2 mile. Heading west on Route 15 toward Cambridge Village, look for Lower Valley Road; the **Gates Farm Bridge** (1897) is a few hundred feet from where the present road crosses the river.

In Waterville and Belvidere: Back on Route 109, continue north to Waterville and, at Waterville Town Hall (on your right), turn left; the **Church Street Bridge** (1877) is in 0.1 mile. Back on Route 109, continue north; the **Montgomery Bridge** (1887) is east of the highway, 1.2 miles north of town hall. Go another 0.5 mile north on Route 109 and turn right; the **Kissin' Bridge** (1877) is in 0.1 mile. Continue north on Route 109, and 1.5 miles from the Waterville Elementary School (just after the bridge over the North Branch), turn left and go 0.5 mile to the **Mill Bridge** (1895). Back on Route 109, continue north 0.9 mile and turn left to find the **Morgan Bridge** (1887). See the "Jay Peak Area" chapter for a description of six more covered bridges another dozen miles north in Montgomery.

In Johnson: Take Route 100C north from its junction with Route 15 for 2.6 miles and turn right; the **Scribner Bridge** (around 1919) is 0.3 mile on your right.

Note: For detailed descriptions of all these sites, see *Covered Bridges of Vermont,* by Ed Barna (The Countryman Press).

GALLERIES Mary Bryan Memorial Art Gallery (802-644-5100), Main Street, Jeffersonville. Open daily 11–5. Built by Alden Bryan in memory of his wife and fellow artist, Mary Bryan, this mini museum has changing exhibits featuring artists who have worked in Jeffersonville.

Vermont Studio Center (802-635-2727), Johnson. Over the past 16 years this nonprofit center has absorbed 20 buildings in the village of Johnson. The lecture hall is a former meetinghouse, and the gallery, exhibiting the work of artists in residence, is in a former grain mill one street back from Main, down by the river. Some 50 professional artists and writers from throughout the country are usually here at any given time. They come to take advantage of the studio space and the chance to learn from each other through lectures and critiques. Inquire about gallery openings and evening slide shows and lectures.

Dibden Center for the Arts (802-635-2356), Johnson State College, Johnson. Open during the academic year, Tuesday through Saturday 10–3. Changing solo and group shows.

SCENIC DRIVES Four loop routes are especially appealing from Jeffersonville:

Stowe/Hyde Park (44-mile loop). Take Route 108 through Smugglers Notch to Stowe Village, drive up the old Stagecoach Road to Hyde Park (be sure to see the old Opera House), and head back through Johnson.

Belvidere/Eden (40-mile loop). From Jeffersonville, Route 109 follows the North Branch of the Lamoille River north to Belvidere Corners; here take Route 118, which soon crosses the Long Trail and continues to the village of Eden. Lake Eden, 1 mile north on Route 100, is good for swimming and boating; return on Routes 100, 100C, and 15 via Johnson.

Jericho/Cambridge (38-mile loop). From Jeffersonville, drive southwest on Pleasant Valley Road, a magnificent drive with the Green Mountains rising abruptly on your left. Go through Underhill Center to the junction with Route 15. At Route 15, either turn right to head back to Cambridge or continue south on Jericho Center Road; return via Jericho and Route 15 to Cambridge Village, then drive back along Route 15 to Jeffersonville.

Jeffersonville/Johnson (18-mile loop). From the junction of Routes 15 and 108, head north on Route 108, but turn onto Route 109 (note the Poland Covered Bridge on your right). Take your first right, Hogback Road, which shadows the north bank of the Lamoille River most of the way into Johnson. Return via Route 15.

HISTORIC HOUSE **The Noyes House Museum** (802-888-7617), Route 100, Morrisville. Open mid-June until September, 1–5 or by appointment. Suggested donation: $3 adult, $1 student. The 18 rooms of this brick, Federal-style house are furnished and filled with varied memorabilia, including an 1,800-piece pitcher and Toby jug collection.

✳ To Do

BICYCLING *Rentals:* Mountain bike rentals are available in Jeffersonville at **Foot of the Notch Bicycles** (802-644-8182) and in Morrisville at **PowerPlay Sports** (802-333-6557), Route 100.

Bicycle touring: **Smugglers Notch Inn** (802-644-2412). The owners can help with local bike routes. **Mannsview Inn** (802-644-8321) offers canoeing/cycling packages.

The **Cambridge Greenway** recreation path runs 1.3 miles along the Lamoille River from Jeffersonville east.

Missisquoi Valley Rail Trail, a 26.5-mile-long recreation path, traverses the northern tier of this region, following the Missisquoi River from Enosburg Falls to Richford. For a map, call the Northwest Regional Planning Commission (802-524-5989).

CANOEING AND KAYAKING The **Lamoille River** from Jeffersonville to Cambridge is considered good for novices in spring and early summer; two small sets of rapids.

A LANDSCAPE PAINTER IN JOHNSON

Kim Grant

Smugglers' Notch Canoe Touring (1-800-937-6266), based at the Mannsview Inn, Jeffersonville, rents canoes and kayaks and offers shuttle service. Paddles are all flat and Class I water.

Green River Canoe & Kayaks (802-644-8336) operates from its location behind Jana's Restaurant in Jeffersonville. Guided canoe and kayaking trips, also instruction and rentals.

See also Sterling Ridge Resort under *Lodging.*

FISHING The stretch of the Lamoille River between Cambridge and Johnson reputedly offers great fly- and spin-fishing for brown trout.

Smugglers' Notch Resort (802-644-8851) offers twice-weekly fly-casting clinics in-season.

T. J.'s Outdoors (802-888-6210), 81 Bridge Street, Morrisville, offers year-round fishing, archery, and muzzle-loader supplies, and fishing guide service May through September.

GOLF Copley Country Club (802-888-3013), Country Club Road, Morrisville, is a nine-hole course open May through October.

HIKING Prospect Rock, Johnson. An easy hike yields an exceptional view of the Lamoille River Valley and the high mountains to the south. Look for a steel bridge to the Ithiel Falls Camp Meeting Ground. Hike north on the white-blazed Long Trail 0.7 mile to the summit.

Belvidere Mountain–Ritterbush Pond and **Devil's Gulch.** These are basically two stretches of the Long Trail; one heads north (3½ hours round-trip) to the summit of Belvidere Mountain, the other heads south (2¾ hours round-trip) to a gulch filled with rocks and ferns. Both are described in the Green Mountain Club's *Long Trail Guide.*

HORSEBACK RIDING ⚘ **Brewster River Horse Center** (802-644-8051), on Edwards Road off Route 108, Jeffersonville, 1.3 miles from Smugglers' Notch Resort, offers guided trail rides and pony rides for kids from June through mid-October.

LaJoie Stables (802-644-5347), on Pollander Road in Cambridge. Horseback riding offered all year.

LLAMA TREKS Northern Vermont Llama Co. (802-644-2257), 766 Lapland Road, Waterville. Treks depart from the Smugglers' Notch Resort and head into the backcountry. Geoff and Lindsay Chandler offer half-day and full-day treks, depending on the season. Snacks are provided with half-day treks, picnic and snack for full-day outings. Call for rates and to reserve. Family rates available.

Applecheek Farm (802-888-4482), 567 McFarlane Road, Hyde Park. Trek on "wilderness trails," with or without a picnic. Trekking season is spring and fall with a break in the heat of summer.

PICNICKING There are several outstanding roadside picnic areas: On Route 108, 0.2 mile north of the junction with Route 15 at Jeffersonville, picnic benches on the bank of the Lamoille; on Route 108 south of Jeffersonville Village on the east side of the highway; on Route 108 in Smugglers Notch itself (see *To See*); on Route 15, just 1.5 miles east of the Cambridge–Johnson line.

SWIMMING Brewster River Gorge, accessible from Route 108 south of Jeffersonville (turn off at the covered bridge).

Smugglers' Notch Resort (802-644-8851; 1-800-451-8752) features an elabo-rate summer water park with eight heated pools and three water slides in sum-mer and a winter pool.

TENNIS Courts at **Smugglers' Notch Resort,** and a summer program of clinics for adults and children and daily instruction at the TenPro Tennis School.

WALKING The **Cambridge Greenway** recreation path runs 1.3 miles along the Lamoille River from Jeffersonville east.

Lamoille County Nature Center (802-888-4965), Cole Hill Road, Morrisville. Two nature trails offer easy walking and the chance to see deer, bear, and a vari-ety of birds, also lady's slippers in early summer. Inquire about programs offered in the outdoor amphitheater.

✳ Winter Sports

CROSS-COUNTRY SKIING **Nordic Ski and Snowshoe Adventure Center** (802-644-8851), Smugglers' Notch Resort. Narrow trails wind up and down through the trees, then climb meadows away from the resort complex, for a total of 27 km of cross-country trails and 20 km of snowshoe trails; rentals; also tele-mark, skate skiing, and snowshoe rentals; lessons and tours; repairs in the warm-ing hut, where there is cocoa by the woodstove.

Smugglers Notch. The stretch of Route 108 that is closed to traffic for snow season is open to cross-country skiers. Guided tours are offered by the Nordic Adventure Center (see above).

DOWNHILL SKIING ✎ **Smugglers' Notch Resort** (802-644-8851; U.S. and Canada: 1-800-451-8752; www.smuggs.com), Jeffersonville. In 1956 a group of local residents organized Smugglers' Notch Ski Ways on Sterling Mountain, a western shoulder of 3,640-foot-high Madonna. In 1963 a high-powered group headed by IBM board chairman Tom Watson gained a controlling interest and began developing the area as Madonna Mountain, a self-contained, Aspen-style resort. Only two owners later, with 550 condominiums, Smugglers' is a major ski resort sporting a natural snow bowl with a satisfying variety of terrain: beginners trails on Morse Mountain (2,250 feet), some world-class trails and glade skiing on Madonna itself, along with intermediate runs that predominate on Sterling Mountain.

The only way to the summit of Madonna, which commands one of the most spectacular views in New England—from Mount Washington to Mount Mansfield—is a 17-minute ride on the longest (and coldest) chairlift in the East, and the way down can be via some of the region's steepest or longest runs. The ideal time to ski this mountain is early March, when it's relatively warm, and midweek, when it's empty. Obviously, this is a place you come, anytime during ski season, for a 5-day ski week—which automatically includes lessons for all family members. *Lifts:* Six double chairlifts, two surface. *Trails:* 70, including two 3.5-mile trails; 25 percent expert, 53 percent intermediate, 22 percent beginner. *Vertical drop:* 2,610 feet. *Snowmaking:* 60 percent. *Facilities:* Mountain Lodge, base lodge with ski shop, rentals, cafeteria, pub. The reception center/ski shop at Morse Mountain has a Village Center, source of rentals and tickets; the complex also includes a ski shop and deli. Top of the Notch warming hut is at the Sterling chair terminal. Snowboarding. *Ski school:* Group and private lessons at Morse and Madonna, beginners at Morse. Children's ski and snowboarding camp. *For children:* Daycare for kids 6 weeks–3 years. Discovery Dynamos Ski Camp for 3- to 5-year-olds—all day with hot lunch and two lessons, games, and races. Adventure Rangers Ski Camp for 6- to 10-year-olds: all day with hot lunch and two lessons; games and races. The Notch Squad is for kids 11–14. Mountain Explorers Ski Program for 15- to 17-year-olds begins at noon daily; lesson and evening activities; teen center. *Rates:* $54 for a 1-day, three-mountain adult lift ticket; youths 7–18, $38. Kids 6 and under ski free. *Note:* Lodging packages greatly reduce ski-week rates.

ICE SKATING **Smugglers' Notch Resort** rink (flooded tennis courts) is lighted at night as part of its FunZone.

SLEIGH RIDES *&* **Applecheek Farm** (802-888-4482), 567 McFarlane Road, Hyde Park. John and Judy Clark's gentle Belgians, Sparky and Sam, take you through the woods by day or night.

LaJoie Stables (802-644-5347), on Pollander Road in Cambridge. Sleigh rides offered all winter.

SNOWMOBILING **Smugglers' Notch Snowmobile Tours** (1-800-347-8266), Junction Hill Road, Jefferson. Evening 1-hour tours through Smugglers Notch. Customized day tours from 2 to 4 hours. Ride on new Polaris machines.

✴ Lodging

RESORT *&* **Smugglers' Notch Resort** (802-644-8851; U.S. and Canada: 1-800-451-8752; UK: 0800-169-8219), 4323 Route 108 South, Smugglers' Notch 05464. More than 550 condominium units in a variety of shapes accommodate a total of 2,400 people. Geared to families and groups (there are meeting facilities), the resort offers a year-round combination of good things: skiing, swimming (the pool is protected by a heated bubble in winter), tennis, and a varied program of summer activities, including a supervised children's schedule of fishing, horseback rides, movies, hikes, and games. Summer tennis and other packages are offered. The resort excels at catering to children, with a variety of very distinct facilities and programs geared to different ages. Treasures, the nursery for newborns and tots, is particularly impressive, as is the program for teens. In winter a Club Smugglers' 5-day ski week includes lodging, skiing, snowboarding, lessons, use of the FunZone, pool, tubing, a dinner out, and other extras from $125 per adult per day, from $109 per youth (7–17); kids 6 and under, free. In summer a comparable program, including Familyfest Camp Programs for youngsters, begins at $1,535 per week for a two-child family. Add 14 percent for combined state tax and service charge. *Note:* Condominium units are all individually owned and vary from fairly basic (just what you want with kids) to luxury units with TV as well as Jacuzzi in the bath. Units also vary widely in location, from roadside to slope-side to up in the woods.

INNS AND BED & BREAKFASTS

Smugglers Notch Inn (802-644-2412; out of state: 1-800-845-3101), 55 Church Street, P.O. Box 280, Jeffersonville 05464. Dating in part from the 18th century, this is a comfortable village inn that's been gentrified without losing its old-fashioned appeal. The living room retains its decorative tin ceiling as well as its brick fireplace, and remains a casual, inviting space with plenty of books and games. A fully licensed, half-circular bar with a copper footrail fills a corner on the way to the columned dining room, which is hung with paintings by artists who have stayed here over the years, a good place for weddings and reunions. The 11 guest rooms all have private bath and country quilts; the room we slept comfortably in was warmed by a gas fireplace. Facilities include an outdoor hot tub and swimming pool. Dining is as simple as walking next door to the Hungry Lion or Lion's Den Pub (see *Dining Out*). Innkeepers Paul, Roberta, and Lori will hand out maps of good local bike routes. $60–125 per room includes a full breakfast.

✍ **Sterling Ridge Resort** (802-644-8265; 1-800-347-8266; www.vermont cabins.com), 155 Sterling Ridge Drive, Jeffersonville 05464. There has been a lot of recent development at Sterling Ridge, including Pond House, a four-bedroom farmhouse that's great for families ($140–220 per night). The main inn, built in 1988, has been divided into three- and four-bedroom suites ($120–200 per night). Back beyond the pond, Scott and Susan Peterson have built 18 one- and two-bedroom log cabins ($80–115 per night, with a 2-night minimum stay), each nicely designed with a fireplace, cathedral ceiling, fully equipped kitchen, and outdoor grill. The inn's 80 acres are webbed with 20 km of trails; facilities include a hot tub and outdoor pool. Mountain bikes are available, and the Petersons own and operate Green River Canoe & Kayaks.

∞ ✿ **Mannsview Inn** (802-644-8321; 1-888-937-6266; www .mannsview.com), 916 Route 108 south, Jeffersonville 05464. The most popular spot in the house is the solarium, a greenery-filled dining area off the open kitchen with a view of the mountains. There's also a library and a billiards room, year-round outdoor Jacuzzi, and common room with big-screen TV. Kelley and Bette Mann offer canoe trips on the Lamoille River. Five guest rooms with private bath, plus two suites with fireplace and Jacuzzi, one of which is appropriate for families. Rates range $65–185 per room double occupancy, with breakfast included. Pets can be housed in a kennel on the premises, and children over 8 are allowed.

Jefferson House (802-644-2030; 1-800-253-9630), 71 Main Street, Jeffersonville 05464. Deborah Brundage offers three bedrooms in a Victorian village house with original woodwork throughout, also a wraparound porch with swings and an upstairs deck. $60–85 double with complete breakfast.

∞ ✍ **Fitch Hill Inn** (802-888-3834; 1-800-639-2903; www.fitchhillinn

.com), 258 Fitch Hill Road, Hyde Park 05655. Handy to many parts of the North Country, this hilltop house owned by Sharon and Gary Coquillette is elegantly maintained. There are six guest rooms, each with private bath and each named for a state (our favorite is Vermont), all nicely furnished and equipped with ceiling fans; three of them can accommodate more than two people. There is ample common room, an outdoor hot tub, and a library of videos for the VCR. $135–205 in high season, $85–155 in low season, includes a full breakfast.

Three Mountain Lodge (802-644-5736), Route 108, Smugglers' Notch Road, Jeffersonville. Originally built in 1966 by the University of Vermont for its outing club, the lodge later housed the UVM and Johnson State College ski teams. It's now primarily a restaurant (see *Eating Out*), but Steve and Colleen Blood now offer a guest cottage adjacent to the lodge for travelers looking for comfortable private accommodations. Nightly rates for the cottage range $65–85 with a maximum occupancy of four.

⊙ ♿ **The Governor's House in Hyde Park** (802-888-6888; 1-866-800-6888; www.onehundredmain .com), 100 Main Street, Hyde Park 05655. Suzanne Boden has completely restored this home to reflect the periods of 1893—when the house was built—and 1759 when the Longfellow House, after which it was designed, was built in Cambridge, Massachusetts. There are seven guest rooms with private bath; a handicapped guest room will be added in 2004. Boden serves an elegant afternoon tea in the library on Thursday and Sunday and alfresco suppers on the lawn when there is a production

at Hyde Park Opera House across the street. Guests are invited to arrive early for lemonade and croquet on the lawn or simply to sit on the back portico and enjoy hors d'oeuvres (BYOB) as the sun sets behind the mountains. Rates range $110–185, including full breakfast.

Village Victorian (802-888-8850; 1-866-266-4672; www.villagevictorian .com), 107 Union Street, Morrisville 05661. An 1890s Victorian in the village of Morrisville, just 7 miles from Stowe. All four guest rooms have queen bed and private bathroom, with a TV/VCR combo in each. Rates of $70–100 include full breakfast.

Also see Berkson Farms in "The Northwest Corner."

TOWN HOUSES Notch Glen Rentals (802-644-5370; www.notch glenrentals.com), 150 Chez Lane, Jeffersonville 05464. Tastefully appointed townhouse units with panoramic views of Smugglers Notch and Mount Mansfield. Available as one-, two-, or three-bedroom units equipped with a full kitchen, dining and living room, and satellite and/or cable TV. One bedroom is available as a separate efficiency with full bath, king-sized bed, and kitchenette, or included as a third bedroom. Located on Route 108 south just 3 miles from Smugglers' Notch Resort, Notch Glen is convenient to antique barns, fine-arts studios, and several gift shops. Rates by the week, the month, or the year.

MOTEL Sunset Motor Inn (802-888-4956; 1-800-544-2347), at the junctions of Routes 100 and 15, Morrisville 05661. Fifty-five comfortable units with easy access to several ski areas and an outdoor pool. The

Charlmont Restaurant is right next door. Rates $54–92.

Brewster River Campground (802-644-2126), 110 Campground Drive, off Route 108, Jeffersonville 05464. Just 20 "low-tech" tent sites, a tepee, and several lean-tos on 20 secluded acres with a fire pit and picnic tables, a modern bathhouse (hot showers); no pets (but there's a local kennel). Tent sites are $20 per night; a lean-to is $30.

✳ Where to Eat

DINING OUT **Hearth & Candle** (802-644-8090), Smugglers' Notch Resort, Jeffersonville. Housed in a New England–style house, one of the first structures built in the condo village, this is the most formal place to eat in town. The atmosphere is upscale English pub. Moderate.

Hungry Lion Restaurant (802-644-5848), at the Smugglers Notch Inn, Route 108 between Jeffersonville and Smugglers. Open daily 4–closing. This restaurant does a full menu of pasta, beef, seafood, poultry, and vegetarian dishes. Entrées range $8–23. Maple-marinated pork chops are a specialty of the house. The **Lion's Den Pub** features microbrews on tap.

See also Persico's Plum & Main, below.

EATING OUT ❦ **Persico's Plum & Main** (802-635-7596), Main Street, Johnson. Open 6 AM–8 PM weekdays, until 9 Friday and Saturday, 8–1 Sunday. Closed Monday. Culinary Institute of America graduate Pat Persico could be writing his own ticket in Stowe, but this Johnson native would rather serve local folks along with the stray skier and leaf-peeper. The breakfast specials might include apple cinnamon griddlecakes with home fries and syrup, or a bacon, cheddar, and onion omelet. The lunch menu covers the basics, but the ingredients are fresh and locally grown and the soup homemade. The dinner menu changes nightly but could include baked fresh haddock with a spinach seafood stuffing or prime rib of beef. BYOB. Inquire about specialty nights (Mexican or Italian, for example).

Dinner's Dunn at the Windridge Bakery (802-644-8219), 158 Main Street, Jeffersonville. Open daily 7–3 for breakfast and lunch. This was a dry-goods store until it became one of New England's outstanding bakeries and coffee shops. Great breakfasts, and homemade soups and sandwiches for lunch. Breads are still a specialty, along with breakfast omelets.

Melben's Restaurant (802-888-3009), 105 Portland Street, Morrisville. Across from the Bijou Theater, Melben's offers moderately priced Italian specialties and fresh seafood.

♿ **Hilary's** (802-888-5352), Route 100, Northgate Plaza, Morrisville. Breakfast, lunch, dinner, and Sunday brunch are all served in this pleasant place that's good for everything from sandwiches to seafood, from vegetarian dishes to steak. Fully licensed.

♪ **Vermont Starry Night Restaurant and Bistro** (802-644-8884), Route 108, Jeffersonville, across from the Village at Smugglers' Notch. Open daily 4:30–9 except Wednesday. A northern Italian menu featuring pastas, fish, and chicken. Entrées $9.50–25.95. Children's menu. Live music every Tuesday.

♪ **Three Mountain Lodge** (802-644-5736), Route 108, Smugglers' Notch Road, Jeffersonville. The restaurant attached to the Three Mountain Lodge features fresh New England seafood, Black Angus beef, vegetarian entrées, homemade pasta, and homemade ice cream. Daily and seasonal specials. Shrimp scampi is $13.95, veal St. Pierre is $18.95, and the Three Mountain Steak, smothered in mushrooms, is also $18.95.

✔ **Jana's** (802-644-5454), at the junction of Routes 15 and 108, Jeffersonville. Open 8 AM–9 PM 7 days a week. A family restaurant, Jana's has a coloring menu for children and a collection of antique sleds. Try a pita rabbit for lunch and Vermont chicken cordon bleu for dinner. Fried baskets, pizzas, and most staples are served.

Cupboard Deli (802-644-2069), junction of Routes 15 and 108, Jeffersonville. Open 5 AM–10 PM weekdays, 6 AM–10 PM weekends. Good for a wide variety of hot and cold subs, deli chili, pizzas, maple baked beans, and other goodies, especially its maple-frosted cinnamon-raisin bread.

✴ Entertainment

Lamoille County Players (802-888-4507); call for summer schedule of productions.

The Cambridge Arts Council stages theater, concerts, and coffeehouses in Jeffersonville. Check local bulletin boards.

Vermont Studio Center Lecture and Reading Series, Johnson. For a schedule of the frequent presentations by artists and writers, call the center (802-635-2727).

✴ Selective Shopping

ANTIQUES **1829 House Antiques** (802-644-2912), Route 15, Jefferson-

ville (2.5 miles east of the village). Open year-round daily except Sunday. Carolyn and Richard Hover's great old barn is filled on three floors with a wide assortment of country furniture and furnishings representing 40 dealers.

Pocketful O' Posies (802-644-2989), 60 Main Street, Jeffersonville. Located in the old Noble Pearl Building, this center represents more than 30 dealers and consigners.

Smugglers' Notch Antiques (802-644-8321), Route 108 south at the Mannsview Inn. This dairy-barn-turned-antiques-center represents 16 dealers and specializes in custom-made and antique furniture. Open daily May through October 10–5, Friday through Sunday from November through April.

The Buggyman Antiques Shops (802-635-2110; 802-635-7664), Route 15, Johnson. Open daily 10–5. A big old barn and 18th-century farmhouse filled with antiques, including wagons, buggies, and sleighs.

Victorian House Antiques (802-635-9549), Johnson. A multidealer and consignment shop.

By Vermont Hands (802-635-7664), Route 15, Johnson (1 mile west of the village), carries fine antiques and some locally made furniture.

ART AND CRAFTS GALLERIES **Quilts by Elaine** (802-644-6635; www .quiltsbyelaine.com), 127 Main Street, Jeffersonville. Open 9–5 daily except Wednesday. Elaine Van Dusen makes great quilts from crib to king sized as well as wall hangings.

Vermont Rug Makers (802-635-2434), Route 100C east of Johnson, and Main Street in Stowe. Handmade rugs from around the world. Open 10–5 except Sunday.

Milk Room Gallery (802-644-5122), Main Street, Jeffersonville. Alison Earl offers custom framing as well as original artwork by 38 local artists.

Boyden Farm, intersection of Routes 15 and 104, just west of Cambridge Village. The second story of this amazing shop/winery (see below) is filled with exquisite, locally made furniture and furnishings. Local crafts arc also displayed downstairs.

Tegu Gallery (802-888-1261), Portland Street, Morrisville. Open Monday through Friday 8–4:30. A new gallery run by River Arts, the Tegu Gallery exhibits the work of regional artists as well as that created by participants in River Arts' workshops.

FARMS AND A WINERY Boyden Valley Winery (802-644-8151), at the intersection of Routes 15 and 104, just west of Cambridge Village. Open Tuesday through Sunday 10–5 from June through December, otherwise Friday through Sunday 10–5. At this fourth-generation working dairy, bordering the Lamoille River, David Boyden has turned an 1878 carriage barn into a microwinery producing both fruit and grape wines. Wine tours and tastings are offered at 11:30 and 1, and the apple wine we brought home was excellent. Maple syrup and Vermont products and crafts (see above) are also sold. Inquire about farm tours.

Applecheek Farm (802-888-4482), 567 McFarlane Road, Hyde Park. Call before coming. A dairy farm with Holsteins and Jerseys, maple sugaring operation; other farm animals include llamas, emus, draft horses, miniature horses. Picnic with llama treks, barbecue with horse and wagon rides.

SPECIALTY STORES Johnson Woolen Mills (802-635-7185; 1-877-635-WOOL; www.johnsonwoolen mills.com), 51 Lower Main Street, Johnson. Open year-round, daily except Sunday 9–5; open Sunday 10–4 from June through January. Although wool is no longer manufactured in this picturesque mill, the fine line of clothing for which Johnson Woolen Mills has long been known is made on the premises. This mill's label can still be found in shops throughout the country, and its famous, heavy green wool work pants, a uniform of Vermont farmers, are especially popular in Alaska. Although there are few discounts at the factory store, the selection of wool jackets and pants—for men, women, and children—is exceptional. The mail-order catalog is filled with sweaters, wool ties, hunting jackets, blankets, and other staples available in the shop.

Three Mountain Outfitters (802-644-8563). Located at Smugglers' Notch Resort. Seasonal sports clothes for all ages as well as toys, shoes and boots, T-shirts, and accessories.

Marvin's Country Store (802-635-2329), Main Street, Johnson, is open Monday through Saturday 9–5:30, Sunday 11–4. This is the retail outlet for the Marvin family's maple products, plus a variety of Vermont gifts.

The Studio Store (802-635-2203; 1-800-887-2203), Pearl Street, Johnson, adjacent to the Vermont Studio Center. Open Wednesday through Saturday 10–6, Sunday noon–5. A fully stocked artist's supply store, independently owned.

Arthur's Department Store (802-888-3125), Lower Main Street, Morrisville. Arthur and Theresa Breault and their daughter, Adrienne, do their buying in New York and Boston; they have created an unexpectedly fine and friendly source of clothing and footwear for men, women, juniors, and children. The Cellar Shop offers genuine bargains.

Vermont Maple Outlet (802-644-5482), 3929 Route 15 between Jefferson and Cambridge. A nice selection of cheese, syrup, handmade jams, and gift boxes.

Forget-Me-Not Shop (802-635-2335), Route 15, 1.5 miles west of Johnson. This eclectic store carries international military surplus clothing and gear, gift items of all sorts, and famous-label clothing at discounted prices. Open daily 9–9.

✳ Special Events

Last weekend of January: **Winterfest**—primitive biathlon (muzzle loaders and snowshoes).

March: **Marchfest.** Four weeks of special events at Smugglers' Notch Resort—Nordic, alpine races, broomball tournaments, crafts shows, folk dances, snow sculpture, fireworks, ball.

First weekend of June: **Vermont Dairy Festival**—arts and crafts, horse pulling, stage shows, 2-hour Saturday parade, country-and-western jamboree Sunday.

July 4: **Celebration,** Jeffersonville—outstanding small-town parade at 10 AM followed by a chicken barbecue, games, crafts, cow-flop bingo, and a frog-jumping contest on the green behind the elementary school. Evening music and fireworks at Smugglers' Notch Resort, food.

September: **Labor Day Festivities** in Cambridge—barbecue on the green, flea market, family road run (3.1 miles) from Jeffersonville to Cambridge along back roads.

The Northeast Kingdom 6

ST. JOHNSBURY, CRAFTSBURY, AND
BURKE MOUNTAIN

JAY PEAK AREA

THE LAKE COUNTRY

Kim Grant

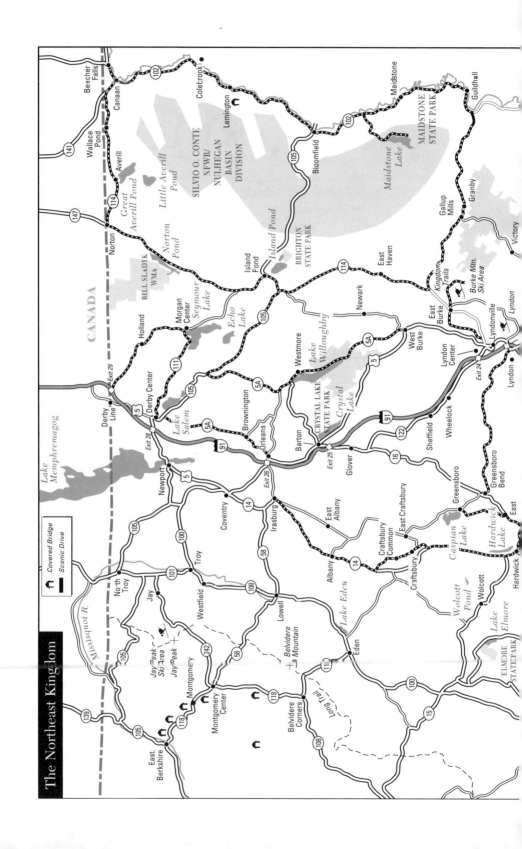

The Northeast Kingdom

Covered Bridge
Scenic Drive

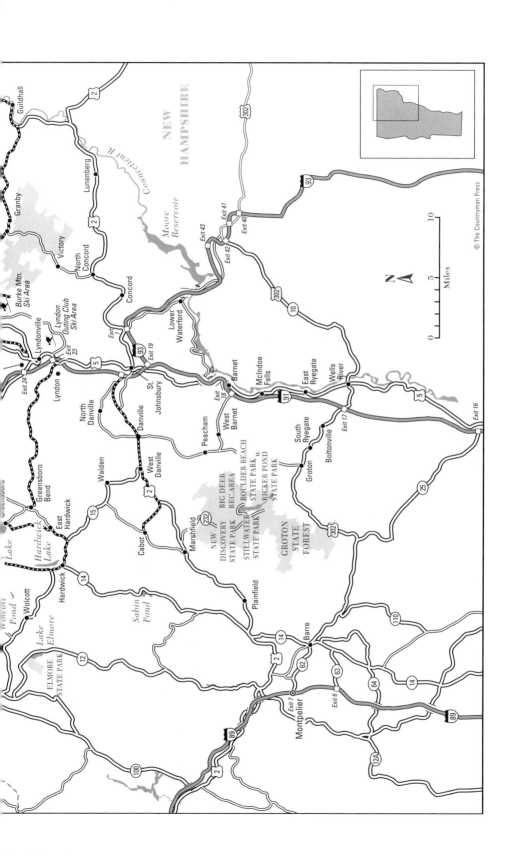

INTRODUCTION

*You know, this is such beautiful country up here. It ought to be called
the Northeast Kingdom of Vermont.*

It was in 1949 that Senator George Aiken made this remark to a group in
Lyndonville. Since then, word has gotten around that that's what Vermont's three
northeastern counties—Orleans, Caledonia, and Essex—should be calling themselves. This is, after all, a world unto itself: the state's most rural and lake-spotted
corner, encompassing more than 2,000 square miles, including 37,575 acres of
public lakes and ponds and 3,540 miles of rivers. Aside from a few dramatic elevations, such as Jay Peak on its northwestern fringe and Burke Mountain at its
heart, this is a predominantly high, open, glacially carved plateau of humped
hills and rolling farmland, with some lonely timber country along the northern
reaches of the Connecticut River.

Neither of the ski areas is large enough to change the look of the surrounding
landscape. In the era of trains and steamboats, there were many more summer
hotels than there are now; yet you can still stay in an unexpected range of

places—from elegant country inns
and full resorts to ski lodges and condominiums, summer cottages and
working farms. And all the amenities
are here: golf, tennis, and horseback
riding as well as plenty of hiking,
fishing, canoeing, and kayaking. Winter sports include ice fishing, tracking
and snowshoeing, some of New England's best snowmobiling, and cross-
country as well as downhill skiing.

Here in this part of Vermont we
feel particularly blessed whenever we
have an excuse to follow farm roads,
because it's in the process of finding
an isolated B&B or craftsperson, a
maple producer or swimming hole

GEORGE AIKEN

that we stumble on the most breathtaking views and people or places of memorable beauty. Frequently we come across traces of the Kingdom's oldest thoroughfare, the 48-mile Bayley-Hazen Military Road, which runs diagonally across the region. It was begun at Wells River on the Connecticut River in 1776 by General Jacob Bayley, and continued in 1778–79 by General Moses Hazen as far as Hazen's Notch (a plaque on Route 58 tells the story). It was a flop as the invasion route but served settlers well after the Revolution when it came time to establish towns in this area. Many communities here boomed in the mid– and late nineteenth century with the advent of railroads.

The Northeast Kingdom has a story to tell. Listen at a lunch counter, in a general store, at a church supper, at a county fair, or during the peerless Northeast Kingdom Foliage Festival. Admittedly it's fading, but you can sharpen your ear with Howard Frank Mosher's beautifully written books—*Northern Borders*, *Where the Rivers Flow North*, and *A Stranger in the Kingdom*. Kingdom-based filmmaker and arts activist Jay Craven has turned two of these into films.

Unfortunately, while this is the single most distinctive corner of the entire state, 2,000 square miles is too large an area to describe without dividing it in three. If you have a particular passion such as canoeing, cross-country skiing, fishing, hiking, or mountain biking, check *To Do* under all three.

GUIDANCE **The Northeast Kingdom Travel and Tourism Association** (802-525-4386; 1-888-884-8001; www.travelthekingdom.com), a nonprofit umbrella organization promoting the area, publishes the useful *Travel Planner* and *Cultural Heritage Tour Map*.

GETTING THERE *By bus:* Check with **Vermont Transit** (1-800-552-8737; www.vermonttransit.com) about schedules to St. Johnsbury from Boston, New York, and Connecticut via White River Junction. At this writing, buses will stop in Lyndonville and Barton on their way north to Newport.

By car: I-93 makes the Northeast Kingdom far more accessible from the southeast than is still generally realized: Bostonians can be in St. Johnsbury in 3 hours. Note that I-91 works like a fireman's pole, a quick way to move north–south through the Kingdom. In snow, beware the high, open, 16-mile stretch of highway between Lyndon Center and Barton known as Sheffield Heights.

MEDICAL EMERGENCY Emergency service is available by calling **911.**

Northeastern Vermont Regional Hospital (802-748-8141), 1315 Hospital Drive, St. Johnsbury. **North Country Hospital** (802-334-7331), 189 Prouty Drive, Newport.

A NORTHEAST KINGDOM FARMSTEAD

Kim Grant

ST. JOHNSBURY, CRAFTSBURY, AND BURKE MOUNTAIN

With a population of less than 7,600, St. Johnsbury is the largest community in the Northeast Kingdom. Thanks to members of the Fairbanks family, who began manufacturing their world-famous scale here in the 1830s, it is graced with an outstanding museum of natural and local history, a handsome athenaeum, and an outstanding academy. The general late-19th-century affluence that St. J (as it is affectionately known) enjoyed as an active rail junction and industrial center has been commemorated in ornate brick along Railroad Street and sloping Eastern Avenue and in the fine mansions along Main Street, set high above the commercial downtown. In the 1960s, when Fairbanks became a division of a conglomerate—which threatened to move the scaleworks south—townspeople themselves raised the money to subsidize a new plant. The point is that this is a spirited community boasting one of the country's oldest town bands (performing Monday nights all summer in Courthouse Park), a busy calendar of concerts, lectures, and plays, and all the shops and services needed by residents of the picturesque villages along the Connecticut River to the south, the rolling hills to the southwest and northwest, and the lonely woodlands to the east. Less than a dozen miles north, the wide main street of Lyndonville is also lined with useful shops. Burke Mountain, a short way up Route 114, is accessible by car as well as by foot in summer and draws skiers from throughout the Northeast in winter.

As Route 2 climbs steeply west from St. J to Danville, a spectacular panorama of the White Mountains unfolds to the east. The village of Danville itself is a beauty, and the back roads running south to Peacham and north to Walden follow ridges with long views. Continue on through Hardwick and north to Craftsbury, where fields roll away like waves to the mountains in the distance.

Craftsbury is a composite of scattered villages, most of which you drive through in a trice. It's Craftsbury Common, with its magnificent common surrounded by white homes, academy, and church, that compels you to stop. Get lost in the surrounding web of well-maintained dirt roads. Eventually you hit a paved, numbered road, and in the meantime you find some of Vermont's most breathtaking farmscape, spotted with small lakes and large ponds. Don't miss Greensboro, an early-20th-century summer compound on Caspian Lake.

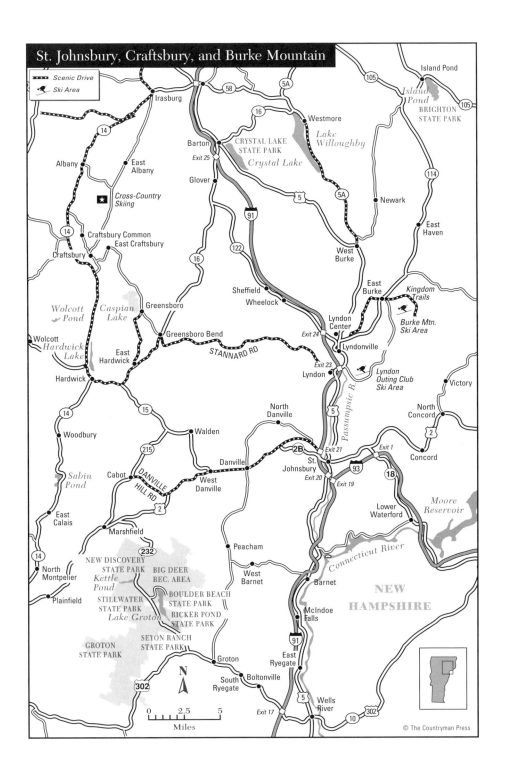

St. Johnsbury, Craftsbury, and Burke Mountain

Scenic Drive
Ski Area

Island Pond

Island Pond

105

BRIGHTON
STATE PARK

Irasburg

58

5A

105

114

14

16

Westmore

Lake Willoughby

Barton

Exit 25

CRYSTAL LAKE
STATE PARK

Crystal Lake

Albany

East Albany

Glover

5

5A

Newark

Cross-Country
Skiing

91

East Haven

Craftsbury Common
East Craftsbury

14

122

West Burke

East Burke

Kingdom Trails

Craftsbury

16

Sheffield
Wheelock

Lyndon Center

Burke Mtn.
Ski Area

Wolcott Pond

Caspian Lake

Greensboro

Exit 24

Lyndonville

Wolcott

Hardwick Lake

Greensboro Bend

STANNARD RD

East Hardwick

Exit 23
Lyndon

Lyndon
Outing Club
Ski Area

Hardwick

14

15

North Danville

5

Passumpsic R.

North Concord

Victory

Woodbury

215

Walden

Exit 21

Exit 1

2

Sabin Pond

Cabot

DANVILLE
HILL RD

Danville

West Danville

2B

St. Johnsbury

Exit 20

93

Exit 19

18

Concord

Moore Reservoir

East Calais

Marshfield

2

Lower Waterford

14

North Montpelier

232

NEW DISCOVERY
STATE PARK
Kettle Pond

BIG DEER
REC. AREA

Peacham

West Barnet

Connecticut River

Barnet

NEW

HAMPSHIRE

Plainfield

STILLWATER
STATE PARK
Lake Groton

BOULDER BEACH
STATE PARK
RICKER POND
STATE PARK

McIndoe
Falls

91

SEYON RANCH
STATE PARK

GROTON
STATE PARK

302

N

Groton

South Ryegate

East Ryegate

Boltonville

5

Wells
River

10

302

Exit 17

0   2.5   5
Miles

© The Countryman Press

GUIDANCE **Northeast Kingdom Chamber of Commerce** (802-748-3678; 1-800-639-6379; www.nekchamber.com), Suite 3, 51 Depot Square, St. Johnsbury 05819. The chamber maintains an outstanding year-round welcome center in its vintage railroad station, open Monday through Thursday 9–6 in summer and fall, Friday, and Saturday 9–8, Sunday 11–3; in winter Monday through Saturday 10–5, Sunday 11–3, a source for lodging, dining, and general information for the region.

✳ Towns and Villages

Barnet (population: 1,690). An old Scots settlement encompassing the villages of McIndoe Falls as well as East and West Barnet and Barnet Center. The village of Barnet itself is on a curve of the Connecticut River, almost lost today in a curious intertwining of I-91 and Route 5. **Goodwillie House** (802-633-2563) in Barnet Center, built in 1790 by a Scottish pastor, served as a stop on the Underground Railroad and now houses the collections of the Barnet Historical Society; unfortunately it's only open by request and on Fall Foliage Day. Drive to West Barnet to find **Harvey's Lake** (good for both fishing and swimming); along the way stop by the 1870s **Ben Thresher's Mill** (open Saturday 10–2 from July through September, and daily during foliage season). The beautiful round red **Moore Barn** sits above the Passumpsic River in East Barnet (north on Route 5 from Barnet). Also see the Karmê Chöling Shambhala Buddhist Meditation Center (www.karmecholing.org) under *Lodging*.

Burke (population 1,571; chamber of commerce: 802-626-4124; www.burke vermont.com). The town includes Burke Hollow and West Burke, but it's the village of East Burke that offers attractive shops, restaurants, and lodging. That's because it's home to Burke Mountain alpine and cross-country ski areas and Burke Mountain Academy as well as Kingdom Trails, best known for mountain biking but also good for hiking and cross-country skiing. Add to all this separate trails for snowmobiling. The library and historical society building (802-626-9823), with its paintings and historical collection, is open Monday, Tuesday, and Thursday 2–5, also by appointment.

Cabot (population: 1,090). Known during the War of 1812 for its distilleries (the whiskey was sold to Canadians), this distinctly upcountry village is now famed for its cheese. The Cabot Farmers Co-op Creamery is Vermont's major producer, and its visitors center is a popular attraction. Cabot is called the mother of the Winooski because the river rises in four of its ponds.

Concord (population: 1,205). Six miles east of St. Johnsbury on Route 2, Concord is a proudly built village with an unusual number of columned houses. The **Concord Museum** (802-695-330) is found upstairs in the tower-topped town hall; there's a picture of St. Johnsbury's Railroad Street, painted in the 1940s, on its stage curtain. A plaque declares this to be the site of the country's first "Normal School" (to train teachers) in 1823, founded by the Reverend Samuel R. Hall, who is also credited with inventing the blackboard. Photos of Concord in the 1890s line the walls in the Mooselook Restaurant east of the village on Route 2. A short way farther along, the 400-acre Miles Pond offers boat access, as does Shadow Lake in Concord Center.

Craftsbury (population: 994). Few places convey such a sense of tranquillity and order as the village of Craftsbury Common. In summer, petunias bloom in the post office window boxes, and the green of the grass contrasts crisply with the white fence. In winter, the general whitewash of this scene contrasts with the blue of the sky. Throughout the year there are nearby places to stay and books to check out at the desk in the new Craftsbury Public Library with its imposing portraits of Ebenezer and Samuel Crafts. Unlike most North Country pioneers, Ebenezer was university educated (Yale, class of 1740). Forced to sell his tavern in Sturbridge, Massachusetts (the still-popular Publick House), due to war debts, he made his way here over the Bayley-Hazen Military Road, eventually bringing his family and 150 of his Sturbridge neighbors this way on sleds. Ebenezer was quick to establish a school here. His son Samuel, a Harvard graduate who served two terms as Vermont's governor, founded the Academy, which still serves as the public high school for the town. The **Sterling College** campus adds to the variety. Many farmers welcome visitors to their sugarhouses during sugaring season in late March and early April and sell syrup from their farmhouses year-round. Inns and B&Bs offer year-round lodging, and Craftsbury Outdoor Center offers one of the most extensive and dependable cross-country ski networks in New England; its summer sculling program is also nationally recognized. The extensive web of well-surfaced dirt roads meandering in all directions is beloved by bicyclists and horseback riders.

Danville (population 2,211). Until 1855, Danville was the shire town of Caledonia County. Its village is exceptionally beautiful, set high on a plateau, with a large green complete with bandstand and Civil War monument. The imposing town hall was built as the county courthouse, and the small, square Passumpsic Savings Bank is one of the safest strongholds around, thanks to devices installed

CRAFTSBURY COMMON

Kim Grant

after it was last held up, in 1935. Danville is headquarters for the American Society of Dowsers. Dowser's Hall (802-684-3417) is open weekdays 9–5; see *To See*. **West Danville** is a crossroads (Routes 15 and 2) village with Hastings Store, a great, old-fashioned general-store-cum-post-office, at its center. One of the world's smallest libraries sits across the road at Joe's Pond (named for a Native American beloved by early settlers), which features a public beach with picnic and sanitary facilities. The water from Joe's Pond is said to empty, eventually, into Long Island Sound, while that from Molly's Pond (a mile south, named for Joe's wife) presumably winds up in the Gulf of St. Lawrence.

Greensboro (population: 770). Shaped like an hourglass, Caspian Lake has a century-old following. The unusual purity of its water is checked three times weekly in-season by its association of cottage owners—who include noted authors, educators, and socialites—all of whom mingle in Willey's Store in the center of Greensboro. There is a public beach and resort facilities maintained by Highland Lodge, also open in winter for cross-country skiing. Greensboro also claims Vermont's oldest (nine-hole) golf course.

Hardwick (population: 3,174; chamber of commerce: 802-472-3397) is a small trading center for the southwestern corner of the Kingdom. Main Street is unexpectedly Victorian, a reminder of the town's heyday as one of the world's largest granite processors. The granite was actually in Woodbury, 5 miles south, whence it arrived by rail. Thousands of skilled European craftsmen moved to town beginning in the 1870s and continuing into the 1920s; a number of French Canadians remain. The Lamoille River runs through town, good for fly-fishing. East Hardwick is also worth finding. **The Hardwick Historical Society** (802-563-2508), housed in the former Hardwick Depot, is open May through September, Monday, Wednesday, and Friday 10–2, and the **Hardwick Town House** (802-472-8800), noted for its hand-painted stage curtains, is a venue for film and live performances, open Wednesday through Saturday 10–3.

THE DANVILLE LIBRARY

Kim Grant

Lyndonville (population 1,227). An up-and-down roll of land encompasses the villages of Lyndonville, Lyndon Center, Lyndon Corner, Red Village, and East Lyndon, and the neighborhoods of Vail Hill, Pudding Hill, Darling Hill, and Squabble Hollow. Lyndon isn't a tourist town, but it offers real, down-home hospitality and five covered bridges. The village of Lyndonville was developed by the Passumpsic River Railroad Co. in the 1860s. Besides a handsome (long gone) station and a number of brick rail shops, the company laid out broad streets, planted elm trees, and landscaped Bandstand Park. **Lyndon**

State College is on Vail Hill (T. N. Vail was the first president of AT&T; he came here to buy a horse and ended up buying a farm, which eventually turned into 20 farms, much of which is now occupied by campus). The **Shores Memorial Museum** (www.shoresmuseum.org; open by appointment: 802-626-1355) in Lyndon Center, the home of Dr. Venila Shores, is now filled with local memorabilia. Lyndonville's famous product is Bag Balm. Band concerts are held Wednesday evenings during summer months in Bandstand Park. The Caledonia County Fairgrounds are the site of frequent events; the Caledonia County Fair itself runs for 5 days in early August.

Christina Tree

Peacham (population: 635). High on a ridge overlooking the White Mountains, this is a tiny but aristocratic village settled just after the Revolution, with a fine new library at the four-corners. Peacham's handsome homes and setting have attracted retired professors, literati, artistic luminaries, and ambassadors. All three Peachams (South, East, and Center) are worth exploring, as are the roads between. The Historical House, an 1820s school, is open July through early October, Sunday and Monday 2–4, also on July 4 and Foliage Day. The latter is when the 1820s blacksmith shop operates and "Ghost Walks," with residents impersonating long-deceased residents, are offered in the hilltop cemetery—which tells its own story and offers one of the best views in the Kingdom any day.

✹ To See

LOCAL ATTRACTIONS The American Society of Dowsers (802-684-3417; www.dowsers.org) is headquartered in Dowser's Hall (open weekdays 9–5), Brainerd Street, just off the common in Danville; the **American Society of Dowsers Bookstore** (802-748-8565; 1-800-711-9497), 430 Railroad Street, St. Johnsbury, sells book about dowsing and dowsing equipment. The ancient art of dowsing is the knack of finding water through the use of a forked stick, a pair of angle rods, or a pendulum. The society has more than 5,000 members throughout the world; its annual convention is held in June at Lyndonville State College. It happens to be headquartered here because in the fall of 1958 some 50 people from different parts of the country congregated in Danville to demonstrate dowsing techniques as part of the Northeast Kingdom Foliage Festival. The founding of the society in 1961 was an outgrowth of these annual demonstrations. Occasional weekend workshops are also offered. In addition to dowsing equipment, the store carries a host of New Age books and tapes on healing,

INSIDE THE ST. JOHNSBURY ATHENAEUM

Christina Tree

MUSEUMS ✎ **The Fairbanks Museum and Planetarium** (802-748-2372; www.fairbanksmuseum.org), 1302 Main, St. Johnsbury. Open year-round, Monday through Saturday 9–5, Sunday 1–5 (closed Monday from mid-October through mid-April). $5 adults, $4 seniors, $3 ages 5–17; $12 families; $3 for planetarium shows, which are Saturday and Sunday at 1:30 year-round. A wonderfully Victorian-style "Cabinet of Curiosities," said to be the oldest science education museum in the nation and the state's only public planetarium, the Fairbanks is much more as well.

"I wish the museum to be the people's school . . . to teach the village the meaning of nature and religion," explained Franklin Fairbanks at the museum's 1891 dedication.

The main hall is capped by a 30-foot-high, barrel-vaulted ceiling, its floor lined with Victorian-style cabinets displaying thousands of stuffed animals: from mice to moose, from bats to bears (including a superb polar bear), birds galore (from hummingbirds to passenger pigeons), reptiles and fish, insects' nests. Founder Franklin Fairbanks was passionate about nature, and the collection represents most native species of mammals and birds as well as many gathered from around the world, a total of 3,000 specimens. The Vermont State Geologic Collection is also displayed, along with an extensive herbarium of New England plants. The balcony, which circles the entire hall level, is lined with historical displays depicting local 19th-century life (including the Civil War) and "ethnological" exhibits drawn from a 5,000-piece collection representing most of the world's far corners. Altogether the museum displays 160,000 objects.

In the planetarium, which seats just 50 people, you learn about the night sky as it appears in the Northeast Kingdom. The museum is also a U.S.

weather observation station, and its daily "Eye on the Sky" forecasts are a fixture of Vermont Public Radio (VPR). The weather station is in the basement, also worth a visit to see exhibits telling the story of the Fairbanks family and their scales. A new interactive kids-geared exhibit opens in 2004. There is

HORACE AND FRANKLIN FAIRBANKS

St. Johnsbury Athenaeum

also a fine little gift shop. The museum archives include a resource library for studies and information about the Northeast Kingdom. There are also ambitious exhibits in the main gallery, changing seasonally. The annual Fairbanks Festival Weekend (late September) features demonstrations of the Kingdom's traditional home industries.

St. Johnsbury Athenaeum and Art Gallery (802-748-8291; www.stjathenaeum.org), 1171 Main Street, St. Johnsbury. Open Monday and Wednesday 9–8, closed Sunday, otherwise 10–5:30. Donation. Completed in 1871 and thoroughly restored in 2003, the athenaeum was conceived and carefully created (not just donated) by Horace Fairbanks, who personally selected the paintings and leather-bound collection of 7,000 books. The art gallery, the big attraction, is said to be the oldest unaltered gallery in the country and has a distinctly 19th-century feel. Smaller canvases and sculptures are grouped around the outsized painting *Domes of Yosemite,* by Albert Bierstadt. Natural light through an arched skylight enhances the effect of looking into the Yosemite Valley. The gallery is at the rear of this fascinating public library, a national historic landmark, which has recently reopened after extensive renovations that included adding 18 feet to the former lecture hall (now open stacks), uncovering arched windows and subtly inserting an elevator, and generally restoring the 1870s look of the galleried reading rooms.

THE FAIRBANKS MUSEUM

chakras, earth mysteries, the esoteric and metaphysical, Reiki, runes, and well-being, not to mention labyrinth T-shirts, crystals, and more.

Bag Balm (802-626-3610; www.bagbalm.com), Route 5, Lyndonville. Developed in 1899 as an antiseptic ointment for cattle, Bag Balm proved particularly effective for chapped udders and is still used by Vermont farmers. In recent years its campy, old-fashioned green tins have begun to appear in Madison Avenue pharmacies and ski resort boutiques, at three or four times the price they fetch locally. The factory is at 184 Williams Street (across the RR tracks and up the hill from the info center in the middle of the village). Tours are offered weekdays, 1–2:20. The company, which has been owned by the same family since 1933, still employs just four workers "on the floor." Bag Balm is sold here, but it's cheaper in Russell's Drugstore, May Store, or Lyndonville Hardware.

✎ **Cabot Creamery Visitors Center** (802-563-2231; 1-800-837-4261; www.cabotcheese.com), Cabot Village (no way can you miss it). Open year-round, daily June through October 9–5, Monday through Saturday the rest of the year, 9–4. Cabot has been judged "best cheddar in the world" at the industry's olympics. Cooperatively owned by dairy farmers since 1919, the center showcases its history with a video and offers a half-hour tour of "Cheddar hall" to view the cheesemaking ($1 per person over age 12 includes samples). The store features all of Cabot's many dairy products, along with other Vermont products. Call ahead to check when cheese is being made and inquire about the week's specials on Cabot products, also about recipes and the Cabot Critters Coloring Book.

DAIRY ASSOCIATION COMPANY, INC.

MAKERS OF

Maple Grove Farms of Vermont (802-748-5141; www.maplegrove .com), 1052 Portland Street (Route 2 east), St. Johnsbury. Open May through October. Guided tours are offered daily 8–4:30 of "the world's oldest and largest maple candy factory." In business since 1915, this is an old-fashioned factory in which maple candy is made from molds. A film in the adjacent museum depicts maple production and displays tools of the trade. A large, neighboring gift store stocks many things besides maple.

Also see *Gardens* under *Selective Shopping*.

COVERED BRIDGES All five within northern Caledonia County are in Lyndonville—one 120-foot, 1865 bridge across the Passumpsic, 3 miles north of town off Route 114; one as you enter town, a genuine 1869 bridge moved from its original site; two in Lyndon Corner (one dating from 1879, the other from 1881, both west off Route 5); the fifth in Lyndon Center on Route 122.

FOR FAMILIES *Note:* The Fairbanks Museum is number one in this category.

✒ **The Great Vermont Corn Maze** (802-748-1399; www.vermontcornmaze .com), Patterson Farm, Wheelock Road, North Danville. Open August and September from 10–5, October from 10–4 (until the second to last Sunday); also 6–9 PM on selected weekends in August and September. Call first if the weather is questionable. $7 ages 12 and over, $5 ages 4–11. The corn maze takes half an hour to more than 2 hours to complete; there's also a "gopher tunnel" and science center. Everyone we've talked to who has found this place has been enthusiastic, but we've also spoken to several people who never did find it. Begin at the blinking light on Route 2 in Danville and head north; it's best to download the map on the web site.

✒ **Maple Leaf Llamas** (802-586-2873), 654 North Craftsbury Road, Craftsbury Common. Open daily year-round. Easy to find. Susan Houston welcomes visitors (call before) to take a walk with one of the couple of dozen llamas housed in her red barns. Farm tours are available, and raw or corded llama fiber is sold.

🐾 ✒ **Stephen Huneck's Dog Chapel and Gallery** (802-748-5593; www .huneck.com), 1356 Spaulding Road, marked from Route 2 east of St. Johnsbury. Open Monday through Saturday 9–5, Sunday 11–4. The full-scale wooden chapel "welcomes all creeds and breeds. No dogma allowed." Seven surrounding acres on "Dog Mountain" are planted in wildflowers, and visitors are welcome to bring (or e-mail) photos of their beloved animals to grace the chapel walls. The gallery, of course, showcases nationally known Huneck's stylish, carved wooden animals and bold, fanciful furniture, panels and jewelry, and books. Dogs welcome.

SCENIC DRIVES **Route 2 West from St. Johnsbury to Danville.** As the road climbs steadily, the White Mountains rise like a white wall in the distance. This actually works better if you are driving east from Danville. Either way, be sure to pull off (there's an eastbound pullout) to appreciate the panorama.

Danville Hill Road. Continue west on Route 2 from West Danville to East Cabot; after Molly's Pond, take the right-hand turn—Danville Hill Road, marked for Cabot. This is a high road with long mountain views; note the Birdman (see *Crafts Shops*) along the way and the Cabot Creamery Visitors Center in Cabot.

Burke Mountain. A 2.5-mile auto road to the summit of Burke Mountain (3,267 feet) commands a sweeping view of the North Country; picnic areas are provided halfway and at the summit. This preserve was formerly the 10,000-acre Darling State Forest, donated to the state in 1933. The road was constructed by the Civilian Conservation Corps. The toll road and campsites in the campground are open May 25 through October 15.

Darling Hill Road from Route 114 in East Burke, 5 miles south to Route 114 in Lyndonville, follows a ridge past a magnificent former estate that once encompassed many old homesteads and still offers great views. The bright yellow 38-room mansion, on a private drive, has been beautifully restored.

Greensboro Village to East Hardwick. The road passes through Hardwick Street (that's the name of the hamlet) and a fine collection of Federal and Greek Revival houses; from Greensboro Village to Hardwick it makes a beeline through high and open farm country; and from Craftsbury Common north to Route 14 through Albany and Irasburg, it follows the rich farmland of the Black River Valley.

Lyndon to Greensboro Bend. An old ridge road with splendid views, 17-mile **Stannard Mountain Road** is unpaved but usually well graveled most of the way. Check locally, though, because there are occasional washouts. The views are best driving west.

✳ To Do

BIKING Craftsbury Outdoor Center (802-586-7767; www.craftsbury.com), Craftsbury Common, rents 21-speed fat-tire bikes and offers instruction and guide service on 200 miles of dirt roads and cross-country ski trails.

Kingdom Trails Association (802-626-0737; www.kingdomtrails.org). The East Burke area is webbed by roughly 100 miles of trails, a composite of systems on Darling Hill, around the village, and on Burke Mountain itself, as well as the Burke cross-country trails, maintained by a conservation organization that includes more than 40 landlords. Pick up a map and a day pass ($6 adult, $3 junior) at **East Burke Sports Shop** (802-626-3215) in the middle of the village. Trails are designated for various nonmotorized uses, but what's famous here are the singletracks for mountain bikers. Hikers have the right-of-way on other trails, but this is clearly mountain biker heaven. Roughly half the trails are maintained for winter cross-country and snowshoe use.

KINGDOM TRAILS IN THE EAST BURKE AREA

Marilyn Pastore

Note: Request the outstanding *Cycling in the Kingdom* map published by the Northeast Kingdom Development Association and available from their web site (www.nvda .net) or from the Northeast Kingdom Travel & Tourism Association (502-525-4386; 1-888-884-8801). Bike rentals are also available from the

Village Shop (802-626-8448) in Lyndonville; "multi-sport vacations," including biking, are offered by **Vermont Adventure Company** (1-866-525-3154; www.vtadventureco.com).

BOATING *Rentals:* **Injun Joe Court** (802-684-3430), Route 2, West Danville; **Harvey's Lake Campground** (802-633-2213), West Barnet; **Village Sport Shop** (802-626-8448), Lyndonville. See also *Camping* and *Canoeing, Kayaking, and Sculling.* This area is pocked with lakes, and launches are shown on the state map.

CAMPING **Groton State Forest** (802-584-3829; www.vtstateparks.com) in Marshfield and Groton. This 25,623-acre preserve offers five separate campgrounds, each an individual state park, all accessed from Route 232. **New Discovery Campground** (802-584-3042) has a total of 47 campsites, 14 of them lean-tos; beach privileges and hiking trails; primitive camping. **Stillwater Campground** (802-584-3822), on the west side of Lake Groton, has a total of 63 tent sites, 16 lean-tos; campers' beach and boat launch; rental boats, dump station. **Ricker Pond Campground** (802-584-3821) has a total of 33 campsites, 22 of them lean-tos, on the south side of Ricker Pond; campers' beach, rental boats, nature trail, dump station. **Big Deer State Park** (802-584-3822) has 28 tent/trailer sites (no hook-ups) near Boulder Beach and Groton Nature Center with many miles of trails. **Kettle Pond** (802-426-3042), on the south side of the pond, has walk-in fishing, group camping, hiking, and snowmobiling. For an overview of Groton State Forest see *Green Space.*

Burke Mountain Campground (802-626-1390; 802-626-3322), a small campground on Burke Mountain with five lean-tos and room for 19 tents, is geared to hikers and bikers.

Also see *Lodging—Private Campgrounds.*

CANOEING, KAYAKING, AND SCULLING East of St. Johnsbury, the **Moore** and **Comerford Reservoirs,** created by dams, are good for canoeing (there are two boat launches in Lower Waterford)—as we found out one evening, listening to birdcalls and watching a baby beaver swim steadily toward a beaver lodge beneath the pines. Below the Comerford Dam, the stretch of the Connecticut River south to McIndoe Falls (now the McIndoe Dam) is excellent, and the portage around the dam isn't difficult. For a canoe-camping guide to the Connecticut from Wells River south, contact the **Upper Valley Land Trust** (603-643-6626).

Other rivers that invite canoeing are the **Passumpsic** and **Moose,** which join the Sleeper at St. Johnsbury. A boat launch on the Moose River can be accessed from Concord Avenue in St. J, and look for a boat launch on the Passumpsic in Passumpsic Village, 5 miles south of St. Johnsbury. **Vermont Adventure Company** (802-525-3154; 1-866-542-7204; www.vtadventureco .com) offers kayaking and canoe tours, rentals on the Connecticut and Barton Rivers, and two secluded lakes and ponds. **Highland Lodge** also has canoes and kayaks for its guests.

Craftsbury Outdoor Center (802-586-7767; www.craftsbury.com), Craftsbury Common, has offered nationally acclaimed summer sculling programs for 27 years. Weekend, 4-day, and weeklong sessions run late May through mid-September. Open to all ages and ski levels. Sessions include tailored coaching, video analysis, demo equipment, and access to the swim beach, massage, nature trails, and mountain biking. $450–900 includes lodging and three daily meals. The center also rents canoes and kayaks for use on Great and Little Hosmer Ponds and on the Black River.

FISHING Fishing is huge here. For regulations, see www.nekchamber.com. Check out **Harvey's Lake** in West Barnet, the **Moore Reservoir, Shadow Lake,** and **Miles Pond** in Concord, **Ricker** and **Levi Ponds** in Groton State Forest, **Lake Elligo** and **Caspian Lake** in Greensboro, and **Little** and **Great Hosmer Ponds** in Craftsbury, as well as the **Lamoille, Passumpsic, Moose,** and **Connecticut Rivers.** Local lakes are also good for salmon, lake and rainbow trout, and perch. There are trout in the streams, too. A handicapped-accessible fishing platform has been constructed in **Passumpsic Village** on the Passumpsic River. The **Lamoille River** in Hardwick is good for trout and perch

Seyon Ranch, a lodge on Noyes Pond in Seyon Ranch State Park (802-584-3829) in Groton State Forest, is a classic old hunting lodge built by wealthy Bostonian Harry Noyes, restored by the state and catering in-season to fishermen, both groups and individuals, offering accommodations for 16 and meals for up to 50; square-trail trout fishing, with flies only, from boats rented at the site. George Willy at the Village Inn in East Burke offers guiding and drift-boat tours.

See also Harvey's Lake Cabins and Campground under *Lodging* and Quimby Country, Seymour Lake Lodge, and *Fishing* in "The Lake Country."

GOLF St. Johnsbury Country Club (802-748-9894; 1-800-748-8899), off Route 5 north, open daily mid-May through October. This is an outstanding PGA-rated, 18-hole course, truly one of the Kingdom's gems. The original nine holes were designed in 1923; nine more were added by Geoffrey Cornish. Amenities include cart rentals and a good restaurant.

SCULLING AT CRAFTSBURY OUTDOOR CENTER
©Amy Wilton Laughing Dog Photography

Mountain View Country Club (802-533-9294), Greensboro, nine holes. Established 1898; open to non-members midweek only. Use of carts permitted only for health reasons.

HAY- AND SLEIGH RIDES On Darling Hill, both the **Wildflower Inn** and the **Inn at Mountain View Farm** offer sleigh rides (see *Lodging*).

HEALTH SPAS St. Johnsbury Academy Field House (802-748-8683), Main Street, St. Johnsbury, has a pool, track, weight room with Nautilus and free weights, and three racquetball courts. These are open to the public at certain hours; call ahead for times and rates.

The Club at Old Mill (802-748-5313), Perkins Street, St. Johnsbury. Indoor tennis, racquetball, aerobics, Nautilus, free weights, sauna, Jacuzzi.

CoachWorks Farm (802-755-6342), Page Pond Road, Albany near Craftsbury Common, is an amazingly sophisticated facility with an indoor lap pool, sauna, steam bath, massage, and weight machines. Day passes are available.

HIKING AND WALKING TRAILS *Note:* See Craftsbury Outdoor Center and Kingdom Trails Association under *Biking.*

Groton State Forest Trail System (802-584-3829). Off Route 232 (which runs north–south, connecting Routes 2 and 302), this 25,623-acre forest is primarily known for camping facilities but also offers an extensive year-round trail system accessing major points of interest. Favorite hikes include the Peacham Bog Natural Area and two trails to the summit of Owls Head Mountain (there's a summer road as well as a trail), where a handsome old CCC wood-and-stone watchtower commands spectacular views. See *Green Space* for an overall description of the forest.

HORSEBACK RIDING DND Stables (802-626-8237) in East Burke. Debby Newland guides riders 12 years of age or older (unless they are experienced) of all abilities on trails that extend from her farm to local snowmobile and cross-country trails, as well as the Kingdom Trails system. Younger children are welcome to ride in the ring. Rides are tailored to the rider (maximum of four) and can be as long as desired ($30 per hour).

Rohan Farm (802-467-3701), East Burke. Brian Kelly offers trail rides and cross-country treks geared to intermediate and better riders over the web of bridle paths on Darling Ridge and the adjacent mountains.

RUNNING Craftsbury Outdoor Center (802-586-7767; www.craftsbury.com), Craftsbury Common, offers 5-, 6-, and 7-day camps late June through July; different sessions focus on training for triathlons, marathons, road racing, Masters running, and just plain fun and fitness. Camps are open to all ages and abilities; $600–800 covers coaching, lodging, and three daily meals.

SWIMMING There are public beaches on **Harvey's Lake** in West Barnet; **Caspian Lake** near Greensboro Village; **Joe's Pond** in West Danville; **Molly's Pond** in Marshfield; **Shadow Lake Beach** (in Glover marked from Route 16); **Miles Pond** in Concord; and within **Groton State Forest,** notably at **Boulder Beach State Park** (802-584-3823; www.vtstateparks.com) and at **Ticklenaked Pond** in Boltonville (off Route 302 west of Wells River). There are also public pools in St. Johnsbury and in Lyndonville.

✳ Winter Sports

CROSS-COUNTRY SKIING Two of New England's outstanding cross-country trail systems are found in this area. Unfortunately, you have to settle on one or the other—given the way the roads run, they're an hour's drive apart.

In the Craftsbury area

Craftsbury Outdoor Center Nordic Ski Center (802-586-7767; www.crafts bury.com), Craftsbury Common, grooms 85 km of its 130 km marked and maintained trail system; it offers rentals, instruction, and lodging packages. The system connects with Highland Lodge (802-533-2647; see *Lodging*) in Greensboro, which offers a total of 60 km of trails, 15 of them well groomed. The only major New England cross-country system that's nowhere near an alpine ski hill, the Craftsbury Outdoor Center/Highland Lodge trails web the kind of red-barn-spotted farmscape that's equated with, but increasingly rare in, Vermont. They traverse rolling fields, woods, and maple and evergreen groves, with stunning views of the distant Green Mountains. Thanks to their elevation and Craftsbury's exceptional grooming, they also represent some of the most dependable cross-country skiing in the Northeast and usually remain skiable well into March and sugaring season. Home to the late-January Bankworth Craftsbury Ski Marathon, one of Vermont's standout winter events. Daily trail passes available.

In East Burke

Burke Mountain Cross-Country (802-626-8338; www.burkexc.com). Groomed trails begin at 1,300 feet and wind through woods that yield to panoramic views. Rentals, lessons, guided tours; 62 km of tracked trails, an 80 km system that connects with the Kingdom Trails network (see *Biking*), some 50 more km of trails that wind through the village and loop along Darling Hill with spectacular views (best accessed from the Wildflower Inn and the Inn at Mountain View Farm). Trail fees required.

CROSS-COUNTRY SKIING AT CRAFTSBURY OUTDOOR CENTER

©Dennis Curran

⊙ ♿ **Seyon Ranch State Park** (802-584-3829; www.vtstateparks.com). This isolated 1890s hunting/fishing lodge deep in Groton State Forest has been winterized and caters to cross-country skiers with 5 miles of groomed trails. See *Lodging*.

See also Hazen's Notch in "Jay Peak Area."

DOWNHILL SKIING AND SNOWBOARDING **Burke Mountain** (802-626-3322; www.skiburke.com), East Burke. "The Vermonter's Mountain" is a big peak with a respectable vertical, known for excellent terrain and reasonable prices. After some bumpy years it seems to be back on an even keel, owned (through an operating company) by Burke Mountain Academy, a prep school for aspiring racers, known for the number of graduates who become Olympic contenders. In recent years snowmaking coverage (abetting a 250-inch annual snowfall) and glade skiing terrain have been substantially increased.

Lifts: One quad chairlift, one double chairlift, one Poma, one J-bar. *Trails and slopes*: 34 trails, nine glades (100 acres). *Elevation:* 3,267 feet. *Vertical drop*: 2,000 feet. *Snowmaking:* 80 percent. *Snowboarding:* Gap Park, a 5-acre technical playland. Snowboarding is permitted on trails. *Facilities:* Sherburne Base Lodge includes a glass-walled restaurant as well as a cafeteria; a mid-lodge serves the upper mountain. Trailside lodging is offered in dozens of privately owned condos (Burke Vacation Rentals: 802-626-1161; Mountainside Property Rentals: 802-626-3548). Also check with the Burke Area Chamber of Commerce (www.burkevermont.com), the best way to compare local lifts and lodging packages, including local motels and B&Bs. *Programs:* Club Den Day Care, open weekends and holiday periods; ski school, rentals. *Rates:* Weekends $45 adult, $35 senior and junior; weekdays $29 adult, $24 senior and junior—but substantially less with lodging.

SNOWMOBILING Given the extent of the trail system, accessibility to the trail from local lodging places, and dependable snow cover, this area is becoming as well known among snowmobilers as it is to cross-country skiers. The trail systems, however, seldom cross. Also see *Snowmobiling* in "The Lake Country."

The Northeast Kingdom Chamber of Commerce (802-748-3678; 1-800-639-6379; www.nekchamber.com) publishes a map listing what's required to sled here and a list of the local clubs from which you must purchase a VAST membership in order to use the trails. Rentals are available from **All Around Power Equipment** (802-748-1413), Route 5 north, St. Johnsbury. Echo Ledge Farm Inn in East St. Johnsbury offers snowmobile storage as well as trail access.

✳ Green Space

Barr Hill Nature Preserve, Greensboro. Turn right at the town hall and go about 0.5 mile to Barr Hill Road (another left). The trails at Barr Hill, managed by The Vermont Nature Conservancy, overlook Caspian Lake. Don't miss the view from the top.

Victory Basin, alias Victory Bog. This 4,970-acre preserve administered by the

Vermont Fish and Wildlife Department includes a 25-acre boreal bog with rare plant life, 1,800 acres of wetlands, 1,084 acres of hardwoods, and 71 acres of clearings and old fields. The dirt road access is via Victory; there are three parking areas: Mitchell's Landing, Lee Hill, and Damons Crossing.

Waterford Dam at Moore Reservoir. New England Power offers guided tours of the huge complex of turbines. There are also picnic sites and a boat launch here. The approach is from the New Hampshire side of the Connecticut River, just below Lower Waterford, Vermont, off Route 135.

In St. Johnsbury

Fred Mold Park, near the confluence of the Passumpsic and Moose Rivers, is a great picnic spot by a waterfall and old mill. **The Arlington Preserve,** accessible from Waterman Circle, is a 33-acre nature preserve with woods, meadows, and rock outcroppings.

Groton State Forest (www.vtstateparks.com). This 25,600-plus-acre forest is the second largest contiguous landholding by the state of Vermont. It's a scenic and rugged place, best known for its five separate campgrounds (see *Camping*) and fishing but also harbors Lake Groton and both Osmore and Ricker Ponds and offers an extensive year-round trail system. The area was intensively logged, beginning in 1873 with the opening of the Montpelier & Wells Railroad that ran through the forest, ending in the 1920s when most of the timber had been cut. Subsequent fires further altered the landscape from evergreens to mostly maple and birch. The naturalist-staffed **Groton Nature Center** (802-584-3823) in **Boulder Beach State Park** (a day-use area featuring a swim beach on Lake Groton), marked from Route 232, is open June through early September and serves as the information source for the forest and the trailhead for the 2.5-mile trail to Peacham Bog. Seyon Ranch State Park (see *Lodging*) is on Noyes Pond in another part of the forest, catering to groups, fishermen, and cross-country skiers.

See also *Biking, Hiking and Walking Trails,* and *Camping.*

✳ Lodging

In the St. Johnsbury area

& **Rabbit Hill Inn** (802-748-5168; 1-800-76-BUNNY; www.rabbithill .com), Route 18, Lower Waterford 05848. Brian and Leslie Mulcahy welcome you to this pillared landmark, an inn since 1795. All 19 rooms and suites are romantic confections, with canopy beds, antiques, and "indulging" bathrooms. Many have working fireplace, Jacuzzi for two, and private porch. All have been painstakingly furnished, complete with a "room diary." Summer swimming and fishing in a freshwater pond, canoeing, and golf privileges; winter cross-country skiing and snowshoeing. $275–435 per couple includes breakfast, afternoon tea, and five-course, candlelit dinner.

🍲 **Broadview Farm** (802-748-9902), 2627 McDowell Road, North Danville 05828. Open Memorial Day through October. This shingle-style country mansion has been in Molly Newell's family since 1901. It's set on 300 acres with a panoramic view of mountains, on a farm road in North Danville that, Molly assures us, was once the Boston–Montreal Road. In the late

19th century, before its shingles and gables, this old farmhouse took in summer boarders, advertising its 2,000-foot elevation as a sure escape from malaria and hay fever. Today the elevation suggests dependable cross-country skiing. Molly has thoroughly renovated the old place, removing 4,000 pounds of radiators, replacing windows, and gutting and redesigning the kitchen, while preserving the fine woodwork, detailing, and maple floors throughout the house. The three guest rooms are furnished with family antiques (check out the great oak set in the Yellow Room). Baths are private or shared; $55–120 double includes a full breakfast.

❧ **The Albro Nichols House** (802-751-8434; www.nekchamber.com/albronicholshouse), 53 Boynton Avenue, St. Johnsbury 05819. This 1840s Federal-style house sits up behind Arnold Park at the head of Main Street, a flowery, quiet setting that's still within strolling distance of St. Johnsbury's museums, galleries, theaters, shops, and restaurants. Margaret Ryan is a former prep school dean and a high school theater director who clues in guests to the Kingdom's cultural scene. The pleasant, square Rose Room with private bath ($80) is on the ground floor; the upstairs rooms (both $60), one with twin beds, the other with a double (this would be a delightful room for a single person, too), share a book-lined sitting room and a bath. Common rooms feature plenty of books and interesting art; a full breakfast is included. *Note:* Rates don't change during foliage season.

✑ **Emergo Farm B&B** (802-684-2215; 1-888-383-1185; www.emergofarm.com), 261 Webster Hill, Danville 05828. Just north of the village, this strikingly handsome farm is a prizewinning, sixth-generation working dairy farm. The upstairs apartment has two bedrooms, full kitchen, sitting room, and bath, ideal for a family or two couples (a pullout in the sitting room sleeps extra kids). Rooms are also available individually with private bath. The farm's 230 acres include a hilltop with panoramic views of much of the Kingdom. Historical and present-day farm tours are offered, and livestock includes Nigerian dwarf goats as well as 130 head of cattle (80 milking cows). $85–140 per room includes a full breakfast, served downstairs in the dining room.

Hamilton House Bed & Breakfast (802-684-9800; 1-866-684-9800; www.thehamiltonhouse.com), P.O. Box 280, Danville 05828. Housing a local bank from 1884 until 1925, this is a handsome house on Danville's handsome village common. There's a hearth in the suitably named Grand Room and a crystal chandelier above the elegant breakfast table, wallpaper on the ceilings as well as walls of the five elaborately decorated guest rooms, each with a private bath and two with gas fireplace. "Elizabeth" is a particularly spacious room with a canopy bed and hearth, and "Abigail" with its sleigh bed is appealing. Your hosts are Shirley La Porte and daughter Nancy Hogue. $109–129 includes breakfast.

❧ **Echo Ledge Farm Inn** (802-748-4750; www.echoledgefarm.com), P.O. Box 75, East St. Johnsbury 05838. Ruth Perkins and her family are your hosts at this bed & breakfast on a farm established in 1793. The five comfortable bedrooms have private baths and are nicely, comfortably furnished. Guests have a wing of the old farmhouse to themselves, a dining area with fridge as well as the living room. Afternoon tea, plenty of books, local menus, and a full breakfast are included in $95. Wine and beer are available. In winter snowmobilers can easily access the VAST Corridor Trail; snowmobile storage is offered (inquire about rentals). The adjacent 200-year-old barn houses antiques and gifts. Paths lead down to the Moose River across Route 2.

The Old Homestead (802-633-4016; 1-877-OLD-HOME; www.theold homestead.com), P.O. Box 150, Barnet 05821. Gail Warnaar plays the oboe and bassoon, sells music for double-reed instruments, and offers five rooms in her 1850s village home, which faces Route 5 and backs on gardens and meadow. Two second-floor rooms (private baths) feature porches overlooking the grounds, while a small first-floor single room with a spool bed (shared bath) is appealing. Common space is comfortable, and musical groups will find rehearsal space. $69–115 includes a breakfast of fruit and fresh-baked bread; reduced rates for weekdays and longer stays.

The Gardeners Rest B&B (802-748-9388; gardenerest@kingcon.com), 682 Daniels Farm Road, Waterford 05819. Brits Margaret and Keith Rowlett are passionate gardeners who are transforming the acres around their vintage 1854 farmhouse into a model English garden, the kind that blazes with color spring through fall and encompasses a shady lane, carefully orchestrated views, pergolas, and a couple of ponds. In all there are 16 acres, much of it in meadow and including a brook. The house sits 0.5 mile off hardtop but just 5 miles from St. J and I-93. It's a beauty, with a downstairs living room (no TV) and bedroom overlooking the garden, also two upstairs rooms with sloping ceilings, all with private bath. $85–115 includes a full breakfast with homemade granola and a hot "savory" or sweet. Not appropriate for children under age 14.

The Inn at Maplemont Farm (802-633-4880; 1-800-230-1617; www.maplemont.com), Route 5, Barnet 05821. Tom and Sherry Tolle's well-kept, large yellow farmhouse sits in a bucolic 43 acres across the road from the Connecticut River. The three guest rooms are pleasant, all with private bath; South Peacham, the ground-floor twin, is particularly attractive. Pet and livestock accommodations are available if you arrange in advance. $80–120 per night includes a hearty breakfast.

Sherryland (802-684-3354), Danville 05828. Caroline Sherry's large, 19th-century farmhouse is on a pleasant country road about a mile south of the village green. Five guest rooms are genuinely homelike. No meals; still only $40 double ($45 for twin beds), $35 single, $5 per cot. Caroline has welcomed generations of guests and says she still enjoys it.

Long Meadow Inn (802-757-2538; 1-800-394-2538), 1886 Ryegate Road (Route 5), Wells River 05081. This stately brick Federal by the river, once a stagecoach stop, is now nicely restored (and extensively fireproofed) by Roy and Ellen Canlon. There are five pretty guest rooms, two with private bath. From $35 (for singles, shared bath) to $65 for a double room with private bath, breakfast included.

In the Burke Mountain–Lyndonville area

⊙⊙ ♂ **The Wildflower Inn** (802-626-8310; 1-800-627-8310; www.wildflowerinn.com), 2059 Darling Hill Road, Lyndonville 05851. This is a fine old farmhouse set high on a ridge with a spectacular view, surrounded by its own 500 acres including gardens and trails maintained for hiking, mountain biking, and cross-country skiing. Jim and Mary O'Reilly have eight children (five boys, three girls), and other children are particularly welcome. There is a big playroom in the main house; a daily (except Sunday) supervised morning arts, crafts, and summer nature program for children ages 4 and up in the big barn; a variety of animals to relate to in the petting barn; a sports complex with basketball, a batting cage, and tennis court and playing field beyond. Adult spaces include an indoor sauna and hot tub, an attractive parlor and library—stocked with games and the kind of books you really want to read. The landscaped pool commands a spectacular view of rolling hills. Dinner is in Juniper's (see *Dining Out*), but for children, there's the option of parent-free dining at Daisy's Diner, a 5:30–9:30 dinner and activity program (summer only). Breakfast is a three-course production, and tea is also served.

Upstairs in the main house, two family suites have great views. There are a total of 24 units (10 rooms and 14 suites), some with and some without views. They include a romantic hideaway with whirlpool bath in the old schoolhouse (with view) and Grand Meadow, a fully equipped two-bedroom retreat with two baths (a Jacuzzi in one) and view. $99–149 for rooms, $129–169 for one-room suites, $149–199 for two-room suites, $169–259 for three-room suites. Rates are per couple B&B plus $25 per teen, $20 per child ages 4–11, and free for ages 3 and under. Singles pay $20–25 less. Christmastime is especially festive here. Ask about special packages.

⊙⊙ ♞ **The Inn at Mountain View Farm** (802-626-9924; www.innmtnview.com), Darling Hill Road, East Burke 05832. Like the Wildflower Inn, this is part of a onetime 9,000-acre hilltop estate owned by Elmer Darling, a Burke native, who built the brick creamery in 1890 to supply dairy products to his Fifth Avenue hotel (it used to churn out 600 pounds of butter a month and 70 pounds of cheese per day). The inn also includes the neighboring "Farm House" and the magnificent red barns and other outbuildings. It's backed by 440 acres that spread across a high ridge and are laced with paths, part of the Kingdom Trails network (see *To Do*) maintained for walking, mountain biking, and cross-country skiing.

AT THE INN AT MOUNTAIN VIEW FARM

Marilyn Pastore

Marilyn Pastore has tastefully decorated the 14 guest rooms (private baths), which are divided between the Creamery and the Farm House with its three "luxury suites," each with fireplace and Jacuzzi. A sauna is accessible to all guests. The centrally air-conditioned Creamery, however, houses the inn's common space: a sitting room with a big old painting of Lake Willoughby, a signboard for the lake's long-defunct dance hall, and a restaurant serving breakfast to guests and open to the public 6 nights a week (see *Dining Out*), featuring seasonal tables set in the perennial gardens and picnic lunches for those who wish. Horse-drawn wagon and sleigh rides are offered, along with donkey walkabouts with two miniature Sicilian donkeys, Molly and Ema. The inn is a favorite for weddings and reunions, given its renovated Morgan barn. $150–235 includes a full breakfast. Pets can be boarded in the barn. Inquire about special packages.

⊚⊛ **The Old Cutter Inn** (802-626-5152; 1-800-295-1943; www.oldcutter inn.com), 143 Pinkham Road, East Burke 05832. Closed April and November. This 1845 farmhouse just minutes from Burke Mountain has been owned and operated by Swiss-born chef Fritz Walther since 1977. It's a spotless, cozy inn with a two-bedroom suite with fireplace plus nine rooms, five with private bath. Its excellent dining room is open to the public every night except Wednesday (when it still serves guests); you can choose between the formal dining room (see *Dining Out*) and a friendly, less expensive pub. The grounds include a heated, landscaped swimming pool and views of Willoughby Gap. The inn can accommodate wed-

ding receptions and rehearsal dinners of up to 44 people. From $69 with shared bath, $79 with private bath, $12 per extra person in room; $175 for a suite. MAP is available, as well as multiday packages; cheaper off-season.

⊚ ⊛ ☀ **The Village Inn of East Burke** (802-626-3161; 802-793-4517; www.villageinnofeastburke.com), Box 186, East Burke 05832. This comfortable, affordable B&B offers many rarely found amenities, like a fully equipped guest kitchen; a truly inviting living room with a fireplace, books, games, and satellite TV; an outdoor Jacuzzi; gardens; and a streamside picnic area. All five rooms have private bath, and some are large enough to accommodate families. Innkeeper George Willy is also a fishing guide who offers drift-boat tours, while Lorraine Willy raises bees and maintains a large organic garden. Both are plugged into all the sporting possibilities of the area. $75 includes breakfast.

⊛ **Branch Brook Bed & Breakfast** (802-626-8316; 1-800-572-7712; bbbb@together.net), P.O. Box 217, Lyndon 05849. This is an exceptional house with long, graceful parlor windows, built in the 1850s, beautifully converted to a B&B by Ted and Ann Tolman. The room with a pencil-post, canopy bed, locally crafted from cherrywood, is worthy of brides; two rooms are tucked under exposed beams, furnished with antiques. All but two of the five have private bath. Prices are $65–85 per couple with a hearty breakfast; Ann Tolman has a food-service background and prides herself on breakfasts prepared on her English Aga cooker. Two of Lyndon's five covered bridges are within walking distance.

Moonlight Inn Vermont (802-626-0780; moonlightinnvt@aol.com), 801 Center Street (P.O. Box 1325), Lyndonville 05851. Shirley Banks welcomes visitors with genuine, western friendliness while Dick Banks is the quiet, capable Vermonter. Their spacious Victorian house on a quiet side street offers comfortable common space and three second-floor guest rooms, one with twins, all with private bath. A serious quilter, Shirley offers lessons and quilting weekends. $85–95 includes a full breakfast.

In the Craftsbury area

🐾 ♪ **Inn on the Common** (802-586-9619; 1-800-521-2233; www.innonthecommon.com), Craftsbury Common 05827. One of the Kingdom's crown jewels is now owned by innkeepers Jim and Judi Lamberti, who established an enviable reputation at the Inn at Essex. The 16 guest rooms are nicely decorated with well-chosen wallpapers, fabrics, antiques, brass and four-poster beds, and original art; five have a woodstove or fireplace, They are divided among three Federal-style buildings, two facing each other and the third one a short walk away, by the village's magnificent common. The main inn also houses an attractive library and one of the region's best restaurants (see *Dining Out*). In summer you can take advantage of the solar-heated pool, the perennial gardens, lawn croquet, and the tennis court. Nearby Craftsbury Outdoor Center is a destination for mountain biking, running, and sculling, and offers some of New England's best cross-country skiing. $240–340 per couple includes a four-course dinner, full breakfast, and gratuity. Pets are $25 by prior reservation.

♪ **Highland Lodge** (802-533-2647; www.highlandlodge.com), Greensboro 05841. Open May 30 through October 16 and December 20 through March 15. A fine, Victorian-era inn, set in 120 acres on the shore of Caspian Lake, that manages to be both airy in warm weather and cozy in winter, now managed by the second generation of Smiths (David, Wilhelmina, and Alex)—hosts whose warmth is reflected in the atmosphere of their public rooms. Common rooms include a comfortable library with desks and armchairs, a game room, a living room with fireplace, and a sitting room with baby grand piano. Upstairs are 11 rooms, all with private bath. There are also 11 cottages (4 remain open in winter). In summer, facilities include tennis courts and a pleasant beach with bathhouse and boats, along with the nature trails on the property and in the adjacent Barr Hill Nature Preserve; in winter the draw is cross-country skiing on the extensive network radiating from the inn's touring center, rising to unusual elevations with superb views. Inside, there is plenty of space to read and get away from other guests, along with nice corners in which to socialize. For children, there's an organized summer program (ages 4–9). $110–145 per person, $35–75 per child depending on age, MAP; inquire about family rates; 15 percent gratuity, as well as breakfast and dinner, is included. Less in May and weekdays in June, September, October, January, and March.

🐾 ♪ **Craftsbury Bed & Breakfast** (802-586-2206; www.scenesofvermont.com/craftsburybb), Craftsbury Common 05827. Open year-round by reservation. Margaret Ramsdell welcomes guests to her farmhouse on Wylie Hill, with views that (even by local standards) are hard to beat. Generally known as Margie's Place, this friendly, informal B&B caters to skiers, bicyclists, and hikers. The two upstairs rooms (sharing a bath) have the longest views, but the four additional ground-floor guest rooms (sharing two baths) are perfectly pleasant. There's an inviting living room, and the door to the big country kitchen—with its glowing soapstone stove, backed by gleaming copper—is always open. In winter (December through early April) guests can ski out the door and onto 100 km of groomed trails maintained by the Craftsbury Outdoor Center. $60–80 includes a full breakfast (maybe cinnamon-apple pancakes or eggs with cheddar cheese).

∞ ♿ **Lakeview Inn** (802-533-2291; www.lakeviewinnbb.com), P.O. Box 95, Main Street, Greensboro 05841. Open March through October. Built in 1872 as a summer boardinghouse by Caspian Lake, this handsome clapboard inn served that purpose right up until the 1980s (it housed the musicians who performed in Summer Music from Greensboro), but it had stood abandoned for 8 years when Kathy Unser and John Hunt took it on, painstakingly restoring it. It has since been added to the National Register of Historic Places. Much of the ground floor is now an informal restaurant (see *Eating Out*), but guests have a downstairs sitting room with a big-screen TV and another inviting upstairs common room with a view of gardens filled with daylilies. The nine attractive guest rooms have private bath, and one is handicapped accessible; a top-floor three-bedroom suite sleeps six.

$135–350 (for the suite) includes a full breakfast.

🐾 **Craftsbury Inn** (802-586-2848; 1-800-336-2848; www.craftsburyinn .com), Route 14, Craftsbury 05826, across from a classic general store in Craftsbury Village. Closed in early November and in April. Billl and Kathy Maire are your hosts at this handsome 1850 Greek Revival–style inn, built as a private residence in the 1850s with a second-story wraparound porch. There are attractive living and game rooms. Upstairs, the 10 guest rooms (6 with private bath) are also nicely decorated, with beds ranging from canopy through twins to a kid's bunk room. This is also a working fiber farm, with llamas, sheep, goats, and rabbits. Kathy spins the yarn, which is hand dyed, and the couple make handcrafted knitting needles. $140–175 per couple MAP, $90–125 B&B; midweek packages and single rates are available.

Whetstone Brook Bed & Breakfast (802-586-6916), 1037 South Craftsbury Road, Craftsbury 05826-4220. An 1826 Vermont classic Cape that, with additions, has been home to six generations of the Wilson family is now Audrey and Bryce Wilson's retirement project, a pleasant B&B. There's a piano in the living room and an Aga stove in the kitchen; the small round tables in the dining room are positioned to view the meadow through the French doors. The upstairs Laura Ashley Room has a private bath, while two more rooms share; the ground-floor Apple Blossom Room has a queen bed and private bath. $79–104 includes a full breakfast.

Somerset House (802-472-5484; 1-800-838-8074), 130 Highland Avenue, Hardwick 05843. An 1890s

Victorian home on a quiet, leafy street in Hardwick. Judy and Roger Waible offer four unfussily appealing guest rooms, with private bath, and perennial flower gardens. A full breakfast includes fresh fruit and a hot entrée. $79–99 double, $65–79 single.

The Kimball House (802-472-6228; www.kimballhouse.com), 173 Glendale Avenue, Hardwick 05843. Sue and Rod Holmes have lived in this big, handsome 1890s "painted lady" since 1979 but have only recently (with their four children grown) converted it to a B&B. All three guest rooms are upstairs (one has twin iron beds) and share a full upstairs bath, one with a shower downstairs. Two rooms have TV. There's plenty of downstairs common space, plus a big wraparound porch and backyard. $79 per couple includes a full breakfast, maybe eggs Benedict.

MOTELS ✐ ✸ **Fairbanks Inn** (802-748-5666; www.stjay.com),

RENEWAL CENTERS FOR BODY AND SPIRIT Karmê Chöling Shambhala Buddhist Meditation Center (802-633-2384; www.karmecholing.org), 369 Patneaude Lane, Barnet 05821. Receptionist: 9–5 weekdays, 1:30–5 weekends. The oldest (founded in 1970) and probably still the best of New England's Buddhist meditation centers, Karmê Chöling follows the Tibetan Buddhist path of understanding one's own mind through meditation. What began as a small center in an old farmhouse now includes 540 wooded, path-webbed acres, six meditation halls, a practice pavilion, an *azuchi* (Zen archery range), a large organic garden, private guest rooms, and dining facilities. The centerpiece remains the original, now expanded farmhouse with its beautiful Main Shrine Room. Casual visitors are welcome (call beforehand), but this is all about 1- to 7-day retreats (many are geared to weekends) on a variety of themes but with the practice of "mindfulness meditation" at their heart. The daily routine begins with a 6:30 wake-up call and continues until 10:30 lights-out. Space to sleep in the Main Shrine is included in the cost of a program; an introductory weekend retreat is $70.

✿ **Craftsbury Outdoor Center** (802-586-7767; www.craftsbury.com), P.O. Box 31, 535 Lost Nation Road, Craftsbury Common 05827. Recreational facilities are the big attractions here, with accommodations for 90 guests divided between two rustic lodges: 9 large doubles and 31 smaller rooms sharing lavatory-style hall bathrooms, 3 larger rooms with private bath, 2 efficiency apartments, and 4 housekeeping cottages sleeping four to eight. Three meals are served, buffet-style, in the dining hall. Guests come for the programs offered: running, sculling, walking, mountain biking, and cross-country skiing, along with winter Elder Hostel programs; or they stay and enjoy the outdoors at their own pace. Facilities include swimming at Lake Hosmer, exercise rooms, sauna, tennis courts, and 320 acres. From $80–175 per person/$140–235 per couple, including three plentiful meals with vegetarian options; family and multiday rates are available. (See also *Biking, Canoeing, Running,* and *Cross-Country Skiing.*)

401 Western Avenue (Route 2 east), St. Johnsbury 05819. This three-story, 45-unit, quite luxurious motel has central air-conditioning, cable, data ports, outdoor heated pool, and fitness center privileges. $79–169 single or double per standard room, more triple and quad and for mini suites; the honeymoon suite is $179–259. Pets accepted in some rooms. Many kinds of discounts honored; children under age 18 stay free.

❧ **Colonnade Inn** (802-626-9316; 1-877-435-5688), 28 Back Center Road, Lyndonville 05851. A two-story, 40-unit motel just off I-91, exit 23. Standard motel rooms, cable TV and phone, continental breakfast. $50 double, $60 for a two-bedded room ($5 per additional person), more during foliage. Bargain-priced ski packages with Burke Mountain. Children stay free.

❧ **Comfort Inn & Suites** (802-748-1500; 1-800-654-6200; www.vtcom fortinnsuites.com), off I-91, exit 20, Route 5 south. A 107-unit high-rise motel with an indoor heated pool, a fitness center, a video arcade, cable, data ports, direct VAST trail access— selected from 1,200 candidates to be "Inn of the Year."

OTHER LODGING ∞ ♿ **Seyon Ranch State Park** (802-584-3829; www.vtstateparks.com). This isolated 1890s hunting/fishing lodge on Noyes Pond, deep in Groton State Forest, is staffed and open year-round, catering to fishermen and cross-country skiers in-season, offering retreats and courting groups in between. There's a living room with fireplace, a dining room, and a meeting space. Five rooms have double and queen beds, and there are bunk rooms with shared

baths, accommodating a total of 16, and serving up to 50 for meals. Inquire about special programs like quilting and cooking. Managers Cory and Shana Drew offer three meals daily. $30 per person, meals extra.

PRIVATE CAMPGROUND Harvey's Lake Cabins and Campground (802-633-2213; www.harveyslakes cabins.com), 190 Camper's Lane, West Barnet 05821. Ten lakefront, furnished (antique funk decor) cabins with kitchen, bath, living area, loft bedrooms, and a campground with 53 wooded sites for RVs and pop-up tents on 35 acres. This is Vermont's oldest private campground. Paddle-boats, swimming, and fishing; also bicycle rentals.

✳ Where to Eat

DINING OUT

In the St. Johnsbury area

Elements (802-748-8400), 98 Mill Street (off Railroad Street), St. Johns-bury. Open for lunch Tuesday through Friday, for dinner Tuesday through Saturday; the bar is open from 4 PM. A former water-powered sawmill with all its wheels and belts still intact makes a great space for this hip new hideaway just off the main drag. A long bar backed by glass blocks divides it into two distinct dining areas (we prefer the bar side). Chef Ryan O'Malley and his wife, sous-chef Allyson O Malley, combine local ingredients (wherever possible) in novel and delicious ways. Nightly specials might range from Black Angus (from a local farm) meat loaf and grilled macaroni and cheese with almonds ($13) to seared venison strip loin with blackberry sauce, red cabbage, and roasted sweet potatoes

($22). We opted for a polenta lasagna with eggplant over roasted vegetables ($15). A "light course" menu also features specialties such as trout cakes served with tomato jam, wasabi, and crème fraîche ($7) and game pâté served with dilly beans and mustard ($6). The idea is to share. For dessert, try the corn bread pudding with dried cranberries, crème Anglaise, and homemade caramel. Everything, with the exception of a chocolate cake, is, we're told, made on the premises.

Creamery Restaurant (802-684-3616), Danville. Open Tuesday through Friday for lunch and dinner, Saturday for dinner only. A former creamery nicely converted into a gracious little restaurant. A blackboard menu features homemade soups, curries, and pad Thais, along with salads, pies, and a choice of meat and seafood dishes. Breads and soups are homemade, and salad comes with all dinners. In contrast to many of the area's more upscale restaurants, chef Robert White has been here long enough to establish a reputation, and owner Marion Beattie has been on board for upward of 30 years. Entrées $14-16; there's a less expensive pub menu downstairs.

Rabbit Hill Inn (802-748-5168; 1-800-76-BUNNY; www.rabbithill .com), Route 18 in Lower Waterford. Open to outside guests by reservation, space permitting. The elegant dining room holds just 15 tables, and both food and atmosphere are carefully orchestrated. There's candlelight and crystal, harp or flute music many nights, and a choice of five-course dinners. You might begin with a shrimp and corn pancake, followed by a salad of local baby greens. Then comes the fruit sorbet with a "splash

of champagne" to cleanse your palate for the entrée: maybe a chicken and root vegetable fricassee or grilled beef tenderloin in white balsamic-blueberry syrup or sautéed gingersnap-crusted scallops. $50 prix fixe includes dessert. Add 18 percent service.

In the Lyndonville–Burke area
River Garden Café (802-626-3514; www.rivergardencafe.com), Route 114, East Burke Village. Open Wednesday through Sunday for lunch and dinner; Sunday brunch is 11–2. A hugely and justly popular place with an attractive decor and wide-ranging menu. Lunch is a large and varied choice of sandwiches, wraps, and salads. Dinner entrées might include pepper-crusted lamb loin, roast salmon served with artichoke hearts, olives, and tomatoes on couscous, or Jamaican jerk chicken with eggplant Parmesan. A café burger or steak sandwich is also available at night. Entrées generally run $15.95–21.95, and the wine list is a point of pride. Breads and desserts are homemade. The café atmosphere is casually elegant, with a year-round back porch and summer patio dining within earshot of the river.

The Old Cutter Inn (802-626-5152; www.oldcutterinn.com), Burke Hollow Road, East Burke. Open for dinner daily except Wednesday, also for Sunday brunch; closed November and April. Owner Fritz Walther prepares a few of his native specialties, like Rahmschnitzel (pork medallions sautéed in butter with shallots, deglazed with white wine, and finished with fresh mushrooms in a light cream sauce). He is also known for his beef Wellington and veal dishes. Less formal fare, like smoked trout, Swiss bratwurst, and forster-schnitten, is served in the Tack Room, a favorite local gathering place. Entrées $15–25, less in the Tack Room.

The Inn at Mountain View Farm (802-626-9924; www.innmtview.com), Darling Hill Road, East Burke. Open for dinner to outside guests (by reservation) except Tuesday. This brick-walled room, once the heart of a working creamery, is an attractive dining room with a varied menu ranging from vegetarian dishes like asparagus with a pasta pillow to leg of lamb. Entrées $14.95–20.95. Specials vary each night, as do the featured wines.

✒ **Juniper's at The Wildflower Inn** (802-626-8310; www.wildflowerinn .com), between Lyndonville and East Burke on Darling Hill Road. Open (except November and April) Monday through Saturday 5:30–9. With a new name, a new slogan ("country fare with flair"), and a new boast ("the largest selection of Vermont brewed beers in the Kingdom"), this is still the inn's delightful old dining space— and it's still a good idea to request a table on the sunporch, overlooking a spread of valley with mountains rolling into the distance. You can still dine on filet mignon ($19.95) but also on grilled meat loaf with bacon-mushroom gravy ($9.95), or roasted vegetables with a griddled lentil scallion cake and red pepper sauce ($10.95). Sandwiches and "junior juniper" plates are also available. Tuesday nights feature BBQ rib specials. All Vermont beer is just $2.50.

In the Craftsbury area
Inn on the Common (802-586-9619; 1-800-521-2233; www.innonthecom mon.com), Craftsbury Common. Open to the public by reservation Tuesday through Saturday evenings. The dining room in this exceptional inn has the feel of an elegant restaurant, and the menu to match. It changes seasonally and offers several choices. On a fall evening you might begin with a frisée and spinach salad with blue cheese, apples, and dried cranberries, then dine on crispy duck breast with wild rice pilaf and apricot brandy sauce. Dessert could be a frozen chocolate mocha terrine with raspberry coulis. Innkeeper Jim Lamberti prides himself on the wine list. Entrées $18.50–21.50.

Highland Lodge (802-533-2647; www.highlandlodge.com), Greensboro. The inn is open late May through mid-October and Christmas week through mid-March. Breakfast, lunch (except Monday), and dinner (by reservation) are served in the inn's attractive dining room and, weather permitting, on the porch. Dinner entrées could include Vermont leg of lamb with roasted garlic sauce, farmed salmon fillet with mustard and tarragon, or triple orange chicken breast. Begin with wild mushroom soup and French walnut rolls and end with bittersweet chocolate cake. Lunch features interesting croissants, salads, and soups as well as the usual sandwiches. Specials, too, can be interesting. Dinner entrées $7.50–23.

EATING OUT

In and around St. Johnsbury
✒ **Surf & Sirloin** (802-748-5412), 264 Portland Street (Route 2 east). Open for breakfast, lunch, and dinner, 6 AM–9 PM daily. This local standby is east of the bridge into town. When we stopped by for lunch, Calvin Belknap had been chef-owner for only a few weeks. No one as yet seemed aware that a guy who had grown up in St. J, gone on to become the execu-

tive chef at the Williamsburg Inn and the Mount Washington Hotel, and been selected one of the country's top chefs three years in a row had come home to offer his kids the same advantage he'd had: an education at St. Johnsbury Academy. As a native son, Calvin is more interested in perpetuating the reputation of a local institution than offering upscale, high-end cuisine—but you have to wonder how long he will be content with a menu that features fried seafood and pork chops. Per our conversation we predict that prices won't rise, but the food may well be worth sampling.

Northern Lights Bookshop & Café (802-748-4463), 378 Railroad Street. Open daily from 9 for bagels, croissants, currant scones, sour cream coffee cake, and assorted omelets; at lunch for homemade soups, salads, and sandwiches; until 5:30 Monday through Thursday, until 7:30 Friday, 5:30 Saturday, and 3 Sunday. Dinner specials Friday night. Espresso, cappuccino, and teas all day. Begun as a bookstore café, this inviting, imaginative space with its booths and artwork now fills a second storefront. The soups are sensational; beer and wine are served.

Danville Restaurant (802-684-3484), 86 Route 2 west, Danville Village. Open for breakfast Tuesday through Saturday 7–11, lunch Tuesday through Friday 11–1:30, dinner Friday and Saturday. Housed in a village home, this family restaurant is good for all three meals at reasonable prices in a friendly atmosphere. Both counter and table service, from hamburgers to full-course meals; daily specials.

Cucina de Gerardo (802-748-6772), 1216 Railroad Street (in the old creamery building). Everyone's favorite place for gourmet pizzas, chicken pesto, and mussels marinara. Far closer to Italy than you might suspect you could come in St. J.

Cindy's Pasta (802-748-4848), Route 5 north of the Green Mountain Mall. Open 6:30 AM–lunch Monday and Tuesday, 6:30 AM–dinner Wednesday through Saturday; closed Sunday. Cindy gets up at 5:30 to start baking the day's breads, and the pasta is all made on premises. Try the seafood scampi or vegetable lasagna. Lunch is salads and sandwiches.

St. Jay Diner (802-748-9751), Memorial Drive (Route 5 north). Open daily for breakfast and lunch, 7:30 AM–2:30 PM. Reliable roadfood.

Anthony's Restaurant (802-748-3613), 321 Railroad Street. Open 6:30 AM–8 PM weekdays, until 9 Friday, from 7 Sunday. Anthony and Judy Proia have run this cheerful family-geared diner since 1979, remodeling it several times to make it handicapped accessible and give it a homier feel. Regulars still gather around the counter, and there are booths as well. Breakfast is big: specialty omelets and about everything else you can think of. "Specials" at all three meals. The fries are homemade, along with the soups; pies are a point of pride.

Mooselook Restaurant (802-695-2950), Route 2, east of Concord. Open 6 AM–8 PM, closed Monday and at 7 PM in winter. This is a better-than-average North Country kind of place: "Most" soups are homemade, and specialties include country-fried steak and Vermont-fried chicken; all meals include soup and choice of potato and vegetable. This is also "home of the slugger," a 7-ounce burger with all the fixings. For visitors the additive is what's on the walls: dozens of vintage-19th-century photos of what this area was all about a more than a century ago.

Kham Thai Cuisine (802-751-8424), 112 Memorial Drive (Route 5 north). Open daily 11–9, until 10 Friday and Saturday. A great addition to local dining options, reasonably priced, reliable.

Black Bear Tavern & Grille (802-748-1428; www.blackbeartavern grille.com), 205 Hastings Hill Road. Open for lunch and dinner. Just north of downtown, adjacent to the Holiday Motel but its own place, locally popular with a gracious, friendly atmosphere and an upscale sports bar. Steaks, seafood, burgers, and sandwiches, all reasonably priced.

Upper Valley Grill (802-584-3101), junction of Routes 302 and 232, Groton. Open 6 AM–9 PM daily. At the junction of two lonely stretches of road, this is a welcome oasis: a general store with a friendly, U-shaped counter in back, good for homemade soups, apple pie, and daily specials.

In the Lyndonville–Burke area
& **F. Scotts** (802-626-5557), Route 5, Lyndonville. Open nightly for dinner from 5. Geared to locals with a large, reasonably priced menu including a $6.95 senior and children's menu. Plenty of parking. This 70-seat restaurant is in a big old house with beautifully carved and finished woodwork and furniture thanks to its previous owner, a founding partner in Lyndonville Furniture. Chef-owner Bill Lewis has been here more than 15 years and is known for such offerings as prime rib, as well as lobster, shrimp, and scallop pie. The most expensive entrée is $14.95. Full liquor license.

Miss Lyndonville Diner (802-626-9890), Route 5 south, Lyndonville. Open from 6 AM until supper, famed for strawberry pancakes with whipped cream for breakfast, pie, homemade French toast, and jumbo eggs. This is one of the famous railroad diners, along with Miss Newport and Miss Bellows Falls, that made their way to Vermont years ago. When they came, they brought with them the best of classic diner fare.

✂ **The Pub Outback** (802-626-1188; www.thepuboutback.com), East Burke, out back of the Bailey's & Burke General Store. Open daily 4–9, later Friday and Saturday. This former cow barn is now a cheerful pub with a full menu, from soups to pitas, veggies, burgers, sandwiches, steaks, pastas, the works. Children's menu. Full bar.

In the Craftsbury area
⊙ **Lakeview Inn Constant Bliss Café** (802-533-2291; www.lake viewinnbb.com), Main Street, Greensboro. Open daily for breakfast, lunch, and light fare until 4; later in summer. This is a meeting spot for miles around, an expansive, comfortable dining room with a bakery and deli serving soups, chili, salads, and such. Definitely worth checking. A good venue for a wedding reception.

For **Warners Gallery, Happy Hours Restaurant,** and **P&H Truck Stop** in Wells River, see "Upper Valley River Towns."

BREWS **The Brick House** (802-472-5512), East Hardwick (posted from Route 16). Open Memorial through Labor Day, noon–4; closed Monday. English-born Judith Kane serves a traditional "Cream Tea" (cucumber sandwiches, scones, ham, and fresh cream) and offers an assortment of teas, cold drinks, and pastries. Reservations suggested, but patrons "are welcome to pop in." Many come just for the gift shop, known for its splendid summer hats as well as jewelry, clothing, books, gardening tools and more. The 3 acres of perennial gardens (www.perennialpleasures.net, open 10–5) represent 900 varieties of plants, featuring heirloom flowers— lemon lilies, golden glow—and medicinal plants.

Trout River Brewing Company (802-616-9396; www.troutriverbrew ing.com), Route 5, Lyndonville. Friday and Saturday 5–8:30, open for hand-tossed pizzas as well as the selection of ales and other selections on draft, brewed on the premises. The three signature beers here are Rainbow Red (medium bodied), Scottish Ale, and Hoppin' Mad Trout; also seasonal specials. Inquire about tours and tastings.

✴ Entertainment

Catamount Arts (802-748-2600; 1-888-757-5559; www.catamount arts.com), 139 Eastern Avenue, St. Johnsbury. The Catamount Arts Center (the former St. Johnsbury Post Office) is the venue for a film series that includes nightly film screenings (7 PM) and two shows on Saturday (7 and 9); also Sunday matinees November through April. The 100-seat auditorium also hosts more than 30 live Showcase Presentations annually and the biweekly Jazz on a Sunday series. Regional artists are featured in the gallery here, and some 3,000 video rentals are available in the lobby. Catamount Arts was established in 1975 as a nonprofit cultural organization serving the region.

Star Theater (802-748-4900; 802-748-9511), 18 Eastern Avenue, St. Johnsbury. Cinemas 1-2-3; first-run movies.

Craftsbury Chamber Players (1-800-639-3443; www.craftsbury chamberplayers.org) has brought chamber music to northern Vermont for upward of 40 years. The series runs mid-July through mid-August, Thursday evening at 8 at the Hardwick Town House; there are also Thursday-afternoon performances alternately at the Presbyterian Church in East Craftsbury and Fellowship Hall in Greensboro. Most performers are faculty members at the Juilliard School of Music in New York City. Also see below.

The Northeast Kingdom Arts Council (www.nekarts.org) is restoring **Hardwick Town House** (802-472-8800), 127 Church Street, Hardwick. An 1860 schoolhouse, it has been the anchor venue for the Craftsbury Chamber Players and also now hosts a variety of programs: film, drama, music, and other live performances. The stage features hand-painted curtains.

🎭 **Vermont Children's Theater** (802-626-8838), Darling Hill Road, Lyndonville. Local youngsters perform amazingly well. Performances the last two weekends in July are by thespians ages 8–12 and, in August, ages 13–18.

🎭 **Circus Smirkus** (802-533-7443; 1-800-532-7443; www.smirkus.org) in Greensboro. A children's circus camp stages frequent performances in July and August.

Band concerts: **St. Johnsbury Town Band concerts,** weekly all summer at the bandstand in Town Hall Park,

Monday 8 PM. **Lyndonville Town Band concerts,** every Wednesday in summer at 8 PM. **Craftsbury band concerts** at the band shell on the common, Sundays at 7 in July and August. In **Greensboro,** concerts on the dock at Caspian Lake are sponsored by the Greensboro Association, summer Sundays at 7:30.

✳ Selective Shopping

ANTIQUES SHOPS **Farr's Antiques** (802-684-3333), just off the Danville green on the Peacham Road. Open daily 10–4. Oak tables, chairs, dressers, and other assorted furniture and furnishings fill three floors of a former granary.

Route 5 Antiques & Collectibles (802-626-5430), Route 5, Lyndonville. Open daily except Tuesday 10–5. A multidealer and consignment shop.

Antiques & Emporium (802-626-3500), 260 Hill Street, Lyndonville. Open daily 10–5 except Tuesday. Another multigroup shop with everything from rugs and clocks to furniture, pottery, and prints.

BOOKSTORES 📖 **Northern Lights Bookshop & Café** (802-748-4463; www.nlightsvt.com), 378 Railroad Street, St. Johnsbury. A bright, lively, full-service bookstore that's a real part of St. Johnsbury's cultural life. The stock is unusually extensive, with many Vermont-based writers, a large children's section, also cards, magazines, and children's toys. The popular café (see *Eating Out*) displays work by local artists (see *Galleries*). Inquire about author's readings and music.

The Galaxy Bookshop (802-472-5533; www.galaxybookshop.com), 7 Mill Street, Hardwick. Since Linda Ramsdell moved her shop into a vintage-1910 bank building, she offers not only ample space for her stock but also probably the only drive-through book and rental audiotape (call ahead) service in the country. Audiotapes? Local farmers listen while driving tractors and doing chores. This is a full-service bookstore specializing in Vermont writers and unusual titles; armchairs invite lingering. The satellite **Stardust Books** (802-586-2200) in the former library on Crafstbury Common is open Saturday 10–1 (coinciding with the farmer's market) and Wednesday 3–6. Inquire about frequent author readings and other special events.

Green Mountain Books & Prints (802-626-5051), 1055 Broad Street, Lyndonville (Route 5 on the corner of the common). Open Monday through Saturday 9–5. Ellen Doyle is the second generation of her family to preside over this book lover's heaven: an unusual mix of new and used books; many new, discounted titles and rare books. Doyle seems to know something about every book in the place. Vermontiana, Native American, and children's books are specialties, but the range is wide and patrons are welcome to sit in a corner for as long as they wish. Bigger than it looks at first: There are separate children's and fiction rooms.

Country Bear Books (802-626-3469; www.countrybearbookshop.com), 63 Depot, Lyndonville. Open daily 9:30–5, closed Sunday. A large stock of new—and used—books, most at discount prices.

Antiquarian Muse (802-472-3536), 144 Main Street, Hardwick. Open weekdays 10–3. A brick house filled with 5,000 used and collectible books for adults and children.

CHEESE For the Cabot Creamery Visitors Center, see *To See*.

Bonnie View Sheep Farm (802-755-6878), 2228 South Albany Road, Craftsbury Common. Neil Urie produces his award-wining cheeses—blue, Camembert, and feta, as well as a hard Vermont Shepherd–style cheese—on the 470-acre farm that's been in the family since 1890. He's not really set up for visitors but not adverse to those who drop by, no easy feat given the maze of dirt roads leading to his farm. It's sublime backcountry, however, and 5 PM is the best time to come. The cheese is sold at local stores.

Jasper Hill Farm (802-533-2566), Garvin Hill Road, Greensboro. Mateo and Andy Kehler make Winnemere cheese (cloth-bound hard cheddar that needs to age for a year), Bayley-Hazen Blue, and Constant Bliss (named for a Union scout from Greensboro killed in the Civil War), all soft, washed-rind cheese, available at Willey's (see *General Stores*).

CRAFTS SHOPS

In the St. Johnsbury area
Northeast Kingdom Artisans Guild (802-748-0158), 430 Railroad Street, St. Johnsbury. Open Monday through Saturday; closed Monday off-season. This cooperative of more than 60 Vermont artists showcases some magnificent work in many media.

Uniquity (802-748-1912), 443 Railroad Street. Open daily 9:30–5:30, 11–4 on Sunday. Locally made quilts, baskets, paintings, candles, household accessories, and gifts, plus a frame shop.

The Peacham Corner Guild (802-592-3332), 643 Bayley-Hazen Road. Open June through mid-October; closed Tuesday, but otherwise 10–5,

Sunday 11–5. Handcrafted gifts, small antiques.

Birdman (802-563-2877), Danville Hill Road between Route 2 and Cabot. Open July through October, Monday through Saturday 8–5; November through June by chance or appointment. Edmund Menard produces small, impressively fantailed birds: Christmas ornaments, a bird necklace, earrings, lapel pins, and more.

Songbird Pottery (802-563-2330), 3764 Mack Mountain Road, West Danville. Open daily 1–4, but call before. Harley and Patricia Strader make functional and decorative glazed stoneware from local materials. Lead-free and dishwasher-safe.

Brigid's Farm (802-592-3062), 123 Slack Street, Peacham. Open except August, Friday through Monday 1–5. A small farm with sheep, Angora goats, and dairy goats with a weaving studio and mittens, hand-spun yarns, spinning wheels, natural dye extracts, and supplies sold.

Snowshoe Farm (802-592-3153), 520 The Great Road, Peacham. Open year-round, but call. Ron and Terry Miller breed alpacas and process their fiber, selling it along with hand-knit or woven alpaca products.

In the Craftsbury–Greensboro area
Mill Village Pottery (802-586-9971), 6 Mill Village Road (on the way to Craftsbury Outdoor Center), Craftsbury Common. Open summer and fall 10–5 daily; usually open off-season, too, but call ahead. Lynn Flory specializes in one-of-a-kind vessels and unusual functional ware such as the "Yunan steamer," a lidded ceramic pot with a conical chimney in its center, designed to retain vitamins and minerals.

The Miller's Thumb (802-533-2960; www.themillersthumb.com), Greensboro Village. Open year-round (except March and April), daily 10–5:30. A former gristmill built in 1792 with a view of Greensboro Brook churning down falls below, through a window in the floor. Owners Anne and Rob Brigham have a great eye for selecting art, crafts, home furnishings, and gift items, many made locally; check out the furniture and clothing upstairs.

Caspian Hot Glass Studio (802-533-7129), top of Brezzy Avenue, Greensboro. Open May through January, daily 10–5. Glassblowers Jacob Barron and Lucas Lonegren work in their sugarhouse-shaped studio and display their original glass lighting and tableware—also ornaments and art glass—in the attached gallery.

GALLERIES *Note:* St. Johnsbury's most famous art gallery is the St. Johnsbury Athenaeum (see *To See*).

Tamarack Gallery (802-525-3041), Whetstone Brook Road and East Craftsbury Road, Craftsbury. Open Memorial Day through Columbus Day, Thursday through Saturday 1–5. An enormous, vintage-1912 barn housing two floors of exhibit space, featuring contemporary fine art and photography.

GRACE Gallery (802-472-6857), 13 Mill Street, Hardwick. Open Tuesday through Thursday 10–3. *GRACE* stands for "Grassroots Art and Community Effort," a 25-year-old program that offers arts workshops and displays the rotating exhibits in the old firehouse.

See also Northern Lights Bookshp & Café under *Bookstores*.

GARDENS **Vermont Daylilies** (802-533-2438), 295 Breezy Avenue, Greensboro. Over 500 varieties of daylilies with display gardens; also potted daylilies, hostas, and garden perennials on sale. The gardens are always open, while the store is open May through September 10–5.

Perennial Pleasures Nursery (802-472-5512; www.perennialpleasures .net), East Hardwick. Sited at the Brick House (see *Brews*) and run by Rachel Kane, this unusual nursery specializes in authentic 17th-, 18th-, and 19th-century restoration gardens. There are 3 acres of flowering perennial and herb gardens, grassy walks, and arbors; more than 375 varieties of plants are available.

Stillmeadow Farm (802-755-6713), 158 Urie Road, South Albany. In the greenhouses at this handsome farm that's been in the same family since the 1830s, Elizabeth Urie sells a variety of vegetable plants and flowers; hanging baskets are a specialty. Open May through July.

☯ **Jeudevine Falls** (802-472-5486; www.vtwaterfalls.com), Route 14, Hardwick, 2.25 miles north of the junction with Route 15. Open Memorial Day through late October. $6 adult, under 14 free. Two waterfalls, one 130 feet high, are lighted at night. In May and June the display of azaleas and rhododendrons is extensive; then come foxgloves and wildflowers, and then an acre's maze of sunflowers. There are also extensive walking paths and a gazebo for weddings; group gatherings encouraged.

GENERAL STORES **Hastings Store** (802-684-3398), West Danville. See West Danville under *Towns and Villages*.

Willey's Store (802-533-2621), Greensboro Village. One of the biggest and best general stores in the state, in business over 100 years; an extensive grocery, produce, and meat section, local dairy products (check out Constant Bliss Cheese, made in Greensboro), hardware, toys, and just about everything else you should have brought for a vacation but forgot. Don't miss the upstairs with its selection of everything from flannel shirts and buttons through yard cloth and boots. Helpful staff will help you find what you are looking for.

Bailey's & Burke General Store (802-626-9250; www.baileysand burke.com), Route 114, East Burke. Open weekdays 6:30 AM–9 PM, Sunday 8–9; closes at 8 in winter. This classic old general store has been nicely fancied up by longtime local residents Jody Fried and Bill Turner. The second-floor gallery has been restored and displays work by local craftsmen. Downstairs are breads, pies, cookies, and coffee cakes baked daily right here; also a gourmet deli featuring specialty pizzas, cheeses, cold cuts, soups, and salads with café tables to eat them at. A selection of wines, coffees, and teas.

Craftsbury General Store (802-586-2811), Craftsbury Village. A genuine, old-style village store.

The Peacham Store (802-592-3310), Peacham Village. Open sporadically. Crafts, collectibles, and specialty foods. Gourmet food to take out.

SPECIAL SHOPS The Farmer's Daughter (802-748-3994), Route 2 east of St. Johnsbury. Open mid-April through mid-November, daily 8–6. Billed as the country's oldest "Gift Barn"—not just because the barn is 180 years old but also because it's been under the same ownership for

43 years. A lot of stuff, much of it hokey but fun.

Moose River Lake and Lodge Store (802-748-2423), 370 Railroad Street, St. Johnsbury. Open except Sunday 10–5; in summer Sunday, too (11–4). Antiques, rustic furniture, and accessories for the home, camp, or cabin: taxidermy specialties, deer antlers and skulls, prints, pack baskets, fishing creels and snowshoes, folk art, an extensive wine collection, and more.

Peter Glenn Ski & Sports (802-748-3433; www.peterglenn.com), 452 Railroad Street, St. Johnsbury. A full four-season sports shop, top quality at good prices.

Samadhi Store and Workshop (802-633-4440), 30 Church Street, Barnet. An offshoot of nearby Karmê Chöling, selling singing bowls and gongs, Japanese yukata robes, teas, Vermont-made raku incense bowls, lacquerware from Japan and Korea, locally made meditation benches and tables, and meditation cushions and yoga mats made on site.

Diamond Hill Store (802-684-9797), Route 2, Danville on the green. This former general store is now a sleek emporium specializing in handmade chocolates, wine, and gifts.

Christina Tree

Through the Woods (802-748-5369), 107 Eastern Avenue, St. Johnsbury. Specializes in crafts and collectibles for the home. An interesting shop with lots of unusual items.

Lyndon Furniture (802-748-5996; www.lyndon.com). David Allard began making furniture in a fieldstone house he was building for his parents but today produces a distinctive line of furniture—beds, tables, many chairs, dining room and bedroom sets—in his Lyndon factory. Request a catalog or check out the online catalog. **Stahler Furniture** (1-800-439-5996) on Route 5, Lyndonville (across from Brooks), is a showcase and prime outlet.

Caplan's Army Store Work & Sportswear (802-748-3236), 457 Railroad Street, St. Johnsbury. Established in 1922 and still in the same family, a serious source of quilted jackets, skiwear, Woolrich sweaters, hunting boots, and such; good value and friendly service.

SUGARHOUSES **Rowell Sugarhouse** (802-563-2756), 4962 Route 15, Walden. Visitors are welcome year-round, 9–5. Maple cream and candy as well as sugar; also Vermont honey and sheepskins.

Goodrich's Sugarhouse (802-563-9917), just off Route 2 by Molly's Pond in East Cabot. A family tradition for seven generations, open to visitors March through December with a full line of award-winning maple products.

Goss's Sugar House (802-633-4743), 101 Maple Lane, Barnet. Gordon and Pat Goss have won a blue ribbon for their syrup at the Caledonia County Fair. They welcome visitors, sell year-round, and will ship.

Harry F. Sweat (802-586-2838), Craftsbury, on the road from the common to Craftsbury Center. There are 3,000 taps; the sugarhouse is open in-season.

Martin Calderwood (802-586-2297), South Albany Road, Craftsbury. Here sap from 1,900 taps is gathered with a tractor and sled. Sugar parties arranged on request.

Fred and Bob Kinsey (802-525-8863), County Road, Albany. Wood-fired boiling, sugarhouse, visitors welcome.

✳ Special Events

February: **Snowflake Festival Winter Carnival,** Lyndonville–Burke. Events include a crafts show, snow sculpture, ski races for all ages and abilities, sleigh rides, music, and art.

March: **Open sugarhouses.**

May: In East Burke the **Annual White-Water Canoe Race** on the Passumpsic River, May 1. **Hardwick Spring Festival** (last weekend) includes a parade, crafts fair, and chicken BBQ. **Annual Vermont Open Studio Weekend** (www.vermontcrafts.com) on Memorial Day weekend.

June: **Lumberman's Day** at Burke Mountain in Lyndonville. **Dowsers National Convention** (802-684-3410), held at Lyndon State College.

June–October: **Farmer's markets,** in downtown St. Johnsbury Saturday 9–1; in Craftsbury Saturday 10–1; in Danville Wednesday 9–1; in Hardwick Friday 3–6.

July: The **July 4 parade** in Cabot is the best around (802-563-2279). **Peacham Independence Day festivities** include a Ghost Walk in the cemetery, with past residents impersonated. **Burklyn Arts Council Summer Craft Fair** (Saturday closest to July 4) in Bandstand Park, Lyndonville. **Antiques and Uniques Fair** in Craftsbury Common. **Stars and Stripes Pageant,** Lyndonville (last weekend)—big auction, parade featuring Bread and Puppet Uncle Sam, barbecue. The **Irasburg Church Fair** is the third Saturday.

♪ *July–August:* **Circus Smirkus** (802-533-7443), Greensboro. A children's circus camp stages frequent performances.

August: **Old Home Days,** Craftsbury Common—parade, games, crafts (802-586-7766). **Caledonia County Fair** (third week), Mountain View Park, Lyndonville—horse, pony, and ox pulling; cattle, sheep, alpaca, rabbit, and swine shows; midway, rides, demolition derby, music.

First weekend of October: **Fall Foliage Craft Fair** in Hardwick.

Saturday after Thanksgiving: **Kirby Quilters Craft Fair** (www.kirbyquilters.com)—huge (fills two gyms at Lyndon State College).

December: **Burklyn Christmas Crafts Market** (the first weekend)—a major gathering of North Country craftspeople and artists in the Lyndon Town School.

December 31: **First Night** celebration in St. Johnsbury.

September–October: **Northeast Kingdom Fall Foliage Festival,** the last week in September or first one in October. Seven towns take turns hosting visitors, feeding them breakfast, lunch, and dinner, and guiding them to beauty spots and points of interest within their borders. In Walden the specialty is Christmas wreath making; in Cabot there's a tour of the cheese factory; in Plainfield, farm tours; in Peacham, a Ghost Walk and crafts fair; in Barnet the exceptional historical society house is open, and guided tours of back roads are outstanding; the finale comes in St. Johnsbury, with a farmer's market and arts and crafts fair. For details, contact the Northeast Kingdom Chamber (see *Guidance*).

BARNET CENTER DURING THE NORTHEAST KINGDOM FALL FOLIAGE FESTIVAL   Christina Tree

JAY PEAK AREA

Jay Peak towers like a sentinel above a wide valley in which the state of Vermont and the province of Quebec meet at three border crossings and mingle in the waters of Lake Memphremagog—and in general ambience. The sentinel itself has fallen to the French. The face of Vermont's northernmost peak is owned by Mont-Saint-Saveur International, and more than half of the patrons at Jay Peak ski area hail from across the border. Montreal is less than 2 hours away.

In summer and fall as well as in winter, a 60-passenger aerial tram hoists visitors to the 3,861-foot summit of Jay Peak. The view sweeps from Mount Washington to Montreal, back across the lake, down the spine of the Green Mountains and southwest across Lake Champlain to the Adirondacks.

In winter, storms sweep down from Canada or roll in from Lake Champlain, showering the clutch of mountains around Jay with dependable quantities of snow. Admittedly, given its exposed position, Jay can be windy and frigid in January and February (we try to visit in March), the reason—along with spectacular snowfall—that regulars are drawn by "off-piste" skiing through glades and into the backcountry beyond. In nearby Hazen's Notch cross-country skiers also find some of the most dependably snowy and beautiful trails in New England.

Walk the length of the border between New England and Canada and you will not find a more distinctive stretch than this western fringe of the Northeast Kingdom. This is big-sky farm and logging country with isolated mountains and unexpectedly high passes. It has a haunting quality. Jay Village is a crossroads with a gas station and general store from which Route 242 climbs steeply 4 miles to the Jay Peak access road, then dips steeply 9 miles down to Montgomery Center. Montgomery, known for its six covered bridges, is 2 more miles to the west, and the Hazen's Notch angles back east over a high woods pass and down through fields into Lowell. An inviting drive in summer, it's open only for the first 4 miles in winter, just far enough to access magnificent snowshoeing and cross-country ski trails.

In contrast to most ski resort areas, this area attracts relatively few transients. Innkeepers, restaurateurs, and shopkeepers are a mix of self-sufficient natives and the interesting kind of people who tend to gather in the world's beautiful back-and-behind places.

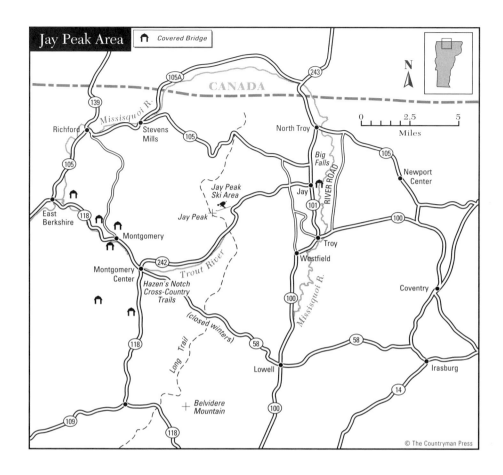

Jay Peak Area

Covered Bridge

CANADA

GUIDANCE Jay Peak Travel Service (802-988-2611; outside Vermont: 1-800-451-4449; www.jaypeakresort.com), Jay 05859, is based at Jay Peak Resort. The Jay Peak Area Association (802-988-2259; 1-800-882-7460; www.jaypeakver mont.com) is staffed by area members.

GETTING THERE *By air:* **Burlington International Airport,** a 1½-hour drive.

By train: **Amtrak** service to St. Albans.

By bus: **Greyhound** and **Vermont Transit** service to Newport; host lodges will generally pick up.

By car: From points south take I-91 exit 26 at Orleans and follow Route 5 north 4 miles to Coventry, then head north on Route 14 and then south on Route 100, 11 miles to Troy. Travel 3 miles north on Route 101 to the turnoff for Jay on Route 242. Believe it or not, this is shorter and less confusing than exiting in Newport.

WHEN TO GO Foliage and winter seasons both begin early here: By the last week in September color is substantial but the inns are empty. The area only fills on winter weekends, when buses from Montreal augment the crowds on the slopes. Midweek is relatively empty all season except during Canadian school vacations (check) but during Presidents' Week (public school vacation in New England) it's the one major mountain that isn't crowded. Given the windchill factor, we like to ski here in March, which can be glorious. For cross-country it's great all winter. July through October is very quiet.

MEDICAL EMERGENCY Emergency service is available by calling **911.**

North Country Hospital & Medical Center (802-334-7331), Prouty Drive, Newport.

✳ To See

Jay Peak summit. The spectacular view from the top is accessible via the new 60-person tram at Jay Peak Resort (802-966-2611), Route 242, Jay. It operates daily during ski season and from the last weekend in June through Labor Day, then in foliage season, mid-September through Columbus Day, 10–4, weather permitting. $10 adults, $6 age 14 and under, $30 family pass.

Hazen's Notch. From Montgomery Center, an unpromising narrow road, Route 58, climbs steeply east, quickly changing to dirt. In winter it's open only for the first 4 miles and is the site of a popular ski touring spot. In summer it's a beautiful road, dappled with sunlight through the thick foliage. Look for a picnic spot near the height-of-land, close to a clear roadside spring. A historic site plaque says the road through the high pass was built by General Moses Hazen in 1778–79, commissioned by George Washington himself. The road was begun in 1776, 48 miles to the southeast at the town of Wells River on the Connecticut River, and was intended to reach St. John, Quebec. It was abandoned on this spot in April 1779 when the news that British patrols might use it as an invasion route (it was meant to work the other way) reached the camp at Hazen's Notch.

Montgomery and its covered bridges. Montgomery boasts a grand total of six Town lattice covered bridges: one right in Montgomery Village over Black Falls Creek; one south on Route 118; another nearby but 3 miles off Route 118 on West Hill on an abandoned side road over a waterfall; another northwest on Route 118 over the Trout River; and two in Montgomery Center, both a mile west of Route 118 over the Trout River (see our area map). Montgomery Village itself is picturesque. It began as a lumbering center and was for a long time one of the world's major producers of timothy grass seed culture. The Montgomery Historical Society's collection is housed in an 1835 wooden church, open June through September at stated hours; the society also sponsors Saturday-evening concerts on the common in July and August.

St. Benoit du Lac (819-843-4080), Austin, Quebec. Open daily. This noncloistered French Benedictine monastery, founded in 1912, is sited on the west shore of Lake Memphremagog in a fjordlike section. It's an impressive building, and the resident monks welcome visitors for daily Mass and vespers (usually at 5 PM), at which Gregorian chant is sung. The monastery shop sells recordings of Gregorian chant, also hard cider, cheese, vestments, and religious articles. The easiest route from Newport is via the North Troy border crossing, then through Mansonville, South Bolton, and Austin.

✳ To Do

BICYCLE TOURING A time-honored and -tested 22.6- or 33.7-mile ride begins at the Black Lantern Inn (see *Lodging*) in Montgomery Village, passes two covered bridges along Route 118 north, and takes you to East Berkshire; you can simply continue to Enosburg Falls, where Lake Carmi offers camping and swimming, or turn onto the Richford Road, and loop back to Montgomery or loop up into Canada.

The **Missisquoi Valley Rail Trail** begins in Richford and runs 26.4 miles west to St. Albans.

MOUNTAIN BIKING Jay Peak (802-988-2611; 1-800-451-4449) maintains a network of trails for experienced mountain bikers via its aerial tramway, which will transport them and their bikes to the 3,861-foot summit from which several routes descend: 20 miles of alpine and 15 miles of cross-country.

CANOEING The 86-mile-long **Missisquoi River** makes a complete loop around Jay, passes briefly through Quebec, and continues across Vermont to empty into Lake Champlain. The upper half of the river near Jay offers spring fast water, and the lower reaches are gentle and broad, good spring and summer ground for beginners and those who enjoy traversing outstanding rural landscape. For canoes and boat rentals, contact the **Missisquoi Riverbend B&B** (802-744-9991), Route 100, Troy; **Raven Ridge Canoe Rental & Guide Service** (1-888-933-4616) in Enosburg also serves this area with canoe and kayak rentals and guiding.

BIG FALLS OF THE MISSISQUOI River Road hugs the river, paralleling Route 101 between Troy and North Troy. You can access the falls from either town or from Vielleux Road off Route 101 at its junction with Route 105. This last is the prettiest route, through farmland and through the covered bridge south of the falls. Look for the unmarked pull-off in a grove of pine trees. The falls, thundering through a deep gorge, are awe-inspiringly magnificent.

BIG FALLS IN THE NORTH TROY AREA   Christina Tree

FISHING The **Trout River** deserves its name. Brook trout can also be found in the **Missisquoi,** and **Lake Memphremagog** harbors smallmouth bass and salmon, among other species. See "The Lake Country" for boat rentals.

GOLF The 18-hole golf course at Jay Peak Resort is due to open in 2005. In the meantime see the Newport and Orleans golf clubs in "The Lake Country."

HIKING The **Long Trail** terminates its 262-mile route at the Canadian border, 10 miles north of Jay Peak, but the trek up Jay itself is what most hikers look for here. The most popular ascent is from Route 242, 1.2 miles west of the entrance to the ski area; the round-trip hike takes 3 hours. For details on this and the section of the trail between Hazen's Notch and Route 242, also for the final, fairly flat leg to the border, see the *Long Trail Guide,* published by the Green Mountain Club, which maintains the trail and four shelters in this area.

✍ **Hazen's Notch Association** (802-326-4799; www.hazensnotch.org), 1421 Hazen's Notch Road (Route 58), Montgomery Center. No trail fee, but contributions appreciated. Twenty miles of a total 40 miles of trails are maintained for hiking, winding through 2,500 acres of privately owned woods and meadows; it's 15 minutes to Bear Paw Pond. The 2-mile-long Burnt Mountain Trail ascends to the 2,700-foot summit of Burnt Mountain, an open summit with 360-degree views that include Hazen's Notch, the Jay Mountains, Mount Mansfield, and Lake Champlain. Inquire about frequent nature walks, fly-fishing workshops, and other special events. Sharon and Rolf Anderson offer nature and ecology day camps for children 6–9, Adventure Day and Overnight Camps for those 10–15.

HORSEBACK RIDING Missisquoi Riverbend B&B (802-744-9991), Route 100 in Troy Village, offers trail rides.

SWIMMING A number of inns have their own pools. The most popular local swimming hole is at Jay Four Corners, downstream from the Route 101 bridge.

TENNIS ✍ **Jay Peak Resort** (802-988-2611) maintains tennis courts in warm-weather months.

✳ Winter Sports

CROSS-COUNTRY SKIING Hazen's Notch Cross-Country Ski and Snowshoeing Center (802-326-4708), Route 58, Montgomery Center. This outstanding touring center offers 45 km of meticulously tracked trails, some with fine views of Jay and the Cold Hollow Mountains, connecting with the Catamount Trail. In business since 1978, when Val Schadinger and Rolf Anderson first laid out the trails, Hazen's Notch offers a rustic, noncommercial atmosphere that has attracted a loyal following. Early and late in the season, this tends to be one of half a dozen cross-country networks in New England that have snow (elevation: 1,000–1,670 feet).

Jay Peak Resort (802-988-2611) maintains 20 km of trails near the base of the mountain.

DOWNHILL SKIING ✦ **Jay Peak** (information and reservations: 802-988-2611; 1-800-451-4449 including Canada; snow conditions: 802-988-9601; www.jay peakresort.com). While there's an easy-intermediate trail (Northway) off the summit, Jay Peak regulars duck into glades right off the top. Jay's 20 glades and extreme chutes are what draw many of its regulars, who like to strike out into 150 acres of backcountry terrain. Unlike regular runs, wooded trails ("glades") cannot be covered by human-made snow and so require a lot of the natural stuff, which is what Jay Peak has in spades: an average of 330 inches annually. That's twice the snow many New England areas receive.

The original trails here are stateside, on a shoulder of Jay Peak. Still considered some of the toughest runs in Vermont, they were carved 30 years ago by local residents. An enterprising Kiwanis group (it included the parish priest) convinced the Vermont Legislature to reroute existing roads up over the high ridge from which Jay's access road arises, thus linking it to northwestern Vermont as well as to the Northeast Kingdom. They also imported an Austrian skimeister to create a true trail system and ski school. Then in the early 1960s the lumber company Weyerhaeuser Corporation acquired the ski area and installed a Swiss-built tramway to Jay's Peak, which it topped with a Sky Haus tram station, a building that emphasizes the crest of the summit and gives it a distinctly Matterhorn-like cap. Weyerhaeuser also built the large, sturdy, Tyrolean-style base complex that still stands and includes a 48-room hotel.

JAY PEAK

Christian Tremblay

Since 1978 the resort has been owned by the Montreal-based owners of Saint-Saveur, a lucrative Laurentian ski area. The original trams have been replaced with sleek cars, lifts have been improved, and condominiums have been proliferating. A 27-hole golf course and greatly expanded base facilities are planned. Weekends can be mobbed by Montrealers, but midweek is frequently wide open, and spring skiing is superb.

Lifts: 60-passenger aerial tramway; two quad chairs, one triple, one double; one T-bar. *Trails and slopes:* 76 trails, glades, and chutes totaling more than 50 miles of skiing, spread over two peaks, connected by a ridge-line. *Off-piste skiing:* 200 acres. *Vertical drop:* 2,153 feet. *Snowboarding:* Permanent half-pipe course; Jay Burton Kids Method Center for kids 12 and under includes trampoline exercises and balance board training among its teaching tools. Board demo center, rentals, instruction for beginners. *Snowmaking:* 85 percent of the total 385 acres. *Snowshoeing:* Weekly snowshoeing walks led by a naturalist. *Facilities:* Austria Haus and Tram Haus base lodges with cafeteria, pub, and ski and rental shop. Sky Haus cafeteria at the summit, nursery and daycare facilities. Rentals. A lighted skating rink and skate rentals. Van service is offered from Burlington International Airport (80 miles away) and from the Amtrak station in St. Albans (a 45-minute drive). *Ski school:* U.S.- and Canadian-certified instructors, adult and junior racing clinics, American Teaching Method (ATM). Telemarking instruction and rentals offered. *For children:* Mountain Explorers for both skiing and snowboarding for 5- to 12-year-old group, kinderschool for ages 2–5. Daycare for ages 2–7. *Rates:* $54 adult, $40 junior (14 and under), but far cheaper with lodging packages.

SLEIGH RIDES **Phil & Karen's Sleigh/Hayrides** (802-744-9928), 143 Kennison Road, Westfield. Old-fashioned sleigh- or hayrides are offered through meadows and along a quiet road, drawn by Belgians Charlie and Duke.

Missisquoi Riverbend B&B (802-744-9991) offers sleigh rides.

SNOWMOBILING The area is webbed with **Vermont Association of Snow Travelers** (VAST) trails; check with the local inns.

✳ Lodging

On-mountain
Jay Peak Travel Service (1-800-451-4449; www.jaypeakresort.com).

✎ **Hotel Jay** (1-800-451-4449), Route 242, Jay 05859. Located right at the lifts, an adequate but tired lodge with 48 big rooms, some with double beds, some queen and some twin beds, color TV, phone, and private bath; a pleasant public dining room, a game room, family room, sauna and Jacuzzi, outdoor pool (summer only). Rates are reasonable, especially in the off-season. In winter a 2-day package including lift, lodging, two breakfasts, and one dinner can be had for $268 per person (except over the holidays). Kids 14 and under stay and ski free.

Condominiums: **Jay Peak Condominiums.** A total of 130 condos and town houses, including some rental units, constructed in clusters: studios and two- and three-bedroom units accommodate from 4 to 10 people; all have fireplace, living room, and fully equipped kitchen. More than 60 rental units in the trailside **Village** with two to five bedrooms are luxurious. From $82 per person in the off-season and from $312 including lifts for 2 nights during ski season.

Off-mountain
INNS **Black Lantern Inn** (802-326-4507; 1-800-255-8661; www.black lantern.com), Montgomery 05470. A white-pillared, brick inn built in 1803 as the Montgomery Village stage stop, this is the area's most appealing place to stay. Innkeepers Deb and Bob Winders offer eight attractive rooms (private baths) and seven suites (one with three bedrooms) divided between the main inn and neighboring Burdette House. Some have fireplace or wood-burning stove and

steam shower or whirlpool bath. The inn itself also offers a small reading/talking area, warmed by a soapstone stove off a cozy taproom; there's a low-beamed, charming dining room (see *Dining Out*). This is not a place for children. Beyond the porch is the village with its six covered bridges, and from the back there is a hot tub under the gazebo with a view of Hazen's Notch. Summer is low season: $104 per room, $141–219 per suite B&B, including tax and gratuity. Ski season: $116 for rooms, from $153 for suites.

English Rose Inn (802-326-3232; 1-888-303-3232; www.theenglish roseinn.com), 195 Mountain Road (Route 242), Montgomery Center 05471. The former Eagle Lodge has a new identity. Gary and Mary Jane Bouchard-Pike (he from Britain, she from Highgate Center) spent 2 years renovating the rambling 1850 farmhouse before opening with 14 redecorated rooms, 3 of them suites (all with private bath). Lacy curtains, Victorian antiques, and knickknacks have been added, and the dining room is now open to the public as Paddington's (see *Dining Out*), but there is still ample common space, including a Victorian parlor with TV and VCR (lots of films), a large library, and a cozy fireplace room. $40–115 in low season, $55–135 in ski season includes a full breakfast and afternoon tea. The high end is for a suite with fireplace and Jacuzzi.

∞ **Inglenook Lodge** (802-988-2880; 1-800-331-4346; www.inglenookver mont.com), Route 202, Jay 05859. This classic family-run lodge near the Jay Peak access road offers a great view. It has 10 large and 8 smaller rooms, catering to families and groups. There's a sunken lounge with circular fireplace, an indoor swimming pool, Jacuzzi, and sauna. $69–89 per couple B&B, $138 MAP. Owner Janice Kruse also manages **Trillium Woods at Jay,** on Route 242 between the village and the mountain. These are town houses holding eight, with Jacuzzi, fireplace, and sauna; $370 per night in ski season, available by the week and month in summer.

The Inn on Trout River (802-326-4391; 1-800-338-7049; www .troutinn.com), P.O. Box 76, Montgomery Center 05471. Built grandly by a lumber baron, this attractive village house offers 10 guest rooms with private bath, and one suite with a brass bed and woodstove. There are also hearths in the dining room, library, and foyer. The innkeepers are Michael and Lee Forman. The **Hobo Cafe** and more formal Lemoine's Restaurant (see *Dining Out*) are open to the public. $43–72 per person B&B. Inquire about the service charge.

BED & BREAKFASTS 🐾 🏃 **Woodshed Lodge** (802-988-4444; 1-800-495-4445; www.woodshedlodge.com), Route 242, Jay 05459. Just 3 miles from Jay Peak, this landmark old lodge is maintained by John and Chris Engler, who cater to families. Three of the seven rooms have private bath (one with whirlpool tub), while four share three baths. There's a sitting room upstairs and a library/TV lounge downstairs. $50–70 per couple in summer, $70–90 in winter includes breakfast plus $10 per extra person, $5 per child; inquire about weekend specials including one dinner.

Phineas Swann B&B (802-326-4306; www.phineasswann.com), Main

Street, Montgomery Center 05471. Michael Bindler and Glen Bartolomeo are the hosts in this bright gingerbread Victorian with its delightful sunroom and wood-burning fireplaces. In the main house four guest rooms are decorated with period antiques and Laura Ashley patterns. $99–139 per room includes full breakfast (like raspberry French toast) and afternoon tea with fresh pastries. There are also two suites with sitting room, fireplace, and Jacuzzi in the Carriage House: $195 for two bedrooms, $145 for one bedroom. Add 13 percent gratuity.

Missisquoi Riverbend B&B (802-744-9991; www.riverbendvt.com), 6198 Route 100, Troy 05868. A Victorian farmhouse on the edge of the village offers 15 acres on the Missisquoi River. Innkeepers Paul Becker and Jim McKenzie enjoy introducing guests to the delights of paddling (canoes available). The house offers two guest rooms with shared bath and two suites with private bath. This is a comfortable, casual place with fireplaces in the living room and library. Birders are particularly welcome; horseback riding and sleigh rides are offered. $78–89 in summer/fall and $89–99 in winter includes a full breakfast.

♦ Idyllwild East Bed & Breakfast (802-988-9830; www.idyllwildeast .com), 1387 Route 101, Troy 05859. Pronooll and Dortha Johnson's contemporary house is remarkably roomy. The three attractive guest rooms (two with shared bath) are off a big entry-level family room with a wood-burning stove and TV. On the second floor is a larger, brighter "great room" with a dining area and eat-in kitchen. Common space also includes a back

deck and more than 3 landscaped acres. $75 single, $95 double with breakfast; family and meal plan rates available.

Couture's Maple Shop and Bed & Breakfast (802-744-2733; 1-800-845-2733; www.maplesyrupvermont.com), 560 Route 100, Westfield 05874-9197. Pauline and Jacques Couture raised six children in this 1892 farmhouse while also maintaining a dairy farm and sizable maple syrup business. Two guest rooms with queen-sized beds and a pullout couch share a bath. The cow barn is out the back door, and the sugarhouse is just up the hill. $85 per couple ($10 per extra person) includes a full breakfast served in the newly renovated farm kitchen.

The Lodge at Jay (802-988-4459; 1-877-204-7039), Route 242, Jay Four Corners 05859. This well-built lodge has been recently renovated and furnished. Facilities include a restaurant and pub and an evolving spa that at present includes a steam room, sauna, and exercise room with massage available on request. There's also an entertainment room with a wide-screen TV. Winter rates are $87–130.75 during the regular season, more for family suites; under 14 free with parents. Inquire about ski-and-stay packages.

Rose Apple Acres Farm (802-988-4300; 1-877-879-9135; fax: 802-988-2309), 721 East Hill Road, North Troy 05859. Closed in winter. Jay and Camilla Meads's comfortable house sits on 52 acres, with lovely views, good for cross-country skiing. It's a real farm with sheep, goats, and horses. Located 10 miles from Jay Peak, near a covered bridge on the Missisquoi River; good for fishing and canoeing. There are two guest rooms, one with private bath. Camilla makes porcelain dolls in her studio (see *Selective Shopping*). The Meads cater to Long Trail hikers with a special rate of $35 per person; they will shuttle hikers to and from the trailhead or bus. Otherwise, rates range $50–60, including breakfast.

✳ Where to Eat

DINING OUT Black Lantern Inn (802-326-4507), Montgomery Village. Dinner is served nightly in-season, less often in spring and summer. Phone to reserve. The low-beamed dining room of this delightful old inn is the setting for candlelight dinners. While the menu changes nightly, you might begin with a spinach- or sausage-stuffed portobello mushroom followed by Black Angus filet mignon stuffed with Green Mountain Blue Cheese and roasted garlic, with strawberries Amaretto for dessert. Entrées range from $12 (for a vegetarian dish) to $22.

North Troy Village Restaurant (802-988-4063), Main Street, North Troy. Open at 5 PM daily except Tuesday. Irene McDermott has earned an enthusiastic following. The attractive dining room in this 1890s village hotel is the scene of memorable meals. The reasonably priced menu is extensive and features seafood and prime rib specials. There's a kids' menu and "mini-meals," like a 5-ounce tournedo (why don't others do this?). Warning: The "Little Bear Cut" is enormous.

Paddington's (802-326-3232), Route 242 between the Jay Peak access road and Montgomery Center. Open Thursday through Sunday 5–9:30. We have only breakfasted here, but chef-owners Gary and Mary Jane Bouchard-Pike both hold culinary school degrees and spent their

lives in the restaurant business before opening the dining room of this old inn (formerly the Eagle Lodge). So it should be good. Specialties include prime rib with Yorkshire pudding, and Cornish pasty (golden flaky crust filled with Vermont cheddar, a blend of fresh herbs, and veggies). Entrées $12.95–21.95, including house salad, vegetables, starch, and fresh-baked bread. Children's menu available.

Lemoine's at the Inn on Trout River (802-326-4391), Main Street, Montgomery Center. Serving nightly in winter, check off-season. The lacy dining room in this handsome old house is the setting for heart-healthy meals featuring entrées like turkey tenderloin with celery sauce, and grilled leg of lamb with pesto and sun-dried tomatoes. Full dinners run $20.50–24.25.

Inglenook Lodge (802-988-2880), Route 202, Jay. The menu changes nightly but this big, cheerful lodge dining room is always a good deal, specializing in complete dinners with a soup and salad bar for $12–20.

Hotel Jay (802-988-2611) at Jay Peak. Dinner is served 6–9, and reservations are a must in winter. In summer, dinner is served only Friday and Saturday. The big, functional dining room is cheery, and the menu features dishes like veal Gruyère and fillet of salmon. Entrées $13.95–21.

EATING OUT The Belfry (802-326-4400), Route 242, between Montgomery Center and the Jay Peak access road. Open nightly 4–late. No reservations, and during ski season you'd better get here early if you want a booth. Built in 1902 as a schoolhouse, this is the area's most popular pub, and the food's good, thanks to longtime manager Chantal Polhtier who now owns it, along with Marty Lumbra, who drives the local school bus. If you've been here a day or two, chances are you will recognize someone in the crowd around the mirrored oak-and-marble back bar. The soup is homemade, and the blackboard lists daily specials, like pan-blackened fish and grilled lamb chops. The set menu features "belfry steak" ("price depends on the chef's mood"), salads, burgers, and deep-fried mushrooms. Inquire about music.

The Lodge at Jay Restaurant and Pub (802-988-4459), Route 202, Jay Four Corners. This newly renovated lodge features a big, already popular restaurant specializing in steak, pasta, and fish with nightly specials in the $11–14 range. **Squidwards Nightclub and Bar** downstairs features a wide choice of beers on tap and weekend entertainment during ski season.

🐟 ✈ **Bernie's** (802-326-4682), Main Street, Montgomery Center. Open 6:30 AM–10 PM, later on weekends. The best place around for lunch, and not bad for dinner, either. Bigger than it looks from its greenhouse-style front, this is a genuine gathering spot for the area. Breakfast options include bagels, smoked salmon, and eggs any style, and the breads (including wheat onion, six-grain, and herb) are baked daily, for sale separately as well as used in sandwiches. Soups are a luncheon specialty, and at dinner the menu ranges from sautéed scampi through pastas. Fully licensed with a pub in back. John Boucher frequently presides behind the counter.

Jay Country Store (802-988-4040), Jay Village. Open daily 6:30 AM–9 PM, Sunday 7:30–8. Sandwiches at the counter and in the sunny solarium are the best in the village, reflecting the quality of the store's deli.

The Old Bobbin Mill Restaurant & Pub (802-744-2233), Route 100, Westfield. Open daily except Monday 7 AM–8 PM, later Thursday through Saturday. Local fiddlers gather for Wednesday breakfast. This a genuine old lumber turned bobbin mill, turned crafts shop, turned pub and restaurant. Menus and servings are large and prices low. A cheeseburger deluxe with the works is $3.50 even at dinnertime. Other choices include Vermont roast turkey with sage dressing and homemade gravy, and hot roast beef, sliced thin and stacked on bread, topped with brown gravy.

Hidden Country Restaurant (802-744-6149), Route 100, Lowell. Open Monday through Saturday 4:30–9 PM, Sunday 8:30–11:30 AM. Begun in 1988 by Joe St. Onge, this restaurant draws diners from throughout the Kingdom. The specialty is prime rib; rolls and desserts are homemade, and the Friday fish fry is famous. There's a trout pond for paid fishing and an eight-hole chip-and-putt golf course.

✳ Selective Shopping

Jay Country Store (802-988-4040), Jay Village. Open daily. The center of Jay Village, selling papers, gas, food, and wine basics, also a deli (see *Eating Out*), plus an interesting assortment of gift items and cards.

Couture's Maple Shop (802-744-733; 1-800-845-2733), 560 Route 100, Westfield. Open year-round, Monday through Saturday 8–6. A long-established maple producer: maple candy, cream, granulated sugar, pancake mix, and salad dressing, as well as syrup; will ship anywhere.

Jed's Maple Products (802-744-2095; www.jedsmaple.com), 475 Carter Road, Westfield. Syrup, candy, and frosted nuts. Inquire about the annual Mud Season Sugar On Snow Party.

The Tickle Trunk (802-988-4731), Cross Road, Jay. Open Friday through Monday 10–5. Full of clocks, books, Victorian and country antiques, vintage clothing, and works by local artists and artisans.

Rose Apple Acres Dolls (802-988-4300), East Hill Road, North Troy. Modern porcelain figures and restoration.

The Pink Lady (802-848-3836), 66 Main Street, Richford. Open daily 10–5. Subtitled "the Richford Antique and Gift Center," this elaborate Victorian mill owner's mansion now offers 21 rooms filled with antiques, art, vintage and new clothing, jewelry, mirrors, lamps, crafts, and more.

Red Barn Studio (802-326-4672), 32 Fuller Bridge Road, Montgomery (behind the Methodist church), is open mid-May through mid-October by chance or appointment, showcasing local artists.

✳ Special Events

Last Sunday of January: **Hazen's Notch Ski Race.**

Mid-February: **Winter Festival**—varied events including a race from the summit of Jay Peak to Jay Village.

July–August: **Concerts on the common,** presented by the Montgomery Historical Society on Saturday evening (802-326-4404).

Mid-August: **Jay Day.**

September: **Concerts on the common** in the Montgomery Village church.

First weekend of October: **Octoberfest,** Jay Peak—big annual arts and crafts fair.

THE LAKE COUNTRY

INCLUDING NEWPORT, BARTON, AND ISLAND POND

The Northeast corner of the Northeast Kingdom is spotted with some of the most beautiful lakes in New England. The largest of these is Memphremagog and the most dramatic, Lake Willoughby. There are many more, however, especially in Essex County, the easternmost and loneliest corner of Vermont, in which publicly owned land has recently increased substantially.

At the height of railroad passenger service, large wooden hotels rose on the shores of several of these lakes. In Newport, at the southern tip of Lake Memphremagog (which stretches more than 30 miles north into Canada), the 400-room Memphremagog House stood next to the railroad station, Newport House was across the street, and the New City Hotel was nearby. Guests came by train from Boston and Philadelphia. Lindbergh came with his *Spirit of Saint Louis,* and there was a racetrack and a paddle-wheeler. The city's past splendor is recalled in archival photos mounted by the Memphremagog Historical Society of Newport in the new State Office Building, where there's also a display on northern Vermont Abenaki people, from Paleolithic through current times. Recently the city has reclaimed its lakefront with a marina and boardwalk.

Less than a dozen miles northeast of Newport is the split-nationality community of Derby Line, Vermont, and Stanstead, Quebec. This is a major border crossing (I-91 continues north as Highway 55), linking with the major east–west highway between Montreal and Quebec City. The international line runs right through the Haskell Opera House in Derby Line—the audience in America attends concerts in Canada.

West of Derby Center you are quickly in little-trafficked lake country: Lakes Derby and Salem, Seymour and Echo all have good fishing, and dozens of smaller ponds have boat launches. Island Pond is a town as well as a lake, and for travelers it looms large on the map because you have to pass through it to get to the empty (of people, but teeming with moose, black bear, and other wildlife), lake-pocked land surrounding the town in every direction. It's the obvious place to stop for lunch or dinner. There's good fishing around Averill and in this lonely stretch of the Connecticut River as it dwindles into a stream.

Lake Willoughby, west of Barton, is one of Vermont's most hauntingly beautiful lakes. Mounts Hor and Pisgah, which rise abruptly from opposite shores,

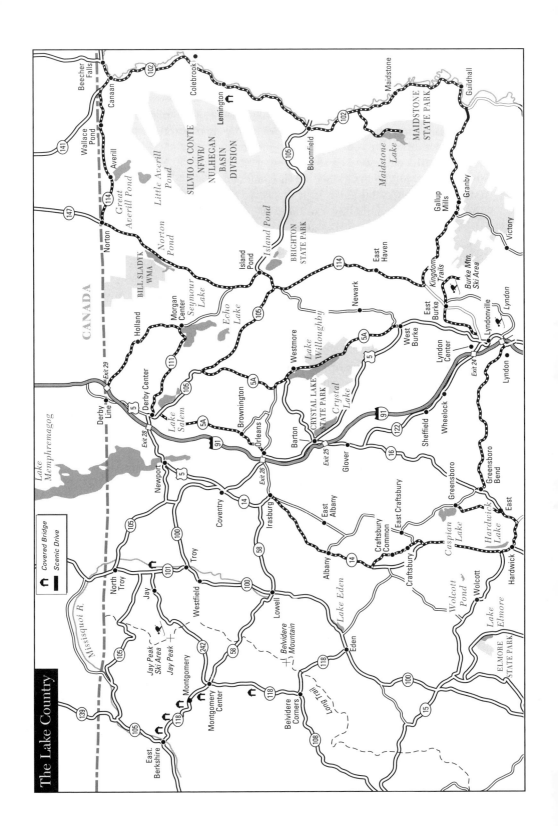

The Lake Country

Covered Bridge
Scenic Drive

create a fjordlike effect when viewed from the public beach in Westmore at the northern end or from the southern tip of the lake. Mostly undeveloped, Willoughby is surrounded for much of its length by state forest, and the water is stocked with salmon and rainbow trout. A well-known resort area in the days of grand hotels and steamboats, it now has a limited, loyal following of sailors, sailboarders (there is always a breeze here), and year-round fishermen.

Barton, this area's southernmost commercial center, also obviously boomed in the late 19th century, when six passenger trains a day stopped in summer, bringing guests to fill the town's big hotels (long gone) or the gingerbread "camps" (still there) on Crystal Lake. Its shops serve the communities of Brownington to the east, Irasburg and Glover to the west, plus the beautiful web of farm roads between West Glover and Albany.

GUIDANCE Vermont North Country Chamber of Commerce (802-334-7782; www.vtnorthcountry.com) maintains a walk-in visitors center on the Causeway in Newport, open daily year-round, in summer and fall 9–5, in winter 9:30–4:30.

The Derby Line Welcome Center (802-873-3311) on I-91 south, with restrooms, at the border serves arriving Canadians.

Barton Area Chamber of Commerce (802-525-1137; www.bartonareacham ber.com), P.O. Box 403, Barton 05822, serves the southern part of this region and has listings of summer lakeside cottages.

Island Pond Chamber of Commerce (802-723-6300; www.islandpondcham ber.org).

GETTING AROUND Two pieces of advice: (1) Avoid driving lonely stretches after dark and if you must, do so slowly, watching for moose, which are difficult to spot at night and deadly if you collide at high speed. (2) Gas up. Pumps are few and far between and tempting woods roads abound.

WHEN TO COME Snowmobilers converge on Island Pond and ice fishers come to many of the lakes in winter; fishermen come in spring, hunters in fall. Otherwise this is summer and fall foliage country.

✳ Villages

Barton Village (population: 742). The hotels are gone, but Crystal Lake remains beautiful, with a clifflike promontory on one side and public beaches at its northern rim. There is golf here, and the town of Barton itself packs an astounding number of services into its small downtown. The Crystal Lake Falls Historical Association maintains the **Pierce House Museum** (802-525-6251) on Water Street, next to the old-fashioned office of the *Barton Chronicle*, an excellent little weekly covering much of Orleans and Essex Counties.

Brownington Village is a crossroads full of outstanding, early-19th-century buildings, the core of a once proud hill town long since eclipsed by such valley centers as Barton, Orleans, and Newport. There are 19th-century flower and heirloom herb gardens behind the Eaton House and a spectacular panorama from the wooden observatory set up in a meadow behind the church. A descriptive walking tour booklet is available at the Old Stone House Museum, the big attraction in the village.

Island Pond (population: 1,260). The crossroads of Vermont's lonely, northeasternmost corner, Island Pond has the look and feel of an outpost.

A sign in front of the city-sized depot reads, PIONEER RAILROAD PLANNER JOHN A. POOR'S DREAM OF AN INTERNATIONAL RAILROAD CONNECTING MONTREAL, CANADA, WITH THE ICE-FREE HARBOR OF PORTLAND, MAINE, BECAME A REALITY ON JULY 18, 1854, WHEN THE fiRST THROUGH TRAINS MET AT THIS GREAT HALFWAY POINT ON THE GRAND TRUNK RAILWAY. During the late 19th century and into the 20th, Island Pond hummed with the business of servicing frequent passenger trains and freight trains transporting logs and wood pulp. No longer. Today it's a funky village on a pond with an island in its center. The Twelve Tribes, a religious community, has rooted here, buying and restoring many of the Victorian houses and operating the town's one big specialty store. Winter is now the season here. Island Pond is the region's snowmobiling capital.

✳ To See

Bread and Puppet Theater Museum (802-525-3031), Route 122, Glover. Open June through November 1, 10–6. The internationally known Bread and Puppet Theater tours in winter, but much of the year the weathered, vintage-1863 dairy barn is open to anyone who stops (free, but donations welcome). It houses one of the biggest collections and some of the biggest puppets in the world: huge and haunting puppet dwarfs, giants, devils, and other fantastic figures of good and evil, the artistic expressions of German-born Peter Schumann who founded the Bread and Puppet Theater in 1962 and moved it to Glover in 1974. Tours are offered June through September on Sundays at 2, but otherwise visitors wander and wonder. Publications and postcards are sold in the shop. Sundays in July and August, performances are staged at 3 PM in the outdoor arena in the neighboring field; inquire about Friday-night performances in the timber-frame theater.

The Old Stone House Museum (802-754-2022; www.oldstonehouse museum.org), off Route 58 east of Orleans in Brownington. Open May 15 through October 15, Wednesday through Sunday 11–5. $5 per adult, $4 county residents, $2 students. This is the Orleans County Historical Society Museum, housed in a four-story granite building dating from 1836, built as a dormitory for a rural academy. The structure resembles the earliest dorms at Middlebury College, from which Alexander Twilight, the

NEWPORT LAKEFRONT

VDT

school's principal and building's architect, graduated in 1823. There is some question about whether Twilight was—as Middlebury College claims—the first African American graduate of an American college. There is no question about the beauty of the building and the historical collections filling 23 rooms: Collections represent the towns in Orleans County and also hold 18th- and 19th-century tools, paintings, furniture, and decorative arts. Pick up a walking tour booklet. Inquire about special, year-round workshops.

Also see Jay Peak summit in "Jay Peak Area."

LAKES **Lake Memphremagog,** Newport. Vermont's second largest lake at 33 miles long—only 5 miles of which are within the United States—Memphremagog stretches north from Newport. See St. Benoit du Lac in "Jay Peak Area" as well as listings under *Boating, Fishing,* and *Swimming.*

Lake Willoughby, Westmore. Vermont's most dramatic lake, nearly 5 miles long and more than 300 feet deep, shaped like a stocking with a foot toward the north and Mount Pisgah and Mount Hor rising to more than 2,500 feet on opposite sides at the southern end. See *Boating, Fishing, Swimming,* and *Lodging.*

Seymour Lake. There is a public beach in the tiny village of Morgan Center, also the spot to rent boats for fishing for landlocked salmon. In winter this lake is peppered with fishing shanties, and there is a system of cross-country trails (ungroomed).

Echo Lake. Much smaller than Seymour Lake and adjoining it on the south, this lake is circled by a dirt road and gently rolling hills. There is also public boat access. Good fishing for trout and landlocked salmon.

Island Pond is actually a small lake with a 20-acre island off the sandy beach and a wooded campground in Brighton State Park. Boating and fishing are both easily accessible.

SEYMOUR LAKE

Christina Tree

Crystal Lake, Barton. Roughly 3 miles long and about 1 mile wide, in places more than 100 feet deep, this glacial lake is beautifully sited between rough-hewn mountains. Crystal Lake State Park (see *Swimming*) is justly popular; summer rental cottages can be found through the Barton chamber of commerce. Also see *Fishing.*

Maidstone Lake, Guildhall. One of Vermont's cleanest, clearest, most remote lakes was designated a state park in 1938. This was wilderness but the Civilian Conservation Corps built fireplaces for camping, along with the lodge and picnic shelter that are still in use (see *Green Space*). The lake offers good trout fishing but is best known as a loon nesting area.

FOR FAMILIES ✔ **Cow Town Elk Ranch** (802-766-5068), Derby Center, intersection of Routes 5 and 105. Visitors welcome anytime. Derby once had so many dairies that it was known as Cow Town, but Doug Nelson's is now the only big dairy operation left (1,000 head); he also raises elk (the herd numbered 300 when we last checked). There's parking and a sign answering the 10 most frequently asked questions. Nelson harvests the velvet for the Asian trade in June, so you might want to come before, when the antlers are at their most majestic. Spring is also calving time. Please don't feed the elk, and be cautious: They're friendly, but they're still wild animals.

SCENIC DRIVES **West Burke to Westmore.** The stretch of Route 5A along Lake Willoughby is one of the most breathtaking anywhere.

Island Pond–Lake Willoughby shortcut. An easy route to navigate from Westmore on Lake Willoughby: Turn north in the middle of the village on Hinton Ridge Road and follow it through high, rolling farmland and forest (never mind name changes) until it reaches a T-intersection. Turn right and right again onto Route 105 into Island Pond. The reverse direction is even more beautiful but tricky at the beginning (left onto Hudson Road off Route 105 and then your second left onto Westmore Road).

✳ To Do

BIKING While the region's formal mountain biking meccas are in St. Johnsbury, this pristine area offers hundreds of miles of dirt and logging roads. Request the excellent bike map for the Kingdom from the Northeast Kingdom Travel and Tourism Association (1-800-884-8001).

BIRDING The most famous birds in the Kingdom are the peregrine falcons that nest on Mount Pisgah on Willoughby Lake. Falcons return in spring, nest during summer, and leave by August. Early morning and late afternoon are the best times to see them from the north end of the west-facing cliff.

Over 100 species of birds have been spotted around Lake Willoughby alone. Maidstone Lake is famed as a nesting area for loons, and the Nulhegan Basin is an important breeding habitat for migratory birds and nesting thrushes and warblers. Boreal forests in the basin support rare species such as spruce grouse, gray

ISLAND POND LOOP This 66-mile loop circles the northeastern corner of Vermont, beginning in Island Pond and heading north on Route 114. The Canadian National Railway's Grand Trunk line from Montreal to Portland, Maine, hugs the highway the full 16 miles to Norton. This railway was once Montreal's winter lifeline to Europe, as goods could not be shipped in or out of the frozen port of Montreal during the coldest months. About halfway to **Norton,** near the south end of long and slender **Norton Pond** (there's a boat launch on Route 114), a gravel road to the left leads into the Bill Sladyk Wildlife Management Area, frequented by hunters, fishermen, and loggers. Just before reaching the tiny village of Norton (opposite slightly larger Stanhope, Quebec), the forest thins out and farmland reappears. Norton is the site of the notorious Earth People's Park, a 1960s-style, loosely governed hippie commune that has survived but has dwindled from hundreds to perhaps two dozen residents. The road passes several farms, a school, and the **Norton Country Store** (open daily 7 AM–9 PM), then swings abruptly eastward to avoid the imposing Canadian port-of-entry.

Continuing eastward along the border, Route 114 reenters the forest, passing a series of lakes, most of which are dotted with hunting and fishing camps. The largest of the lakes is **Great Averill Pond.** For directions to the boat launch, stop by the **Lakeview Store** (open daily 8–7), where owner Priscilla Roy sells the wool that she spins, also weaving supplies and locally handcrafted items. East of the store a road leads to Quimby Country, one of Vermont's oldest and most interesting resorts. Shortly after passing Big Averill, you leave the St. Lawrence watershed and begin a rapid descent into the Connecticut River Valley. Halfway from Averill to Canaan, the road skirts the south shore of sizable **Wallace Pond,** almost entirely within the province of Quebec.

Canaan, 14 miles east of Norton, is a pleasant pocket of civilization with a handsome green, Fletcher Park, with a lovely Greek Revival building in its far corner. Built as a tavern in 1846 and said to have served for a while as the northernmost U.S. stop on the Underground Railroad, this is now the **Alice M. Ward Memorial Library** (802-266-7135), worth a stop to see the Cannan Historical Society's changing exhibits upstairs.

In Bessie's Diner, across from the green on Route 114, a framed tintype depicts Canaan as the village was when a covered bridge spanned the Connecticut River here, connecting it with West Stewartstown, New Hampshire. Today you barely notice the river, here just a fledgling stream spanned by a brief bridge. Turn north along this stream if you want to see the village of Beecher Falls, 2 miles north. The small, sagging village is dominated by the huge Ethan Allen Furniture plant (closed at this writing) and is a Canadian border crossing. Across another brief bridge is Stewartstown, New Hampshire.

In reality these far corners of Vermont and New Hampshire form a region of their own, a fishing, snowmobiling, and moose-watching mecca known by various names but most accurately as the Connecticut Lakes. You might want to detour north on Route 3 in New Hampshire (Vermont ends at Beecher Falls). A state-operated information center (with restrooms) south of Pittsburg orients visitors to the series of four lakes strung along the 22 semiwilderness miles north of town. This stretch of Route 3 is known as "Moose Alley" for reasons easy to grasp if you drive it on a summer evening. Fishing lodges and rental camps, salted away around these lakes, way outnumber lodging options contained in the entire vast area of Vermont covered by this chapter, but you see few from the road. Die-hard Connecticut River buffs may want to hike in to its source, a small pond accessible via a path beside the Route 3 border station (restrooms).

From Canaan the loop turns south on Route 102, through river-bottom farmland, through Lemington, and past the impressively long Columbia covered bridge, which demands a photo stop. This stretch of the river valley alternately narrows and widens, and the road tunnels through forest, broken occasionally by farms, fields, and glimpses of impressive mountains. In Bloomfield (the store may or may not be open) the Grand Trunk railroad line angles east across the road, heading for Portland. Here our route turns west on Route 105 (it's 16 miles back to Island Pond).

For another great detour, however, continue at least the mile down Route 102 to **Brunswick Springs,** once the site of a mineral springs resort. Said to be a sacred Abenaki site, the resort's buildings repeatedly burned and are all gone, but the springs still run pure. Another 4 miles south on Route 102 (and 5 miles in on a dirt road) brings you to Maidstone State Park, offering camping and swimming as well as fishing. The Connecticut River widens noticeably the farther south you drive on Route 102, and views of the White Mountains are increasingly dramatic. If you continue another 7 miles south to Guildhall, you are informed by a billboard-sized sign that the town was "discovered" in 1754, chartered in 1761, and settled in 1764, making it the oldest town in northeastern Vermont (by contrast, Norton was not settled until 1860). An attractive, square green is flanked by historically interesting buildings: a tiny courthouse, church, town hall (the Guild Hall, 1798), and an ornate 1909 Classical Revival library with stained-glass windows. An unassuming white-clapboard house serves as a county lockup.

Two miles downriver from Guildhall, a town road marked GRANBY runs west off Route 102, beginning as a paved road but becoming gravel well before reaching the tiny hamlets of Granby and Gallup Mills, about 8 miles from Route 102. This is wild, wooded, and boggy country, good for spotting moose and bear. Lumber camps and sawmills once peppered this area, and there was even a steam railway. The road finally descends about 8 miles west of Granby to reach Route 114, joining it a couple of miles north of East Burke. Take Route 114 some 12 miles north through rolling, mixed farm- and forestland to its junction with Route 105, 2 miles west of Island Pond.

jay, Wilson's warbler, olive-sided flycatcher, rusty blackbird, black-backed wood-pecker, and three-toed woodpecker. **Northeast Kingdom Outfitters** (802 754-9471; www.northeastkingdomoutfitters.com) offers wildlife walking expeditions in this area. See *Green Space* for more about the venues.

BOATING With thousands of miles of rivers and streams and the lion's share of the Kingdom's more than 37,000 acres of lakes and ponds, this area offers some of the best paddling in the Northeast. The DeLorme *Vermont Atlas and Gazetteer* shows put-ins.

Vermont Leadership Center (802-723-6551; www.vtlc.org), 10 Mile Square Road, East Charleston (5 miles west of Island Pond), offers rental canoes on the Clyde River, also guided canoe expeditions on a variety of waters. **Vermont Adventure Company** (802-525-3154; 1-866-542-7204; www.vtadventure co.com) offers kayaking and canoe tours, rentals on the Connecticut and Barton Rivers, and two secluded lakes and ponds. **White Caps Campgrounds** (802-467-3345) at the southern end of Lake Willoughby rents canoes and kayaks. Aluminum boats (14 feet) with small motors, also pontoons and sailboats, may be rented at **Newport Marine** (802-334-5911) at Eastside Restaurant Docks, Farrants Point, on Lake Memphremagog in Newport. Boats are also available at **Brighton State Park** in Island Pond (see *Green Space*), **Anglin' Boat Rentals** on Crystal Lake in Barton (802-525-3904), and **Nulhegan Guiding** (802-895-4328) in Island Pond.

On the Connecticut River, Canaan is a good place to put in, but there are several rapids at the start. Canoeing is also good below Colebrook, New Hampshire, for 3 miles but then rather fast for an equal distance. (See also *Fishing*.)

FISHING This is a fly-fishing mecca, drawing serious fishermen to wilderness brooks and ponds as well as rivers and lakes. Most general stores sell 3-day fishing licenses (see *Fishing* in "What's Where" for fishing regulations). Check in the *Vermont Atlas and Gazetteer* for local access points to ponds. Rental boats, bait, and tackle are available at the sites listed under *Boating*. The pamphlet *Vermont Guide to Fishing*, prepared by the Vermont Fish and Wildlife Department, available locally, tells where to find what. **Northeast Kingdom Outfitters** (802-754-9471; www.northeastkingdomoutfitters.com) offers fly-fishing schools as well as drift-boat fishing tips and guide service. **Osprey Fishing Adventures** (603-922-3800). Ken Hastings of Columbia, New Hampshire, is the fishing guru for this stretch of the river. Guides can also be found through the Vermont Leadership Center (see *Green Space*), through the **Vermont Outdoor Guide Association** (1-800-425-8747; www.voga.org), and through local fishing-geared lodging, listed below.

In May head for the **Willoughby Falls Wildlife Management Area.** From Orleans drive east on Route 58 for 0.2 mile. At the BROWNINGTON sign bear left and drive 0.1 mile to the Vermont Fish and Wildlife parking area. Between the last week in April and the second week in May, wild rainbow trout climb the falls here, jumping high to clear the whitewater to reach their spawning ground. **Willoughby** is known as the prime fishing lake; check out the **Clyde River** for

brook trout and landlocked salmon, the **Barton River** for trout and perch. **Lake**
Memphremagog is good for smelt, smallmouth bass, and walleyes, in addition
to salmon and trout, but also has plenty of milfoil. **Seymour Lake** is (at this
writing) milfoil-free and known for bass and lake trout. **Holland Pond** and
Echo Lake are known for rainbow trout, and **Norton Pond** is known for fighting pike. Ice fishing is particularly popular on Memphremagog and Seymour
Lake. There is a state fish hatchery in Newark; **Newark Pond** has an access and
is good for yellow perch along with trout. The **Willoughby River** is known,
especially in early spring, for rainbow trout, as are the **Barton** and **Black
Rivers.** The **Clyde River,** recently acclaimed as the first river in the country to
have a dam removed for environmental reasons, is known for landlocked Atlantic
salmon.

Lodging geared to fishermen includes Seymour Lake Lodge in Morgan, which
offers advice and free boats to its guests, and Quimby Country, a self-contained
resort that includes 70-acre Forest Lake, 0.5 mile from 1,200-acre Great Averill
Pond, both lonely and remote but good for trout and salmon; rowboats can be
rented here by the day. Also see Crystal Lake B&B in Barton and the Village Inn
of East Burke in the "St. Johnsbury" chapter, and check out *Green Space* as well.

GOLF Newport Country Club (802-334-2391), off Mount Vernon Street, overlooking the lake. Eighteen holes, rentals, instruction, restaurant; April through
November.

Dufferin Heights Golf Club (819-876-2113), Stanstead, Quebec. May through
November. Nine holes, cart rentals, restaurant.

Orleans Country Club (802-754-2333), Route 58, near Lake Willoughby. April
through November; 18 holes, rentals, instruction.

Barton Golf Course (802-525-1126), Telfer Hill Road, Barton. April through
September, 18 holes, cart rentals, low fees.

Grandad's Invitational, Newark. This nine-hole course is a local legend. Ask
around for directions and leave your fee in the mailbox.

HIKING AND WALKING Mount Pisgah and **Mount Hor,** Lake Willoughby.
Named respectively for the place where the Lord sent Moses to view the
Promised Land and for the place Moses' brother Aaron died after the Lord commanded him to go there, these twin mountains, separated by a narrow stretch of
lake, form Willoughby Gap. Both are within the 7,000-acre Willoughby State
Forest and offer well-maintained hiking trails. Mount Pisgah (2,751 feet) on the
east side of the lake (access marked from Route 5A) has fairly short climbs yielding spectacular views of the White Mountains; trails up Mount Hor (2,648 feet)
begin on the Civilian Conservation Corps road, 1.8 miles west of its junction
with Route 5A, and also offer panoramic views of the Green Mountains to the
west. For details, consult *50 Hikes in Vermont* (Backcountry Guides) and *Day
Hiker's Guide to Vermont* (Green Mountain Club).

Wheeler Mountain. The trail begins on Wheeler Mountain Road, which leaves
the north side of Route 5, 8.3 miles north of West Burke and 5 miles south of

Barton Village. From the highway, the unpaved road climbs 1.9 miles to the trailhead.

Bald Mountain. There are excellent views from the newly restored fire tower at the summit of this, the tallest peak in the Willoughby Lake area. Trails ascend to the summit from both the north (Lookout's Trail, 2.8 miles) and the south (Long Pond Trail, 2.1 miles). From the north side of Bald Mountain, you can hike on trails and wilderness roads all the way to the summit of Mount Hor; Haystack Mountain (a side trip) has excellent views and two trails. Details can be found in *Day Hiker's Guide to Vermont* (see *Hiking and Walking* in "What's Where").

Bluff Mountain (elevation: 2,380 feet) looms over Island Pond to the north. It's a popular climb, with spectacular views. The trail starts from Route 114, north of the village. Inquire locally for directions.

Monadnock Mountain (elevation: 3,140 feet), in Lemington, towers over the Connecticut River and Colebrook, New Hampshire. A trail runs west, beginning as a driveway off Route 102 near the bridge to Colebrook. An abandoned fire tower crowns the summit.

HORSEBACK RIDING **Perry Farm** (802-754-2396) in Brownington offers hour-long trail rides at $25 per person.

Galluping Acres Riding Stable (802-754-2337), Ticehurst Road, Brownington. Open year-round, 10–dusk. Horseback riding through woods and fields on back roads, also wagon pulled by Belgians.

SCUBA DIVING **Willoughby Lake Divers** offers some rental gear and air fills at Northern Exposure (see *Eating Out*) in Westmore. For special tours contact Tharon Faulkner: 802-467-3104.

SWIMMING In Newport try **Prouty Beach,** a public facility on Lake Memphremagog. On Seymour Lake there is a public beach in Morgan Center. There are state facilities at Island Pond, a large beach that is sandy and shallow for quite a way out, great for children. **Crystal Lake State Beach** (802-525-6205), 90 Bellwater Avenue, Barton (just east of the village off Route 15), is open daily late May through September, with lifeguard, bathhouse (built of stones quarried on the lake and built in the late 1930s by the CCC), and picnic facilities; and **Pageant Park,** a mile farther east on Route 16, is a town-owned park open daily until 10 PM, also with a bathhouse and camping (primarily tenting). May Pond, also along Route 16 in Barton, is a great spot for swimming, canoeing, and kayaking. Lake Willoughby has small public beaches at both its northern and southern tips. **Boulder Beach Day Use Area** (802-584-3820) in Groton State Forest has a public beach, picnic area, snack bar, and bathhouse.

✳ Winter Sports

CROSS-COUNTRY SKIING **Vermont Leadership Center** (802-723-6551), 10 Mile Square Road, East Charleston (5 miles west of Island Pond), is a 600-acre preserve with 40 km of groomed skiing and snowshoeing trails. Rentals and guided tours are offered.

Sugarmill Farm (1-800-688-7978), Route 16, Barton. Eleven kilometers of marked trails meander through the farm; 800- to 1,400-foot elevations.

DOGSLED TOURS **Hardscrabble Dogsled Tours** (802-626-9895), based in Sheffield, offers tours ranging in length from an hour to a day.

DOWNHILL SKIING See Burke Mountain and Jay Peak in their respective chapters.

SNOWMOBILING *Northeast Kingdom Snowmobile Map* is free from the Northeast Kingdom Chamber of Commerce (1-800-639-6379). Island Pond is the snowmobiling capital of the Kingdom, from which groomed VAST (Vermont Association of Snow Travelers: 802-229-0005) trails radiate in all directions. The local Brighton Snowmobile Club maintains a snow phone: 802-723-4316. **Kingdom Cat Corp.** (802-723-9702; www.kingdomcat.com) on Cross Street in Island Pond is the snowmobile rental operation in the area, and offers guided tours.

SLEIGH RIDES **Perry Farm** (802-754-2396) in Brownington offers hay- and sleigh rides for groups of up to 10 people. At **Galluping Acres** (802-754-2337), Brownington Center, wagon and sleigh rides are offered.

✳ Green Space

Note: For more information on Vermont state parks, visit www.vtstateparks.com.

Brighton State Park (802-723-4360), Island Pond, 2 miles east on Route 105 to State Park Road. Open mid-May through mid-October. Campsites are nestled in a stand of white birch trees on Spectacle Pond: 63 tent/trailer sites, 21 lean-tos, and a rental cabin. The park includes frontage on the south shore of Island Pond, where there's a day-use area that features a sandy beach, a bathhouse with restrooms, and rental boats. Hiking trails include a leisurely hike to Indian Point and wildlife. Watch for moose and loons.

Maidstone State Park (802-676-3930), RR 1, Box 388, Brunswick 05905. Open Memorial Day through Labor Day. Five miles south of Bloomfield on Route 102, then 5 miles on dirt road, this is the most remote Vermont state park and retains much of its wilderness forest of maple, beech, and hemlock. The park's camping and day-use facilities are on Maidstone Lake, one of the most pristine lakes in Vermont. It's home to lake trout, rainbow trout, and brookies. Moose sightings and the call of the loon are common. There's a beach, picnic area, picnic shelter, hiking trails, and 45 tent/trailer sites, 37 lean-tos.

Vermont Leadership Center (802-723-6551), 10 Mile Square Road, East Charleston (5 miles west of Island Pond), is a 600-acre preserve with 40 km of walking/skiing and snowshoeing trails traversing neighboring private property. Aside from its formal nature hikes, guided canoeing, and frequent outreach programs, the center also serves as an informal clearinghouse for local canoe, fishing, tracking, and nature guides.

Bill Sladyk Wildlife Management Area, off Route 114, south of Norton Pond: 9,500 forested acres, also accessible via a gravel road past Holland Pond from Holland Village, 11 miles east of Derby. A detailed map is available from the Fish and Wildlife Department in Waterbury (802-241-3700).

Silvio O. Conte National Fish and Wildlife Refuge, Nulhegan Basin Division (802-962-5240; www.nulhegan.com), 5360 Route 105, Brunswick. Mailing address: P.O. Box 2127, Island Pond 05846. In 1999 when the Champion International Corporation announced plans to sell its holdings in Essex County, the U.S. Fish and Wildlife Service purchased this 26,000-acre tract (roughly 10 miles in diameter) that's home to rare animals and migratory birds. The Vermont Agency of Natural Resources acquired some 22,000 adjoining acres to form the West Mountain Wildlife Management Area; another 84,000 acres surrounding these preserves continue to be logged but with easements to protect their development. Over 100 species of birds nest in the Nulhegan Basin, which is home to moose, black bear, beaver, fisher, white-tailed deer, and coyote. The Nulhegan River and its tributaries harbor brook trout, bullhead, chain pickerel, chub, and more. The refuge is open to hunting, fishing, trapping, bird-watching, and hiking. It includes 40 miles of gravel roads, 17 miles of wooded pathways, and the Mollie Beattie Bog interpretive boardwalk (handicapped accessible). No biking. Request a map.

✳ Lodging

In Newport/Derby Line
Water's Edge B&B (802-334-7726; www.watersedgebnb.com), 324 Wishing Well Avenue, Newport 05855. Several miles north of downtown Newport, Pat Bryan's contemporary house sits right on the edge of Lake Memphremagog. Common space is tasteful and includes a deck. The three guest rooms include a queen room with a lake view ($75), a splendid corner queen with two windows on the lake ($90), and a suite with a sitting area and gas stove ($125). All rooms have private bath and TV. In summer guests have use of the canoe, rowboat, and dock; in winter there's snowmobile and ice-fishing access right out the front door. Bird-watching year-round. Rates include a full breakfast. Residents include two big, gentle dogs, and Shadow, a small black cat.

The Birchwood B&B (802-873-9104; www.together.net/~birchwd),

502 Main Street, Derby Line 05830. Betty and Dick Fletcher's handsome 1920s village house has three spacious, antiques-furnished (the couple owns an antiques store), immaculate bedrooms with private bath: the Double Bed Chamber (antique pineapple bed), the blue-and-white Queen Canopy Chamber, and the green-and-pink Twin Bed Room. The fireplace in the formally furnished living room is frequently lit, and guests gather around the long formal dining table for full, candlelit breakfasts. $95–100 includes breakfast.

In the Barton Area
🐾 ♪ **Crystal Lake B&B** (802-525-4670; www.crystallakebb.com), P.O. Box 333, 202 Lakeside Lane, Barton 05822. Open Memorial Day through Halloween. This trim white house sits right on the western shore of the lake with a deck overhanging it and views across its width and length. The three rooms with private bath are bright,

nicely furnished, two with water views. There's a knotty-pine-walled living room with a piano, gas fireplace, and comfortable seating, and guests can fish and swim from the dock; boats and canoes can be rented. A loft apartment in the neighboring building with four windows on the water is ideal for a family or longer stay. Dewey and Glenn Rogers have lived in many places around the world and now divide their year between this "piece of paradise" and Florida. Some people just know how to live! $99 per couple, $88 single includes breakfast. The apartment goes for $550 per week.

⊙ **Maple Manor B&B** (802-525-9591; www.maple-manor.com), 77 Maple Lane, West Glover 05875. This elaborate mansion with more than a touch of fantasy is an anomaly in the surrounding farmscape, a 250-acre estate specializing in elaborate weddings. The original farmhouse has been expanded and fitted with French doors, a conservatory, and many large windows through which the light streams. Both the common rooms and three guest rooms are exuberantly decorated. $125–225 per night includes a three-course candlelit breakfast served at the formally set dining room table, overlooking the flower gardens and pool. The top floor of the equestrian barn can accommodate groups of up to 200 for wedding receptions. Sleigh rides are offered in winter.

✔ **Rodgers Country Inn** (802-525-6677; 1-800-729-1704; www.virtual vermont.com/rodgers), 582 Rodgers Road, West Glover 05875. Not far from Shadow Lake, this 350-acre farm has been in Jim Rodgers's family since the 1800s. The farmhouse has

five guest rooms sharing three baths. Common space includes an enclosed porch, living rooms, and a game room with a TV and VCR. Nancy Rodgers serves meals family-style in the large kitchen/dining area. $45 per adult, $22.50 per child under 12 ($250/$135 per week), includes an ample breakfast and dinner. B&B rates available. Snowmobilers welcome.

On Lake Willoughby
& **WilloughVale Inn on Lake Willoughby** (802-525-4123; 1-800-594-9102; www.willoughvale.com), RR 2, Box 403, Westmore 05860. This special lakeside inn just keeps getting better and better. The original farmhouse/restaurant here has been replaced by a new inn, tastefully built along traditional lines with windows that maximize the spectacular lake view. It is now owned and operated by the Gameroff family, who also own the Green Mountain Inn in Stowe. Recently the size of its restaurant (see *Dining Out*) has been reduced to increase common space and add luxury suites with lake views. Guest rooms in the inn itself include three "luxury suites" with fireside Jacuzzi and private porch, one with a living/dining room and kitchen, and seven attractive rooms with private bath, phone, and TV (one handicapped accessible). There are four housekeeping cottages (one and two bedrooms) with fireplaces across the road, right on the lake. A taproom and light dinners are available; breakfast is also available for guests. Standard rooms with queen beds in the main inn begin at $79 midweek in winter and spring and $129 in summer and fall; the Lupine Room, with four-poster and Jacuzzi, ranges $119–159; weekdays are cheaper than

weekends, and weekly rates are offered. The Pisgah Cottage with a Jacuzzi, living room with fireplace, pullout sofa bed, and eat-in kitchen as well as deck and private dock is $159 midweek in low season, $229–249 in high. The other cottages are the same or slightly less, with weekly rentals in summer $1,398–1,478. Canoe, bicycle, and snowshoe rentals are available on the premises. Inquire about packages with meals and lodging, also lifts and lodging (with nearby Burke).

Fox Hall (802-525-6930), mailing address: 145 Fox Hall Lane, Barton 05822. The main house of a turn-of-the-20th-century mansion, which served for many decades as a girls camp, has been turned into a comfortable bed & breakfast. Common space is ample, and the eight guest rooms—some round, four with private bath—are furnished with antiques. All offer views of Lake Willoughby. The 76 acres include lake frontage and a dock. Guests have access to canoes and a floating raft. But they may never want to leave the wide old porch, which commands one of the most dramatic views in Vermont, right down Willoughby Gap. $79–109 in summer and fall; less in winter.

In Irasburg/Albany
Brick House (802-754-2108), P.O. Box 33, Irasburg 05845. Roger and Jo Sweatt welcome you to their 1875 brick house just off the common in this small, very Vermont village. There are three guest rooms, one twin bedded (or king) with private bath, and two (one with a lace-topped canopy bed and the other with a brass bed) sharing a bath. A breakfast, which might include Jo's crustless mushroom quiche, is included in $50–80 double.

Village House Inn (802-755-6722), P.O. Box 228, Route 14, Albany 05820. This fine Victorian village house with a wraparound porch is a full-service inn with eight crisply decorated bedrooms (private baths) just minutes from Craftsbury Common and adjacent to the Catamount cross-country ski trail. Kate Fletcher serves a full breakfast, included in $89 per couple. The dining room (see *Dining Out*) fills much of the first floor. Handy to VAST trails and to Craftsbury cross-country trails.

In the North Country
🍴 🐾 ✎ ♿ **Seymour Lake Lodge** (802-895-2752; www.seymour lakelodge.com), Route 111, Morgan 05853. Brian and Joan Du Moulin both grew up right around here (on opposite sides of the border) and maintain a casual, homey lodge that retains its vintage-1915 character, the kind that's increasingly hard to find. They offer nine rooms (two with private bath). A two-bedroom suite with laundry facilities, phone, TV, and fridge is handicapped accessible. Guests also have access to the kitchen (fridge, freezer, stove, microwave) and the BBQ so they can cook their own lunch and dinner. Breakfast is served 7–9. The Du Moulins also operate an antiques shop on the premises. The inn is open for winter ice fishing and snowmobiling (it's on the VAST trail) or cross-country skiing on the lake; in summer and fall it caters to fishermen, bicyclists, and families, and in late fall to sportsmen. Use of canoes, kayaks, and a sailboat is free to guests, and there's a swim beach across the road. Small rental boats for fishing are available. The game room includes a TV and VCR, a Ping-Pong table, and darts, and a

computer jack is available. $55–80; $10 per extra person. Inquire about the apartment with wood-burning stove, sleeping up to five. Children are welcome, and two rooms are delegated to accept pets.

Lakefront Inn & Motel (802-723-6507; www.thelakefrontinn.com), Cross Street, Island Pond 05846. A two-story motel and a main building housing the lobby and suites with one, two, or three bedrooms (some with fireplace) in the center of the village overlooking the pond. Four of the 20 units have built-in kitchenette. A floating dock is reserved for motel guests, and a heated multi-bay garage is available for guests to work on servicing their snowmobiles in winter. Just across the way are public tennis courts, a beach, a picnic area, a boat launch, a lighted ice hockey rink, and a children's playground. Robert and Sharon Dexter charge $79 per room, $295 per efficiency for two people in winter (high season), $10 per extra person. Summer rates are lower.

Lake Salem Inn (802-766-5560; www.lakesaleminn.com), 1273 Route 105, Derby 05829. This attractive inn with its columned porch is set on 7 acres overlooking Lake Salem. Joe and Mo Profera offer four guest rooms, all with private bath. The spacious first-floor "library" ($125) has a queen-sized sleigh bed and a sitting area, the "Zen Room" ($115) is airy and tranquil, and both the Wyoming Room and the Hideaway have lake views and private decks ($155). Common space includes a TV, books, and games; there's a back deck and boat dock. Rates include a full breakfast, and dinner (Joe used to own an Italian restaurant) is available on request. No children, please.

Note: Summer rental cottages are listed with the Newport and Barton Chambers of Commerce. See *Guidance.*

SEYMOUR LAKE LODGE IN MORGAN

Christina Tree

☃ ✍ **Quimby Country** (802-822-5533; www.quimbycountry.com), P.O. Box 20, Averill 05901, is about as north (less than 3 miles from Canada) and as east (10 miles from New Hampshire) as you can get in the Kingdom. This unique 1,050-acre resort is a 19th-century lodge and grouping of 20 cabins overlooking 70-acre Forest Lake. It is also 0.25 mile from 1,200-acre Great Averill Pond, 4 miles from 400-acre Little Averill, and surrounded by its own woodland, which, in turn, is surrounded by more woodland, much of it now conservation land. Begun as a fishing lodge, Quimby Country evolved into a family-oriented resort under the proprietorship of Hortense Quimby, attracting a large following in the process. Fearful that the place might change when it came up for sale upon Miss Quimby's death, a number of regular guests formed a corporation and bought it. When the place is in full operation, late June through late August, it's about families and returnees. Rates are $128–149 per adult, $62–91 per child depending on age and week, with all three meals and a supervised children's program geared to ages 6–15 that includes swimming, hiking, overnight camping, and rainy-day activities. Reasonable rates during spring fishing season (May 10 through June 27), and again August 30 through foliage season when cottages are available on a housekeeping basis and it's quiet enough to hear the leaves fall. This is a great place for birders, walkers, good conversation, and family reunions.

QUIMBY COUNTRY

Christina Tree

CAMPGROUNDS See Brighton State Park and Maidstone State Park in *Green Space*.

✳ Where to Eat

DINING OUT

In and around Newport

Lago Trattoria (802-334-8222), 95 Main Street, Newport. Open Tuesday through Sunday from 5 PM. Chef-owner Frank Richardi claims not to fry anything except calamari, a departure for downtown Newport, as is the sophisticated modern Italian decor. The menu includes pastas and staples like chicken Marsala and cacciatore. Try the semiboned, slowly roasted duck with apricot glaze, served with butternut squash ravioli, maple-roasted root vegetables, and marinated beans. Pizzas from $8.50, otherwise entrées $13–22.

The East Side (802-334-2340), 47 Landing Street, Newport. Open for lunch and dinner weekdays, breakfast on weekends. Closed Monday. Formerly The Landing, this is a large old landmark with a seasonal outdoor deck and dock. The reasonably priced lunch menu might include lamb stew and biscuits or grilled chicken salad; the dinner menu is also moderately priced. The night's special might be marinated center-cut pork chop, deep-fried oysters, or Yankee pot roast. Many locals come just for dessert (try the pecan ribbon). Live entertainment Friday and Saturday.

The Village House Inn & Restaurant (802-755-6722), Route 14, Albany. Open Friday and Saturday by reservation. Kate Fletcher offers a limited but dependable and reasonably priced menu. You might begin with butternut squash soup, then dine on pork escallops sautéed with lemon, capers, and white wine.

Near Lake Willoughby

WilloughVale Inn (802-525-2123; www.willoughvale.com), Route 5A, Westmore. Open nightly in July and August and Labor Day through Columbus Day; Thursday through Saturday during the Christmas and ice-fishing seasons, but call to check. The Willoughby Room and less formal Tap Room both overlook Lake Willoughby, and the food is fine. Begin with wild mushrooms sautéed with shallots, fresh herbs, and white wine, baked in puff pastry, then dine on maple-barbecued chicken or fresh vegetable lasagna. Entrées $14.95–20.95. You can always also get a burger or smoked chicken quesadilla.

In Essex County

☙ **Quimby Country** (802-822-5533), Route 114, Averill (see *Lodging*). Open to the public for dinner by reservation only, offering a rotating menu of two entrées, plus a children's entrée; Sunday-night buffet. Moderate.

Loon's Landing (802-723-LOON), 135 Main Street, Island Pond. Open for lunch and dinner. Closed Monday off-season. Just opened when we stopped by, this pleasant restaurant was obviously doing something right. Prices are reasonable: $11.99 for a grilled pork chop. Beer and wine served.

EATING OUT

In and around Newport

The Brown Cow (802-334-7887), 900 East Main Street, Newport, open daily 6 AM–7 PM except Sunday, when it's 7–1. This is a nice spot to linger over breakfast (served all day); sandwich and salad lunches, reasonably priced dinners. Homemade ice cream on homemade pie.

Miss Newport Diner (802-334-7742), East Main Street, Newport. Open 5 AM–11 PM daily except Saturday, when it closes at 10:30 PM. Blueberry pancakes and fresh muffins are the specialty, along with homemade soup and friendly natives; choice of stools and booths.

Derby Cow Palace (802-766-4724), Main Street (Route 5), Derby. Open at noon on weekends, from 3 PM weekdays. This is the most recent venture for Doug Nelson, owner of the largest local dairy operation and of Cow Town Elk Ranch. Needless to say, the pleasant log restaurant specializes in beef, from burgers to prime rib. Fully licensed, with a bar menu.

Rosewood Café (802-334-26236; 1-800-410-2625), in the back of Newport Natural Foods. Open daily 9–5:30. This cozy café in the back of a natural foods shop is a real find: soups, hot entrées, wraps, and bread, as well as daily specials.

Café Sante (819-876-2576), 237 Dufferin, Stanstead, Quebec. Open Tuesday through Saturday 7–2, Friday night 5:30–9. Just across the border, a true little bistro with a blackboard menu, specializing in vegetarian dishes and occasional live music. BYOB.

La Vielle Douane (819-876-2776), 232 Dufferin, Stanstead, Quebec. Literally "the old customs" house, steps across the border from Derby Line, this is your standard Greek eatery featuring souvlaki and pizza, but it has a full family restaurant menu and it's fun to order "truite arc-en-ciel" instead of rainbow trout. Fully licensed.

Martha's Diner (802-754-6800), Routes 5/14, Coventry. Open Monday through Friday 5 AM–2 PM, Saturday 5–1, Sunday 6–noon. A classic chrome diner with classic diner food.

In Island Pond

🦌 🍴 **Jennifer's Restaurant** (802-723-6135), Cross Street. Open daily for breakfast, lunch, and dinner, with a children's menu. The town's gathering spot, a cheery restaurant known for good food, especially seafood—which even coastal residents find inexplicably outstanding. Hearty breakfast sandwiches, and roast turkey, surf and turf for dinner. Beer and wine served.

Friendly Pizza (802-723-4616), 31 Derby Street (Route 105). Closed Monday, otherwise open from 11 until at least 9 PM. John Koxarakis offers a wide variety of pizzas, also steaks, spaghetti, sandwiches, grinders, and Greek salad in his small eatery on the southern fringe of the village.

In Canaan

🦌 🍴 **Bessie's Diner** (802-266-3310), 166 Gale Street. Open weekdays except Mondays from 6, Saturday from 7, and Sunday from 8; closes at 8 every night. Admittedly we're suckers for cheap and friendly, but Vernon and Bonnie Crawford's place is so pleasant and wholesome—ditto for the food—that we can't rave enough. On our last visit we went for the special: cabbage soup and a tuna fish casserole (real tuna with rice, beans, and onions). The menu includes burgers, 30 different kinds of sandwiches, open-faced bagelwiches (try the Grump-Fish), subs, and wraps. Poutines (Quebec-style french fries with gravy and cheese curds) are a specialty, and a wide and reasonably priced choice is available at dinner. Service is fast and friendly. Wine and beer. **Cow**

Licks, an ice cream window, operates summers.

Northland Restaurant and Lounge (802-266-9947). A large, clean, comfortable place offering three squares. The spacious adjoining bar/lounge/dance floor hosts rock and country-rock bands Saturday evening.

In the Barton area

Candlepin Restaurant (802-525-6513), Route 5 north of Barton. Open 7 days a week featuring family-style breakfast, lunch, and dinner. Just minutes off I-91, this is the best place to eat around the Barton area, known for seafood specialties, staples like Vermont roast turkey with dressing and cranberry sauce, and homemade pie. The daily lunch special: chowder, a BLT, and homemade fries plus tea is under $6. It's a big, friendly place with booths; beer and wine served.

Northern Exposure (802-525-3789), Route 5A, Westmore on Lake Willoughby. Open in summer Monday through Saturday 6 AM–9 PM, Sunday 8–8; in winter weekdays 6–6, Saturday 7–6, Sunday 8–6. It's just nice to know that this place is there where you need it with pizzas (call ahead) as well as a deli good for grinders, steak-n-cheese, chili, and soup of the day. In summer the ice cream shop features Hershey's.

✷ Entertainment

♿ **Haskell Opera House** (819-873-3020), in Derby. This splendid vintage-1904 theater has perfect acoustics, three antique sets, a rare roll-up curtain depicting scenes of Venice, and a rococo interior. Its season runs late April through mid-October and includes performances by a resident theater company, opera, dance, and a variety of outstanding concerts. **QNEK Productions** (802-334-8145), the summer resident theater company at the Haskell, offers reasonably priced evening and matinee productions of musicals and other stock Broadway hits. Tickets for opera house performances are also available at the Woodknot Bookshop, Newport (802-334-6720).

Piggery Theater (819-842-2431), North Hatley, Quebec. June through August, summer theater.

Bread and Puppet Theater Museum (802-525-3031), Route 122, Glover. The internationally known Bread and Puppet Theater with its huge and haunting puppet dwarfs, giants, and devils performs Sundays in July and August at 3 PM outdoors; inquire about Friday-night performances in the timber-frame theater. Also see *To See*.

Waterfront Cinemas (802-334-6572), 137 Waterfront Plaza, Newport. First-run films on three screens.

✷ Selective Shopping

Bogner Factory Outlet (802-334-0135), 150 Main Street, Newport. Looking more like a boutique than the outlet it is—for the nationally known ski- and sportswear partially made in town.

Woodknot Books (802-334-6720), 137 Main Street, Newport. Open 9–5 except Sunday, Friday until 6. A good selection of books and magazines.

The Great Outdoors (802-334-2851), 177 Main Street, Newport. In summer the store features an extensive array of fishing gear and sells fishing licenses; four-season sporting goods. Rental bikes, kayaks, and canoes, also rental in-line skates, snowshoes, cross-country skis, and snowboards.

Country Thyme (802-766-2852; 1-800-334-7905; www.countrythyme vermont.com), 60 Route 111, Derby (near the junction of Routes 111 and 5). Every inch of the ground floor in Kay Courson's house is crammed with gifts, toys, specialty foods, Christmas decorations, and more.

In Island Pond
Simon the Tanner (802-723-4452), Cross and Main Streets. Open daily except Saturday, closing at 3 on Friday, otherwise 9–5, until 8 on Thursday. This is an unlikely spot for such a huge shoe store, but here it is selling a wide variety of name-brand shoes— Birkenstock and Clarks sandals, Dansko and Stegmann clogs, Doc Martens, work boots, winter boots, Tubbs snowshoes, and a big selection of athletic shoes, all at below-usual prices. There's also a bargain basement. Candles, specialty food, wrought iron, natural soaps, and body care products made by the Twelve Tribes, an international sect that

STEVE STACEY'S "CHISEL & SAW" CREATIONS

Christina Tree

rooted in Island Pond several decades ago, restoring a number of houses and winning the respect of the community.

Chisel & Saw (802-723-4915), Route 114, Island Pond. Steve Stacey's colorful chain-saw carvings fill his roadside garden. The dancing bears, Buddhas, and merlins are all for sale; visitors welcome.

In the Barton–Glover–Irasburg area
Currier's Quality Market (802-525-8822), Glover. Open year-round daily, Monday through Saturday 6–9, Sunday 9–6. James and Gloria Currier's general store is a must-stop if just to see the 948-pound (stuffed) moose and variety of formerly live animals lurking in the aisles and festooned from the rafters in this old-style emporium. In addition to staples and a good deli counter with hot specials, this is a major sporting goods store, selling fishing and hunting licenses and stocking extensive gear.

Evansville Trading Post (802-754-6305), Route 58 between Orleans and Lake Willoughby. Open early May through October. A crafts cooperative for Clan of the Hawk, the local Abenaki Indian band. The 39-acre tribal grounds are the scene of a big powwow the first weekend in August and a crafts show the last week in July.

Steffi's Studio (802-754-6012), Irasburg green. Steffi Huess crafts gold and silver jewelry, and sells it along with other local arts and crafts right from the front room in her home.

Castle Shoppe and Café (802-754-2057), 4887 Burton Hill Road, Irasburg. Open year-round on weekends, 11–5. Sara Gregoire's striking,

European-castle-like house show-cases antiques (for sale), from porcelain to many styles of furniture; she also serves home-baked pastries in the café. (Leave the Irasburg common with the white church on your right, take a left at the next church, and then bear left at the Y in the road.)

Norman Dion's (802-754-8770), Irasburg. Closed Tuesday, Wednesday, and Sunday mornings. The warehouselike complex on your right before you get to the Castle (see above). This is a local institution, a vast collection of trash and treasure, well known to antiques dealers from near and far.

Labour of Love Gardens (802-525-6695), Route 16, Glover Village. An acre of public gardens is behind the house, on the Barton River, mid-May until frost, plus antiques and crafts.

Lake Parker Country Store (802-525-6985; 1-800-893-6985), Main Street, West Glover. By Lake Parker. Good for basics plus sandwiches and baked goods. This is a prime outlet for prizewinning Bonnie View Farm sheep cheese, made in nearby South Albany.

Sugarmill Farm Maple Museum (802-525-3701), Route 16 south of Barton Village. Mid-March through mid-November. The Auger family has turned its former dairy farm into a combination maple museum, working maple operation, dairy parlor, and gift shop selling its own syrup and locally crafted items. Attractions include a tractor-drawn wagon trip through the orchards, a covered bridge, a film on sugaring, a sugarhouse, vintage farm and sugaring tools, and picnic tables. Ben & Jerry's is served year-round; sugar-on-snow in-season.

Sugarwoods Farm (802-525-3718), 2287) Route 16, Glover. Open May through September, 8–4:30; February through April, Saturday 8–1. A major outlet for maple syrup, candy, and sugaring equipment.

In Averill
Lakeview Store (802-822-5570), Route 114, Averill. Open daily 8–7. A no-nonsense general store except for the fabulous wools and some hand-crafted items: bowls, sweaters, baskets, also weaving supplies. Pick a fleece at nearby Swanson Oldfarm and the store's owner, Priscilla Roy, will spin it.

✳ Special Events
February: **Newport Winter Carnival. Island Pond Snowmobile Races.**

March: **Sugaring** throughout the region.

June: **Antique Gas/Steam Engine Show** at the Old Stone House Museum in Brownington (www.oldstone housemuseum.org).

July: **Memphremagog International Aquafest**—a swim race from Newport to Magog in Canada (32 miles), also a waterskiing tournament, parade, public suppers, and more.

August: **Orleans County Arts and Crafts Fair** (first Saturday) in Barton (802-334-7325); **International Car Show** in Newport (802-334-6079); **Orleans County Fair** (last week; 802-525-555) in Barton, an old-fashioned event at the extensive fairground—horse, pony, and ox pulling, harness racing, stage shows, demo derby, tractor pull, arts, crafts, and agricultural exhibits. **Clan of the Hawk Pow Wow** at the Evansville

Trading Post (see *Selective Shopping*). **Old Stone House Day**—open house, picnic lunch, crafts demonstrations at the museum in Brownington Village (www.oldstonehousemuseum .org). **North Country Moose Festival** (last week). Based in Colebrook, New Hampshire, a series of colorful events on both sides of the Connecticut River.

INDEX

INDEX